Divine Madness

Divine Madness

By

Harry Eiss

CAMBRIDGE
SCHOLARS
PUBLISHING

Divine Madness, by Harry Eiss

This book first published 2011

Cambridge Scholars Publishing

12 Back Chapman Street, Newcastle upon Tyne, NE6 2XX, UK

British Library Cataloguing in Publication Data
A catalogue record for this book is available from the British Library

ISBN (10): 1-4438-3298-7, ISBN (13): 978-1-4438-3298-4

To Meghan, David and Colleen Ross

May life be a secret garden
Where enchantment is still possible

Lila is Sanskrit for *play*, the *play* of the gods. It is the *self-generating genesis* of *Bliss*, created by *Bliss* for the purpose of *Bliss*. It is the uninhibited, impulsive sport of Brahman, the free spirit of creation that results in the spontaneous unfolding of the cosmos to be found in the eternity of each moment. It is beyond the confining locks and chains of reason, beyond the steel barred windows looking out from the cages of explanation, beyond the droning tick-tick-tick of the huge mechanical clocks of time.

Come, let us enter the realm of the *madman* and the finely wrought threads of Clotho as they are measured out by Lachesis and cut by Atropos to create the great tapestry of life, including the intricate, intertwining designs of *dementia* with the *trickster,* the *shaman,* the *scapegoat,* the *shadow,* the *artist* and the *savior.*

Come, let us join in the *divine madness* of the gods.

****

Elwood P. Dowd: "Well, I've wrestled with reality for 35 years, Doctor, and I'm happy to state I finally won out over it."
—Mary Chase, *Harvey*, Oct. 15, 1950

****

Wer Uber gewisse dinge den Verstand nicht verliert, der hat keinen zu verlieren. (He who does not lose his mind over certain things has no mind to lose.)
—Gotthold Ephraim Lessing in his play *Emilia Galotti* (1772), IV, vii.

TABLE OF CONTENTS

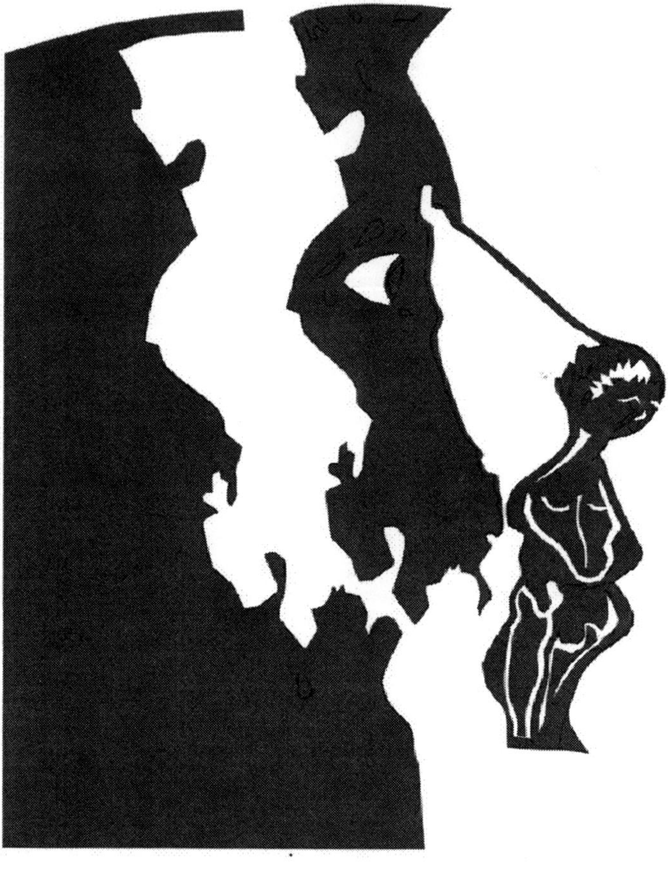

Whisperer

In the time when Johann Casimir was Duke of Coburg, his Master of the Stables was named G. P. von Z. This master of the stables first resided in the street called Spitalgasse, *afterward in a dwelling subsequently inhabited by D. Frommann and then in a large villa outside town, which was called* Rosenau. *Finally he took up residence in the castle, where he also acted as captain of arms. A ghost forced him to these frequent moves. In appearance this spirit looked exactly like his living wife so that each time when he entered a new dwelling and sat at his table he often doubted whether he was in the presence of his true wife. For the spirit followed him out of each house and everywhere. When his wife once again suggested moving into new living quarters to avoid the ghost, the apparition began to cry out in a loud voice: "Go where you will. I will follow you, even to the ends of the earth!" This was not an idle threat for when the Master of the Stable moved out, the doors of the houses he left behind slammed shut with ferocious force. From then on the spirit was never seen in the abandoned house but only in the new residence.*

Every day when the true wife dressed herself, the ghost appeared in the same clothing regardless of whether it was a fancy dress or an every-day dress and the colour of the fabric didn't matter. This is why the wife never went about her household tasks alone, but was always accompanied by a servant. The spirit often appeared between eleven and twelve o'clock. If a priest or man of the cloth was present, the ghost did not appear. When once Johann Pruescher the Father Confessor had been invited and the noble man and his wife and sister accompanied him down the stairs, the spirit began to climb the stairs from below at the same time. Through the wooden rail it gripped the young maid's apron and disappeared when she began to scream. Once the spirit lay on its side over the threshold to the kitchen. When the cook asked "What do you want?" the spirit responded "I shall have your mistress." But the mistress of the house never experienced any harm. Things did not go as well for the young maid, the sister of the noble man. One time the spirit hit the girl so hard in the face that her cheek swelled up and the girl had to return to her father's house. Finally the spirit retreated and it became peaceful in the house once more.

— Brothers Grimm, #260

CREDITS

I want to thank Noreen Parker for her valuable, intelligent editing help with this work. It would not have the professional quality it has without her efforts.

I also want to thank Joel Rudinger for his exceptional illustrations, which could stand on their own as superb works of art and most certainly add to the textures of the book.

PREFACE

Rape of Sedna

In Inuit mythology, Sedna is the creator-goddess of all the sea animals. When a central Eskimo hunts for seals swimming under the fields of ice or for whales in his walrus skin umiaq far out at sea, he asks Sedna to feed his family. If he honors the animal's spirit and pours fresh water into its mouth when it has been killed, Sedna will send him another at a later time of need. But if he does not honor the spirit of the animal and neglects to give it water, Sedna will rise in anger and with-hold her gifts. Then it is bad luck for the hunter. For at all times, one must be worthy.

It is also said that when famine strikes, the spirit of the village shaman swims to the bottom of the sea to ask Sedna to send his people food animals. If she allows him to comb luck out of her watery hair, they will find food and survive.

—Joel Rudinger
Sedna: Goddess of the Sea

Joel Rudinger and I sat at a small, round table, one of those high tables with tall chairs that prevent the feet from touching the floor. He had come to Eastern Michigan University to discuss his book *Sedna: Goddess of the Sea* with my World Mythology and Critical Approaches to Literature classes, and now we were taking a break to have a light lunch at the new Student Union, an impressive building with a two-story wall of windows overlooking a pleasant man-made double pond that had a picturesque, white walking bridge over its short connecting channel and three water sprouts in each bay sending glistening water sprays some thirty feet into the blue, sunlit sky.

"So, how was the cruise to Alaska?"

"Good, a bit of a journey into my past."

"I remember you mentioning that the ship had a number of deck hot tubs, and when it got into the Arctic Circle it was possible to sit in them and watch the Aurora Borealis."

"The Northern Lights are only visible at night. During the summer, there is daylight twenty-two hours a day, so while the aurora was alive and well, none of the ship passengers saw it. However, during my four years in Alaska I saw it often. I remember well one time I saw a full blown display of greens and whites and violet undulating waves emanating from the newly discovered Van Allen Radiation Belt. It was in 1962 and I was driving my new 1962 VW Beetle from college to Fairbanks. I was so mesmerized by the astral display of lights that I drove left of center and was immediately pulled over by a Fairbanks police car and given a $100 traffic violation fine.

"Did you find evidence of the Sedna story across the straight in Russia as you hoped?"

"Didn't get the chance to talk with them as much as I wanted."

"Well, what did you find?"

"Here's the story. Susan and I took a ten day vacation on a 120 passenger Cruise-West ship from Whittier, Alaska, to Kodiak, then to Dutch Harbor in the Aleutian chain and finally into the Bering Sea. We had permission to enter Russian waters and visit two communities, Providenia and New Chappalina, where I hoped to ask some Siberian natives if they knew the Sedna narrative. Didn't want to use the word "myth" or "legend" with regards to Sedna since either word would imply a fiction, and if, in fact, Siberian Yup'ik Eskimos still held some kind of ritualistic belief relationship with her, it could be insulting.

Providinia was a small town with paved streets, eight story weatherworn concrete apartment buildings, unmarked stores, a small hillside cemetery, a large statue of Lenin, and a social hall. Most of the townspeople were white Russian. I did not see many Eskimos in the streets of the town, although natives and young Caucasian dancers performed for the people of our cruise ship in the social hall. Providinia had, at one time, serviced a military outpost a few miles north of town, but that outpost had been decommissioned after the Cold War.

However, we did take a rocky bumpy hilly jaw-jumping teeth rattling ride in some kind of old large boxy springless transport bus to the small native village New Chappalina, where the population was 95% Yup'ik. There we attended another concert/performance, and the natives had set up a gymnasium with craftsmen selling their carvings at ridiculous prices ($1500 for a little stone carving, a souvenir from Siberia for rich tourists). Only five people spoke to us in English, a fisherman who was demonstrating his fishing techniques, an older woman who translated for a young man with sled dogs, our two tour guides who had come with us from Providenia, and a woman who introduced the show. There were few natives who spoke English, and the adult whites in Providinia walked by us without eye contact. One little five-year-old girl walking alone down the middle of one of the streets in town said to me in perfect English, "hello," but other than a general store shopkeeper who was looking to sell some wares, and the local tour director who was paid by Cruise West, we had minimal contact with the people. So, no, I didn't get much of a response from the Siberian population. I had little opportunity to ask because we were also under constant scrutiny by the Russian police. To be honest, I think more people spoke English than they let on, since that part of Siberia can probably pick up Alaska TV stations, and some may have had satellite.

Just before I left on the trip, I was in contact with a Canadian researcher named Neil Christopher. In an email to me in 2008, he wrote, "I am jealous of your opportunity to visit some Siberian sea coast villages. According to what I have read (and several interviews) you should be able to find a version of the sea mother in that region. I think in the book Kappianaqtut I listed some names recorded in Siberia and the Bering Strait region."

Looking into Christopher's book, *Kappianaqtut*, the one Siberian reference I found was "Nulirah," "old woman." An Asiatic name for her is "Nulirahak" or "the big woman." A good number of different native names come from the eastern parts of northern Canada, such as Baffin Island, and Greenland. All this means that even if I would have been free to mingle with the general populations, they probably would not have known the name Sedna. However, this is conjecture on my part. A synopsis of her story might have been recognizable.

Of greater importance, though, was my discovery of the story knife that shows up in the book. Native girls often carried "snow" knives. Anyway, the ancient carved ivory story knives I found in a native museum in Barrow in 2007 were an exciting discovery since I instantly saw their use in my narrative.

I had gotten to know Joel through the years as we gave presentations at a number of Popular Culture Association conferences throughout the United States and Canada, and his experiences in Alaska, introduction to the Inuit world of folktale and myth, and eventual publication, *Sedna: Goddess of the Sea* had led me to invite him to visit my classes to help facilitate my students' comprehension of the reality and power of sacred rituals and texts, and how they allow us to connect with the world of the spirit.

Joel was sparked to write the book because other versions of the story, most notable the one by the San Souci brothers misrepresented it, turning it into a silly, shallow insult. In the hope of getting my students to understand why this other version of the story was missing the point and why the real versions of the story were so important, I had pushed Joel to give his own interesting story of how he came to know the real depth and power of it and the whole world of Inuit mythology and spirituality. He would later write it down in a book I edited:

> In June, 1960, I was to graduate with a major in zoology, but my interests had begun to switch from parasites and microscopes to literature and creative writing. Spearheading this change was an Invertebrate Anatomy class research paper on Professor Karl Von Frisch's theory on how bees (*hymenoptera*) communicated and navigated by polarized light. The paper was well researched and it had earned a grade of A. But as Professor Ed Karlin held it out to me, with a dramatic gesture, he took it back and, with his Parker fountain pen, added a thick black minus after the A. He told me that it was an excellent paper, that he enjoyed reading it, it was well researched, but it was not written in scientific language. "It is not a scientific paper," he said. "It is a twenty-five page poem, and I suggest you change your major, because you do not, and probably will never, think like a scientist. But you write well. Go into English!" He was a wise man. In my heart, I knew he was correct. And the next day, I gave all my precious hand-prepared slides of stained tissues simples of cross-sectioned parasites to a classmate who was blissfully looking forward to a career of teaching high school biology.
>
> I sent out letters to several universities to see if I could get into a graduate English program. Having read the article in the magazine, I also wrote to the University of Alaska to see if they had a Masters program in English. A week later, I got a response from the U of A in Fairbanks

saying that they did, indeed, have a brand new program. An application to the Graduate School was included.

Three weeks later, I sent them the unimpressive results of my Graduate Record Exam, filled out the application, sent official transcripts with my pitiful twenty-four credit hours of English, and—as if it was meant to be—a week later the Dean of Students wrote to tell me that my application had been accepted! I was hired as a graduate teaching assistant in the Department of English at the University in Alaska starting the day after Labor Day in 1960.

I stopped by my invertebrate anatomy professor's office to tell him the good news, but he was no longer there. He was, in fact, home in bed dying of cancer. He would pass away soon after I left Ohio. He was the first of many helpers and guides who showed up to alter and redirect the course of my life, a life leading ultimately to Sedna, the Inuit sea goddess.

Now that I was starting a new direction, I was about to leave behind everything familiar. My parents were surprisingly supportive, especially my mother. My friends thought my plans were exciting. I boxed up my dictionary and a few other books, sold my black mother-of-pearl drum set for $200, and my 6 cylinder 1954 emerald green, stick-shift, mint-condition two-door Buick with the white wall tires for $600, bought a new Smith Corona portable manual typewriter, a large steamer trunk, two new white dress shirts wrapped in cellophane, a heavy green checkered sport coat, and a black tie to teach in. I bought a one-way flight to Fairbanks and was ready to go. The steamer truck and boxes of books were sent ahead by train. I followed a week later. The first thing I wanted to see was the building pictured in the magazine. I knew, of course, that there would be no moose hanging from the window, but still I thought, maybe. . . .

When I walked into my Freshman composition classroom in the Bunnell Building on the U of A campus, there sat thirty students. Many were native Alaskans. But, if truth be told, cultural curiosity was not high on my agenda. I was struggling, teaching two composition classes while taking three high level classes of my own as a graduate student. I had no care, no time for social life, temperatures dipped regularly to minus 30, and winter nights were twenty-two hourse long. At one point, I kept a suicide journal. It was not an easy time. In short, I had lost my vision.

At the end of my first year at the university, I was homesick and decided to return to Ohio. But my life was to be affected by another unexpected Helper and Guide, Dr. Charles Keim, Professor of Journalism. Chuck Keim had shared with me the process of writing his biography of Dr. Otto Geist and had given me a tour of his writing studio over his garage. He was also a hunting guide, and in April 1961, he asked if I would like to be a "packer" for big game outfitter Hal Waugh. Chuck was going to work for him as a guide in the Post Lake region of the Alaska Range that summer and Hal needed a "packer" for his hunting party out in the mountains. A packer, as I found out, was one who packed out the meat on his back when a moose, sheep, caribou, or bear was killed at a distance from Base Camp. Although I had already sent all my books and clothes back to Ohio, my two crisp white dress shirt still in cellophane, remembering my initial reason for coming to Alaska—to experience new things and build life memories—I said yes. The next day I was told that I had the job.

The Post Lake packer job would not begin until August and my teaching contract was over in May. Needing to find work between times, I went to the Fairbanks Office of Unemployment and found that the Alaska Railroad needed extra gang laborers for the summer. I went to the ARR employment office, filled out an application, and was told to be ready to go to work as a "gandy dancer" the following Monday. The only clothes I now owned were Army surplus pants and shirts; a gray, felt wide-brimmed Dobson hat; and a pair of Red Wing boots. On Monday, I arrived at the railroad station, got on a gang car, and was transported sixty miles to a siding where several railroad cars were sidelined and waiting. There was a dining care and several sleeping cars divided into small cubicles, one double bunk bed per cubicle. When I stepped off the train, I looked around. I was the only white guy, except for Billy the foreman. Everyone else was an Alaskan or Canadian native.

The work was hard, prying up heavy creosoted ties and tamping new gravel under them with a long handled shovel to level the track. We got up at three in the morning to beat the blankets of mosquitoes that swarmed up from the tundra in black, whining, undulating clouds exactly at 2:30 in the afternoon. If we worked a few minutes late and didn't get back into the cars, I would be literally covered; my shirt, pants, gloves, and hat were black with live blood-sucking insects. I noticed that the natives didn't seem to be bothered by them. The mosquitoes would hover by the thousands over them but never land. Their skin had developed a natural repellant. It was only Billy and me who had a problem. And Billy had a very private stash of repellant.

Horace Smoke was my roommate in the sleeping car. He was a forty year old Athabascan Indian from Yukon Territory, Canada. In the afternoons, after the mosquitoes had risen and we had taken refuge in the dining car, he would tell me stories of his life. He had been a dog musher back home and had twice won the Yukon Quest. Horace told me the prize was $10,000 for first place, huge money in the 1950's and early 60's, but in the summers, he came to Alaska to work on the railroad. The pay was good and he could send money back to his family. Horace told me stories of hunts, some tall tale "stretchers" I suspect, and made a few allusions to some colorful characters who lived in the tundra, but I did not yet understand the importance of his stories. Horace was unknowingly setting the stage for things to come. He was quietly showing me how traditional stories were inseparable from cultural values. He was, to some extent, another Helper and Guide, although I would not know that until years afterwards.

As a work-soft college student and a native of suburban Toledo, Ohio, I had never done any hard maual labor. I had seen prison chain gangs working along the roads in Florida and Georgia, but I had never translated their activity into physical pain. Suffice it to say that after two and a half tortuous weeks of blood-sucking mosquitoes, heaving gravel with wrist-twisting, long handled shovels, pry-barring up heavy ties still spiked to the rails, my body rebelled, and I quit. The other laborers were wiry, strong, and hardened. They had done this type of tough work all their lives. The next day, I flagged down the commuter train as it came around the bend and rode back to Fairbanks thankful to be alive and relatively undamaged.

Back in Fairbanks, I found work on the university garden crew until my packer job began in August. I flew to Anchorage, picked up the chartered float plane by the airport, and was flown out to Post Lake on the North Fork of the Kuskokwim River, 250 miles from nowhere. The base camp consisted of a cook tent, three crew tents, three tents for the client-hunters, two canvas latrines, a meat drying rack, and a food cache on eight foot pylons, all spread out on the tundra's muskeg. This was my home for the next forty days. This is where I saw brown bears, moose, Dall sheep, caribou, fox, wolves, golden eagles, ravens, magpies, and ptarmigan. The mountains went from green to white as the snows came. Post Lake went from blue to white as the ice began to form. Before the snow came, the slopes of the mountains were covered with blueberries. Sometimes I would stand at a fording place at the river's edge just looking, surrounded by vast silent beauty. One day while waiting to cross the Kuskokwim with a pack of food on my back and a concern for grizzlies up-stream—not another human within five miles—I saw the snow-capped mountains in front of me shift. It was a pure moment of elusive grace. It was magic. This was the moment and the place that I discovered indefinable spiritual existence. This was the place and the moment I fell in love with Alaska. My vision had returned.

I resumed my graduate studies and was ready to graduate in May 1964. I had written a creative thesis, the university's first, and since I had just been accepted into the University of Iowa's Graduate Writers' Workshop, I thought it would be fun to have some of my poems translated into Eskimo. I knew a young education major named Cecila Ulroan. She was from Hooper Bay, a Yup'ik village on the Bering Sea. Cecelia agreed to translate a few of my poems into the Yup'ik language and let me record her translation. I gave her three of my poems, made a date for that weekend for her to come to my apartment for supper, and afterwards I would record her voice on my Wollensok reel-t-reel field tape recorder. Cecilia did a good job translating. Then, when she was finished, she looked up and said, "Would you like me to sing you a song in my native language?" And so she sang a few songs in Yup'ik about snowballs and picking berries. Then she asked if I would like to hear a traditional story from her village. "Yes," I said. And she told me the story of "The Fiery Hand," a monster that floated through the air across the Bering Sea to eat disobedient children.

> As I listened, I felt that this was yet another life-changing moment. Horace Smoke had told me stories of his life and village; this was the first I had heard a real Alaskan folktale-legend. It opened up a new world of imagination. I was hooded like a salmon with a mouthful of chum. (pp. 40-44)

Joel's career would lead him from his Master of Arts Degree at the University of Alaska and a Master of Fine Arts degree in poetry from the University of Iowa to a Doctorate from Bowling Green State University, which hired Dr. Ray Browne in 1968 to create a program in Popular Culture while Joel was there. Since Joel had a strong background in folklore, Dr. Browne hired him to teach a senior level course in it, and then, when Joel completed his dissertation, he got hired at the new Firelands branch campus in Huron, Ohio, which resulted in him teaching the Firelands courses in children's literature. And this is where he encountered the San Souci version of the Sedna story, and it sparked his own research and eventual picture book of the story.

His version is a hard-hitting, honest presentation of the Inuit world, a harsh environment where the raw forces of nature are fully capable of presenting that combination of stunning beauty and frightening horror that brings a real sense of the sublime, a viseral experience of the *grace* Joel wrote about. I wrote the following for the back cover of the book:

> Sedna appears in many forms, some friendly, some frightening, even horrific. She is the Inuit creator-goddess, and her stories connect the Inuit with the cold, often cruel world that surrounds them, a world that cannot escape the forces of nature and the closeness of life with its often dangerous textures. The mythic spirits of this world are not refined or distant, but are rough-hewn and real. And it is the water and its moods that drive the life of the Inuit. So it is fitting that Sedna lives deep in its threatening and mysterious caverns. Sometimes beautiful, sometimes macabre, she expresses the sublime, a world beyond comprehension, beyond ethos, beyond all human clarification, a world of the spirit, a world to be appeased, to be obeyed, to be supplicated
>
> Joel Rudinger gives us a mythical Sedna true to the harsh Inuit world where she first appeared. The dark shadows of the story remain. The betrayals of her father Ootuk are portrayed in graphic detail, and the scene of him forcing death upon her by repeatedly stabbing her hands until she must succumb to a cold watery grave gains power in its straight-forward folk tale language. The raw, honest language is matched by the primitive simplicity of the silhouette illustrations cut from black paper. The feel of the language and the feel of the illustrations match the feel of the story, and the reader enters for a time this dark mythic level of existence.

> Tired of all of the glossy, commercialized, and cleaned-up versions of folk tales, I was immediately taken by this rich embracement of the deeper levels that such stories are meant to contain.

The story, as are all true myths, is an expression of the deeply ingrained archetypes that support our lives, links between the literal, physical world and the sensed, invisible, spiritual world that gives it meaning. The loss of this connection, this real purpose of the myths is what drove Joel to try and recapture it for a culture that was in the process of denying its validity. Later in his discussion for my book, he wrote:

> There are suggestions that in some Inupiaq communities, Sedna is no longer being credited with being the great mother of the sea mammals, the spiritual being who has for a score of generations given sustenance to hungry Eskimo communities. On a recent National Geographic special, televised on February 5th, 2009, the documentary "Whale Hunters" was shown of a recent subsistence whale capture. After a bowhead whale had been killed and dragged onto the ice near the Alaskan village of Barrow, men, women, and children gathered together to give thanks. As I watched the community gather at the edge of the sea, I waited with anticipation to hear their thanks to Sedna for her bounteous gift. However, that was not what happened. Instead, they all stood at the edge of the ice as the leader proclaimed loudly over the Arctic Ocean, "Thank you, God, for the gift of this whale you have given us. This is for your glory only, in Jesus' name, Amen." As I sat silent in my chair, I asked myself: What will be the future of this wonderful legend? Will the Inuit children of the current generation forget about Sedna and all that she has meant to their culture for thousands of years? Will they never know her story or its meaning? Will she, like Zeus and Athena and Ztlas and Persephone, become a folk legend they descover by accident in a history book or a literature class instead of hearing of her from their fathers? I mention this National Geographic documentary because in its own way it is part of the changing history of the Sedna legend. It has all the same ritual, but the benefactor has changed. Perhaps the greatest variation of a tale is the disintegration and disappearance of that tale. We can only hope that Jesus and Sedna can co-exist within this ancient culture and both keep their separate and distinct cultural presences alive. (p. 63)

All about us the student union clattered with the voices and other noises of a busy student population pulling chairs up to high tables to dig into hamburgers stacked with bacon and tomatoes and lettuce and cheese and mayonnaise and ketchup and mustard and pickles, and french fries drenched in oil and sprinkled with salt, and thick, rich vanilla, strawberry and chocolate malts filled with processed sugar and eggs. Some pulled textbooks and looseleaf notebooks out of their backpacks. Many listened to music through their earphones. Others talked on cell phones. But we didn't notice.

"I'm pleased you have a passage in your book about the spirit of the village shaman swimming to the bottom of the sea to ask Sedna to send the sacred food animals, hoping she will allow him to comb out her hair in supplication to the worlds of nature and the spirit, a necessary show of respect for the sacred animals that give up their lives that men might survive."

"Yes," Joel replied and smiled.

****

Noreen Parker and I were newly in love, and we had driven down the California coast to visit her former mother-in-law.

Noreen took a drink of her Arnold Palmer, a mixture of lemonade and ice tea. "So, there is a ghost at the Hotel del Coronado?"

"Yes," her former mother-in-law, Jennea, continued.

I sipped my Tangaray Martini. This was interesting. "Please, tell us."

"Well," she continued, "the story goes, a woman registered here . . . I believe it was 1892 . . . sometime in the1890s, as Lottie Bernard. She was alone and apparently ill, but told the front desk not to worry about it, because her brother was a doctor and would be arriving shortly. When asked why she had no luggage, she said she'd been traveling with her brother, but he had to unexpectantly depart the train in Orange, and when he did, he inadvertently took all of the luggage claim checks with him, leaving her no way to retrieve her bags when she checked into the Del.

Later that evening, she told the bell boy she was not feeling well, said she had stomach pains. Today, people suspect she was pregnant. At any rate, the next day, she went to the drugstore, and was obviously in distress."

"And no one helped her?" Noreen asked.

"Apparently some offered, but she refused, claiming her doctor brother would be arriving shortly."

"And her brother?" I prompted.

"Never arrived. Today, most don't believe there was a brother."

"Then what happened?" Noreen asked.

"Well, apparently, she continued to stay in her room, have the bell boy bring her various items, towels, medicine, even whiskey, for a couple of days. I believe he even gave her a sponge bath, not so unusual in those days—at least that's what I've been told."

"Hmmm," I muttered. "The gay-nineties!"

"She mainly kept to herself. Then, a couple evenings after her arrival, after checking with the front desk about any telegrams, she went back to her room. No one took much notice. No one heard anything in the night. But she was discovered the next morning on the steps, dead. There was a large pistol next to her and a pool of blood, and it was pronounced a suicide."

"Did they ever discover what was going on?" I asked.

"No one ever quite figured it out. The best guess is that she was really a woman named Kate Morgan from Iowa, the wife of a gambler named Tom Morgan who had gotten her pregnant and deserted her. But that's just speculation."

"So," Noreen said, "it's *her* ghost that haunts the Del?"

"Yes. A number of guests have reported seeing her ghost. The hotel tried to downplay it, and they changed the room numbers to try and cover it up."

"What does she do?" I asked.

"Well, . . . let's see . . . I guess workers have seen flickering lights in her room, a television turning itself on-and-off, strange breezes, . . . hmm . . . scents, sounds, objects moving . . ., doors opening and closing . . . the usual things that people find with ghosts."

"Do you know of specific sightings?" Noreen asked.

"Well, one couple said they felt someone brush against them in their room and later the blankets were ripped right off of the bed while they were sleeping, and they saw this vague female form at the end of the bed. They were told the next day that they had slept in Kate Morgan's room, and they felt certain she had been with them. . . .

Another time, some lady doctor from Minnesota saw a woman in a "period costume" walking down the stairs toward the ocean, and in the darkness this lady turned and looked directly at her, somehow clearly revealing her face through the night over a fairly lengthy distance. Then, the next morning, she saw a picture of Kate Morgan in a brochure at the hotel gift shop and realized it was the woman she had seen the night before. She was certain she had seen Kate Morgan's ghost. . . . You know, standard ghost stories."

"Interesting," I said. "Are there *many* reports? Common?"

"Well, let's see. . . Jennea took a dainty sip of her Raspberry iced tea before continuing her story. "There was a doorman who reported bringing a couple to the room and finding an indentation of a woman in the bed. He tried to smooth the linens out, but found it impossible. This kind of indentation in the bed has actually been a fairly common experience. And reports of guests hearing whispers, and the fan getting turned on or off by itself.

"So there are lots of these experiences?" I asked.

"Yes. Many describe her in detail, and they all seem to see the same dark-haired, good-looking woman wearing a long dress from that time, tight fitting, high collar, expensive. Although there are variations. I've heard of some seeing a blonde girl as well." She shrugged her shoulders and took another sip of tea.

It wasn't an overly busy day at the Del. We were sitting in the Ocean Terrace Lounge, and most of the tables were unused. But we could see through the windows to Promenade Deck and the sand beyond, where a number of people were enjoying the sun, playing volleyball, walking along the large rocks, or just lounging in lawn-chairs with umbrellas. Fortunately, we had large fans slowly turning above us to help keep us cool.

The famous Hotel del Coronado. I wondered--is it possible there is a ghost slipping in-and-out of this historic gathering place of the rich and famous?

If I am to believe in ghosts, then I have to believe in things beyond explanation, beyond what logic and science can explain away. I have to enter into that age-old dialogue about existence, about reality and the possibility that there are many realities. What is real? Is reality only the physical world that I experience with my eyes and my ears, my touch and my taste? My smell? Is the world of the dream anything more than random chemical activity in the brain of a homo sapien that needs to revitalize itself in some kind of biological cycle? Do spirits, souls, doppelgangers, angels--supernatural beings of any kind actually exist? Is it possible to experience a *real* miracle? Or is it all just some kind of trick of the mind? Ultimately, I need to ask if God is nothing more than a desperate creation by humans to give life meaning and value.

After my conversation at the Hotel del Coronado, I looked up what I could find about it's famous ghost. And there most certainly was some woman who was shot there and died. Beyond that, it becomes speculation. And Noreen's mother-in-law was correct. There are a lot of sightings. Some of the others include: On February, 2000, a guest who stayed in the haunted room (#3327), wrote: "Kate Morgan woke us both up with her crying—scary, but interesting!" and subsequently reported receiving calls on his pager from number 3327. In 1993, guests in the room reported the television turning itself on and off and its cabinet doors abruptly closing. In October, 1992, Sharon Whitley stayed in the room, and reported an unused towel becoming rumpled and covered with lipstick, lights flickering, static on the phone line, hearing voices, and a feeling by both her and her friends of someone watching them. Numerous experiences have also been reported in room 3519: Parapsychologist and director of the Office of Scientific Investigation and Research in Los Angeles, Christopher Chacon, used infrared cameras and various other equipment to find 37 abnormalities and designated the room a place of a "classic haunting." In 1992, the *Home Show* filmed a visit and caught an ashtray moving and a glass shattering on tape. In 1883 a Secret Service agent reported loud noise, footsteps, and talking in the room above—only to find out there is no room above. Others have reported unexplained experiences throughout the hotel. Concierge staff have heard muffled conversations and the sounds of a young girl whispering from otherwise empty spaces. One twice saw a "dusty" looking man in late 1940s clothing. A salesperson in the Gift Shop reported books "jumping" off the shelves, a sales sign slammed onto the counter, falling off the wall twice, and another occasion a clock was reported flying off its shelf (in each case, shoppers in the store corroborated the experiences). Another reported postcards and books flying, not falling, but flying off the shelf. In October, 2001, a couple staying in room 3284 reported the television suddenly coming on, changing channels by itself, and seeing six human apparitions dressed in old-fashioned clothes, "all laughing and having a good time." A family staying in room 3343 reported witnessing their mother's strange reflection in the bathroom mirror, her eyes the size of Orphan Annie's and looking like bull's eyes. In 1992, a nine-year-old girl woke up to see a transparent woman in a white nightgown standing near her bed. Another couple reported seeing the ghost of a "beautiful blond girl dressed in layered and tapered cream chiffon," who floated between them in their guestroom.

Those interested in reading up on the Hotel del Coronado and it's ghosts will find the following sources worthwhile: the Heritage Department, Hotel del Coronado, 1500 Orange Avenue, Coronado, CA 92118; the San Diego Historical Society; the San Diego Public Library; the San Diego State University; and Save Our Heritage Organization.

****

On December 29, 1987, Janet Lunn posted a letter to me about the ghosts, both fictional and real, that she was living among in her house, the same house that served as the setting for her novel *The Root Cellar*:

> I love this house. I loved peopling it with the ghosts of Rose, Will, Susan, Sam and the rest. They are good company for the other ghosts—most of whom are only footsteps on the stairs—and have settled very comfortably

> here. The house is as I described it in the book. There is, alas, no root cellar. There was once, of course, but with the barns, drive sheds and other out buildings, it has long since disappeared. My husband said often that we would have to either paint one on the surface of the ground behind the house or dig one, as visiting children have been bitterly disappointed. Also, there is no creek running through the back yard. There is the bay, however, not called Hawthorn Bay. It is Pleasant Bay. This whole area was once called Hawthorn Point, which is why I gave the bay that name. Sadly the Hawthorns are almost all gone now. The last of them suffered terribly three winters ago and are hanging on by a few die-hard branches.

Janet and I had been friends for many years, generally visiting with one-another in a café near some literature conference where we were speaking. In 1988, I drove up into Kitchener, Ontario, where she was the current "writer-in-residence," to visit her. And we corresponded, not by emails, by letters during a time before emails would largely replaced them.

We talked about dualities, reflections, the sense of place and how storytellers supply the invisible essence, the heritage of a landscape. Her book, *Shadow in Hawthorne Bay,* was an expression of just this idea, and within it the idea of the *story* being the transmitter, preserver, and even creator of a tradition, a heritage, a culture. Stories, she would say, form a long conversation handed down from one teller to another, from the old ones to the young ones, and stories carry with them the history, the beliefs, and the life blood of a community. In talking specifically about *Shadow in Hawthorne Bay*, she would point out that the stories in Scotland are old and have gone through many storytellers, that the culture is a mature one. However, she would continue, in Canada, the stories are nonexistent or very new, the culture is young, still waiting for the storytellers, the new old ones, to begin the needed story of its vast, rugged landscape and the people who would struggle to make it their home. That is how she concluded *Shadow in Hawthorne Bay,* having Mary kneel over Duncan's grave and talk to him, to his spirit:

> "It is well, Duncan," she said. "And it will be well, for it is meant to be. It is not the same here for me as it was at home—as it was not the same for you. The burns that rush so swiftly down our hillsides are not the creeks that wander through these deep woods. The high hills are not these low lands and the spirits of our rocks and hills and burns, the old ones who dwell in this unseen world, are not here.
>
> But we are not to grieve. The old ones came to our hills in the ancient times. It began somewhere. It began there long ago as it begins here now. We are the old ones here."

PART I:

EMPATHY

Guilt

I found in the caves of the Unconscious demons and were-wolves, strange faces of forgotten gods, and devils, while my mind played unceasingly on everything it remembered of myths and magic. Folds of bedclothes suddenly became the carven image of Baal; a crumpled pillow appeared as the horrible visage of Hecate. I was transported into an atmosphere of miracle and witchcraft, of all-pervading occult forces, although I had taken no interest whatever in these subjects prior to my illness.

—John Custance, *Wisdom, Madness and Folly*

The Scapegoat

1 Who has believed our report?
  and to whom has the arm of the LORD been revealed?
2 For he shall grow up before him like a tender plant,
  and as a root out of dry ground: he hath no form or comeliness;
  and when we shall see him, there is no beauty that we should desire him.
3 He was despised and rejected of men;
  a man of sorrows, and acquainted with grief.
  and we hide as it were our faces from him;
  he was despised, and we esteemed him not.
4 Surely he hath borne our griefs,
  and carried our sorrows:
  yet we did not esteem him,
  stricken, smitten of God, and afflicted.
5 But he was wounded for our transgressions,
  he was bruised for our iniquities;
  the chastisement of our peace was upon him,
  and with his stripes we are healed.
6 We all, like sheep, have gone astray;
  we have turned every one to his own way;
  and the LORD hath laid on him
  the iniquity of us all.
7 He was oppressed, and he was afflicted,
  yet he opened not his mouth;
  he is brought like a lamb to the slaughter,
  and as a sheep before her shearers is dumb,
  so he openeth not his mouth.
8 He was taken from prison and from judgment:
  and who shall declare his generation?
  for he was cut off out of the land of the living;
  for the transgression of my people was he stricken.
9 And he made his grave with the wicked,
  and with the rich in his death;
  because he had done no violence,
  neither was any deceit in his mouth.
10 Yet it pleased the LORD to bruise him;
  he has put him to grief;
  when thou shalt make his soul an offering for sin,
  he shall see his seed, he shall prolong his days,
  and the pleasure of the Lord shall prosper in his hand...

11 He shall see of the travail of his soul,
and shall be satisfied;
by his knowledge shall my righteous servant justify many,
for he shall bear their iniquities.
12 Therefore will I divide him a portion with the great,
and he shall divide the spoil with the strong;
because he hath poured out his soul unto death;
and he was numbered with the transgressors;
and he bore the sin of many,
and made intercession for the transgressors.

Isaiah 53, *King James Bible* (1)

In *The Ones Who Walk Away from Omelas*, Ursula K. Le Guin presents the reader with a common motif, a community that is festive and happy and without pain or suffering, so long as a few, in this case, one of them lives a life of lonely, horrific torment. (2) She credits the following quote from William James for her inspiration: "If the hypothesis were offered us of a world in which Messrs. Fourier's and Bellamy's and Morris's utopias should all be outdone, and millions be kept permanently happy on the one simple condition that a certain lost soul on the far-off edge of things should lead a life of lonely torment . . . how hideous a thing would be [the enjoyment of this happiness] when deliberately accepted as the fruit of such a bargain." (3) This is the motif of the *scapegoat*, found in such characters as Snowball in George Orwell's *Animal Farm* (4), and Darcy in *Pride and Prejudice.* (5)

Le Guin concludes her story by adding another dimension to this motif, pointing out that "at times one of the adolescent girls or boys who go to see the child does not go home to weep or rage, does not, in fact, go home at all." Instead some of these adolescents, and later she includes some of the older people as well, simply walk away from Omelas, their exposure to the suffering child making their idyllic world no longer desirable. This cannot help but suggest the exit from the most idyllic world of all, Eden, the garden where Adam and Eve lived without the knowledge of good and evil (or of the dual planes of existence—physical and spiritual), a purely childlike innocence without meaning or value. But when given the chance, the temptation to do so, they *knowingly* bite of the forbidden fruit and gain the knowledge of good and evil. This knowledge of something other than pure joy, pure happiness, and pure festival is the fall from innocence into the world of the adult human, a world where meaning and value and the dual planes of visible and invisible exist.

This *realization and acceptance of the horror* of a world without self-responsibility, without ethical sensitivity, without meaning and value is the added silence between the words that touches the reader with the knowledge of both the sorrow and nobility of human existence. "These people go out into the street, and walk down the street alone. They keep walking, and walk straight out of the city of Omelas, through the beautiful gates. They keep walking across the farmlands of Omelas. Each one goes alone, youth or girl, man or woman. Night falls; the traveler must pass down village streets, between the houses with yellow-lit windows, and on out into the darkness of the fields." This indeed is the human journey out of the sunlit world of childhood into the dark, shadowy world of the adult, a world that includes the ultimate unknown darkness of death and the knowledge of our own ignorance. "Each alone, they go west or north, towards the mountains. They go on. They leave Omelas, they walk ahead into the darkness, and they do not come back. The place they go towards is a place even less imaginable to most of us than the city of happiness. I cannot describe it at all." And we all walk with them, at least those of us who have the courage to face the human condition. And what do they or we know about this place they and we walk toward? According to Le Guin, "It is possible that it does not exist." Nonetheless, there is a strange comfort in the concluding sentence, "But they seem to know where they are going, the ones who walk away from Omelas."

William James' point in the passage that inspired Ursula La Guin to write *The Ones Who Walk Away from Omelas* is not just that there is an ethical dimension to the concept of a *scapegoat* but that the *natural* negative response to such a situation is *inborn*, is *innate.* This raises some interesting possibilities in terms of the original humans as represented in the Garden of Eden in *Genesis.* (6) Were they created with *innate* ethical sensitivity? The story suggests that they were not, yet they knew it was *wrong* to disobey God before they disobeyed. Or did they? Maybe it was simply a matter of knowing they would be *punished*, a form of power ethics, which really is no ethics at all, as it is driven by the *instinct* for self-preservation or gratification (depending which side of the equation one is on), common to all living things, and does not involve anything beyond mere physical existence, is actually a denial of meaning and value. If not born or, rather, created with ethical sensitivity, then perhaps Adam and Eve were created with the capacity for it, with some innate ethical organ or brain potential that just needed something to initiate it, to spark it. If so, it is curious that it is Satan who is responsible for this initiation of ethical sensitivity. And God condemns it and condemns humans to lives of hardship and temporality for gaining it. It is also worth noting that ethical existence is gained as the result of curiosity and disobedience (taking on *self-responsibility*—even though both Adam and Eve do try to blame Satan in his guise as the tempter, the snake).

What about a scientific model? The best science has come up with are the ever-changing interpretations of Darwin's theory of evolution, a theory that suggests human ancestry goes back through a chain of mutations or evolutions from some form or forms of pre-human existence. (7) Most paleontologists and archeologists believe that the evolutionary biting of the forbidden fruit occurs, not with the creation of crude tools or weapons (these are meant for their practical, literal value), but with *cave wall paintings*, thus exhibiting a belief in the *invisible world of the mind*, a form of thinking and knowing beyond mere literal, practical existence, for these paintings cannot literally have a practical purpose. Furthermore, it is likely that they were more than mere decoration, especially since they are high on the walls and ceilings of caves that would have had no natural light. They are, in fact, paintings that would have been extremely difficult to execute—needing both some kind of platform to stand on and some kind of lighting, a fire, involving both danger and work for no practical purpose, unless there is a belief that there is some kind of other reality, an invisible reality that interacts with and influences the visible reality. In other words, if the paintings were merely meant to be pretty or some kind of casual doodling, there would be no point in creating them in such an unfriendly environment. The dark, mysterious, underground environment, then, must have suggested feelings of forces beyond the corporeal, sunlit world above ground, and it is very likely the paintings were understood as a means of having influence on the physical world, a means of contacting, of supplicating, satisfying, perhaps worshipping spiritual forces, forces beyond phenomenal existence, most likely meant to help with and justify the killing and eating of the wild beasts they depict. And this assumption is further justified because many of them have been traced over multiple times, suggesting a ritualistic repetition, and the main scenes are of hunting.

France is the landscape. The first to emerge is Altamira. In the 1860s, a poacher on the estate of Senor Don Marcelino Santiago Tomas Sanz de Sautuola followed his dog, which had gotten lost in pursuit of a wounded fox, into a small hole. Within it stretched the huge, painted caves of *the beginnings of human consciousness*. There was no immediate rush to explore and unravel this hidden world. However, a few years later Don Marcelino was made aware of the caves and decided to play at archeology and geology. After having the entrance enlarged, he was able to recover some bone fragments of long extinct animals, which he showed to his friend, Vilanova y Piera, Professor of Geology at the University of Madrid, who confirmed that the bones were from the European Stone Age, and had been split by prehistoric man to extract their marrow.

Again, there was no rush to further explore the caves, but in 1879, Don Marcelino realized that the prehistoric objects on display at the Universal Exhibition of Paris from the Dordogne were of the same materials his own caves held. The next spring, he further explored his caves, discovering among the bones flints that he recognized as belonging to Lartet's Magdelanian Culture, and further back, the bones of a giant bear, some marks on the walls, and what appeared to be the pigment that made them in a shell.

While he was exploring, his daughter Maria with her dog Robot wandered off to entertain herself and discovered a huge cave vault with paintings on the ceiling of a herd of bison. Realizing that these bison were extinct, thus confirming a prehistoric origin of the paintings, Don Marcelino hired an artist to make copies and in 1880 published a scientific monograph on his amazing cave.

However, the initial reaction from the scientific community was one of disbelief and a suggestion that it was all a hoax. Don Marcelino had little interest in taking on the academic community, and his friend Vilanova y Piera was unable to persuade it to reconsider its initial reaction.

It was not until 1895 that French historian Emile Riviere was able to respark interest. He noticed that the markings in Don Marcelino's caves matched those found in a Dardogne cave, La Mouthe, that had been unopened until its excavation, thus, giving it a stronger proof against tampering, and a new rush of archeology began to discover and open up other similar caves. The only caves of these new ones to emerge on as grand a scale as Altamira were the caves at Lascaux (coincidentally, once again, discovered as the result of following a dog).

Now the evidence was overwhelming, and the scientific community had to accept the artistic imagination of these early humans. (8)

Jacob Bronowski, in attempting to comprehend these cave wall paintings, to make sense out of why these early humans would bother to go to such extremes, writes,

> The cave paintings act as a kind of telescope tube of the imagination: they direct the mind from what is seen to what can be inferred or conjectured. Indeed, this is so in the very action of painting; for all its superb observation, the flat picture only means something to the eye because the mind fills it out with roundness and movement, a reality by inference, which is not actually seen but is imagined. (9)

Joseph Campbell calls them temple caves, for "a temple is a landscape of the soul." He explains,

> When you walk into a cathedral, you move into a world of spiritual images. It is the mother womb of your spiritual life—mother church. All the forms around are significant of spiritual value. Now, in a cathedral, the imagery is in anthropomorphic form. God and Jesus and the saints and all are in human form. And in the caves the images are in animal form. But it's the same thing, believe me. . . . The message of the caves is of a relationship of time to eternal powers that is somehow to be experienced in that place. (10)

Furthermore, he elaborates,

> If a *differentiating* feature is to be named, separating human from animal psychology, it is surely this of the subordination in the human sphere of even economics to mythology. And if one should ask why or how any such unsubstantial impulsion ever should have become dominant in the ordering of physical life, the answer is that in this wonderful human brain of ours there has dawned a realization unknown to the other primates. It is that of the individual, conscious of himself as such, and aware that he, and all that he cares for, will one day die. (11)

Rollo May writes:

> It is absurd to think of artists simply as "painting nature," as though they were only anachronistic photographers of trees and lakes and mountains. For them, nature is a medium, a language by which they reveal their world. What genuine painters do is to reveal the underlying psychological and spiritual conditions of their relationship to their world . . . For in the art the underlying spiritual meaning of the period is expressed directly in symbols. This is not because artists are didactic or set out to teach or to make propaganda; to the extent that they do, their power of expression is broken; their direct relation to the inarticulate, or, if you will, "unconscious" levels of the culture is destroyed. They have the power to reveal the underlying meaning of any period precisely because the essence of art is the powerful and alive encounter between the artist and his or her world. (12)

Several intertwining aspects of existence and of human existence are at play here, all of them ultimately resulting from a realization of duality, of *self* and *other*. In the Garden of Eden story, the realization of duality includes an *ethical* dimension (involves biting the forbidden fruit from the tree of *the knowledge of good and evil*). It also involves going against the *other* (in this case God), which, if one considers it, is the only way of establishing *self*, of being an individual, because anything in existence that never thinks for itself, never makes a decision, cannot be separate from whatever is determining its existence. It also involves *curiosity*, the desire to know that which is *forbidden*, even though it is said to be dangerous, horrifying, and harmful. Thus, the desire to *know*, the drive to *knowledge* is more powerful than the fear of even death. Again, if one considers it, this must be the case, for *self* can only exist if there is also *non-self* or *non-existence*—the *birth of consciousness, self-realization*, then must also be the birth of death. Knowledge and oblivion are necessary companions.

This also demands dual worlds, dual realities, the reality of the body and the reality of that which is beyond the body, the natural world and the supernatural world. Humans, then, experience both the reality of the brain (the natural, physical body organ) and mind (the ephemeral supernatural world that goes beyond the limitations of the body; in the mind one can travel through time and space even to future events that have never happened and will never happen in the natural world of the body—yet they still *exist*, and their existence is more important than the natural existence of the body).

> At first
> Senseless as beasts I gave men sense, possessed them of
> mind . . .
> In the beginning, seeing, they saw amiss, and hearing,
> heard not,
> but like phantoms huddled
> In dreams, the perplexed story of their days
> Confounded.
>
> Aeschylus (13)

This is a central passage from Aeschylus' tragedy about the myth of Prometheus stealing fire from the gods and giving it to humans, providing a common interpretation of it as an expression of the passing on of knowledge and independence to humans (the birth of human consciousness). Rollo May writes:

> The Greek myth closest to the story of Adam is that of Prometheus, who stole Fire from the gods and gave it to human beings for their warmth and productivity. The enraged Zeus, noting one night from a glow on earth that the mortals had fire, seized Prometheus, bore him off to the Caucasus, and chained him to a mountain peak. The torture devised by Zeus' skillful imagination was to have a vulture feast by day on Prometheus' liver, and then, when the liver had grown back during night, the vulture would tear at it again the next day, thus ensuring perpetual torment for the pathless Prometheus. (14)

Fire symbolizes enlightenment (sentience, self awareness, knowledge) and power, a means of controlling nature (thus, the birth of consciousness, and the control over the physical world through consciousness). This is a dramatic, violent transformation, a birth of light out of darkness. It was thought in Greek culture that the liver was the organ where consciousness existed, thus the night, symbolic of the other world (the world of the dream and existence beyond the sunlit world of the body) is the time when it makes sense for the liver to grow back. Rollo May continues:

> So far as punishment goes, Zeus had an edge over Yahweh in cruelty. For the Greek god, smoldering in anger that man should now have fire, crammed all the diseases, sorrows and vices into a box in the form of moth-like creatures, and had Mercury take the box to the earthly paradise (very much like the Garden of Eden) in which Pandora and Epimetheus lived in untroubled happiness. When the curious woman opened it, out flew the creatures, and mankind was visited with these never-ending afflictions. These demonic elements in the gods' dealings with man certainly do not present a pretty picture. (15)

This is the same consequence as that suffered by Adam and Eve; the birth of consciousness includes the knowledge of separation, and sets in motion the differentiation, the existence of two realities, one natural, the other supernatural. And humans exist in both.

And this is the key, the two realities intersecting in the human brain/mind (body/spirit or soul). *Bodhi* is a Sanskrit term that means to be enlightened or awakened, and is the basis for Siddhartha's new name *Buddha* (the enlightened one) upon his awakening to a higher consciousness. It is similarly used in Christian mysticism to convey the saint's condition of being lit by a higher power--the merging of the human and the divine in *theosis*. Interestingly, in Eastern Christian theology, it is this merging of the divine (of the spirit, the supernatural) and the human (physical, natural), this complimentary unity of the creator and the created that leads to self-realization, the realization of the self, once again placing humans in the role of existing in both natural and supernatural worlds.

This, in turn connects self realization with creativity. Rollo May concludes his comparison of the Garden of Eden and the Prometheus myth with this wrinkle:

> As the Adam story is the myth of self-consciousness, Prometheus is the symbol of creativity--the bringing of new ways of life to mankind. (16)

Since self-consciousness involves separation, involves thinking for oneself instead of passive obedience to directives from another, it must, then, also involve creativity, the bringing of something different into existence, the birthing of a new idea, a new way of seeing, of living, of understanding existence itself. On a psychological development chart, the distinguishing factor between a child and an adult might be said to be when a person goes from psychological obedience, submission, dependency on others to taking self-responsibility, thinking for one-self. As a child, we learn the truths that our culture lives by, whether they be ethical, spiritual, or simply practical. But, as an adult, we must question those truths, must decide as individuals if we agree with them or want to attempt to change them. If so, then we are taking part in change, which is the term for bringing something new into existence. In this sense, then, we become creators. And in the myth of Prometheus stealing the fire of the gods and giving it to humans, it might be said that fire becomes the symbol of creativity.

While the Christian Garden of Eden story might focus on self-consciousness, it cannot avoid the connection of self-consciousness with creativity. For, even if it is God who forces Adam and Eve out of the Garden, by discovering their own uniqueness, they have already exited it.

In *The Giver*, Lois Lowry expands on the idea of the *scapegoat*. (17) Here the *scapegoat* comes in the position of the *Receiver*, a person selected to take in all of the suffering of the community, to take in, in truth, all of the impractical feelings and traditions and history of the community, so that the rest might live lives without pain or sorrow. The *Receiver's* role is not as demeaning as the "imbecilic" child in Omelas, much the opposite, the *Receiver's* job "is the most honored" in the community; but it is one filled with taking on the pain and suffering of others. Interestingly, it is in some ways a reversal, because the *receiver* is the wise person trying to absorb all of the knowledge of good and evil into himself so that the community can return to a Garden of Eden existence, and *not have to take responsibility* for making difficult decisions.

At one point Jonas, the *Receiver in Training* asks the current *Receiver* (now designated the *Giver*) "'why can't *everyone* have the memories? I think it would seem a little easier if the memories were shared. You and I wouldn't have to bear so much by ourselves, if everybody took a part.' The Giver sighed. 'You're right,' he said. 'But then everyone would be burdened and pained. They don't want that. And that's the real reason The Receiver is so vital to them, and so honored. They selected me—and you—to lift that burden from themselves.'" (18)

In truth, all of the community other than the *Receiver* live lives of childhood innocence and obedience; and if they break a rule, there are strict punishments in place, including public humiliation and the often used final *release* (a euphemism for killed—though the people other than the *Committee of the Elders* and the *Receiver* do not realize this, wondering just where people go who are *released*, similar to a child's inability to understand death). There is *no self-responsibility,* and anyone inadvertently taking on the hint of self-responsibility is immediately punished. It is obedience that is desired, *not free will.* The closest thing to *free will* is a period of time called the *volunteer* hours, time set aside for children from eight to twelve to choose where to volunteer—the purpose being to demonstrate to the council of elders what roles to assign children for their adult lives at the *Ceremony of Twelve,* which marks the end of childhood and the beginning of adulthood; and the idea here is that the children will choose tasks that fit the abilities they have been born with, thus the choice is not so much a choice as a predetermined ability (at least in theory); if a child should choose tasks that don't suit the child's best abilities, the *Committee of the Elders* will force the child into the occupation that best suits it, or the child/adult will disappear (here there are suggestions of either release or escaping to other communities).

Sexual desire is eliminated through the use of pills. Once children reach the age when they begin experiencing the *stirrings*, indicated by *sexual dreams* (and it is required that all reveal any dreams they have in what amount to family confessions every evening), the pills are introduced, and are taken until old age, when the stirrings no longer occur. Instead of sex and the entire emotional trauma of it driving procreation, certain women, *birthmothers* are assigned the role of birthing children. They are treated the way breading stock would be treated, taken into the *Birthing Center* for three years, during which time they are impregnated three times, and then they become Laborers for the rest of their lives, until they enter the House of the Old. And it is clear they are looked down upon by the rest of the community. Furthermore, it is clear that the desired qualities of a birthmother are those of Inger, chosen to be one—she "was a nice girl though somewhat lazy, and her body was strong." (19). In other words, this form of selective breeding values physical strength over intelligence and initiative.

It reminds me of H. G. Wells' Eloi, a society of small, elegant, androgynous, and very childlike people in his book *The Time Machine.* They do no work, have no curiosity, live off of the abundant plants that surround them, and every so often disappear. They are simply stock for the Morlocks, an apelike people living underground and running the machinery that provides the *paradise* for the herds of livestock (the Eloi) living above ground.

The children the women in *The Giver* birth are then assigned to families, one boy and one girl to each. The elders name the children and make the assignments. The parents have no say. They simply apply for a child, and one is chosen for them. In truth, the parents have little say in whom they marry. While it is true they apply to the committee for a desired mate, it is the committee that decides. Interestingly, when Jonas is given the memories, the sense of *love* from the *Giver* he throws away his pills.

Each year in December (an appropriately symbolic month, as it is the month of the winter solstice, which is the time when the days reach the end (or death) of becoming shorter and the beginning (or birth) of becoming longer (the reason December is the final month of the year; the same reason Christ's birth takes place when it does), *The Ceremony of Twelve* takes place. Actually, it's a two-day ceremony that works its way slowly through all of the children one age at a time, cumulating in the final age, the age of what might be called the *coming of age*, twelve, when the children are given their assignments in life, determined by the *Committee of Elders*, and are put into whatever training program is required for their adult professions, or more correctly, since their professions are connected to their entire lives, their adult lives.

Jonas is the child the book focuses on. There are two early indications that Jonas is unique, his very unusual blue eyes, eyes that seem to have more "depth" to them, and an experience he has of "seeing" an apple differently while he is playing catch with it. Then comes his moment at *The Ceremony of Twelve*, his turn to be given his life's occupation, and we find out that he has been chosen to be the next *Receiver*. It is at this moment that the Chief Elder lists for us the qualities a *Receiver* must have:

> *"Intelligence,"* she said. "We are all aware that Jonas has been a top student throughout his school days.
>
> *"Integrity,"* she said next. "Jonas has, like all of us, committed minor transgressions." She smiled at him. "We expect that. We hoped, also, that he would present himself promptly for chastisement, and he has always done so.
>
> *"Courage,"* she went on. "Only one of us here today has ever undergone the rigorous training required of a Receiver. He, of course, is the most important member of the Committee: the current Receiver. It was he who reminded us, again and again, of the courage required.
>
> "Jonas," she said, turning to him, but speaking in a voice that the entire community could hear, "the training required of you involves pain. Physical pain.
>
> He felt fear flutter within him.

"You have never experienced that. Yes, you have scraped your knees in falls from your bicycle. Yes, you crushed your finger in a door last year."

Jonas nodded, agreeing, as he recalled the incident, and its accompanying misery.

"But you will be faced, now," she explained gently, "with pain of a magnitude that none of us here can comprehend because it is beyond our experience. The Receiver himself was not able to describe it, only to remind us that you would be faced with it, that you would need immense courage. We cannot prepare you for that.

"But we feel certain that you are brave," she said to him.

He did not feel brave at all. Not now.

"The fourth essential attribute," the chief Elder said, "is *wisdom.* Jonas has not yet acquired that. The acquisition of wisdom will come through his training.

"We are convinced that Jonas has the ability to acquire wisdom. That is what we looked for.

"Finally, The Receiver must have one more quality, and it is one which I can only name, but not describe. I do not understand it. You members of the community will not understand it, either. Perhaps Jonas will, because the current Receiver has told us that Jonas already has this quality. He calls it the Capacity to See Beyond." (20)

Here the *scapegoat* clearly becomes the person capable of connecting the two realities, that of physical existence and that of spiritual existence (natural and supernatural); and partakes of the same qualities as those of the *psychic,* the *artist,* the *shaman*, and the *savior.* And though Jonas is afraid and wants to deny his chosen role, he remembers his experience with the apple and knows he indeed has the capacity to experience something beyond explanation, something the other members of the community cannot experience or truly comprehend, knows he has the *capacity to see beyond.*

It is also important that "the Receiver-in-training cannot be observed, cannot be modified. That is stated quite clearly in the rules. He is to be alone, apart, while he is prepared by the current Receiver for the job." (21) This *separateness,* it has already been indicated, is not just during training, and the current *Receiver* has already been depicted sitting among the Elders, but even in their midst "seemed oddly separate from them." (22) It is even more emphasized in Jonas' immediate psychological response: "Now for the first time in his twelve years of life, Jonas felt separate, different. He remembered what the Chief Elder had said: that his training would be alone and apart. But his training had not yet begun and already, upon leaving the Auditorium, he felt the apartness." (23) Later he will find that the *Receiver* is actually in a room with a *lock* on it to keep others out.

This separation, this apartness, this feeling of being different, of being outside the community is a key element of a *scapegoat*. There is an uneasy *forbidden* quality about a *scapegoat*, a combination of respect and disgust. As Jonas is told when he asks about a previous Receiver in training who failed, "we are never to speak the name, or to use it again for a new child. Jonas was shocked. A name designated Not-to-Be-Spoken indicated the highest degree of disgrace." (24) And when he asks what happened to her, he is told "uncomfortably" that no one knows. Yet, his mother ends the conversation, "You've been greatly honored, Jonas. Greatly honored." (25)

And upon opening his folder, the folder prepared especially for the *Receiver*, he and the reader discover that the rules he will now be expected to obey are separate from those for the rest of the community, again emphasizing his *other* status. The first two prevent him from socializing with the others: 1. Go immediately at the end of school hours each day to the Annex entrance behind the House of the Old and present yourself to the attendant; 2. Go immediately to your dwelling at the conclusion of Training Hours each day. The third one gives him the option to be "rude," something he and all of the other members of the community have been strictly trained never to be, and to question any other person in the community about anything and expect an answer. The fourth prohibits him from discussing his training with anyone else. The fifth prohibits him from dream-telling (suggesting that his new position will involve dreams, even though he has not been prone to them so far in his life). The sixth is also a foreshadowing; it says he cannot apply for medication for any illness or injury related to his training (the constant references to his training being painful and perhaps too much for him to handle suggest the "tests" required of a standard "hero's adventure"; higher levels of knowing, of wisdom, of spirituality must be *earned*). The seventh rule says he cannot apply for release (again suggesting that he might want to because the training will be so difficult). And the eighth and final rule says he *can* lie (an interesting reversal of demands for honesty the rest of the community must obey).

I have not been complete in my designation of Jonas' position; the complete title is *The Receiver of Memories*, and Jonas is told upon his first meeting with his predecessor that the *memories* are not just his own personal *memories*, but they are the *memories* of the entire world (it is no coincidence and perhaps even heavy-handed that the Receiver's room is walled with books, hundreds of books that are forbidden to all of the other members of the community—suggesting the same connections of books to thinking and knowing and individuality, and the desire of the community to prevent that as Ray Bradbury's *Fahrenheit 451*). (26)

The Giver also connects *memory* to *wisdom*. The *Receiver,* now the *Giver*, says: "When you receive the memories. You have the capacity to see beyond. You'll gain wisdom, then, along with colors." (27) And as Jonas is introduced to painful memories and asks why it is necessary to experience them, the *Giver* explains *that painful memories are necessary to gain wisdom*. Furthermore, the Giver says: "Oh, your instructors are well trained. They know their scientific facts. Everyone is well trained from his job. It's just that . . . without the memories it's all meaningless." (28) At another point he says, "You do understand, don't you, that this *is* my life? The memories?" (29)

Another quality attached to gaining the ability to see colors (and to have wisdom) is the ability to choose, the opposite of the Sameness the community embraces: as Jonas says, "If everything's the same, then there aren't any choices! I want to wake up in the morning and *decide* things! (30) But, as the *Giver* points out, the problem with having the ability, the right to make a *choice* is that one might make the wrong choice—it is "not safe."

Jonas' first lesson when he begins his training and first meets the current *Receiver* consists of the *Receiver* transmitting the sensation of sliding down a snow covered hill, and it is done through touch, done *inexplicably*, and the mythic, the spiritual, the super-natural connection is assumed. In other words, the physical, scientific, natural truths are broken. The *Receiver* is the one capable of making this connection! A *scapegoat*, then, is a person capable of escaping or transcending the natural laws, the laws of nature.

In the end, Jonas takes Gabriel, a baby scheduled to be released, and escapes the community, letting loose all of the memories he holds back on this community, and suggesting that even though memories can be both painful and dangerous, it is better to have them than to live meaningless lives that do not know love or the sorrows of infanticide and euthanasia. Just as we feel it is right and good when some of the inhabitants of Omalas walk away from their bright, happy, festival world into a dark, unknown world that includes sorrow, suffering and death, we join with Jonas in his escape, even if it might be to his death, and we want the community to have to face its own memories, to have to take up the burdens it has avoided for so long. The *scapegoat* in both cases has been a means of avoiding taking self-responsibility, a way to remain in the innocent, meaningless, boring world of the child.

Shirley Jackson's *The Lottery*, published in *The New Yorker*, June 26, 1948, contrasts the commonplace activities of a contemporary rural village in America with an annual rite known as the lottery. (31) No one in the village remembers the reason for this lottery, but there is a strong suggestion that at one time it was meant to be a fertility rite, to insure the crops will grow. On June 27, the adults assemble for the annual event and the children began gathering stones. The head of each family draws a small slip of paper. Bill Hutchinson gets the one with the black spot, meaning his family has been chosen. Then each member of his family draws a slip, and it's his wife, Tessie, who gets the mark. The ritual then demands that she be stoned to death by the rest of the village. Here the *scapegoat* has no special qualities, good or bad, but is simply chosen the result of *fate*.

Though there are some in the village who are beginning to question the ritual, on the whole it is simply done without question based on a tradition so strong that it no longer even needs a reason or justification and has passed from the realm of sacrifice into one of blindly following a meaningless and thus horrific tradition.

The rubric *scapegoat* comes from the Biblical story of Yom Kippur (Day of Atonement) related in Leviticus 16. According to Jewish tradition, God inscribes each person's fate for the coming year into a "book" on Rosh Hashanah, and waits until Yom Kippur to "seal" the verdict. During the Days of Awe, a Jew tries to amend his or her behavior and seek forgiveness for wrongs done against God (*bein adam leMakom*) and against other human beings (*bein adam lechavero*). The evening and day of Yom Kippur are set aside for public and private petitions and confessions of guilt (*Vidui*). At the end of Yom Kippur, one considers one's self absolved by God. This ritual of atonement and repentance involves the sacrificing of a goat, a *scapegoat*:

> 16:1 And the Lord spake unto Moses after the death of the two sons of Aaron, when they offered before the Lord and died;
> 16:2 And the Lord said unto Moses, Speak unto Aaron thy brother, that he come not at all time into the holy place within the vial before the mercy seat, which is upon the ark; that he die not: for I will appear in the cloud upon the mercy seat.
> 16:3 Thus shall Aaron come into the holy place: with a young bullock for a sin offering and a ram for a burnt offering.
> 16:4 He shall put on the holy linen coat, and he shall have the linen breeches upon his flesh, and shall be girded with a linen girdle, and

with the linen mitre shall he be attired: these are holy garments; therefore shall he wash his flesh in water, and so put them on.
16:5 And he shall take of the congregation of the children of Israel two kids of the goats for a sin offering, and one ram for a burnt offering.
16:6 And Aaron shall offer bullock of the sin offering, which is for himself, and make an atonement for himself, and for his house.
16:7 And he shall take the two goats, and present them before the Lord at the door of the tabernacle of the congregation.
16:8 And Aaron shall cast lots upon the two goats; one for the Lord, and the other lot for the scapegoat.
16:9 And Aaron shall bring the goat upon which the Lord's lot fell, and offer him for a sin offering.
16:10 But the goat, on which the lot fell to be the scapegoat, shall be presented alive before the Lord, to make atonement with him, and to let him go for a scapegoat into the wilderness.
16:11 And Aaron shall bring the bullock of the sin offering, which is for himself, and shall make an atonement for himself, and for his house, and shall kill the bullock of the sin offering which is for himself.
16:12 And he shall take a censor full of burning coals of fire from off the altar before the Lord, and his hands full of sweet incense beaten small, and bring it within the vail:
16:13 And he shall put the incense upon the fire before the Lord, that the cloud of the incense may cover the mercy seat that is upon the testimony, that he die not:
16:14 and he shall take of the blood of the bullock, and sprinkle it with his finger upon the mercy seat eastward; and before the mercy seat shall he sprinkle of the blood with his finger seven times.
16:15 Then shall he kill the goat of the sin offering, that is for the people, and bring his blood within the vail, and do with that blood as he did with the blood of the bullock, and sprinkle it upon the mercy seat, and before the mercy seat:
16:16 And he shall make an atonement for the holy place, because of the uncleanness of the children of Israel, and because of their transgressions in all their sins: and so shall he do for the tabernacle of the congregation, that remaineth among them in the midst of their uncleanness.
16:17 And there shall be no man in the tabernacle of the congregation when he goeth in to make an atonement in the holy place, until he

come out, and have made an atonement for himself, and for his household, and for all the congregation of Israel.
16:18 And he shall go out unto the altar that is before the Lord, and make an atonement for it; and shall take of the blood of the bullock, and of the blood of the goat, and put it upon the horns of the altar round about.
16:19 and he shall sprinkle of the blood upon it with his finger seven times, and cleanse it, and hallow it from the uncleanness of the children of Israel.
16:20 And when he hath made an end of reconciling the holy place, and the tabernacle of the congregation, and the altar, he shall bring the liver goat:
16:21 And Aaron shall lay both his hands upon the head of the live goat, and confess over him all the iniquities of the children of Israel, and all their transgressions in all their sins, putting them upon the head of the goat, and shall send him away by the hand of a fit man into the wilderness:
16:22 And the goat shall bear upon him all their iniquities unto a land not inhabited: and he shall let go the goat in the wilderness.
16:23 And Aaron shall come into the tabernacle of the congregation, and shall put off the linen garments, which he put on when he went into the holy place, and shall leave them there:
16:24 And he shall wash his flesh with water in the holy place, and put on his garments, and come forth, and offer his burnt offering, and the burnt offering of the people, and make an atonement for himself, and for the people.
16:25 And the fat of the sin offering shall he burn upon the altar.
16:26 And he that let go the goat for the scapegoat shall wash his clothes, and bathe his flesh in water, and afterward come into the camp.
16:27 And the bullock for the sin offering, and the goat for the sin offering, whose blood was brought in to make atonement in the holy place, shall one carry forth without the camp; and they shall burn in the fire their skins, and their flesh, and their dung.
16:28 and he that burneth them shall wash his clothes, and bathe his flesh in water, and afterward he shall come into the camp.
19:29 And this shall be a statute forever unto you: that in the seventh month, on the tenth day of the month, ye shall afflict your souls, and do no work at all, whether it be one of your own country, or a stranger that sojourneth among you:

> 16:30 For on that day shall the priest make an atonement for you, to cleanse you, that ye may be clean from all your sins before the Lord.
> 16:31 I shall be a sabbath of rest unto you, and ye shall afflict your souls, by a statue forever.
> 16:32 And the priest, whom he shall anoint, and whom he shall consecrate to minister in the priest's office in his father's stead, shall make the atonement, and shall put on the linen clothes, even the holy garments:
> 16:33 And he shall make an atonement for the holy sanctuary, and he shall make an atonement for the tabernacle of the congregation, and for the altar, and he shall make an atonement for the priests, and for all the people of the congregation.
> 16:34 And this shall be an everlasting statute unto you, to make an atonement for the children of Israel for all their sins once a year. And he did as the Lord commanded Moses. (32)

The ritual based on this Biblical passage goes as follows: Two goats are procured, similar in respect of appearance, height, cost, and time of selection. With one of these on his right and the other on his left, the high priest, who is assisted in this rite by two subordinates, puts both his hands into a wooden case, and takes out two pieces of paper, one inscribed "for Yahweh" and the other "for Azazel." The high priest then lays his hands with the papers upon the two goats and says, "A sin-offering to Yahweh"; and the two men accompanying him reply, "Blessed be the name of His glorious kingdom forever and ever." He then fastens a scarlet woolen thread to the head of the goat "for Azazel"; and laying his hands upon it again, recites the following confession of sin and prayer for forgiveness: "O Lord, I have acted iniquitously, trespassed, sinned before Thee: I, my household, and the sons of Aaron Thy holy ones. O Lord, forgive the iniquities, transgressions, and sins that I, my household, and Aaron's children, Thy holy people, committed before Thee, as is written in the law of Moses, Thy servant, 'for on this day He will forgive you, to cleanse you from all your sins before the Lord; ye shall be clean.'" This prayer is responded to by the congregation present. A man is selected, preferably a priest, to take the goat to the precipice in the wilderness; and he is accompanied part of the way by the most eminent men of Jerusalem. Ten booths have been constructed at intervals along the road leading from Jerusalem to the steep mountain. At each one of these the man leading the goat is formally offered food and drink, which he refuses. When he reaches the tenth booth those who accompany him proceed no further, but watch the ceremony from a distance. When he comes to the precipice he divides the scarlet thread into two parts, one of which he ties to the rock and the other to the goat's horns, and then pushes the goat down. The cliff is so high and rugged that before the goat has traversed half the distance to the plain below, its limbs are utterly shattered. Men are stationed at intervals along the way, and as soon as the goat is thrown down the precipice, they signal to one another by means of kerchiefs or flags, until the information reaches the high priest, whereat he proceeds with the other parts of the ritual.

The scarlet thread is symbolically referenced in Isaiah 1:18:

> 1:18 Come now, and let us reason together, saith the Lord: though your sins be as scarlet, they shall be as white as snow; though they be red like crimson, they shall be as wool. (33)

The *Talmud* states that during the forty years that Simon the Just was high priest, the thread actually turned white as soon as the goat was thrown over the precipice: a sign that the sins of the people are forgiven. In later times the change to white was not invariable: a proof of the people's moral and spiritual deterioration that was gradually on the increase, until forty years before the destruction of the Second Temple, when the change of color was no longer observed.

Azazel is a puzzle. In one etymology, it is a combination of *azaz* (rugged) and *el* (strong, powerful, of God). In this sense it is used to refer to a mountain, the strongest of mountains, and in this sense for the Jews to use it to refer to the large, rugged mountain the scapegoat was thrown down.

Another possible etymology suggests the word is the combination of Uza and Azael, two of the fallen angels referenced in Genesis, 6:2, 4:

> 6:2 That the sons of God [angels] saw the daughters of men that they were fair; and they took them wives of all which they chose. . . .
> 6:4 There were giants in the earth in those days; and also after that, when the sons of God [angels] came in unto the daughters of men, and they bare children to them . . . (34)

If this is correct, then the sacrifice of the goat atones for the sin of fornication, of which these angels were guilty, and then by extension for any sin.

> And Azazel taught men to make swords and knives and shields and breastplates; and made known to them the metals [of the earth] and the art of working them; and bracelets and ornaments; and the use of antimony

> and the beautifying of the eyelids; and all kinds of costly stones and all colouring tinctures. And there arose much godlessness, and they committed fornication, and they were led astray and became corrupt in all their ways. (35)

Many contemporary scholars believe the idea suggested by Abraham Ibn Ezra (1089-1164) and stated by Nachmanides (1194-1270) that Azazel is a *se'irim*, a goat-like spirit, one of the *jinn* that haunt the desert, to which the Israelites often offered sacrifice. Thus, instead of recognizing Azazel as a deity, the sending of the goat was (as stated by Nachmanides) a symbolic expression of the idea that the people's sins and their evil consequences were to be sent back to the spirit of desolation and ruin, the source of all impurity. The fact that the two goats were presented to God before the one was sacrificed and the other sent into the wilderness, was proof that Azazel was not ranked with God, but regarded simply as the personification of wickedness in contrast with the righteous government of God. The rite, resembling, on the one hand, the sending off of the epha (about a bushel of hay) with the woman embodying wickedness in its midst to the land of Shinar in the vision of Zachariah (36), and, on the other, the letting loose of the living bird into the open field in the case of the leper healed from the plague (37), was, indeed, viewed by the people of Jerusalem as a means of ridding themselves of the sins of the year. In the same sense, the crowd, called Babylonians or Alexandrians, pull the goat's hair to make it hasten forth, carrying the burden of sins away with it (38), and the arrival of the shattered animal at the bottom of the valley of the rock of Bet Ḥadudo, twelve miles away from the city, was signalized by the waving of shawls to the people of Jerusalem, who celebrated the event with boisterous hilarity and amid dancing on the hills (39). Evidently the figure of Azazel was an object of general fear and awe rather than, as has been conjectured, a foreign product or the invention of a late lawgiver. More as a demon of the desert, it seems to have been closely interwoven with the mountainous region of Jerusalem.

This is supported in the *Book of Enoch*, which brings Azazel into connection with the Biblical story of the fall of the angels, located on Mount Hermon, a gathering-place of demons (40). Azazel is represented in the *Book of Enoch* as one of the leaders of the rebellious Watchers in the time preceding the flood; he taught men the art of warfare, of making swords, knives, shields, and coats of mail, and women the art of deception by ornamenting the body, dyeing the hair, and painting the face and the eyebrows, and also revealed to the people the secrets of witchcraft and corrupted their manners, leading them into wickedness and impurity; until at last he was, at the Lord's command, bound hand and foot by the archangel Raphael and chained to the rough and jagged rocks of Ha Duduael (Beth Ḥadudo), where he is to abide in utter darkness until the great Day of Judgment, when he will be cast into the fire to be consumed forever (41).

The story of Azazel as the seducer of men and women was also familiar to the rabbis, as may be learned from Tanna d. b. R. Yishma'el: "The Azazel goat was to atone for the wicked deeds of Uza and Azazel, the leaders of the rebellious hosts in the time of Enoch" (42).

Since Azazel occupied a place in Mandæan, Sabean, and Arabian mythology (43) renders it probable that Azazel was a degraded Babylonian deity. Origen (44) identifies Azazel with Satan (45); with Samael; and the Zohar Aḥare Mot, following Naḥmanides, with the spirit of Esau or heathenism; still, while one of the chief demons in the Cabala, he never attained in the doctrinal system of Judaism a position similar to that of Satan.- (46) by which Sulamith administers an oath to the daughters of Jerusalem. The critics were probably thinking of a Roman faun. Since this goat, carrying the sins of the people placed on it, is sent away to perish, *"scapegoat" has come to mean a person, often innocent, who is blamed and punished for the sins, crimes, or sufferings of others, generally as a way of distracting attention from the real causes.*

In Christian theology, the story of the *scapegoat* in Leviticus is interpreted as a symbolic prefiguration of the self-sacrifice of Jesus, who takes the sins of humanity on himself, having been driven into the 'wilderness' outside the city by order of the high priests. (47) Christianity, then, slides the notion of the *scapegoat* into a doctrine of *atonement* in its stress that Jesus died not just to *absorb* but to *atone* for the sins of mankind. Christian doctrine has, in turn, developed three major theories of how *atonement* might work. The first of these was put for by the early Church, especially by Origen (48), and claims that the crucifixion of Christ was a *ransom*, most commonly a *ransom* paid to Satan to satisfy his claim on the souls of humanity resulting from the first sin by Adam and Eve, which could only be absolved through a *ransom* paid to the Devil to free human souls. In this view, God tricks Satan by using his own son Christ, who is able to escape death into life everlasting. Once Satan accepts Christ's death as ransom, justice is satisfied, and God is able to free humans from Satan's hold. In this case, *redemption* is a form of exchange, of buying back. It is supported by such passages from the Bible as Mark 10:45; "For even the Son of Man did not come to be served, but to serve, and to give his life as a ransom for many" (49); and 1 Timothy 2:5-6; "For there is one God and one mediator between God and men, the man

Christ Jesus, who gave himself as a ransom for all men—the testimony given in its proper time." (50)

The second theory, coming mainly from Anselm of Canterbury and traditionally taught in Catholic, Lutheran, and Reformed churches, claims that the crucifixion of Christ was a *satisfaction*--a restitution, a mending of what has been broken, a payback for what was taken, a balancing out of an injustice. In this view, Christ's death is a substitute for the sins of mankind, according to Thomas Aquinas and John Calvin, a punishment meant to satisfy the demands of divine justice.

The word *atonement* does not appear in the *Authorized Version of the New Testament* except in Romans 5:11, where in the *Revised Version* the word *reconciliation* is used. (51) It does, however, appear a great deal in the *Old Testament*, meaning *at-one-ment*, i.e., the state of being *at one* or being *reconciled*, so that *atonement is reconciliation*. On the one hand, it can mean the result or effect of Christ's death (in which case it would lead to the third view); but the word is also used to denote how this *reconciliation* is brought about-- the death of Christ itself; and in this sense it means *satisfaction*-- to make an *atonement* is to make *satisfaction* for offences (52), and, in terms of the human race, to *reconcile*, to propitiate God in its behalf, to *sacrifice* one-self for all humans, to be a *scapegoat* so that they might be freed from sin.

Christ, then, *rectifies* the disturbed relations between God and man, removing the separation caused by the original sin so that reconciliation is possible. The reconciliation is mutual, not only that of sinners toward God, but also that of God toward sinners, affected by the sin-offering he himself provided, so that consistently with the other attributes of his character his love might flow forth in all its fullness. The primary idea presented to us in different forms throughout the Scripture is that the death of Christ is a *satisfaction* of infinite worth rendered to the law and justice of God, and accepted by him in place of the very penalty man had incurred. It must also be constantly kept in mind that the *atonement* is not the cause but the consequence of God's love to guilty men (53). The *atonement* may also be regarded as necessary, not in an absolute but in a relative sense, i.e., if man is to be saved, there is no other way than this which God has devised and carried out (54). This is God's plan, clearly revealed; and that is enough for us to know.

The third theory, coming from early Christianity and the teachings of St. Augustine, and put forth by Peter Abelard and Hastings Rashdall, claims that the crucifixion of Christ was a *moral influence*, an act of exemplary obedience meant to affect those who were informed of it. Joseph Campbell explains:

> Abelard's idea was that Christ came to be crucified to evoke in man's heart the sentiment of compassion for the suffering of life, and so to remove man's mind from blind commitment to the goods of this world. It is in compassion with Christ that we turn to Christ, and the injured one becomes our Savior. . . It is the suffering that evokes the humanity of the human heart.
>
> Moyers: So you would agree with Abelard that mankind yearning for God and God yearning for mankind met in compassion at the cross?
>
> Campbell: Yes. (55)

In each of the three theories, Christ is *willingly sacrificing himself* for humanity, *willingly suffering* to *absolve* humans for their sins or, in the third view, to *influence* them to move beyond sin to *salvation* through *empathy*, and thus he can be said to be taking on the role of a *scapegoat*.

Definitions of *sacrifice* include the terms *forfeit* and *forfeiture*, the act of surrendering something as a *penalty for a mistake or a fault or a failure of some kind*. This definition, then, does make Christ's Crucifixion an act of *sacrifice*, and, in fact, fits all of the three major interpretations of Christ's Crucifixion as one of *atonement*.

Another definition of *sacrifice* is to *give up*, to *endure the loss of*. Again, this can fit the concepts of *atonement*, depending on how one understands, how one interprets Christ *giving up his life and suffering on the Cross*. Certainly he is *suffering on the Cross*. No important interpretations of the event deny that, and the graphic depictions of the physical sufferings emphasize the wounds inflected upon him. However, a question can be raised about how certain Christ is in terms of *his own salvation*, in terms of entering a better existence. It seems absurd to suggest he might not be certain, as his endless statements and actions throughout his life indicate an absolute knowledge, certainly a belief he is indeed the son of God and will be *rewarded* for his *suffering* with a very pleasant eternal life.

Here is where the seemingly strange moment of doubt on the Cross becomes crucial. St. Matthew and St. Mark write: "And about the ninth hour Jesus cried with a loud voice, saying, *Eli, Eli, lama sabachthani?* That is to say, My God, my God, why hast thou forsaken me?" (56). This can be interpreted in different ways, one of them that he is expressing doubt about his own beliefs, about his own salvation. If this is so, then his entire life is one *not of knowledge* but of *faith* (a belief in that which is beyond proof) and *heroism* (self-sacrifice, the giving up of one's self for something greater than or other than oneself).

However, if Christ *knows* he will not die to an eternal nothingness but be reborn, *resurrected* to a better life, his *sacrifice* is less and the *heroism of it* is brought into question. It really is not much of a *sacrifice* or act of *heroism* if one gives up something because he *knows* he is getting something better.

Consider, for example, another famous act of *heroism* in the form of a *scapegoat*, that of *Oedipus Rex* (the following discussion is taken from my book *Insanity and Genius*). (57)

Oedipus solved the Riddle of the Sphinx, demonstrating his intelligence and releasing his city from its control. Thus Thebes saw Oedipus as a *savior* and made him its king.

However, a problem remained. Apollo had put a plague on Thebes, and it was thought that the plague would remain until the person responsible for murdering the former king, King Laius was found and brought to justice.

Oedipus vowed to once again save his city. He condemned this murderer as evil and pushed forward to find him. Curiously, others were not sure he should do this. His wife, the queen, once married to Laius, urged him not to continue with his search. The great blind seer Teiresias told him to let it go.

Why? It made no sense to Oedipus. Evil had been done, and the city remained under a plague. Certainly he as the king was obligated to save his people, to discover truth, to right the wrong.

But then came the astonishing discovery. Oedipus himself was the man who had murdered Laius, and seemingly for not a very good reason, seemingly simply out of anger and pride. Now came the moment of truth. The moment in life when one faces the ultimate challenge, the ultimate horror inside oneself. The key was knowledge, not just any knowledge, but *self-knowledge*, the truth about who and what one is.

The gods had demanded that he do what he did. He had been *fated* to kill his father and marry his mother. That was not of his own making. Yet it was considered *ethically* evil to murder one's father and wed one's mother. He had said it, time and again; the man who murdered Laius was evil and must be punished. He had condemned himself to damnation.

But, now, now that he knew, now he had gained some power he did not have prior to this, the power that comes from *the knowledge of self*, now he could decide (be in charge of his own actions, his own ethos, now he was in a position to think for himself, to take *self-responsibility, the only way to give life meaning and value)*. The choice was harsh, seemingly unfair. He could remain as king of Thebes, perhaps justify this action by saying the punishment was unfair. He had not known after all that it was his father he had killed, that he had married his own mother. Thus, he could deny his own darkness, his own Shadow desires (what Freud later named after him as the desire to kill one's father and marry one's mother; the Oedipus Complex, a standard stage in male development). The city would remain under a plague, condemned by Apollo, continuing as a wasteland, a place where frightening entities lived in the shadows of each person, and appeared literally in the form of punishment from the gods, but no one would be to blame for it. It was simply the human condition being lived out in the city of Thebes. It had been fated by the gods, a fate issued because of the sins of a previous generation.

Oedipus chose not to follow this line of reasoning. Instead, in what must be seen as an act of heroism, of self-sacrifice, he condemned himself, banned himself from Thebes, and in so doing took all of the darkness, all of the evil shadows of human existence into himself, freeing Thebes to be reborn in its original innocence.

Sigmund Freud thought this a perfect story to represent his views of early childhood desires to kill one's father and have sex with one's mother. For Sigmund Freud, this became the initial emergence into consciousness, the initial and basic drive to life that all of the others grew out of. He wrote:

> If *Oedipus Rex* moves a modern audience no less than it did the contemporary Greek one, the explanation can only be that its effect does not lie in the contrast between destiny and human will, but is to be looked for in the particular nature of the material on which that contrast is exemplified. There must be something which makes a voice within us ready to recognize the compelling force of destiny in the Oedipus, while we can dismiss as merely arbitrary such dispositions as are laid down in *Die Ahnfrau* or other modern tragedies of destiny. And a factor of this kind is in fact involved in the story of King Oedipus. His destiny moves us only because it might have been ours—because the oracle laid the same curse upon us before our birth as upon him. It is the fate of all of us, perhaps, to direct our first sexual impulse towards our mother and our first hatred wish against our father. (58)

This psychological combination of self-consciousness, of gaining the knowledge of whom and what one is with the potential toward evil matches a standard interpretation of the Garden of Eden.

"In Adam's fall we sinned all" begins the famous Puritan alphabet used to teach children that humans are all born in sin as result of Adam and Eve's original fall from grace. (59)

In the minds of these God fearing Puritans that original sin meant that all mortal flesh was infected with an innate sinfulness! Ann Bradstreet, one of the acclaimed Puritan poets, expresses it in a poem titled "Childhood":

Stained from birth with Adam's sinful fact,
Thence I began to sin as soon as act:
A perverse will, a love to what's forbid,
A serpent's sting in pleasing face lay hid:
A lying tongue as soon as it could speak
    And fifth commandment do daily break. (60)

Condemned by God himself because of that initial weakness, the Puritans saw life as but a continual battle against the forces of evil within, and only the most stringent discipline, the most masochistic existence could bring salvation. As Cotton Mather was known to preach, it was better for a child to be whipped than damned! (61)

After all, the *King James Bible* makes it clear in *Genesis*:

6. And when the woman saw that the tree *was* good for food, and that it *was* pleasant to the eyes, and a tree to be desired to make *one* wise, she took of the fruit thereof, and did eat, and gave also unto her husband with her: he did eat. 7. And the eyes of them both were opened, and they knew that they *were* naked; and they sewed fig leaves together, and made themselves aprons.
8. And they heard the voice of the Lord God walking in the garden in the cool of the day: and Adam and his wife hid themselves from the presence of the Lord God amongst the trees of the garden.
9. And the Lord God called unto Adam, and said unto him, Where *art* thou?
10. And he said, I heard thy voice in the garden, and I was afraid, because I *was* naked; and I hid myself.
11. And he said, Who told thee that thou *wast* naked? Hast thou eaten of the tree, whereof I commanded thee that thou shouldest not eat?
12. And the man said, "The woman whom thou gavest *to be* with me, she gave me of the tree, and I did eat.
13. And the Lord God said unto the woman, What *is* this *that* thou hast done? And the woman said, "The serpent beguiled me, and I did eat.
14. And the Lord God said unto the serpent, Because thou hast done this, thou *art* cursed above all cattle, and above every beast of the field; upon they belly shalt thou go, and dust shalt thou eat all the days of thy life:
15. And I will put enmity between thee and the woman, and between thy seed and her seed; it shall bruise thy head,
and thou shalt bruise thy his heel.
16. Unto woman he said, I will greatly multiply thy sorrow and thy conception; in sorrow thou shalt bring forth children, and thy desire *shall by* to thy husband, and he shall rule over thee.
17. And unto Adam he said, Because thou hast hearkened unto the voice of thy wife, and hast eaten of the tree,

of which I commanded thee, saying, Thou shalt not eat of it: cursed *is* the ground for thy sake; in sorrow shalt thou eat *of* it all the days of thy life; thorns also and thistles shall it bring forth to thee; and thou shalt eat the herb of the field: in the sweat of thy face shalt thou eat bread, till thou return unto the ground, for out of it wast thou taken: for dust thou *art*, and unto dust shalt thou return.
20. And Adam called his wife's name Eve; because she was the mother of all living.
21. Unto Adam also and to his wife did the Lord God make coats of skins, and clothed them.
22. And the Lord God said, Behold, the man is become as one of us, to know good and evil: and now, lest he put forth his hand, and take also of the tree of life, and eat, and live forever:
23. Therefore the Lord God sent him forth from the Garden of Eden, to till the ground from whence he was taken.
24. So he drove out the man; and he placed at the east of the garden of Eden cherubim, and a flaming sword which turned every way, to keep the way of the tree of life. (62)

It was clear. Life was a curse! Children were a curse! Because Adam and Eve had eaten the forbidden fruit of the tree of the knowledge of good and evil, God had condemned them and all of their children to an eternal suffering, and, since all that now remained to separate humans and God was the fruit on the tree of eternal life, humans were forbidden to come near it.

The curse had been cast! Innocence had been lost, and once lost could never be regained! How unfortunate! What a horrible fall from grace!

But wait! How fortunate! A wondrous fall! The birth of meaning and value! The birth of human existence! The birth of mind! The human mind! In the human brain!

The intersection of two planes of existence!
The Fall from Grace IS the miracle of human existence!

The King James *Bible* tells us that before this fall Adam and Eve "were both naked, the man and his wife, and were not ashamed." (63) That is, they were both innocent to shame, both without a sense of good or evil. It was simply a state of animal existence. The human brain did not have a map for judging good and evil.

Thus, the first humans to be were unable to be either loyal and obedient or disloyal. They simply did what they were told to do. It did not matter who told them, as they could not distinguish good from evil. So, when snake told Eve to bite of the fruit because it was good, she could only see that snake was right and bite of it.

"Genesis" tells us:

> 1. Now the serpent was more subtle than any beast of the field which the Lord God had made. And he said unto the woman, Yea, hath God said, Ye shall not eat of every tree of the garden?
> 2. And the woman said unto the serpent, We may eat of the fruit of the trees of the garden:
> 3. But of the fruit of the tree which *is* in the midst of the garden, God hath said, Ye shall not eat of it, neither shall ye touch it, lest ye die.
> 4. And the serpent said unto the woman, Ye shall not surely die:
> 5. For God doth know that in the day ye eat thereof, then your eyes shall be opened, and ye shall be as gods, knowing good and evil.
> 6. And when the woman saw that the tree *was* good for food, and that it *was* pleasant to the eyes, and a tree to be desired to make *one* wise, she took of the fruit thereof, and did eat, and gave also unto her husband with her: and he did eat. (64)

It is not surprising that it is the woman who is first tempted to bring about the transformation, since it is obvious in nearly all of the natural world that the female is the giver of life, the one who literally brings new life into being, and, thus, she is also the one who births the new level of existence out of the old.

Bill Moyers questions Joseph Campbell: "It does seem that this story has done women a great disservice by casting Eve as responsible for the Fall. Why are women the ones held responsible for the downfall?"

Joseph Campbell replies simply: "They represent life. Man doesn't enter life except by women, and so it is woman who brings us into this world of pairs of opposites and suffering." (65)

And it is not surprising that it is a snake that tempts this transformation, as the snake is the creature who transforms, shedding its skin to be reborn. According to Ania Teillard, the snake is "an animal endowed with magnetic force. Because it sheds its skin, it symbolizes resurrection. Because of its sinuous movement '(and also because its coils are capable of strangling)' it signifies strength. Because of its viciousness, it represents the evil side of nature."(66) Heinrich Zimmer claims that the snake is the life force, determining both birth and rebirth. (67) Carl Jung claims that snakes are a well documented representation of transformation and renovation, a firm archetype, suggesting as an example the Egyptian Uraeus as the expression of the Kundalini (the Yoga concept of the snake as the coiled ring in at the bottom of the spinal cord that uncoils and climbs through all of the chakras up the spinal column to the third eye of Shiva, giving man the sense of the eternal; thus, representing the necessary sexual energy capable of spiritual awareness) on a higher plane. (68) J. E.

Cirlot points out that Philo of Alexandria (representing a common view of ancient writers) "believed that when the snake shakes off its skin it likewise shakes off its old age, that it can both kill and cure and that it is therefore the symbol and attribute of the aggressive powers, positive and negative, which rule the world. (This is a Gnostic and Manichean idea of Persian provenance.) He decided finally that it is the 'most spiritual of animals'." (69)

The snake is also a creature of the swamp, the fertile birthing place of life, the place where earth mixes with water (water being the most powerful place of transformation, because it is the natural life-giving amniotic fluid of the womb, because it is the dominant element in living beings, and, in a tautology, because it is the place of the birth of life, as opposed to a desert, which is without life). J. E. Cirlot refers to Enel (70) in pointing out that the snake is "used, as are other reptiles, to refer to the primordial—the most primitive strata of life. In the *Book of the Dead* (XVII), the reptiles are the first to acclaim Ra when he appears above the surface of the waters of Nou (or Nu or Nun)." Marcia Eliade points out that, in India, snake cults or cults of the spirit of the snake are connected with the symbolism of the waters of the sea. Snakes are guardians of the springs of life and of immortality, and also of those superior riches of the spirit that are symbolized by hidden treasure. (71)

And the snake has obvious phallic qualities in its shape, its texture (slippery), its ability to be both soft and hard, its sinuous movements, its threatening tongue, its ability to spit out poison, its resemblance to a ligament, and its undulating body patterns.

Furthermore, the snake has close associations with women and seduction beyond Eve. According to Pail Diel the snake not only symbolizes personal sin, but the principle of evil inherent in all of life, as represented, for example, in the serpent of Midgard. (72) Eliade refers to Gresmann (166) who claimed that Eve was an archaic Phoenician goddess of the underworld who represented the snake, and Eliade supports this by referencing many Mediterranean deities who are shown carrying a snake (i.e., Artemis, Hecate, and Persephone), and further relating these to Cretan priestesses, and to Medusa and the Erinyes, mythic females with snakes for hair. (73)

Very interesting in context of all of this is a huge amount of myth or folklore surrounding Lilith, especially the specific versions involving the dual creation stories in Genesis. Genesis 1:27 reads, "So God created man in his own image, in the image of God he created him; male and female he created them." Here Adam and his wife are made from clay or dust, equal and adult.

The creation story in Genesis 2 has God create Adam, and then, showing some pity on Adam because Adam is lonely, create his wife Eve from his rib. Here man and woman certainly are not created at the same time or given equal status. While Biblical scholars and clergy have come up with numerous explanations for this discrepancy (and some others in the two stories), an important body of stories has evolved outside of the Bible that claim Adam had two wives. His first wife was Lilith.

Lilith, created equally and at the same time as Adam, considered herself his equal and refused to submit to him, most specifically refused to assume the standard missionary position beneath him for sex, thus violating the command to be fruitful and multiply. Instead, she left him. The various stories give various ways she left (one is that she simply spoke the Holy Name of God and disappeared).

But her disappearance didn't mean she was gone, and a whole body of stories developed around her as the negative female, one who consorted with the fallen angels and other demons, perhaps bore and killed children of Adam, and in terms of the fall from innocence in the Garden of Eden, either as the snake that tempted Eve or the one who prompted it to do so. (74)

J. E. Cirlot also points out connections of the snake to the tree, which, he says, "being unitary, may be said to correspond to the masculine principle, in which case the ophidian would represent the feminine. Thus, the tree and the serpent are, in mythology, prefigurations of Adam and Eve (if the above story is incorporate, better stated as prefigurations of man and woman). Furthermore" Cirlot continues, "by analogy, we also have here a situation of symbolic Entanglement—the snake curled round the tree (or round the staff of Aesculapius)—and a symbolic image of moral dualism." (75)

The garden is also a place of growth and transformation, and this is God's garden, so the transformation would naturally be a growth into a spiritual or mental world. Also, since man was made from clay, the physical substance, but "God created man in his *own* image, in the image of God created he him," (Genesis 1, 27) man must have within him the spiritual, the mental level of existence.

The invisible world of meaning and value, the world of the human mind, joins with the visible world, the literal, physical world, in the brain. In other words, the mind is the reality beyond the limitations of matter, and the brain is where this mental world enters into and patterns the visible world of matter. It is, then, in the human mind/brain that the mapping out of meaning and value take place, and, thus, that is where the world of physical existence obtains an *ethical* and a *spiritual* quality. Physical existence (life) has meaning and value simply and solely because of this interaction in the human mind/brain. The mapping out of meaning and value is the purpose of human existence, and the fulfillment of it is the highest experience possible. Thus, denying mere meaningless physical existence for a higher mental or spiritual existence brings the highest *joy*, and *joy* here is meant as that experience of the wonder of the universe and the knowledge of being a central part of that wonder. *Joy is the realization of self, the affirmation of life.* (*Genius and Insanity,* pp. 94-101)

Let us return to *Oedipus Rex*. In our rush to interpret and elaborate on it, we have forgotten something very important.

On level of id or libido, Sigmund Freud's ideas work. The male child competes with his father for his mother, and wishes to replace his father (just as each generation must replace the previous generation). Thus, Oedipus kills his father and marries his mother. While Sigmund Freud's theories concerning the Oedipus Complex are more complicated than this, and such oversimplification is often done by his detractors to distort his point, this general straight-forward interpretation remains, and the fact that he chose this particular story to use for the ultimate example of the theory at the very least means he set himself up for this interpretation. Furthermore, his main discussion of it in *Totem and Taboo*, comparing humans to apes, suggests exactly this. (76)

But a closer look at the play itself offers a much different view of the human condition. What gets forgotten, purposely or out of a careless viewing or reading of the play, is that Oedipus killed his father and married his mother out of ignorance (perhaps out of instinctual drives, but certainly not out of any kind of conscious intent). He did not do it willingly or knowingly. Once he discovered what he had done, through the gaining of *self*-knowledge, the knowledge of whom and what he was, he was empowered to think for himself, to have *self*-responsibility. And he was given a horrible decision. Either he could deny the responsibility of saving his city (i.e., the human community), or he could banish himself from the city, accepting responsibility for something he was fated to act out. He, after all, was not the one who initiated the problem. His father, Laius had raped a young boy, and the boy's father, Pelops had asked the gods to deny Laius a son or to be destroyed by that son. Or Oedipus could take on the responsibility of redeeming his father (thus, human existence) through self-sacrifice.

Here, then, comes the crucial realization. The drive to kill one's father is not of the world of higher knowledge, or of the higher functions of the human mind; rather it is of the lower, animal instinctual drives. This fits exactly with Freud's connection of the entire concept with the actions of apes (suggesting that the literal killing of the father ape by his sons is being done by humans psychologically and symbolically in the Oedipus Complex). Rather, the Oedipus drama suggests that by gaining higher knowledge of what it means to be human (by opening the mind to decisions beyond the ignorant drives of mere flesh, humans can in fact overcome, gain control over, or at least accept responsibility for this drive). This, then, is the challenge, which is to both have the desire (the animal drive to life), and to gain control over it with the higher ethical psychic entities, what might be called in Freudian terms the super-ego. Indeed, this is closer to the focus of Freud's Oedipus Complex than the simple desire to replace the father. What Freud emphasized is the *ambivalence* of the two desires. Thus, the father is not merely to be killed by the son, but redeemed as well (later in his career, Freud would struggle with this in the realm of Eros and Thanatos).

Remember, it all begins with a *fall* from *grace*, from *innocence,* represented in the Judeo/Christian mythos as a *sin* against God (the father). Thus, the original human father Adam needs redemption, which gets accomplished in the death of a *son*, Jesus Christ (interesting discussion could take place at this point about the image of God as father, perhaps a father also needing to be both killed and resurrected on whatever levels of existence; and Nietzsche's dramatic claim that God is dead because humans have killed him comes immediately to mind).

In fact, each generation redeems the previous one on several levels: certainly on the simple physical level of the continuation of the species; but also on the higher levels of connecting with the previous generation (through compassion and empathy) and what ethical, spiritual realizations are passed on. It is, as just mentioned, in the willing sacrifice of Christ that all previous generations of humans going all the way back to Adam and Eve, who represent the birth of human consciousness, which is clearly connected to the birth of an ethos, after all the fruit comes from the Tree of the Knowledge of Good and Evil, are redeemed; while, at the same time, Christ is redeeming his father (God), is reconnecting God with human existence.

Salvation, then, comes from redemption, not from patricide. And Oedipus, rather than suggesting that the most important drive in humans is that of survival, or the drive to life, suggests it is the drive to meaning and value.

It is worth emphasizing that salvation is not a one-way connection. Not only are humans reconnected to the world of God, but God is reconnected to the physical world of humans. The world beyond physical existence and the world of physical existence complete each other. The *self* and the *knowledge of the self* are equated.

Let me repeat: In Sophocles' *Oedipus Rex* Oedipus is born *fated* to kill his father and marry his mother. He has no choice in this. And, as much as everyone in the drama attempts to outwit fate, it cannot be done, and Oedipus fulfills his horrific fate. This is the realm of the body, of the physical universe outside of the human mind. But then comes salvation. By seeking knowledge (which is, in fact, knowledge of who and what he is, or self-knowledge) Oedipus empowers himself, because he puts himself into an ethical and spiritual position, a position to give his seemingly fated and meaningless life both meaning and value on the ethical level of right and wrong, and on the spiritual level of salvation. He chooses (free will) to sacrifice himself to save his city. It is a heroic decision. He could have chosen to remain as king of Thebes, in which case the plague would have remained. Instead, he condemned himself in order to have the plague lifted and save his city, his people, human existence. This self-sacrifice is the ultimate gift given to humans. It is the chance to have a life of meaning and value, a chance to outwit the meaningless plane of physical existence and put a pattern, an ethical map and a spiritual map, on the universe.

While the Chorus, upon the revelation to Oedipus of the truth of his crimes insists that he "were better dead than alive" (77) he, while fully realizing and accepting the horror of what he has done, without hesitation replies, "Do not counsel me anymore. This punishment / That I have laid upon myself is just." (78)

Here the *self* is confirmed without denying the *other*, the environments of the visible world of physical existence and of the invisible world of fate. *Self* exists, but not separate from an environment. Furthermore, meaning and value comes into existence through sacrificing the *self* to the *relationship* of the *self* to the *environment*. Neither *self* nor *fate* is totally in control. One cannot exist without the other.

It amounts to sacrificing the *self* as more important than the *other*, in which case ethos would be denied, because life without a context would simply become self-gratification. This is a denial of ethos and spirituality because there is no truth beyond physical existence; only the selfish desires of the individual on a physical level would be recognized. Ethos and spirituality only exists, or exists for humans if humans allow it. If there is no judgment beyond gratifying the body desires, or the desires of the individual psyche, then there is no universal ethos or spiritual world, at best only the separate ethos of each individual human, and that ethos is at best simply an instinctual response to the environment, in which case ethos, if it can be called that, has no choice, only a blind following of one's instincts. And since ethos is by definition a matter of judgment, of distinguishing Good and Bad, Right and Wrong, it does not exist.

If ethos does exist, then it takes shape in the human mind/brain (certainly in human existence; this becomes a tautology). The question here is not if it originates there or arrives there from some outside source (a God, which can lead to everything being fated, and thus life being a meaningless following out of this God's desires, i.e., no self-responsibility, or not, depending on whether or not the God is all-powerful), or a particular structuring of the brain that results in humans having no choice but to consider certain things as Good and other things as Evil (ultimately such a situation can also lead to life being meaningless, as the structures of science and logic can be said to predetermine everything, and thus humans have no choice but to live out pre-programmed scientific and logical principals, or not, depending on whether or not science and logic can reduce all of existence to patterns that must be followed).

If, rather than saying that ethos does not exist because there is no free will or choice involved in human existence, ethos is denied by going beyond it, by saying that there is something more important or at least more powerful than even the values of an ethos, i.e., Soren Kierkegaard's teleological suspension of the ethical, that does not deny ethos in the same sense of it not existing. Rather, it says ethos does exist, but that there are higher truths than the ethical truths, truths that have to do with the *numinous*, the *sublime,* the realizations of *faith*, ultimately, the truths of *salvation*—the highest truths of meaning and value in human existence, truths that *humans can experience but never fully comprehend*.

The goal in life is not to avoid such truths, not to avoid a terrifying confrontation with the sublime or the numinous, but to have the chance to face them with human nobility, for they are the moments to experience the epiphanies that give human life a special place in the cosmos.

Indeed, it is not the final lines of Creon or the Chorus that define a man. They are but the landscape. It is Oedipus rising above this barren condemnation when he says "But let me go Creon! Let me purge my father's Thebes of the pollution" that resonates, that stays with the audience, that makes everyone relate, feel the desolation and admire the man capable of rising above it. (79)

In William Shakespeare's *Hamlet*, the same realization of the harshness of human existence, the demands of "fate" are not denied, but instead become the chance for meaning, the key to what is best in a human. In his introduction to *Hamlet*, Edward Hubler writes:

> In a tragedy, the hero normally comes to the realization of a truth of which he had been hitherto unaware. This is, as Aristotle has it, "a change

from ignorance to knowledge" . . . . In Hamlet and King Lear, for instance, there is a transformation in the character of the hero. Toward the end of his play Lear is the opposite of what he had been at the beginning. He has been purged of his arrogance and pride, and the pomp and circumstance of kingship, on which he had placed great store, is to him no more than an interesting spectacle. What matters now is the love of the daughter he had rejected in the first scene. When we first meet Hamlet he is in a state of depression. The world to him is "an unweeded garden" from which he would willingly depart. He has found corruption not only in the state but in existence itself . . . . By the final scene, however, his composure has returned. He no longer appears in slovenly dress; he apologizes to Laertes, and he treats Claudius with courtesy up to the point at which Gertrude's death discloses the king's treachery and compels him to the act of vengeance.

All this is not simply a return to Hamlet's former self. In the course of the action he has grown in stature and wisdom. He is no longer troubled by reasoning doubts, for he knows now that reason is not enough. An over reliance on reason and a belief in untrammeled free will are hallmarks of the Shakespearean villain; the heroes learn better. In the beginning of the final scene Hamlet is still beset from without and within—"thou wouldst not think how ill all's here about my heart; but it is no matter." And it does not matter, because he has now come to put his trust in providence. Earlier in the scene he had said,

> Our indiscretion sometime serves us well
> When our deep plots do pall, and that should learn us
> There's a divinity that shapes our ends,
> Rough-hew them how we will.
> (V.ii.8-11)

This is not, as has been said, "a fatalist's surrender of his personal responsibility." It is the realization that man is not a totally free agent. With this realization Hamlet faces the fencing match and the king's intrigues without concern for self. What matters at the end of an important tragedy is not success or failure, but what a man IS. Tragedy of the first order moves into the realm of the human spirit, and at the close we contemplate the nature of man. In this respect Shakespeare and the Greeks are the same, but they reach the end by widely divergent paths . . ..

Melodrama such as TITUS uses horror and grief as entertainment, bringing them as close to the spectator as it can. Tragedy uses them as truth. These, it says, are part of our human heritage, and we must face them. And in the end, partly because they are faced, they lose their terror, and the tragedy passes beyond them. It is not surprising, then, that the greatest tragedies are those involving the greatest horrors, for facing a great horror demands greatness of spirit. This greatness of spirit is what we contemplate at the end of a Shakespearean tragedy. At the close of the

> tragedy we are not so much concerned with Hamlet or Othello as individuals, as with the spirit of man triumphant in defeat . . . .
>
> What matters now is not so much what a man DOES but what he IS. . . . It might be the voice of Hamlet before the fencing match: "If it be now, 'tis not to come. . ."
>
> Hamlet's remarks on the bones [while talking to the skull of Yorick] are his last comment on the discrepancy between appearance and reality. He is coming to accept reality for what it is. Then as the generalization continues, a funeral procession enters, and Hamlet learns who is to be Buried today. He has seen the body of an old friend dug up to make room for the body of the woman he loves. He has looked on death at what is for him its worst. It is after the graveyard scene that the man who had continually brooded on death is able to face it. It seems axiomatic that any horror becomes less horrible once we have looked squarely at it When we see Hamlet again he can defy augury, for the augurs can foretell only such things as success or failure; but there is nothing, except himself, to prevent a man from facing his own private horror and rising above it. And so it is with Hamlet. When Horatio offers to cancel the fencing match "if your mind dislike anything," he is able to reply, "Not a whit, we defy augury. There is special providence in the fall of a sparrow. If it be now 'tis not to come; if it be not to come, it will be now; if it be not now, yet it will come. The readiness is all. Since no man of aught he leaves knows, what is't to leave betimes? Let it be." "Readiness" here means both submitting to providence and being in a state of preparation. It is not that death does not matter; it matters very much indeed, but readiness matters more. Shakespeare's tragic heroes do not renounce the world. The dying Hamlet is concerned about the welfare of the state and his own worldly reputation. Such values are never denied, but at the end of the tragedies they are no longer primary values. At such moments the central thing is the spirit of man achieving grandeur. (80)

And we suffer with him, are attracted to him, somehow understand the greatness of his decision, for it is the potential greatness in each of us.

But it is even more complex than this. For Soren Kierkegaard, Oedipus's self-sacrifice, the sacrifice of a Tragic Hero (Soren Kierkegaard uses Agamemnon's sacrificing of his daughter Iphigenia to appease the gods as the example) is a subordination of the individual to the universal (certainly on the level of a universal ethos), a denial of the individual (ethos). Soren Kierkegaard's Abraham, on the other hand, goes against the universal, the ethos of his community for a unique, personal relationship to his God. He is, in fact, denying everything else, logic, compassion, the entire history and mythology of his world, most importantly his own human nature, all of which condemn his actions, and he is not doing it for some benefit for either himself or his community (which would deny

Kierkegaard's whole point). This is the opposite of the rebellion of the Garden of Eden, a denial of that gaining of the knowledge of Good and Evil, a return to pure innocence and obedience, carrying with it the ability to completely believe in God, and in that belief the belief that the killing of Isaac is not going to result in Isaac's death, but that, contrary to all logic and all conscious knowing, Isaac will regain his same living self after the act is completed or certainly that it is a possible outcome (faith here carrying with it a belief in the impossible).

This is more of a leap of faith then even the Biblical story gives us, as in the Biblical version, God intercedes before the act is completed, and there is no proof of the miracle of faith, only an assumed proof that Abraham had true faith in the belief that he was not going to fail his existential test at the moment of realization.

But here we encounter more complications. Are we not putting thoughts into Abraham's mind? Are we not guessing at his reasons? How do we know he believed Isaac would not die? Soren Kierkegaard actually begins his discussion with four different scenarios, four different versions of the thoughts of Abraham.

Does not Soren Kierkegaard give us more of a reason not to embrace faith than to embrace it? Are Abraham's actions not too pure, too innocent to be possible, or desirable? Can they carry any self-responsibility? Can they not be viewed as a denial of *self* through an absolute obedience to God? If all of the *self* is denied for faith, isn't *self* denied? It's one thing to go beyond logic and all of practical and rational knowing in favor of intuition and the kind of knowing beyond reason, another to go beyond all forms of knowing, including compassion for no reason other than obedience. Oedipus and Agamemnon sacrificed themselves, went against their deep desires for something more important than them, for meaning and value as humans comprehend it (for a "universal order"). For them, all of the knowledge of their mind, all of human mythology and history came into play, including the fall from innocence (represented for them in such stories as that of Prometheus giving fire to humans). They were doing their best to act in accordance with their understanding of what was best, and they were using all of their knowledge and intelligence (both logical and intuitive) to make their decisions. It is, in fact, through the insistence on gaining self-knowledge that Oedipus is able to gain meaning and value and stand up to the gods, deny them complete power.

It is clear that Soren Kierkegaard sets up Abraham as taking self-responsibility in terms of denying all influences from everything beyond pure faith, including both human nature and ethical considerations. However, the question becomes whether there is anything left.

If one says that this voice of God he hears is some form of knowing and thinking (whether it be explicable or inexplicable), then that form becomes the key to self-responsibility, but that, in turn, denies pure faith, or, rather, becomes a definition of faith. Faith becomes listening to that inexplicable voice within (or that part of the brain/mind that some voice from without communicates with), and immediately the various disciplines of inquiry begin to identify just what that voice is, because that voice, then, becomes the key to a definition of human. And it is an existence beyond all other forms of knowing. Thus, all of human knowing, conscious and unconscious, other than that irrational voice, is at best worthless, and human existence becomes simply obedience, and thus meaningless. The paradox is clear. Either the value of human existence comes from complete obedience (which is a denial of self-responsibility, and thus a contradiction), or complete Faith is ultimately a denial of self-responsibility, and thus needs to be considered in the sense of one end of a continuum that needs to be balanced by some personal "I," which in turn involves forms of knowing and makes decisions for itself. Thus, it is the tension between believing in that which is beyond knowing and knowing itself that becomes the key to human existence.

A person of pure faith, what Soren Kierkegaard calls a *knight of faith* would be pure only if he denied all else, if the universal were completely eliminated in the relationship of I to God. Soren Kierkegaard, however, admits, not being able to do this himself, and in opposition to what Existentialism becomes, still maintains an impure relationship to the social world around him in addition to the essential relationship to God.

But wait. Perhaps this is a misinterpretation of Soren Kierkegaard. Is it not the absolute obedience after all, but rather the struggle that matters. It is a "sickness," a "fear" and a "trembling" that Soren Kierkegaard emphasizes. And isn't "existentialism" defined in terms of the I/Other relationship, the encounter? Reality exists not in the I nor in the Other, but in the encounter of the two, in the act of living. But again, we come to something of a tautology here. Existence is existence. It does, however, open the door to the idea that the meaning of life is in the journey of life. And thus, "existence" might be replaced on one side of the equation with meaning. Again, here, we end up defining human existence in terms of meaning and value. (*Insanity and Genius*, pp. 133-141)

Returning to Christ's moment of doubt: *Eli, Eli, lama sabachthani?* that is to say, My God, my God, why hast thou forsaken me?"(81), it is now possible to see Christ as that exact encounter, as the entity where the I and the Other come together, the I being that reality which is known and the Other being that reality which is beyond knowing. In this sense, it might be said that the *scapegoat* is the means to *salvation*.

Kenneth Burke coined the expression, "scapegoat mechanism," which claims that humans solve conflicts by blaming them on a third party, in his books *Permanence and Change* (82), and *A Grammar of motives* (83). In a psychological sense, this mechanism involves the use of *projection* or *displacement* to focus feelings of aggression, hostility, frustration, and the like on another individual or group that is innocent or if not completely blameless certainly not deserving of the degree of blame inflicted. Rene Girard developed Burke's theories, claiming that human history prior to the Crucifixion of Christ has been driven by this mechanism, a result of humans being driven by desire for that which another has or wants (what he calls mimetic desire), and that this causes a triangulation of desire and results in growing conflict, to the point where society is at risk. Then the *scapegoat mechanism* kicks in, and a person or group is singled out as the cause of the trouble. This person or group, then, is driven out or killed, and the cause of the conflict is resolved by putting the blame on this scapegoat or scapegoats. The cycle then begins anew. However, according to Girard, this cycle is broken in the Crucifixion of Christ by showing it from the victim's perspective, where the victim's sacrifice is actually a transformation, a resurrection, where it is the condemner, not the *scapegoat*, who is guilty. (84)

Now we are finding that the *scapegoat* is one with the *savior*, the person who rescues another from danger, harm, a miss-spent life, sin, because it is through the *scapegoat* or *savior* that *salvation* is achieved. In other words, the *scapegoat* not only takes others' sins or failings upon himself, he offers the means to a better existence. *Salvation* is achieved through the *scapegoat as savior*.

Notes

1. "Isaiah" 53, *King James Bible,* 1611; Thomas Nelson Inc.; Camden, New Jersey, 1970.
2. "*The Ones Who Walk Away from Omelas,*" *New Dimensions 3, 1973.*
3. "The Moral Philosopher and the Moral Life," *International Journal of Ethics*, volume 1, number 3, April ,1891, pp. 330-354.
4. *Animal Farm,* George Orwell, London: Penguin Group, 1946.
5. *Pride and Prejudice*, Jane Austin, Egerton, 1813; rpt., Bantam, 1983.
6. "Genesis," *King James Bible,* 1611; Thomas Nelson Inc.; Camden, New Jersey, 1970.
7. *The Origin of Species*; rpt., Gramercy, 1995.

8. *The History of Archeology: Great Excavations of the World*, John Romer, Checkmark Books: New York, 2001.
9. *The Ascent of Man*, Little, Brown: Toronto, 1973, p. 56.
10. *The Power of Myth*, Doubleday: New York, 1988, p. 101.
11. *Myths to Live By*, Bantam, Books: New York, 1972, p. 20.
12. *The Courage to Create*, Bantam Books, New York, 1975, p. 53-4.
13. *Prometheus Bound*, from Classical Greek times, actual date unknown; this translation comes from Carl G. Jung, p. 135. The drama is the first in a trilogy; the other two, *Prometheus Unbound* (parts remain), and *Prometheus the Firebearer*, have been lost.
14. Rollo May's quote; *Man's Search for Himself*, New York: W. W. Norton, 1953, p. 158.
15. Rollo May's quote; *Man's Search for Himself*, New York: W. W. Norton, 1953, p. 158.
16. Rollo May's quote; *Man's Search for Himself*, New York: W. W. Norton, 1953, p. 158.
17. *The Giver*, Lois Lowry, New York: Bantam Doubleday Dell, 1993.
18. *The Giver*, Lois Lowry, New York: Bantam Doubleday Dell, 1993, pp. 112-113.
19. *The Giver*, Lois Lowry, New York: Bantam Doubleday Dell, 1993, p. 53.
20. *The Giver*, Lois Lowry, New York: Bantam Doubleday Dell, 1993, pp. 62-63.
21. *The Giver*, Lois Lowry, New York: Bantam Doubleday Dell, 1993, p. 61.
22. *The Giver*, Lois Lowry, New York: Bantam Doubleday Dell, 1993, p. 61.
23. *The Giver*, Lois Lowry, New York: Bantam Doubleday Dell, 1993, p. 65.
24. *The Giver*, Lois Lowry, New York: Bantam Doubleday Dell, 1993, p. 67.
25. *The Giver*, Lois Lowry, New York: Bantam Doubleday Dell, 1993, p. 67.
26. *Fahrenheit 451*, Ray Bradbury, Ballantine, 1953.
27. *The Giver*, Lois Lowry, New York: Bantam Doubleday Dell, 1993, p. 95.
28. *The Giver*, Lois Lowry, New York: Bantam Doubleday Dell, 1993, p. 105.
29. *The Giver*, Lois Lowry, New York: Bantam Doubleday Dell, 1993, p. 103.
30. *The Giver*, Lois Lowry, New York: Bantam Doubleday Dell, 1993, p. 97.
31. "*The Lottery*," Shirley Jackson, *The New Yorker*, June 26, 1948.
32. "Leviticus" 16, *King James Bible,*1611; Thomas Nelson Inc.; Camden, New Jersey, 1970.
33. "Isaiah" 1:18, *King James Bible,*1611; Thomas Nelson Inc.; Camden, New Jersey, 1970.
34. "Genesis," 6:2, 4, *King James Bible,*1611; Thomas Nelson Inc.; Camden, New Jersey, 1970.
35. *The Book of Enoch* 8 1-3a, ancient Jewish writings, ascribed to Enoch, the great-grandfather of Noah, not currently part of the Canon of Scripture used by Jews, except the Beta Israel canon; nor by any Christian group, except the Ethiopian Orthodox Church canon. Western scholars believe that its older sections, especially the *Book of the Watchers* date from about 300 BC and the latest part, *Book of Parables*, probably about the end of the 1st century BC. Ethiopian scholars, however, generally hold that Ge'ez is the language of the original from which the Greek and Aramaic copies were made, because that it is the only

language in which the complete text has yet been found. Western scholars, however, suggest that, since there are fragments in Aramaic from the *Dead Sea Scrolls* and a few Greek and Latin fragments, these were the likely sources, perhaps partially Aramaic and partially Hebrew, similar to Daniel. A short section of 1 Enoch (1En 1:9) is quoted in the New Testament (Jude 1:14-15), and there apparently attributed to "Enoch the Seventh from Adam" (1En 60:8). It is argued that all the writers of the New Testament were familiar with it and were influenced by it in thought and diction.
36. “Zechariah,” 5: 6-11, *King James Bible,* 1611; Thomas Nelson Inc.; Camden, New Jersey, 1970.
37. “Leviticus,” 10:7, *King James Bible,* 1611; Thomas Nelson Inc.; Camden, New Jersey, 1970.
38. “Yoma,” vi. 4, 66b; "Epistle of Barnabas," vii. Yoma is Hebrew for “Day,” and is the fifth tractate or volume of *Seder Moed* ("Order of Festivals") of the *Mishnah* and of the *Talmud*, and mainly deals with the laws of the Jewish holiday Yom Kippur, on which Jews atone for their sins from the previous year. It consists of eight chapters and has a Gemara ("Completion") from both the Jerusalem Talmud and the Babylonian Talmud.
39. “Yoma,” vi. 6, 8; Ta'an. iv. 8.
40. *Enoch* xiii.; compare Brandt, "Mandäische Theologie," 1889, p. 38.
41. *Enoch* viii. 1, ix. 6, x. 4-6, liv. 5, lxxxviii. 1; see Geiger, "Jüd. Zeit." 1864, pp. 196–204.
42. “Yoma,” 67b.
43. see Brandt, "Mandäische Theologie," pp. 197, 198; Norberg's "Onomasticon," p. 31; Adriaan Reland’s "De Religione Mohammedanarum," p. 89; Kamus, s.v. "Azazel" (demon identical with Satan); Delitzsch, "Zeitsch. f. Kirchl. Wissensch. u. Leben," 1880, p. 182.
44. "Contra Celsum," vi. 43.
45. Pirḳe R. El. (l.c.).
46. Compare "the roes and the hinds," Cant. ii. 7, iii. 5.
47. Also see John 1:29 and Hebrews, Ch. 9-10.
48. Origen, also known as Origen Adamantius, c. 185–254, was one of the most distinguished writers of the early Christian Church. Tradition has it that he was an Egyptian who taught in Alexandria, reviving the Catechetical School of Alexandria where Clement of Alexandria had taught. At first, the patriarch of Alexandria supported Origen but later expelled him for being ordained without the patriarch's permission. He relocated to Caesarea Maritima and died there after being tortured during a persecution.
49. “Mark,” 10:45, *King James Bible,*1611; Thomas Nelson Inc.; Camden, New Jersey, 1970.
50. “1 Timothy,” 2:5-6, *King James Bible,*1611; Thomas Nelson Inc.; Camden, New Jersey, 1970.
51. “Romans,” 5:11. Atonement is used here in the *King James Bible,*1611; Thomas Nelson Inc.; Camden, New Jersey, 1970.
52. Ex. 32:30; Lev. 4:26; 5:16; Num. 6:11, *King James Bible,*1611; Thomas Nelson Inc.; Camden, New Jersey, 1970.

53. John 3:16; Rom. 3:24, 25; Eph. 1:7; 1 John 1:9; 4:9, *King James Bible,*1611; Thomas Nelson Inc.; Camden, New Jersey, 1970.
54. Ex. 34:7; Josh. 24:19; Ps. 5:4; 7:11; Nahum 1:2, 6; Rom. 3:5, *King James Bible,*1611; Thomas Nelson Inc.; Camden, New Jersey, 1970.
55. *The Power of Myth: Interviews with Bill Moyers*, ed. Sue Flowers, Doubleday: New York, p. 140.
56. Matt., xxvii, 46; Mark, xv, 34, *King James Bible,*1611; Thomas Nelson Inc.; Camden, New Jersey, 1970.
57. *Insanity and Genius*, Harry Eiss, Cambridge Scholars Press: Newcastle, England, 2008, pp., 94-101, 133-141.
58. *The Interpretation of Dreams,* trans. by James Strachey, Avon books, pp. 295-296.
59. *From Instruction to Delight: An Anthology of Children's Literature to 1850,* Patricia Demers & Gordon Moyles, Oxford Univ. Press, 1982, pp. 31-32, contains a reproduction of one of the illustrated versions of this popular alphabet poem, this one from *The New England Primer* (c. 1683-1830).
60. From *The Works of Anne Bradstreet,* ed., J. Hensley (Cambridge, Mass: Harvard Univ. Press, 1967, p. 54.
61. *From Instruction to Delight: An Anthology of Children's Literature to 1850,* Patricia Demers & Gordon Moyles, Oxford Univ. Press, 1982, p. 42.
62. "Genesis," 3:6-24, *King James Bible: Red Letter Version,* Riverside: Iowa Falls, Iowa, 1971, p. 3.
63. Genesis," 3:6-24, *King James Bible: Red Letter Version,* Riverside: Iowa Falls, Iowa, 1971, p. 3.
64. "The Journey Inward," *The Power of Myth: Interviews with Bill Moyers*, ed. Sue Flowers, Doubleday: New York, p. 55.
65. Il Simbolismo dei Sogni, Milan, 1951; trans. J. E. Cirlot, Diccionario De Simbolos Tradicionales; trans. Jack Sage, *A Dictionary of Symbols*, Routledge & Kegan Paul: London, 1962, p. 287.
66. *Myths and Symbols in Indian Art and Civilization*. New York: , 1946.
67. *Psychology and Alchemy* (collected works), 12). London, 1953.
68. *A Dictionary of Symbols*, 2nd ed., ed. J. E. Cirlot, Trans. by Jack Sage, Routledge & Kegan Paul: London, 1976, p. 287.
69. *La langue sacree*. Paris, 1931: *A Dictionary of Symbols* 2nd ed., ed. J. E. Cirlot, Trans. by Jack Sage, Routledge & Kegan Paul: London, 1976, p. 287.
70. *Tratado de historie de las religions*. Madrid, 1954; *A Dictionary of Symbols* 2nd ed., ed. J. E. Cirlot, Trans. by Jack Sage, Routledge & Kegan Paul: London, 1976, p. 286.
71. *Le Symbolisme dans la mythologie grecque*, Paris, 1952; *A Dictionary of Symbols* 2nd ed., ed. J. E. Cirlot, Trans. by Jack Sage, Routledge & Kegan Paul: London, 1976, p. 286.
72. *Mystische Reste in der Paradieserzahlune*, Archive f. Rel. X, 345.
73. *Tratado de historia de las religions,* Madrid, 1954. *A Dictionary of Symbols* 2nd ed., ed. J. E. Cirlot, Trans. by Jack Sage, Routledge & Kegan Paul: London, 1976.
74. *The Alphabet of Ben Sira* is the source most refer to for the origin of this story. It didn't appear until Medieval times, but various sources for the elements in it

have been found dating back to Jewish beliefs and to passages in the Bible. There are many sources discussing Lilith, including the following: Siegmund Hurwitz, *Lilith*, Switzerland: Damion Press, 1992; *Lilith's Cave: Jewish tales of the Supernatural*, Howard Schwartz, San Francisco: Harper& Row, 1988; Raphael Patai, *The Hebrew Goddess*, 3rd enlarged edition, New York: Discus Books, 1978; *The Witch Book*, Raymond Buckland, Visible ink Press, November 1, 2001.
75. *A Dictionary of Symbols* 2nd ed., ed. J. E. Cirlot, Trans. by Jack Sage, Routledge & Kegan Paul: London, 1976, p. 288.
76. *Totem and Taboo: Some Points of Agreement between the Mental Lives of Savages and Neurotics*, trans., James Strachey, W. W. Norton, 1950.
77. *Oedipus Rex*, Final Scene, line 139.
78. *Oedipus Rex*, Final Scene, line 140-141.
79. *Oedipus Rex*, Final Scene, lines 222-223.
80. *The Complete Signet Classic Shakespeare,* ed. Sylvan Barnet, Harcourt, Brace, Jovanovich, 1972.
81. Matt., xxvii, 46; Mark, xv, 34, *King James Bible,*1611; Thomas Nelson Inc.; Camden, New Jersey, 1970.
82. *Permanence and Change: An Anatomy of Purpose,* 1935; 3rd ed., Univ. of Calif., 1984.
83. *A Grammar of Motives,* 1945; Univ. of Calif., 1989.
84. *The Scapegoat,* Rene Girard, trans. Yvonke Freccero, John Hopkins Univ., 1986.

SHADOWS IN THE FOG

The fog comes
on little cat feet.
It sits looking
over harbor and city
on silent haunches
and then moves on.
—Carl Sandburg (1)

Look Too Close

In the mists of the fog, the ethereal dance of water and air, the ever elusive swirl of appearance, reality, illusion, hope and fear, it is possible to glimpse the eternal moment when the infinite and the finite intersect in love and hate, being and becoming, creation and destruction, possible to hear whispers of the early dreams of the fertile swamps, the sounds of water and earth becoming mud, becoming clay, becoming and becoming and becoming, possible to sense the elusive truths of God, the touch of his hands as he molds the wet clay into solid form, possible to feel his breath, his spirit, his sense of wonder, possible both to know and not know the truths beyond truth, the meanings beyond meaning, the rising tides of the moon that crash against the solid sunlit sands of the body, the logical, rational, blind and thirsty world of the hard, dry earth, the ephemeral thoughts mysteriously flowing into the dry cells of the brain, given life by the evanescent shadows of the spirit, possible to join with the currents of the life-giving rivers of the mind, the ever-changing rivers of human desire and need, of human unity and separation, of human discovery-and-loss of self.

Daphne du Maurier's novel *The Scapegoat* uses the term *scapegoat* more in the sense of a *doppelganger,* a double of a living person, a look-alike person, often seen as an *evil twin* or a form of *bilocation*, an instance where a person exists (or appears to exist) in two places at the same time. (2) In Norse mythology, a *vardoger* is a ghostly double that precedes a living person and can be seen performing their actions in advance.

Jean Paul created the term in his three volume novel *Siebenkas*. (3) Firmian Stanislaus Siebenkas is unhappily married and consults his friend Leibgeber (his doppelganger), who convinces Siebenkas to fake his death and begin a new life, where he meets Natalie, falls in love, and gets married.

Shahar Arzy and colleagues at University Hospital, Geneva, Switzerland, applied electrical stimulation of a patient's left temporoparietal junction, and the patient immediately felt the presence of another person, a *doppelganger*, next to her, a person she described as young, of indeterminate sex, silent, motionless, and with a body posture identical to her own. A second electrical stimulation resulted in her unpleasant sensing the presence of a man with his arms wrapped around her. A third stimulation was applied while having her perform a language test with a set of flash cards, and in this case she sensed the presence of a sitting person who attempted to prevent her from taking the test. (4) Such tests suggest that the left temporoparietal junction of the brain evokes the sensation of a self image, and if it is injured or in some way not functioning as it should, this self image might be replaced with the sensation of a duplicate self nearby; certain forms of schizophrenia, especially paranoid schizophrenia involving delusions of persecution and alien control also have been known to cause this feeling of a duplicate self, a *doppelganger.* (5)

On August 15, 1822, Mary Shelley, wrote a letter to Maria Gisborne describing her husband Percy Bysshe Shelley having a nightmare in the morning hours of June 23, 1822, where he claimed to have met his own doppelganger. He claimed to have dreamt about the house falling in a flood, and then,

> ... talking it over the next morning he told me that he had had many visions lately — he had seen the figure of himself which met him as he walked on the terrace & said to him — "How long do you mean to be content" — No very terrific words & certainly not prophetic of what has occurred. But Shelley had often seen these figures when ill; but the strangest thing is that Mrs. Williams saw him. Now Jane, though a woman of sensibility, has not much imagination & is not in the slightest degree nervous — neither in dreams or otherwise. She was standing one day, the day before I was taken ill, [15 June] at a window that looked on the Terrace with Trelawny — it was day — she saw as she thought Shelley pass by the window, as he often was then, without a coat or jacket — he passed again — now as he passed both times the same way — and as from the side towards which he went each time there was no way to get back except past the window again (except over a wall twenty feet from the ground) she was struck at seeing him pass twice thus & looked out & seeing him no more she cried — "Good God can Shelley have leapt from the wall? Where can he be gone?" Shelley, said Trelawny — "No Shelley has past — What do you mean?" Trelawny says that she trembled exceedingly when she heard this & it proved indeed that Shelley had never been on the terrace & was far off at the time she saw him. (6)

Coincidentally (or not), Percy Bysshe Shelley's drama *Prometheus Unbound* contains the following passage in Act I: "Ere Babylon was dust, / The Magus Zoroaster, my dear child, / Met his own image walking in the garden. / That apparition, sole of men, he saw. / For know there are two worlds of life and death: / One that which thou beholdest; but the other / Is underneath the grave, where do inhabit / The shadows of all forms that think and live / Till death unite them and they part no more...." (7)

Izaak Walton claimed that English metaphysical poet John Donne saw his wife's doppelgänger in 1612 in Paris, on the same night as the stillbirth of their daughter.

> Two days after their arrival there, Mr. *Donne* was left alone, in that room in which Sir *Robert*, and he, and some other friends had dined

> together. To this place Sir *Robert* returned within half an hour; and, as he left, so he found Mr. *Donne* alone; but, in such ecstasy, and so altered as to his looks, as amazed Sir *Robert* to behold him in so much that he earnestly desired Mr. *Donne* to declare befallen him in the short time of his absence? to which, Mr. *Donne* was not able to make a present answer: but, after a long and perplext pause, did at last say, *I have seen a dreadful Vision since I saw you: I have seen my dear wife pass twice by me through this room, with her hair hanging about her shoulders, and a dead child in her arms: this, I have seen since I saw you.* To which, Sir *Robert* replied; *Sure Sir, you have slept since I saw you; and, this is the result of some melancholy dream, which I desire you to forget, for you are now awake.* To which Mr. *Donnes* reply was: *I cannot be surer that I now live, then that I have not slept since I saw you: and am, as sure, that at her second appearing, she stopped, looked me in the face, and vanished.* (8)

Izaak Walton first provides this in the edition of *Life of Dr John Donne* published in 1675, and is attributed to "a Person of Honour... told with such circumstances, and such asseveration, that... I verily believe he that told it me, did himself believe it to be true." However, while it is true at the time Donne was extremely worried about his pregnant wife, and was going through severe illness himself, R. C. Bald points out that Walton's account "is riddled with inaccuracies. He says that Donne crossed from London to Paris with the Drurys . Donne still confined to her bed in Drury House. Actually, of course, Donne did not arrive in Paris until more than three months after he left England, and his wife was not in London but in the Isle of Wight The still-born child was buried on 24 January.... Yet as late as 14 April Donne in Paris was still ignorant of his wife's ordeal." (9) In January, Donne was still at Amiens. His letters do not support the story as given. (10)

According to Carl Sandberg,

> A dream or illusion had haunted Lincoln at times through the winter. On the evening of his election he had thrown himself on one of the haircloth sofas at home, just after the first telegrams of November 7 had told him he was elected President, and looking into a bureau mirror across the room he saw himself full length, but with two faces.
>
> It bothered him; he got up; the illusion vanished; but when he lay down again there in the glass again were two faces, one paler than the other. He got up again, mixed in the election excitement, forgot about it; but it came back, and haunted him. He told his wife about it; she worried too.
>
> A few days later he tried it once more and the illusion of the two faces again registered to his eyes. But that was the last; the ghost since then wouldn't come back, he told his wife, who said it was a sign he would be

> elected to a second term, and the death pallor of one face meant he wouldn't live through his second term.-(11)

Sandberg's source was Noah Brooks' *Washington in Lincoln's Time* (12) Noah Brooks claimed that Lincoln told it to him on November 9, 1864, at the time of his re-election, and that he had printed an account "directly after." He also claimed that the story was confirmed by Mary Todd Lincoln, and partially confirmed by Private Secretary John Hay (who thought it dated from Lincoln's nomination, not his election). Brooks' version is as follows (in Lincoln's own words):

> It was just after my election in 1860, when the news had been coming in thick and fast all day and there had been a great "hurrah, boys," so that I was well tired out, and went home to rest, throwing myself down on a lounge in my chamber. Opposite where I lay was a bureau with a swinging glass upon it (and here he got up and placed furniture to illustrate the position), and looking in that glass I saw myself reflected nearly at full length; but my face, I noticed had *two* separate and distinct images, the tip of the nose of one being about three inches from the tip of the other. I was a little bothered, perhaps startled, and got up and looked in the glass, but the illusion vanished. On lying down again, I saw it a second time, plainer, if possible, than before; and then I noticed that one of the faces was a little paler — say five shades — than the other. I got up, and the thing melted away, and I went off, and in the excitement of the hour forgot all about it — nearly, but not quite, for the thing would once in a while come up, and give me a little pang as if something uncomfortable had happened. When I went home again that night I told my wife about it, and a few days afterward I made the experiment again, when (with a laugh), sure enough! the thing came back again; but I never succeeded in bringing the ghost back after that, though I once tried very industriously to show it to my wife, who was somewhat worried about it. She thought it was a "sign" that I was to be elected to a second term of office, and that the paleness of one of the faces was an omen that I should not see life through the last term. (13)

Near the end of Book XI of his autobiography, *Dichtung und Wahrheit* (*Truth and Fiction*), Johann Wolfgang von Goethe wrote:

> Amid all this pressure and confusion I could not forego seeing Frederica once more. Those were painful days, the memory of which has not remained with me. When I reached her my hand from my horse, the tears stood in her eyes; and I felt very uneasy. I now rode along the foot-path toward Drusenheim, and here one of the most singular forebodings took possession of me. I saw, not with the eyes of the body, but with those of

> the mind, my own figure coming toward me, on horseback, and on the same road, attired in a dress which I had never worn, — it was pike-gray [*hecht-grau*], with somewhat of gold. As soon as I shook myself out of this dream, the figure had entirely disappeared. It is strange, however, that, eight years afterward, I found myself on the very road, to pay one more visit to Frederica, in the dress of which I had dreamed, and which I wore, not from choice, but by accident. However, it may be with matters of this kind generally, this strange illusion in some measure calmed me at the moment of parting. The pain of quitting for ever noble Alsace, with all I had gained in it, was softened; and, having at last escaped the excitement of a farewell, I, on a peaceful and quiet journey, pretty well regained my self-possession. (14)

There are numerous doppelganger examples appearing at the moment of death. Christina Hole records the strange appearance of Vice-Admiral Sir George Tryon's doppelganger (or ghost) in Victorian England. It is said he walked through the drawing room of his family home in Eaton Square, London, looking straight ahead, not exchanging a word to anyone, in front of several guests at a party being given by his wife on June 22, 1893 while he was supposed to be in a ship of the Mediterranean Squadron, maneuvering off the coast of Syria. Subsequently it was reported that he had gone down with his ship, the HMS *Victoria*, that very night, after it had collided with the HMS *Camperdown* following an unexplained and bizarre order by him to turn the ship in the direction of the other vessel. (15)

Christina Hole follows this example with one concerning John Otway Wynyard, who died in England October 15, 1785. His doppelganger ghost was seen by his broth George and Captain Sherbroke while they were serving in the thirty-third Regiment in Canada. They were in the sitting room reading about four o'clock in the afternoon. Sherbroke looked up from his book and saw a stranger standing in the room. He was about twenty-years-old, looked ill, and wore light indoor clothing more suited to England than Canada. He called to George, who recognized his brother, and they watched together as the ghost walked into the bedroom, which had no other exit. Immediately following it in, they found the bedroom empty. George was certain something had happened to his brother, but there was no way of knowing until the English mail arrived above a ship from England. When it did, Captain Sherbroke received a letter that George's brother had, indeed, died at the moment the doppelganger appeared to him.

Christina Hole follows this with yet a third. This one concerns Lord Lyttleton, who died November 17, 1779 in Epsom. Three days before his death he was awakened by the sound of a bird fluttering in the bed curtains and saw the ghost of a women in white standing by his side. When he asked her if he would be alive in two months, she told him he would die within three days. The next morning he told his guests about this, what he thought was a dream.

Three days later he went to Pitt Place, his house in Epsom, taking a number of his friends with him. He felt well, and declared he had "bilked" the ghost. Just after eleven, he went to bed. However, while his servant Stuckey was helping him undress he suddenly put his hand to his side, collapsed and died.

It was later discovered that he must have taken the warning more seriously than he said, for he had previously arranged to spend that weekend at Dartfort with his friend, Peter Andrews, but had changed his mind without letting Andrews know. Andrews went to bed early that evening. Between eleven and twelve he woke to see Lyttleton, dressed in his personal bed-gown, looking at him through the curtains of the bed. Thinking it was a joke of some sort, he threatened to throw something at Lyttleton if he did not go away. But Lyttleton's ghost said, "It's all over with me, Andrews." Andrews, still not believing, threw his slippers at him, whereupon, Lyttleton retreated to the dressing-room, which had only one entrance. When Andrews followed him, he found the room empty. Upon investigation, he found his bed-gown hanging in its usual place, apparently unused, and his servants claimed no one had visited the previous evening. Still suspecting a joke was being played on him, he ordered the servants not to admit anyone and went back to bed. The next day he received news that Lyttleton had died at the same time he had seen him in his room.

In his novella *The Double,* Fyodor Dostoevsky immediately presents his main character as a man caught in an uncertain duality:

> It was a little before eight o'clock in the morning when Yakov Petrovich Golyadkin, a titular councilor, woke up from a long sleep. He yawned, stretched, and at last opened his eyes completely. For some two minutes, however, he lay in his bed without moving, like a man who is not yet quite certain whether he is awake or still asleep, whether all that is going on around him is real and actual, or the continuation of his confused dreams. (16)

Is he waking from a dream or falling into a dream, in "never-never land" or "the capital city of Petersburg"? After a few minutes he is reassured by the familiar surroundings, the "dirty green, smoke-begrimed, dusty walls," the "mahogany chest of drawers and imitation mahogany chairs, the table painted red, the ottoman upholstered in reddish oilcloth with little green flowers," the "clothes taken off in haste overnight and flung in a crumpled heap on the sofa." But, then, are these familiar because they are part of his *real* life or because they are part of some *hallucinatory nightmare*?

Once he had pulled himself into this world, "he leaped out of bed in one bound" and "ran straight to a little round looking glass" to reassure himself that he looked like himself, and his thoughts betray his uneasiness, as he confirms that "there's nothing wrong," that "so far all goes well." And the dualities of a mirror can hardly be ignored.

Then, the subtle reversal of awaking slides into the narrative as a subordinate clause, "although he was barefoot and in the attire in which he was accustomed to go to bed, he ran to the window and with great interest began looking for something in the courtyard." So which is it? Has he just entered the dream? Or is he just leaving it?

Other phrases are sprinkled in to suggest something isn't quite right; he has "scattered and wandering thoughts," is "extremely absent-minded," and his mood shifts rapidly, "laughter" being "replaced by a strange, anxious expression."

There is also an emphasis on him dressing, worrying about whether his clothes will fit, with a special emphasis on making sure his boots fit (suggestive of the cliché "if the shoe fits wear it). And "it was also noticeable that during his master's inspection Petrushka watched him with strange expectancy, and with marked curiosity followed every movement he made," raising questions of why, of whether or not there might be something "different" or "unusual" about him.

This uneasy straddling of realities, of "real" and "imagined" worlds continues as Golyadkin got into his hired carriage and "rubbed his hands convulsively and went off into a quiet, noiseless chuckle, like a man who has succeed in playing a splendid trick." Just what is going on here? Is he simply going through a daily routine, perhaps a bit disoriented, or is he indeed a doppelganger not quite himself? But then the sentence concludes "and immediately after his access of gaiety, however, laughter was replaced by a strange, anxious expression on the face of Mr. Golyadkin." He continues to perform for any who might see him "at once assuming a decorous and sedate air when he thought anyone was looking at him." Then shortly, "he was startled by a most unpleasant sensation and, frowning like some poor devil whose corn has been accidentally stepped on, he huddled hastily, even fearfully, into the darkest corner of his carriage." Does this man have bipolarism?"

What he saw to cause him to retreat into the shadows were two of his colleagues, who "were also, it seemed to Mr. Golyadkin, extremely perplexed at encountering their colleague in this way." We are told he is worried they will find it unusual, but he reassures himself: "Why, what is there strange about it? A man in a carriage, a man needs to be in a carriage, and so he hires a carriage." But his reassurance is immediately undermined, and we are told "Mr. Golyackin broke off suddenly, petrified," because a man in a "droshky" pulled by a "pair of Kazan horses, very familiar," happened to see him and "appeared to be extremely astonished at the unexpected sight and, bending out as far as he could, looked with the greatest curiosity and interest into the corner of the carriage in which our hero made haste to conceal himself."

Realizing it is his boss, Golyackin takes us yet again directly into the crux of things: "To bow or not to bow? To hail him or not? To recognize him or not?" our hero wondered in indescribable anguish, "or shall I pretend that I am not myself, but somebody else strikingly like me, and look as though nothing were the matter? Just . . . not me, not me and that's all," said Mr. Golyadkin, taking off his hat to Andrey Filippovich, and keeping his eyes fixed upon him. "Don't . . . don't mind me," he whispered with an effort; "just don't mind me. It's not me at all, Andrey Filippovich, it's not me at all, not me, and that's all."

Something strange is going on here. And then Golyackin demonstrates he is aware of it, concerned about it, and decides to immediately seek out the doctor he just visited for the first time but a week ago for his own "peace of mind." He will "Make believe that" he "is all right, and . . . simply looked in as" he "passed."

Upon reaching the door of the doctor's office, he debated knocking or simply putting off the visit, but decided to "assume an air of propriety," of "undue familiarity," and after a bit of indecision, pulled the cord to ring the bell. When the doctor finished with previous patients and found Golyackin waiting, he was not happy, "assumed a strange and, one may almost say, a displeased expression." We soon find that Dr. Krestyan Ivanovich has prescribed a "change of habits." We read on as Golyackin stumbles through a confusing explanation of how he is not good at being the kind of man the doctor has told him to be, at, in other words, assuming a new role or identity. Golyackin stresses that he has "no taste for contemptible duplicity," that he only puts "on a mask at a masquerade," and doesn't "wear one before people every day."

As the interview continues, the stumbling, insecure Golyackin does seem to change, becoming more confident, speaking "distinctly and clearly, weighing his words with a self-confident air and reckoning on their probable effect," but we see the other Golyackin, the stumbling, bumbling one is not completely replaced, as he finishes his speech "with anxiety, with great anxiety, with extreme anxiety" and waits "timidly" for the doctor's reply. As the exchange continues, this back-and-forth personality continues, and soon he noticed that "a queer change came over him."

The doctor is caught up in it, confused by it. For a time they stare at each other "motionless." Then Golyackin begins to cry! And claims "I have enemies; I have malicious enemies who have sworn to destroy me."

The interview shifts into Golyackin relieving himself of rumors he has heard, innuendoes, then leaves the doctor in a confused state, walks down the stairs and out to his carriage, looks up to see the doctor looking down at him, and says to himself, "That doctor is stupid."

We cannot be sure what is happening, but we know either Golyackin is having some kind of mental breakdown or we are caught in the fragments of multiple realities.

Chapter III begins with the subtle (or not so subtle) "Mr. Golyadkin spent the whole morning madly bustling about. Note the particular word chosen: *madly*. Impossible to say that such a pregnant word is not purposely intended to carry its multiple meanings. The chapter takes us quickly through Golyackin making large purchases at several stores (though putting everything on hold without deposit), sitting down for a meal, during which he anxiously waits for time to pass, inadvertently encountering the same two co-workers he had passed earlier in the day, and doing his best to socialize with them, leading up to his attempt to put into place the doctor's orders to be a different man, a social man, including, again, the doppelganger suggestions: "You all know me, gentlemen, but hitherto you've known only one side of me. . . . Hitherto, gentlemen, you have not known me." His bold manner, so different than they have known, cause them to laugh out loud at him.

Then he heads to dinner at Olsufy Ivanovish's, where he assumes he is one of the honored guests, but instead he is dismissed, not allowed to enter. Confused, he first takes his rented carriage home, then decides to go instead to a modest restaurant, dismiss the rented carriage, take a private room and order dinner. "He felt very ill and his brain was in a state of utmost confusion and chaos."

Then the great dinner party Golyackin was denied entrance to gets described, and a grand affair it is. When we return to Golyackin, we find that he has not given up on it. He stands just outside, looking in, eventually gathers the courage needed, and simply walks into it. In bold, audacious manner, he strikes up conversations, immediately annoying each of the guests he attempts to solicit, eventually tries to dance with the featured guest Klara Olsufyevna, who screams, and is escorted out.

The clock strikes midnight (with all of its symbolism), and "Mr. Golyadkin was killed—killed entirely, in the full sense of the word, and if he still preserved the ability to run, it was simply through some sort of miracle, a miracle in which at last he himself refused to believe." Then comes the description of his own insanity in the form of a storm, a midnight storm that he is lost in, alone in:

> It was an awful November night—wet, foggy, rainy, snowy, fraught with colds in the head, fevers, swollen faces, quinseys, inflammations of all kinds and descriptions—fraught, in short, with all the gifts of a Petersburg November. The wind howled in the deserted streets, lifting up the black water of the canal above the righs, and perkily brushing against the lean lanterns on the embankment, so that they chimed in with the howling in a thin, shrill creak, keeping up the endless squeaky, jangling concert with which every inhabitant of Petersburg is so familiar. It was both snowing and raining. Lashed by the wind, the streams of rain water spurted almost horizontally, as though from a fireman's hose, pricking and stinging the face of the luckless Mr. Golyadkin like a thousand pins and needles. In the stillness of the night, broken only by the distant rumbling of carriages, the howl of the wind, and the creaking of the lanterns, there was the dismal sound of the splash and gurgle of water, streaming from every roof, every porch, every gutter, and every cornice, onto the granite of the pavement. There was not a soul, near or far, and, indeed, it seemed that there could not be any at such an hour and in such weather. And so only Mr. Golyadkin, alone with his despair, was trotting mincingly along the pavement of Fontanka, in haste to reach as soon as possible his flat on the fourth story in Shestilavochny Street. (17)

And we are informed that "If any disinterested spectator could have glanced casually at Mr. Golyadkin's painful progress, he too would instantly have grasped the awful horror of his pitiful plight and would certainly have said that Mr. Golyadkin looked as though he wanted to hide somewhere from himself, as though he were trying to run away from himself! Yes! It was really so. One may say more: Mr. Golyadkin wanted not only to run away from himself, but to be obliterated, to cease to be, to turn into dust." (18)

Then, while he stands near the "black turbulent waters" of the canal, "completely exhausted," suggesting to us that he is likely contemplating suicide, he indeed meets his doppelganger. It is a curious meeting in the swirling storm. A man passes by, a man who seems somehow familiar. Golyadkin follows him. He goes straight to Golyadkin's own dwelling, gets Petrushka, who obviously believes him to be Golyadkin, lets him in, and Golyadkin "dashed into his lodging."

> All that he had dreaded and surmised had come to pass in reality. His breath failed him, his head was in a whirl. The stranger, also in his coat and hat, was sitting before him on his bed, and with a faint smile and slightly screwed-up eyes, nodded to him in a friendly way. Fr. Golyadkin wanted to scream, but could not, to protest in some way, but his strength failed him. His hair stood on end, and he almost fell down with horror. And, indeed, there was good reason. He recognized his nocturnal friend. The nocturnal friend was none other than himself—Mr. Golyadkin himself, another Mr. Golyadkin, but absolutely the same as he himself—in short , what is called his double in every respect. . . . (19)

Can't be more direct and absolute than this. But . . . This ends the chapter, and immediately at the beginning of the next chapter, we are led to the likelihood it was a dream, the dream of a very *paranoid* man:

> Precisely at eight o'clock next morning Mr. Golyadkin woke up in his bed. At once all the extraordinary incidents of the previous day and the wild, incredible night, with all its almost impossible adventures, presented themselves to his imagination and memory in all their terrifying fullness. Such intense, diabolical malice on the part of his enemies, and, above all, the final proof of that malice, froze Mr. Golyadkin's heart. But at the same time it was all so strange, incomprehensible, wild, it seemed so impossible, that it was really hard to credit the whole business. Mr. Golyadkin himself would have been indeed ready to admit that it was all incredible raving, a passing derangement of the imagination, a darkening of the mind, if he had not fortunately known by bitter experience to what lengths spite will sometimes carry a man, what a pitch of ferocity an enemy may reach in avenging an injury to his honor and pride. Besides, Mr. Golyadkin's bruised limbs, heavy head, aching back, and bad cold bore vivid witness to the reality of his expedition of the previous night, and to some extent of all that had happened on that occasion. And, indeed, Mr. Golyadkin had known long, long before that *they* were getting up something, that there was someone else with *them*. But, having thought it over thoroughly, he made up his mind to keep quiet, to submit and not to protest against it for the time being. "Perhaps they only intend to frighten me," he reflected, "and when they see that I don't mind, that I make no protest, but keep perfectly quiet and bear with it meekly, they'll give it up, they'll give it up of themselves, give it up of their own accord." (20)

When his servant Petrushka comes in to serve the morning tea, he shows no signs of noticing anything unusual the night before, but "He knows, he knows, he knows all about it, the scoundrel!" Mr. Golyadkin grumbled to himself," his paranoia clear (unless it really did happen). Gathering up his courage, Mr. Golyadkin goes to work, expecting to be confronted over his actions the previous night. However, no one bothers with him. No one seems to have experienced what he did. Then his boss, the very Andrey Filippovich he expects to be in trouble with, comes in to seat a new employee near him, and pays Golyadkin no attention at all. So, we must believe the events of the previous day must have all been only real in the psychotic mess of his own mind.

But then, when Golyadkin sees who this new worker is he realizes it is the same double or doppelganger he met the previous night, or, if not, then yet another doppelganger: "What is this? Is it a dream?" he wondered. "Is it reality or the continuation of what happened yesterday? How is that? And by what right is all this taking place? Who has permitted the existence of such a clerk, who has authorized this? Am I asleep, am I dreaming?" (21)

Trying to sort this out, Golyadkin decides to ask his co-worker Anton Antonovich about the amazing coincidence. At first, Anton shows little interest, and is only slowly led to admit that the new worker does indeed look very much like Golyadkin. As the conversation continues Anton admits more and more how similar they look, but he has no interest, shows little concern about it, and eventually simply leaves to continue his work. Golyadkin takes this reaction as part of the plot against him, saying to himself "So that's the sort of game that's going on here!" (22)

Not sure what to do next, he ends up deciding to do nothing for the moment. The work day ends, and he goes into somewhat upbeat into the cool Russian air. "Yet something was fretting him, not exactly anguish, but at times he had such a gnawing at his heart that he did not know how to find relief." (23) Then his doppelganger appears beside him, they talk hesitatingly, and Golyadkin invites the man to his home "utterly unable to grasp what was happening to him." (24)

We get a clever phrase to begin chapter vii: "He recovered himself a little." (25) Such double entendres continue, as the scene plays out. Petrushka lets in the doppelganger Mr. Golyadkin and shows no signs that there is anything unusual, causing our hero (as Dostoevsky often refers to him) ever more anxiety about the whole world of his acquaintances being in on some kind of trick against him (and again suggesting he is paranoid). He notices that his double visitor is also anxious, shy, even "scared," and makes the comparison that "he was at that moment rather like the man who for want of his own clothes, has put on somebody else's" (which he goes on to state don't fit quite right). Then our hero accidentally drops his hat on the floor, and our double immediately picks it up, brushes it off, and replaces it (as if it were his own hat that he had dropped). Mr. Golyadkin decides this poor stranger needs him. Again, it is emphasized that this stranger has Mr. Golyadkin's same name, Yakov Petrovich, and comes from the same district he came from.

As the evening continues Mr. Golyadkin becomes more and more happy with his double, and ends up seeing him as a fellow comrade, a brother. He invites the man to live with him helps him get into bed. However, after the man has fallen asleep, he looks in on him and has some doubts, even condemns the man for taking on his name—in other words, at the last moment before sleep, his happy welcoming of this strange stranger gets overturned by negative thoughts.

This leads into the next chapter, where he finds upon waking up the next morning that his newly made friend, his double, has already departed, taking his bed with him. And his servant Petrushka has apparently mistaken his double for him!

Then things go from bad to worse. Our hero Mr. Golyadkin goes to work, where he meets his double Yakov Petrovich, the same double who came to work the previous day, the same double who slept at his house the previous night, but this double barely recognizes him from the previous day, and has no memory of the meeting the previous night!

Struggling to clarify it, Golyadkin uses the term "mask," "I am simply developing a theory, that is, I am advancing the idea, Anton "Antonovitch, that persons who wear a mask have become far from uncommon, and that nowadays it is hard to recognize the man beneath the mask." (26) At this point Dostovesky begins distinguishing the two Golyadkin's as Golyadkin, Sr., and Golydkin, Jr. As the scene at the office continues, Golydkin, Jr., outdoes Golydkin, Sr., in accomplishing tasks, and chides him when he tries to clarify what is going on. The chapter ends with the two of them leaving work. It concludes, "It seemed as though all were lost for Mr. Golyadkin." (27)

Then we follow him seeming indeed lost. He reaches his home, but decides not to stay and eat there, goes to Audri Filippovich's house, decides to eat at a nearby restaurant, finds his double has already eaten there and he is being charged for the double's meal, leaves, ends up home again, writes a letter to his double and orders his servant to take the letter to the office and find out the address and deliver it, heads to work, changes his mind and goes back home, falls asleep, and when he awakes finds his servant has returned and fallen asleep. Having decided he should not have written the letter, he wakes his servant and asks what became of his errand. The servant, however, says he was never sent on this errand! So what has been going on here? Has it all been a dream, some kind of terrible nightmare? When Golydkin pushes Petrushka, his servant plays along with the game, saying he did ask for the double's address, found out it was the same as Golydkin's, and end it by mixing in "Good folk live honestly, good folk live without cheating, and they don't come in twins. . . ." So, perhaps, just perhaps, Petrushka has seen this double, perhaps this double really does exist.

And so we continue to follow our delusional man, and all of Dostoevsky's clever double entendres, as Golydkin condemns himself, "I'm my own enemy! I'm my own murderer! . . . My own murderer, that's what I am!" (28).

Then he sees what he thinks might be "an illusion, a figment of his imagination," (29)

What Golydkin sees is a letter sitting on his table, and at first we think it probably the same letter he sent Petrushka to deliver, and in the circular dualities taking place we suspect is the same letter he mailed out, come back to him. However, it is not. Instead, it is a letter from Vahrameyev, confirming that Petrushka came to him to deliver the letter Golydkin sent with him, and his story was so impossible that Vahrameyev thought him drunk, and in addition Vahrameyev no longer wishes to have anything to do with Golydkin, as Golydkin's actions of late have been "fraudulent" and dishonorable, and especially disrespectful to a woman named Karolina Ivanovna. In response, Golydkin immediately composes a letter professing his innocence and ignorance of what he has been accused.

When we first began this strange story, we immediately realized something wasn't right, either the world was out of joint or Golydkin was lost in a dream, or some such mixture of reality and illusion was taking place, and we followed the endless dualities, the double entendres, the confusing encounters with a double or doppelganger, the seemingly paranoid suggestions that the entire world was working against Golydkin. One moment we thought it obvious that Golydkin is psychotic, the next that his paranoia had some basis in reality, perhaps, just perhaps had some justification.

By now we are beginning to wonder just how long Dostoevsky is going to lead us through this confusing, irrational labyrinth of delusions and sanity; and ultimately, if he is going to clarify it or simply leave it as an enigma.

In the end, perhaps unfortunately, he will resolve it.

But there is still a bit more before he is ready to do that. So we read on, watching as Golydkin's suspicions spiral more and more out of control until it seems it must be simply a matter of him being insane. We watch him run down his doppelganger in a taxi, convince him to have lunch, a chance for both he and us to sort out just what's been going on. But the glib doppelganger-double ends up convincing Golydkin that it is *he* who has wronged the double, rather than the reverse, and Golydkin ends up apologizing and trying to create a friendship. But then, just as quickly the double rushes off, leaving Golydkin stuck with the bill for the meal, and Golydkin again feels betrayed (as do we for we know no more than before the meeting). Then, as we read through his continually confusing attempts to sort it out, Golydkin ends up back at another social gathering similar to the one where he earlier made a fool of himself and got escorted out; and the same thing happens this time, only this time his double is also there to contribute to the general disregard for him.

Now what? Well, he hires a cab to take him to Izmailovsky Bridge, and we are inundated with phrases suggesting he is about to commit suicide in the symbolic cold, snow of winter by jumping into the also symbolic water; he turns "cold all over," (30), and thinks to himself "I am done for . . . I have vanished there can be no doubt any longer." He has exchanges with his hired cabby, who keeps asking him "Won't you soon be going, sir?" leading up to the ramblings of a sad man who appears indeed to have given up:

> Suddenly Mr. Golyadkin started. The soaked red beard of his cabman appeared over the woodstack again. . . .
>
> "I am coming directly, my friend. I'm coming at once, you know, at once," Mr. Golyadkin responded in a trembling and weak voice.
>
> The cabman scratched the back of his head, stroked his beard, and moved a step forward . . . then stood still and looked at Mr. Golyadkin.
>
> "I am coming directly, my friend; you see, my friend . . . I . . . just a little, you see, only a second . . . you see, my friend. . . ."
>
> "Won't you be going anywhere at all?" the cabman asked, at last resolutely confronting Mr. Golyadkin.
>
> "I'm coming directly, my friend, I am waiting, you see, my friend. . . ."
>
> "Yes sir. . . ."
>
> "You see, my friend, I . . . What village do you come from, my friend?"
>
> "We are under a master. . . ."
>
> "And have you a kind master?"
>
> "He's not bad. . . ."
>
> "Yes, my friend; you stay here, my friend, you see. . . . Have you been in Petersburg long, my friend?"
>
> "I've been driving a cab for a year now. . . ."
>
> "And are you getting on all right, my friend?"
>
> "Not bad."
>
> "To be sure, my friend, to be sure. You ought to thank Providence, my friend. You should look for a good man. Good people are none too common nowadays, my friend. A good man would wash you, give you food and drink, my good fellow, a good man would. But sometimes you

see tears shed by the wealthy, my friend—a lamentable example; that's how it is, my friend. . . ."

The cabman seemed to feel sorry for Mr. Golyadkin.

"Well, your honor, I'll stay on. Will your honor be waiting long?"

"No, my friend, no; I . . . you know . . . er . . . I won't wait any longer, my good man. . . . What do you think, my friend? I rely upon you. I won't stay here any longer."

"Aren't you going to drive anywhere?"

"No, my friend, no: and I'll make it worth your while, my friend . . . that's how it is. How much do I owe you, my dear fellow?"

"What you hired me for, please, sir. I've been waiting here a long time; you won't wrong a man, sir."

"Well, here, my friend, here."

At this point Mr. Golyadkin gave six whole rubles to the cabman, and made up his mind in earnest to waste no more time, that is, to clear off with a whole skin, especially since the matter had been settled and the cabman dismissed, and there was nothing more to wait for. He walked out of the yard, through the gate, turned left and, without looking around, took to his heels, breathless and rejoicing. "Perhaps it will all be for the best," he thought, "and perhaps in this way I've steered clear of trouble." Indeed, Mr. Golyadkin suddenly, all at once, felt unusually light-hearted. "Oh, if only it could turn out for the best!" thought our hero, though he put little faith in his own words. "I know what I'll do . . ." he thought. "No I'd better try the other tack. . . . Or wouldn't it be better to do this?" In this way, hesitating and seeking for the solution of his doubts, our hero ran as far as Semyonovsky Bridge;" (31)

But then, just when he is ready to end it all, he changes his mind, and the above sentence concludes, "but, having reached it, he rationally, prudently, and conclusively decided to return." And much to our surprise, or perhaps no longer so surprising for we have watched the reversions enough to no longer be surprised by them, he is greeted back to the party as if he is the most admired guest of them all! He is overcome with both confusion and joy. He is "reconciled with mankind and his destiny, and at the moment filled with love, not only for Olsufy Ivanovich, not only for the guests as a whole, but even for his noxious twin (who seemed now to be by no means noxious, and not even to be his twin at all, but a person very agreeable in himself and in no way connected with), our hero, in a voice broken with sobs, tried to express his feeling to Olsufy Ivanoich, but was too much overcome by all that he had gone through, and could not utter a word; he could only, with an expressive gesture, point silently at his heart. . . ." (32) This happy emergence from his misery continues until, yet again:

> Then something quite unexpected occurred. . . . The door opened noisily, and on the threshold stood a man, the very sight of whom turned Mr. Golyadkin's heart to ice. He stood rooted to the spot. A cry of horror died away in his chocking throat. (33)

Yes, the person sends chills through our hero Mr. Golyadkin, and right when everyone else in his world has suddenly embraced him. Who could it be? Well, "Mr. Golyadkin knew this personage very well. He had seen him before, had seen him that day. . . . It's . . . . it's Krestyan Ivanovich Rutenspitz, doctor of medicine and surgery . . ." (p. 174). Indeed, it is the same doctor Mr. Golyadkin visited early in the story, and now it is all revealed. Mr. Golyadkin has in fact been under the care of this doctor because Mr. Golyadkin has some form of mental disease. What we have been witness to is the rapid disintegration of his mind.

And now, as he emerges, at least briefly, from this psychosis, he again recognizes his physician, and "Tears started from Mr. Golyadkin's eyes." And he says, "In that case I'm ready . . . I have full confidence . . . and I entrust my fate to Krestyan Ivanovich. . . ." (34) But then his confidence shifts to fear: "When he came to himself, he saw that the horses were taking him along an unfamiliar road. Dark woods wound to the right and the left of it; the place was desolate and deserted. Suddenly he almost swooned: two fiery eyes were staring at him in the darkness, and those two eyes were glittering with malignant, hellish glee. "That's not Krestyan Ivanovich! Who is it? Or is it he? It is. It is Krestyan Ivanovich, but not the old Krestyan Ivanovich, it's another Krestyan Ivanovich! It's the terrible Krestyan Ivanovich!" (35)

We follow our hero's thoughts as he flip-flops back-and-forth from joy to fear, from intimation of the reality outside his mind to his psychotic nightmare reality inside, and the novella concludes:

> "Krestyan Ivanovich, I . . . I believe . . . I'm all right, Krestyan Ivanovich," our hero was beginning timidly in a trembling voice, hoping by his meekness and submissiveness to propitiate the terrible Krestyan Ivanovich a little.
>
> "You will get quarters at public expense, viz. firewood, light, and service, which you don't deserve," Krestyan Ivanovich's answer rang out, stern and terrible as a judge's sentence.
>
> Our hero cried out and clutched his head. Alas! He had had a presentiment of this for a long time. (36)

This kind of *doppelganger* is a psychic double, an entity within the invisible world of one man, and a man obviously unbalanced. This leads to an interpretation of the novella based on psychological concepts. The doppelganger is being presented not as symbolic psychological double, but as a real psychological double. One possible psychological explanation for such a situation is the concept of *projection.*

In Freudian psychology, *projection* is a form of *paranoia*, which in turn is one of what he calls the *neuroses of defense,* "pathological aberrations of normal psychical affective states," specifically of *mortification*:

> The determining element of paranoia is the mechanism of projection involving the refusal of belief in the self-reproach. Hence the common characteristic features of the neurosis: the significance of the voices as the means by which other people affect us, and also of gestures, which reveal other people's mental life to us; and the importance of the *tone* of remarks and *allusions* in them—since a direct reference from the *content* of remarks to the repressed memory is inadmissible to consciousness. (37)

Paranoia is a perception of self-importance and of persecution, justified through a systematic, organized delusion, a *projection* of one's own *fears* onto others, into a fleshed-out reality that has somehow lost touch with literal reality, a form of *hallucination* that remains *justifiable*, that can be defended if one only buys into the premise of the alternative world. (38)

In terms of *projection,* Freud writes," The purpose of paranoia is thus to ward off an idea that is incompatible with the ego, by projecting its substance into the external world." For example, a woman frightened by new experiences of sexual desire suddenly believes her neighbors are gossiping about her, calling her a slut or a whore, thus *projecting* the self reproach of being a slut into the outside world. "The alcoholic will never admit to himself that he has become impotent through drink ... So his wife is to blame. . . .The official who has been passed over for promotion requires that there is a conspiracy against him and that he be spied on in his room. Otherwise he would have to admit his shipwreck. . . . The *grande nation* cannot face the idea that it could be defeated in war. Ergo it was not defeated; the victory does not count. It provides an example of mass paranoia and invents the delusion of betrayal." (39)

According to Melanie Klein projection also consists of the fantasies the individual has about what he has done. In other words, it travels through time, recreating the past. (40)

Richard J. Romenthal elaborates:

> Projection is a mental mechanism whereby aspects of the self are attributed to others. It is an essential component of empathy and identification, and it may be used as a mechanism of defense in which a person attempts to get rid of unacceptable impulses and aspects of the self by externalizing them

> on to other people or on to the environment. There is a continuing relationship with the projected aspects of the self and with the person or object into which they are projected. The individual may feel persecuted by these others or in identification with them. He may feel a need to control them, or conversely, may feel controlled by them. Excessive use of projective mechanisms may leave an individual feeling internally depleted, and such an inner sense of impoverishment renders him less able to protect himself from the intrusiveness of others. It will also leave him uncertain as to his own psychic boundaries, where he ends and the other begins, resulting in a confusion between inner and outer reality (fantasy versus reality, dream versus life). (41)

Freud's term for the *uncanny* is *das unheimliche*, which he contrasts with *heimlich* ("homely" or "familiar") and *heimisch* ("native"), and claims "what is 'uncanny' is frightening precisely because it is not known and familiar." (42) Tracing of the etymology of the term leads him to conclude: "heimlich is a word the meaning of which develops in the direction of ambivalence, until it finally coincides with its opposite, unheimlich. Unheimlich is in some way or other a sub-species of Heimlich." (43) He then ascribes this total reversal in the meaning of the *uncanny* to a process of *repression*, stating "for this uncanny is in reality nothing new or alien, but something which is familiar and old-established in the mind and which has become alienated from it only through the process of repression." (44)

He argues on the authority of Otto Rank that at the narcissistic stage in the *ego's* development, the *ego* invents a *double*, someone or an object it can identify with. The invention of this *double* is initially a defense mechanism, "an insurance against the destruction of the ego." (45) Yet, as the *ego* passes the narcissistic stage, the *double* loses its original function, reverses its position: "From having been an assurance of immortality, it becomes the uncanny harbinger of death." (46)

Thus, the quality of uncanniness can only come from the fact of the *double* being a creation dating back to a very early mental stage, long since surmounted—a stage, incidentally, at which it wore a more friendly aspect. Once the *ego* passes its narcissistic stage, instead of being a needed protection, the *double* becomes a thing of terror, just as, after the collapse of their religion, the gods turned into demons. (47)

Furthermore, since there is in the unconscious mind a strong compulsion to repeat as a result of instinctual impulses, "whatever reminds us of this inner 'compulsion to repeat' is perceived as uncanny." (48)

Decades before Freud began trying to understand this *psychological double* and the dangers of *repression*, Edgar Allan Poe gave us a wonderful expression of it in his story *William Wilson* (49)

Since the story is going to deal with the struggle between the *ego* and its *double*, in Jungian terms the *ego* and the *shadow*, it is interesting that Poe's first person narrator begins by stressing how he refuses to give his *real* name, as if somehow that will prevent him from "sullying" the purity of the page with his *"real appellation."* He then spends a good deal of time detailing out his family character, emphasizing that his parents are not intelligent, but that he has inherited an excitable temperament. After stressing that at least partially because of their weak mental and physical qualities his parents could not control his "evil propensities," he emphasizes that he take responsibility, saying "I was left to the guidance of my own will, and became, in all but name, the master of my own actions."

Having such a negative view of his family, it is not surprising that he feels fortunate in escaping his home environment as a child where he attended a school which he goes to great length to describe as a "gothic prison," with a principal who acts as a church pastor in enforcing the severe rules.

Nevertheless, even with his negative attitude, he turns out to be an exceptional student in all aspects, clearly superior to the others.

But now is when the real story begins. There is one student, curiously, obviously in terms of the theme of the story, having his same name, his same build, same dress style, and having joined the school the same day he did. Later, he will mention that this *double* was born on the same day as well. The older students believe them to be brothers. Interestingly, the only difference is that this *double* can never raise his voice above a whisper.

This other William Wilson immediately becomes his rival, though not surprisingly, the narrator admits a bit of admiration and even attraction for this otherwise enemy. However, the relationship moves ever more negative, eventually resulting in a scuffle, after which our narrator becomes even more obsessed with his *double*, eventually sneaking into his bedroom with the idea of playing a practical joke, shinning a light on him, seeing a different face in the darkness, and rushing out of the room in terror.

After several months secluded from the school to recover, he returns to his studies, but at a different school, hoping to be done with his *double.* At this school he falls into a drinking binge, until, during a particularly drunken revelry, he is visited yet again by this frightening *double*.

He changes schools again, this time moving to Oxford. Here he chooses a new vice, gambling, and becoming skilled at it, he plies his trade on a weak-minded classmate named Glendinning, luring him into some large losses. However, in his moment of evil triumph, again his *double* arrives, this time revealing him to be a scam artist and ruining his reputation at the school and throughout England.

We next find our narrator in Rome, attending a masquerade ball at the palace of Duke Di Broglio. This time the vice he is involved in is adultery, and he is determined to steal the duke's wife away from him. As he searches through the costumed guests for her, he feels that same hand on his arm he has felt before, and hears the same whispered *William Wilson*. Of course, his *double* wears the same costume he has one, a Spanish cloak with a black silk mask. His double draws him into a side room, where he becomes enraged and stabs him. At that moment, he is horrified to find the room transforms, and a mirror replaces the body of his now bleeding double, who speaks, "In me didst thou exist—and, in my death, see by this image, which is thine own, how utterly thou hast murdered thyself."

Poe has presented us with the disastrous consequences of the Freudian concept of the *repressed, unconscious alter-ego.* In this case, he gives us a *projection*, an instance where the *psychological double is projected into the outside environment.* By having his protagonist travel across Europe, he emphasizes that this is a mental, not a physical condition. And by stressing that it is not the result of a childhood environment or specific incident suggests that it cannot be explained away that easily. He also limits the possibility it is inherited to that tendency to excitability in his family, and stresses that the parents were simple and boring, were in other words not prone to the same mental misbalance. Furthermore, Poe indicates that his narrator feels more than just hate or fear of this *double*. In fact, he feels a certain attraction.

Al-Tayyib Salih's *Season of Migration to the North* has an unnamed narrator (a different way of connecting the narrator and the dark *alter ego* than Poe's *doubling* of the *fictitious pseudonym* attempt to remove the *self* of the narrator), suggesting that this narrator is in fact the dark *shadow* character of himself, Mustafa. (50)

The novel begins: "It was, gentleman, after a long absence—seven years to be exact, during which time I was studying in Europe—that I returned to my people." During this absence, he missed his homeland, a village in a bend of the Nile, and this is described in wonderfully poetic language. Interestingly, he writes that "because of having thought so much about them during my absence, something rather like a fog rose up between them and me . . . but the fog cleared and I awoke." This symbolism of a "fog" and of it taking place while he was "asleep" suggests there will be some kind of mixture between the "real" and the "dream" or "unreal" worlds taking place, suggests, perhaps, we are going to see it all through a veiled psychological cloth.

Among all of the pleasant familiars of his home village, there is a disturbing change:

> Suddenly I recollected having seen a face I did not know among those who had been there to meet me. I asked about him, described him to them: a man of medium height, of around fifty or slightly older, his hair thick and going grey, beardless and with a moustache slightly smaller than those worn by men in the village; a handsome man.
>
> "That would be Mustafa," said my father.
>
> Mustafa who? Was he one of the villagers who'd gone abroad and had now returned?
>
> My father said that Mustafa was not a local man but a stranger who had come here five years ago, had bought himself a farm, built a house and married Mahmound's daughter—a man who kept himself to himself and about whom not much was known.

This Mustafa "had said nothing. He had listened in silence, sometimes smiling; a smile which, I now remember, was mysterious, like some talking to himself." But two days later, Mustafa comes to the narrator's house to meet him. Mustafa is very polite, but, as with Poe's narrator, this narrator finds fault, finds him too polite, and this narrator also has an overly high opinion of himself, as he says, "I had in those days, if the truth be told, a rather high opinion of myself." Again, as in Poe's story, this other self, this alter-ego, immediately gets the upper hand, responding to the narrator's faining modesty about his doctorate by saying "We have no need of poetry here. It would have been better if you'd studied agriculture, engineering or medicine." The narrator is "furious," thinks to himself, "Look at the way he says 'we' and does not include me, though he knows that this is my village and that it is he—not I—who is the stranger." And again, as with Poe's narrator, the dislike is mixed with an attraction, and he tells us that he finds Mustafa a combination of an attractive "weakness" that "prevails" over a "feminine beauty."

Mustafa's mystery is emphasized when the narrator asks him where he comes from and tells him that the narrator's grandfather Mahjoub has already revealed he is from Khartoum, causing Mustafa to be "slightly taken aback," as if this is not true, as if he is afraid of being found out. Then, just to make sure we realize there is something not quite honest about it all, he says, "Your grandfather knows the secret." And leaving both the narrator and the reader to ponder this, he leaves, and this scene ends.

Then comes a scene where Mahjoub forces Mustafa to get drunk by threatening to get divorced if he does not, and Mustafa reluctantly does. Once drunk, Mustafa recites an English poem in perfect English, startling the narrator, and again alerting the reader to the fact that something strange is going on here, as Mustafa should not even be able to speak English, much less to have memorized an English poem. When the narrator later confronts Mustafa about this, Mustafa denies it, and the narrator is left to ponder the mystery.

He doesn't have to wait long, as the next night Mustafa invites him over and, after receiving a promise from him not to tell anyone in the village, hands him a bundle of papers that include a birth certificate and two passports, one of them filled with stamps from many countries. Then he begins his story:

As it turns out, he was born in Khartoum, his father dead before his was born, his mother cold, unemotional. And pointedly, he says, "I had felt from childhood that I—that I was different—I mean that I was not like other children of my age: I wasn't affected by anything, I didn't cry when hit, wasn't glad if the teacher praised me in class, didn't suffer from the things the rest did. I was like something rounded, made of rubber: you throw it in the water and it doesn't get wet, you throw it on the ground and it bounces back."

Then a man in a uniform riding a horse appeared and took him to school. Here, Mustafa says, "I discovered in my brain a wonderful ability to learn by heart, to grasp and comprehend. On reading a book it would lodge itself solidly in my brain. No sooner had I set my mind to a problem in arithmetic than its intricacies opened up to me, melted away in my hands as though they were a piece of salt I had placed in water. I learnt to write in two weeks, after which I surged forward, nothing stopping me. My mind was like a sharp knife, cutting with cold effectiveness. I paid no attention to the astonishment of the teachers, the admiration or envy of my school mates. The teachers regarded me as a prodigy and the pupils began seeking my friendship, but I was busy with this wonderful machine with which I had been endowed. I was cold as a field of ice, nothing in the world could shake me."

He continued to excel in school, until the headmaster told him he needed to another country to continue his studies, and Cairo, Egypt was chosen. His mother, again without emotion, gave him some money, and he departed. Interestingly, he mentions meeting a "man wearing clerical garb and with a large golden cross round his neck" on the train trip. This is immediately followed by his arrival, where he emphasizes his first sexual stirrings upon meeting Mrs. Robinson. She notices that he is overly serious and suggests he should learn to forget his "intellect." He says, "and on the day they sentenced me at the Old Bailey to seven years' imprisonment, I found no bosom except hers on which to rest my head." In addition to the connections of his sexual desires with a mother figure and the established duality between the two large categories of thinking (intellect and emotion or left and right cerebrum or conscious and unconscious), the "seven years" time period jumps off the page—identical to the narrator's seven years spent in England. He will connect his first experiences with this world of the heart, with that kind of knowing that goes beyond the "intellect," in a later sentence: "From her I learnt to love Bach's music, Keats' poetry, and from her I heard for the first time of Mark Twain." Shortly, Mustafa puts any guessing aside and says directly that he desired her. At the same time he also says "I was wrapped up in myself."

Then, after spending three years with the Robinson's, Mustafa heads for England "and tragedy," still a "hard, cold feeling" in his breast and a "sharp knife inside [his] skull." The whole scene is couched in a metaphor that stretches throughout the novel:

> And when the sea swallowed up the shore and the waves heaved under the ship and the blue horizon encircled us, I immediately felt an overwhelming intimacy with the sea. I knew this green, infinite giant, as though it were roving back and forth within my ribs. The whole of the journey I savoured that feeling of being nowhere, alone, before and behind me either eternity or nothingness. The surface of the sea when calm is another mirage, ever changing and shifting, like the mask on my mother's face. Here, too, was a desert laid out in blue-green, calling me, calling me.

Also intertwined here is the metaphor of a journey. The entire novel is set up with the journey to England connected to the life journey. This life journey is what Joseph Campbell calls the Hero's Adventure. It involves leaving the known, secure world (the world of the child), facing the various tests of life, and return to the known world, only now a changed person (an adult).

Then he meets Jean Morris. He says: "Everything which happened before my meeting her was a premonition; everything I did after I killed her was an apology, not for killing her, but for the lie that was my life." As linear time does in dreams, the time frame here gets a bit confusing, as he says he is twenty-five when he meets her. By this time, he has fallen into a heartless man who parties, drinks, and has sex with a stream of women. He sees these women as "prey." Just to highlight his evil ways, he outlines Ann Hammond, one of his victims: "One day they found her dead. She had gassed herself. They also found a small piece of paper with my name on it. It contained nothing but the words: "Mr. Sa'eed, may God damn you."

It is becoming easy to connect up Mustafa's cold hatred on women with his mother's cold feelings toward him. Freud's theories about childhood experiences fit perfectly.

Woman after woman Mustafa conquerors and drives to suicide. But Jean Morris is different. She is not easily conquered, and this is what drives him to her. It is a war going on, each wanting to destroy the other. So they marry, not out of love, but out of hate.

Jean Morris is Mustafa's *anima*, his female counterpart, and the two of them continue their love/hate relationship towards their desires for death:

> When night brought us together in bed, I wanted to possess her. "Not now," she said, turning her back on me. "I'm tired." For two months she wouldn't let me near her; every night she would say "I'm tired" or "I'm unwell." No longer capable of taking any more, one night I stood over her with a knife in my hand. "I'll kill you," I told her. She glanced at the knife with what seemed to me like longing. "Here's my breast bared to you," she said. "Plunge the knife in." I looked at her naked body which, though within my grasp, I did not possess. Sitting on the side of the bed, I bowed my head meekly. She placed her hand on my cheek and said in a tone that was not devoid of gentleness: "My sweet, you're not the kind of man that kills." . . . . I pushed her violently from me. "I hate you," I shouted at her. "I swear I'll kill you one day." . . . Then, in a voice of simulated tenderness, she said: "I too, my sweet, hate you. I shall hate you until death."

It is the conquering that matters, the need to make the other surrender. Mustafa says, "The moments of ecstasy were in fact rare; the rest of the time we spent in a murderous war in which no quarter was given." And it is all mixed into the sexual desire; sexual desire and the desire for oblivion are intermixed, cannot be separated. Finally comes the moment:

> I found her stretched out naked on the bed, her white thighs open. Though her lips were formed into a full smile, there was something like sadness on her face; it was as though she was in a state of great readiness both to give and to take. On first seeing her my heart was filled with tenderness and I felt that Satanic warmth under the diaphragm which tells me that I am in control of the situation. Where had this warmth been all these years? "Was anyone with you" I said to her in a confident voice I thought I had lost for ever. "There was no one with me, "she answered me in a voice affected by the impact of mine. "This night is for you alone. I've been waiting for you a long time." I felt that for the first time she was telling me the truth. This night was to be the night of truth and of tragedy. I removed the knife from its sheath and sat on the edge of the bed for a time looking at her. I saw the impact of my glances live and palpable on her face. We looked into each

other's eyes, and as our glances met and joined it was as though we were two celestial bodies that had merged in an ill-omened moment of time. My glances overwhelmed her and she turned her face from me, but the effect was apparent in the area below her waist which she shifted from right to left, raising herself slightly off the bed; then she settled down, her arms thrown out languorously, and resumed looking at me. I looked at her breast and she too looked at where my glance had fallen, as though she had been robbed of her own volition and was moving in accordance with my will. I looked at her stomach and as she followed my gaze a faint expression of pain came over her face. As my gaze lingered, so did hers; when I hurried she hurried with me. I looked long at her white, wide-open thighs, as though massaging them with my eyes, and my gaze slipped from the soft, smooth surface till it came to rest there, in the repository of secrets, where good and evil are born. I saw a blush spread up her face and her eyelids droop as though she had been unable to control them. Slowly I raised the dagger and she followed the blade with her eyes; the pupils widened suddenly and her face shone with a fleeting light like a flash of lightning. She continued to look at the blade-edge with a mixture of astonishment, fear, and lust. Then she took hold of the dagger and kissed it fervently. Suddenly she closed her eyes and stretched out in the bed, raising her middle slightly, opening her thighs wider. "Please, my sweet," she said, moaning: "Come—I'm ready now." When I did not answer her appeal she gave a more agonizing moan. She waited. She wept. Her voice was so faint it could hardly be heard. "Please darling."

"Here are my ships, my darling, sailing towards the shores of destruction. I leant over and kissed her. I put the blade-edge between her breasts and she twined her legs round my back. Slowly I pressed down. Slowly. She opened her eyes. What ecstasy there was in those eyes! She seemed more beautiful than anything in the whole world. "Darling," she said painfully, "I thought you would never do this. I almost gave up hope of you." I pressed down the dagger with my chest until it had all disappeared between her breasts. I could feel the hot blood flushing from her chest. I began crushing my chest against her as she called out imploringly: "Come with me. Come with me. Don't let me go alone."

"I love you," she said to me, and I believed her. "I love you," I said to her, and I spoke the truth. We were a torch of flame, the edges of the bed tongues of Hell-fire. The smell of smoke was in my nostrils as she said to me "I love you, my darling," and as I said to her "I love you, my darling," and the universe, with its past, present and future, was gathered together into a single point before and after which nothing existed."

The unnamed narrator discovers the above passage amongst Mustafa's papers after Mustafa has died. Mustafa has left the narrator in care of his wife and family, and with a key to a secret room. After Mustafa's wife has been forced to marry Wad Rayyes, an old man in the village, and killed him and herself when he attempted to have sex with her (a crude version of what happened above), the narrator decides to unlock this secret room, and upon entering it, he is immediately connected to Mustafa: "I struck a match. The light exploded on my eyes and out of the darkness there emerged a frowning face with pursed lips that I knew but could not place. I moved towards it with hate in my heart. It was my adversary Mustafa Sa'eed. The face grew a neck, the neck two shoulders and a chest, then a trunk and two legs, and I found myself standing face to face with myself."

Heinrich Heine published the following poem in *Buch der Lieder*:

Still ist die Nacht, es ruhen die Gassen,
In diesem Hause wohnte mein Schatz;
Sie hat schon längst die Stadt verlassen,
Doch steht noch das Haus auf dem selben Platz.

Da steht auch ein Mensch und starrt in die Höhe,
Und ringt die Hände, vor Schmerzensgewalt;
Mir graust es, wenn ich sein Antlitz sehe –
Der Mond zeigt mir meine eigne Gestalt.

Du Doppelgänger! Du bleicher Geselle!
Was äffst du nach mein Liebesleid,
Das mich gequält auf dieser Stelle,
So manche Nacht, in alter Zeit? (51)

Translated in English:

The night is quiet, the streets are calm,
In this house my beloved once lived:
She has long since left the town,
But the house still stands, here in the same place.

A man stands there also and looks to the sky,
And wrings his hands overwhelmed by pain:
Upon seeing his face, I am terrified—
The moon shows me my own form!

O you Doppelganger! You pale comrade!
Why do you ape the pain of my love
Which tormented me upon this spot
So many a night, so long ago?

In 1828 Franz Schubert gave this poem the title *Das Doppelganger*, and made it the thirteenth song in his work, *Schwanengesang*, one of several chillingly dark songs of this period, this one coming to an extraordinary climax, conveying madness at the realization of rejection and imminent death. (52)

This song of lost love has a sparse, funeral like accompaniment. Not surprisingly, it is in the key of B minor, the key of submission, of defeat, in this case of an agonized acceptance of loss. It begins with a haunting, four bar ostinato of a chord progression of I, Vb, Ib, Vc, which repeats several times throughout, and the empty chords create a despairing sense of foreboding to match the dark streets and moonlit sky. In bars one and four the chords are completely bare, doubled fifths. The second chord has not fifth, and the third chord has not root. Furthermore, the leading note A is doubled two octaves below, and instead of leading to the tonic jumps to a diminished 4th. After five repetitions of this ostinato, it appears a sixth time (bars 56-59) with a major triad on the flattened supertone C natural, changing the effect of the B minor. Throughout F sharp is featured, both as an inner pedal note and in the vocal line, which continually resolves, corresponding to the poem's expression of despair. The dissonance of the vocal line (as exhibited in bar 16 on the word "long") matches the lover's pain.

The second ostinato (bars 9-12) has an unconventional harmony created by flattening the leading note (A natural in chords Vb and III) and following it with a two bar piano interlude (bars 13-14) which brings together both forms of the leading note—A natural and A sharp. In the third statement of the second ostinato, (bars 29-33), the final chord changes from C sharp to C natural, so that V7c of B minor becomes the augmented 6th of E minor, formed by using the flattened submediant (C natural in E minor) above which is placed an augmented 6th (A sharp) with a major 3rd (E) and an augmented 4th (F sharp). Instead of resolving to a dominant harmony (V or 1c-V) the progression sinks back to the beginning ostinato in B minor. The next time it appears, the augmented 4th is replaced by a perfect 5th (G). Fittingly, bars 43-47 modulate into D# minor, the key of fear, distress and the supernatural to musically suggest the doppelganger. It ends with a postlude, beginning with the first ostinato and ends with a plagal cadence and tierce de Picardie, the minor third of the D chord getting raised to D#, and ending at B major.

In 1913, Hanns Heinz Ewers wrote the script for a German silent horror film, *Der Student von Prag* (*The Student of Prague*, also known as *A Bargain with Satan*), a reworking of the Faust legend which also included the first portrayal of a *double* role by an actor on the screen. (53)

This film sparked Otto Rank to write a study of the *double*, the first such study to incorporate literary, psychological, mythical, and ethnological sources and illustrations of it. He begins his study with the following detailed plot summary of the film:

> Balduin, the most dashing student and the best fencer at the University of Prague, has dissipated all his money and is weary of his profligate activities. Crossly, he turns aside from his cronies and their diversion with the dancer Lyduschka. Then a sinister old man, Scapinelli, approaches him and offers help. Roaming through the forest and conversing with this strange adventurer, Balduin witnesses a hunting accident of the Count von Schwarzenberg's young daughter, whom he rescues from drowning. He is invited to her castle, where he meets her cousin and fiancé, Baron Waldis-Schwarzenberg. Although he behaves awkwardly and has to leave in discomfiture, he has made such an impression upon the count's daughter that, from then on, she indicates frostily to her fiancé that he should keep his distance.
>
> At his lodgings Balduin practices fencing positions in front of his large mirror and then falls into disconsolate reflections about his unpleasant situation. Scapinelli appears and offers him wealth upon the signing of a contract that will permit Scapinelli to take from Balduin's room whatever he pleases. Balduin laughs, points to the bare walls and primitive furnishings, and happily signs the document. Scapinelli looks inquisitively about the room, apparently finding nothing that will suit him, until he finally points to Balduin's *mirror image*. The student willingly goes along with the supposed joke but is numbed with astonishment when he see his *alter ego* detach itself from the mirror and follow the old man through the door and out upon the street.
>
> Now an elegant gentleman, the former impoverished student has gained entry into circles where he again sees the much-admired count's daughter. At a ball he has the chance to confess his love to her on the castle terrace. This moonlit idyll, however, is interrupted by her fiancé and is overheard by Lyduschka, who now crosses Balduin's path as a flower girl and follows him incessantly on perilous roads. Balduin is abruptly torn away from the sweet thoughts of the first success of his suit by the apparition of his reflection which, leaning against a column, appears on the parapet of the veranda. Believing that his eyes have deceived him, he is jolted from semi-consciousness only by the approach of his friends. As he departs, Balduin slips a note into his beloved's handkerchief, which she had dropped; the note asks her to come to the Hebrew cemetery the next night. Lyduschka furtively follows the count's daughter to her room in order to learn the contents of the note; but she finds only the handkerchief and Balduin's stickpin, which he had used as a fastener.
>
> On the next evening the princess [*sic*] hurries to the rendezvous; Lyduschka, who sees her by chance, follows her like a shadow. In the deserted cemetery the lovers stroll in the splendid moonlight. They pause

atop a small knoll, and Balduin is just about to kiss his beloved for the first time when he stops short, staring horrified at his double who has suddenly revealed himself behind one of the headstones. While Margit flees in terror of the uncanny apparition, Balduin vainly tries to capture his likeness, who has disappeared just as suddenly as he came.

Meanwhile, Lyduschka has taken the handkerchief and Balduin's tiepin to Margit's fiancé, who decides to challenge Balduin to a duel with sabers. Since Waldis-Schwarzenberg pays no heed to the warnings of Balduin's skill in fencing, the old Count Schwarzenberg, who is already indebted to Balduin for the rescue of his daughter, decides to ask that the life of his future son-in-law, and only heir, be spared. With some reluctance Balduin gives his word not to slay his opponent. But in the forest on the way to the duel, his earlier self comes toward him, holding a bloody saber and wiping it clean. Even before Balduin comes to the spot where the duel is to take place, he sees from a distance that his other self has already slain his opponent.

His desperation increases still more when, from now on, he is no longer admitted into the count's house. He makes a futile attempt to forget his love in wine; while playing cards, he sees his double opposite him; and Lyduschka entices him, but with no success. He must see his beloved again; and one night—on the same path which Lyduschka earlier had used—Balduin sneaks into the room of Margit, who has not yet forgotten him. Sobbing, he casts himself at her feet. She forgives him and their lips meet in the first kiss. Then, at an accidental movement, she notices in the mirror that his image is not reflected next to hers. Terrified, she asks the reason, and he covers his head in shame as his mirror-image appears grinning at the door. Margit swoons at the sight, and Balduin escapes in terror, followed at every step by the gruesome shadow. So pursued, he flees through the streets and alleyways, over walls and ditches, through meadow and forest. Finally, he comes upon a carriage, throws himself into it, and urges the coachman to the greatest possible speed. After a rather long drive at a furious pace, Balduin believes that he is safe, gets out, and is about to pay the coachman, when he recognizes his reflection in the man. In frenzy he rushes on. He sees the spectral figure on all street-corners and must plunge past it into his house, where he securely locks all the doors and windows.

On the point of putting an end to his life, he places his loaded pistol in readiness and prepares to write down his last will and testament. But again, his double stands grinning before him. Bereft of all control over his senses, Balduin seizes the weapon and fires at the phantom, which disappears at once. He laughs with relief and, believing that he is now rid of all torments, uncovers his hand-mirror—formerly wrapped carefully with cloth—and views himself for the first time in a long while. In that same moment he feels a keen pain in the left part of his chest, is aware that his shirt is soaked with blood, and realizes that he has been shot. In the next instant he collapses to the floor, dead. The smirking Scapinelli appears, in order to tear up the contract over the corpse.

The last scene shows Balduin's grave beside a body of water, shaded by a huge weeping willow. His double is sitting on the mound of the grave with the uncanny black bird [raven?], the constant companion of Scapinelli. The beautiful verses of Musset ("December Night") elucidate:

> Wherever you go, I shall be there always,
> Up to the very last one of your days,
> When I shall go to sit on your stone. (54)

Otto Rank put together his study of the *double* early in his career and early in the development of psychology, so it is not surprising that he does not have the mature language of psychology to unravel the various implications of the *double* or *shadow* or *doppelganger* aspects. Nevertheless, he does suggest the interesting connection of the *double* with intimacy between Balduin and Countess Margit, noting that "the eerie double must disturb only 'all hours of sweet company' of the couple, and that he becomes visible only to them," and stressing that "his interventions become more terrifying in proportion as the demonstrations of their love become more fervent." In fact, as Rank emphasizes, "At Balduin's avowal of love on the terrace, his mirror-image appears, so to speak, as a silent figure of warning; at the meeting of the lovers at night in the cemetery, he interrupts their growing intimacy by preventing their first kiss; and finally, in the decisive meeting of reconciliation, which is sealed by an embrace and a kiss, he forcefully separates the lovers forever." Rank's conclusion is that "Balduin is prevented from loving a woman by his own personified self; and, just as his mirror-image follows him to the meetings with his beloved, so does Lyduschka follow the count's daughter like a shadow." In other words, the *double* or more properly the *shadow* is that aspect of both Balduin and Margit's psyches that prevents them from consummating a love for another. (55) Though Otto Rank doesn't go into it in detail, the connection of this *double* with *eros* and *amore* foreshadows Jung's theories of the *shadow*, and its connections with desires beyond the social *persona* of the *ego*. As Freud and Jung both point out, the drives of the *id* include the drive to life (*eros*) and the drive to chaos and destruction (*thanatos*). Later in his study, Rank will put a different spin on this, suggesting that the inability to love (whether it be *eros, amore*, or *agape*) has to do with *narcissism*, a psychological defect.

The story also employs the symbolism of the *mirror* as representing the *double,* the *other,* the *shadow* the life force of the *unconscious* aspect of the psyche, and it is obvious why this works. When we look into a mirror, we see *our own reflection*, though in *reverse*. We do not see through a mirror, as we do a window, and, thus, we are prevented from seeing outside of ourselves, for our eyes only see our own image (in reverse). This can lead to a *narcissistic* view, dangerous not only because we lose a true sense of ourselves in the context of the environment outside of ourselves but also because we see ourselves in *reverse*, see our *shadow* and might confuse it with our *ego*, our public *persona,* or, perhaps even more likely, because we see our *persona* and assume it is all there is (the reflection, which is not the truth, gets substituted for the truth beyond the reflection, the truth within the mirror).

This *reflected illusion* works the same with the light of the *moon* which is but a *reflection* of the sun's light, and with the *reflections* off the surface of the *water*. One must be careful not to get caught in the *illusion*.

If we are fooled and see only the *reflection* and not the world within the *other reality* of the mirror, we can misjudge ourselves, can see only our public face as is represented in the reflexion. However, if we see *into* the mirror, enter *into* that world, we find the *truth* behind the *appearance*. This is expressed in a simple, straight-forward manner in the Brothers Grimm version of *The Little Snow White*, where Snow White's Step-mother, the new Queen looks into her mirror for answers to her own beauty (her own essence). It gets played out in the memorable exchanges:

> "Looking-glass, Looking-glass, on the wall.
> Who in this land is the fairest of all?'
>
> "Thou, O Queen, art the fairest of all."

But then, when this is no longer so, the mirror tells her:

> "Looking-glass, Looking-glass, on the wall,
> Who in this land is the fairest of all?"
>
> "Thou art fairer than all who are here, Lady Queen.
> But more beautiful still is Snow-white, as I ween." (56)

Here the *mirror* is the *gateway* to the truth the Queen cannot otherwise know. It is her inner voice, her unconscious telling her public voice, her conscious the truth beyond the appearances, the truth of the deeper, richer realities of meaning and value. This is the same truth creative people have tried to express throughout the millennium, the truth of beauty, not that superficial physical beauty, but the beauty of truth, the truth of beauty that humans sense and know beyond explanation.

Throughout temporal and physical human existence, *mirrors* have represented this. The Latin term for *mirror* is *speculum*, the basis of *speculate*, originally tied to the activity of scanning the sky, the stars with a *mirror*. Interestingly, the Latin word for star is *sidus*, the base for con*sider*ation, which means to study all of the stars, as they are reflected in *mirrors*. In other words, *mirrors* are connected to the higher truths, to knowledge, and to the heavens, i.e., the spiritual world beyond explanation. By extension, the reflections of the celestial truths, in Christian terms, the truths of Heaven, the Word of God, in a mirror suggest that a mirror contains or at very least reflects the essence of creation. One is looking into the very birth of everything when one looks into a mirror. And this actually works in terms of contemporary science, as various "mirrors" are being employed by the leading astronomers to see into the moment of creation, the cosmological understanding of the beginning of everything, the scientific correspondence to the biblical Genesis.

In 2 Corinthians, 3: 18, St. Paul states, "But we are all, with open face beholding as in a glass the glory of the Lord, are changed into the same image from glory to glory, even as by the Spirit of the Lord." (57) And since we see the glory of God in this glass (mirror), he continues: "Therefore, seeing we have this ministry, as we have received mercy, we faint not; But have renounced the hidden things of dishonesty, not walking in craftiness, nor handling the word of God deceitfully; but by manifestation of the truth commending ourselves to every man's conscience in the sight of God." (58) In other words, the *mirror* is a place to experience, to see the "manifestation of the truth."

With this in mind, *mirrors*, especially darkened or smoking *mirrors*, have been used as a means of divination. The belief is that, if one looks into a *mirror* long enough, visions will appear. The Aztecs made polished black obsidian *mirrors* specifically for this purpose. For Taoism, the *magic mirror* reveals evil influences, drives them away, and offers protection against them. "According to legend, Pythagoras had a magic mirror which he, like the Thessalian witches, would turn towards the Moon before reading the future in it." Congolese fortune-tellers sprinkle a mirror with chalk dust, thinking it the emanation of the spirits, and the patterns that result. Shamans in central Asia perform divinization from the images lighted up by the sun or the moon, the moon regarded as reflecting all that takes place on Earth. (59)

Having the water serve as the mirror, as in the story of Narcissus, gives all of this an additional dimension, as the ever-changing water also represents the unconscious. Therefore, when we look into the water, we are looking into our own unconscious (and again, our reflection is a reverse of our *persona*, is, in other words, the *shadow* part of us. (60)

The *black bird (raven)* at the end of the story is a symbol of both maturity (knowledge) and death (as seen in endless works such as Edgar Allan Poe's *The Raven* and clearly expressed in the Garden of Eden story, where the *knowledge* of Good and Evil carries with it the loss of innocence, of childhood, and the loss of eternal life, where, in other words, both *birth* and *death* are brought into existence and are connected to the gaining of *knowledge*; and as an aside, *self-responsibility*). The *Weeping Willow* is an almost too obvious representation of the sad side of nature, that life must include death. And in killing his *double*, his *shadow* in the mirror, Balduin also kills himself, for, of course, we are *dual*, and cannot survive without our *double*.

Lest we forget, all of this in framed by the Faustian contract with Scapinelli, who has gained control over Balduin's *double*, this dark, mirror-image of himself and separated him into two incomplete entities that struggle against each other until they kill each other and resolve the contract.

This Faustian contract comes out of German folklore, centered on the idea of some worldly man, a highly successful scholar, making a deal with Satan, exchanging his *soul* for some combination of unlimited knowledge and earthly pleasure. In earlier versions of the story, after an established period of years (often twenty-four) Faust is condemned in the end to an eternal Hell. The first printed version I've come across of it is a little chapbook bearing the title *Historia von D. Johann Fausten*, 1587, a publication that gets re-edited and borrowed from throughout the 16th century. Other early versions include *Das Wagnerbuch*, 1593, *Das Widmann'sche Faustbuch* ,1599, *Dr. Fausts großer und gewaltiger Höllenzwang*, Frankfurt, 1609, *Dr. Johannes Faust, Magia naturalis et innaturalis*, Passau, 1612), *Das Pfitzer'sche Faustbuch* (1674), *Dr. Fausts großer und gewaltiger Meergeist* (Amsterdam 1692), *Das Wagnerbuch*, 1714, and *Faustbuch des Christlich Meynenden*, 1725. The first chapbook got translated to English as *The Historie of the Damnable Life, and Deserved Death of Doctor John Faustus*, and was the main source of Christopher Marlowe's important, controversial drama, *The Tragical History of Doctor Faustus* (c. 1604) performed by The Admiral's Men twenty-five time from October, 1594 to October, 1597, likely was revived for several additional performances. (61)

In the prologue, Marlowe compares Faustus to Icarus, suggesting the theme of hubris, and has Faustus say he has used up all possible disciplines (logic simply a tool for arguing, medicine worthless except it allow for raising the dead, law as being too upstanding and above him, divinity as useless because all humans are sinful and resulting in a divinity of *que sera, sera.* In the end, he calls upon his servant Wagner to bring fourth two famous magician (angels), Valdes and Cornelius, who represent the "good" angel and the "bad" angel. In the end he is persuaded to give his life to the study of magic.

As something of an aside, two scholars appear and note Faustus's absence, suggesting his fall into the art of Magic might be his downfall.

Then he summons a devil, and unaware that Lucifer and other devils observe him, creates a magic circle and speaks an incantation to revoke his baptism. Then Mephistopheles appears before him. Faustus cannot tolerate the hideous looks of him and commands he change form, which he does. This emboldens Faustus, and he tries to bind Mephistopheles to his service, but he cannot because Mephistopheles already serves Lucifer. Mephistopheles also informs Faustus that it was not his power that summoned him, but rather the result of Faustus rejecting the scriptures, which always opens the way for Satan to appear and claim the person's soul.

Then Mephistopheles provides a brief history of Satan and the rest of the devils, pointing out that Hell has no circumference but instead is a state of mind. Then, through Mephistopheles, Faustus makes his bargain with Satan. He will be given twenty-four years of life on Earth with Mephistopheles as his servant, but then must give his soul to Lucifer and spend the rest of eternity condemned to Hell. He is required to sign off on this deal with his own blood, and upon cutting his arm he finds it immediately heals with the warning "Man Flee," a warning he ignores, and the deal is made.

Faustus begins his twenty four years of power asking Mephistopheles a number of questions about science, to which Satan is evasive and demonstrates that he is untrustworthy. Then the good and bad angels reappear and the good one urges Faustus to repent and revoke his oath, but he remains firm in his own damnation. Next Lucifer puts the seven deadly sins before Faustus, who recognizes but ignores them. The rest of the play shows Faustus dissipating his remaining time, finally seeming to repent, but in the end having to go with Mephistopheles to Hell.

In one version of the play, Faustus is carried off the stage by devils. In the other version, his friends throw him a final party, a religious ceremony hinting at salvation.

In terms of Christianity, the play has resulted in a lengthy, continuing debate over predestination, especially the Calvinist beliefs, one side viewing it as a demonstration that man has no real choice, the other that it satirizes this view. In terms of psychology and Otto Rank's perspectives, Satan represents the *double* of God, the dark, *shadow* side.

Probably the most important version of this story, a two-part, closet drama that expands it beyond a simple Christian morality play and includes references from such far-ranging sources as Roman and Hellenic poetry, philosophy and literature, comes from Johann Wolfgang von Goethe. (62)

In this version Faust, frustrated with his studies, power, and life experiences, quests for the true essence of life (*was die Welt im Innersten zusammenhalt).* Mephistopheles, representing Satan, learns of Faust and makes a deal with him. Mephistopheles will serve Faust until the instant Faust achieves the zenith of human happiness, at which point Mephistopheles will take his soul. Faust believes this moment will never arrive and is willing to make the bargain.

The first part involves Faust's lustful relationship with Gretchen, a naïve young woman, resulting in Gretchen and her family being destroyed by Mephistopheles' lies and Faust's desire, though in the end Gretchen is saved. Faust, on the other hand, is left to grieve in shame.

It is, actually, a complex story, taking place in numerous settings, beginning in Heaven, where we find that Mephistopheles makes a wager with God, betting he can corrupt God's favorite human, Faust, turn him away from righteous pursuits. Then it shifts to Faust's study, where Faust decides that scientific, humanitarian and religious learning are nothing more than vanity, and turns to magic in quest of infinite knowledge. Frustrated, he ponders suicide, but puts it aside when he hears the echo of a nearby Easter celebrations. He goes for a walk with his assistant Wagner, and is followed home by a stray dog.

Back in his study, the dog transforms into Mephistopheles, and the deal is struck. When Mephistopheles tells Faust to sign the pact with blood, Faust complains that his word of honor should be good enough, but in the end gives into Mephistopheles and signs it with a drop of his own blood.

After a few happenings, Faust meets Gretchen (aka Margaret). He is attracted to her, and uses jewelry and the help of her neighbor Martha (and Mephistopheles) to seduce her. She administers a sleeping potion to her mother (who dies from it) in order to gain privacy that Faust can visit her. Then she discovers she is pregnant. Her brother condemns Faust, challenges him, and dies at his hands (again with the help of Mephistopheles). Gretchen drowns the illegitimate child and is convicted of murder. Faust tries to save her from death by freeing her from the prison, but she refuses to escape. Faust and Mephistopheles flee the dungeon, and voices from Heaven announce that she will be saved.

The second part is an allegorical poem. Goethe moves the drama out of the smaller world into a much larger landscape, and brings in a number of classical allusions. The romantic story is forgotten, at least for a time. Faust wakes in a field of fairies, and a whole new, much larger cycle of adventures and purposes takes place in five acts, each representing a different theme. This time Satan and Faust enter and gain control over the world of politics and the classical gods, meeting with Helena of Troy (the most beautiful woman in the world), and upon taming the forces of both war and nature, Faust has his zenith of happiness, and dies.

At this moment, Mephistopheles attempts to seize Faust's soul, but the angels intercede in the name of the Grace of God, which they claim Faust deserves because he has tried hard to achieve and because Gretchen, who has forgiven him herself, intercedes. In the final scene, Faust's soul goes to Heaven in the presence of God in the form of the "Holy Virgin, Mother, Queen, Goddess—The Eternal Feminine," representing the Goddess as victorious over Mephistopheles.

Thomas Mann's novel, *Doktor Faustus: Das Leben des deutschen Tonsetzers Adrian Leverkühn, erzählt von einem Freunde (Doctor Faustus: The Life of the German composer Adrian Leverkuhn as Told by a Friend),* (63) adapts the central idea of making a pact with Satan to represent the corrupted soul of Germany under Hitler. In it, his main character is Adrian Leverkuhn, a talented composer who makes his pact with a Mephistophelean character.

It is narrated by Adrian Leverkuhn's childhood friend, a schoolmaster named Serenus Zeitblom; and is, in essence, an extended reflection by Serenus Zeitblom on Adrian Leverkuhn's life, set in the context of Nazi Germany (the same time Mann is writing the novel).

Adrian Leverkuhn begins as a student of theology, but gives that up for his passion for composing music. His compositions, while technically well done, lack energy and imagination. In a "confession" written years later, he states that he "voluntarily" contracted syphilis from a prostitute, expecting his artistic inspiration to deepen as a result of him becoming mad from the disease. Then, in a scene similar to Ivan Karamazov's mental breakdown in Fyodor Dostoevsky's final novel, *The Brothers Karamazov,* Satan appears, convinces Adrian Leverkuhn that even though he can only see Satan because he is mad that does not mean he does not exist, and promises him artistic success if he agrees to give up on human love. The result is a twenty-four year career where he becomes the most brilliant German composer of his time. As he reaches his artistic peak, he becomes more and more obsessed with the Apocalypse and the Last Judgment. Sensing his madness heading towards a complete mental breakdown, in a self-conscious imitation of Faust, he calls his friends to witness his final demise, and after a performance of his masterwork, "The

Lamentation of Doctor Faustus," he confesses his demonic pact before his collapses into incoherence, and lives out the last decade of his life in a childlike state, under the care of his mother.

Consistent with other versions of the story, Adrian Leverkuhn yearns for the love of a woman, and in this case he falls for one and has a friend court her for him. This is doomed to failure, and in the end she falls in love with the friend instead of him. As he comes to the end of his career, a five-year-old nephew comes to live with him in the country, and he feels a great love for this boy, but again it is doomed to failure, and the boy suddenly dies of meningitis.

On a social and political level, the novel is meant to express the decline of the German culture during the Nazi era, a time when humanism is replaced by nihilism and a violent primitivism. Mann cleverly expresses this connection in his narrator, Serenus Zeitblom's comments throughout. Curiously, though he condemns him, Serenus Zeitblom continues to idolize Adrian Leverkuhn throughout his life and mourns him after his death. And the dual nature of the German character is meant to be represented, the humanist and the logical, each needing the other.

It is clear that Adrian Leverkuhn's character as a composer is based on Arnold Schoenberg, whose musical innovation was the twelve-tone-system, and who is often considered the greatest German composer of the twentieth century, demonstrated by Mann purposely describing Adrian Leverkuhn's compositions in detail based on Schoenberg's music. It is also clear that Mann used Nietzsche as a source. Nietzsche contracted syphilis as a young man, but still went on to achieve creative genius before succumbing to madness and dying in a mental institution.

In the end, a major difference between this version of Faust and the other major ones is that the central character clearly does not achieve any kind of redemption.

In all of the stories of Faust, the *double* is Satan or some messenger of Satan, some representative of Satan, and when this is the case, the psychological *double* or *shadow* becomes a *mythological* one, Satan representing God's darker side, his *spiritual double*.

John Milton's *Paradise Lost* is probably the most imposing work representing this, and it is interesting how his picture of Satan, especially through the first three books of the work, depicts Satan as an attractive rebel, even as a heroic character, a point that many respected writers and critics have noted since. (64) William Blake, who illustrated several of Milton's works, including *Paradise Lost,* in his own work *The Marriage of Heaven and Hell,* offered a symbolic reading of *Paradise Lost*, including the assertion "The reason Milton wrote in fetters when he wrote of Angels

& God, and at liberty when of Devils & Hell, is because he was a true Poet and of the Devil's party without knowing it!" (65)

There is most certainly a charisma to Satan's fearlessness as represented in his bold confrontation with Chaos and Death, his leadership qualities—even able to rally his fallen angels after the huge defeat in the Angelic War by arguing that God rules as a tyrant and that *all* angels should rule as gods (Book 5, lines 794-802), his magnificent appearance (the most beautiful of all of the angels in Heaven), and his willingness to stand up to God, even if it means eternal damnation. It has been said that he is presented in the image of the heroes of Classical Literature, perhaps filled with too much hubris and yet also perhaps justified their demands. (66) However this arrogance is interpreted, it is an example of the *anti-hero,* who does not submit to authority. (67)

Furthermore, he casts himself as an innocent victim, demoted instead of promoted. When he says, "Better to reign in Hell than to serve in Heaven" (Book I, l. 263), we can understand that as the plea of all subjected people. When he calls his band of rebel angels to a forum and includes them in deciding strategy, saying, "[B]y what best way . . . Whether of open war or covert guile, / We now debate; who can advise, may speak" (Book II, 11. 40-42), and then they vote on their course of action, and Satan asks for volunteers, it is a democratic process, not the dictatorship form of leadership of God. And, in fact, when none volunteer, Satan takes on the task himself, both impressing and embarrassing his followers: "Towards him they bend/With awful reverence prone; and.../Extol him equal to the highest in heaven" (Book II, ll. 477-479).

When he shares his feelings of pain and alienation upon reaching Earth in Book IV, we are likely to have sympathy and even empathy. He pauses on his journey at Mt. Niphates, and "torments inwardly" (Book Iv, 1. 88), revealing his capacity for heroic insight. He wonders, "[I]s there no place/Left for repentance, none for pardon left?" (Book IV, ll. 79-80), and decides, based upon his own experiences, there is not: "So farewell hope, and with hope farewell fear,/Farewell remorse: all good to me is lost" (Book IV, lines 108-109). In other words, Satan, as would any true hero, experiences a profound existential despair but pushes forward anyway, remaining faithful to his own ideals, even though they go against those of the rest of the world.

However, such critics as C. S. Lewis (68), who sees Satan as pure evil, and Stanley Fish (69), who sees Milton tricking the reader into seeing his own evil by becoming attracted to Satan, point out that this is not a hero in the sense of a hero's quest, but a hero in the sense of a failed hero's quest, and as the work progresses, we are likely to note that much of what Satan says partakes of self-deception—saying, for example, that "angels are self-begot, self-raised," rather than created by God (Book V, line 860), and that his form devolves from a glorious comet or meteor into a humble cherub, a cormorant, a toad, and finally a serpent or snake. His great intellect also deteriorates, until he is deluding himself, beginning to believe Earth is more beautiful than Heaven, tricking himself into thinking he would rather live on Earth than in the unparalleled grandeur of Heaven. Though his mind cannot stop an incessant flow of thoughts, he has lost any concept of morality and is blinded to God's Grace.

In the end, one's interpretation should not involve what John Milton was trying to do, but what he did. And then, not whether or not God and Satan and the rest of the cast in *Paradise Lost* match a particular religion or a particular interpretation of the *Bible,* but what is *expressed* in terms of *poetry*, as it is not, after all, a religious text, nor is it some form of historical or non-fiction writing. It is a work of creative and imaginative writing. As such, Satan becomes a "larger than life" *double* or *shadow* of God, representing the *anti-establishment*, the *individual*, the *maverick* rebelling against the *system,* the *structure,* the *authority,* the *powers that be.* Such a rebellion might or might not be justified (that is a different philosophical and religious discussion), but it always is a demand for the freedom of the individual. So, just as the Classical Greek Heroes raised their fists to the gods and in doing so demonstrated a huge hubris (and often received strong punishment from the gods for their actions), Satan does that here.

Just to highlight that this is an *interpretation* of the Biblical story, a very different *interpretation* of the same story comes from the Muslim version out of Persia, where *Iblis/Shaytan* (the Islamic names of Satan) is condemned to Hell by *Allah* (God) for *loving* him too much, a sophisticated relationship that works well if seen from Jungian psychology, where *Allah* is the mythological equivalent of the *ego* and *Iblis* is the mythological of the *shadow*, forming a relationship that needs to be balanced for the *self* to be complete. On the mythological level, this suggests that a balanced duality is necessary as well; in fact, *Allah* and *Iblis* need each other, at least for human comprehension, there needs to be a duality. Keep in mind that it is not necessarily an ethical duality, not necessarily Good versus Evil. Perhaps thinking of it in the terms as an *anima-animus* duality helps clarify this. One is not Good, the Other Evil; rather, they are two different parts to the whole.

According to the *Qur'an*, *Allah* created *Iblis* out of "smokeless fire" (along with all of the other *jinn*) and created man out of "clay." The primary characteristic of the *Iblis*, besides hubris, is that he has no power other than the power to cast evil suggestions into the hearts of *humans* and *jinn*, although the *Qur'an* does mention appointing *jinn* to assist those who are far from *Allah* in a general context. "We made the Shayatin (devils) Auliya' (protectors and helpers) for those who believe not." (70)

In basic Islamic teachings, *Allah* created at least three intelligent races: *angels*, *jinns*, and *humans*, but only granted *jinns* and *humans* free will to choose between good and evil. (71) According to the *Qur'an*, *Iblis* was a devoted *jinn*. (72) However, the *Oxford Dictionary of Islam* (73) and *The New Encyclopedia of Islam* (74) claim he was a disobedient *angel.*

In either case, when *Allah* created *humans* (Adam), He commanded all of the *angels*, including *Iblis* to bow down to Adam, whom he considered his highest creation. All of the *angels* did, except *Iblis.*

According to Joseph Campbell, *Iblis* so loved *Allah* that he could not bow to any other. Here is how he explains it to Bill Moyers:

> Moyers: And yet one of my favorite myths is the story from Persia that Satan was condemned to hell because he loved God so much.
>
> Campbell: Yes, that's a basic Muslim idea about Satan being God's greatest lover. There are a number of ways of thinking about Satan, but this is based on the question, why was Satan thrown into hell? The standard story is that, when God created the angels, he told them to bow to none but himself. Then he created man, whom he regarded as a higher form than the angels, and he asked the angels to serve man. And Satan would not bow to man.
>
> Now, this is interpreted in the Christian tradition, as I recall from my boyhood instruction, as being the egotism of Satan. He would not bow to man. But in the Persian story, he could not bow to man because of his love for God—he could bow only to God. God had changed his signals, do you see? But Satan had so committed himself to the first set of signals that he could not violate those, and in his—I don't know if Satan has a heart or not—but in his mind, he could not bow to anyone but God, whom he loved. And then God says, "Get out of my sight."
>
> Now, the worst of the pains of hell, insofar as hell has been described, is the absence of the Beloved, which is God. So how does Satan sustain the situation in hell? By the memory of the echo of God's voice, when God said, "Go to hell." That is a great sign of love.
>
> Moyers: Well, it's certainly true in life that the greatest hell one can know is to be separated from the one you love. That's why I've liked the Persian myth. Satan is God's lover—
>
> Campbell: --and he is separated from God, and that's the real pain of Satan. (75)

Other interpretations of this version focus more on the *hubris* of *Iblis*, not in terms of being equal to *Allah*, but in terms of being superior to *humans*. When *Allah* asked *Iblis*, "What prevented thee from prostrating when I commanded thee?" *Iblis* said: "I am better than he: Thou didst create me from fire, and him from clay." (76)

The initial story put forth in the film *A Student of Prague* (discussed above, prior to the discussions of Faust), with its myriad psychological and mythological implications, is Otto Rank's set up for his discussion of the *double*, where he will begin by exploring appearances of it in literature,

He immediately plunges into E.T.A. Hoffmann's "The Story of the Lost Reflection," what he considers to be the inspiration for Ewers film script. (77)

This delightful tale might well be called a morality story, as it fits the general qualities of the morality plays common in medieval drama during the 14-16 centuries, where the characters are two-dimensional and the plot generally revolves around the struggle for men's souls.

In this story a first person narrator immediately sets the stage:

> I was delirious with fever: the cold of death pierced my very heart, and heedless of the fury of the storm I ran through the streets hatless and cloakless like one escaped from a madhouse. The weathercocks screaked on the roof-tops like scared owls, and the gusts of the night wind followed one another through the air like the distant sound of the eternal wheels that register the fall of the years into the gulf of time. And yet this was the eve of the very merry festival of the New Year. (78)

Then, immediately, the devil is characterized as a trickster figure, one who "every year chooses just this moment to play me some trick of his own peculiar fashion." With this in place, our protagonist heads out to the annual "soiree" the "counselor of justice" holds each New Year's Eve.

Here he meets Julia, a woman he knew and fell in love with years ago. After indicating at length how exquisite and beautiful she is and how she overwhelms him to such a degree that he is "motionless and dumb" in her presence, he describes her attempt to get him to drink a "delicious sherbet," the same drink he accepted from her hand many times in the past. Then, just as he is in the middle of rhapsodizing about Julia and his undying love for her, her "hideous" husband with "long spider legs" and "toad's eyes" appears and she rushes from the room, leaving our narrator crushed with despair.

He rushes "out of that accursed house like a madman," and runs through the streets and the "fury of the storm" until he reaches Huntsmen Tavern. "Parched with a violent thirst," he drops on a bench, breathless and "quite blown," orders a "pot of beer and some tobacco," and is soon drunk. Another man (whom we will soon find out is named Peter Schlemihl) joins him and begins smoking a pipe and spreading out a "great quantity of herbs" on the table. Then a third man (we will later learn is Erasmus) appears, this one concerned that the landlord cover any *mirrors* in the room. This aversion to *mirrors* gets emphasized when our narrator offers the man a "steel snuff-box polished like a mirror," and the man thrusts it away from him, exclaiming, "The devil fly away with your accursed looking-glass!"

As we will see throughout the story, the *mirror* is emphasized as that symbolic reflection of the truth of the "other" world, a world that reveals whether or not a man retains his *reflection*, which clearly, in this story represents his *soul.*

This final man to join the gathering is clearly depraved to the point where "his features [are] discomposed, and he [is] pale as a corpse." He is, in fact, a fallen man, a man who has given away his *soul.*

The three of them talk and the conversation turns to the "metaphysics of happiness." Both the other men "shudder" when the narrator tells them of his recent experiences, and then, when the conversation resumes, it turns pointedly to that of a young painter. "'He catches a likeness with admirable art,' said the tall dry man; 'his portraits lack nothing but speech; they are so full of life that you might think them a reflection taken out of a mirror.'" And the story proceeds with its delightful, if heavy-handed emphasis on the symbols. "'What a stupid thing to say!' exclaimed the little brown man, throwing himself about in his chair. 'How can anyone imagine that an image reflected in a mirror could be taken away from? By who, I ask you, unless the devil took a hand? Yes, yes, master professor, you great judge of matters artistic, just you make me touch with my finger a reflection taken out of any mirror you please, and I will cut you a caper a hundred feet in the air on the spot!'"

So now it is stated clearly though ironically that the *devil* is the one with the power to take a man's *reflection* (his *soul*), and that the *mirror* is what will reveal that it is gone. The conversation continues in this manner until the man who represents the devil's victim leaves and we are told directly who he is: "'What is the matter, dear sir?' I said, in a tone full of pity. 'The matter!' he [replies], sobbing, 'the matter! Alas! That little man you saw there a moment ago is a wicked sorcerer who has just pursued me into the last refuge where I imagined I might forget my horrible misfortune of having lost my . . . Adieu, sir, adieu!'"

"And the stranger [gets] up and swiftly [reaches] the door, passing all the way through the whole tavern without casting the smallest shadow on the walls." The narrator then rushes home, but the landlord will not let him in and says, "'The good God preserve my house from such ghosts! I would as soon pour out a drink for the devil in person!'"

The narrator then goes to the Golden Eagle, a place of lodging owned by his good friend, Mr. Matthew, and he is given a room. However, rather than a place of refuge, it turns out to be a place where the strange happenings continue. First, he looks into a large *mirror*, and he sees his adored Julia in the depths of it. He reaches out to her, but then he hears someone sighing from his bed, and it turns out to be the very *sorcerer* he just sat with in the tavern. He wakes the man, who has been having a bad dream about a woman named Giulietta, and now agrees to tell his story. He gets out of the bed, puts on a dressing-gown and sits in a chair by the fireplace, revealing as he passes the *mirror* that he has no *reflection*. Then he says, "'I am more to be pitied than Peter Schlemihl. Schlemihl sold his shadow: it was his own fault, his own doing, and besides, he had his price. But I, dear sir, I had given my reflection for love, to HER, to Giulietta!'"

If it hasn't already highlighted itself, now it is becoming evident that the other factor in all of this mix of *mirrors* and *shadows* and *souls* and *bargains with the devil*, is the temptation of a woman, the *woman as temptress*. Each of these men are giving away or selling their souls for love of a woman.

After his emotional outburst, the little man throws himself on the bed and is quickly asleep; and the narrator follows suit. Then he wakes, or rather half-wakes an hour before dawn and sees the little man writing by the light of two candelabra. The narrator falls into a "kind of hallucination," where Julia is again offering him a drink, but the little man urges him not to accept her bribe. "'What are you afraid of? [says] Julia. 'Are you not altogether mine, *you and your shadow?*'" As he struggles to decide, the little man and Peter Schlemihl begin to laugh. The room fills with people, and narrator wakes up.

The little man is gone, but he has left his writing on the table, and it becomes the main story within this morality tale.

It turns out that the little man's name is Erasmus Spicker, who begins his story finding himself in "seventh heaven," with a loving wife and son, Rasmus. He has just reached a position in life where he can afford to travel to Florence, so he fills a "leather belt with gold pieces," and gets into a "berlin to go and visit romantic Italy." There he meets up with his countrymen in the "midst of every kind of voluptuous delight," and he throws himself into "their orgies" and shares their adventures. However, when they all arrange to meet at a villa on the outskirts of the city and each of them brings a mistress, he does not. When asked why, his proclaims his fidelity to his wife and family. The rest of them tease him, and one of the women says with a smile, "'Here is a sage whose soul Giulietta might make him lose!" Then the beautiful Giulietta appears and "placing herself with enchanting coquetry beside Erasmus, by her airs and graces" she makes all of the other young men jealous of him. And she seduces him:

> At the sight of Guilietta Erasmus [feels] a devouring fire shoot through his veins. When he [finds] her so close to him the intoxication of desire [inflames] his imagination. The lovely Italian [rises], [takes] a goblet, and [offers] it to him. He [drains] the treacherous drink at a draught, and [falls] at the feet of the siren. "Oh!" he [cries], "'tis thou, thou alone in all the world that art worthy of love, angel of heaven! 'Tis thou I sought for in my young man's dreams! I have found thee now at last, my soul and my God!"

Then, having seduced him, Guilietta turns cold and leaves him to suffer in his desire for her. Deserted, he makes his way to his street escorted with but a little page. "All at once a tall dry man with a hooked nose and a sardonic mien, clad in a crimson doublet with steel buttons, [appears] in front of Erasmus and [says], laughing, in a bleating voice: 'Aha, Master Spicker, have we escaped out of some old book engravings with that costume of the olden times, that plumed bonnet and that rapier? Do you want the street urchins to run hooting after you? You had best get back quickly into your book.' 'Eh! What has my costume to do with you?' [cries] Erasmus; and elbowing the rascal who was thus teasing him he [tries] to pass him by, but the man in red [stops] him and [says] in very loud tones 'Gently, my master, do not go so fast, and don't push people; this is not the hour to visit the fair Giulietta!'"

Erasmus' anger comes to the surface and he looks to seize and choke this man who is goating him on, but the man disappears. The footboy tells Erasmus the man is the "marvelous doctor of Florence, Signor Dapertutto."

Over the next day Guilietta and Signor Dapertutto continue to entice Erasmus, until Guilietta is accosted by a "very ugly little Italian" who makes Erasmus jealous, and this quickly leads to a fight. When the Italian draws a stiletto, Erasmus seizes him and throws him to the ground so violently that he dies. His jealousy has caused him to kill a man, and now he must leave quickly before he is arrested. But he hesitates, struggling between his love for Guilietta and his wife. Now Guilietta has him. She says, "What you wish is impossible! But at the least leave me your *reflection*, my beloved, that I may not remain forever bereft of you wholly.' 'My reflection?' [cries] Erasmus. And at the same time he [draws] Giulietta in front of the mirror, which [reproduces] their amorous posture. 'How could you keep my reflection?' 'Dear friend,' [says] Giulietta, 'this fugitive appearance that we call a reflection, and which all polished surfaces give, can be detached from the person and belong to the being you love best on earth. Will you refuse me this souvenir? Would you deprive me of the poor pledge that might remind me of our too-fleeting happiness?' 'Yours, yours, now and forever!' [cries] Erasmus in a frenzied delirium of love. 'Take my reflection, and may no power of heaven or hell avail to take it from you!' These words [exhaust] his strength; he [swoons] in the embraces of the lovely Italian; and it [seems] to him that his image [detaches] itself from his *ego*, his individuality, that it [joins] itself closely to that of Guilietta, which [holds] out his arms to it, and both [flee] away into the perspective of the mirror and [are] lost in a strange fantastic mist."

Then Erasmus gets immediately picked up by his nemesis, Signor Dapertutto, who, if Erasmus will give himself "unreservedly," will save him by carrying out "certain operations with [his] reflection." When Erasmus explains he has given up his shadow, Dapertutto laughs. Realizing who he is, Erasmus hits him, and escapes back to his own country (Germany) with the help of his friend, Frederick.

However, his countrymen realize he has no *reflection*, and they assume he must be in cahoots with the devil. He spends the next few days trying to "slip quietly away," but word of his condition spreads rapidly. His family welcomes him lovingly, until they also realize he has no *shadow*, and then they, too, become terrified of him.

Amazingly, Erasmus has not yet freed himself from his love for Giulietta, and he again cries out for her. Out of nowhere, Dapertutto appears and offers to take him to her, if he will drink from a phial. Erasmus suspects the plan is to poison him and refuses, but continues to struggle about it because he is so madly in love, until he sees a turtle-dove peck at the stopper of the phial and fall dead, leaving no doubt.

Though he has been saved from this elixir of poison, he still despairs for Giulietta, and one night she appears. He begs her to take him back. "'My good Erasmus,' [she says], putting an arm round her lover's neck, and fixing a look full of fascination upon him, 'no one wishes you to commit the crime that appalls you so; but if you desire, my beloved, to be the eternal husband of my beauty, take this parchment and write these words: 'I give to Depertutto full power to break the bonds that chain me to earth; it is my sole wish and desire henceforth to belong to Giulietta, whom I have freely chosen to be the mate of my body and of my soul for all eternity.'"

Then Depertutto appears behind Giulietta, dressed, as usual in red (to symbolize the devil), a vein bursts in Erasmus' left hand, and he is pushed to sign off with his own blood.

But this is a story where the soul gets another chance. "Erasmus [dips] the pen in the blood, and [is] bending over to write, when a white ghost [rises] up from the floor and [interposes] between him and Giulietta. 'In the name of the Saviour,' [says] the ghost, sobbing, 'do not proceed!' It [is] the ghost of his mother. Erasmus [casts] the pen at her feet, and [tears] up the document. Giulietta's eyes [dart] baleful fires; her lovely face [dissolves], and from all her body there [gush] greenish sparks. Erasmus Spicker [makes] the sign of the cross, and Guilietta and Dapertutto [vanish] growling in a whirlwind of solphurous smoke that [puts] out the lights.

However, it is not, ultimately, a happy ending. When Erasmus returns to his wife and she realizes all he has been through, she welcomes him back. But she finds that the *mirror* will not give him back his *reflection*, and she tells him he must do more *penance*. He returns to Florence to seek out his *reflection*, meets up with Peter Schlemihl, and the two of them travel together for a time, each seeking his *shadow*, but then they also separate to wander off alone, two lost people searching for their *souls*.

An important motif of this story and of many of these stories about the struggles of a man between his *ego* and his *shadow*, are the *duplicity* of *women*, the *devil* or *angel* relationship with women. In this story, we are told that Erasmus has a very good, loving relationship with his wife. However, once he is put into a situation where he is tempted, he rather easily succumbs. And Guilietta is clear and very consciously the *woman temptress*, the woman at the service of the devil (in Jungian terms, this is the *anima* assisting the *shadow* to undermine the *ego*). She doesn't accidentally or unknowingly tempt Erasmus, but very clearly purposely uses her charms to control him and lead him into Hell by gaining possession of his *shadow*.

Erasmus, then, gets caught in a kind of *purgatory*, a twilight zone where he struggles with his desires for the demonic woman, represented as the woman who is very physically attractive (sexually attractive), who flatters him and builds up his *ego*, and the moral woman who demands a kind of obedience to a higher set of rules that he needs to live up to, a woman who demands his fidelity, not because he is attracted to her, but because it is how he proves himself a good man. There is an obvious conflict between the Freud's *super-ego* and *id*, between Christian *agape* and *eros,* between Jung's *ego* and *shadow/anima.*

The men in this story have lost their *shadow* and become weak, frightened, dislikeable men, suggesting a man does need his *shadow*. It is obvious that eliminating a man's dark side, his potential for going against the established rules of correct behavior is not the solution. At the same time, it is clear that succumbing to the dark side of a relationship with a woman also enfeebles the man. So the solution resides somewhere in a more complex mixture of these opposites. A man must retain his *shadow*, must satisfy his desires for the dark woman (who might be psychologically designated as the *shadow anima*), but must not let her take control, must instead have the strength to both experience and yet resist her, the strength to both satisfy his desires and yet not give into them. It is clear in this story that the moment the man gives into the dark woman she has no more interest in him. She has won the battle. At the same time, a man needs the angelic woman (perhaps designated as the *ego anima*), but again must not give into her, not allow her to become the dominate force. If she wins, the man is weak and worthless, an object of ridicule.

All of this opens an interesting discussion on the woman's psychological counterpart, her seeming desire to both control and yet not be allowed to control a man, her own struggles with her *shadow* and with her opposite psychic entity, her *animus*. Obviously some women have clearly chosen to be completely the *angelic woman* (a nun comes to mind) or the *demonic woman* (a whore or prostitute). Of course, these are symbolic categories, and in truth, in the real world, neither nuns nor whores and prostitutes are so one-dimensional, but they are largely controlled by the psychic entity they represent. A psychologically healthy woman, in other words, must also find a way to include and balance both the angelic and demonic aspects.

Otto Rank concludes his remarks on this story by observing the similarity of it with the previously discussed *A Student of Prague* in "the equivalence of the mirror and shadow as images, both of which appear to the ego as its likeness." (79) As I have discussed, this is exactly what is happening, the *reflection* in the *mirror* being the likeness, but in truth the opposite of the image it reflects, the *ego* the persona of the conscious world, and the *shadow* the life force of the unconscious world, equal and both necessary for a fully functioning psyche.

Otto Rank uses Hans Christian Andersen's wonderfully enigmatic story *The Shadow* as an example of this same motif in other stories, in this case, similar to Al-Tayyib Salih's *Season of Migration to the North* and Edgar Allan Poe's *William Wilson,* offering a *double* or *shadow* that constantly follows and foils the *self,* but in this story also suggesting that poetry (all of the arts) is the connection between the sunlit world of consciousness and the moonlit world of that which is beyond conscious knowing, or more precisely, the world of logic and reason and explanation and the world beyond that. (80)

In a light tone, Andersen begins by telling us about a "learned man who had come straight from a cold climate to a hot one," so hot he and all of the other people there found it necessary to stay indoors during the day with doors and shutters closed against the heat. This heat was so powerful it caused the man and his shadow to shrink, to become thin, and not to be able to revive until the sun went down. Andersen writes, "As soon as the lamp was brought into the room the shadow stretched itself all along the wall, right up to the ceiling; it was obliged to stretch in order to get its strength back." The man would accomplish the same stretching to regain his strength by going out on his balcony at night, after the sun went down, as did the rest of the town. The result is that in this town the normal life of the day and night are reversed, and the symbolism of day and night are employed to represent the conscious world of literal existence and the unconscious world of the dream.

One house directly opposite "the house of the learned stranger" had a peculiar quality. No one ever appeared on the balcony, though the door to it was always open, and the inside was always dark, though music came from within that the learned stranger found wonderful. He asked the landlord about this apartment and was told that no one knew who had taken the house, no one was ever seen there, and as for the music, "'It's just as though someone were sitting and practicing a piece he couldn't get on with—always the same piece."

This is not a *real* place, not the world of *literal* existence, but, rather, it is of the *once-upon-a-time* reality of a *parable*, a *dream,* and a *myth*. Not only has the story immediately emphasized this land as a curiously hot, unreal place, a place where light and shadow, day and night take on larger meanings, and the learned man (the stranger to this land) has an overly emphasized relationship with his shadow, but now there is this enigmatic, other-worldly house with an inexplicable, enchanting music. Certainly this is one of those sacred places where the visible world of the senses intersects the invisible world of the spirits.

Then, the story continues, "one night the stranger woke up" and saw a "curious blaze of light" coming from this mysterious house. "All the flowers shone like flames in the loveliest colours, and there amidst the flowers stood a graceful slender girl: she too seemed to glitter, and the sight of her quite dazzled his eyes." But when he woke, it all disappeared; only the "sound of music so soft and enchanting that it could easily make you give way to romantic thoughts" remained. He thought it was a "sort of magic."

Could this house represent his own inner world, his *dream* world? Could this woman be a part of his own *unconscious*? Certainly the imagery suggests it. It is the world of the night and the moon. What does music have to do with it? Music is also of that world, the world beyond logic and reason and the clear rational truths of the sun. And it has an allure, an attraction, is "enchanting" and "romantic." Perhaps this mysterious woman he only sees as he is waking up, as he is still in something of a *dream* state, is his own *anima*, an incarnation of a *desiderata*. Remember, he was only able to glimpse her briefly while waking from a dream.

Then, one evening, while he sat in his balcony with a light burning behind him, his shadow appeared on the wall of the mysterious house:

> "I believe my shadow is the only living thing to be seen over there," said the learned man. "Look how nicely it sits among the flowers. The door is standing half-open—what a chance for the shadow to pop inside, have a look round and then come and tell me what it has seen! Now then, make yourself useful!" he said in fun. "Kindly step inside . . . Well, aren't you going?" and he gave the shadow a nod, and the shadow nodded back. "That's right, go along—but mind you come back." The stranger stood up, and the shadow over on the neighbour's balcony did the same. And the stranger turned round, and so did the shadow. Anyone watching carefully could have seen quite well that the shadow went in at the half-open balcony door at the very moment that the stranger went into his room and dropped the long curtain behind him.

The next morning, when the man went out on his balcony to drink his coffee and read the papers, he found his shadow was not there and realized it had, indeed, gone off and left him. His initial annoyance came because he remembered a story, well known to everyone in the cold country he was from, about a man without a shadow, and he realized that when he returned home he better not let anyone know his shadow had left him, because if they found out they would simply think him an imitator. One thing this alerts us to is that others have visited this *other world,* and had a similar experience. Whatever this strange place is, it is possible to travel there and return changed, return without a shadow.

That evening, he again found he had no shadow, and now there could be no doubt. However, since things grew fast in the hot country, he was able to regrow a new shadow. "So the learned man went home and wrote books about what is true and good and beautiful in the world; and days and years went by—yes, many years." The true, the good, and the beautiful are of the world of the arts, the reality beyond the truths of logic and reason, the truths of math and science, so it is clear this man has traveled to the realities of the arts, the form of knowing beyond explanation.

"Then one evening he was sitting in his room, and there came a gentle knock at the door." It turned out to be a very thin person, a person who made him feel very uncomfortable, and with good reason, because he soon learned it was his former shadow, who claimed, "I've now such a body of my own that I've positively got flesh—and cloths too." Indeed, this shadow had done well for himself and now wished to purchase his freedom.

In a line dripping with irony, the learned man said, "Upon my soul, you take my breath away." The two of them sat and talked, the shadow insisting on buying his way out of any debt he might owe the man, the man in turn insisting the shadow owes him nothing, he is simply an old friend the man wishes well. The learned man's only request was for the shadow to tell him what was in the house across from the balcony and how he came to be where he is.

"'Well, now you shall hear the whole story,' said the Shadow, stamping his patent leather boots down on the sleeve of the learned man's new shadow which lay there at his feet like a poodle."

Now a rich texture gets added to the tapestry:

> "Whom do you think I found living over there in the neighbour's house?" said the Shadow. "The fairest of the fair—Poetry! I was there for three weeks, and it meant as much as living for three thousand years and reading all that man has imagined and written down. Believe me, that is so. I have seen everything and I know everything."
>
> "Poetry!" cried the learned man. "Yes, yes, in the large towns she often lives like a hermit. Poetry! Yes, I caught a glimpse of her for one short second, but my eyes were full of sleep. She stood on the balcony, glittering as the Northern Lights glitter. Go on, my good fellow; go on! You were on the balcony, you went in at the door, and then--?"

The man wanted to know all there is to know about Poetry, but the Shadow was slow to respond, and was more interested in pointing out that now he was independent, well-informed, in good standing, and excellently connected—deserving to be addressed by the man with more respect. The man agreed, but insisted on knowing more about this "antechamber" of Poetry:

> "What did the inner rooms look like? . . . Was it like being in the green forest? Or in some holy church? Were the halls like the starlit sky when one is standing on the mountain heights?"

Here, Andersen is connecting the realities of poetry (the arts) with nature and religion. The entire story is clearly written from the perspective of the Romantic Movement views that connect up poetry with nature and the higher truths of religion, the belief that the poet is a form of prophet who can lead less sensitive, less artistic people to see the higher truths through his poetry.

As the man (expressing our own desires) pushed to know more, the Shadow (now capitalized) continued to play it coy. The man persisted: "Yes, but what did you see, sir? Were all the gods of antiquity striding through those great halls? Were the heroes of old doing battle there? Were the darling children at play, and did they tell you their dreams?"

The Shadow then revealed its connection to that world, the world of the night and the dream and the arts. "'I was there, I repeat, and you must understand that I saw everything there was to see. Had you come across, you would not have become a man; but I did.'" And here we struggle to grasp the relationship of the shadow to the arts, the mysterious world of the night and the moon, the world the conscious ego cannot fully enter. The shadow continued. "'And I also learnt to know my innermost nature, as I received it at birth, my relationship to Poetry. No, when I was with you, I never gave it a thought; but at sunrise and at sunset, you remember, I always grew remarkably large—in the moonlight I stood out almost plainer then yourself. In those days I didn't understand my own nature; in the antechamber it dawned upon me—I was a man . . .'"

As a man/shadow, this Shadow then went about the world, hiding at first because he had no clothes, noticeably hiding under a woman's skirt, looking into rooms and seeing what others cannot or should not. "'I saw," added the Shadow, "what none are supposed to know, but what all are dying to know—trouble in the house next door . . . If I had a newspaper, it would have had plenty of readers! But I used to write direct to the person in question, and there was panic wherever I went. They were terribly afraid of me—and, oh! so fond of me. The professors made me a professor, the tailors gave me new clothes; I was well provided for. The master of the mint made me coins, and the women said I was handsome. And that's how I became the man I am."

This is what the world of "poetry" is all about, those truths of the world of the shadow, those desires, needs, wishes, hopes, knowings of the world beyond the sun, beyond the conscious world of logic and reason.

Then the Shadow left the man for a time, and the man continued to write about the *true* and the *good* and the *beautiful*, but, he said, "'no one bothers his head about that sort of thing. It makes me quite desperate, for it means so much to me.'"

Here it is obvious that Andersen is expressing that same sentiment stated so clearly by John Keats in his poem "Ode on a Grecian Urn": Beauty is truth, truth beauty; That is all ye can know on earth and all ye need to know." And since we realize what Andersen is expressing, the progression of the story is obvious:

> "It wouldn't worry me," said the Shadow. "I'm getting fat—which is just what one should try to be. I'm afraid you don't understand the world, and you're getting ill. You should travel. I'm going abroad this summer; won't you come with me? I should so like a traveling companion. Come with me, as my shadow! It will be a great pleasure to have you with me, and I'll pay your expenses."
>
> "Surely that's going a bit far," said the learned man.
>
> "It depends how you take it," said the Shadow. "It'll do you a world of good to travel. If you will be my shadow, you shall have everything on the trip for nothing."

Reading this symbolically, the journey is the journey of life, and the shadow, the part of the psyche that connects up with the reality of poetry is the place to find truth and good and beauty, just what the man desires. So, he should let his shadow lead the way. However, he doesn't; he declines the offer.

"Things went badly for the learned man. He was dogged by care and sorrow, and his ideas about the true and the good and the beautiful were to most people about as attractive as roses to a cow. He ended by falling quite ill."

Wonderfully, ironically, his friends remark, "'Why, to look at, you're no more than a shadow."

The Shadow returned and this time persuaded the man to travel with him, and the fact that he told the man he "must go and take the waters" carries with the strong symbolism of *water*, the fluid, liquid world of the unconscious, the supernatural, the means to rebirth (as in Baptism). As they traveled, the learned man took on the role of the shadow and suggested they were now equal and should travels as friends. However, the Shadow would not have it, and said so. "And from then on the Shadow treated his former master as an inferior."

The symbolic properties of water continued as the learned man and the Shadow traveled to a "watering-place" (to help the Shadow grow his beard which wouldn't grow, an indication of him not really being a man) where a "beautiful princess" who "suffered from the complaint of over-sharp sight," noticed that the Shadow posing as a man had no shadow of his own. The Shadow responded that she had far too clear sight and should be gone because the spa had cured her, but she decided she liked the man without a beard (the Shadow) and stayed. Sight is an important symbol, and involves seeing on levels beyond mere physical sight; the reason this princess could see the Shadow did not really have a shadow is because she has a kind of sight beyond that of a normal person.

The Princess and the Shadow then danced the night away and fell in love. The dance floor is the symbolic stage of life, and here it is the place where the Princess (who is the same beautiful woman first seen in the man's waking dream at the beginning of the story, the life force of the world of Poetry), and the Shadow (that elusive twilight part of a man) come together. In other words, man enters the world of poetry through his shadow self.

The Princess, however, remembered her huge country filled with people to rule over, so she wanted to be sure this "wise man" who "dances beautifully" really was what he appeared to be, and she began asking him difficult questions, causing him to become confusing:

> "You can't answer that!" cried the Princess.
>
> "I learned that in the nursery," said the Shadow. "I believe even my shadow [the learned man] over there by the door can answer that."
>
> "Your shadow!" said the Princess. "That would be very remarkable."
>
> "Well, I won't say for certain that he can," said the Shadow, "but I should imagine so. He has now been with me so many years, listening to me all the time—I should imagine he can. But may I draw your Royal Highness's attention to one thing: he takes such pride in passing for a human being that, to get him into the right mood (which he has to be, if he is to answer well), he must be treated exactly the same as a human being."
>
> "I do like that," said the Princess.
>
> So then she went up to the learned man by the door and chatted with him about the sun and the moon and about people, both inside and out, and his answers were wonderfully shrewd and sound.
>
> "What a man this must be, when his mere shadow is as wise as that!" she thought. "And what a blessing it would be for my people and kingdom, if I chose him as a husband! I'll do it."

It's all fitting together, but it's all complicated. The learned man has a connection with the reality beyond mere physical existence through his shadow, the part of him that exists in that world, the world of the moon and the dream, and the learned man, who has tried so hard to understand and explain truth and beauty and the good, can ultimately only really come to know it by his shadow dancing with poetry (ultimately, all of the arts).

Ironically, the story will now move quickly into the Shadow and the Princess getting married, but in this marriage the Shadow demands that the learned man completely give himself to the role of being the Shadow's shadow. The learned man refuses. The Shadow condemns him, calls him Mad (with all of the connotations of the mad artist, which overlaps the various other men who have entered the world of the shadow—shamans, saviors, and the like), and the learned man is put to death.

In his brief discussion of this story, Otto Rank emphasizes how the *shadow* or *double* peruses the man, determined to "foil" him, resulting in "a catastrophic effect in the relationship of love." (81) If one believes Carl Jung's theories placing the *anima* and *shadow* in close proximity within the *unconscious*, then the common association of *the other* as *shadow-involving-an-anima* relationship makes sense, and the connections of both *shadow* and *anima* with the *libido-drive-of-the-id*, the natural drive to procreation, the life force flesh out a psychic map that makes sense. The *conscious* world of the *ego*, while it is a shallow one of social and public *personas* without the *unconscious* world of the *shadow, anima,* and *id*, when balanced with them results in a *self*, a complete psyche that is both driven by the higher values of reason and logic and form in combination with the intuitive drives and knowing beyond them of the *unconscious* and able to know and exist in a world that goes beyond them, is able to experience the agony and the ecstasy as one and the same, the *mysterium tremendum*, the *sublime—God*.

In 1887, Guy de Maupassant wrote *The Horla* in the form of a first person journal, beginning with the narrator, sane and happy:

> May 8. What a lovely day! I have spent all the morning lying on the grass in front of my house, under the enormous plantain tree which covers and shades and shelters the whole of it. I like this part of the country; I am fond of living here because I am attached to it by deep roots, the profound and delicate roots which attach a man to the soil on which his ancestors were born and died, to their traditions, their usages, their food, the local expressions, the peculiar language of the peasants, the smell of the soil, the hamlets, and to the atmosphere itself.
>
> I love the house in which I grew up. From my windows I can see the Seine, which flows by the side of my garden, on the other side of the road, almost through my grounds, the great and wide Seine, which goes to Rouen and Havre, and which is covered with boats passing to and fro.
>
> On the left, down yonder, lies Rouen, populous Rouen with its blue roofs massing under pointed, Gothic towers. Innumerable are they, delicate or broad, dominated by the spire of the cathedral, full of bells which sound through the blue air on fine mornings, sending their sweet and distant iron clang to me, their metallic sounds, now stronger and now weaker, according as the wind is strong or light.
>
> What a delicious morning it was! About eleven o'clock, a long line of boats drawn by a steam-tug, as big as a fly, and which scarcely puffed while emitting its thick smoke, passed my gate.
>
> After two English schooners, whose red flags fluttered toward the sky, there came a magnificent Brazilian three-master; it was perfectly white and wonderfully clean and shining. I saluted it, I hardly know why, except that the sight of the vessel gave me great pleasure. (82)

However, the next entry just four days later immediately begins his frightening mental odyssey into a less pleasant, less comfortable world, a world where inexplicable entities with powers beyond the explanations of logic and science hold court. It is important to note that he attempts to clarify his illness as not so much a physical illness but, rather, a spiritual illness:

> May 12. I have had a slight feverish attack for the last few days, and I feel ill, or rather I feel low-spirited.
>
> Whence come those mysterious influences which change our happiness into discouragement, and our self-confidence into diffidence? One might almost say that the air, the invisible air, is full of unknowable Forces, whose mysterious presence we have to endure. I wake up in the best of spirits, with an inclination to sing in my heart. Why? I go down by the side of the water, and suddenly, after walking a short distance, I return home wretched, as if some misfortune were awaiting me there. Why? Is it a cold shiver which, passing over my skin, has upset my nerves and given me a fit of low spirits? Is it the form of the clouds, or the tints of the sky, or the colors of the surrounding objects which are so change-able, which have troubled my thoughts as they passed before my eyes? Who can tell? Everything that surrounds us, everything that we see without looking at it, everything that we touch without knowing it, everything that we handle without feeling it, everything that we meet without clearly distinguishing it, has a rapid, surprising, and inexplicable effect upon us and upon our organs, and through them on our ideas and on our being itself.

It is clear, this narrator is going to struggle with the "invisible" world that is "full" of "unknowable forces," forces we paradoxically *sense* beyond our *senses*, forces of the spiritual world that exists both within and without us, the world of madness and salvation. His journal continues:

> 2
>
> How profound that mystery of the Invisible is! We cannot fathom it with our miserable senses: our eyes are unable to perceive what is either too small or too great, too near to or too far from us; we can see neither the inhabitants of a star nor of a drop of water; our ears deceive us, for they transmit to us the vibrations of the air in sonorous notes. Our senses are fairies who work the miracle of changing that movement into noise, and by that metamorphosis give birth to music, which makes the mute agitation of nature a harmony. So with our sense of smell, which is weaker than that of a dog, and so with our sense of taste, which can scarcely distinguish the age of a wine!

> Oh! If we only had other organs which could work other miracles in our favor, what a number of fresh things we might discover around us!
>
> May 16. I am ill, decidedly! I was so well last month! I am feverish, horribly feverish, or rather I am in a state of feverish enervation, which makes my mind suffer as much as my body. I have without ceasing the horrible sensation of some danger threatening me, the apprehension of some coming misfortune or of approaching death, a presentiment which is no doubt, an attack of some illness still unnamed, which germinates in the flesh and in the blood.

First, in the manner of a good logical approach to discovering the source of the illness, it is necessary to eliminate scientific or medical reasons, to eliminate physical reasons:

> May 18. I have just come from consulting my medical man, for I can no longer get any sleep. He found that my pulse was high, my eyes dilated, my nerves highly strung, but no alarming symptoms. I must have a course of shower baths and of bromide of potassium.

Then it's time to suggest possible *mental* reasons, *unnatural* feelings of "menace" and "fear" in the "night," that moonlit world filled with ghosts and other spirits that shun the conscious world of the sun, that world of sleep and the mysteries of the dream:

> May 25. No change! My state is really very peculiar. As the evening comes on, an incomprehensible feeling of disquietude seizes me, just as if night concealed some terrible menace toward me. I dine quickly, and then try to read, but I do not understand the words, and can scarcely distinguish the letters. Then I walk up and down my drawing-room, oppressed by a feeling of confused and irresistible fear, a fear of sleep and a fear of my bed.

3

> About ten o'clock I go up to my room. As soon as I have entered I lock and bolt the door. I am frightened - of what? Up till the present time I have been frightened of nothing. I open my cupboards, and look under my bed; I listen - I listen - to what? How strange it is that a simple feeling of discomfort, of impeded or heightened circulation, perhaps the irritation of a nervous center, a slight congestion, a small disturbance in the imperfect and delicate functions of our living machinery, can turn the most light-hearted of men into a melancholy one, and make a coward of the bravest? Then, I go to bed, and I wait for sleep as a man might wait for the executioner. I wait for its coming with dread, and my heart beats and my legs tremble, while my whole body shivers beneath the warmth of the

> bedclothes, until the moment when I suddenly fall asleep, as a man throws himself into a pool of stagnant water in order to drown. I do not feel this perfidious sleep coming over me as I used to, but a sleep which is close to me and watching me, which is going to seize me by the head, to close my eyes and annihilate me.
>
> I sleep - a long time - two or three hours perhaps - then a dream - no - a nightmare lays hold on me. I feel that I am in bed and asleep - I feel it and I know it - and I feel also that somebody is coming close to me, is looking at me, touching me, is getting on to my bed, is kneeling on my chest, is taking my neck between his hands and squeezing it - squeezing it with all his might in order to strangle me.
>
> I struggle, bound by that terrible powerlessness which paralyzes us in our dreams; I try to cry out - but I cannot; I want to move - I cannot; I try, with the most violent efforts and out of breath, to turn over and throw off this being which is crushing and suffocating me - I cannot!

Now, in the reality or unreality of the dream the *other*, the dangerous entity of this *other world* appears. Here is the mystery, and it is a frightening mystery, one that promises to *strangle, suffocate* and *paralyze* the narrator. Is it real? Is it some dark psychic force?

4

> And then suddenly I wake up, shaken and bathed in perspiration; I light a candle and find that I am alone, and after that crisis, which occurs every night, I at length fall asleep and slumber tranquilly till morning.

The world of *nature*, what would seem to be the place to oppose the *unnatural* world of the *spirits*, is instead a place to encounter them. It is the world beyond the consciously controlled world of the city, that civilized world where logic and science hold sway. It is where the protagonists of folk tales go to get in touch with the spirits, both inner and outer, and transform psychologically, emotionally, spiritually, and physically, where they go to receive their just rewards (positive or negative). It is where our narrator goes seeking his own psychic health:

> June 2. My state has grown worse. What is the matter with me? The bromide does me no good, and the shower-baths have no effect whatever. Sometimes, in order to tire myself out, though I am fatigued enough already, I go for a walk in the forest of Roumare. I used to think at first that the fresh light and soft air, impregnated with the odor of herbs and leaves, would instill new life into my veins and impart fresh energy to my heart. One day I turned into a broad ride in the wood, and then I diverged toward La Bouille, through a narrow path, between two rows of exceedingly tall

> trees, which placed a thick, green, almost black roof between the sky and me.
>
> A sudden shiver ran through me, not a cold shiver, but a shiver of agony, and so I hastened my steps, uneasy at being alone in the wood, frightened stupidly and without reason, at the profound solitude. Suddenly it seemed as if I were being followed, that somebody was walking at my heels, close, quite close to me, near enough to touch me.
>
> I turned round suddenly, but I was alone. I saw nothing behind me except the straight, broad ride, empty and bordered by high trees, horribly empty; on the other side also it extended until it was lost in the distance, and looked just the same - terrible.
>
> I closed my eyes. Why? And then I began to turn round on one heel very quickly, just like a top. I nearly fell down, and opened my eyes; the trees were dancing round me and the earth heaved; I was obliged to sit down. Then, ah! I no longer remembered how I had come! What a strange idea! What a strange, strange idea! I did not the least know. I started off to the right, and got back into the avenue which had led me into the middle of the forest.

Indeed, our narrator has been fortunate here, as it is easy to get lost in the physical, psychological and spiritual forest he has entered. He indeed seems on the edge of insanity, on the edge of never finding his way back to that avenue leading to the conscious, sane world of the city.

5

> June 3. I have had a terrible night. I shall go away for a few weeks, for no doubt a journey will set me up again.
>
> July 2. I have come back, quite cured, and have had a most delightful trip into the bargain. I have been to Mont Saint-Michel, which I had not seen before.

This time the journey is into the spiritual world, the world of the church--a beautiful abbey on a rock, on a hill, on an island in the middle of a bay, each of these a symbol of the spiritual world, the same world as the unconscious, the world beyond the *natural* world; it is the *supernatural* world:

> What a sight, when one arrives as I did, at Avranches toward the end of the day! The town stands on a hill, and I was taken into the public garden at the extremity of the town. I uttered a cry of astonishment. An extraordinarily large bay lay extended before me, as far as my eyes could reach, between two hills which were lost to sight in the mist; and in the middle of this immense yellow bay, under a clear, golden sky, a peculiar hill rose up, somber and pointed in the midst of the sand. The sun had just

disappeared, and under the still flaming sky stood out the outline of that fantastic rock which bears on its summit a picturesque monument.

At daybreak I went to it. The tide was low, as it had been the night before, and I saw that wonderful abbey rise up before me as I approached it. After several hours' walking, I reached the enormous mass of rock which supports the little town, dominated by the great church. Having climbed the steep and narrow street, I entered the most wonderful Gothic building that has ever been erected to God on earth, large as a town, and full of low rooms which seem buried beneath vaulted roofs, and of lofty galleries supported by delicate columns.

I entered this gigantic granite jewel, which is as light in its effect as a bit of lace and is covered with towers, with slender belfries to which spiral staircases ascend. The flying buttresses raise strange heads that bristle with chimeras, with devils, with fantastic animals, with monstrous flowers, are joined together by finely carved arches, to the blue sky by day, and to the black sky by night.

6

When I had reached the summit, I said to the monk who accompanied me: "Father, how happy you must be here!" And he replied: "It is very windy, Monsieur"; and so we began to talk while watching the rising tide, which ran over the sand and covered it with a steel cuirass.

Here he hears the stories, the *legends* that tell of happenings beyond what reason and logic can grasp.

And then the monk told me stories, all the old stories belonging to the place - legends, nothing but legends.

One of them struck me forcibly. The country people, those belonging to the Mornet, declare that at night one can hear talking going on in the sand, and also that two goats bleat, one with a strong, the other with a weak voice. Incredulous people declare that it is nothing but the screaming of the sea birds, which occasionally resembles bleatings, and occasionally human lamentations; but belated fishermen swear that they have met an old shepherd, whose cloak covered head they can never see, wandering on the sand, between two tides, round the little town placed so far out of the world. They declare he is guiding and walking before a he-goat with a man's face and a she-goat with a woman's face, both with white hair, who talk incessantly, quarreling in a strange language, and then suddenly cease talking in order to bleat with all their might.

"Do you believe it?" I asked the monk. "I scarcely know," he replied; and I continued: "If there are other beings besides ourselves on this earth, how comes it that we have not known it for so long a time, or why have you not seen them? How is it that I have not seen them?" He replied: "Do we see the hundred-thousandth part of what exists? Look here; there is the wind, which is the strongest force in nature. It knocks down men, and blows down buildings, uproots trees, raises the sea into mountains of water, destroys cliffs and casts great ships on to the breakers; it kills, it whistles, it sighs, it roars. But have you ever seen it, and can you see it? Yet it exists for all that."

7

I was silent before this simple reasoning. That man was a philosopher, or perhaps a fool; I could not say which exactly, so I held my tongue. What he had said had often been in my own thoughts.

July 3. I have slept badly; certainly there is some feverish influence here, for my coachman is suffering in the same way as I am. When I went back home yesterday, I noticed his singular paleness, and I asked him: "What is the matter with you, Jean?"

"The matter is that I never get any rest, and my nights devour my days. Since your departure, Monsieur, there has been a spell over me."

However, the other servants are all well, but I am very frightened of having another attack myself.

July 4. I am decidedly taken again; for my old nightmares have returned. Last night I felt somebody leaning on me who was sucking my life from between my lips with his mouth. Yes, he was sucking it out of my neck like a leech would have done. Then he got up, satiated, and I woke up, so beaten, crushed, and annihilated that I could not move. If this continues for a few days, I shall certainly go away again.

One's physical breath is also one's spiritual breath, one's essence. A kiss on the mouth is an exchange of one's spirit or soul with another.

July 5. Have I lost my reason? What has happened? What I saw last night is so strange that my head wanders when I think of it!

As I do now every evening, I had locked my door; then, being thirsty, I drank half a glass of water, and I accidentally noticed that the water-bottle was full up to the cut-glass stopper.

Now there is physical evidence—if we believe our narrator, who, we suspect, is on the edge of insanity.

Then I went to bed and fell into one of my terrible sleeps, from which I was aroused in about two hours by a still more terrible shock.

Picture to yourself a sleeping man who is being murdered, who wakes up with a knife in his chest, a gurgling in his throat, is covered with blood, can no longer breathe, is going to die and does not understand anything at all about it - there you have it.

8

Having recovered my senses, I was thirsty again, so I lighted a candle and went to the table on which my water-bottle was. I lifted it up and tilted it over my glass, but nothing came out. It was empty! It was completely empty! At first I could not understand it at all; then suddenly I was seized by such a terrible feeling that I had to sit down, or rather fall into a chair! Then I sprang up with a bound to look about me; then I sat down again, overcome by astonishment and fear, in front of the transparent crystal bottle! I looked at it with fixed eyes, trying to solve the puzzle, and my hands trembled! Somebody had drunk the water, but who? I? I without any doubt. It could surely only be I? In that case I was a somnambulist - was living, without knowing it, that double, mysterious life which makes us doubt whether there are not two beings in us - whether a strange, unknowable, and invisible being does not, during our moments of mental and physical torpor, animate the inert body, forcing it to a more willing obedience than it yields to ourselves.

Oh! Who will understand my horrible agony? Who will understand the emotion of a man sound in mind, wide-awake, full of sense, who looks in horror at the disappearance of a little water while he was asleep, through the glass of a water-bottle! And I remained sitting until it was daylight, without venturing to go to bed again.

July 6. I am going mad. Again all the contents of my water-bottle have been drunk during the night; or rather I have drunk it!

But is it I? Is it I? Who could it be? Who? Oh! God! Am I going mad? Who will save me?

July 10. I have just been through some surprising ordeals. Undoubtedly I must be mad! And yet!

On July 6, before going to bed, I put some wine, milk, water, bread, and strawberries on my table. Somebody drank - I drank - all the water and a little of the milk, but neither the wine, nor the bread, nor the strawberries were touched.

9

On the seventh of July I renewed the same experiment, with the same results, and on July 8 I left out the water and the milk and nothing was touched.

Lastly, on July 9 I put only water and milk on my table, taking care to wrap up the bottles in white muslin and to tie down the stoppers. Then I rubbed my lips, my beard, and my hands with pencil lead, and went to bed.

Deep slumber seized me, soon followed by a terrible awakening. I had not moved, and my sheets were not marked. I rushed to the table. The muslin round the bottles remained intact; I undid the string, trembling with fear. All the water had been drunk, and so had the milk! Ah! Great God! I must start for Paris immediately.

July 12. Paris. I must have lost my head during the last few days! I must be the plaything of my enervated imagination, unless I am really a somnambulist, or I have been brought under the power of one of those influences--hypnotic suggestion, for example--which are known to exist, but have hitherto been inexplicable. In any case, my mental state bordered on madness, and twenty-four hours of Paris sufficed to restore me to my equilibrium.

Yesterday after doing some business and paying some visits, which instilled fresh and invigorating mental air into me, I wound up my evening at the Theatre Francais. A drama by Alexander Dumas the Younger was being acted, and his brilliant and powerful play completed my cure. Certainly solitude is dangerous for active minds. We need men who can think and can talk, around us. When we are alone for a long time, we people space with phantoms.

I returned along the boulevards to my hotel in excellent spirits. Amid the jostling of the crowd I thought, not without irony, of my terrors and surmises of the previous week, because I believed, yes, I believed, that an invisible being lived beneath my roof. How weak our mind is; how quickly it is terrified and unbalanced as soon as we are confronted with a small, incomprehensible fact. Instead of dismissing the problem with: "We do not understand because we cannot find the cause," we immediately imagine terrible mysteries and supernatural powers.

10

Yet again "reason" gets undermined, as "in this world one is certain of nothing, since light is an illusion and noise is deception."

July 14. Fete of the Republic. I walked through the streets, and the crackers and flags amused me like a child. Still, it is very foolish to make merry on a set date, by Government decree. People are like a flock of sheep, now steadily patient, now in ferocious revolt. Say to it: "Amuse yourself," and it amuses itself. Say to it: "Go and fight with your neighbor," and it goes and fights. Say to it: "Vote for the Emperor," and it votes for the Emperor; then say to it: "Vote for the Republic," and it votes for the Republic.

Those who direct it are stupid, too; but instead of obeying men they obey principles, a course which can only be foolish, ineffective, and false, for the very reason that principles are ideas which are considered as certain and unchangeable, whereas in this world one is certain of nothing, since light is an illusion and noise is deception.

At this point, our narrator turns surprisingly sane, becomes our own questioning voice in what follows:

July 16. I saw some things yesterday that troubled me very much. I was dining at my cousin's, Madame Sable, whose husband is colonel of the Seventy-sixth Chasseurs at Limoges. There were two young women there, one of whom had married a medical man, Dr. Parent, who devotes himself a great deal to nervous diseases and to the extraordinary manifestations which just now experiments in hypnotism and suggestion are producing.

He related to us at some length the enormous results obtained by English scientists and the doctors of the medical school at Nancy, and the facts which he adduced appeared to me so strange, that I declared that I was altogether incredulous.

"We are," he declared, "on the point of discovering one of the most important secrets of nature, I mean to say, one of its most important secrets on this earth, for assuredly there are some up in the stars, yonder, of a different kind of importance. Ever since man has thought, since he has been able to express and write down his thoughts, he has felt himself close to a mystery which is impenetrable to his coarse and imperfect senses, and he endeavors to supplement the feeble penetration of his organs by the efforts of his intellect. As long as that intellect remained in its elementary stage, this intercourse with invisible spirits assumed forms which were commonplace though terrifying. Thence sprang the popular belief in the supernatural, the legends of wandering spirits, of fairies, of gnomes, of ghosts, I might even say the conception of God, for our ideas of the Workman-Creator, from whatever religion they may have come down to us, are certainly the most mediocre, the stupidest, and the most unacceptable inventions that ever sprang from the frightened brain of any human creature. Nothing is truer than what Voltaire says: 'If God made man in His own image, man has certainly paid Him back again.'

11

"But for rather more than a century, men seem to have had a presentiment of something new. Mesmer and some others have put us on an unexpected track, and within the last two or three years especially, we have arrived at results really surprising."

My cousin, who is also very incredulous, smiled, and Dr. Parent said to her: "Would you like me to try and send you to sleep, Madame?"

"Yes, certainly."

She sat down in an easy-chair, and he began to look at her fixedly, as if to fascinate her. I suddenly felt myself somewhat discomposed; my heart beat rapidly and I had a choking feeling in my throat. I saw that Madame Sable's eyes were growing heavy, her mouth twitched, and her bosom heaved, and at the end of ten minutes she was asleep.

"Go behind her," the doctor said to me; so I took a seat behind her. He put a visiting-card into her hands, and said to her: "This is a looking-glass; what do you see in it?"

She replied: "I see my cousin."

"What is he doing?"

"He is twisting his mustache."

"And now?"

"He is taking a photograph out of his pocket."

"Whose photograph is it?"

"His own."

That was true, for the photograph had been given me that same evening at the hotel.

"What is his attitude in this portrait?"

"He is standing up with his hat in his hand."

She saw these things in that card, in that piece of white pasteboard, as if she had seen them in a looking-glass.

12

The young women were frightened, and exclaimed: "That is quite enough! Quite, quite enough!"

But the doctor said to her authoritatively: "You will get up at eight o'clock to-morrow morning; then you will go and call on your cousin at his hotel and ask him to lend you the five thousand francs which your husband asks of you, and which he will ask for when he sets out on his coming journey."

Then he woke her up.

On returning to my hotel, I thought over this curious séance and I was assailed by doubts, not as to my cousin's absolute and undoubted good faith, for I had known her as well as if she had been my own sister ever since she was a child, but as to a possible trick on the doctor's part. Had not he, perhaps, kept a glass hidden in his hand, which he showed to the young woman in her sleep at the same time as he did the card? Professional conjurers do things which are just as singular.

However, I went to bed, and this morning, at about half past eight, I was awakened by my footman, who said to me: "Madame Sable has asked to see you immediately, Monsieur." I dressed hastily and went to her.

She sat down in some agitation, with her eyes on the floor, and without raising her veil said to me: "My dear cousin, I am going to ask a great favor of you."

"What is it, cousin?"

"I do not like to tell you, and yet I must. I am in absolute want of five thousand francs."

"What, you?"

"Yes, I, or rather my husband, who has asked me to procure them for him."

I was so stupefied that I hesitated to answer. I asked myself whether she had not really been making fun of me with Dr. Parent, if it were not merely a very well-acted farce which had been got up beforehand. On looking at her attentively, however, my doubts disappeared. She was trembling with grief, so painful was this step to her, and I was sure that her throat was full of sobs.

13

I knew that she was very rich and so I continued: "What! Has not your husband five thousand francs at his disposal? Come, think. Are you sure that he commissioned you to ask me for them?"

She hesitated for a few seconds, as if she were making a great effort to search her memory, and then she replied: "Yes - yes, I am quite sure of it."

"He has written to you?"

She hesitated again and reflected, and I guessed the torture of her thoughts. She did not know. She only knew that she was to borrow five thousand francs of me for her husband. So she told a lie.

"Yes, he has written to me."

"When, pray? You did not mention it to me yesterday."

"I received his letter this morning."

"Can you show it to me?"

"No; no - no - it contained private matters, things too personal to ourselves. I burned it."

"So your husband runs into debt?"

She hesitated again, and then murmured: "I do not know."

Thereupon I said bluntly: "I have not five thousand francs at my disposal at this moment, my dear cousin."

She uttered a cry, as if she were in pair; and said: "Oh! oh! I beseech you, I beseech you to get them for me."

She got excited and clasped her hands as if she were praying to me! I heard her voice change its tone; she wept and sobbed, harassed and dominated by the irresistible order that she had received.

"Oh! oh! I beg you to - if you knew what I am suffering - I want them to-day."

14

I had pity on her: "You shall have them by and by, I swear to you."

"Oh! thank you! thank you! How kind you are."

I continued: "Do you remember what took place at your house last night?"

"Yes."

"Do you remember that Dr. Parent sent you to sleep?"

"Yes."

"Oh! Very well then; he ordered you to come to me this morning to borrow five thousand francs, and at this moment you are obeying that suggestion."

She considered for a few moments, and then replied: "But as it is my husband who wants them - "

For a whole hour I tried to convince her, but could not succeed, and when she had gone I went to the doctor. He was just going out, and he listened to me with a smile, and said: "Do you believe now?"

"Yes, I cannot help it."

"Let us go to your cousin's."

She was already resting on a couch, overcome with fatigue. The doctor felt her pulse, looked at her for some time with one hand raised toward her eyes, which she closed by degrees under the irresistible power of this magnetic influence. When she was asleep, he said:

"Your husband does not require the five thousand francs any longer! You must, therefore, forget that you asked your cousin to lend them to you, and, if he speaks to you about it, you will not understand him."

Then he woke her up, and I took out a pocket-book and said: "Here is what you asked me for this morning, my dear cousin." But she was so surprised, that I did not venture to persist; nevertheless, I tried to recall the circumstance to her, but she denied it vigorously, thought that I was making fun of her, and in the end, very nearly lost her temper.

15

There! I have just come back, and I have not been able to eat any lunch, for this experiment has altogether upset me.

July 19. Many people to whom I have told the adventure have laughed at me. I no longer know what to think. The wise man says: Perhaps?

July 21. I dined at Bougival, and then I spent the evening at a boatmen's ball. Decidedly everything depends on place and surroundings. It would be the height of folly to believe in the supernatural on the Ile de la Grenouilliere. But on the top of Mont Saint-Michel or in India, we are terribly under the influence of our surroundings. I shall return home next week.

July 30. I came back to my own house yesterday. Everything is going on well.

August 2. Nothing fresh; it is splendid weather, and I spend my days in watching the Seine flow past.

August 4. Quarrels among my servants. They declare that the glasses are broken in the cupboards at night. The footman accuses the cook, she accuses the needlewoman, and the latter accuses the other two. Who is the culprit? It would take a clever person to tell.

August 6. This time, I am not mad. I have seen - I have seen - I have seen! - I can doubt no longer - I have seen it!

I was walking at two o'clock among my rose-trees, in the full sunlight - in the walk bordered by autumn roses which are beginning to fall. As I stopped to look at a Geant de Bataille, which had three splendid blooms, I distinctly saw the stalk of one of the roses bend close to me, as if an invisible hand had bent it, and then break, as if that hand had picked it! Then the flower raised itself, following the curve which a hand would have described in carrying it toward a mouth, and remained suspended in the transparent air, alone and motionless, a terrible red spot, three yards from my eyes. In desperation I rushed at it to take it! I found nothing; it had disappeared. Then I was seized with furious rage against myself, for it is not wholesome for a reasonable and serious man to have such hallucinations.

16

But was it a hallucination? I turned to look for the stalk, and I found it immediately under the bush, freshly broken, between the two other roses which remained on the branch. I returned home, then, with a much disturbed mind; for I am certain now, certain as I am of the alternation of day and night, that there exists close to me an invisible being who lives on milk and on water, who can touch objects, take them and change their places; who is, consequently, endowed with a material nature, although imperceptible to sense, and who lives as I do, under my roof –

August 7. I slept tranquilly. He drank the water out of my decanter, but did not disturb my sleep.

I ask myself whether I am mad. As I was walking just now in the sun by the riverside, doubts as to my own sanity arose in me; not vague doubts such as I have had hitherto, but precise and absolute doubts. I have seen mad people, and I have known some who were quite intelligent, lucid, even clear-sighted in every concern of life, except on one point. They could speak clearly, readily, profoundly on everything; till their thoughts were caught in the breakers of their delusions and went to pieces there, were dispersed and swamped in that furious and terrible sea of fogs and squalls which is called MADNESS.

I certainly should think that I was mad, absolutely mad, if I were not conscious that I knew my state, if I could not fathom it and analyze it with the most complete lucidity. I should, in fact, be a reasonable man laboring under a hallucination. Some unknown disturbance must have been excited in my brain, one of those disturbances which physiologists of the present day try to note and to fix precisely, and that disturbance must have caused a profound gulf in my mind and in the order and logic of my ideas. Similar phenomena occur in dreams, and lead us through the most unlikely phantasmagoria, without causing us any surprise, because our verifying apparatus and our sense of control have gone to sleep, while our imaginative faculty wakes and works. Was it not possible that one of the imperceptible keys of the cerebral finger-board had been paralyzed in me? Some men lose the recollection of proper names, or of verbs, or of numbers, or merely of dates, in consequence of an accident. The localization of all the avenues of thought has been accomplished nowadays; what, then, would there be surprising in the fact that my faculty of controlling the unreality of certain hallucinations should be destroyed for the time being?

17

I thought of all this as I walked by the side of the water. The sun was shining brightly on the river and made earth delightful, while it filled me with love for life, for the swallows, whose swift agility is always delightful in my eyes, for the plants by the riverside, whose rustling is a pleasure to my ears.

By degrees, however, an inexplicable feeling of discomfort seized me. It seemed to me as if some unknown force were numbing and stopping me, were preventing me from going further and were calling me back. I felt that painful wish to return which comes on you when you have left a beloved invalid at home, and are seized by a presentiment that he is worse.

I, therefore, returned despite of myself, feeling certain that I should find some bad news awaiting me, a letter or a telegram. There was nothing, however, and I was surprised and uneasy, more so than if I had had another fantastic vision.

August 8. I spent a terrible evening, yesterday. He does not show himself any more, but I feel that He is near me, watching me, looking at me, penetrating me, dominating me, and more terrible to me when He hides himself thus than if He were to manifest his constant and invisible presence by supernatural phenomena. However, I slept.

August 9. Nothing, but I am afraid.

August 10. Nothing; but what will happen to-morrow?

August 11. Still nothing. I cannot stop at home with this fear hanging over me and these thoughts in my mind; I shall go away.

August 12. Ten o'clock at night. All day long I have been trying to get away, and have not been able. I contemplated a simple and easy act of liberty, a carriage ride to Rouen - and I have not been able to do it. What is the reason?

August 13. When one is attacked by certain maladies, the springs of our physical being seem broken, our energies destroyed, our muscles relaxed, our bones to be as soft as our flesh, and our blood as liquid as water. I am experiencing the same in my moral being, in a strange and distressing manner. I have no longer any strength, any courage, any self-control, nor even any power to set my own will in motion. I have no power left to WILL anything, but someone does it for me and I obey.

Now the stage is set and *the other* takes charge:

18

August 14. I am lost! Somebody possesses my soul and governs it! Somebody orders all my acts, all my movements, all my thoughts. I am no longer master of myself, nothing except an enslaved and terrified spectator of the things which I do. I wish to go out; I cannot. HE does not wish to; and so I remain, trembling and distracted in the armchair in which he keeps me sitting. I merely wish to get up and to rouse myself, so as to think that I am still master of myself: I cannot! I am riveted to my chair, and my chair adheres to the floor in such a manner that no force of mine can move us.

Then suddenly, I must, I MUST go to the foot of my garden to pick some strawberries and eat them - and I go there. I pick the strawberries and I eat them! Oh! my God! my God! Is there a God? If there be one, deliver me! Save me! Succor me! Pardon! Pity! Mercy! Save me! Oh! What sufferings! What torture! What horror!

August 15. Certainly this is the way in which my poor cousin was possessed and swayed, when she came to borrow five thousand francs of me. She was under the power of a strange will which had entered into her, like another soul, a parasitic and ruling soul. Is the world coming to an end?

But who is he, this invisible being that rules me, this unknowable being, this rover of a supernatural race?

Invisible beings exist, then! How is it, then, that since the beginning of the world they have never manifested themselves in such a manner as they do to me? I have never read anything that resembles what goes on in my house. Oh! If I could only leave it, if I could only go away and flee, and never return, I should be saved; but I cannot.

August 16. I managed to escape to-day for two hours, like a prisoner who finds the door of his dungeon accidentally open. I suddenly felt that I was free and that He was far away, and so I gave orders to put the horses in as quickly as possible, and I drove to Rouen. Oh! how delightful to be able to say to my coachman: "Go to Rouen!"

19

I made him pull up before the library, and I begged them to lend me Dr. Herrmann Herestauss's treatise on the unknown inhabitants of the ancient and modern world.

Then, as I was getting into my carriage, I intended to say: "To the railway station!" but instead of this I shouted - I did not speak; but I shouted - in such a loud voice that all the passers-by turned round: "Home!" and I fell back on to the cushion of my carriage, overcome by mental agony. He had found me out and regained possession of me.

August 17. Oh! What a night! What a night! And yet it seems to me that I ought to rejoice. I read until one o'clock in the morning! Herestauss, Doctor of Philosophy and Theogony, wrote the history and the manifestation of all those invisible beings which hover around man, or of whom he dreams. He describes their origin, their domains, their power; but none of them resembles the one which haunts me. One might say that man, ever since he has thought, has had a foreboding and a fear of a new being, stronger than himself, his successor in this world, and that, feeling him near, and not being able to foretell the nature of the unseen one, he has, in his terror, created the whole race of hidden beings, vague phantoms born of fear.

Having, therefore, read until one o'clock in the morning, I went and sat down at the open window, in order to cool my forehead and my thoughts in the calm night air. It was very pleasant and warm! How I should have enjoyed such a night formerly!

There was no moon, but the stars darted out their rays in the dark heavens. Who inhabits those worlds? What forms, what living beings, what animals are there yonder? Do those who are thinkers in those distant worlds know more than we do? What can they do more than we? What do they see which we do not? Will not one of them, some day or other, traversing space, appear on our earth to conquer it, just as formerly the Norsemen crossed the sea in order to subjugate nations feebler than themselves?

20

We are so weak, so powerless, so ignorant, so small - we who live on this particle of mud which revolves in liquid air.

I fell asleep, dreaming thus in the cool night air, and then, having slept for about three quarters of an hour, I opened my eyes without moving, awakened by an indescribably confused and strange sensation. At first I saw nothing, and then suddenly it appeared to me as if a page of the book, which had remained open on my table, turned over of its own accord. Not a breath of air had come in at my window, and I was surprised and waited. In about four minutes, I saw, I saw - yes I saw with my own eyes - another page lift itself up and fall down on the others, as if a finger had turned it over. My armchair was empty, appeared empty, but I knew that He was there, He, and sitting in my place, and that He was reading. With a furious bound, the bound of an enraged wild beast that wishes to disembowel its tamer, I crossed my room to seize him, to strangle him, to kill him! But before I could reach it, my chair fell over as if somebody had run away from me. My table rocked, my lamp fell and went out, and my window closed as if some thief had been surprised and had fled out into the night, shutting it behind him.

So He had run away; He had been afraid; He, afraid of me!

So to-morrow, or later - some day or other, I should be able to hold him in my clutches and crush him against the ground! Do not dogs occasionally bite and strangle their masters?

August 18. I have been thinking the whole day long. Oh! Yes, I will obey Him, follow His impulses, fulfill all His wishes, show myself humble, submissive, a coward. He is the stronger; but an hour will come.

August 19. I know, I know, I know all! I have just read the following in the "Revue du Monde Scientifique": "A curious piece of news comes to us from Rio de Janeiro. Madness, an epidemic of madness, which may be compared to that contagious madness which attacked the people of Europe in the Middle Ages, is at this moment raging in the Province of San-Paulo. The frightened inhabitants are leaving their houses, deserting their villages, abandoning their land, saying that they are pursued, possessed, governed like human cattle by invisible, though tangible beings, by a species of vampire, which feeds on their life while they are asleep, and which, besides, drinks water and milk without appearing to touch any other nourishment.

Now the break with reality comes full force. Our narrator can no longer distinguish his own "dreams," his own nightmares from the external world. The literal, physical world becomes his nightmare, a form of paranoid schizophrenia (unless it does exist outside of him in the literal world—in which case the entire world is mad!).

21

"Professor Don Pedro Henriques, accompanied by several medical savants, has gone to the Province of San-Paulo, in order to study the origin and the manifestations of this surprising madness on the spot, and to propose such measures to the Emperor as may appear to him to be most fitted to restore the mad population to reason."

Ah! Ah! I remember now that fine Brazilian three-master which passed in front of my windows as it was going up the Seine, on the eighth of last May! I thought it looked so pretty, so white and bright! That Being was on board of her, coming from there, where its race sprang from. And it saw me! It saw my house, which was also white, and He sprang from the ship on to the land. Oh! Good heavens!

Now I know, I can divine. The reign of man is over, and he has come. He whom disquieted priests exorcised, whom sorcerers evoked on dark nights, without seeing him appear, He to whom the imaginations of the transient masters of the world lent all the monstrous or graceful forms of gnomes, spirits, genii, fairies, and familiar spirits. After the coarse conceptions of primitive fear, men more enlightened gave him a truer form. Mesmer divined him, and ten years ago physicians accurately discovered the nature of his power, even before He exercised it himself. They played with that weapon of their new Lord, the sway of a mysterious will over the human soul, which had become enslaved. They called it mesmerism, hypnotism, suggestion, I know not what? I have seen them diverting themselves like rash children with this horrible power! Woe to us! Woe to man! He has come, the - the - what does He call himself - the - I fancy that he is shouting out his name to me and I do not hear him - the - yes - He is shouting it out - I am listening - I cannot - repeat - it - Horla - I have heard - the Horla - it is He - the Horla - He has come! –

Ah! the vulture has eaten the pigeon, the wolf has eaten the lamb; the lion has devoured the sharp-horned buffalo; man has killed the lion with an arrow, with a spear, with gunpowder; but the Horla will make of man what man has made of the horse and of the ox: his chattel, his slave, and his food, by the mere power of his will. Woe to us!

22

But, nevertheless, sometimes the animal rebels and kills the man who has subjugated it. I should also like - I shall be able to - but I must know Him, touch Him, see Him! Learned men say that eyes of animals, as they differ from ours, do not distinguish as ours do. And my eye cannot distinguish this newcomer who is oppressing me.

Why? Oh! Now I remember the words of the monk at Mont Saint-Michel: "Can we see the hundred-thousandth part of what exists? Listen; there is the wind which is the strongest force in nature; it knocks men down, blows down buildings, uproots trees, raises the sea into mountains of water, destroys cliffs, and casts great ships on to the breakers; it kills, it whistles, it sighs, it roars, - have you ever seen it, and can you see it? It exists for all that, however!"

And I went on thinking: my eyes are so weak, so imperfect, that they do not even distinguish hard bodies, if they are as transparent as glass! If a glass without quicksilver behind it were to bar my way, I should run into it, just like a bird which has flown into a room breaks its head against the windowpanes. A thousand things, moreover, deceive a man and lead him astray. How then is it surprising that he cannot perceive a new body which is penetrated and pervaded by the light?

A new being! Why not? It was assuredly bound to come! Why should we be the last? We do not distinguish it, like all the others created before us? The reason is, that its nature is more delicate, its body finer and more finished than ours. Our makeup is so weak, so awkwardly conceived; our body is encumbered with organs that are always tired, always being strained like locks that are too complicated; it lives like a plant and like an animal nourishing itself with difficulty on air, herbs, and flesh; it is a brute machine which is a prey to maladies, to malformations, to decay; it is broken-winded, badly regulated, simple and eccentric, ingeniously yet badly made, a coarse and yet a delicate mechanism, in brief, the outline of a being which might become intelligent and great.

23

There are only a few - so few - stages of development in this world, from the oyster up to man. Why should there not be one more, when once that period is accomplished which separates the successive products one from the other?

Why not one more? Why not, also, other trees with immense, splendid flowers, perfuming whole regions? Why not other elements beside fire, air, earth, and water? There are four, only four, nursing fathers of various beings! What a pity! Why should not there be forty, four hundred, four thousand! How poor everything is, how mean and wretched - grudgingly given, poorly invented, clumsily made! Ah! The elephant and the hippopotamus, what power! And the camel, what suppleness!

But the butterfly, you will say, a flying flower! I dream of one that should be as large as a hundred worlds, with wings whose shape, beauty, colors, and motion I cannot even express. But I see it - it flutters from star to star, refreshing them and perfuming them with the light and harmonious breath of its flight! And the people up there gaze at it as it passes in an ecstasy of delight!

What is the matter with me? It is He, the Horla who haunts me, and who makes me think of these foolish things! He is within me, He is becoming my soul; I shall kill him!

August 20. I shall kill Him. I have seen Him! Yesterday I sat down at my table and pretended to write very assiduously. I knew quite well that He would come prowling round me, quite close to me, so close that I might perhaps be able to touch him, to seize him. And then - then I should have the strength of desperation; I should have my hands, my knees, my chest, my forehead, my teeth to strangle him, to crush him, to bite him, to tear him to pieces. And I watched for him with all my overexcited nerves.

I had lighted my two lamps and the eight wax candles on my mantelpiece, as if, by this light I should discover Him.

Now comes the mirror, that symbolic world of truth beyond literal existence. Surely, it is his own frightening *shadow*, his own *other*, his own *reflection* he struggles to keep from destroying him.

24

My bed, my old oak bed with its columns, was opposite to me; on my right was the fireplace; on my left the door, which was carefully closed, after I had left it open for some time, in order to attract Him; behind me was a very high wardrobe with a looking-glass in it, which served me to dress by every day, and in which I was in the habit of inspecting myself from head to foot every time I passed it.

So I pretended to be writing in order to deceive Him, for He also was watching me, and suddenly I felt, I was certain, that He was reading over my shoulder, that He was there, almost touching my ear.

I got up so quickly, with my hands extended, that I almost fell. Horror! It was as bright as at midday, but I did not see myself in the looking-glass! It was empty, clear, profound, full of light! But my figure was not reflected in it - and I, I was opposite to it! I saw the large, clear glass from top to bottom, and I looked at it with unsteady eyes. I did not dare advance; I did not venture to make a movement; feeling certain, nevertheless, that He was there, but that He would escape me again, He whose imperceptible body had absorbed my reflection.

How frightened I was! And then suddenly I began to see myself through a mist in the depths of the looking-glass, in a mist as it were, or through a veil of water; and it seemed to me as if this water were flowing slowly from left to right, and making my figure clearer every moment. It was like the end of an eclipse. Whatever hid me did not appear to possess any clearly defined outlines, but was a sort of opaque transparency, which gradually grew clearer.

At last I was able to distinguish myself completely, as I do every day when I look at myself.

I had seen Him! And the horror of it remained with me, and makes me shudder even now.

25

August 21. How could I kill Him, since I could not get hold of Him? Poison? But He would see me mix it with the water; and then, would our poisons have any effect on His impalpable body? No - no - no doubt about the matter. Then? - then?

August 22. I sent for a blacksmith from Rouen and ordered iron shutters of him for my room, such as some private hotels in Paris have on the ground floor, for fear of thieves, and he is going to make me a similar door as well. I have made myself out a coward, but I do not care about that!

September 10. Rouen, Hotel Continental. It is done; it is done - but is He dead? My mind is thoroughly upset by what I have seen.

Well then, yesterday, the locksmith having put on the iron shutters and door, I left everything open until midnight, although it was getting cold.

Suddenly I felt that He was there, and joy, mad joy took possession of me. I got up softly, and I walked to the right and left for some time, so that He might not guess anything; then I took off my boots and put on my slippers carelessly; then I fastened the iron shutters and going back to the door quickly I double-locked it with a padlock, putting the key into my pocket.

Suddenly I noticed that He was moving restlessly round me, that in his turn He was frightened and was ordering me to let Him out. I nearly yielded, though I did not quite, but putting my back to the door, I half opened it, just enough to allow me to go out backward, and as I am very tall, my head touched the lintel. I was sure that He had not been able to escape, and I shut Him up quite alone, quite alone. What happiness! I had Him fast. Then I ran downstairs into the drawing-room which was under my bedroom. I took the two lamps and poured all the oil on to the carpet, the furniture, everywhere; then I set fire to it and made my escape, after having carefully double locked the door.

26

I went and hid myself at the bottom of the garden, in a clump of laurel bushes. How long it was! How long it was! Everything was dark, silent, motionless, not a breath of air and not a star, but heavy banks of clouds which one could not see, but which weighed, oh! so heavily on my soul.

I looked at my house and waited. How long it was! I already began to think that the fire had gone out of its own accord, or that He had extinguished it, when one of the lower windows gave way under the violence of the flames, and a long, soft, caressing sheet of red flame mounted up the white wall, and kissed it as high as the roof. The light fell on to the trees, the branches, and the leaves, and a shiver of fear pervaded them also! The birds awoke; a dog began to howl, and it seemed to me as if the day were breaking! Almost immediately two other windows flew into fragments, and I saw that the whole of the lower part of my house was nothing but a terrible furnace. But a cry, a horrible, shrill, heart-rending cry, a woman's cry, sounded through the night, and two garret windows were opened! I had forgotten the servants! I saw the terror-struck faces, and the frantic waving of their arms!

Then, overwhelmed with horror, I ran off to the village, shouting: "Help! Help! Fire! Fire!" Meeting some people who were already coming on to the scene, I went back with them to see!

By this time the house was nothing but a horrible and magnificent funeral pile, a monstrous pyre which lit up the whole country, a pyre where men were burning, and where He was burning also, He, He, my prisoner, that new Being, the new Master, the Horla!

Suddenly the whole roof fell in between the walls, and a volcano of flames darted up to the sky. Through all the windows which opened on to that furnace, I saw the flames darting, and I reflected that He was there, in that kiln, dead.

27

Dead? Perhaps? His body? Was not his body, which was transparent, indestructible by such means as would kill ours?

If He were not dead? Perhaps time alone has power over that Invisible and Redoubtable Being. Why this transparent, unrecognizable body, this body belonging to a spirit, if it also had to fear ills, infirmities, and premature destruction?

Premature destruction? All human terror springs from that! After man the Horla. After him who can die every day, at any hour, at any moment, by any accident, He came, He who was only to die at his own proper hour and minute, because He had touched the limits of his existence!

No - no - there is no doubt about it - He is not dead. Then - then - I suppose I must kill myself!

Clearly external and internal realities have gotten so intertwined here that it is not possible to know what the real reality is, and that's the point.

One man's savior is another's madman.

****

> "It is not proven that Elizabeth's personal equilibrium was set off balance by the slant of the office floor, nor could it be proven that it was Elizabeth who pushed the building off its foundations, but it is undeniable that they began to slip at about the same time."
> —Shirley Jackson, *The Bird's Nest* (83)

In psychology, an *alter ego* is similar, even equated, to a psychological *doppelganger*, a second self. If taken into the realm of *Dissociative Identity Disorder* (DID) it refers to multiple personalities in the same person. It originated in psychology at the beginning of the twentieth century, and was largely replaced by the designation of *schizophrenia*. However, today, as *schizophrenia* and other mental aberrations have become more clearly understood, DID has established itself as a unique group of mental conditions.

It is generally used in popular reference to refer to someone with two distinct *personas*, whether the person is aware of them or not. And it became a standard ploy of the super-heroes of the DC comic books, especially of the "Pre-Crisis" years (the first fifty years prior to the *Crisis on Infinite Earths* twelve-issue American comic book limited series (identified as a "12-part maxi-series") and crossover event, produced by DC Comics in 1985 to simplify its continuity, remove the concept of the Multiverse in the fictional DC Universe, and depicted the deaths of such long-standing superheroes as Supergirl and the Barry Allen incarnation of the Flash).

Superman with his alter-ego Clark Kent begins this common DC alter-ego ploy, and it is an interesting one, as, he is certainly aware of his two roles at all (or most) times, and he carefully plays both roles to fool the world. In fact, much of the storyline involves his struggles to prevent others (especially Lois Lane) from knowing he is both Superman and Clark Kent, the justification generally being that he doesn't want to endanger his friends and adopted family, though, if one stops to think about it, it seems unnecessary and fraught with more problems than it solves.

One interesting thing it does, however, is provide an endless storyline relationship with a woman, Lois Lane, who works on at the Daily Planet with the purposely inept Clark Kent, but who is in love with the stunning

Superman. This *ménage a trios* offers a somewhat innocent version of a psychological study of what women want in a male. Clark Kent, who seems to love Lois Lane, takes on the *persona* of an overly awkward, bumbling man, yet a kind, thoughtful one, one constantly doing things in his self-effacing way to help her. However, he obviously just can't get it right in her eyes, and she sees him in a condescending way as a well-meaning but incapable friend, something of a nuisance, perhaps something of a loveable, helpless puppy, but someone for whom she would never even consider the possibility of being in love. Superman, however, can do no wrong. She is head-over-heels in love with him. He, on the other hand, is a modern day knight sworn to the quest, the knightly duty of saving the world, not with the heavy emphasis on the Christianity of the original knights of King Arthur's Round Table, but, rather the *American* ethos, and he won't allow himself the luxury of falling in love. It's clear what Lois Lane wants in a man, not so clear what Superman wants in a romantic relationship.

It's possible to discuss at length this curious relationship, not so much in terms of the *ego-shadow-anima* relationships, but in terms of the struggle between *agape* (that love of God obedience to the established Christian religion, obedience to the Christian *credo*), *amore* (that individualized love where a knight does his good deeds in the name of a woman, but does not consummate it physically—the *Tristan and Iseulde* story is the classic representation of this), and *eros* (sexual, physical love—the drives of the libido). If Superman is attracted to Lois Lane in the sense of *amore and or eros*, he hides it well, and, at any rate, he must give it up in order to fulfill his role as a modern day savor (again, not so much a Christian savor, though there is a an inclusion of God in his ethical paradigm, but more of a secular savor serving the American Way), and though he somehow always manages to save both Lois Lane and the world, he has to put saving her second to saving the world. (84)

Also, there is no real dark side to Superman, no *shadow.* On the other hand, Bruce Wayne and Batman form a clear division between the *ego persona* and the *shadow*, which is a perfect set up for an exploration of why the *shadow* is the empowered male, capable of both evil and good. Yes, it is the shadowy world of the "bat" that draws us into this super-hero, and if anything, the major flaw in the comic strip and subsequent movies is that they don't explore this more. It's always there, that psychological darkness that drives Batman, but at the same time, it's kept in the background.

Unlike Superman, Batman is a human without super powers, and his drive is established on the basis of a psychological trauma from his childhood. Bob Kane and Bill Finger decided that Batman's dark adult persona would be the result of seeing his parents murdered when he was a child. This leads not only to his desire to fight crime, but to his persona as a vigilante, a man who works outside the law. He is psychologically a *shadow*, a personality of the night, the world of the dream or nightmare, a frightening *bat*man—a man who knows the dark drives of the human psyche and can outdo even the most demented villains in their own territory.

His *alter-ego* is an extremely successful public playboy, living off of his parents' fortune, a *persona* he adopts to keep people from guessing at his dark other self. Notably, in spite of his cultured, shallow public face, he is a generous humanitarian, constantly giving money to good causes and doing positive things for his community. Furthermore, this public Batman is also a ladies' man, a flirt, and he has numerous affairs, though none become serious. For a while, there is also a Batgirl, but that relationship also doesn't carry much depth or material for analysis. In fact, the only relationship outside of his own duality is with his sidekick Robin, and that has garnered a lot of speculation concerning indications of homosexual tendencies. But again, not even Robin is a central character, and at times, there is no sidekick at all. This is not a series about relationships outside the psyche; this is a series about an inner duality, a man struggling with his own demons.

All of the DC characters have inconsistencies through the decades, and tone of Batman varies wildly, from dark, mysterious and graphic to light, ironic, and campy. However, in the end, it is the dark, shadowy Batman that holds the most interest, and his own psychological struggles to work outside the law and outside of accepted standards of morality are what attract us to him. This is a *powerful shadow* unleashed, capable of being as cruel as its criminal foes, only barely staying on the good side of the equation by a powerful *ego*; and the tensions do not come from the possibility of succumbing to some outside personality or force but clearly from the possibility of succumbing to his own inner darkness.

Having stressed this, it also should be noted that the various representations of him do not take advantage of it nearly as much as they should, and even in the brilliant movie version *The Dark Knight*, it is ultimately not Batman but a stunning portrayal of his enemy The Joker that pushes this nightmarish shadowy vision of a chaotic, demented world to its macabre conclusion, coming as close to expressing the horror of modern life as possible in a film where Batman wins for the conscious persona of law and order, and unfortunately is given an excuse for being outside the law—i.e., he is really a good guy, but has to suffer being misrepresented as a bad guy, an heroic form of self-sacrifice. (85)

As with the DC Comic superheroes, the Marvel Comic Hulk and David Banner alter-ego series varies throughout its run, the most interesting depiction beginning with issue #245 (March, 1980), when Bill Mantlo took over, and in his "Crossroads of Eternity" issues (#300-313) explored the idea that Banner experienced child abuse. When Peter David took over the series in May, 1987 (#331), he further altered the beginning relationship between Banner and Hulk, expanding the abuse into having Banner suffering from dissociative identity disorder (DID).

According to the WebMC Mental Health Center online, DID (also known as multiple personality disorder) is a standard outcome of severe trauma during early childhood, and/or repetitive physical, sexual or emotional abuse. While all people experience momentary disassociation (daydreaming or just losing one's thought process), DID is a more dramatic disassociation, thought to be a defense mechanism, a means of separating oneself from some situation or experience that is too violent, painful or traumatic to incorporate into normal brain functions, similar to *dissociative amnesia, dissociative fugue,* and *depersonalization disorder.* It is characterized by the presence of two or more distinct identities or personality states that alternate dominating a person's behavior. Often there is an inability to remember important personal information and differing memories of the same events.

The different identities (called *alters*), have distinct ages, sexes, races, postures, gestures, and even speech patterns. They might even be animals. When a person moves back-and-forth between these personalities, it is called *switching*, and the process can take place over seconds or over days. As is to be expected, people with DID often experience depression, mood swings, suicidal tendencies, sleep disorders, anxiety, panic attacks, compulsions, ritualized behavior, phobias, hallucinations, and eating, alcohol, and drug problems. They also are inclined to headaches, amnesia, time loss, trances, and out-of-body experiences. They might become self-abusive, and exhibit other negative traits, such as stealing and reckless driving. They might even be aware of these actions and how they are wrong but be unable to stop themselves. There is often a feeling of depersonalization (a sense one is detached from one's own body), derealization (a sense the world is not real or is unclear or distant).

Today, *schizophrenia* is distinguished from DID by being defined as a severe mental illness involving chronic and recurrent psychosis, hearing and seeing hallucinations, thinking or believing things with no basis in reality (having delusions), but not experiencing multiple personalities.

Furthermore, while suicide is a risk with *schizophrenia*, it is not as common as with DID.

In the Hulk comics, the transformation of Bruce Brenner into his alter-ego results from strong emotions, and the Hulk acts as something of a physical embodiment of his id, driven by basic emotions and unable to make sophisticated ethical distinctions (thus neither good nor bad). Stan Lee, in originating the character, referenced *Frankenstein* and *Dr. Jekyll and Mr. Hyde*, explaining, "I had always loved the old movie *Frankenstein*. (86) And it seemed to me that the monster, played by Boris Karloff, wasn't really a bad guy. He was the good guy. He didn't want to hurt anybody. It's just those idiots with torches kept running up and down the mountains, chasing him and getting him angry. And I thought, 'Wouldn't it be fun to create a monster and make him the good guy?" (87)

The most famous real life instance of multiple personalities is that of Shirley Ardell Mason, and it might ironically raise the most questions about the legitimacy of the DID prognosis. It reached an international audience because of Flora Rheta Schreiber's novel, *Sybil*, a fictionalized version that sparked two movies, the first a well done television movie that garnered much praise, the second a well acted but seemingly pointless remake. (88)

The book begins with a list of Sybil's personalities (her *alters*), and the year each began (changing the name for each): Sybil Isabel Dorsett (1923), the main personality; Victoria Antoinette Scharleau (1926), nicknamed Vicky, self-assured and sophisticated; Peggy Lou Baldwin (1926), assertive, enthusiastic, and often angry; Peggy Ann Baldwin (1926), a counterpart of Peggy Lou but more fearful than angry; Mary Lucinda Saunders Dorsett (1933), a thoughtful, contemplative, and maternal homebody; Marcia Lynn Dorsett (1927), an extremely emotional writer and painter; Vanessa Gail Dorsett (1935), intensely dramatic; Mike Dorsett (1928), one of Sybil's two male selves, a builder and a carpenter; Sid Dorsett (1928), the second of Sybil's two male selves, a carpenter and a general handyman; Nancy Lou Ann Baldwin (date undetermined), interested in politics as fulfillment of biblical prophecy and intensely afraid of Roman Catholics; Sybil Ann Dorsett (1928), listless to the point of neurasthenia; Ruthie Dorsett (date undetermined), a baby and one of the less developed selves; Clara Dorsett (date undetermined), intensely religious and highly critical of Sybil; Helen Dorsett (1929), intensely afraid but determined to achieve fulfillment; Marjorie Dorsett (1928), serene, vivacious, and quick to laugh; The Blonde (1946), a nameless perpetual teenager with an optimistic outlook; and finally the new Sybil (1965), a fully integrated "cured" person.

In the *"Preface,"* Flora Rheta Schreiber claims to have meet and become friends with Sybil, to have worked with her and Dr. Wilbur for a period of ten years putting the book together, and to have gotten affirmation from Sybil and Dr. Wilbur that Sybil's characters and the psychiatric facts are all accurately represented in the book.

Then, consistent with a well written work of fiction, the book begins in the middle of a dramatic mental breakdown. Sybil is psychologically lost in both space and time, fragmented. But we try to follow the scattered narrative, soon finding her realizing she needs to see a psychiatrist, and having Dr. Cornelia Wilbur recommended by her family doctor. It is 1954. Sybil is a college student who has suffered dramatic physical and psychological abuse as a child. She complains of spells, loses time, fades in and out of consciousness, sometimes for days, reemerging in unfamiliar cities, wearing clothes she cannot remember owning. At first, Dr. Wilbur thinks she is suffering from a case of hysteria, but then, one day, Sybil walks into Dr. Wilbur's office with a new personality, and in a confident voice declares, "Sybil couldn't come, you can call me Vicky."

As the sessions continue, Dr. Wilbur realizes that Sybil has endured a "nightmarish" childhood. Her mother who was mentally ill and had a history of sexually abusing children, would insert objects into Sybil's body, force her to drink laxatives and suffer through enemas until she was seven, hang her from the ceiling, choke her, leave her in a corn crib to smother, beat her, and permanently scare her with a button hook. Her Fundamentalist father was passive and distant, and did nothing to protect her.

The prognosis, then, is that Sybil's various personalities were developed as a coping mechanism to endure her childhood trauma.

As the book continues, Sybil's *alters* gradually become co-conscious, communicative, and willing to share responsibilities, ultimately able to compose music and produce art. Wilbur attempts to help Sybil merge these personalities, partially through the use of hypnosis, at first convincing her that they are all the same age, then finally bring them all together under a new, optimistic self (The Blonde), who is, in the final passage, a single, psychologically healthy person.

In the book and subsequent films, the truth is bent for the fictional punch. For example, it is put forth in these versions that she became a recluse, but that simply was not true. Instead, she continued to exhibit her paintings, taught art, designed toys, and owned her own business, and was a devout member of her local Seventh Day Adventist church, well known and well liked (few people even knowing that she was the real Sybil).

Furthermore, the psychiatric community itself questions the process and conclusions of Shirley's psychiatrist, tending to believe that Shirley's multiple personalities were more the result of leading suggestions from the psychiatrist than from Shirley's own psychic manifestations. In other words, it might be true that Shirley suffered anxiety and some form of schizophrenia, but it is likely that she did not have multiple personalities.

Dr. Herbert Spiegel and Robert W. Reiber, upon listening to tapes of conversations between Flora Schreiber and Shirley's psychiatrist Cornelia B. Wilbur, concluded that Dr. Wilbur, who used hypnosis, suggested the personalities to Shirley, and that the book was more of a fictional fabrication than a representation of the reality. Furthermore, the American Psychological Association recommends that the case no longer be cited as a classic example of Multiple Personality Disorder. (89)

The most famous case of DID (at the time referred to as Multiple Personality Disorder) prior to Shirley Ardell Mason, is that of Chris Costner Sizemore, made famous by the 1957 film *The Three Faces of Eve* (for which Joanne Woodward won an Oscar). (90)

In the film, Eve White is a shy wife and mother who experiences terrible headaches and occasional blackouts, eventually leading her to see psychiatrist Dr. Luther, who puts her under hypnosis and reveals her "alter," Eve Black, a wild, fun-loving opposite. Eve Black knows all about Eve White, but Eve White knows nothing about Eve Black. When her husband is exposed to Eve Black, he abandons her and their daughter Bonnie. Eve Black attempts to kill Bonnie, and Eve White is placed in an asylum, where Dr. Luther continues to work with her. He considers both personalities to be incomplete and pushes her to remember some traumatic event in her childhood in the hope of finding a cure. It turns out that her beloved grandmother died when she was six, and following family custom, she was required to kiss the dead body at the viewing, a practice that so horrified her she split into two distinct personalities.

Eventually a third personality appears, the more stable Jane, and once she is able to remember the childhood experience, Jane begins to piece her life together, eventually eliminating Eve White and Eve Black altogether, becoming whole and psychologically healthy. She marries a man named Earl and reunites with her daughter Bonnie.

Chris Costner Sizemore, under the pseudonym Evelyn Lancaster, wrote about it in *The Final Face of Eve* (1958), then followed that up with *I'm Eve* (1977), revealing her true identity, and followed that up with *A Mind of My Own* (1989). (91) The real life case this is based on has more validity than *Sybil*, and the film was carefully crafted to match the actuality.

It is thought that the film was brought out at least partially because of Shirley Jackson's excellent fictionalized representation of DID in her novel, *The Bird's Nest.* (92) The title comes from a nursery rhyme:

> Elizabeth, Beth, Betsy and Bess.
> They all went together to find a bird's nest.
> They found a nest with five eggs in it.
> They each took out one, and left four in it.

If it hasn't already clicked for you, the point of this nursery rhyme, and thus, of the book, is that the four names are all simply different names for the same person.

The book begins in a matter-of-fact tone describing Elizabeth Richmond's matter-of-fact life, stressing the ordinariness of it and of her:

> Elizabeth Richmond was twenty-three years old. She had no friends, no parents, no associates, and no plans beyond that of enduring the necessary interval before her departure with as little pain as possible. Since the death of her mother four years before, Elizabeth had spoken intimately to no person, and the aunt with whom she lived required little of her beyond a portion of her weekly pay and her prompt presence at the dinner table. Although she had arrived daily at the museum for two years, since her employment the museum had been in no way different; the letters signed "per er" and the endless listings of exhibits vouched for by E. Richmond were the outstanding traces of her presence. There were half a dozen people who spent their time in the same office, and half a dozen others who occupied other offices on the third floor, and all of these knew Elizabeth, and said" Good morning" to her, and even "How are you today?"—this on particularly bright spring mornings—but those of them who, in philanthropy or mortal kindness, had endeavored to become more friendly with her had found her blank and unrecognizing. She was not even interesting enough to distinguish with a nickname; where the living, engrossed daily with the fragments and soiled trivia of the disagreeable past, or the vacancies of space, kept a precarious hold on individuality and identity, Elizabeth remained nameless; she was called Elizabeth or Miss Richmond because that was the name she had given when she came, and perhaps if she had fallen down the hold in the building she might have been missed because the museum tag reading Miss Elizabeth Richmond, anonymous gift, value undetermined, was left without a corresponding object. (pp. 6-7)

This very bland woman lives with her Aunt Morgen, "the type of woman freely described as 'masculine,' if she had been a man she would have cut a very poor figure indeed. If she had been a man she would have been middle-sized, weak-jawed, shifty-eyed, and clumsy; fortunately, having been born not a man, she had turned out a woman, and had of necessity adopted from adolescence (with what grief, perhaps, and frantic railings against the iniquities of fate, which made her sister lovely) the personality of the gruff, loud-voiced woman so invariably described as "masculine." Her manner was free, her voice loud, she loved eating and drinking and said she loved men; she took toward her sober niece an attitude of avuncular heartiness, and among her few friends she was regarded as fairly dashing because of her fondness for blunt truths and her comprehensive statements about baseball." (pp. 10-11)

The two women live together in a friendly, but not overly warm relationship, with a boring routine in place that doesn't require much from either of them. However, we quickly learn that Elizabeth is prone to headaches, and the first night we see them together, we sense something strange about Elizabeth. After her aunt has fixed her a water bottle for her sore back, fetched some blue pills to help her sleep, and left her in her bedroom, certainly thoughtful actions, Elizabeth surprises herself and us:

> Bad old woman, Elizabeth thought, and then was surprised at herself: Aunt Morgen had been very kind to her. "Bad old woman," and she realized that she had spoken it aloud. Suppose she hears me, Elizabeth thought, and giggled. "Bad old woman," she said, very loudly indeed. (p. 15)

Our bland woman has some kind of other personality! Not only that, but she has opened and taken home with her a curious letter she received at work: "dear lizzie," the letter read, "your fool's paradise is gone now for good watch out for me lizzie watch out for me and don't do anything bad because I am going to catch you and you will be sorry and don't think I wont know lizzie because I do—dirty thoughts lizzie dirty lizzie." (p. 6) Not only does this letter not fit in with her carefully controlled world, but for some reason she takes it home with her and saves it in a special box in her closet with another letter, one written by her mother before she died.

Things become even more disjointed, for the next morning Elizabeth is accosted by Aunt Morgen, upset that she has snuck out during the night. Elizabeth denies it, seems honestly to not believe it, yet the feel of their exchange is that Aunt Morgen is not making it up.

This scene is followed by a quick succession of more letters from dirty lizzie, and more accusations from Aunt Morgen about Elizabeth going out in the middle of the night, always denied by Elizabeth, but she continues to keep the letters in her secret red valentine box. Then, as we're absorbing this strange situation, Aunt Morgen bursts into the Elizabeth's room while she is sitting on her bed counting her letters. Aunt Morgen has been calling for Elizabeth, but gotten no answer and thinks something must be wrong. Elizabeth seems to be totally unaware of any problem. But there is an empty brandy bottle on the table, and Aunt Morgen says Elizabeth "stinks of the stuff." Elizabeth, however, remains calm, unaware of any impropriety, unaware of having drunk any liquor.

Then there is a visit from Mr. and Mrs. Arrow, where Elizabeth is obviously going-in-and-out of consciousness, of being aware of her actions and then being unaware of them; and it is clear that when she is unaware, she is doing things that are not appropriate. Her aunt takes her to see Dr. Ryan, the family doctor she has often seen as she was growing up. He doesn't think there is anything wrong with Elizabeth, but on a whim decides to recommend another doctor for her to visit, one he insists is not a psychoanalyst, an "odd duck" who might be able to figure out what's wrong.

The novel then begins the next chapter in the voice of this new doctor, this Dr. Wright, who begins by letting the reader know he is a simple, straight-forward, honest general practitioner. But he is going to tell us about this woman, who he calls Miss R. And now we follow his introduction to her and his decision to hypnotize her. She at first resists, but as her visits to him continue, she allows it, and slowly, he begins to see other personalities emerge under hypnosis, personalities that oppose the quiet, overly unassuming woman who first appeared at his office:

> I watched her in horror, the smile upon her soft lips coarsened, and became sensual and gross, her eyelids fluttered in an attempt to open, her hands twisted together violently, and she laughed, evilly and roughly, throwing her head back and shouting, and I, seeing a devil's mask where a moment before I had seen Miss R.'s soft face, thought only, it cannot be Miss R.; this is not she. (p. 55)

The visits soon reveal yet a third personality, and our simple, commonsense doctor, after considering the possibility of "demonic possession," turns refers us to a more informed medical expert to give us the official diagnosis:

> "Cases of this kind are commonly known as 'double' or 'multiple personality,' according to the number of persons represented, but a more correct term is *disintegrated* personality, for each secondary personality is a part only of a normal whole self. No one secondary personality preserves the whole physical life of the individual. The synthesis of the original consciousness known as the personal ego is broken up, so to speak, and shorn of some of its memories, perceptions, acquisitions, or modes of

> reaction to the environment. The conscious states that still persist, synthesized among themselves, form a new personality capable of independent activity. This second personality may *alternate* with the original undisintegrated personality from time to time. By a breaking up of the original personality at different moments along different lines of cleavage, there may be formed several different secondary personalities which may take turns with one another." (93)

Then the doctor's narrative takes us into a number of exchanges between him and the various personalities of Elizabeth, highlighting the nursery rhyme that serves as the center for the book, and suggesting that Elizabeth's relationship with her mother, and the affect of her mother's death, is somehow involved with her mental disassociation. The doctor begins to feel inadequate, and when Elizabeth gets physically sick, he turns his attentions away from her. But, then, one night her aunt contacts him, saying Elizabeth refuses to see anyone but him. He tries to decline, but feels forced to go to her house. And it is the Betsy personality now in control of Elizabeth. This section ends with the doctor trying to get Betsy to let Elizabeth back out.

The next chapter is titled "Betsy," and it is a wonderfully written description of Betsy having taken over, stolen about $100 from the aunt and boarded a train to New York, where she is completely lost, and realizes she is seeking her mother. She speaks openly to strangers, putting herself in dangerous situations, and wanders completely lost through New York in her search. The exchanges are a brilliant expression of this childlike delusional persona. I am going to provide one of them here as an example:

It is her first morning in New York. She has checked into a hotel room and realizes she is hungry, so she goes downstairs to the hotel dining room:

> She was not awed by the size or the whiteness of the dining room, after having seen the satin bedspreads upstairs, and all tables not Aunt Morgen's were equally strange to her. She sat down, thinking with humor that if she stepped on the waiter's foot, or dropped her pocketbook, or perhaps missed the chair altogether, sitting down, she could always slip off and leave Lizzie to cope. She unfolded her napkin and looked around, and sat back in the soft chair with satisfaction. Each thing, she thought pleasurably, is nicer than the last; everything gets better and better.
>
> With an enormous feeling of delighted wickedness she ordered an Aunt-Morgen-ish glass of sherry, and did not notice the waiter's hesitation over whether she was as old as she looked, and entitled to be served, or as

old as she acted, and must necessarily be refused; the waiter, however, was in the last analysis philosophical, and concluded that a woman was more likely to look her age than to act it, so that Betsy was served with sherry and she sipped it gracefully, quite as professionally as Aunt Morgen might. Because it was not possible, in this most charming of worlds, for anything to be either mistaken or out of sorts, when Betsy desired company she looked up at the first person passing her table and said "Hello."

"Hello," he said, surprised, and hesitating by the table.

"Sit down, please," Betsy said politely.

He opened his eyes wide, glanced beyond her at the empty which had been his objective, and then laughed. "All right," he said.

"I feel funny sitting here alone," Betsy explained. "No one to talk to, or anything. At home there was always Aunt Morgen there and even when she didn't talk I could have someone to look at. Someone I knew, that is," she said.

"Of course," he said, sitting down. "Have you been here long?" he asked, taking up his napkin.

"I just got here this morning, and the bus driver told me to be careful, so of course I am, but I thought you looked all right to talk to." He seemed a very civil man, not so old as Doctor Wrong [her name for Doctor Wright], but older than Robin, and not at all uncomfortable at talking like this to someone he had not met before. "You weren't outside my window a little while ago?" she asked him suddenly, "climbing across a ledge?"

He shook his head, surprised. "I'm not spry enough," he said.

"*I* could if I wanted to. Lizzie gets faint, but of course I never do."

"Who is Lizzie?"

"Lizzie Richmond. I brought her with me, and she wants to get out, but she can't." She stopped and looked at him suspiciously. "I wasn't going to tell anyone about Lizzie," she said.

"It doesn't matter," he said. "I won't tell.

"Anyway, my mother's going to get rid of Lizzie—we're not going to have *her* around all the time, after the trouble we've already had, getting rid of Robin and all."

"Are you having lunch?" He took the menu from the waiter, smiling at her, and Betsy said, "This is the first time I've ever been in a restaurant," and wiggled happily. "And I'm *extremely* hungry," she added.

"Then we had better make this a special lunch," he said. "Shall I choose for you?" He held the menu toward her, and said, "Or would you rather order something for yourself?"

Betsy took the menu and glanced at it briefly and then handed it back. "Lizzie speaks French," she said, "but of course *I* never bothered to take it up much, so you'd better choose. Only lots of things, please. Everything exciting." She hesitated. "Nothing," she said, "nothing like . . . macaroni, or pickles, or sandwiches, or things like that. Things Aunt Morgen makes."

"Well" he said profoundly. He regarded the menu in deep thought. "No pickles," he said, debating, "no sandwiches." Finally, with the waiter standing by, and both of them nodding reassuringly at Betsy, he ordered smoothly and quite as though he very frequently had occasion to order lunches for young ladies who wanted everything exciting, and no pickles. While she listened to the lovely words which meant foods so exciting she did not even know the order in which they would be served, and listened to the music coming distantly from some upper corner of the room and listened to the fine harmonious sound of forks touching knives, and cups touching saucers, Betsy told herself, this is what it is going to be like all the time, now.

"There," he said at last, handing the menu to the waiter. "I think you're going to like everything. Now, tell me—I don't even know your name."

"I'm Betsy. Betsy Richmond. My mother's name is Elizabeth Richmond, Elizabeth Jones before she was married. I was born in New York."

"How long ago?"

"I forget," she said vaguely. "Is that for me?" The waiter set a fruit cup before her, and she took the cherry from the top with her fingers and put it into her mouth. "My mother left me with Aunt Morgen," she went on indistinctly, "but she didn't go with Robin."

"The one you had such trouble getting rid of?"

Betsy nodded violently, swallowed, and said, "But I don't have to remember that part, I decided in the bus. One bad thing about Robin ought to be enough, don't you think?"

"I should think so," he said. "Seeing as you got rid of him, anyway."

She giggled, lifting her spoon. "*And* I got rid of Aunt Morgen, *and* I got rid of Doctor Wrong, *and* I'm going to get rid of Lizzie, and I'm the gingerbread boy, I am."

"I wonder if Aunt Morgen will be worried about you," he said carefully.

She shook her head again. "I wrote her a postcard with a picture on it and I said I wasn't coming back, and anyway they'll be looking for Lizzie, not me. Can I have some more fruit?"

"He'll be bringing you something else in a minute."

"I can pay for it—I have plenty of money." When she saw that he was smiling she thought, and then said acutely, "That was wrong, wasn't it? That was wrong to say—why?"

"I invited you to lunch, sort of," he said. "That means that I am going to pay, so you mustn't say anything about paying. You must wait, and then be very gracious about my paying."

"Gracious," she said. "You mean 'Thank you *so* much'? Like Aunt Morgen?"

"Exactly like Aunt Morgen,"he said. "Where is your mother now?"

"I don't know just where she is. I'm still finding out. Like the man down on the ledge. [She previously watched a man walking on a ledge from her motel room.] They're going to have to tell me because I'll just keep asking and looking and looking and asking and asking and looking and looking and—" She stopped abruptly, and there was a silence. When she looked up, he was placidly finishing his fruit. "Sometimes," she said with great caution, "I get mixed up. You'll just have to excuse it."

"Of course," he said without surprise.

"So you see," Betsy said, looking with deep satisfaction into a bowl of clear soup in which, far down, small strange shapes moved, and stirred, and stared, and strode.

"Who are you?" asked Elizabeth, blankly.

"How do you do?" he said. "I'm a friend of yours."

Betsy looked up, gasping, and moved far back in her chair, and scowled at him. "Don't you listen to her," she said. "She tells lies."

"All right," he said, and moved his spoon in his soup.

"I don't want any soup," Betsy said sullenly.

"All right," he said. "It's good, though, I always like soup."

"Aunt Morgen likes soup," Betsy said. "All the time."

"And pickles?"

Betsy giggled, in spite of her annoyance. "Old Aunt Pickle," she said.

"Old Doctor Pickle," he said.

"Old Lizzie Pickle."

"Elizabeth Jones that was?"

"What?" said Betsy.

"Elizabeth Pickle before she was married," he said.

"You stop that right now," Betsy said furiously. "You just stop talking like that. I'll tell my mother."

"I'm sorry," he said. "It was a joke."

"My mother doesn't like jokes. Not mean jokes, and when Robin made mean jokes my mother told him to stop and when you make mean jokes you sound like Robin."

"And you'll get rid of me?"

She laughed. "That was smart, how I got rid of Robin," she said, and then, breathlessly, "Oh!" turning to look at a tray of pastries being wheeled past her chair. "Can I have one?"

"First eat your lunch. Your nice soup."

"I want cake," said Betsy.

"Your mother wouldn't want you to have dessert first."

Betsy was quiet suddenly. "How do you know?" she said. "How do you know what my mother would want?"

"She *certainly* wouldn't want you to be sick. That would be silly."

"That's right," Betsy said joyfully, "Mother's Betsy can't be sick, Betsy is Mother's baby and she mustn't cry, and Aunt Morgen said stop spoiling the child."

I think," he said slowly, "that we don't like Aunt Morgen, do we, you and I? I don't think Aunt Morgen is so much."

"Aunt Morgen says to make the child stop fawning on Robin all the time. Aunt Morgen says the child is too old to scramble around with Robin like that. Aunt Morgen says the child knows more than is good for her."

"Old Aunt Pickle," he said.

"I want cake," Betsy said, and he laughed, and gestured to the waiter with the dessert wagon. "Only one," he said, "and then you eat the rest of your lunch I ordered for you. We're not going to have you sick, remember."

"Not *me*," said Betsy, bending lovingly over the tiny rich cakes, her eyes sparkling with the reflections of whipped cream and chocolate and strawberries; "it's Lizzie who gets sick," she said; one had bananas and one had chopped nuts and one had cherries; Betsy sighed.

"And you say they'll be looking for Lizzie?"

"Maybe the little square one," Betsy said. "Just to start. I choose the little square one," she said to the waiter. "Because then later I can try another kind and if any of them are very very good I can come back and have them again, after I've tried them all. Because I live right upstairs," she said parenthetically to the waiter, "so I can keep coming back and coming back. So I choose—"

She broke off as the headwaiter came to their table. "Telephone for you, Doctor," he said.

"Doctor?" said Betsy, rising. "Doctor?" She snatched at her pocketbook, and said in anger, "You're just Doctor Wrong in another face and you tried to fool me—"

"Wait a minute, please," he said, putting out a hand to stop her, but she brushed past him, her lips trembling and her hands shaking with anger. "It was mean of you," she said, "and I'll tell my mother you pretended to be friends, and now I can't have the little square one." She started off, and then remembered. "Thank you *so* much for paying," she said, bowing her head graciously, and then, almost running, left the restaurant and went through the hotel lobby into the street. (pp. 109-114)

First, Robin appears to be the name of her mother's lover, with suggestions that he was not the best of men and might have even had some kind of sexual relations with Elizabeth. It's possible that this name was chosen because Robin is a common name for the Devil. The name also fits the eggs in the nest analogy that umbrellas the entire novel.

Second, her childlike personality fits people with this unusual mental makeup. Today, such people might not be classified as DID, but though they might well have extremely high intellectual abilities, they have gaps in their thinking; they are disjointed, lost, fragmented. I have known such a person well, and can vouch for the accuracy of this depiction. Her mind is complex, and fascinating, although she is a tortured soul. She is a brilliant actress, a beautiful writer and person. I use her as an example because my experience knowing this person has allowed me to realize that one can have profound idiosyncrasies and complexes of the mind and still function, albeit often with extreme difficulty, in the real world, and create masterful art, perhaps because of these complexes of mind. The hope always is that through maturation or a life catharsis, there is a synthesis or coming together of "self."

Third, remember, Elizabeth is actually twenty-three-years-old. This makes it hard to buy into her extremely child-like appearance and actions, and the fact that the people she encounters constantly see her as a child. However, again, I have known a person much other than her, capable of becoming similarly childlike, and with a bit of hesitation I can believe she looks young enough for it to all work, especially since those she encounters seem to be amused by her childlike qualities. In any case, this literal journey to New York is also, and more importantly, a representation of a psychological journey, a journey that involves a disconnect with reality, a journey into a mind that is fragmented, a mind struggling to piece itself together. Each of her encounters is similar to the one above in that she is childlike, overly open, telling these strangers all about herself, innocently putting herself in situations where she can be abducted, raped, robbed, even murdered—she is extremely vulnerable, and we fear for her safety throughout, while at the same time we are intrigued by her, are struggling to piece her together ourselves. And we are aware that the literal, physical danger is matched by the psychological danger, the danger of being forever fragmented, perhaps even of committing suicide. And this is especially reinforced when her various personalities get violent with each other, attempting to strangle her, and she "wakes up" in a doctor's office, with Aunt Morgen and Doctor Wright notified of her whereabouts (she was discovered in the motel hallway "beaten, scratched, and half-strangled" with a memo in her pocketbook containing their phone numbers). The dialogue here is vague and scattered, but we are informed that the wounds on her neck were "self-inflicted." And Dr. Wright (referred to as a *little* man) says he knows who caused her wounds.

The next chapter returns to Dr. Wright's narration. He is annoyed with her as Betsy and with the entire affair, and suggests that readers must also be getting bored with it, but, of course, he will continue "quickly" to his conclusion. Of course, he doesn't. Instead we get to join him as he interacts with the four personalities:

> Elizabeth the numb, the stupid, the inarticulate, but somehow enduring, since she had remained behind to carry on when the rest of them went under; Beth, the sweet and susceptible; Betsy, the wanton and wild, and Bess, the arrogant and cheap. (p. 153)

The sessions continue, the four personalities emerging and disappearing, some aware of some of the others, each working against the others for dominance. Dr. Wright does his best to get them to realize each other and to merge into one mentally sound individual. It becomes an intriguing, ever-changing puzzle to try and follow and sort out.

As this chapter continues, Aunt Morgen becomes more and more this somewhat frightening outside personage each of the persons inside Elizabeth and Dr. Wright himself are a bit afraid to confront. But finally the doctor decides he needs to talk with her, explain Elizabeth's condition, and get her to help him resolve the mental breakdown. He schedules a visit to her house, and the result is a comic scene where the two of them get drunk on her brandy, and she ends up blathering about how bad Elizabeth's mother was and how she had to do her best to try and take care of both the mother and daughter. Mixed into this ever less sane ranting is a confusing narrative about how Elizabeth's mother died. Aunt Morgen's drunken revelations finally push the doctor to leave in disgust, vowing to be done with both Elizabeth and her aunt.

Then the narrative continues with Aunt Morgen confronting Elizabeth, Beth, Betsy, and Bess over the next few days, including an amusing scene where each of them in turn takes a bath unaware that the others have also done so, and finally Aunt Morgen calls Dr. Wright and threatens him into coming to the house. Everything becomes more and more hectic, until finally it all comes to a head with Aunt Morgen and Dr. Wright physically restraining Elizabeth until all of her personalities merge.

The final chapter has a happy quality about it, and it's clear Elizabeth has gotten rid of her alter egos. She is happy, and feels good that she is "all alone." When she visits Dr. Wright, he points out that she still has a long way to go to be fully healed, but it is obvious she has now overcome her split personalities, and the emphasis is that she has no name, as is highlighted in a somewhat maudlin ending that suggests Dr.Wright and Aunt Morgen are amazingly going to become a couple:

> "This child is without a name," the doctor said across her to Morgen. "Did you know?"
>
> Morgen thought, and then laughed. "I guess she is," she said, "but I hadn't noticed." She laughed again, and pressed her niece's arm. "If you're taking on a new name, how about Morgen this time?"
>
> "Victoria?" suggested the doctor.
>
> "Morgen Victoria," Morgen amended generously.
>
> "Victoria Morgen," said the doctor.
>
> She laughed, too, holding both their arms. "I'm happy," she said, just as she had that afternoon. "I know who I am," she said, and walked on with them, arm in arm, and laughing. (pp. 275-276)

The emphasis throughout the final chapter that Elizabeth, or whatever her name is to become, has *no name*, that there is a lack of identity once the personalities within her leave suggests the much larger contexts of philosophy since Rene Descartes' famous enquiry into how we know we exist, which is considered the beginning of modern philosophy . He is perhaps best known for the philosophical statement "*Cogito ergo sum*" (French: *Je pense, donc je suis*; English: *I think, therefore I am;* or *I am thinking, therefore I exist* or *I do think, therefore I do exist*), found in Part IV of *Discourse on the Method* (1637 – written in French but with inclusion of "Cogito ergo sum") and Part I of *Principles of Philosophy* (1644 – written in Latin).

Creative people and celebrities have often taken on a form of *alter ego*, a public or professional persona, a role other than their real life role. Examples are endless. One easy indication of this is to change one's name, something that has been standard in the Hollywood movie world from the beginning of the nineteenth century:

Edie Adams - Elizabeth Edith Enke, Maud Adams - Maud Wickstrom, Nick Adams - Nicholas Adamshock, Ben Affleck - Benjamin Geza Affleck, Eddie Albert - Edward Albert Heimberger, Alan Alda - Alphonso D'Abruzzo, Jane Alexander - Jane Quigley, Fred Allen - John Sullivan, Woody Allen - Allen Konigsberg, June Allyson - Ella Geisman, Don Ameche - Dominic Felix Amici, Julie Andrews - Julia Wells, Jennifer Aniston - Jennifer Anastassakis, Laura Antonelli - Laura Antonaz, Eve Arden - Eunice Quedens, Beatrice Arthur - Bernice Frankel, Jean Arthur - Gladys Greene, Fred Astaire - Frederick Austerlitz, Christopher Atkins - Christopher Bauman, Frankie Avalon - Francis Thomas Avalonne.

Lauren Bacall - Betty Joan Perske, Kevin Bacon - Kevin Norwood Bacon, Christian Bale - Christian Charles Philip Bale, Kaye Ballard - Catherine Balotta, Eric Bana - Eric Banadinovic, Anne Bancroft - Anna-Maria Louisa Italiano, Antonio Banderas - José Antonio Dominguez Bandera, Brigitte Bardot - Camille Javal , Rona Barrett - Rona Burstein, Gene Barry - Eugene Klass, John Barrymore - John Blythe, Kathy Bates - Kathleen Doyle Bates, Orson Bean - Dallas Burrows, Tony Bennett - Anthony Dominick Benedetto, Jack Benny - Benjamin Kubelsky, Tom Berenger - Thomas Michael Moore, Halle Berry -Halle Maria Berry, Milton Berle - Milton Berlinger, Joey Bishop - Joseph Gottlieb, Jack Black - Thomas Black, Jr., Amanda Blake- Beverly Louise Neill, Robert Blake - Michael Gubitosi, Cate Blanchett - Catherine Elise Blanchett, Orlando Bloom - Orlando Jonathan Blanchard Bloom, Victor Borge - Borge Rosenbaum , Ernest Borgnine - Ermes Effron Borgnino, David Bowie - David Robert Jones, Marlon Brando - Marlon Junior Brandeau,

Fanny Brice - Fanny Borach , Jeff Bridges - Jeffrey Leon Bridges, Charles Bronson - Charles Buchinski, Mel Brooks - Mel Kaminsky, Yul Brynner - Yul Taidje Kahn, Jr., Sandra Bullock - Sandra Annette Bullock, George Burns - Nathan Birnbaum, Ellen Burstyn - Edna Gilhooley, Richard Burton - Richard Walter Jenkins, Steve Buscemi - Steven Vincent Buscemi, Red Buttons - Aaron Chwatt.

James Caan - James Langston Edmund Caan, Nicolas Cage - Nicolas Kim Coppola, Michael Caine - Maurice Micklewhite, Rory Calhoun - Francis Timony Durgin, Jim Carrey - James Eugene Carrey, Cyd Charisse - Tula Ellice Finklea, Charo - María del Rosario Pilar Martínez Molina Baeza, Cher - Cherilyn Sarkisian, George Clooney - George Timothy Clooney, Lee J. Cobb - Leo Jacoby, Claudette Colbert - Lily Chauchoin, Mike Connors - Krekor "Kirk" Ohanian, Robert Conrad - Conrad Robert Falk, Lou Costello - Louis Francis Cristillo, Kevin Costner - Kevin Michael Costner, Daniel Craig - Daniel Wroughton Craig, Joan Crawford - Lucille Le Sueur, Michael Crawford - Michael Dumble-Smith, Bing Crosby - Harry Lillis Crosby, Tom Cruise - Thomas Mapother IV, Tony Curtis - Bernard Schwartz.

Matt Damon - Matthew Paige Damon, Rodney Dangerfield - Jacob Cohen, Bobby Darin - Walden Robert Cassotto, Geena Davis - Virginia Elizabeth Davis, Doris Day - Doris von Kappelhoff, Daniel Day-Lewis - Daniel Michael Blake Day-Lewis, Jimmy Dean - Seth Ward, Yvonne De Carlo - Peggy Middleton, Sandra Dee - Alexandra Zuck, John Denver - Henry John Deutschendorf Jr., Johnny Depp - John Christopher Depp II, John Derek - Derek Harris, Danny DeVito - Daniel Michaeli, Cameron Diaz - Cameron Michelle Diaz, Leonardo DiCaprio - Leonardo Wilhelm DiCaprio, Angie Dickinson - Angeline Brown, Matt Dillon - Matthew Raymond Dillon,Troy Donahue -Merle Johnson, Jr., Diana Dors - Diana Fluck, Kirk Douglas - Issur Danielovitch, Mike Douglas - Michael Delaney Dowd, Jr., Kirsten Dunst - Kirsten Caroline Dunst.

Clint Eastwood - Clinton Eastwood, Jr., Barbara Eden - Barbara Huffman, Vince Edwards - Vicent Edward Zoino, Ron Ely - Ronald Pierce, Dale Evans - Frances Octavia Smith, Chad Everett - Raymond Cramton.

Douglas Fairbanks - Douglas Ullman, Colin Farrell - Colin James Farrel, Will Ferrell - John William Ferrell, Stepin Fetchit - Lincoln Perry, Sally Field - Sally Mahoney, W.C. Fields - William Claude Dukenfield, Peter Finch - William Mitchell, Rhonda Fleming - Marilyn Louis, Joan Fontaine - Joan de Havilland, Glenn Ford - Gwyllyn Samuel Newton Ford, John Ford - Sean O'Fearna, John Forsythe - John Freund, Jodie Foster -

Alicia Christian Foster, Jamie Foxx - Eric Marlon Bishop,Tony Franciosa - Anthony Papaleo, Connie Francis - Concetta Franconero.

Greta Garbo - Greta Gustafsson, John Garfield - Julius Garfinkle, Judy Garland - Frances Gumm, James Garner - James Scott Bumgarner, Paul Giamatti - Paul Edward Valentine Giamatti, Mel Gibson - Mel Columcille Gerard Gibson, Whoopie Goldberg - Caryn Johnson, Bobcat Goldthwait - Robert Francis 'Bobcat' Goldthwait, John Goodman - John Stephen Goodman Eydie Gorme - Edith Gormezano, Cary Grant - Archibald Leach, Hugh Grant- Hugh John Mungo Grant, Peter Graves - Peter Aurness, Rocky Graziano - Rocco Barbella, Joel Grey - Joe Katz, Jake Gyllenhaal - Jacob Benjamin Gyllenhaal.

Buddy Hackett - Leonard Hacker, Gene Hackman - Eugene Allen Hackman, Tom Hanks - Thomas Jeffrey Hanks

Jean Harlow - Harlean Carpentier, Woody Harrelson - Woodrow Tracy Harrelson, Naomie Harris - Naomie Melanie Harris, Rex Harrison - Reginald Carey, Josh Hartnett - Joshua Daniel Hartnett, Ethan Hawke - Ethan Green Hawke, Helen Hayes - Helen Brown, Rita Hayworth - Margarita Cansino, Charlton Heston - Charles Carter, Steven Hill - Solomon Krakovsky, Hulk Hogan - Terry Jene Bollea, William Holden - William Franklin Beedle, Jr., Billy Holiday - Eleanora Fagan, Judy Holliday - Judith Tuvim, Bob Hope - Leslie Townes Hope, Robert Horton - Meade Howard Horton, Jr., Leslie Howard - Leslie Stainer, Harry Houdini - Ehrich Weiss, Rock Hudson - Roy Scherer Jr., Helen Hunt - Helen Elizabeth Hunt, Tab Hunter - Arthur Andrew Gelien.

Burl Ives - Burle Icle Ivanhoe.

David Janssen - David Meyer, Don Johnson - Donald Wayne, Al Jolson - Asa Yoelson, Jennifer Jones - Phyllis Isley, Louis Jourdan - Louis Gendre.

Danny Kaye - David Kaminsky, Boris Karloff - William Henry Pratt, Diane Keaton - Diane Hall, Howard Keel - Harold Leek, Nicole Kidman - Nicole Mary Kidman, Larry King - Larry Zeigler, Keira Knightley - Keira Christina Knightley, Ted Knight - Tadeus Wladyslaw Konopka, Ben Kingsley - Krishna Banji.

Cheryl Ladd - Cheryl Stoppelmoor, Frankie Laine - Frankie LoVecchio, Veronica Lake - Constance Ockleman - Dorothy Lamour - Mary Kaumeyer, Mario Lanza - Alfredo Cocozza, Michael Landon - Eugene Orowitz, Larry the Cable Guy - Daniel Lawrence Whitney, Stan Laurel - Arthur Jefferson, Jude Law - David Jude Heyworth Law Steve Lawrence - Sidney Leibowitz, Heath Ledger - Heathcliff Andrew Ledger, Gypsy Rose Lee - Rose Louise Hovick, Janet Leigh - Jeanette Morrison, Jerry Lewis - Joseph Levitch, Hal Linden - Harold Lipshitz,

Little Richard - Richard Penniman, Carole Lombard - Jane Peters, Jack Lord- John Joseph Ryan, Sophia Loren - Sophia Scicoloni, Peter Lorre - Laszio Lowenstein, Bela Lugosi - Bela Ferenc Blasko.

Moms Mabley - Loretta Mary Aitken, Shirley MacLaine - Shirley Beatty, Elle MacPherson - Eleanor Gow, Tobey Maguire - Tobias Vincent Maguire, Lee Majors - Harvey Lee Yeary II, Karl Malden - Mladen Sekulovich, Jayne Mansfield - Vera Jane Palmer, Fredric March - Frederick Bickel, Rocky Marciano - Rocco Francis Marchegiano, Dean Martin - Dino Crocetti, Chico Marx - Leonard Marx, Groucho Marx - Julius Marx, Gummo Marx - Milton Marx, Harpo Marx - Adolph Marx, Zeppo Marx - Herbert Marx, Walter Matthau - Walter Matuschanskayasky, Ewan McGregor - Ewan Gordon McGregor, Audrey Meadows - Audrey Cotter, Jayne Meadows - Jayne Cotter, Ethel Merman - Ethel Zimmerman, Ray Milland - Reginald Truscott-Jones, Ann Miller - Lucille Collier, Guy Mitchell- Albert George Cernick, Marilyn Monroe - Norma Jean Baker, Yves Montand - Ivo Levi, Demi Moore- Demetria Gene Guynes, Garry Moore- Thomas Garrison Morfit, Julianne Moore- Julie Anne Smith, Rita Moreno - Rosita Alverio, Harry Morgan - Harry Bratsburg, Bill Murray - William James Murray.

Sam Neill - Nigel John Dermot Neill, Chuck Norris - Carlos Ray, Kim Novak - Marilyn Pauline Novak.

Hugh O'Brian - Hugh Krampke, Maureen O'Hara - Maureen Fitzsimons, Gary Oldman - Leonard Gary Oldman.

Al Pacino - Alfredo James Pacino, Patti Page - Clara Ann Fowler, Jack Palance - Walter Palanuik, Gwyneth Paltrow - Gwyneth Kate Paltrow, Bert Parks - Bert Jacobson, Guy Pearce - Guy Edward Pearce, Minnie Pearl - Sarah Ophella Colley Cannon, Gregory Peck - Eldred Gregory Peck, Bernadette Peters - Bernadette Lazzaro, Lou Diamond Phillips - Lou Upchurch, Joaquin Phoenix - Joaquin Rafael Phoenix, Edith Piaf - Edith Gassion, Slim Pickens - Louis Lindley, Mary Pickford - Gladys Smith, Brad Pitt - William Bradley Pitt, Natalie Portman - Natalie Hershlag, Stephanie Powers - Stefania Federkiewicz.

Anthony Quinn - Antonio Rudolfo Oaxaca Quinn.

Tony Randall - Leonard Rosenberg, Ahmad Rashad - Bobby Moore, Johnnie Ray - John Alvin, Martha Raye - Margaret Theresa Yvonne Reed, Donna Reed - Donna Belle Mullenger, Della Reese - Delloreese Patricia Early Keanu Reeves - Keanu Charles Reeves, Paul Reubens (Pee-Wee Herman) - Paul Reubenfeld, Burt Reynolds - Burton Leon Reynolds, Jr., Debbie Reynolds - Mary Frances Reynolds, Joan Rivers - Joan Sandra Molinsky, Harold Robbins - Frances Kane, Tim Robbins - Timothy Francis Robbins, Julia Roberts - Julia Fiona Roberts, Edward G. Robinson

- Emmanuel Goldenberg, Ginger Rogers - Virginia McMath, Roy Rogers-Leonard Slye, Mickey Rooney - Joe Yule Jr., Meg Ryan - Margaret Mary Emily Anne Hyra, Winona Ryder - Winona Horowitz.

Telly Savalas - Aristotelis Harris Savalas, Peter Sellers - Richard Henry Sellers, Jane Seymour - Joyce Frankenberg, Omar Sharif - Michael Shalhoub, Charlie Sheen - Carlos Irwin Estevez, Christian Slater - Christian Michael Leonard Hawkins, Buffalo Bob Smith - Robert Emil Schmidt, Ann Sothern - Harriet Lake, Sissy Spacek -Mary Elizabeth Spacek, Kevin Spacey - Kevin John Fowler, Robert Stack - Robert Modini, Sylvester Stallone - Sylvester Gardenzio, Jean Stapleton - Jeanne Murray, Barbara Stanwyck - Ruby Stevens, Connie Stevens - Concetta Ingolia, James Stewart - James Maitland Stewart, Sharon Stone - Sharon Vonne Stone, Gale Storm - Josephine Cottle, Meryl Streep - Mary Louise Streep, Hilary Swank - Hilary Ann Swank.

Robert Taylor - Spangler Arlington Brugh, Danny Thomas - Muzyad Yakhoob, Billy Bob Thornton - William Robert Thornton, Uma Thurman - Uma Karuna Thurman, Tina Turner - Annie Mae Bullock, Twiggy - Leslie Hornby.

Peter Ustinov - Peter Alexander von Ustinow.

Roger Vadim - Roger Vladimir Plemiannikov, Rudolph Valentino - Rudolpho D'Antonguolla, Abigail Van Buren - Pauline Ester Friedman, Jean-Claude Van Damme - Jean-Claude Camille François Van Varenberg.

Christopher Walken - Ronald Walken, Andy Warhol - Andrew Warhola, Denzel Washington - Denzel Jermaine Washington, Jr., David Wayne,- Wayne McMeekan, John Wayne - Marion Michael Morrison, Sigourney Weaver - Susan Alexandra Weaver, Clifton Webb - Webb Parmalee Hollenbeck, Johnny Weissmuller - Peter Jànos Weissmuller, Raquel Welch - Raquel Tejada, Tuesday Weld - Susan Kerr Wells, Nathaniel West - Nathaniel Wallenstein Weinstein, Gene Wilder - Jerome Silberman, Bruce Willis - Walter Willison, Kate Winslet - Katherine Elizabeth Winslet, Shelley Winters - Shirley Schrift, Reese Witherspoon - Laura Jeanne Reese Witherspoon, Elijah Wood - Elijah Jordan Wood, Natalie Wood - Natalia Nikolaevna Zakharenko, Jane Wyman - Sarah Jane Fulks.

Gig Young - Byron Barr.

Renée Zellweger - Renée Kathleen Zellweger, Catherine Zeta-Jones - Catherine Jones.

Some reasons for the name changes are obvious, and the main one is that these people wanting to put forth a popular, attractive persona are employing standard marketing techniques. Since Hollywood is an American institution aimed mainly at an American audience (certainly the case for the first half of the century), the names need to work well in the language of the targeted group--Americans, who speak English, and not just English but an American form of English. So names that come from other cultures, from other languages, have a foreign quality, which generally (though not always) will make the persona less attractive simply because it is different. Also, since these names come from other languages, they are often difficult to pronounce, not a good thing when one wants to be memorable.

The main group here is the Jews. Would *all American persona* Kirk Douglas lose some of that image if he were known as Issur Danielovitch? Would *all American* Steve Lawrence *be* an all American singer if his name were Sidney Leibowitz? Is Winona Ryder the same persona as Winona Horowitz? How about thinking of Danny Thomas as Muzyad Yakhoob? Other ethnic groups with their own languages and names have the same situation. Try thinking of John Denver as Henry John Deutschendorf Jr. or Raquel Welch as Raquel Tejada or Jean-Claude Van Damme - Jean-Claude Camille François Van Varenberg.

Some name changes want to give the macho male a name to match. Would John Wayne be as powerful a male if he were Marion Michael Morrison? Would Michael Caine be as much of a ladies' man if he were Maurice Micklewhite? Is Rock Hudson as much of a heart-throb if he is Roy Scherer Jr.? How about Jack Palance as Walter Palanuik? Is ultra sophisticated Cary Grant as much so if he is Archibald Leach?

It works in a similar way for females. Is Connie Stevens as much of a typical American teen-ager if her name is Concetta Ingolia? How about Natalie Wood as Natalia Nikolaevna Zakharenko or Barbara Eden as Barbara Huffman or Marilyn Monroe as Norma Jean Baker? What happens to the persona of Edie Adams as Elizabeth Edith or Jean Harlow as Harlean Carpentier?

These name changes are only a part of creation of an alter ego. Everything about these alter egos gets glamorized. A whole new personality is created, filled with glamour and sophistication and wealth. Peasants are turned into royalty.

It gets even more complicated, because the real people are playing at being movie and television stars, who, in turn, are playing roles on television and in movies. And it gets hard to go against the image, to go against the persona on the big screen, hard to avoid being type-cast, not only in the roles one gets, but in life.

Jack Carlton Moore is an example of how the various alter egos get intertwined. He was born in Chicago, Illinois, and began entertaining as an eight-year-old circus acrobat, appearing in the Century of Progress

Exposition in Chicago in 1934 as part of a trapeze act. As a young man, he worked as a model for John Robert Powers. In the later thirties, he began supplementing his modeling as a stunt man and bit player in Hollywood. In 1940, Hollywood producer Edward Small persuaded him to simplify his name to Clayton Moore, and he appeared in some B westerns and Republic Studio cliffhangers. Then he served in the U.S. Army Air Forces during WWII, where he made training films with the First Motion Picture Unit. (94)

George Trendle, who was the creator/producer of *The Lone Ranger* radio show saw Clayton Moore in the *Ghost of Zorro* serial, and cast him in the role of The Lone Ranger for the television version of the show, the first Western written specifically for television, and ABC's first hit series, earning an Emmy nomination in 1950. Moore starred in 169 episodes. However, after two years, Moore left the show over a pay dispute. He continued to act in various Westerns and Serials, and eventually reunited with ABC and continued until 1957. In addition to the television show, he starred in two feature-length Lone Ranger movies, and later did some acting in such other series as *Snake River Trapper* and *The Adventures of Kit Carson.*

After completing the second Lone Ranger movie, *The Lone Ranger and the Lost City of Gold*, 1958, Moore began a series of some forty personal appearances, various TV guest spots, and some classic commercials as the Lone Ranger. Then, in 1979, Jack Wrather (who owned the rights to the Lone Ranger character), obtained a court order prohibiting Moore from making any future appearances as the Lone Ranger. Wrather planned a new movie of the Lone Ranger and didn't want a 65-year-old man representing his new version. However, Moore had become so associated with the role that this proved to be a public relations disaster. Moore got around the restrictions by changing his costume slightly (wearing wraparound sunglasses instead of a mask) and counter-suing Wrather. Moore eventually won his suit and was able to resume his appearances as the Lone Ranger, which he did until just before his death in 1999, claiming he fell in love with the Lone Ranger character and wanted to make his personal life match the values expressed by the Lone Ranger Creed. He became so intertwined with the character that he is the only person on the Hollywood Walk of Fame to have his character's name included along with his own on his star.

William Lawrence Boyd was born in Hendrysburg, just east of Cambridge, Ohio, to day laborer Charles William Boyd and Lida Wilkens. After his father's death, he moved to California and took odd jobs as an orange picker, a surveyor, a tool dresser, an auto salesman, and an extra in such films as *Why Change Your Wife?* He enlisted in the army during WWI, but was exempted because of a weak heart. Thus, he was available to continue his acting, and he became a leading man in silent films, eventually staring in Cecil B. DeMille's *The Volga Boatman* in 1926, and appearing in such other Radio Pictures films as *The King of Kings*, *Skyscraper,* and *Lady of the Pavements*. However, his successful contract with Radio Pictures ended in 1931 when his picture was mistakenly used in a newspaper story about the arrest of another actor, William "Stage" Boyd, on gambling and liquor charges. As a result, he was broke and without work. (95)

Then came his alter-ego. In 1935, he was offered the supporting role of Red Connors in *Hop-Along Cassidy*, a movie based on the rough, hard-drinking, swearing, smoking wrangler Hopalong Cassidy character created by Clarence E. Mulford for a series of pulp fictions books. Instead of taking the supporting role, Boyd went for the lead, and got it.

It was to become his new role in life. Though he never branded a cow or mended a fence, could not bulldog a steer, and even disliked Western music, he now took on the persona of what was to become one of the most famous cowboys of all time, the rival of the likes of Roy Rogers and Gene Autry. Over the next twelve years, he made 66 films as this character, producing the final twelve himself. And, helping to created the whole genre of Hollywood Cowboys, in an interesting example of the entertainment industry establishing an entire *false* (or especially for a study such as the one in this book, an *alternate*) reality, a version of history that has only slight references to the real history.

Realizing the potential of television, Boyd purchased the rights to the Hopalong Cassidy character, books, and films for $350,000, and in 1949 released the films to television, where they were very successful. He also saw the potential in merchandising Hopalong Cassidy watches, trash cans, cups, dishes, Topps trading cards, a comic strip, comic books, radio shows and cowboy outfits. America loves success stories, and in 1950, Boyd/Hopalong appeared on the covers of both *Look* and *Time* magazines.

When the character was transferred from pulp fiction to film, he was modified, reinvented, no longer the rough, unAmerican villain, he became the Upright American Cowboy, fighting in the most honest ways against the bad guys. And just as Clayton Moore identified with his character, William Boyd took on his creation, often dressing as a cowboy in public. As with all of the other successfully created cultural cowboys, Boyd became very wealthy from his new persona, and he emphasized his Hopalong Cassidy ethics by refusing to license products he thought were unsuitable or dangerous and insisted his fans be allowed to attend his personal appearances free.

He knew the persona held a double-edged reality, and when Cecil B. DeMille offered him the role of Moses in *The Ten Commandments*, Boyd turned it down, realizing his identification with Hopalong was so strong that no viewing audience could ever accept him in another role. However, he was glad to have a cameo as Hopalong in the 1952 circus epic, *The Greatest Show on Earth.*

In *real* life Boyd married five times (to Laura Maynard, Ruth Miller, Elinor Fair, Dorothy Sebastian and Grace Bradley). Elinor Fair bore him a son, but the boy died at nine months. After retiring from the screen, Boyd invested in real estate, settled in Palm Desert, California, and refused interviews and photographs, knowing that they would only disillusion his millions of fans. He died in 1972 from complications of Parkinson's disease.

November 5, 1911, Leonard Franklin Slye was born to Andrew Slye and Mattie Wolmack Slye in Cincinnati, Ohio, in a tenement on 2nd Street. Unhappy with their jobs and life in general, his dad and his dad's brother Will built a 12-by-50 foot houseboat from salvage lumber, and on July, 1912, the family headed down the Ohio River to Portsmouth, where they purchased land, and as a result of a flood, were able to float their houseboat right onto the property and use it as their house. In 1919, they purchased a farm in Duck Run, about twelve miles north of Portsmouth and built a six-room house. Since this farm could not support the family, Leonard's father Andrew took a job at a shoe factory in Portsmouth, living there during the week and only returning home on weekends with gifts for the family following paydays, one of which was a horse that Leonard immediately began learning how to care for and ride. (96)

When Leonard was 17, the family moved to Cincinnati, where his father again got a job in a shoe factory. However, finances remained tight, and Leonard quit school to join his father in the factory. He tried to finish high school at night, but found he could not stay awake and gave up the attempt. In 1929, Leonard's older sister Mary moved to Lawndale, California with her husband, and soon the entire family followed. Their first visit lasted only four months, but in the spring of 1930 they moved there permanently. Father and son quickly found work as truck drivers for a construction project, but one morning upon reporting for work they found their employer had gone bankrupt. It was the time of the Great Depression, and the family now found themselves living among the masses of refugees who travelled from fruit picking job to fruit picking job and lived in the make-shift worker campsites.

All during this time, Leonard, now referred to simply as Len, entertained himself, his family, and the other workers by playing his guitar and singing. One night his sister Mary suggested he try out for the Midnight Frolic radio program amateur talent contest. Reluctantly, he did, and dressed in a Western shirt she made for him, he performed, singing, yodeling, and playing his guitar. It resulted in an invitation to join a local country music group, The Rocky Mountaineers, which he did in August of 1931.

Things that could never have been predicted were coming together. In 1932 Leonard (generally now known simply as Len) met Lucille Ascolese while on tour. In the same year, a palomino colt named Golden Cloud was foaled in Santa Cietro. In May of 1933 Len, now 21, proposed to Lucille, 19, via a radio broadcast. Then he went on tour with the O-Bar-O Cowboys, and in June of that year met Grace Arline Wilkins, who traded him a lemon pie for singing *Swiss Yodel* on the local radio station. Success, however, was not immediate. After four years with little happening, in 1934, he formed a new group, Sons of the Pioneers, with Bob Nolan and Tim Spencer. This group hit it big with such songs as *Cool Water* and *Tumbling Tumbleweeds*, resulting in Len's first film appearance in 1935, after which he got steady work, including a large supporting role (still under the name Leonard Slye) in a Gene Autry movie.

Len and Lucille divorced in 1935, and Len and Grace Arline Wilkins married in 1936. By 1938, Republic's big Western star, Gene Autry was having contract disputes, and Republic wanted to be ready to replace him, so they held auditions. Len snuck into one of them and got signed to a seven-year contract. He appeared as Dick Weston in *Wild Horse Rodeo*, where he sung one song. Then nothing happened until Gene Autry failed to report for the beginning of his next film. Republic was ready, and put their newly renamed replacement Roy Rogers into the lead role in *Under Western Stars*. It was an immediate hit, and a new star was born.

Before filming began on it, Republic gave Roy his choice of their best horses, and the third one he tried was a "beautiful golden palomino" that turned "on a dime and gave you some change." Smiley Burnette, Roy's sidekick in his first two films, suggested the horse was quick as a "trigger," and the name was decided.

After the success of *Under Western Stars*, Republic starred Roy in a series of historical Westerns--*Rough Riders Roundup, Days Of Jesse James, Frontier Pony Express*, and *Young Buffalo Bill*. He immediately established himself as a major Western star. In addition to his string of Western movies, early in 1940 he received excellent reviews for his role as

Claire Trevor's younger brother in the film *The Dark Command*, which also starred John Wayne and Walter Pidgeon.

In this same year he got a clause into his contract with Republic allowing him to own the rights to his likeness, voice and name, and as with Hopalong Cassedy, he amassed a fortune from merchandizing—action figures, cowboy adventure novels, play sets, a comic strip and Dell Comics series—for a time second only to Walt Disney in this marketing. At the same time, his group, The Songs of the Pioneers continued performing, and as of this printing, still do (though, of course, the original members have long since died).

In 1941, Roy and Grace adopted Cheryl Darlene. In 1943, they had a daughter, Linda Lou. In 1946 they had a son, Roy Jr. (Dusty), but Arline died of complications from the birth. Roy had met Dale Evans in 1944 when the two were cast in a movie together, and now that Roy was no longer married, they reunited and married on New Year's Eve, 1947.

His movie career was stunning. In the *Motion Picture Herald* Top Ten Money-Making Western Stars poll, he was listed for fifteen consecutive years from 1939 to 1954, holding first place from 1943 to 1954.-He appeared in the similar *Box Office* poll from 1938 to 1955, holding first place from 1943 to 1952. (In the final three years of that poll he was second only to Randolph Scott.) And he appeared in the *Top Ten Money Makers Poll* of all films in 1945 and 1946. Furthermore, he was a television idol for children, with most of his postwar films done in Trucolor, a far superior technique to the general black-and-white B-movies of the time.

In 1950, Roy and Dale had daughter Robin Elizabeth, but she had Down Syndrome, and died from complications of the mumps shortly before her second birthday. (Dale Evans wrote about this in her book *Angel Unaware*). Both Roy and Dale were outspoken Christians, and they actively worked for various children's charities; again establishing the high ethical and spiritual image of the Hollywood Cowboy Image. And again, he appeared in numerous shows as his Roy Rogers alter-ego, on rare occasions taking on other cowboy roles, but avoided taking any roles that went against his created persona.

This alter-ego is perhaps the most famous of the many Cowboy Heroes created by Hollywood in the process of creating an entire other reality, the entire world of Western America that more people comprehend as the real history than the real history itself—raising endless, important questions about reality. Certainly, in a sense, this reality created by pulp fiction, radio, television, and Hollywood films is real, and it informs the conscious and unconscious understanding of the world of far more people than the historic world of Western America.

Furthermore, it is a world that carries a clear ethical and spiritual center, a pattern of values and meaning that the real, the historic Wild West did not, at least not on such a precisely evident map. We might well ask if reality has any ethical and spiritual form or shape, or if it only takes on meaning because the human mind shapes it into a reality with meaning. Does God provide meaning and value through the human mind? Or is it already there and the human mind simply a somewhat ineffective organ trying to grasp it? In other words, which is more real, the historic wild west or the wild west filtered through the human mind?

There were many Western alter-egos created, from Tom Mix and Gene Autry to perhaps the most towering Cowboy of all, John Wayne. Some of the early celebrities and movie creations were, in an almost eerie situation, the actual historic figures.

Tom Mix (born Thomas Hezikiah Mix, January 6, 1880) was Hollywood's first Western megastar, making a reported 336 films 1910-1935. He was perhaps the only Cowboy Star who really was a cowboy, learning to ride horses and working on a local farm as a child, and later working a variety of cowboy jobs in the Oklahoma Territory, including the Miller Brothers 101 Ranch, where he stood out as a skilled horseman and expert shot, winning the 1909 Riding and Rodeo Championship. Apparently, he was interested in entertaining from a young age, and there is a story that he was caught by his parents practicing a knife throwing act in hopes of joining the circus. He enlisted in the Army in 1898 for the Spanish-American War, but deserted, perhaps as a result of marrying Grace Allan in 1902. He was never court-martialed or punished in any way for his desertion. His marriage only lasted one year, and in 1905, he married Kitty Jewel Perinne, again divorcing within a year, marrying Olive Stokes in 1909, and again divorcing and marrying Victoria Forde (a co-star in several of his westerns) in 1918. As is normal with the larger-than-life characters from the Wild West, truth and fiction get entangled. For example, he claimed to have been the son of a cavalry officer and to have attended the Virginia Military Institute, neither of which is true. (97)

He began his film career as supporting cast member for the Selig Polyscope Company in 1910 with the film *Ranch Life in the Great Southwest*, where he demonstrated his skills as a cattle wrangler. The film was a success, making him an immediate star. He made over 100 films with Selig before they went broke, and then he signed with Fox Film Corporation, where he made more than 160 additional films, these having more of a storyline than his previous films, and provided the initial

Hollywood image of the good, clean-cut cowboy who always "saved the day" from the obvious villains. As also became custom, he had his intelligent and handsome horse, in his case named Tony, who also became a celebrity. While this would not necessarily be the case with future Hollywood Cowboys, Tom Mix always did his own stunts (and was frequently injured). Other Cowboy standards also got put in place—the glamorous cowboy costumes, the set (a standard cowboy town with saloon, jail, bank, doctor's office, surveyor's office, and hotel—all on one dusty main street with hitching posts and water troughs for the horses). The inclusion of Indians was accomplished here by having an Indian village just outside of this town. And then, there was the countryside, a simulated desert, mountains, a large corral, and a ranch house on the prairie.

In 1929, Mix worked his final year of silent pictures for Film Book Office of America (FBO), a studio run by Joseph P. Kennedy Sr., and coincidentally served as a pallbearer for Wyatt Earp. He divorced Forde in 1931, and married his fifth wife, Mabel Hubbard Ward in 1932. During the early thirties he acted in nine talking pictures for Universal Pictures, but his injuries had caught up with him, and his last picture, *The Miracle Rider* was in 1935. After that, he finally did fulfill his childhood dream, and began appearing in the Sam B. Dill circus, which he eventually purchased.

Texas governor James Allred named him an honorary Texas Ranger, and he took his show on a promotional trip to Europe. His daughter, Ruth, who had also appeared in a few of his films, managed the circus while he was out of the country, but it quickly failed, and they had a falling out. It is estimated he made over six million dollars in his career. His image had become so popular that Ralston-Purina produced a Tom Mix radio series, *Tom Mix Ralston Straight Shooters*, which ran for nearly twenty years, indicating how much his alter-ego had taken on a life of its own, because he never appeared on it, and, of course, a radio show could not demonstrate any of his rodeo skills. In other words, it was a show based on a character that had taken over the real man. The alter ego was a creation with a different past and life style than the real Tom Mix (though both had some similar cowboy skills).

On the afternoon of October 12, 1940, Tom Mix drove his 1937 Cord 812 Phaeton off of Arizona State Route 79, where it rolled into a gully, pinning him underneath. A large aluminum suitcase filled with money, traveler's checks and jewels flew forward from the back, striking him in the head, shattering his skull, and breaking his neck. So the real life Tom Mix had a dramatic death, but certainly not the kind of death his cowboy alter ego might have (mythic cowboys don't drive cars). However, because of his famous persona, a stone memorial marks the site of his death, and the gully has been name Tom Mix Wash.

He was the original Hollywood Cowboy, designated as the "King of the Cowboys," and he would help football player John Wayne get a job moving props in the back lot of Fox Studios when John Wayne's injury ended his athletic career. Accolades abound. He has a star on the Hollywood Walk of Fame, his cowboy boot prints, palm prints, and even his horse Tony's hoof prints in the famous Grauman's Chinese Theatre sidewalk, and has been inducted into the Western Performers Hall of Fame. In addition, there are Tom Mix museums in Dewey, Oklahoma and Mix Run, Pennsylvania. The Beatles even included him on the cover of their famous *Sergeant Pepper's Lonely Hearts Club Band* album.

And as the realities of Tom Mix get ever more complex, he has been played by Bruce Willis in the 1988 film *Sunset* (where James Garner played another iconic Cowboy, Wyatt Earp), referred to in the *Beverly Hillbillies* television show, where Jed Clampett wanted to go to Beverly Hills because he wanted to live in the same place as Tom Mix. Woody Allen even included film footage of him attending a party at Hearst Castle in Allen's film *Zelig.* Daryl Ponicsan reconfigured him in the novel *Tom Mix Died for Your Sins*; Clifford Irving offered a pseudo-autobiography of him in *Tom Mix and Poncho Villa*; James Horwitz visits Tom Mix Wash and leaves his childhood cowboy boots at the foot of the monument in his book *They Went Thataway*; Philip Jose Farmer resurrects him in *The Dark Design* and *The Magic Labyrinth*; and Father Mulcahy even uses a Tom Mix pocket knife to perform emergency surgery in the television show *MASH.* Philip K. Dick names an underground blunder the Tom Mix in his science fiction novel *The Penultimate Truth*; the ghost of Tom Mix haunts a Hollywood couple in *The Ghosts of Edendale*; and in *Batman/Houdini: The Devil's Workshop* Tom Mix is a high profile figure in Gotham society.

The list goes on. He is mentioned as a pall bearer for Wyatt Earp in the end credits for George P. Cosmatos film *Tombstone*. *Doctor Who* has an episode titled "The Gunfighters" where the Doctor wonders why everyone wants to dress like Tom Mix. The United States Postal Service has commemorated him on a postage stamp. In the television series *Bewitched,* an episode titled "Serena's Youth Pill" has Darin telling his boss Larry Tate that a magic drink will help him grow up to be more like Tom Mix.

The grandson of a Methodist preacher, Orvon Grover Autry was born September 29, 1907, to Delbert Autry and Elnora Ozment near Tioga, Texas. In the 1920s the family moved to Ravia, Oklahoma, where Orvon worked on his father's ranch. During these years, he often played guitar and sang at the local dances. (98)

After graduation, he continued his performing while working as a telegrapher for the St. Louis-San Francisco Railway, where famous humorist Will Rogers heard him and encouraged him to pursue a professional career. Once he had enough money to travel, he headed to New York to do just that, auditioning for Victor Talking Machine, which became RCA Victor. The owner, Shilkret turned him down because he had just hired two other singers and had no need of a third. Shilkret suggested he go sing on the radio to get some experience and gave him a letter of introduction to do just that.

By 1928, he was being billed on Tulsa radio station KVOO as "Oklahoma's Yodeling Cowboy," and by 1929 he was being recorded by RCA Victor. That same year he signed a recording deal with Columbia Records, began working on WLS-AM radio in Chicago, Illinois. At this time he recorded a number of "hillbilly" prohibition songs such as *Do Right Daddy Blues* and *Black Bottom Blues*. His first hit, *That Silver-Haired Daddy of Mine* came in 1932, the same year he married May Spivey.

In 1934, he began his film career with his singing partner Burnette in *Old Santa Fe* as part of a singing quartet, and then took on a starring role in the following year in a twelve-part serial, *The Phantom Empire*. His career took off, and by 1940, he had made forty-four B-grade Westerns for Republic Pictures under his own name, with his horse Champion, and his friend Burnette as his sidekick. These were all films featuring him as a "singing" Cowboy. He would be the top Western Star through the later thirties, and vie with Roy Rogers for that position through the forties and fifties (excepting 1943-5, when he was serving in the U.S. Army Air Corps). In addition, his *Gene Autry Flying "A" Ranch Rodeo* CBS radio show debuted in 1940 and would continue until 1956. His horse Champion even had a show, *The Adventures of Champion*. In 1950 he produced and starred in his own television show on CBS, and began a number of guest appearances on such other shows as *Jubilee USA*. In 1951, he formed his own production company, and in 1953 purchased Monogram Movie Ranch, renaming it Melody Ranch after one of his movies, and used it for location shooting for his future movies. He would eventually sell it, and it has since become a museum.

Most importantly for the concerns of this book, he was important in establishing the Hollywood Cowboy image, even creating the *Cowboy Code*:

1. Never shoot first, hit a smaller man, or take unfair advantage;

2. Never go back on his word, or a trust confided in him;
3. Always tell the truth;
4. Be gentle with children, the elderly and animals;
5. Not advocate or possess racially or religiously intolerant ideas;
6. Help people in distress;
7. Be a good worker;
8. Keep himself clean in thought, speech, action and personal habits;
9. Respect women, parents and his nation's laws;
10. Be a patriot.

And the real Gene Autry, as with Tom Mix, did have some legitimacy as a Cowboy, owning a string of rodeo stock in Ardmore, Oklahoma, owning part of and later all of the World Championship Rodeo Company, purchasing Montana's top bucking horses in 1954 and becoming the livestock for most of the major rodeos for the next twelve years. These activities as an owner resulted in him being inducted into the Professional Rodeo Cowboys Association Pro Rodeo Hall of Fame in 1979. Owning, however, is not the same thing as being, and certainly Autry's professional persona as the Cowboy was a fictional creation.

When he retired from show business in 1964, he had made close to 100 films and recorded over 600 records, many of the songs ones he had written himself, and interestingly, the biggest hits not Cowboy songs but ones that have become Christmas classics: *Rudolph the Red Nosed Reindeer, Here Comes Santa Claus Right Down Santa Clause Lane,* and *Frosty the Snowman.*

His business acumen (and huge celebrity) also allowed him to be involved in many things the Hollywood Cowboy would not. He purchased the California Angels baseball team in 1961, and served as vice president of the American League from 1983 until his death. He also owned KTLA, a television station in Los Angeles, and several radio stations. In fact, he was listed in *Forbes* famous 400 richest Americans for many years.

His celebrity status is unquestionable, and he is the only celebrity to have five stars on the Hollywood Walk of Fame, one for each of the five possible categories (motion pictures, radio, recording, television, and live theater).

As the Hollywood Cowboy took shape over the first half of the twentieth century, Marion Robert Morrison was to become *the* iconic symbol of it. He was born in Winterset, Iowa, May 29, 1907, to Clyde Leonard Morrison, the son of American Civil War veteran Marion Mitchell Morrison, and Mary "Molly" Alberta Brown. His middle name was soon changed to Mitchell when his parents decided to name their next son Robert. (99)

The family moved to Palmdale and then in 1911 to Glendale, California, where the father worked as a pharmacist. Marrion had a large Airedale Terrier named Duke, and a local fireman began to call him Little Duke, a nickname that would stick with him the rest of his life. He had a normal childhood and adolescence, notably because of his future holding a job for a time at a local ice cream shop for a man who shod horses for Hollywood studios. He was an active member of the Order of DeMolay, a youth organization associated with the Freemasons, played football for the 1924 champion Glendale High School team, applied for the U. S. Naval Academy, but was rejected, instead attended the University of Southern California (USC) on a football athletic scholarship, but lost it due to an injury and dropped out.

He began working at local film studios, and, as mentioned above, Western Cowboy star Tom Mix got him a summer job working in the prop department (in exchange for football tickets). This led into bit parts in movies and importantly established a friendship with legendary director John Ford. He is reported to have also met legendary *cowboy* Wyatt Earp at this time.

After a few bit parts in Fox Film movies, one of which (*Words and Music,* 1929) credited him as Duke Morrison, he got his first starring role in *The Big Trail* (1930), and director Raoul Walsh gave him the screen name of John Wayne (he had no say in this, was not even present when the decision was made). It was a major movie, the first big-budget outdoor spectacle of the beginning sound era, and made at a then huge cost of over $2 million, including hundreds of extras and wide angle views of the American southwest. However, the film did not do as well as hoped at the box office, partially because few theaters were equipped to show the film in its innovative widescreen format, and it was considered a flop. This, unfortunately, for John Wayne moved him back into minor roles, including one in *The Deceiver* (1931), playing a corpse. Throughout the thirties, he appeared in about eighty low budget westerns, including a role in *Riders of Destiny* where he was one of the early singing cowboys (albeit the result of dubbing in someone else's voice). One benefit for him was learning the various riding skills and other stunts of Hollywood Cowboys.

Then came his breakthrough role in John Ford's classic *Stagecoach* (1939), the beginning of him starring in over twenty of Ford's Films, including *She Wore A Yellow Ribbon, The Quiet Man, The Searchers, The Wings of Eagles,* and *The Man Who Shot Liberty Valance*.

In 1941, he co-starred with Harry Carey in his first color film, *Shepherd of the Hills*, and the following year appeared in his only film with Cecil B. DeMille, *Reap the Wild Wind* (a rare instance where he played against character in the role of a man with questionable values). He had an image he intended to maintain, and even turned down such major roles as the starring role in *All the King's Men* (for which Broderick Crawford won an Oscar) because he believed the script was un-American. He also held grudges, and refused the leading role in *The Gunfighter* (which was then given to Gregory Peck) because Harry Cohn, the chief of Columbia Pictures had mistreated him years before when he was still an unknown.

Though he began and remained the ideal Hollywood Cowboy, John Wayne made numerous films outside of this genre as well, mostly playing similar larger-than-life masculine men in such war films as *Flying Tigers, Flying Leathernecks, Island in the Sky, The Wings of Eagles, Jet Pilot,* and the highly acclaimed *The High and the Mighty*.

His portrayal of Ethan Edwards in *The Searchers* (1956) is often considered to be his best. (He even named his youngest son after the character). He was nominated for an Oscar as a producer for *The Alamo* (1960), though the film was a financial flop, and also produced and directed *The Green Berets* (1968), in an attempt to provide a patriotic film during a time of anti-war sediment, but it again was not the success he hoped for.

Perhaps, if the film had come at a different point in history, it would have been more accepted by the public, but it was as much of a political film as an artistic endeavor, and the country was not in the mood for John Wayne's strong conservative views. In 1969, he gave his most memorable performance as Rooster Cogburn in *True Grit*, where he portrayed the rough, crusty, as always larger-than-life cowboy he had developed through his career, and won an Oscar for it. His final film was *The Shootest* (1976), ironically portraying J. B. Books, a man dying of cancer, the illness that Wayne would succumb to three years later (the result of being a chain-smoker most of his life). By the time he was done, he had starred in over 142 films, and still holds the record for appearances on the top ten money making Western Stars list, twenty-five times.

Though he was a strong patriot, a conservative, and supported the U. S. involvement in various wars, he dodged going to war himself during WWII, and that stigma remained with him, causing people to wonder about the sincerity of his many performances as a war hero. Certainly, here we have a clear instance of confusion between the *real* Marion Morrison and the *alter-ego* John Wayne. He also got himself into trouble in a May 1, 1971 interview for *Playboy* with his comments that the government did not owe the Native Americans anything for taking their lands in the past. Other conservative comments through the years also caused problems. He condemned people on welfare, and stated he believed in white supremacy until Blacks get educated enough to be responsible.

He was married three times and divorced twice, fathering four children with Josephine Alicia Saenz and three with Pilar Pallete. He also had numerous affairs, including one with Marlene Dietrich that lasted for three years. He was, by all accounts, an alcoholic, and according to Sam O'Steen's memoir of him, *Cut to the Chase*, studio directors knew to shoot Wayne's scenes before noon, because by afternoon he "was a mean drunk."

He died on June 11, 1979, less than a month after receiving the prestigious Congressional Gold Medal. At the ceremony, Robert Aldrick, then president of the Directors Guild of America, stated:

> It is important for you to know that I am a registered Democrat and, to my knowledge, share none of the political views espoused by Duke. However, whether he is ill disposed or healthy, John Wayne is far beyond the normal political sharp shooting in this community. Because of his courage, his dignity, his integrity, and because of his talents as an actor, his strength as a leader, his warmth as a human being throughout his illustrious career, he is entitled to a unique spot in our hearts and minds. In this industry, we often judge people, sometimes unfairly, by asking whether they have paid their dues. John Wayne has paid his dues over and over, and I'm proud to consider him a friend and am very much in favor of my Government recognizing in some important fashion the contribution that Mr. Wayne has made.

On June 9, 1980, Wayne was posthumously awarded the Presidential Medal of Freedom by Jimmy Carter (at whose inaugural ball Wayne had appeared "as a member of the loyal opposition," as Wayne described it in his speech to the gathering). Thus Wayne received the two highest civilian decorations awarded by the United States government.

Wayne rose beyond the typical recognition for a famous actor to that of an enduring icon who symbolized and communicated American values and ideals, mainly, though not entirely, in the alter ego of the Hollywood Cowboy. By the middle of his career, he had developed a larger-than-life image, and as his career progressed, he selected roles that would not compromise his off-screen image. In his last film *The Shootest* (1976), he refused to allow his character to shoot a man in the back as was originally scripted, saying "I've made over 250 pictures and have never shot a guy in the back. Change it."

The Hollywood image of John Wayne took on such huge dimensions that Japanese Emperor Hirohito asked to meet him in 1975 (as the symbolic representation of his country's former enemy. And even though he did not serve himself, many veterans have said they signed up to serve as a result of watching his movies. Even several army gear got named after him: the P-38 named the John Wayne can-opener, the paper towels named John Wayne Toilet Paper because they are tough and don't take shit from anyone, the C-ration cracker called "John Wayne Crackers" because only those tough as him could eat them. Even a mountain pass used by army tanks at Fort Irwin got named John Wayne Pass. Endless public places are named in his memory, including John Wayne Airport in Orange County, California, the John Wayne Marina in Sequim, Washington, the John Wayne Elementary School in Brooklyn, New York, and the John Wayne Pioneer Trail in Washington state's Iron horse State Park. In Maricopa, Arizona, part of the Arizona State highway 347 is named John Wayne Parkway. And at his birthplace in Winterset, Iowa, there is the John Wayne Birthplace Museum.

John Wayne, the *alter ego* of Marion Robert Morrison, had become the epitome of the Hollywood Cowboy, a man filled with a certain kind of American ethos, and the entire fictionalized world of Hollywood's Wild West was the attraction, a fantasy once-upon-a-time world, one that had its share of hardships and bad people, but one where right and wrong were easy to sort out, and one where the American version of the Good Guy won.

While the real John Wayne only partially matched this iconic image, that wasn't important. The fictional world was more real and more important than the real world.

Clint Eastwood Jr. would be the final huge Hollywood Western Star. He was born in San Francisco on May 31, 1930 to Clinton Eastwood Sr., a steelworker, and his wife, Ruth Eastwood-Belden. During his childhood the family moved around northern California, finally settling in Oregon. After graduating from high school, Clint moved to Seattle, where he worked for a time as a lifeguard, before entering the military in 1951, after which he moved to Los Angeles, where he found work digging swimming pools, and began auditioning for bit parts in B-movies, getting uncredited parts in *Tarantula* (1955) and *Revenge of the Creature* (1955), then credited roles in *Francis in the Nave* (1955), *The First Traveling Saleslady* (1956), *Lafayette Escadrille* (1958), and *Ambush at Cimarron Pass* (1958). His breakthrough came with the television series *Rawhide* (1959), where he starred as Rowdy Tates for six years. (100)

Then he really entered the Hollywood Cowboy Movie Star category by ironically making Spaghetti Westerns in Italy: *A Fistful of Dollars* (1964), *For a Few Dollars More* (1965), and especially *The Good, The Bad, and the Ugly* (1966). These made him an instant international star, and major roles followed: *Coogan's Bluff* (1968), *Hang 'Em High* (1968), *Paint Your Wagon* (1969), *Kelly's Heroes* (1970), and *Two Mules for Sister Sara.* (1970)

He both starred in and directed *Play Misty for Me* (1971), and starred in *Dirty Harry* (1971), which led to three sequels, *Magnum Force* (1973), *The Enforcer* (1976), *Sudden Impact* (1983), and *The Dead Pool* (1988).

His westerns (such as *High Plains Drifter,* 1973, which he also directed) fit into the new category of "revisionist" westerns, where the Hollywood version of the Wild West was indeed getting revised to make it better fit the real Wild West.

He continued to mix genres, much as John Wayne did, starring in *Thunderbolt and Lightfoot* (1974), what is generally considered the quintessential western, *The Outlaw Josey Wales* (1976), *The Gauntlet* (1977), the comedy *Every Which Way But Loose* (1978) and its sequel *Any Which Way You Can* (1980) with Clyde the orangutan, *Firefox* (1982), *Tightrope* (1984), *Pale Rider* (1985), and *Heartbreak Ridge* (1986).

In the late eighties, his films declined in quality, with such bombs as the comedy *Pink Cadillac* (1989) and cop adventure *The Rookie* (1990). But he rebounded with his western, *Unforgiving* (1992), earning an Oscar for directing and producer, and a nomination for best actor. This was followed by a well received secret service movie, *In the Line of Fire* (1993), a popular love story, *The Bridges of Madison County* (1995), the popular *Absolute Power* (1997) and *Space Cowboys* (2000). Mixed in were a couple of flops, *True Crime* (1999) and *Blood Work* (2002).

Then came probably the best film of his career, *Million Dollar Baby* (2004), a box office hit that won him an Oscar for best picture, along with nominations for best actor and director. The next film he acted in was *Gran Torino* (2008), and that made him the oldest leading man to reach #1 status at the box office ever.

Clint Eastwood, Jr., is the transitional Hollywood Cowboy Star, and the way his career and his alter-ego are handled demonstrate that the once-upon-a-time Hollywood Western and Cowboy Hero have changed dramatically. No longer is the real person tied so clearly to his alter ego. Now, he can separate from it, can play multiple roles, both within westerns and outside of them. While it is true that Clint Eastwood does much the same thing John Wayne did in playing to a type character, in both cases a rough, macho man image, the characters' ethical qualities are not as clean in Clint Eastwood's characters as in John Wayne's. In fact, ethical Good and Evil have become muddled, just as they have in the real world.

Hollywood Westerns with their created Western Cowboy Heroes became a huge genre of the film industry, developing their fictional reality out of the pulp fictions, radio plays and real historic characters of the West for most of the first half of the nineteenth century before those more concerned with the *real* history of the West gained the upper hand and broke the spell, insisting on highlighting how the *real* world, the *real* wild west was being misrepresented, no longer interested in understanding imaginative reality for what it is, no longer allowing the higher truths to exist (at least not in such stark, unrealistic dualities as symbolized by white and black cowboy hats), and so Hollywood began putting out films such as *Dances with Wolves* that attempted to be more faithful to the historic west or turned to other genres. Clint Eastwood is in many ways the key transitional figure, the last huge western star, yet one that is both iconic and yet more human in his complexity.

Other categories of entertainment are also centered on *alter-egos*. Professional wrestling has given us numerous larger-than-life *alter egos*, the likes of The Rock (Dwayne Johnson), Diesel (Kevin Nash), Edge (Adam Copeland), Sergeant Slaughter (Robert Remus), and Hulk Hogan (Terry Gene Bollea). Hip-hop artists commonly do the same: 50 Cent (Curtis James Boo Boo Jackson III), Master P (Percy Miller), Babyface (Kenneth Brian Edmunds), Lil Bow Wow (Shad Gregory Moss), and LL Cool J (James Todd Smith). Some, such as Eminem (Marshall Bruce Mathers III) and T.I. (Clifford Joseph Harris, Jr.) have used the alter-egos Slim Shady and T.I.P. to explore divisions in their personalities. T.I.'s album, *T.I. vs. T.I.P.*, even directly appropriates a Jekyll and Hyde plot.

Rock-and-Roll artist David Bowie took on two *alter-egos* for his public personas, Ziggy Stardust and The Thin White Duke. Shock rockers Alice Cooper (Vincent Damon Furnier) and Marilyn Manson (Brian Warner) became known almost exclusively by their *alter-egos*. Brian Warner made it a point not to be seen in public with his horror make-up. Sometimes artists have taken on an alter-ego for a specific album, as in the case of Christina Aguilera being Xtina. At times, entire rock-and-roll groups have taken on *alter-egos*. *Kiss* is a perfect example. The Beatles took this a step further, consciously adopting an *alter-ego group, Sgt. Pepper's Lonely Hearts Club Band,* the album often considered the most important ever released.

At the time, albums were simply collections of songs that had little to do with one-another other than that the same artist had recorded them, and the featured song was expected to carry the album.

The Beatles, however, became such a huge influence they could get away with something different. For a time, they had been releasing singles without bothering to gather them into albums. They also decided to stop touring. Instead, they secluded themselves in their studio from December 6 and April 3, experimented with a number of drugs, including marijuana, cocaine, and LSD, and began creating an album that was meant to be a complete, united work.

How it all came together has been the subject of many, many studies, and just who is responsible for the various pieces of it will forever remain guesswork. However, the initial concept seems to have come mainly from Paul McCartney. In a *Playboy* interview (Dec., 1984), he stated: "[Sgt. Pepper] was an idea I had, I think, when I was flying from L.A. to somewhere. I thought it would be nice to lose our identities, to submerge ourselves in the persona of a fake group. We would make up all the culture around it and collect all our heroes in one place. So I thought, a typical stupid-sound name for a Dr. Hook's Medicine Show and Traveling Circus kind of thing would be Sgt. Pepper's Lonely Hearts Club Band. Just a word game, really." [In *Beatles in Their Own Words*, he elaborated] "After you have written that down you start to think: 'There's this Sgt. Pepper who has taught the band to play, and got them going so that at least they found one number. They're a bit of a brass band in a way, but also a rock band because they've got the San Francisco thing.'" (101)

There are other versions. According to Pete Shotton and Ringo Starr, it wasn't Paul, but Mal Evans who both coined the name Sgt. Pepper's Lonely Hearts Club Band, and also suggested that this fictitious group be presented as the Beatles' alter egos. (102)

John Lennon was not into it, saying "Sgt. Pepper is called the first concept album, but it doesn't go anywhere. All my contributions to the album have absolutely nothing to do with this idea of Sgt. Pepper and his band; but it works 'cause we *said* it worked (103).

This concept of it working or being something because its creator or creators say it is actually fits it even more into the whole realm of concept art (and raises interesting questions about what *reality* is).

When Peter Blake began working on the cover, he said that "Paul explained that [the concept] was like a band you might see in a park. So the cover shot could be a photograph of them as though they were a town band finishing a concert in a park, playing on a bandstand with a municipal flowerbed next to it, with a crowd of people around them. I think my main contribution was to decide that if we made the crowd a certain way the people in it could be anybody." (104)

As it turned out, when Blake asked the Beatles to pick some onlookers for the scene, they picked the most well-know people they could think of. John Lennon even wanted to include Jesus, but he was vetoed here (he had already gotten himself and the group in trouble with comments about Jesus). Mahatma Gandhi also got nixed for fear of offending India.

In the end, Peter Blake explained: "All the figures which you see behind the Beatles only filled a space about two feet deep, and then there was a line of figures in front of them which were the waxworks. The actual Beatles stood on a platform about four feet deep in all with the drum in front of them, and in front of that there was a flowerbed which was pitched at an angle, maybe ten feet deep. So that from front to back the whole thing was only about fifteen feet deep." (105)

At this time, another mixture of reality and illusion was taking place, the "Paul is dead" hysteria, and this cover has been interpreted and reinterpreted by those looking for clues to that. The hand above Paul's head is supposedly a sign of death; the Beatles are supposedly standing around his freshly dug grave; the yellow hyacinth bass guitar supposedly marks his grave; the black clarinet Paul holds symbolizes death; and even the fact that Harrison's finger on the back cover is point to the first line of *She's Leaving Home*, which is "Wednesday morning at 5 o'clock as the day begins" is thought to indicate the time of his death. Suggestions have been made that Paul is being represented by an actor named William Campbell, who had plastic surgery to look like him; the inside photo of Paul with an arm patch reading O.P.D. (Ontario Police Station) is interpreted as Officially Pronounced Dead, and the photo of Paul on the back has him facing away. On and on. (106)

Comic performers have also found *alter-egos* valuable. The Marx Brothers performed throughout their careers as their vaudeville characters. Arthur Adolph Marx (Harpo) consistently took on his impish non-speaking character, the same character in film after film. His brother Julius Marx (Groucho) would play (and be credited as) Groucho, whether he was cast a professor (as in *Horse Feathers*), a veterinarian (*A Day at the Races*), or a president (*Duck Soup*). Such stand-up comedians as Don Rickles (Mr. Warmth) and Jackie Mason (Hartounian) developed their comic *alter-egos* into distinct personalities. Andy Kaufman took this into multiple characters, the Foreign Man (later Latka Gravas), Tony Clifton, and an impersonation of Elvis Presley. The biopic *Man on the Moon* depicts him as a man whose true identity was difficult to isolate, even by his close friends, because of the prevalence of these alter-egos which he switched into off stage as well as on. Paul Rubins did much the same thing with his Pee Wee Herman *alter-ego*, staying in character off screen, and when he was caught masturbating during his personal life off screen his career came crashing down because it did not match his public persona.

Peter Jeremy William Huggins became one of the more interesting cases of this mixing of *real* and *alter* egos. He was born to Lord Lieutenant of Warwickshire, heir of the Cadbury chocolate fortune November 3, 1933, educated at Eton, where he claims to have been an "academic disaster," attributing this to dyslexia. Nevertheless, he excelled at singing as a member of the college choir and decided to become an actor, much to his father's chagrin. In fact, his father was so distraught over it, he demanded Peter change his name so as not to dishonor the family name. With his new name, Brett Jeremy got his training at the Central School of Speech and Drama in London, made his professional acting debut at the Library Theatre in Manchester, 1954, and his London stage debut with the Old Vic Company in Shakespeare's *Troilus and Cressida*, 1956. Later that year he took on the role of the Duke of Aumerie in *Richard II* on Broadway. Throughout the rest of the 1950s, he continued his career as a regular in the Old Vic and National Theatre casts. Beginning in the 1960s, he continued his acting on British television, starring in numerous series, most famously as D'Artagnan in the 1966 adaptation of *The Three Musketeers* and as Bassanio in *The Merchant of Venice* with Laurence Olivier playing the role of Shylock. He also performed in movies, notably as Freddie Eynsford-Hill in *My Fair Lady*, curiously because of his own vocal abilities, having his singing dubbed in.

He was known for his precisely honed diction, at least partially the result of surgery to correct a birth speech impediment (rhotacism) that previously kept him from properly pronouncing the "R" sound. One result of this was his insistence on doing speech exercises daily.

While he was a well known, successful actor who took on many roles (numerous productions of Shakespeare's works), the role that defined both him and his career came in a series of Granada Television films made between 1984-1994, the definitive performance of the role of Sherlock Holmes for his generation, perhaps the definitive performance of that persona ever. Indeed, Sherlock Holmes became Brett's *alter-ego* in a dramatic psychological mixture of manic depression and obsession.

The films were adapted by John Hawkesworth and others from Sir Arthur Conon Doyle's famous works, and Brett appeared in 41 episodes acting with Edward Hardwicke as Dr. Watson, a character Brett had ironically played in a Los Angeles production, *The Crucifer of Blood*, with Charlton Heston as Holmes, 1980.

The concept of the series from the beginning was to represent the most authentic, accurate Holmes ever, and Brett took this to the extreme, conducting extensive research and being ever alert to any discrepancies between the scripts and the original stories. He put together a 77 page

"Baker Street File" on everything from Holmes' mannerisms to his eating and drinking habits that he keep on the set for reference. He also applied the idea of an actor becoming the character he played, prophetically saying "some actors are becomers—they try to become their characters. When it works, the actor is like a sponge, squeezing himself dry to remove his own personality then absorbing the characters like a liquid."

His insistence on *becoming Sherlock Holmes* quickly took on an obsessed quality. He began using Holmes' eccentric hand gestures and short, violent laughter, took on Holmes dramatic way of thrusting himself to the ground just to look for a foot-print, began leaping over furniture or jumping on the parapet of a bridge without regard for his own safety. In truth, some of Holmes' obsessive and depressive personality traits matched Brett's own. Both were prone to outbursts of passionate energy followed by periods of lethargy.

As the series of films continued, he became ever more obsessed. Instead of leaving his character behind him when the day's work was done, he kept him always close and began having nightmares about him. Then he began referring to Holmes not by name but instead as "You Know Who" or "Him" as in "Watson describes You Know Who as a mind without a heart, which is hard to play, hard to become, so what I have done is invent an inner life." For example, he filled the hollowness of Holmes by imagining what You Know Who's nanny looked (she was covered with starch) and decided Holmes didn't see his mother until he was eight.

This extreme obsession with *becoming* Holmes on screen began crossing the line. When other actors went for lunch, Brett sat alone on the set, studying the script. On holidays and weekends, he read the original stories over and over, determined to catch even the slightest nuances of the character. Ironically, he once said, "Some actors fear if they play Sherlock Holmes for a very long run the character will steal their soul, leave no corner for the original inhabitant."

In 1985, Brett's second wife, Joan Sullivan, whom he called his soul mate (noting that they had the same birthday), died shortly after Brett finished filming Holmes' death in *The Final Problem*. He would have trouble during the next film, *The Return of Sherlock Holmes*, exhibiting dramatic mood swings, eventually being hospitalized and diagnosed as a manic-depressive. Lithium tablets were prescribed, and he pushed to get back to his portrayal of Holmes. A two hour adaptation of *The Sign of Four* was filmed. But Brett's condition was obviously getting rapidly worse. The lithium slowed him down and put on weight. He was retaining huge amounts of water. His heart was also giving way (had swollen to twice its normal size). He was unable to breath and needed an oxygen mask on the set. But he was obsessed and refused to stop the performance. He knew his driving desires were killing him, but it didn't matter. All that mattered was *being* Sherlock Holmes. Which he did until he died September 12, 1995.

Perhaps the person who managed not just *an alter-ego* but a complete *multiple personality persona* to the point of denying his *self* (similar to that of Elizabeth at the end of *The Bird's Nest*), and the one who most tied this loss of identity to the entire artistic and intellectual world of the time is Robert Allen Zimmerman, born in Duluth, Minnesota, on May 24, 1941, the son of Abram Zimmerman and Beatrice Stone, part of a small, close-knit Jewish community. When he turned six, his father got polio, and the family moved to his mother's nearby town on Hibbing, where he spent the rest of his youth, listening to blues, country, and early rock-and-roll on the radio, forming his own bands while in high school and dreaming of becoming a performer similar to Little Richard.

He moved to Minneapolis in 1959 and began attending the University of Minnesota, where his early interest in rock-and-roll shifts to folk music. He would later explain:

> "The thing about rock'n'roll is that for me anyway it wasn't enough ... There were great catch-phrases and driving pulse rhythms ... but the songs weren't serious or didn't reflect life in a realistic way. I knew that when I got into folk music, it was more of a serious type of thing. The songs are filled with more despair, more sadness, more triumph, more faith in the supernatural, much deeper feelings. (107)

He began performing in coffee houses around Dinkytown (the college town around the University of Minnesota), and took on his *alter-ego* name, Bob Dylan (after the poet Dylan Thomas), explaining: "You're born, you know, the wrong names, wrong parents. I mean, that happens. You call yourself what you want to call yourself. This is the land of the free." (108) He would officially change his name to Bob Dylan in 1962.

After a year of college, he dropped out. In January, 1961, he headed to New York City to see his current idol, Woody Guthrie, who was seriously ill from Huntington's Disease in Greystone Park Psychiatric Hospital. Dylan would later write about Guthrie that he "was the true voice of the American spirit." (109)

Dylan began performing in the clubs of Greenwich Village, performing harmonica on a recording by Carolyn Hester, which caught the attention of the album's producer John Hammond, who signed him to Columbia Records that October. Dylan's first album, simply titled *Bob Dylan* (1962), was a collection of traditional folk, blues, and gospel songs with two original compositions. It did not sell well, and was considered a failure. Hammond, however, continued to support Dylan.

Indicative of Dylan's multiple personas, he recorded several songs at this time under the *alter-ego* of Blind boy Grunt for *Broadside Magazine*, recorded as a piano player under the *alter-ego* Bob Landy on a 1964 anthology album, *The Blues Project*, and played harmonica on Ramblin' Jack Elliott's 1964 album *Jack Elliot* as *alter-ego* Tedham Porterhouse.

In 1962, Dylan signed a management contract with Albert Grossman, whom Dylan compared to Elvis Presley's manager Colonel Tom Parker. Grossman and Hammond did not get along, and in the end Hammond was the one to *go. Dylan's second album was produced by Tom Wilson.*

After about a year performing in England, where he first performed his famous *Blowin' in the Wind* song (one that took its melody from a traditional slave song, *No More Auction Block*), he recorded his second album, *The Freewheelin' Bob Dylan* (May, 1963), much of which consisted of protest songs, several of which would get recorded by other artists (most famously Peter, Paul and Mary, who were instrumental in making *Blowin' in the Wind* THE anthem for the protest movements of the 1960s). In fact, partially simply because Dylan's own singing was so unique (many would say was bad, often off key, pretty much always nasal, certainly with an edge), he gained his popular audience mainly through recordings of his songs by other people. Joan Baez, who became his lover for a time, recorded several, and often performed with him onstage. (110) Others included The Byrds, Sonny and Cher, The Hollies, The Association, Manfred Mann, and The Turtles. The album also included one of his best loved ballads, *Don't Think Twice, It's All Right,* a song that most believe is the result of his sorrow over the break-up with his first serious girl-friend, Suze Rotolo. As with *Blowin' in the Wind*, he took the melody from a traditional folk song (*Scarlet Ribbons for Her Hair*).

A Hard Rain's a-Gonna Fall, another famous protest song on the *Freewheelin'* album took the melody of the folk ballad *Lord Randall* and has been considered the first song to mark a new direction in popular music, blending a stream-of-conscious, imagery attack on social conditions with a traditional folk song form. (111) *Rolling Stone Magazine* called it "The greatest protest song by the greatest protest songwriter of his time: a seven-minute epic that warns against a coming apocalypse while cataloging horrific visions—gun toting children, a tree dripping blood—with the wide-eyed fervor of John the Revelator." (112) The album also demonstrated numerous other characteristics of Dylan's repertoire, humor, surreal imagery, and talking blues, and influenced the entire direction of popular music. George Harrison (of the Beatles) said: "We just played it, just wore it out. The content of the song lyrics and just the attitude—it was incredibly original and wonderful." (113)

In May, 1963, Dylan raised his social, political profile when he walked off *The Ed Sullivan Show* because he was informed that CBS Television's *head of program practices* had decided his planned song, *Talkin' John Birch Paranoid Blues*, was libelous to the John Birch Society and had to be replaced with a different song. Dylan had recorded "Talkin' John Birch Society Blues" for his *Freewheelin* album, but the song was replaced by later compositions, including "Masters of War." (114)

At this time, Dylan and Baez had become leading voices in the civil rights movement, and sang together at the March on Washington, August 28, 1963, orchestrated by Martin Luther King, Jr. where Dylan performed *Only a Pawn in Their Game* and *When the Ship Comes In*. (115)

Dylan's third album, *The Times They Are a-Changin'*, in addition to his strident title song, included other more cynical songs, many dealing with contemporary, real life events, including *Only A Pawn in Their Game* (based on the murder of civil right worker Medgar Evers), and *The Lonesome Death of Hattie Carroll* (based on the murder of black hotel barmaid Hattie Carroll by white socialite William Zantzinger). *Ballad of Hollis Brown* and *North Country Blues* were not about specific events, but nonetheless dealt with the darkness of the breakdown of farming and mining communities. In addition, there were two love songs, *Boots of Spanish Leather* and *One Too Many Mornings*. Again, all of these would get recorded by other artists, especially *The Times They Are a-Changin'*.

Daniel Mark Epstein writes:

> Andersen, one of the big four singer-songwriters of the Greenwich village scene (along with Dylan, Ochs, and Paxton), believes that folk music provided the sound track for the pageantry of the early sixties. "Young people growing up during those times were ready for change . . . spearheading this was the singer-songwriter movement."And Dylan was at the cutting edge of it. "The whole thing burst apart when Kennedy got killed." (116)

He had indeed established himself at the center of the folk protest movements, had in many ways been *the* artist most responsible for bringing folk music to popular consciousness. However, as he always did, he dodged away from this *persona*, and when he was given the prestigious Tom Paine Award by the National Emergency Civil Liberties Committee shortly after the assassination of John F. Kennedy, he appeared drunk and proceeded to attack the committee, even going so far as to defend Lee

Harvey Oswald as something of an Everyman. Part of Dylan's speech went: "There's no black and white, left and right to me anymore; there's only up and down and down is very close to the ground. And I'm trying to go up without thinking of anything trivial such as politics." (117)

Dylan's next album, *Another Side of Bob Dylan*, recorded in one evening in 1964, is more poetically complex, contains less straight-forward protest and social commentary, and suggests his future directions in rock-and-roll. It has been suggested that *It Ain't Me Babe,"* seemingly a simple song about rejecting a lover, is actually meant as a rejection of his role as leader of the protest movements. (118) While *Chimes of Freedom* fits into his protest songs, it moves much further into metaphorical, surrealistic images, and *My Back Pages* seems to be a self-critique on his earlier songs. *Spanish Harlem Incident* and *To Ramona* are love songs, and *I Shall Be Free* and *Motorpsycho Nightmare* are humorous surrealistic songs. Rock-and-Roll tendencies are clear in *Black Crow Blues* and *I Don't Believe You (She Acts Like We Never Have Met).*

Everything about him is changing rapidly in the mid-sixties. His down-to-earth jeans and work shirts are replaced by stylistic pants and shirts, almost carnival in nature; his shoes become the black, pointed boots popularized by the Beatles. His hair becomes a version of the Afro! And he starts wearing sunglasses. Indeed, a completely new *persona* is being consciously created. And his characteristically obscure responses to reporters become pronounced. For example, when asked about a move he was planning to make, he told television show host Les Crane it would be a cowboy horror movie, and when asked if he would play the cowboy, he responded, "No, I play my mother!" (119)

It is obvious that Bob Dylan is finding ways to avoid getting pinned down to any specific role. He is consciously dodging a *self.* He is the joker, the trickster, the enigma. And it is precisely this non-persona, created ironically by taking on multiple personas, that makes him so important.

A dramatic event is going to confirm it. But first he sends out a warning, featuring electric instruments on his next album, *Bringing it all Back Home* (April, 1965) The first single on it, *Subterranean Homesick Blues,* has the feel of Chuck Berry's *Too Much Monkey Business.* (120) *Rolling Stone Magazine* says, "Dylan delivers a proto-rap barrage of one-liners sending up America's mixed-up confusion." (121) The backside of the album was done with simple acoustic guitar and harmonica accompaniment, and consisted of four long songs, the most well known *Mr. Tambourine Man*, mainly because The Byrds had an electric hit with it. David Crosby says that the Byrds recording of it was "the first time anyone put really good poetry on the radio." (122) *Rolling Stone Magazine* writes about another classic song from the album, *It's All Over Now Baby Blue*, pointing out that: "The song is his devastating farewell to innocence, kicking Baby Blue out into the street, whether that means the end of a friendship or his abandonment of the folk scene." (123) *It's Alright Ma (I'm Only Bleeding)*, is also highly acclaimed. *Rolling Stone Magazine* says it "is dazzling, with an incredibly complicated rhyme scheme and a melody that barrels along on two notes until the flourish at the end of each verse," and rates it his seventh best song ever. (124)

Then came the event. Bob Dylan had performed at the Newport Folk Festival in 1963 and 1964, but this year was the headliner, and was determined to perform electric music, going against the firm folk music refusal to use electric instruments because they go against the whole designation of folk music. Bob Dylan, however, was going to turn on the very group that had originally embraced him. He put together a pickup band consisting mainly of members of the Paul Butterfield Blues Band, Mike Bloomfield (guitar), Sam Lay (drums), and Jerome Arnold (bass), plus Al Kooper (organ) and Barry Goldberg (piano). Accounts vary as to just what all went wrong, with the main focus on folk singer icon Pete Seeger's response, suggesting he even attempted to rip out the electric chords to stop the performance. Others, including band member Kooper, claim the problem was more the simple fact that the sound quality was very poor. Whatever the specific reasons, Dylan only played three songs and got booed off the stage. When he returned to the stage with just an acoustic guitar, he played *It's All Over Now Baby Blue,* what *Rolling Stone Magazine* calls his "hard-ass response." (125)

The response to his performance from the folk community was strongly negative. Ewan MacColl wrote: "Our traditional songs and ballads are the creations of extraordinarily talented artists working inside disciplines formulated over time . . . 'But what of Bobby Dylan?' scream the outraged teenagers . . . Only a completely non-critical audience, nourished on the watery pap of pop music, could have fallen for such tenth-rated drivel." (126)

Just four days later, Dylan recorded *Positively 4th Street*, a song filled with vengeance and paranoia and generally interpreted as his response to being rejected by his former friends in the folk community.

Then came what is often considered not only Dylan's greatest song, but perhaps the greatest song of all time, *Like a Rolling Stone.* (127) It peaked at #2 in the United States and #4 in the United Kingdom charts. But it has been credited with altering popular music forever. Bono (lead singer for the group U2) stated for *Rolling Stone Magazine* that "Bob Dylan's sneer on "Like a Rolling Stone" turns wine to vinegar. It's a black eye of a pop song. The verbal pugilism on display here cracks open songwriting for a generation and leaves the listener on the canvas. "Like a Rolling Stone" is the birth of an iconoclast that will give the rock era its greatest voice and vandal." (128) Bruce Springsteen, in his speech during Dylan's inauguration into the Rock and Roll Hall of Fame, said that it was a "snare shot [that] sounded like somebody'd kicked open the door to your mind." (129)

It was the main song on his next album, *Highway 61 Revisited*, titled after a road that led from Dylan's Minnesota home all the way to New Orleans. The title song of the album, *Highway 61 Revisited* is a "series of star-crossed characters (most famously, God and Abraham)" going down "America's 'blues highway,' while spitting venom at a series of American hypocrisies (phony patriotism, crass commercialism)." (130) All of the songs, except for *Desolation Row*, had the new mixture of electric and folk, supported by Mike Bloomfield's blues guitar and Al Kooper's organ riffs. *Desolation Row* was quintessential Dylan over-long (it is eleven minutes) parade of odds-and-ends from history (Einstein, Nero, Ezra Pound, T. S. Eliot), the Bible (Noah, Cain and Abel), fiction (Ophelia, Romeo, Cinderella), and allegory (Dr. Filth and his nurse). Mick Jagger said that it is "a wonderful collection of imagery—a fantasy Bowery—that really gets your imagination working." (131) *Ballad of a Thin Man* is the quintessential expression of a world where nothing fits, where people trying to apply traditional logic and values cannot comprehend the absurdity of the post-modern world swirling around them. A tour followed, and the reactions were mixed, many still upset over Dylan's new *persona*.

Studio efforts were also uneven, and in an attempt to rectify matters, Dylan's producer Bob Johnston set up sessions in Nashville with a number of top-of-the-line performers in addition to Dylan's sidemen Robertson and Kooper. The result is *Blonde on Blonde* (1966), the album some consider Dylan's best. *Rolling Stone Magazine* rates one of its songs, *Just Like a Woman*, Dylan's fourth best ever, saying it is "a complex portrait of adoration and disappointment, written as vengeance but sung as regret." (132) Some consider *Visions of Johanna* Dylan's best song. *Rolling Stone Magazine* rates it ninth, and writes that it is "a tour de force, a breakthrough not only for the writer but for the very possibilities of songwriting. An extended, impressionistic account of a woozy New York City night, rich in pictorial detail and erotic longing, the five long verses zigzag between Dylan's acute dissection of one woman, the tangible and available Louise, and his longing for an absent ideal." (133)

On November 22, 1965, Dylan secretly married Sara Lownds, though Dylan denied it in public. (134) In the spring of 1966, Dylan and his electric band toured Australia and Europe with Dylan playing "unplugged" for the first half and then with his band for the second half. Fans still were not ready to accept his new direction, and the tour closed with a famous confrontation between Dylan and his audience at the Manchester Free Trade Hall in England. (135) Dylan's dialogue with the Manchester audience is recorded (with subtitles) in Martin Scorsese's documentary *No Direction Home.*

July 29, 1966, Dylan crashed his 500cc Triumph Tiger 100 motorcycle on a road near his home in Woodstock, New York, throwing him to the ground. Though the extent of his injuries was never fully disclosed, Dylan said that he broke several vertebrae in his neck. Given Dylan's refusal to let people into his true self (if there is a true self), it's only to be expected that no one ever found out just what happened. No ambulance was called to the scene and Dylan was not hospitalized. Considering how pressure-filled his life had become, his biographers suggest that the crash offered him a much-needed chance to escape from the pressures. (136) Dylan confirmed this when he stated in his autobiography, "I had been in a motorcycle accident and I'd been hurt, but I recovered. Truth was that I wanted to get out of the rat race." (137) In the wake of his accident, Dylan withdrew from the public and, apart from a few select appearances, did not tour again for eight years. (138)

This is one of many intersections in Dylan's life that might be highlighted, because his multiple, changeable alter-egos are going to fragment into a kaleidoscope of reflected images. Once he was enough recovered from his accident, he began working editing film footage of his 1966 tour for *Eat the Document*, a follow-up to *Don't Look Back.* ABC television was given a rough cut of it, but it was rejected as simply incomprehensible. (139) In 1967 he recorded a number of songs with his back up group, the Hawks, at his home and in the basement of the Hawks nearby house, named "Big Pink," many of which got recorded by other groups (i.e., Julie Driscoll, *This Wheel's on Fire*; The Byrds, *You Ain't Goin' Nowhere,* and *Nothing Was Delivered*; and Manfred Mann, *The Mighty Quinn*). Columbia released an album of them in 1975, *The Basement Tapes*; and many of them appeared on various bootleg recordings through the years, eventually resulting in the release of a five-CD set titled *The Genuine Basement Tapes*, a total of 107 songs and alternate takes. The Hawks would rename themselves The Band and record *Music from Big Pink*, versions of some of these songs they first worked on with Dylan.

Dylan first recorded *I Shall Be Released* at this time and later released it in *Greatest Hits, Vol. 2* (1971). Allen Ginsberg about these songs, "In '68 [Dylan told] . . . me how he was writing shorter lines, with every line meaning something. . . . And from that time came some of the stuff . . . like *I Shall Be Released*. . . . There was to be no wasted breath." (140)

In October of 1967, Dylan returned to the recording studio in Nashville, and put together *John Wesley Harding*, a contemplative collection of shorter songs that drew on the American West and the *Bible*, notably promoting the Judeo-Christian tradition, and including the famous song *All Along the Watchtower*, which included lyrics from *Isaiah* (21: 5-9). In a somewhat ironic situation typical of Dylan and his songs, it would get recorded by perhaps the most famous of the psychedelic performers (exactly what this album is counterpointing), Jimi Hendrix, and Hendrix's version would be the one Dylan himself would claim is the definitive one. (141) *Rolling Stone Magazine* would write about it: "You could say that jokes and theft are the twin poles of Dylan's art, and this 12-line masterpiece about a joker (who believes he's being robbed) and a thief (who thinks everything's a joke) penetrates straight to the core of his work." (142)

Woody Guthrie died October 3, 1967, and Dylan made his first live appearance in twenty months at a memorial concert held in Carnegie Hall on January 20, 1968, backed by The Band.

In 1967, Dylan released *Nashville Skyline,* pushing into yet another genre of music and putting forth yet another personality. The album is a collection of mainstream country songs, and Dylan sings in the most mellow voice of his entire career. The hit single from the album is *Lay Lady Lay*. Lenny Kravitz, writing years later remembers how it was his introduction to Dylan, a very different Dylan than he would experience later in life:

> I first heard "Lay, Lady, Lay" when I was six or seven, riding around New York in the back seat of my parents' old VW Bug, listening to WABC. It was the first Bob Dylan song I remember loving. Later, when I heard another one of his songs, I wondered, "Where's that low, crooning voice?" He's singing it in a very different voice from his normal one. I thought this guy sounded like that all the time! . . . The beautiful thing about Dylan is that he is such a chameleon. He's got so many characters inside of him, like a painter with limitless amounts of color. (143)

The album included a duet with Johnny Cash, and Dylan would appear on the first episode of Cash's new television show, singing duets with him of *Girl from the North Country*, *I Threw It All Away,* and *Living the Blues*.

The famous Woodstock Festival was about to happen, but Dylan, always going against the tide, rejected offers to appear and instead went to England to be featured at the Isle of Wight rock festival, August 31, 1969. His performing and recording at this time was very uneven, and there were suggestions that perhaps his motorcycle head injuries had affected him. His next album was a doubt LP titled *Self-Portrait*, which only included a few new songs, and it got poor reviews. His next album, released later that year, *New Morning* got mixed but better reviews. In November of 1968, he had co-written *I'd Have You Anytime* with George Harrison (who recorded it and Dylan's *If Not For You* on his *All Things Must Pass* Album), and now Dylan made a surprise appearance at Harrison's 1971 *Concert for Bangladesh.*

His scattered, uneven activities and career continued. March 16-19, 1971 he recorded *Watching the River Flow* and a new version of *When I Paint My Masterpiece*. On November 4 of the same year he recorded a rare new protest song, *George Jackson*, which mourned the killing of Black Panther George Jackson in San Quentin Prison. In September of 1972, he contributed piano and harmony to Steve Goodman's album *Somebody Else's Troubles*, notably under a pseudonym (Robert Milkwood Thomas). The same year he signed on to write songs and background music and to play the role of Alias in Sam Peckinpah's film *Pat Garret and Billy the Kid*, a box office flop, but including *Knockin' on Heaven's Door*, one of Dylan's most popular songs. According to *Rolling Stone*, when Jerry Fielding, a composer brought in to help Dylan with the movie's music, first heard it, he thought "It was shit." Of course, Dylan, as usual, had the last laugh, and he also had now written and recorded a number of *cowboy songs*, yet another genre.

In 1972 his contract with Columbia Records ended, and he signed on with David Geffen's Asylum Records. His first album for them was *Planet Waves*, and he used The Band as his backing group. The album included two versions of another of his more popular songs, *Forever Young* which he claimed to have written for one of his boys (some speculate is that it was for Jakob, others that it was for Jesse; some speculate it was not for his son at all but was for Neil Young in reference to his hit *Heart of Gold*). *Rolling Stone Magazine* says "Lyrics such as 'May you have a strong foundation/When the winds of changes shift" are as universal and uplifting as Dylan has ever written." (144)

At the same time as this album came out, Columbia Records released *Dylan*, a collection of studio outtakes, mostly cover songs Dylan had recorded while still under contract to them.

In January, 1974, Dylan returned to touring. Backed by The Band, he went on a high-profile forty concert tour. *Before the Flood*, a live double album was released by Asylum Records. Dylan, however, was already unhappy with Asylum because he felt they had messed up the ticket sales of his tour and because *Planet Waves* had not sold well. So he returned to Columbia Records, who subsequently reissued the two Asylum albums under their own imprint.

By the time the tour was over, so was Dylan's relationship with his wife. He filled a small red notebook with songs about relationships and quickly recorded a new album, *Blood on the Tracks* (September, 1974). Later, he re-recorded several of the songs with production assistance from his brother David. When it was released in early 1975, it received mixed reviews. However, as time passed, it began to receive many positive reviews, and there are some who think it his best album. Rick Moody stated that it is the "truest, most honest account of a love affair from tip to stern ever put down on magnetic tape." (145) Bill Wyman said "*Blood on the Tracks* is his only flawless album and his best produced; the songs, each of them, are constructed in disciplined fashion. It is his kindest album and most dismayed, and seems in hindsight to have achieved a sublime balance between the logorrhea-plagued excess of his mid-'60s output and the self-consciously simple compositions of his post-accident years."(146) *Rolling Stone Magazine* rated the opening song, *Tangled Up in Blue*, his third best ever, saying it is a "perfect crossroads . . . where emotional truths meet the everlasting comfort of the American folk song." *Rolling Stone Magazine,* May 5, 2011, p. 58.

That summer, Dylan wrote another of his social, political songs, this one an 8:32 minute ballad about boxer Rubin "Hurricane" Carter, who had been imprisoned for the triple murder committed in Paterson, New Jersey in 1966. After visiting Carter in jail, Dylan was convinced he had been wrongly imprisoned, and performed the song at every date of his Rolling Thunder Revue Tour, a tour that featured many, many performers from the resurgent Greenwich Village folk scene, including T-Bone Burnett, Ramblin' Jack Elliott, Joni Mitchell, David Mansfield, Roger McGuinn, Mick Ronso, Joan Baez, and Beat poet Allen Ginsberg, who had become a huge fan of Dylan.

Halfway through the tour, Dylan released another album, *Desire*, featuring a number of travelogue-like narrative songs. The second half of the tour was documented in a television special and LP, both titled *Hard Rain,* and in 2002, *Live 1975,* an album of the first half of the tour came out. Dylan released a nearly four-hour film *Renaldo and Clara* that mixed in footage of the tour in 1978, but it was poorly received, and later that year he rereleased it in a much shorter version.

In November, 1976, he appeared at The Band's farewell concert, along with many other guests, including Joni Mitchell, Muddy Waters, Van Morrison, and Neil Young. Martin Scorsese chronicled it in *The Last Waltz*, released in 1978. It included about half of Dylan's set.

In 1976 Dylan also wrote and performed *Sign Language* with Eric Clapton for Clapton's album *No Reason to Cry.*

In 1978, Dylan assembled an eight piece band and three back-up singers to go on a 114 show tour of the Far East, Europe, and the U. S., recording the concerts in Tokyo and releasing them as a live double album, *Bob Dylan at Budokan.* Reviews were generally poor for both the tour and album, but the tour grossed over $20 million, which Dylan claimed he needed because of the cost of his divorce. In April and May, he recorded *Street-Legal*, another album that received mixed reviews, mainly because it suffered from poor sound recording and mixing.

It was time for a new Bob Dylan persona. The Jewish boy raised in a small, close knit town in northern Minnesota, who had wanted to be the latest version of Little Richard, the latest version of Woody Guthrie, the foremost protest and social folk singer of his generation, the rock star, the country singer, the . . . , decided to take five months at the beginning of 1979 and attend Bible school. He emerged a *born-again Christian.* (147)

And he was sincere (is that a contradiction when talking about Bob Dylan?). Two albums of Christian gospel music followed. *Slow Train Coming* (1979) featured the guitar accompaniment of Mark Knopfler (of Dire Straits), and was produced by Jerry Wexler, who recalled Dylan laying an evangelical trip on him, to which he replied: "Bob, you're dealing with a sixty-two-year old Jewish atheist. Let's just make an album." (148) The album they made earned Dylan a Grammy Award for Best Male Vocalist for the best known song on it, *Gotta Serve Somebody.* The second album, *Saved* (1980) was not so well received. As usual, Dylan was unfazed. From the fall of 1979 through the spring of 1980, Dylan refused to play his past secular music.

Not surprisingly, not everyone bought into his new persona. John Lennon, for example, in response to *Gotta Serve Somebody* came out with the song *Serve Yourself.* By the fall of 1980, Dylan was beginning to move back into his secular music, mixing it with his Christian songs.

However, he released *Shot of Love* in 1981, with the song *Every Grain of Sand*, which Bono says is "like one of the great Psalms of David." (149) *Rolling Stone Magazine* says: "Equal parts Blakean mysticism and biblical resonance, the song abandons the self-righteousness that plagued Dylan's religious work to offer a desperate prayer for salvation." (150)

In 1983, he released *Infidels*, a well received album, but his work throughout the decade would continue to have the same uneven quality that had been coming out for years. Between July, 1984 and March, 1985, he recorded *Empire Burlesque*. He sang on the USA for Africa fundraising song, *We Are the World*, and appeared at the Live Aid concert, July 13, 1985.

In April, 1986, he even did a bit of rap or hip-hop music on the opening verse of *Street Rock* for *Kingdom Blow*, an album by Kurtis Blow. Dylan's next studio album, *Knocked Out Loaded*, came out July, 1986. It covered songs by Little Junior Parker and Kris Kristofferson, a traditional hymn (*Precious Memories*), collaborations with Tom Petty, Sam Sheppard, and Carole Bayer Sager, and two of his own compositions. Again, it had mixed reviews, and was his first not to make the Top 50 since *Freewheelin'* (1963). However, some have since praised the eleven minute *Brownsville Girl* co-written with Sam Sheppard as a work of genius. Erlewine, Stephen Thomas. (151)

Throughout 1986 and 1987, he toured extensively with Tom Petty and the Heartbreakers, and also toured a bit with the Grateful Dead, resulting in a live album *Dylan & the Dead,* that got terrible reviews. In 1987, he starred in and contributed two songs to Richard Marquand's movie, *Hearts of Fire,* as usual for his film work, a flop. In January of 1988, he was inducted into the Rock-and-Roll Hall of Fame. In May, he released *Down in the Groove,* another poor reviewed album. This disappointment, however, was followed by the successful band he co-founded with George Harrison, Jeff Lynne, Roy Orbison, and Tom Petty, *The Traveling Wilburys,* which had a hit multi-platinum album, *The Traveling Wilburys, Vol.1*, featuring some of Dylan's songs that were described as his most accessible in years. Unfortunately, Roy Orbison died in December, 1988; but the remaining four recorded a second album May, 1990, with the confusing title, *Traveling Wilburys, Vol. 3.*

As usual, he had other projects going at the same time. June 7, 1988, he began touring with a small, ever evolving backup band in what came to be known as The Never Ending Tour. He also put out his own album, *Oh Mercy*, produced by Daniel Lanois, which was praised as his best of the decade. One of the songs, *Most of the Time*, was later prominently featured in the film *High Fidelity*; another, *What Was it You Wanted?* got interpreted as commentary on fans and critics, and a third, *Ring Them Bells* struck listeners as a re-affirmation of his faith.

Then, in 1990, he recorded *Under the Red Sky,* backed by the likes of George Harrison, Slash, David Crosby, Bruce Hornsby, Stevie Ray Vaughan, and Elton John. However, despite these huge talents, the album got bad reviews and sold poorly. Nevertheless, by now an icon, in 1991, he was awarded a Grammy Lifetime Achievement Award, and performed his song *Masters of War* as commentary on the Gulf War currently taking place against Saddam Hussein. *The Bootleg Series, Vol. 1*-3, came out in 1991, and included *Blind Willie McTell,* one of his few masterpieces from the early eighties. Next came two albums full of old folk and blues songs, *Good as I Been to You* (1992) and *World Gone Wrong* (1993). In November, 1994, he recorded two live shows for MTV Unplugged, which resulted in a similarly titled album. He later said he wanted to perform a set of traditional songs, but Sony executives insisted on a greatest hits package. In 1994, Random House published *Drawn Blank,* a collection of his drawings. Macintyre, James (August 10, 2007). (152)

He began recording a new album in January, 1997, but was hospitalized with a life-threatening heart infection and not only stopped the recording sessions for a time but also cancelled a planned European tour. However, he recovered quickly, and performed for Pope John Paul II the following fall. By September, his new album was ready to be released, and *Time Out of Mind*, a collection of darker songs came out to positive reviews that won him his first solo Album of the Year Grammy Award. The same year, President Bill Clinton presented him with a Kennedy Center Honor tribute, saying: "He probably had more impact on people of my generation than any other creative artist." (153)

He entered the new millennium by winning his first Oscar for the dark song *Things Have Changed,* for the movie *Wonder Boys.* His next album, *Love and Theft*, came out September 11, 2001, and again was well received and nominated for several Grammy awards. It included *Mississippi*, which Sheryl Crow says is Dylan writing like a short-story writer, like Steinbeck or Mark Twain—creating a story, but making these classical, sweeping statements." *Rolling Stone Magazine,* May 26, p. 63. In 2003, he was involved in the CD project *Gotta Serve Somebody: The Gospel Songs of Bob Dylan*, and released yet another poor film, *Masked & Anonymous*, which, however bad it might have been, had a perfect title for the real Bob Dylan.

October, 2004, he published the first part of his autobiography, *Chronicles: Volume One,* a confusing work that gave a lot of space to his first year in New York (1961-1962) and virtually ignored the mid-sixties, and then, curiously devoted chapters to the 1970 album *New Morning* and the 1989 album *Oh Mercy.* Nevertheless, it reached number two on the

New York Times Best Sellers Lists and was nominated for a National Book Award. The following year, Martin Scorsese can out with an acclaimed film biography of Dylan, *No Direction Home*, which received a Peabody Award, April, 2006, and a Columbia-DuPont Award, January, 2007.

On May 3, 2006, Dylan took on yet another role, this time as a DJ hosting a well received *Theme Time Radio Hour* for *XM Satellite Radio*, where he played classic and obscure songs from the 1930s to the present day revolving around chosen themes.

On August 29, 2009, he released *Modern Times*, another well received album that entered the U. S. charts at number one, the first one to do so since *Desire*, 1976. It was nominated for three Grammy Awards and won for Best Contemporary Folk/Americana Album. Dylan also won Best Solo Rock Vocal Performance for *Someday Baby*. *Rolling Stone Magazine* named it Album of the Year. On the same day it was released, iTunes Music Store released *Bob Dylan: The Collection*, a digital box set containing all of his albums, a total of 773 tracks plus 42 rare and unreleased tracks.

In August, 2007, Todd Haynes released an award-winning film biography of Dylan, *I'm Not There*, a brilliant representation of Dylan's kaleidoscopic, harlequin, chameleon life. Six different actors (one a woman and one a black boy) represent Dylan (Christian Bale, Cate Blanchett, Marcus Carl Franklin, Richard Gere, Heath Ledger, and Ben Wishaw). The title is appropriately taken from a previously unreleased Dylan song from 1967, and it is a perfect phrase to apply to Dylan, who has spent a life creating and recreating himself in different personas to ultimately deny any one real person. One might well ask, as in the case of Elizabeth in *A Bird's Nest*, if a *real* person exists behind the multiple personalities, behind the masks. In a comment on why six actors were employed to portray different facets of Dylan's personality, Haynes wrote:

> The minute you try to grab hold of Dylan, he's no longer where he was. He's like a flame: If you try to hold him in your hand you'll surely get burned. Dylan's life of change and constant disappearances and constant transformations makes you yearn to hold him, and to nail him down. And that's why his fan base is so obsessive, so desirous of finding the truth and the absolutes and the answers to him - things that Dylan will never provide and will only frustrate.... Dylan is difficult and mysterious and evasive and frustrating, and it only makes you identify with him all the more as he skirts identity. (154)

Dylan continued his elusive career, hotter than ever, On October 1, 2007, Columbia Records released the triple CD retrospective album

Dylan, anthologizing his entire career under the Dylan 07 logo. As part of this campaign, Mark Ronson produced a re-mix of Dylan's 1966 tune *Most Likely You Go Your Way (And I'll Go Mine),* which was released as a maxi-single, the first time Dylan had sanctioned a re-mix of one of his classic recordings.

And yet another Dylan appeared. Actually, it had already surfaced in 2004, when Dylan appeared in a television advertisement for Victoria's Secret lingerie. This raised a few eyebrows; the leader of the movements against the big business, commercialized world was making commercials? For Victoria's Secret? Now, three years later, in October 2007, he participated in a multi-media campaign for the 2008 Cadillac Escalade. Then, in 2009, he gave the highest profile endorsement of his career, appearing with rapper Will.i.am in a Pepsi advertisement that debuted during the telecast of Super Bowl XLIII. The advertisement, broadcast to a record audience of 98 million viewers, opened with Dylan singing the first verse of *Forever Young* followed by Will.i.am doing a hip hop version of the song's third and final verse. Hard for Dylan to dodge around this new persona as a man simply wanting to make money!

And the release of Volume 8 of his *Bootleg Series, Tell Tale Signs: Rare and Unreleased, 1989-2006*, in two CD set ($18.99) or more expensive three-CD version with a 150 page book ($129.99) brought a number of complaints about “rip-off packaging.” (155). Nevertheless, it was also an acclaimed collection, praised by critics for revealing Dylan’s amazing breadth of creativity. (156)

In October, 2007, his persona as a visual artist also got more attention. An exhibit of his art, *The Drawn Blank Series*, opened at the Kunstsammlungen in Chemnitz, Germany, showcasing more than 200 watercolors and gouaches made earlier in 2007 from the original drawings, and premiering the release of the book *Bob Dylan: The Drawn Blank Series*, which includes 170 reproductions from the series.

Then Dylan released *Together Through Life* (April 28, 2009), the result of an arrangement with film director Olivier Dahan to write a song for his movie, *My Own Love Song*. Nine of the ten songs on it are credited as being co-written with Robert Hunter. It received favorable reviews, though was not considered a very important addition to his work. However, because Dylan was so hot, it debuted at number one on the Billboard 200, making Dylan the oldest artist (67) to accomplish that.

Then came yet another side to Dylan, a Christmas album, *Christmas in the Heart* (October 13, 2009), what appears to be a fairly straight-forward rendition of such standards as *Little Drummer Boy*, *Winter Wonderland,* and *Here Comes Santa Claus*, profits going to the charities Feeding

America, Crisis, and World Food Program. When asked by journalist Bill Flanagan why he had performed the songs in such a traditional style, he responded: "There wasn't any other way to play it. These songs are part of my life, just like folk songs. You have to play them straight too." (157)

October 18, 2010, Volume 9 of the *Bootleg Series: The Witmark Demos*, made up of 47 demo recordings of songs taped between 1962-1964 came out. In the same week Sony released *Bob Dylan: The Original Mono Recordings*, a box set of his eight earliest albums in their original mono mix. April 12, 2011, Legacy Recordings released *Bob Dylan in Concert—Brandeis University, 1963*.

While everyone who had any material from Dylan's past was cashing in, Dylan was continuing his Never Ending Tour that had begun in 1988, playing roughly 100 dates a year. As critics and fans have come to expect, each performance is unique, depending on Dylan's mood that night. He has shown almost no interest in bonding with his audience and seems often completely unaware they are even in the building. Also, his singing tends to become, as Neil McCormick states, "a one-dimensional growl with which he chews up, mangles and spits out the greatest lyrics ever written so that they are effectively unrecognizable." (158)

In January, 2011, he took his tour to the Orient, including China, which generated controversy because of China's human rights problems, and because it was assumed they would censor him. However, according to Dylan, they did not.

From September, 2010, through April, 2011, *The Brazil Series,* forty of his acrylic paintings were exhibited in the National Gallery of Denmark.

As of this writing, Dylan continues his multi-faceted life and career, ever the enigma.

His views on religion have been especially confusing. He was born Jewish, then seemed to have little concern for organized religion, other than using the *Bible* as a source of allusions, until after his motor-cycle accident, and his seemingly sudden conversion to Christianity in 1979. However, by 1984, he was distancing himself from his born-again label, directing saying to Kurt Loder of *Rolling Stone Magazine*, "I've never said I'm born again. That's just a media term. I don't think I've been agnostic. I've always thought there's a superior power, that this is not the real world and that there's a world to come." When Loder ask if he belonged to any specific church or synagogue, Dylan laughingly replied, "Not really. Uh, the Church of the Poison Mind." (159) In 1997, he told David Gates of *Newsweek*:

> Here's the thing with me and the religious thing. This is the flat-out truth: I find the religiosity and philosophy in the music. I don't find it anywhere

> else. Songs like "Let Me Rest on a Peaceful Mountain" or "I Saw the Light"—that's my religion. I don't adhere to rabbis, preachers, evangelists, all of that. I've learned more from the songs than I've learned from any of this kind of entity. The songs are my lexicon. I believe the songs. (160)

In a *New York* Times interview of the same year, he told journalist Jon Pareles that he subscribes to no organized religion. (161) Interestingly complicating all this even more, he has been associated with the Chabad Lubavitch movement, and has privately participated in Jewish religious events, including the Bar Mitzvahs of his sons. At the same time, he has continued to perform traditional Christian songs, and in a 2004 interview with Ed Bradley for *60 Minutes* claimed that "the only person you have to think twice about lying to is either yourself or God, and told Bill Flanagan in 2009, "I am a true believer." (162)

In my book *Insanity and Genius*, I discuss the brilliant yet clearly insane artist Richard Dadd, who believed he was sent by Isis to murder evil people, and brutally carried out the perceived assignment to kill his father. However, while living out the remainder of his life in an asylum, he created *The Fairy-Feller's Masterpiece,* a complex painting that provides an intricate interweaving of realities, leaving us to sort through and question our own comprehension of reality. As a result, he became an enigma, a person whose *self* disappears into multiple images, a fractured mirror of shards, each refracting an enticing and yet frustrating piece of the human puzzle. He became a joker, communicating in a mysterious language of figurative meanings, each demanding attention, each questioning the others, each multiplying the mysteries of life until a thick, rich, liquid tapestry engulfs reality and denies clarity in an intoxicating hallucinogenic dream.

This is what Bob Dylan does, eluding his *self* until we are all forced to face the eternal ocean of silence behind the music and struggle to swim through the endlessly criss-crossing waves on the surface of the water, always knowing the real truths lie deep beneath the surface.

Notes

1. *Chicago Poems*, Harcourt, 1944.
2. *The Scapegoat,* Daphne du Maurier, 1957; rpt. Univ. of Pennsylvania, 2000.
3. *Siebenkas,* Jean Paul, 1796; rpt. (German), Reclam Philipp Jun, 1983.
4. "Brain electrodes conjure up ghostly visions," Nature News, nature.com, Sept. 20, 2006.
5. See *The Psychology of Anomalous Experience: A Cognitive Approach*, Graham F. Reed, Prometheus Books, Rev Sub. edition September 1988.
6. Betty T. Bennett. *The Letters of Mary Wollstonecraft Shelley.* Johns Hopkins University Press, Baltimore, 1980. Volume 1, page 245.
7. Shelley, Percy. *Prometheus Unbound.* London: C and J Ollier, 1820.
8. Walton, Izaak. *Life of Dr. John Donne.* Fourth edition, 1675.
9. Bald, R.C. *John Donne: a Life.* Oxford University Press, 1970.
10. Bennett, R.E. "Donne's Letters from the Continent in 1611-12." *Philological Quarterly,* xix (1940), 66-78.
11. Sandburg, Carl. *Abraham Lincoln: The Prairie Years.* Harcourt, Brace and Co., New York, 1926. Volume 2, Chapter 165, pp.423-4.
12. Noah Brooks, *Washington in Lincoln's Time,* Century Books: New York, 1895.
13. Noah Brooks, *Washington in Lincoln's Time.* Century, New York, 1895. Reprinted as *Washington, D.C., in Lincoln's Time.* Edited by Herbert Mitgang. Quadrangle Books, Chicago, 1971. University of Georgia Press, Athens, 1989. First ed., pages 220-221. Mitgang's ed., pages 198-200.
14. *The Autobiography of Wolfgang von Goethe.* Translated by John Oxenford. Horizon Press, 1969.
15. Christina Hole, *Haunted England, A Survey of English Ghost Lore*, B. T. Batsford. 1941, pp. 21–22.
16. Fyodor Dostoevsky, *The Double,* 1846; rpt., Doubleday, Coustance Garnett, trans., 1960.
17. Fyodor Dostoevsky, *The Double,* 1846; rpt., Doubleday, Coustance Garnett, trans., 1960, pp. 43-44.
18. Fyodor Dostoevsky, *The Double,* 1846; rpt., Doubleday, Coustance Garnett, trans., 1960, pp. 44-45.
19. Fyodor Dostoevsky, *The Double,* 1846; rpt., Doubleday, Coustance Garnett, trans., 1960, pp. 51-52.
20. Fyodor Dostoevsky, *The Double,* 1846; rpt., Doubleday, Coustance Garnett, trans., 1960, p. 52.
21. Fyodor Dostoevsky, *The Double,* 1846; rpt., Doubleday, Coustance Garnett, trans., 1960, p. 57.
22. Fyodor Dostoevsky, *The Double,* 1846; rpt., Doubleday, Coustance Garnett, trans., 1960, p. 62.
23. Fyodor Dostoevsky, *The Double,* 1846; rpt., Doubleday, Coustance Garnett, trans., 1960, p. 64.
24. Fyodor Dostoevsky, *The Double,* 1846; rpt., Doubleday, Coustance Garnett, trans., 1960, p. 65.

25. Fyodor Dostoevsky, *The Double,* 1846; rpt., Doubleday, Coustance Garnett, trans., 1960, p. 66.
26. Fyodor Dostoevsky, *The Double,* 1846; rpt., Doubleday, Coustance Garnett, trans., 1960, p. 81.
27. Fyodor Dostoevsky, *The Double,* 1846; rpt., Doubleday, Coustance Garnett, trans., 1960, p. 90.
28. Fyodor Dostoevsky, *The Double,* 1846; rpt., Doubleday, Coustance Garnett, trans., 1960, p. 107.
29. Fyodor Dostoevsky, *The Double,* 1846; rpt., Doubleday, Coustance Garnett, trans., 1960, p. 107.
30. Fyodor Dostoevsky, *The Double,* 1846; rpt., Doubleday, Coustance Garnett, trans., 1960, p. 162.
31. Fyodor Dostoevsky, *The Double,* 1846; rpt., Doubleday, Coustance Garnett, trans., 1960, p. 167.
32. Fyodor Dostoevsky, *The Double,* 1846; rpt., Doubleday, Coustance Garnett, trans., 1960, p. 171.
33. Fyodor Dostoevsky, *The Double,* 1846; rpt., Doubleday, Coustance Garnett, trans., 1960, p. 174.
34. Fyodor Dostoevsky, *The Double,* 1846; rpt., Doubleday, Coustance Garnett, trans., 1960p. 175.
35. Fyodor Dostoevsky, *The Double,* 1846; rpt., Doubleday, Coustance Garnett, trans., 1960, p. 176.
36. Fyodor Dostoevsky, *The Double,* 1846; rpt., Doubleday, Coustance Garnett, trans., 1960, p. 176.
37. Draft K, a letter to Fliess, Jan. 1, 1896.
38. See Rycroft, Charles, *A Critical Dictionary of Psychoanalysis* London: Penguin, 1968; J. Laplanche and J-B Pontalis, *The Language of Psychoanalysis* trans: Donald Nicholson-Smith London: Hogarth Press and the Institute of Psychoanalysis, 1973, p. 296.
39. Draft H, a letter to Fliess, pp. 109-110, Jan. 24, 1895.
40. M. Klein, "Notes on Some Schizoid Mechanisms," *Developments in Psychoanalysis*, London, Hogarth Press, 1946.
41. "Dostoevsky's Use of Projection: Psychic Mechanism as Literary Form in 'The Double,'" Univ. of Calif., Los Angeles.
42. Freud, Sigmund. "The Uncanny." The Standard Edition of the Complete Psychological Works of Sigmund Freud. Translated by James Strachey et al. Volume 17. London: The Hogarth Press, 1955, p. 220.
43. Freud, Sigmund. "The Uncanny." The Standard Edition of the Complete Psychological Works of Sigmund Freud. Translated by James Strachey et al. Volume 17. London: The Hogarth Press, 1955, p.226.
44. Freud, Sigmund. "The Uncanny." The Standard Edition of the Complete Psychological Works of Sigmund Freud. Translated by James Strachey et al. Volume 17. London: The Hogarth Press, 1955, p. 241.
45. Freud, Sigmund. "The Uncanny." The Standard Edition of the Complete Psychological Works of Sigmund Freud. Translated by James Strachey et al. Volume 17. London: The Hogarth Press, 1955, p. 235.

46. Freud, Sigmund. "The Uncanny." The Standard Edition of the Complete Psychological Works of Sigmund Freud. Translated by James Strachey et al. Volume 17. London: The Hogarth Press, 1955, 235.
47. Freud, Sigmund. "The Uncanny." The Standard Edition of the Complete Psychological Works of Sigmund Freud. Translated by James Strachey et al. Volume 17. London: The Hogarth Press, 1955, p. 236.
48. Freud, Sigmund. "The Uncanny." The Standard Edition of the Complete Psychological Works of Sigmund Freud. Translated by James Strachey et al. Volume 17. London: The Hogarth Press, 1955, p. 238.
49. *Tales of Mystery and Imagination*, Burton's Gentleman's Magazine, 1839; rpt., *Tales of the Grotesque and Arabesque*, 1840; rpt. Octopus Books, 1981.
50. 1966; trans., Heinemann Educational Books, 1969.
51. 1827 (October): *Buch der Lieder* ("Book of Songs").
52. Brian Newbould, *Schubert: The Music and the Man*. University of California Press, 1997.
53. The film was remade in 1926, 1935, and 2004 under the same title *The Student of Prague.* Nazi martyr Horst Wessel, then a member of the same Corps (student fraternity) of which Ewers had been a member, appears as an extra in a 1926 version of the movie, also written by Ewers.
54. Otto Rank, "Der doppelganger," *Imago: Zeitschrift fur Anwendung der Psychoanalyse auf die Geisteswissenschaften,* 1914; rpt., *The Double,* trans., Harry Tucker, Jr., Univ. of North Carolina, 1971, pp. 4-6.
55. Otto Rank, "Der doppelganger," *Imago: Zeitschrift fur Anwendung der Psychoanalyse auf die Geisteswissenschaften,* 1914; rpt., *The Double,* trans., Harry Tucker, Jr., Univ. of North Carolina, 1971, pp. 6-7.
56. *The Complete Grimm's Fairy Tales*, Pantheon Books, 1944, pp. 249-259.
57. 2 Corinthians, 4: 1-2, p. 138, The Holy Bible, King James Version; rpt., Thomas Nelson, 1970.
58. 2 Corinthians, 4: 1-2, p. 138, The Holy Bible, King James Version; rpt., Thomas Nelson, 1970.
59. Jean Chevalier and Alian Gheerbrant, *A Dictionary of Symbols,* 1969; trans. by John Buchanan-Brown, Penguin, 1996, p. 659.
60. Tony Crisp, *Dream Dictionary,* Barnes & Noble, 2002, p. 277 and p. 430.
61. rpt., Dover, 1994. Other important versions of the Faust story not discussed here include: Gotthold Lessing, *D. Faust* (fragment, 1784); Friedrich Maximilian Klinger, *Faust Leben, Taten und Höllenfahrt*, 1791; Adalbert von Chamisso, *Faust: Ein Versuch,* 1804, and *Peter Schlemihls wundersame Geschichte,* 1813; Christian Dietrich Grabbe, *Don Juan und Faust*, 1829; Nikolaus Lenau, *Faust: Ein Gedicht*, 1836; Woldemar Nürnberger. Josephus Faust: Ein Gedicht, 1847; Heinrich Heine. *Doktor Faust: Ein Tanzpoem, nebst kuriosen Berichten über Teufel, Hexen und Dichtkunst*, 1851; Vischer, Friedrich Theodor, *Faust: Der Tragödie dritter Teil*, 1862; and Paul Valéry. *Mon Faust*, 1945; Some of the important musical compositions based on the legend include: Hector Berlioz, *The Damnation of Faust*, 1846, a dramatic cantata based on a French version of Goethe's work by Gerard de Nerval, also staged as an opera; Charles Gounod, *Faust*, 1859, an opera based on part one of Goethe's work, libretto by Jules Barbier

and Michel Carré; Franz Liszt, *The Mephisto Waltzes,* four waltzes composed by Franz Liszt in 1859-62, 1880–81, 1883 and 1885. Numbers 1-2 were composed for orchestra, later arranged for piano, piano duet and two pianos; 3 and 4 were written for piano only. Of the four, the first is the most popular and has been frequently performed in concert and recorded. *The Bagatelle sans tonalité (Bagatelle without tonality; also Bagatelle ohne Tonart)* is sometimes included with Liszt's *Mephisto Waltzes*. The manuscript bears the title *Fourth Mephisto Waltz*, and may have been intended to replace the *Fourth Mephisto Waltz*. Critics point out the similarity in tonal center between these two pieces (D major) as confirmation of their composition shortly after one other in 1885, as well as Liszt's initial intent with the *Bagatelle*. One other composition to be considered is the *Mephisto Polka* which, while not a waltz, follows the same program as the other Mephisto works.

62. *Der Tragödie erster Teil* (translated as: *Faust: The First Part of the Tragedy*), 1829, and *Faust. Der Tragödie zweiter Teil: Faust: The Second Part of the Tragedy*, 1832; trans., Walter Kaufmann, 1962.

63. 1947; rpt., Vintige, 1997.

64. 1667; rpt., New York: Oxford Univ., 2004.

65. William Blake, *The Marriage of Heaven and* Hell, 1790-1793; rpt., Oxford, 1975; see also "Paradise Lost", *The Broadview Anthology of British Literature, A (Concise ed.),* J. Black, ed., Peterborough, Ontario: Broadview Press, March, 2007, pp. 996–1061.

66. W. H. Marshall, "Paradise Lost: Felix Culpa and the Problem of Structure," *Modern Language Notes* 76 (1), January, 1961, pp. 15–20.

67. *Milton's Satan*, Paul Stevens, Univ. of Toronto, http://gypsyscholarship.blogspot.com/2010/12/paul-stevens-miltons-satan.html.

68. *A Preface to Paradise Lost: Being the Ballard Matthews Lectures Delivered at University College*, North Wales, 1941; Oxford, 1961.

69. *Surprised by Sin,* Harvard University Press; 2 edition, March 15, 1998; and *How Milton Works*, Belknap Press of Harvard University Press, October 15, 2003.

70. *Qur'an* 7: 27; ed., Sayed A. A. Razwy, Trans., Abdullah Yusuf Ali, published by Tahrike Tarsile; 25th edition, January 1, 2009.

71. *Qur'an*, 10:44 and 7:12; ed., Sayed A. A. Razwy, Trans., Abdullah Yusuf Ali, published by Tahrike Tarsile; 25th edition, January 1, 2009.

72. *Qur'an*, 18:50, 15:27, and 38:76; ed., Sayed A. A. Razwy, Trans., Abdullah Yusuf Ali, published by Tahrike Tarsile; 25th edition, January 1, 2009.

73. Esposito, 2003, p. 279.

74. Cyril Glasse, Altamirz, 2001, p. 189.

75. *The Power of Myth: Joseph Campbell with Bill Moyers,* Betty Sue Flowers, ed., Doubleday, 1988, pp. 255-256.

76. *Qur'an,* 7: 11-12; ed., Sayed A. A. Razwy, Trans., Abdullah Yusuf Ali, published by Tahrike Tarsile; 25th edition, January 1, 2009.

77. *The Adventures of New Year's Eve, Das verlorene Spiegelbild* ("The Lost Reflection") from *Die Abenteuer der Silvester-Nacht* ("The Adventures of New Year's Eve"), 1814; rpt., *Tales of Hoffman*, G.G. Harrap, 1932, pp. 123-148.

78. *The Adventures of New Year's Eve*, *Das verlorene Spiegelbild* ("The Lost Reflection") from *Die Abenteuer der Silvester-Nacht* ("The Adventures of New Year's Eve"), 1814; rpt., *Tales of Hoffman*, G.G. Harrap, 1932, p. 123.
79. Otto Rank, "Der doppelganger," *Imago: Zeitschrift fur Anwendung der Psychoanalyse auf die Geisteswissenschaften,* 1914; rpt., *The Double,* trans., Harry Tucker, Jr., Univ. of North Carolina, 1971, p. 10.
80. *Hans Christian Andersen: Eighty Fairy Tales, trans., R.P. keigwin, Pantheon Books, 1982,* pp. 193-202.
81. Otto Rank, "Der doppelganger," *Imago: Zeitschrift fur Anwendung der Psychoanalyse auf die Geisteswissenschaften,* 1914; rpt., *The Double,* trans., Harry Tucker, Jr., Univ. of North Carolina, 1971, p. 11.
82. *The Horla,* 1887; rpt., *The Horla and Other Stories*, Wildside Press, 2007.
83. Farrar, Straus and Young, 1954.
84. Michael J. Hayde, *Flights of Fantasy*. Albany: BearManor Media., 2009; Tom De Haven, *Our Hero: Superman on Earth*. New Haven, 2009.
85. Les Daniels, *Batman: The Complete History*, Chronicle Books, 1999; and Bill Boichel, "Batman: Commodity as Myth." *The Many Lives of the Batman: Critical Approaches to a Superhero and His Media*. Routledge: London, 1991.
86. SimchaWeinstein, *Up, Up, and Oy Vey!*. Baltimore, Maryland: Leviathan Press. June 19,2006, pp. 82–97.
87. Tom DeFalco, *The Hulk: The Incredible Guide*. London: DK Publishing, May 5, 2003, p. 200.
88. *Sybil*, Flora Rheta Schreiber, Warner, 1974.
89. M. Pendergrast, *American Journal of Clinical Hypnosis, vol.* 50, 1996, pp. 273–283*; Victims of memory: sex abuse accusations and shattered lives*, Upper Access Books, p. 153; Joan Acocella, *Creating Hysteria: Women and Multiple Personality Disorder*. New York: Jossey-Bass, 1979.
90. Released on DVD by 20th Century Fox; Studio Classics, 2004.
91. Chris A. Costner, Chris, *A Mind of My Own: The Woman Who Was Known As "Eve" Tells the Story of Her Triumph over Multiple Personality Disorder*. William Morrow & Co, 1989.
92. Farrar, Straus and Young, 1954.
93. Morton Prince, *The Dissociation of a Personality,* 1905.
94. *I Was That Masked Man*, by Clayton Moore with Frank Thompson, Taylor Publishing Company, 1996.
95. Grace Bradley Boyd and Michael Cochran, *Hopalong Cassidy: An American Legend* Gemstone, York, Pennsylvania, 2008.
96. Robert W. Phillips, *Roy* Rogers, MacFarland Press, 1995; Robert W. Phillips, *Roy Rogers: A Biography, Radio History, Television Career Chronicle, Discography, Filmography, Comicography, Merchandising and Advertising History, Collectibles Description, Bibliography, and Index*, McFarland, 1995, pp. 13-15.
97. Robert S. Birchard, *King Cowboy: Tom Mix and the Movies*, Burbank: Riverwood Press, 1993; Ben Ohmart, *It's That Time Again* Albany: BearManor Media, 2002; David W. Menefee, *The First Male Stars: Men of the Silent Era* Albany: Bear Manor Media, 2007; Olive Stokes Mix with Eric Heath, *The*

Fabulous Tom Mix, New York: Prentice-Hall, Inc., 1957; Paul E. Mix, *The Life and Legend of Tom Mix*, New York: A. S. Barnes and Company, 1972; Jeanine Basinger, *Silent Stars*, 1999; Richard D. Jensen, "The Amazing Tom Mix: The Most Famous Cowboy of the Movies" iUniverse, Inc, 2005.
98. Holly George-Warren, Holly. *Public Cowboy no. 1 : The Life and Times of Gene Autry*. New York: Oxford University Press. 2007; Thomas A. DeLong, *The Mighty Music Box*, Amber Crest Books, Los Angeles, California; *The Encyclopedia of Oklahoma History and Culture; Autry, Gene; Nathaniel Shilkret: Sixty Years in the Music Business*, Scarecrow Press, Lanham, Md., 2005; Phil Hardy, *The Encyclopedia of Western Movies,* London: Octopus, 1985.
99. Randy Roberts and James S. Olson, *John Wayne: American*. New York: Free Press, 1995; James T. Campbell, "Print the Legend: John Wayne and Postwar American Culture". *Reviews in American History*, Volume 28, Number 3, September 2000, pp. 465–477; Donald Shepherd and Robert Slatzer, with Dave Grayson. *Duke: The Life and Times of John Wayne*. New York: Doubleday, 1985; Harry Carey Jr., *A Company of Heroes: My Life as an Actor in the John Ford Stock Company*. Lanham, Maryland: Scarecrow Press, 1994; Donald and Christopher Anderson. *John Wayne's The Alamo: The Making of the Epic Film*. New York: Carol Publishing Group, 1995; Scott Eyman, *Print the Legend: The Life and Times of John Ford*. New York: Simon & Schuster, 1999; Todd. *Howard Hawks: The Grey Fox of Hollywood*. New York: Grove Press, 1997; Maurice Zolotow, *Shooting Star: A Biography of John Wayne*. New York: Simon & Schuster, 1974; Jim Beaver, "John Wayne". *Films in Review*, Volume 28, Number 5, May 1977, pp. 265–284; Carolyn McGivern, *John Wayne: A Giant Shadow*. Bracknell, England: Sammon, 2000; Michael Munn, *John Wayne: the man behind the myth*, Robson, 2009; Ronald L. Davis, *Duke: The Life and Times of John Wayne*. University of Oklahoma Press, 2001.
100. Leonard Engel, *Clint Eastwood, Actor and Director: New Perspectives*. Salt Lake City: University of Utah Press, 2007; ,*The Biography of Clint Eastwood*. London: Plexus, 2007; Douglas Thompson, Douglas, *Clint Eastwood: Billion Dollar Man*. London: John Blake, 2005.
101. *Beatlesongs,* William J. Dowlding, Fireside, 1989, pp. 159-160.
102. *The Big Beat: Conversations with Rock' Greatest Drummers,* Max Weinberg, 1984; *rpt., Beatlesongs,* William J. Dowlding, Fireside, 1989, pp. 159-160.
103. Sept., 1980, *Playboy Interview*.
104. *It Was Twenty Years Ago Today*, Derek Taylor, Fireside, 1987; rpt., *Beatlesongs*, p. 156.
105. *It Was Twenty Years Ago Today*, Derek Taylor, Fireside, 1987; rpt., *Beatlesongs*, p. 156.
106. *The Long and Winding Road: A History of the Beatles on Record*, Neville Stannard, Avon, 1984; *It Was Twenty Years Ago Today*, Derek Taylor, Fireside, 1987; rpt., *Beatlesongs*, pp. 157-158.
107. *Biograph,* Cameron Crowe, 1985.
108. Leung, Rebecca (June 12, 2005). " "Dylan Looks Back". CBS News.
109. Dylan, *Chronicles, Volume One*, pp. 244–246.
110. Joan Baez entry, Gray, *The Bob Dylan Encyclopedia*, pp. 28–31.

111. Ricks, *Dylan's Visions of Sin*, pp. 329–344.
112. *Rolling Stone, May 26, 2011, p. 58.*
113. *Mojo* magazine, December 1993.
114. Heylin, *Bob Dylan: Behind the Shades Revisited*, pp. 114–115.
115. Heylin, *Bob Dylan: A Life In Stolen Moments*, p. 49.
116. Daniel Mark Epstein, *The Ballad of Bob Dylan: A Portrait*, HarperCollins, 2011, p. 115.
117. Shelton, *No Direction Home*, pp. 200–205.
118. Shelton, *No Direction Home*, p. 222.
119. Heylin, *Bob Dylan: Behind the Shades Revisited*, pp. 178–181.
120. Heylin, 2009, *Revolution In The Air, The Songs of Bob Dylan: Volume One*, pp. 220–222.
121. *Rolling Stone Magazine*, May 26, 2011, p. 60.
122. *Rolling Stone Magazine,* May 26, 2011, p. 59.
123. *Rolling Stone Magazine,* May 26. 2011, p. 60.
124. *Rolling Stone Magazine,* May 26, 2011, p. 59.
125. *Rolling Stone Magazine,* May 26, 2011, p. 60; Heylin, *Bob Dylan: Behind the Shades Revisited*, pp. 208–216. "Exclusive: Dylan at Newport—Who Booed?" *Mojo*. October 25, 2007. Jackson, Bruce (August 26, 2002). "The myth of Newport '65: It wasn't Bob Dylan they were booing," *Buffalo Report*, February 23, 2008.
126. *Sing Out!*, September 1965, quoted in Shelton, *No Direction Home*, p. 313.
127. *The Rolling Stone 500 Greatest Songs of All Time*. Rock List Music.
128. *Rolling Stone Magazine,* May 26, 2011, p. 56.
129. Springsteen's Speech during Dylan's induction into the Rock and Roll Hall of Fame, January 20, 1988; Quoted in Bauldie, *Wanted Man*, p. 191.
130. *Rolling Stone Magazine*, May 26, p. 61.
131. *Rolling Stone Magazine,* May 26, 2011, p. 60.
132. *Rolling Stone Magazine,* May 26, 2011, p. 26.
133. *Rolling Stone Magazine*, May 26, 2011, p. 60.
134. Sounes, *Down the Highway: The Life Of Bob Dylan*, p. 193; Shelton, *No Direction Home*, p. 325.
135. "Live 1966". nme.com. September 6, 1998.
136. Sounes, *Down the Highway: The Life Of Bob Dylan*, p. 215; Sounes, *Down the Highway: The Life Of Bob Dylan*, pp. 217–21.
137. Dylan, *Chronicles, Volume One*, p. 114.
138. Heylin, 1996, *Bob Dylan: A Life In Stolen Moments*, p. 143.
139. Sounes, *Down the Highway: The Life Of Bob Dylan*, p. 216.
140. *Rolling Stone Magazine,* May 26, 2011, p. 59.
141. *Biograph*, 1985, Liner notes & text by Cameron Crowe.
142. *Rolling Stone Magazine*, May 26, 2011, p. 59.
143. *Rolling Stone Magazine*, May 26, 2011, p. 65.
144. *Rolling Stone Magazine*, May 26, 2011, p. 64.
145. Hedin, *Studio A: The Bob Dylan Reader*, p. 109.
146. "Bob Dylan," Salon.com. May 5, 2001.
147. Sounes, *Down The Highway: The Life Of Bob Dylan*, pp. 323–337; Heylin, *Bob Dylan: Behind the Shades Revisited*, pp. 490–526; Dylan Interview with

Karen Hughes, (*The Dominion*, Wellington, New Zealand), May 21, 1980; reprinted in Cott (ed.), *Dylan on Dylan: The Essential Interviews*, pp. 275–278.
148. Heylin, *Bob Dylan: Behind the Shades Revisited*, pp. 501–503.
149. *Rolling Stone Magazine,* May 26, p. 60.
150. *Rolling Stone Magazine,* May 26, p. 60.
151. *Knocked Out Loaded.*
152. "Dylan's drawings to go on display—alongside Picasso's," *The Independent*, London.
153. *Remarks by the President at Kennedy Center Honors Reception*, Clinton White House. December 8, 1997.
154. Haynes in Weinstein Company press notes for "I'm Not There," quoted in *Footnote fetishism & "I'm Not There"* by Jim Emerson.
155. Edna Gundersen, (July 29, 2008). "Dylan Reveals Many Facets on 'Tell Tale Signs'". *USA Today*; "Tell Tale Signs," *The Sunday Times* (London). Michael Gray expressed his opinion in his *Bob Dylan Encyclopedia blog* "Tell Tale Signs Pt. 3, Money Doesn't Talk," Bob Dylan Encyclopedia blog. August 14, 2008.
156. Allan Jones, September 30, 2008, "Album Review: Bob Dylan — The Bootleg Series. Vol. 8," *Uncut*;
http://www.uncut.co.uk/music/bob_dylan/reviews/12229.
157. Flanagan, Bill (interviewer) (November 27, 2009). " "Bob Dylan: The Interview"," Big Issue Scotland.
158. McCormick, Neil (April 27, 2009). "Bob Dylan – live review"," London: The Telegraph.
159. *Rolling Stone Magazine*, June 21, 1984.
160. David Gates, "Dylan Revisited," *Newsweek,* Oct. 6, 1997.
161. Jon Pareles, "A Wiser Voice Blowin' In the Autumn Wind," Sept. 28, 1997.162. Flanagan, Bill (interviewer) (November 27, 2009). "Bob Dylan: The Interview," Big Issue Scotland.

GUARDIAN ANGELS

An angel came as I lay in bed;
I will give you wings—the angel said;
I will give you wings that you may fly
To the country of Heaven above the sky.

My beautiful angel flew away,
He came not again by night or by day;
Angels are busy with many things,
And he has forgotten to send the wings. (1)

X-ray Surprise

George Bailey is unhappy, considering suicide. His dream has been to travel the world, but he has repeatedly given it up to help others while waiting for his younger brother Harry to graduate from high school and replace him at the Bailey Building and Loan Association, the business that nearly runs the town. Now it is Christmas Eve and everything has fallen apart.

Family and friends pray for him, and miracle-upon-miracle, their prayers reach Heaven. Clarence Odbody, Angel Second Class, is told he can earn his wings if he saves George. Then Franklin and Joseph, the head angels, take us on a flashback through George's life, so we can see what a kind, unselfish man he has been. When he was twelve, he lost the hearing in one ear in the process of saving Harry from drowning upon falling through the thin ice on a frozen pond. Later, he prevented druggist Mr. Gower from accidentally filling a child's prescription with poison.

The night Harry graduates, George's absent-minded Uncle Billy and Harry tell George his father has had a fatal stroke. Then, a few months later, Henry F. Potter, a heartless slumlord and majority shareholder in Bailey Building and Loan tries to persuade the board of directors to stop providing home loans for the working poor, but George manages to talk them out of it on the agreement that George himself run the business. Sacrificing his desires, he agrees and gives his own college money to his brother, who agrees to take over the business when he returns. However, when Harry graduates and returns home, he has changed his plans. He is married and has been offered an excellent job in the company of his wife's father. George cannot expect Harry to give up this job, and so George continues to run the loan company.

George does, finally, marry his high school sweetheart Mary, and they plan to go on a honeymoon with $2,000 they have saved up. However, yet again, life interferes. There is a "run on the bank," and that $2,000 is needed to save it from collapsing. Time passes. George and Mary raise four children. George starts up Bailey Park, an affordable housing project where they and the other residents do not have to pay Henry F. Potter's high rents. Potter tries to lure George away, offering a $20,000 salary and business trips to New York and Europe, but George refuses.

WWII comes. Henry F. Potter runs the local draft board. George cannot enlist because of his bad ear. Harry, however, becomes a fighter pilot and earns the Medal of Honor for shooting down fifteen enemy aircraft, including two targeting a U. S. transport ship full of troops.

Then Christmas Eve, 1946, arrives. Scatter-brained Uncle Billy runs into Henry F. Potter on his way to the bank to deposit $8,000 for the Building and Loan Company and proudly shows Potter the front-page article about Harry's Medal of Honor. Potter grabs the newspaper, and when he finds the $8,000 inside, he keeps it. Later, Uncle Billy realizes it is gone, and a frantic search begins. Coincidentally, a bank examiner is set to inspect the books that same day, so George appeals to Potter for a loan to save the company. However, of course, Potter turns him down and personally swears out a warrant for his arrest for bank fraud.

Finally, after a lifetime of set-backs, George has reached the breaking point. He yells at his family, and storms out to have a drink at a bar owned by his friend Martini, crashes his car into a tree during a snowstorm, and staggers to a bridge with the intention of committing suicide, thinking he is worth more dead than alive because of a $15,000 life insurance policy.

Just as he is about to leap, Clarence appears, jumps in, and pretends to be drowning. Good Samaritan George rescues Clarence, and Clarence reveals himself to be George's *guardian angel.*

At first, George doesn't believe him, and wishes bitterly that he had never been born. This is the chance Clarence needs to show George an *alternate reality*, a history of his home town Bedford Falls (in the alternate reality, it becomes Pottersville, a town filled with sleazy nightclubs and pawn shops). Without George, Bailey Park never got built, Gower was sent to prison for poisoning the child and became a derelict when he was released, Martini lost his bar, Violet became a dancer at a local club and got arrested as a pickpocket, Uncle Billy got put in an insane asylum for years, Harry died because George was not there to save him, and all of the soldiers Harry saved, died, without him to save them. Mrs. Bailey became a bitter widow running a boarding house, and Mary became a spinster librarian.

Clarence's plan works, and George begs God to let him live. His prayer is answered. He runs home joyously. The bank examiner and policemen are there waiting to arrest him. But then Mary, Uncle Billy, and a crowd of townspeople arrive with more than enough donations to save George and the Building and Loan Business. In addition, George's friend Sam Wainwright sends him a line of credit for $25,000, Harry arrives in his military uniform and gets all the people to sing Auld Lang Sane, and George finds a gift from Clarence, a copy of *The Adventures of Tom Sawyer* with an inscription, "Dear George: Remember no man is a failure who has friends. Thanks for the wings! Love, Clarence." A bell on the Christmas tree rings and George's daughter Zuzu remember that it signifies that an angel has earned his wings. (2)

The belief that God sends a *guardian angel* to watch over each of us was common in Classical Greek philosophy, and is alluded to by Plato in *Phaedo* when Cebes says it seems true that "God is our guardian." (3) The

Old Testament has numerous references to *guardian angels*, which Leo Trepp (and others) claim leads back to Zoroastrian origins (4), where they are known as Arda Fravaš (Holy Guardian Angels). According to Zoroastrian beliefs, each of us is accompanied by a *guardian angel*, which acts as a guide throughout life. They originally patrolled the boundaries of the ramparts of heaven, but volunteer to descend to earth to stand by individuals to the end of their days. References to such *guardian angels* in the *Old Testament* include Job 33:23-6: "If there be a *messenger* with him, an interpreter, one among a thousand, to show unto man his uprightness"; Daniel 10:13: "but lo, *Michael*, one of the chief princes, came to help me." (5) In this second passage, the angel Michael is named, and in the *New Testament Book of Jude,* 9, he is called an *archangel. The Book of Enoch* (part of the Ethiopian Orthodox Tewahedo Church canon) says that God will "set a *guard* of holy angels over all the righteous" (1 *Enoch,* 100:5). New Advent claims that the concept of a *guardian angel* is clearly present in the *Old Testament*, where God saw his angels as his ministers who would carry out his desires, at times, special commissions in the dealings with men. In *Genesis* 28-29 angels deliver Lot from danger; in *Exodus* 32:34, God tells Moses, "My angel shall go before thee." *Psalms,* 9 1:11 contains the line "For he shall give his angels charge over thee, to keep thee in all thy ways." *Hebrews* 1:14 states it directly: "Are they not all ministering spirits, sent forth to minister for them who shall be heirs of salvation?"

References to *guardian* angels also exist in *The New Testament.* In *Matthew* 18:10, Jesus says of children, "Take heed that ye despise not one of these little ones: for I say unto you, That in heaven their angels do always behold the face of my Father which is in heaven." *Hebrews* 1:14 says "Are they not all ministering spirits, sent forth to minister for them who shall be heirs of salvation?"

After Peter was escorted out of prison by an angel, he went to the home of "Mary the mother of John, whose surname was Mark." (*Acts* 12) The servant girt Rhoda recognized his voice and ran to tell the others. However, they replied "Thou art mad. . . . "It is his *angel*." (*Acts* 15) This has commonly been interpreted as his *guardian angel*, as in Raphael's fresco, *The Deliverance of Saint Peter*, in the Vatican. There is also the angel who succored Christ in the garden, *Luke,* 22: 43: "And there appeared an angel unto him from heaven, strengthening him."

Though there is a controversy among the Church Fathers whether or not each of us has a *guardian angel* (thus, it is not included as an *article of faith* in the catechism), there is the famous claim by St. Jerome that this concept is in the *mind* of the Church, and he says, "How great the dignity of the soul, since each one has from his birth an angel commissioned to guard it." (6)

In the twelfth century, Honorius of Autun became the first Christian theologian to provide a scheme for guardian angels, claiming that each soul is assigned a guardian angel the moment it is put into a body. Later, the Scholastic Theologians elaborated and put a whole taxonomy of angelic guardians in place. Thomas Aquinas placed guardian angels at the lowest level of angels, and his views became the most popular, though others, such as Duns Scotus believed that any angel might accept this role. Pope John Paul II, referred to the idea of a guardian angel twice in his Regina Caeli address in 1997: "Let us invoke the Queen of angels and saints, that she may grant us, supported by our guardian angels, to be authentic witnesses to the Lord's paschal mystery." (7)

Jean Daniélou states that later theology can be proved to have borrowed the doctrine of the *guardian angel* for Jewish Christianity. Clement of Alexandria writes in *Eclogae Propheticae* that "Scripture says that little children who are exposed are entrusted to a guardian angel, which brings them up and makes them grow; and they shall be like the faithful here who are a hundred years old." (XLI.1). The *Apocalypse of Peter* says that "Aborted infants are entrusted to a guardian angel so that having obtained a share in the gnosis [teachings of Christianity] they may arrive at a better destiny." Danielou also notes that Jewish Christian theology includes an angel of peace, who receives the soul as it leaves the body and leads it to Paradise. (8)

Christian mystics such as St. Gemma Galgani and Maria Valtorta have claimed interactions with personal *guardian angels,* in addition to having visions of Jesus and Mary. In *The Book of Azariah* Maria Valtorta claimed her *guardian angel* Azariah gave her comments on each Sunday's Missal. (9)

Traditional Catholic prayers also refer to *guardian angels:*

Angel of God, my guardian dear
to whom God's love commits me here.
Ever this day/night be at my side
to light, to guard, to rule and guide.
Amen. (10)

In Latin:

Angele Dei,
qui custos es mei,
me, tibi commissum pietate superna,

illumina, custodi,
rege et guberna.
Amen. (11)

An Eastern Orthodox prayer to the Guardian Angel:

O Angel of Christ, my holy Guardian and Protector of my soul and body, forgive me all my sins of today. Deliver me from all the wiles of the enemy, that I may not anger my God by any sin. Pray for me, sinful and unworthy servant, that thou mayest present me worthy of the kindness and mercy of the All-holy Trinity and the Mother of my Lord Jesus Christ, and of all the Saints. Amen. (12)

The concept of *guardian angels* has been a common literary device dating back to at least Medieval Drama in such morality plays as *The Castle of Perseverance,* and overlap this book's discussion of the tradition of the Faust legend in such works as Christopher Marlowe's *The Tragical History of Doctor Faustus,* where Faust has a *good angel* and a *bad angel.*

In the seventeenth century Sir. Thomas Browne wrote:

Therefore for Spirits I am so farre from denying their existence, that I could easily believe, that not only whole Countries, but particular persons have their Tutelary, and Guardian Angels: It is not a new opinion of the Church of Rome, but an old one of Pythagoras and Plato; there is no heresay in it, and if not manifestly defined in Scripture, yet is it an opinion of a good and wholesome use in the course and actions of a man's life, and would serve as an Hypothesis to salve many doubts, whereof common philosophy affordeth no solution. (13)

By the 19th century, the literary depiction of a *guardian angel* represented it mainly as a force protecting the believer from performing sin, in Freudian psychological terms, a *super-ego*. This, in turn, led to such popular parodies as Lord Byron's *Don Juan*,

"Oh! she was perfect past all parallel—
Of any modern female saint's comparison;
So far above the cunning powers of hell,
Her guardian angel had given up his garrison." (14)

Obviously, this satiric depiction of the *guardian angel* undermines the whole concept. For his representative of it as a cunning woman, Lord Byron is drawing on Alexander Pope's satire, *The Rape of the Lock*, where for the purpose of satirizing alchemy Pope pretended to have a new alchemy. In it there are *sylphs*. Pope did not make up these beings. They come from Paracelsus (1493-1541), who describes *sylphs* as invisible beings of the air; others have compared them to *fairies*. Pope decided they would make for excellent representatives of the folly of alchemy. And to this purpose, he depicted them as the mystically, chemically condensed humors of *peevish women*. Accordingly, women who are full of spleen and vanity turn into *sylphs* when they die because their spirits are too full of dark vapors to ascend to the skies. Belinda, the heroine of Pope's poem, is attended by a small army of *sylphs*, who foster her vanity and guard her beauty. In a wonderfully humorous scene, Pope has the Baron attempt to cut off a lock of Belinda's hair, while the *sylphs* interpose their airy bodies between the blades of the scissors to prevent it (but have absolutely no affect at all). (15) As an aside, the main *sylph*, Ariel, has the same name as Prospero's servant in Shakespeare's *The Tempest*. (16)

Contemporary use of *guardian angels* in literature and film often combines the serious views with a bit of humor. Clarence in *It's a Wonderful Life* is meant to be taken seriously, but at the same time, he is a somewhat inept, comic persona.

In more recent times, Michael Landon's hit television series, *Highway to Heaven* (1984-89) featured a traveling angel, something of a personal angel to a different person each episode. Michael Landon starred as Jonathan Smith, an angel sent down to earth "on probation," and his human companion Mark Gordon, played by Victor French. Each new episode was an assignment from *The Boss* (God) that required Jonathan and Mark to use their humanity (and if necessary a bit of supernatural aid) to help some troubled soul overcome such problems as prejudice, physical disability, sickness, and greed—all handled with politically correct sensitivity and a bit of humor, generally the result of the more sensible, compassionate, and naïve Jonathan and the more practical, cynical and pragmatic Mark. Just as was the case with Clarence, Jonathan's mission on Earth was to do enough good so that he could *earn his wings* and presumably, ascend to heaven. An interesting spin occurs because Jonathon and Mark become such close friends that Mark doesn't want to lose his friend to *The Boss,* and sometimes tries to prevent it from happening. (17)

A similar popular television series, *Touched by an Angel* (1994-2003) starred Roma Downey as an angel named Monica and Della Reese as her supervisor Tess. Each episode had Monica bringing guidance and messages from God to people at a crossroads. In the second season John Dye began showing up as *the angel of death*. As with *It's a Wonderful Life* and *Highway to Heaven*, the main angel is trying to climb the ladder, in this case the main goal is to be promoted from a rookie caseworker to a supervisor. During the seventh season, Valerie Bertinelli joins the cast as a new angel Gloria, who is trainee under Monica and Tess. In the series finale, Monica is up for promotion to supervisor, pending the outcome of a difficult case in which she must defend Zack (played by Scott Bairstow), an innocent drifter accused of causing a boiler explosion that killed most of the children at a school two years ago in the small town of Ascension, Colorado. The explosion killed most of the children, leaving the citizens devastated. Many of Monica's previous assignments appear and help her with the trial. But the persecuting attorney (played by David Ogden Stiers) is really Satan in disguise, Monica loses, and Zach is convicted. Of course, it cannot end with Satan winning. After the trial, Monica gets the citizens to realize their mistake and see that Zack's return to the town actually helped them. They begin going back to church, welcomed by the pastor they had once abandoned. Their change of heart, however, cannot free Zack, so Monica visits him in jail and reveals that she is an angel. She then promises him that she will become his *guardian angel*, forgoing all future assignments and the coveted promotion, to protect him from harm in prison. When she returns in the morning, however, the cell is empty. The citizens decide not to search for him, and it is revealed that Joey inadvertently caused the explosion after Satan tricked him into turning the boiler to high to warm some kittens he'd found. Confused, Monica returns to the desert, where she finds Tess and Zack, learns that Zack was actually God, and that her defending him was a test, which she passed by being willing to sacrifice herself for him. Monica is promoted to supervisor. As she leaves, she says her goodbyes to Gloria, and to Andrew, who gives her a pocket watch to remember their friendship. Tess is also promoted, going to her new job at the feet of God. (18)

Angels in the Outfield puns on the baseball team California Angels to provide a sentimental update of a 1951 film where foster child Roger (played by Joseph Gordon-Levitt) has been abandoned by his irresponsible father who promises to get his act together when the last place baseball team wins the pennant. Roger prays for help, and his prayers are answered in the form of angel Al (Christopher Lloyd), and with the help of angels invisible to all except Roger (they look like glowing special effects) the team starts making miraculous fielding plays. It is a positive, uplifting film that stays generally close to the Bible with an expected happy ending.

The 1951 version is a bit more realistic. In it, the team is the Pittsburgh Pirates, and the orphan is a young girl. Both movies have a rough, but likeable team manager. In this case it is the manager; McGovern who begins hearing the voice of an angel, promising him help if he mends his ways (learns to keep his temper under control).

In *Michael*, Vartan Malt (played by Bob Hoskins) edits the *National Mirror*, a tabloid specializing in unusual stories about celebrities and strange tales of ordinary folks. When he hears a woman is harboring an angel in a small town in Iowa, he sends out Frank Quinlan (played by William Hurt), a reporter whose career is in bad shape, Huey Driscoll (played by Robert Pastorelli), a photography about to lose his job, and Dorothy Winters (played by Andie MacDowell), a supposed angel expert. When they arrive at the farm of Pansy Milbank (played by Jean Stapleton), they meet Michael, who does have angel wings. However, Michael is more into enjoying his last change to take on a human form and experience the pleasures of the senses. He smokes, stuffs himself with sweets (and is noticeably overweight), uses rough language, has poor hygiene, and likes women. After Pansy unexpectedly dies, Frank and Huey decide to take Michael to Chicago with them and let him lose to have some fun. Then the film follows Michael, Frank, Huey, Dorothy, and Sparky the dog on their trip. Along the way Michael slowly reveals that his mission is to get Frank and Dorothy together even though they are both really leery of love because of bad past experience. Sparky gets hit by a truck and killed, but Michael uses up his last miracle to bring the dog back to life, and it becomes apparent that Michael is indeed becoming less and less powerful. Finally, after numerous misadventures, the group reaches Chicago, and Michael gets to fulfill his wish to see Sears Tower before disappearing. After Dorothy and Frank go their separate ways, Michael returns with Pansy in tow and successfully completes his mission to get Dorothy and Frank together. It is a fun movie that celebrates life, basically saying that humans should appreciate their sensual existence (which even the angels envy). Again, however, it is a depiction of an angel that is a far from perfect or superior being.

In 1947, Cary Grant, Loretta Young, and David Niven) starred in *The Bishop's Wife*, a romantic comedy based on a 1928 novel of the same name. In it Bishop Henry Drougham (played by David Niven) prays for help building a new cathedral. A suave angel named Dudley (Cary Grant) appears, initially revealing his identity only to Brougham, who assumes the angel is a response to his prayer. However, he is actually there to help Brougham and his unhappy, neglected wife Julia (Loretta Young) reconnect and in general to positively influence everyone. And everyone, except Brougham, is easily charmed by this classy angel, even agnostic Prof. Wutheridge (Monty Woolley). Eventually, Dudley persuades the wealthy parishioners, particularly Mr. Hamilton (Gladys Cooper), to contribute funds, but not to build the cathedral, instead to feed and clothe the needy (much to Brougham's chagrin). Along the way, Dudley performs light miracles—redecorating the Christmas tree in seconds, saving an old church by restoring interest in the boys' choir, and having a typewriter automatically type up Brougham's sermon to reflect the more Christian stance Dudley has put in place. There is an unexpected twist, as Dudley becomes attracted to Julia, which makes Brougham jealous. Eventually, Brougham stands up to Dudley, Dudley leaves, all memory of him is erased, and everything ends happy.

In 1996, Penny Marshall directed *The Preacher's Wife*, a sentimentalized version of the already sentimental *The Bishop's Wife*, this time set in a Black Baptist church. Reverend Henry Biggs (played by Courtney B. Vance) is the devoted, hard-working pastor of a struggling church in a poor section of New York City. Membership is down, money is tight, the furnace is broken, and real estate mogul Joe Hamilton (played by Gregory Hines) wants to buy up the property and build condominiums. Henry Biggs marriage is suffering because he is so focused on his job, so in a moment of desperation he prays for help. The result is Dudley (an angel played by Denzel Washington). He doesn't believe Dudley is really an angel, but is willing to take whatever help he can get. As things develop, Dudley meets Biggs wife Julie (played by Whitney Houston) and finds himself falling for her. While the plot plays out, Whitney Houston sing a number of songs (it is close to a musical), and in the end with the help of the angel, everything works out. Once again, the focus isn't so much on spiritual salvation as on a romantic connection between humans, and the angel is a well meaning, good hearted, yet very human being.

In 1997, ABC put out *Teen Angel*, a teen comedy that got pulled after sixteen episodes. In it Marty DePolo (Mike Damus) dies from eating a six-month-old hamburger, and God's cousin Rod appoints him his best friend's guardian angel. It's all played for comedy, with the angel using his powers to perform various minor miracles, intentionally or not, undermining any serious views of God and angels in the name of a quick laugh; in this vein, Marty the angel steals Cupid's arrows to help Steve bag a girl, brings in Cleopatra to help Steve write history papers, and grants Steve a golden voice for choir tryouts.

Teen movie *Grease* has a wonderfully ironic performance by Frankie Avalon as a guardian angel to Frenchy, who has left Rydell to pursue her dream of being a beautician, but has had difficulty in all of her classes at beauty school, eventually dying her hair bubblegum pink. She is at odds with what to do until her guardian teen angel Frankie Avalon appears to her and sings *Beauty School Dropout,* a lecture to go back to high school in the form of a humorous send up of the famous beach movies Frankie Avalon starred in.

In 1998, Nicolas Cage and Meg Ryan starred in *City of Angels*, yet another movie where angels would rather be humans. It takes place in Los Angeles, where Seth (Nicolas Cage) is a guardian angel, one of many. His particular responsibility is to appear for humans just before they die and escort them to death. For the purposes of this story, angels such as Seth have trouble understanding humans and their ways. On his latest mission, Seth encounters Maggie Rice (Meg Ryan), who works hard to try and save a man's life and demonstrates a lot of sorrow when she fails to do so. Seth is curious about her and becomes ever more preoccupied with her, finally deciding to become visible to her (though he cannot provide her with any details about himself and his life). Of course, as time goes on, they find they have a mutual attraction, even though Maggie is currently attached to one of her colleagues. Then Seth meets Nathaniel Messinger (Dennis Franz), one of Maggie's patients, who knows Seth is an angel because he, too, was once an angel, but decided to become a human through a process called "falling." Seth begins to think he might want to do the same thing so he can have a fully physical and emotional relationship with Maggie. She realizes he cannot be injured and confronts him; but fails to believe he is an angel and sends him away. Nathaniel then explains the situation to Maggie, telling her that Seth is considering making the same move. Seth, in fact, does this by jumping from the top of a skyscraper. When he awakens after the fall, he experiences all of the human feelings and sensations, beginning with physical injury and pain.

Now he begins to change, to become more human. He finds his way to the hospital in search of Maggie, but hears she has gone to her uncle's mountain cabin for a vacation. Without any money and ignorant about things, he gets mugged and has his boots taken by a gang, but manages to hitch a ride to Lake Tahoe, and shows up at Maggie's door cold and wet, with a split lip. She realized he has become human, tends to his wounds, and they make love. Then, the next morning, while Seth takes a shower and enjoys his first sensations of running hot water, Maggie rides her bike to a local store to buy him some pears. On her way back, all happy, she closes her eyes and opens her arms wide to experience the autumn sun and her future with Seth. However, it all ends when a truck pulls in front of her. Seth senses she is in trouble and runs to her, arriving just in time for her to tell him she sees angels. After she dies, Seth, sad and alone, is visited by his angel friend Cassiel, who asks him if he regrets his decision to become human, and he utters the line that the entire movie has been leading up to: "I would rather have had one breath of her hair, one kiss of her mouth, one touch of her hand, than eternity without it."

He continues to mourn and attempts to adjust, while continuing mourning for Maggie. In the end, the final scene, Seth is at the beach where the angels meet at dawn and sunset to commune with eternity. Then, with all of the angels watching, Seth expresses his joy over being human. This is the key; angels in these films consistently express a desire to be human, to accept the limitations of human life because they find the joys worth the sorrows.

The images of angels also get undermined. They are usually good but often inept, at times rough and crude and very un-angelic. A clear example of this is the television series *Saving Grace* (TNT, 2007-2010). It centers on Grace Hanadarko (played by Holly Hunter), a heavy drinking, cigarette smoking, promiscuous Oklahoma City detective who meets up with her last chance, guardian angel upon running down and killing a pedestrian while drunk. In desperation she calls out for God's help, and Earl, a rough, tobacco-chewing angel appears, complete with wings, to tell her that she is heading straight for Hell, and asks her if she is ready to change her ways and seek God. Then he, the dead pedestrian, and the entire accident scene disappears, as if it never happened, except for a convenient small spot of the victim's blood on her blouse, which enables her to trace the victim, who turns out to be an inmate on death row who is also visited by angel Earl on a regular basis. The series follows Grace as she investigates homicides and other major crimes with her fellow officers, and continues to have one-night stands and drink heavily. Not surprisingly, her rough exterior holds a loving, compassionate interior, which gets exhibited endlessly in her love for her nephew Clay. Angel Earl continues to show up and attempt to lead Grace away from her self-destructive actions and turn to God, and throughout the series there are discussions about faith and how difficult it is to have it in our imperfect world.

The above are but a few examples of *guardian angels* in movies and television. The lines between when these *angels* can be considered *guardian angels* or some other form of angelic encounter get difficult to untangle; but the representations over the last century are fairly similar in representing them in an either very un-angelic light or in a humorous light. Popular songs, especially early rock-and-roll songs (*Johnny Angel, Devil in Disguise, Angel of the Morning, My Little Angel,* on and on) tend to use *angel* more as a metaphor for an extra-ordinary human—exceptionally attractive and desirable, often someone's love interest.

Third Man Syndrome or Factor is similar to experiencing a *guardian angel*, except that is more of psychological experience that doesn't necessarily have anything at all to do with Christianity or any other organized religion. Some unseen, sensed *presence*, a spirit of some sort, provides comfort or help during a traumatic experience. Sir Ernest Shackleton described this experience during the final portion of his trek over the mountains and glaciers of South Georgia, saying "it seemed to me often that we were four, not three." (19) Climber Reinhold Messner and polar explorers Peter Hillary and Ann Bancroft have reported this same experience, as has aviator Charles Lindberg. Peter Suedfeld and John Geiger have done a study and found that these experiences are most often associated with climbers, but are also common among shipwreck survivors and polar explorers. (20) Nancy White has suggested that this experience might be the source of a belief in *guardian angels.* (21) Geraldine McCaughrean's novel *The White Darkness* has teen-age heroine Sym, lost in a doomed Antarctic expedition, guided to safety by her *third man* friend, the imaginary Captain Lawrence Oates. (22)

Notes

1. Rose Fyleman, *Picture Rhymes from Foreign Lands,* Lippincott, 1935.
2. *It's a Wonderful Life,* RKO Pictures, 1947; DVD, 2006.
3. Plato, *Phaedo; Plato Selections*, translated, Raphael Demos, Charles Scribners, 1927 p. 154.
4. Leo Trepp, *A History of the Jewish Experience*. p. 55, Zarathushtra.com.
5. *Holy Bible, King James Version.*
6. "Guardian Angel," *New Advent Catholic Encyclopedia.*
7. Vatican website.
8. *Eclogae Propheticae*, XLVIII, 1; *The Theology of Jewish Christianity. The Development of Christian Doctrine before the Council of Nicaea. Volume One.* Translated and edited by John A. Baker. (Chicago: The Henry Regnery Company) p. 186.
9. Michael Freze, 1989 *They Bore the Wounds of Christ* OSV Press, page 272; Maria Valtorta, *The Poem of the Man God*; Rudolph M. Bell, 2003 *The Voices of Gemma Galgani: the Life and Afterlife of a Modern Saint* University of Chicago Press, p. 47 and p. 185. pages 47 and 185; Maria Valtorta 1972, *The Book of Azariah*, 1972.
10. *Beliefnet Christian Children's Prayers*, beliefnet.com.
11. *Compendium of the Catechism of the Catholic Church*, Vatican.
12. Guardian Angels, Wikipedia.
13. *Religio Medici*, part 1, paragraph 33.
14. 1824 (unfinished at Byron's death); rpt., *Don Juan,* Penguin Classics, 1988, Canto I, xvii.
15. Alexander Pope, *Rape of the* Lock, 1717; rpt., Bibliolife, 2008.
16. William Shakespeare, *The Tempest, 1611;* rpt, Simon and Brown, 2011.

17. John O'Connor, "TV Review: Highway to Heaven with Landon," *New York Times*, September 19, 1984.
18. *Touched by an Angel*, William and Robin Sheets, Zondervan, 1997.
19. Shackleton, Ernest Henry (1914). *South: The Endurance Expedition,* Frank Hurley, Fergus Fleming. Penguin Classics, p. 204.
20. Peter Suedfeld and John Geiger, (2008) "The sensed presence as a coping resource in extreme environments" In: Ellens, J. Harold (ed.), Miracles God, Science, and Psychology in the Paranormal (Vol.3) Praeger.
21. Nancy J. White, "Third Man theory of otherworldly encounters, *The Star*, January, 30, 2009.
22. Harper Teen, 2007.

THE DANCE OF LIGHT AND SHADOW

[Primeval men] could walk upright as men now do, backwards or forwards as they pleased, and they could also roll over and over at a great pace, turning on their four hands and four feet, eight in all, like tumblers going over and over with their legs in the air; this was when they wanted to run fast.... Terrible was their might and strength, and the thoughts of their hearts were great, and they made an attack upon the gods.... Doubt reigned in the celestial councils. Should they kill them and annihilate the race with thunderbolts, as they had done the giants, then there would be an end of the sacrifices and worship which men offered to them; but, on the other hand, the gods could not suffer their insolence to be unrestrained. At last, after a good deal of reflection, Zeus discovered a way. He said: 'I have a plan which will humble their pride and improve their manners; men shall continue to exist, but I will cut them in two and then they will be diminished in strength and increased in numbers; this will have the advantage of making them more profitable to us. They shall walk upright on two legs, and if they continue insolent and will not be quiet, I will split them again and they shall hop about on a single leg.'

—Plato (1)

Perfection

As a pale yellow sun sinks softly towards the horizon, the ripples on the surface of the ocean dance, an interplay of sun and shadow on the eternal, enigmatic water of life--the sparkling light a shimmering waltz made possible by the quiet, dark water that gives it substance. A category similar to *doppelganger* is that of a *soul mate* or *twin mate* or *twin flame*. These *mates* are sometimes thought to be real individuals who fit us well, or, more important for this discussion, some kind of mystic or psychic second half, the other half of our soul, that we need to connect up with to become whole. According to Theosophy, God created androgynous souls, souls equally male and female. Other theories suggest that souls split into separate genders, perhaps because of karma while inhabiting earth, seen as a separation from God; and over a number of reincarnations, they have sought one another, but will only become reunited when they return to their ultimate being. (2)

In psychology, Jung provides two possible categories of such a duality, the *ego/shadow* and the *anima/animus*.

He establishes the dividing line between pre-human and human in evolution at the point where *consciousness* appears, not as a replacement to the *pre-conscious* form of thinking, that "animal" "instinctual" phylogenetic heritage we evolved out of, but as an outward-looking expression of our personality. In *Two Essays on Analytical Psychology*, he hints that this differentiation is expressed in the Greek myth of Prometheus, where the gift of fire represents the mastery over nature *and* the realization of impending death (the gaining of *self* and the loss of *self*). (3)

Furthermore, the division of the psyche into *conscious* and *unconscious* works not only on a personal level but also on a universal level, forming the *collective* experience of the species. In other words our mental make-up works the same way our physical make up works. We are born pre-programmed to grow into a general physical pattern. We all will have bodies roughly the same shape and size and made up of the same organs. This works the same for the brain (the physical organ that holds the mind or psyche). What we need to do to grow into our adult physical selves is to nourish and exercise our bodies. It works the same psychologically. Our brains are structured so we can only think in certain ways. And in order to think as adults we need to nourish and exercise our brains. The mind or psyche is what the brain does. And just as we can only do certain other physical activities, lift so much, run so fast, bend our arms and fingers in certain directions, and so on, the mind can only think in certain ways. There are, then, certain universal mental patterns, universal ways humans can and do think. These universal mental patterns, Jung calls *archetypes*. He writes:

> Archetypes resemble the beds of rivers: dried up because the water has deserted them, though it may return at any time. An archetype is something like an old watercourse along which the water of life has flowed for a time, digging a deep channel for itself. The longer it flowed the deeper the channel, and the more likely it is that sooner or later the water will return. (4)

Human consciousness flows similar to the water, shaping the stream bed and being shaped by the previous flow. Each generation's mental patterning is both molded by and reshapes the universal patterns. For example, all humans have a mother, and the mother archetype gets shaped by each generation of humans into a universal understanding of what a mother is, a mother archetype. In the end, various mother images, such as the Earth Mother (who gives birth and has other motherly interactions with Nature) becomes an archetype or a part of what is called the *Mother Complex* (a mental structure that develops surrounding the archetype of the mother); or the Blessed Virgin (again a female that gives birth, but now birthing the spiritual out of the physical (and forming another part of the *Mother Complex).*

These archetypes become parts of the *collective unconscious*, the universal human unconscious, the repository of the phylogenetic human experience, and they are understood, are revealed *symbolically*, because that is how the *unconscious thinks*.

While it complicates his theories, Jung also puts forth the concept of *conscious archetypes.* These are archetypes perceived consciously in the objective world, the world outside the inner world of the psyche. And the main one is Jung's version of the *ego*, which for him is the directing force of the psyche, but an imperfect one because it exists in the conscious world and responds only to conscious needs, to perceived expectations and restraints of social pressures. It does this through the *persona*, a mask or social façade we put on to satisfy expectations (or, rather, perceived expectations) of those around us, expectations of the *collective consciousness.*

If our *ego* fails to distinguish between itself and the *persona*, then we lose our *self*, we become our *mask*, we, in a sense, fool ourselves into thinking we are the *persona* we wear. Nevertheless, as much as the *persona* is problematic, it is necessary and is a part of our inherited psyche.

Deep within the *unconscious*, the instincts and animal drives begin to form into what Jung calls the *shadow*, the *alter-ego*, a force that is not driven by the demands of the *conscious*, social world outside us. In its full development, it is the powerful individual untamed by society, the rebel, the independent "I" unhampered by concerns about what others think. Jung writes about his realization of this force:

> It was night in some unknown place, and I was making slow and painful headway against a mighty wind. Dense fog was flying along everywhere. I had my hands cupped around a tiny light which threatened to go out at any moment. Everything depended on my keeping this little light alive. Suddenly I had the feeling that something was coming up behind me. I looked back and saw a gigantic black figure following me. But at the same moment I was conscious, in spite of my terror, that I must keep my little light going through night and wind, regardless of all dangers. (5)

Upon awakening, he realized this frightful, dark entity was his own *shadow* reflected in the mist by the flickering candle. Timothy R. O'Neill writes: "The candle is the flickering, uncertain light of consciousness; the spectral shadow is the other self, the vestige of Man's evolution, the dark side of his nature. The weakness of modern Man is his personification of the shadow of his own nature as a frightful fiend, and the unwillingness to turn his head." (6)

Samuel Coleridge expresses this same looming shadowy entity in *The Rime of the Ancient Mariner*, when his travelling protagonist "no more turns his head/because he knows a frightful fiend doth close behind him tread." (7) He begins the poem with a quote from T. Burnet:

> I can easily believe that there are more invisible than visible beings in the universe. But of their families, degrees, connections, distinctions, and functions, who shall tell? How do they act? Where are they found? About such matters the human mind has always circled without attaining knowledge. Yet I do not doubt that sometimes it is well for the soul to contemplate as in a picture the image of a larger and better world, lest the mind, habituated to the small concerns of daily life, limit itself too much and sink entirely into trivial thinking. But meanwhile we must be on watch for the truth, avoiding extremes, so that we may distinguish certain from uncertain, day from night. (8)

Though scholars have long debated the confusing allusions and obscure meanings of the poem, this introductory quote and Coleridge's own notes added in 1817 clearly connect this "looming shadow" with the spiritual world. It is the *Spectra of the Brocken*, a phrase that comes from an experience climbers sometimes have on Brocken Peak, the highest peak of Germany's Harz Mountains. If the sun is close to the horizon behind a climber looking down from a high ridge or peak, a ghostly figure can be seen in the mist directly opposite the sun, its head sheathed in shimmering rings. It is an unnerving apparition, a ghostly *shadow* of one's self. Sometimes this apparition can be huge, and its rainbow-like rings give it an unearthly, spiritual appearance, as if experiencing an entity from some "other" realm.

By connecting the *psychic shadow* to this specter, to this experience we can have in nature where we feel the presence of some other, some spiritual world, we comprehend our *psychic shadow* as a connection to the *other*, as an entity that exists in that ancient river of existence where the mysterious world of the *individual dream* and the spiritual world of the *archetypal dream* flow together.

Robert Louis Stevenson's, *The Strange Case of Dr. Jekyll and Mr. Hyde*, offers a clear exploration of the dual nature of humans. His main character Dr. Jekyll postulates that "man is not truly one, but truly two," and the human soul is a battleground where an *angel* and a *fiend* struggle for control. (9) He hopes that his potion will separate and purify each, but instead all it does is bring the dark side, Mr. Hyde into the forefront of existence, and as time continues this *shadow* character takes over more and more until Dr. Jekyll ceases to exist at all, suggesting that perhaps humans' essential nature is animalistic, primitive, and driven by instinct (one of the characters, Utterson describes Hyde as a *troglodyte*), and the *angelic* side is only very tentatively able to keep this *primitive* side under control with the laws of civilization.

This dichotomy of civilization and nature or a primitive wilderness is cleverly emphasized in the nightmarish landscapes Stevenson gives us within Victorian London, where dark streets twist and coil or lie draped in ominous fog, and in the descriptions of the chilling nightmares of Utterson: "He would be aware of the great field of lamps of a nocturnal city. . . . The figure [of Hyde] . . . haunted the lawyer all night; and if at any time he dozed over, it was but to see it glide more stealthily through sleeping houses, or move the more swiftly . . . through wider labyrinths of lamp-lighted city, and at every street corner crush a child and leave her screaming." Such language creates a primordial world, a frightening animalistic vision where even the veneer of civilization is ill equipped to keep away the irrational drives of dark sides of human nature and the terrifying ghosts of the supernatural world.

However if Mr. Hyde is merely animalistic, driven by instincts, why would he enjoy his evil so much? Animals wouldn't take such joy in their actions, nor would they commit them for no apparent purpose. Thus, there is a sense in which Mr. Hyde is aware of the rules of morality, and his crimes are more of a deliberate desire to break them than a primitive unawareness of the evil he does, suggesting that perhaps evil is a purposeful, even necessary aspect of being human, and of human civilization, that in fact a human psyche and by extension the universal human psyche gains some kind of reward or satisfies some need in going against what it considers correct behavior. This gets emphasized by having Hyde's two most detailed crimes be committed against seemingly innocent and harmless people, a small female child and a much loved, meek old man, neither capable of harming anyone.

There is a sense that Stevenson is not clarifying the duality. Is it one of civilization versus nature (a common philosophical discussion of the time relating to Jean Jacque Rousseau's concepts of the "noble savage," and clearly expressed in Edgar Rice Burroughs' *Tarzan* only 26 years later), or one of good versus evil (an ethical duality), or one of Freud's *superego* versus *id* (a psychological duality), or Jung's *ego* versus *shadow* (an archetypal psychological duality) or perhaps more likely at the time a Christian one of God versus Satan (a religious duality).

Certainly one's public face (in Jungian terms, one's *persona* or *ego*) is important for the characters; both Utterson and Enfield avoid gossip, as they believe it destroys one's reputation. Utterson also attempts to shelter Jekyll from the police enquiries in the role of a friend attempting to help preserve Jekyll's respectability. Throughout the novel, Utterson indicates his desire to preserve a sense of order and decorum, regardless of the evil that might be lurking underneath it. Thus, right or wrong, there is the suggestion that civilized behavior must be kept in place, even if it is shallow and dishonest, perhaps because, if it isn't, the dark, animalistic world beneath it will be unleashed, and that would be much worse.

This *persona* is represented in Jekyll's dual dwellings, his wealthy and comfortable home, and curiously adjoined laboratory, which is described as "a certain sinister block of building . . . [that] bore in every feature the marks of profound and sordid negligence." The respectable, prosperously appearing main house matches the similarly respectable, prosperous Dr. Jekyll; the decaying and neglected laboratory the similarly decadent and corrupt Mr. Hyde.

Certainly the *shadow* is closely related to the *id* (Jung believes the *shadow develops out of the id*, so Stevenson's representation works in those terms).

> When Bilbo opened his eyes, he wondered if he had; for it was just as dark as with them shut. No one was anywhere near him. Just imagine his fright! He could hear nothing, see nothing, and he could feel nothing except the stone of the floor.

> Very slowly he got up and groped about on all fours, till he touched the wall of the tunnel; but neither up nor down it could he find anything: nothing at all, no sign of goblins, no sign of dwarves. His head was swimming, and he was far from certain even of the direction they had been going in when he had his fall. He guessed as well as he could, and crawled along for a good way, till suddenly his hand met what felt like a tiny ring of cold metal lying on the floor of the tunnel. It was a turning point in his career, but he did not know it. He put the ring in his pocket almost without thinking; certainly it did not seem of any particular use at the moment. (10)

If we are to believe such luminaries in the world of psychology as Sigmund Freud, Carl Jung, Bruno Bettelheim, and Clarissa Estes, such philosophers as Immanuel Kent, Soren Kierkegaard, and Friedrich Nietzsche, such mythologists as Joseph Campbell, David Leeming, and Rollo May, such literary critics as Northrop Frye, and such neurologists as Joseph Bogen, M.S. Gazzaniga, Richard Perry, who won a Nobel Prize for his work, and Ronald Meyers (the lists in each field can go on at some length), then stories such as *The Hobbit* are expressing the deepest meanings and values of human existence by transforming them into a *symbolic* form that our conscious (or right cerebrum) can handle, and the critic's job is to attempt to explain the *symbolism* in order to uncover these deep meanings, much as a psychiatrist would attempt to interpret a dream.

The complete story of *The Hobbit* fits nicely into the standard *Mono Myth* (as described by Northrop Frye) or *Hero's Story* (as explained by Joseph Campbell), which depicts the most central and basic pattern of human life, and can be summarized as consisting of three parts: departure, where the main character leaves the known world or level of psychological development and enters into a knew, unknown world; fulfillment, which involves various tests and insights, all having to do with psychological and spiritual development; and return, where the hero crosses back over into the known world as a psychologically and spiritually changed person.

The first chapter of *The Hobbit* fits obviously into the departure, what Joseph Campbell denotes as "the call to adventure" or "crossing over the threshold" portion of the hero's story. The final chapter is the equally obvious return from the adventure. And the chapters in-between all involve the various tests and insights Bilbo encounters that result in his development. But the entire hero's adventure is just too much to cover in this presentation, which, instead will focus on just one part of it, one of the psychological tests Bilbo must pass in order to complete the journey, the test that involves the current discussion of the duality of the *shadow/id* and *ego*.

This takes place in Chapter Five, titled "Riddles in the Dark," a symbolically rich presentation of Bilbo's encounter with and incorporation of his id or shadow psychic entity, and his resulting empowerment. He enters the dark tunnels alone, scared, weak, and lost. At the end he emerges back into the world of light with a newfound sense of *self* ready to face the challenges to come.

The chapter begins, as quoted earlier, with Bilbo plunged into a dark tunnel beneath a mountain, and separated from the dwarves and Gandalf. He knows that goblins reside here, and he is terrified. He crawls about in the dark and discovers a ring. Eventually, he stumbles into some icy water and realizes that he has reached an underground lake. The reader is told that Gollum, a slimy water creature lives here.

Gollum approaches Bilbo and startles him. With the prize of eating Bilbo at state, Gollum challenges Bilbo to a riddling contest, a game Gollum vaguely remembers playing as a child before he became the creature he now is. A deal is struck. If Gollum wins, he gets to eat Bilbo (a symbolic representation of one's *shadow* swallowing one's *self*); if Bilbo wins, Gollum will show him out of the mountain (symbolically the path out of one's unconscious to the above land world of the conscious).

The riddling contest begins, each of them asking and solving riddles for a time. Finally, it comes to Bilbo to ask a riddle and he cannot think of one. So he simply tells Gollum to guess what he has in his pocket. Gollum is given three guesses, actually takes four, but cannot guess that it is the ring Bilbo has found. Thus, Gollum is required to show Bilbo the way out, but says he first must get some things from his rock island.

On his island, Gollum is distraught because he cannot find his precious birthday present. Bilbo gets impatient and tries to help Gollum find what is missing. Gollum tells the hobbit it is none of his business, and thinks, perhaps Bilbo might, indeed, have the missing present, which is, in fact, the ring in Bilbo's pocket (a ring the reader already knows can make its owner invisible). Gollum wants it specifically to do just that so he can eat Bilbo.

Finally, in frustration, unable to find his precious ring, Gollum simply comes after Bilbo, and without realizing the power of it, Bilbo carelessly slips on the ring, becoming invisible, and enabled to follow Gollum up and out of the mountain, where he jumps over Gollum, dodges around the goblins, and escapes into the forest.

That's the literal, prosaic plot summary of the chapter or test. On the deeper levels, it is a story incorporating Joseph Campbell's "belly of the whale" archetype. Campbell states: "The story of Jonah in the whale is an example of a mythic theme that is practically universal, of the hero going into a fish's belly and ultimately coming out transformed . . . a descent into the dark . . . [or unconscious] as water is the unconscious." (11). It actually is even more direct than this, as it is also the decent into mother earth (a cave or tunnel symbolizing the womb, and water symbolizing the amniotic fluid), and thus, on the psychological level, into the deepest portions of the unconscious, the dark tunnels of the mind, where, as Freud says, the most important and powerful needs, desires, and meanings of life reside, a place of transformation, just as is the womb.

Bilbo has stumbled into the darkest passages of his mind, and is obviously lost and frightened by them (i.e., is innocent and childlike when he enters; does not yet have a fully developed psychological *self*). This deep underground world of the *unconscious* is where the *self* is to be found, and the circular ring is the most powerful symbol of *self.* Carl Jung has written extensively on this (and has detailed discussions of the Mandela, the sacred circle in relation to it). In Jung's book *Man and His Symbols*, Aniela Jaffe, in discussing this sacred circle, writes: "Dr. M. L. von Franz has explained the circle (or sphere) as the symbol of the *Self.* It expresses the totality of the psyche in all its aspects, including the relationship between man and the whole of nature. Whether the symbol of the circle appears in primitive sun worship or modern religion, in myths or dreams, in the mandalas drawn by Tibetan monks, in the ground plans of cities, or in the spherical concepts of early astronomers, it always points to the single most vital aspect of life—its ultimate wholeness." (12).

And the ring has even more connections, as it is worn on the hand, and the hand is the messenger of the heart (think of palm reading), which is the symbolic place of the *self.* To further consider the extensions of this, think of some of the important *symbolic* gestures involving hands, from greeting others to praying. Schneider considers the hand especially important "because it is the corporeal manifestation of the inner state of the human being" and because "it expresses an attitude of mind in terms other than the acoustic," i.e., through gesture. (13)

Thus, Bilbo has gone into the tunnels of his unconscious and, without realizing it, gained possession of his deepest *self* (symbolized by the ring). This then is a dangerous happening, especially since Bilbo has no idea of the power and importance of the landscape he has entered. For if he does not have the necessary strengths to handle this encounter, he could simply get lost or swallowed by these psychic caves forever (much as has happened to Gollum).

To emphasize this as a place of transformation, Bilbo happens upon an underground lake, and water is the most powerful symbol of transformation there is. If you believe in evolution, the entire human race evolved out of water. Furthermore, each individual life evolves out of the amniotic fluid of the womb. And as Otto Rank discusses in *The Myth of the Birth of the Hero*, everyone is a hero in birth, undergoing a tremendous psychological and physical transformation from that of a tiny water creature completely dependent on another into an air-breathing mammal who must now begin the journey of life into a completely independent human being. (14) As Cirlot states, "Immersion in water signifies a return to the preformal state, with a sense of death and annihilation on the one hand, but of rebirth and regeneration on the other, since immersion intensifies the life-force." (15) This also applies to psychological and spiritual death-rebirth (as in baptism). St. John Chrysostom writes: It represents death and interment, life and resurrection. . . . When we plunge our head beneath water, as in a sepulcher, the old man becomes completely immersed and buried. When we leave the water, the new man suddenly appears." (16)

But what of the creature in the water, in this case, Gollum? Tolkien writes that Gollum is "a small slimy creature . . . as dark as darkness, except for two big round pale eyes in his face." (17) One can easily visualize him as a reptilian creature, a primitive creature, as Glietman states, "the most primitive portion of the personality, [wanting only to] eat, drink, eliminate, [and] be comfortably warm." (18) Campbell states: "Psychologically, the whale [i.e., creature in the water] represents the power of life locked in the unconscious. Metaphorically, water is the unconscious, and the creature in the water is the life or energy of the unconscious, which has overwhelmed the conscious personality and must be disempowered, overcome and controlled." (19)

This life force in the water can represent several aspects of the unconscious, some negative, some positive, and all dependent on how the rest of the psyche interacts with them. It is easy to see Gollum here as an *id* (Freud's libido or drive to life force, amoral, capable of both creation and destruction), and/or as a *shadow* entity (Jung's dark force in the psyche, a driving force that empowers (again capable of either creation or destruction). Both designations work and neither denies the other, but, rather, thickens the meanings of the other. Carl Jung writes: "Whether the shadow becomes our friend or enemy depends largely upon ourselves . . . the function of the shadow is to represent the opposite side of the ego and to embody just those qualities that one dislikes most in other people (20).

In order to transform from a child into an adult, we must encounter the id/shadow entities within ourselves and gain control over them. If we do not, we remain disempowered children.

Now things are beginning to come together in Bilbo's descent into the mountain. He has gone deep inside his psyche, the tunnels under the mountain, to where his essence (the ring) is to be found, and stumbled on the psyche waters of transformation, where the life force (the id) and the empowering *shadow* live in the form of Gollum.

Some other things the reader does not yet know, and will not find out unless he reads the subsequent *Lord of the Rings Trilogy* thicken what's going on here. As it turns out, the deformed creature stuck in the underground tunnels with his "birth" "day" present (the ring, i.e., his self) is in actuality a hobbit, the same as Bilbo. But Gollum, since he was unable to incorporate his *self*, succumbing to temptation upon first finding the ring, has gotten lost or forever condemned to his own nightmare, the underground tunnels and lake of his own unconscious (same as a person going into the dream or nightmare world and not being able to get back out; a failed hero's story or, as Campbell discusses at length, a form of schizophrenia. (21)

Gollum, thus, has been exiled from the bright light of the surface world, both the psychic and literal communities he was a part of as a child. Rollo May explains this banishment: "One had to surrender his mythic center when he was exiled from his city. . . . Exile generally destroyed the psychic life of the person exiled; he was broken literally by being without a country." (22) Thus, we have Gollum, broken and friendless, homeless and alone in the dark, living on his slimy rock island in the gloomy caves of the mountain and talking only to himself.

This, then, is both literally and psychologically the creature (condition) that could swallow Bilbo (i.e., his own dark side, his own *shadow*).

Now begins the riddling contest, and such contests always involve in one-way-or- another discovering the riddle to one's self. Bruno Bettelheim describes riddles as having connections to rites of passage, giving the example of *The Clever Little Tailor*, who guesses the answer to a riddle and then marries a princess. With this in mind, we are reminded of the most famous riddle of them all, the riddle of the Sphinx from Oedipus Rex, whose answer is man, which by inclusion refers to Oedipus himself. In fact, the entire play revolves around Oedipus's, and thus man's search for self-knowledge, which, in turn, empowers him, allowing him to finally take some self-responsibility and attain both heroic status and salvation through an act of self-sacrifice.

These riddling contests are often represented physically in various forms of combat, such as the jousts of knights, where the winner is always the one who is the most Christian, again, the physical contest representative of the spiritual and psychological state.

The actual riddles, then, are going to represent some psychological/ethical/spiritual qualities in the two contestants. With this in mind, it should be noted that Bilbo's riddles reveal a certain humanity that Gollum's lack, and Gollum's a futility, despair, not to be found in Bilbo's. Interestingly, Gollum is able to rather quickly answer Bilbo's riddles, suggesting that Gollum has more in common with Bilbo than we have been given to know (and we will find out what this is in *The Lord of the Rings*).

The contest ends up involving four riddles from each, with Bilbo finally winning after breaking the rules and asking a question.

Bilbo's first riddle is actually a very common childhood riddle:

Thirty white horses on a red hill,
First they champ,
Then they stamp,
Then they stand still.

Gollum knows the answer and immediately guesses teeth, even revealing that he has only six himself. This seems at first curious, since Gollum doesn't have the right number of teeth, and thus would have to reach beyond his current situation to figure it out (of course, once we find out Gollum was once a hobbit, his quick answer makes more sense).

The obvious level of meaning involving eating here certainly relates to Bilbo's childhood before his adventure (and his numerous daily meals have been highlighted in the initial chapter of the story). The rite of passage beyond the initial feeding at the mother's breast (Freud's oral stage of development) is also represented in the final line, where the eating stops.

Gollum's first riddle is:

Voiceless it cries,
Wingless flutters,
Toothless bites,
Mouthless mutters.

Bilbo comes up with the answer, the wind. Notice the despairing quality of the images, the oxymoron juxtapositions, the suggestions of *nothingness* in repetition of the denying "less" syllables, voiceless, wingless, toothless, and mouthless, and the negative actions of cries, flutters, bits, and mutters.

Bilbo knows the answer, the wind, an entity without substance or form, much like Gollum's current psyche.

Bilbo then riddles:

An eye in a blue face

Saw an eye in a green face.
"That eye is like to this eye,"
Said the first eye,
"But in low place
Not in high place."

Gollum again manages to guess the answer, sun on the daisies, revealing, again, that he has lived above ground.

Plotinus claimed that the eye would not be able to see the sun if, in a manner, it were not itself a sun. Given that the sun is the source of light and that light is symbolic of the intelligence and of the spirit, then the process of seeing represents a spiritual act and symbolizes understanding. (23) Thus, the eye is the passage to the soul or self, and the two eyes here are an obvious reference to the two characters, one from the world of light (and though it's a bit reductive, an obvious connection to the super-ego), one from the world of the earth (and connected to the plant and physical world; once again, though a bit reductive, having a connection to the id or libido, the life force); and the connection between the two is necessary for a total healthy psyche (in other words, Bilbo needs Gollum as much as Gollum needs Bilbo). And, since both know the answer to this riddle of life, again, they are connected and, thus, capable of union.

Even the colors are important, the blue face referring to the sky is a spiritual or intellectual color (again related to the super-ego). Jolan de Jacobi, referring to Jung's color symbolism, says that Jung sees "blue, the colour of the rarefied atmosphere, of the clear sky," as standing for "thinking." (24), and green as representing vegetation, thus connected with life, but also with the transitoriness of life, including death.

Gollum's next riddle goes:

It cannot be seen, cannot be felt,
Cannot be heard, cannot be smelt.
It lies behind stars and under hills,
  And empty holes it fills.
It comes first and follows after,
  Ends life, kills laughter.

Once again, it's worth nothing the negative words and images here, the repetition of "cannot," the denial of the senses, the final line, "ends life, kills laughter."

Bilbo again guesses the answer, the dark. The obvious negative qualities of dark need little elaboration. As Cirlot states, "the darkness introduced into the world, after the advent of light, is regressive; hence, too, the fact that it is traditionally associated with the principle of evil and with the base, unsublimated forces. (25). However, it's not quite so simple as this, because dark is also the matter or landscape out of which all came, and, thus, is the source of life, the primordial chaos or ocean. It is also connected with the night and the dream, and, thus, with the unconscious. And, as Freud and his followers have stressed, the unconscious is the most important part of the psyche, and, in fact, the place where the human mind escapes all of the contexts of environment and establishes a reality of self. Connecting all this up with the underground cave, the tunnels, and the water, it is easy to see the powerful psychic world Bilbo has entered, and how it will either swallow him (much as it has swallowed Gollum), or empower him, should he learn to navigate it and gain control over its energy (i.e., the id, the libido, the drive to life).

The importance of Bilbo being able to come up with the answer here cannot be overstated. It means that he does on some level relate to this world; and naming things is a standard symbol of gaining control over them (as an aside, that's a central element in the story of *Rumplestiltskin*, where he represents the id that the miller's daughter must incorporate and gain control over by naming in order to transform into an adult).

Bilbo counters with:

A box without hinges, key, or lid,
Yet golden treasure inside is hid.

Gollum has some trouble with this one, but, again is able to connect and guess the answer, which is eggs.

The symbolism partakes of the obvious connection of an egg with birth, with potential, with a state of transformation, with, in fact, the world of the id, and in terms of transformation on all levels, with birth into the world of the spirit (the connection of the egg with Easter carries this symbolism for Christianity).

Of course, for humans (for most animals), the eggs are in the womb, which we have already seen is symbolized by the underground tunnels of Mother Earth, or, in a psychological sense, the unconscious, the birthplace of all of our psychic life.

Again, if we are alert to it, the imagery and subject matter are life-giving, rather than Gollum's life-denying riddles.

Gollum comes back with:

Alive without breath,
As cold as death;
Never thirsty, ever drinking,
All in mail never clinking.

Now it's getting harder for Bilbo, but he gets some help from his own watery darkness, and a fish jumps out of the water, keying him to answer correctly fish.

Notice yet again, the negative quality of the riddle. I don't think it's necessary to dwell on that, as it must be obvious by now.

The center of this riddle is the fish, which, as Campbell says, is the life force of the water (remember the early discussion of the whale). This is the encounter with the world of nature and the body. Campbell states, "Metaphorically, water is the unconscious, and the creature in the water is the life or energy of the unconscious, which has overwhelmed the conscious personality and must be disempowered, overcome and controlled." (26)

As with the previous discussing of gaining control over some psychic force by naming it, here Biblo gains control over this, or at least is able to connect with it, incorporate it, symbolically, by naming it.

Bilbo's last riddle:

No-legs lay on one leg, two-legs sat near
On three-legs, four-legs got some.

Gollum easily comes up with the answer, and a rather complex one it is: Fish on a little table, man at table sitting on a stool, the cat has the bones.

Here we have some complex connections with previous riddles, the fish, the eating or consuming, even the connection of absorbing or making the fish a part of oneself. Interestingly, there is also an unavoidable connection with the Riddle of the Sphinx from *Oedipus Rex* (because of the use of various numbers of legs to represent or symbolize the answer), opening a huge door of meanings, including the connection with the answer, which is man or self. Without taking the time to go into it, it is hard to avoid mentioning the connections with Freud's Oedipus complex here and how he stresses this as central to human development. The story of Oedipus Rex is strongly centered on the empowerment that comes from self-knowledge, the knowledge of who and what one is, which is, in reality, what Oedipus seeks throughout the play, and what, in reality, is going on in this riddling contest between Bilbo and Gollum.

Now we come to the final riddle from Gollum:

This thing all things devours;
Birds, Beasts, Trees, Flowers;
Gnaws iron, bites steel;
Grinds hard stones to meal;

Slays kings, ruins towns;
And beats high mountains down.

Again, Bilbo is saved by his own, as of yet unknown, but nonetheless evident qualities, as there is more to him than he realizes (which we have been told over and over again by Gandalf), and thinking he simply asking for more time to think, he gets the answer, which is in fact time.

Time is such an important aspect of all of life, and has so many levels of meaning that anything said about it must acknowledge much more remains to be said. It is one of the most important restrictions on human existence, and at the same time one of the most important landscapes of the human psyche (we mentally live in time, escaping the present into both past and future in our minds), yet at the same time, we know that we only have a short time to exist physically, and, thus, time is both the liberator and prison guard of human existence.

Time is what ends eternity, and eternity is the escape from time. But these huge concepts are too much to dwell on here. In a more concrete sense, the realization of the limits of time is perhaps the most important one in terms of the transformation from a child to an adult (and is specified in the life cycle involving birth and death; one must have the other, and, as Freud struggled to clarify later in his career, Eros, or the drive to life, is not alone, but operates in conjunction with thanatos, the drive to death.

In other words, in guessing this, perhaps even more so in guessing it from some part of himself other than the conscious mind, Bilbo is exhibiting an ability and also a desire to move beyond childhood into adulthood.

This is the crucial moment. Bilbo has entered into a frightening place of transformation, taken on the "test" of a battle with his id, and must trust his intuitive abilities to succeed. These are the qualities that go beyond the intellect, beyond the conscious mind, and we have already seen how he has somewhat accidentally plugged into them. But now it's time to break the rules, to actually cheat and take self-responsibility.

Bilbo goes directly to his symbolic center, his heart, his soul, his self. The ring he has found (remember the earlier discussion of the symbolism of this).

But isn't this unfair to Gollum? After all, Bilbo has broken the rules. According to Jorge J. E. Gracia, Gollum shouldn't have even tried to answer the question, should have refused and asked for a proper riddle. Gracia states, "Once he had accepted the question and tried to answer it, even though he demanded three guesses, which is unusual, he was bound by his promise. Gollum, like all hobbits, attaches great weight to riddle contests." (27) Again, I refer you back to a previous discussion here, that elaborating on the importance of the riddle contest and obedience to its results. Basically, Bilbo had cheated, but Gollum had the chance to refuse the question. However, Gollum's natural curiosity (and probably his desire to lose; i.e., his underlying hobbit ethos) led him to join in his own defeat.

With this final success, the result of breaking the rules, of going against the *public persona*, the respectable Baggins *persona,* the *ego,* Bilbo has gained control over this dangerous *id* or *shadow*, and is empowered. We see this immediately, as he is able to get his *id/shadow* to lead him out of the mountain, back to the world of light, and his ability to become invisible allows him to easily escape the goblins. Richard Purtill states, "The ring of invisibility that Bilbo 'accidentally' finds on his adventure is again a mark of his increased power, evidenced by his ability to trade riddles with Gollum and make the creature guide him out of the caverns." (28). It has obviously saved his life, and will continue to do so in the rest of the story.

But in Jungian terms, this empowerment is a delicate balancing act. The *ego* must not be denied or lost when one allows the *shadow* to emerge. They need to balance each other for a healthy *self.*

J. R. R. Tolkien's *The Lord of the Rings* ties this struggle to the power of the *ring* and allows us to watch it play out.

Crouching near Sam and Frodo (who clutches the ring) while they sleep, Sméagol, originally a normal Hobbit, but now driven mad and twisted by the power of the ring, struggles with his *shadow self*, Gollum, who was made powerful until the ring was lost, but now without his ring is but a withered, piteous creature living in the caves beneath the Misty Mountains, a creature compelled to regain his "precious" at all costs, just as a drug addict seeks yet another hit of his self-destroying drug.

> GOLLUM: (with an evil expression) We wants it. We needs it. Must have the precious.
> They stole it from us. Sneaky little hobbitses. Wicked, tricksy, false!
> SMEAGOL: (sweetly) No! Not master.
> GOLLUM: Yes precious. First they will cheat you, hurt you, LIE.
> SMEAGOL: Master's my friend!
> GOLLUM: You don't have any friends, nobody likes you!
> SMEAGOL: (covering his ears) I'm not listening, I'm not listening.
> GOLLUM: You're a liar and a thief.
> SMEAGOL: No!
> GOLLUM: Mur-der-er.
> SMEAGOL: Go away!
> GOLLUM: Go away? (Gollum laughs manically as Sméagol begins crying)

SMEAGOL: I hate you, I hate you.
GOLLUM: Where would you be without me? Gollum! Gollum saved us! It was me!
We survived because of me! (Sméagol stops crying)
SMEAGOL: (sitting up) Not anymore.
GOLLUM: What did you say?
SMEAGOL: Master looks after us now, we don't need you anymore. Leave now, and
never come back!
GOLLUM: What?
SMEAGOL: LEAVE NOW AND NEVER COME BACK! (Gollum screams in
frustration)
SMEAGOL: LEAVE NOW AND NEVER COME BACK! (Silence)
(Sméagol hesitates and looks around, then realizes that Gollum has left, and he begins to dance and jump around) We told him to go away... and away he goes! Gone, gone, gone!
Sméagol is free! (29)

It would be nice if it were this simple, but in truth, as we must expect, Sméagol is not free. He has succumbed to his *shadow* (it has gained control over his *self).*

While Carl Jung did not offer extensive discussions of the female counterpart to the male *shadow,* William Wyler directed a brilliant exploration of it in *The Letter*, a 1940 film based on a Somerset Maugham story by the same name. (30)

It begins with a view of the appropriately symbolic moon at night in the "uncivilized" British colony of Malay. The exotic "oriental" music confirms the mysterious, *shadowy* world of this rubber plantation where the corrupt European landlords will play out the spiritual, ethical and psychological darkness that winds through their lives, and the dark nightmarish world of the sleeping natives is lovingly caressed by the slow moving camera that draws us into it.

We see a rubber tree with scored bark in the shadows, and we hear the sap dripping into a bucket. The camera pulls back to show us that it is but one of many, and serves as both a literal and symbolic representation of the crude conquering and abuse of nature by Imperialist Europe. It is a juxtaposed confrontation between the corrupt sunlight world of the European *persona*, the world of the *ego*, driven by the *male psyche*, the *conscious* world of Apollo, and the dangerous dark, native, Oriental *persona*, the world of the shadow, driven by the *female psyche*, the *unconscious* world of Apollo's twin sister Artemis, goddess of the moon. As A. Stevens points out, the moon is "conceived of as feminine in our tradition, as it is in most traditions, and commonly associated with the Mother archetype, the Queen of Heaven." (31) It will receive featured treatment throughout the film, an image used again and again to symbolize the dark *shadow* side of the feminine psyche.

The tree, with its roots growing ever deeper into the earth and its branches reaching toward the sun, symbolizes the coming together of the *conscious* and *unconscious* worlds (similar to the tree in the Garden of Eden), and the attempt to control and steal the sap, the life blood or life force of these rubber trees, represents the attempt by European civilization to control and use (and abuse) the rich dark psychic world of nature. Since women and Mother Earth (Nature) have the same life giving qualities, and thus, as Gomes and Kanner say, "despoiling the Earth and subjugating women are intimately connected." (32) As we will see later, Leslie Crosbie's powerful *shadow* and her inability to control it stem from an inability to continue to conform to the European *persona* expected of her. She and the tree are intertwined, and she cannot deny the life force surging through her from her psychic roots deep in the swampy earth of her *unconscious*. She will represent, as R. A. Johnson states, a situation where "We divide the self into an ego and a shadow because our culture insists we behave in a particular manner. This is our legacy from having eaten of the fruit of the tree of knowledge." (33) Leslie's *self* can no longer maintain the needed balance. Her *shadow* has been so denied by the world she lives in that it rebels against it, demanding satisfaction.

But that is yet to come. Now, in the first frames of the film, the camera seduces us into a dark dream, flirting with us, as if the camera itself is a form of the *female shadow* and knows we cannot resist its allure. We are aware we are far from the city lights and noisy confusion of civilization with all of its rules about what is good and bad, rules that deny us our own drives and desires, our own *shadows*. It is as if we have found some dark satanic world that both entices and frightens us, a place where people who have already tasted the forbidden fruit move among the shaded bars of our own nature. Then a gun shot from within the plantation owner's house rudely breaks the languid scene, and a man comes stumbling out the front door onto the porch. Dressed in black, the plantation owner's wife Leslie (played by Bette Davis) follows, coldly shooting him again and again. The camera pans up to her face and then juxtaposes it with the moon as the clouds cross temporarily in front of it. When the moon reappears it casts her shadow over the man she has just murdered. Dogs bark. The black workers gather. Leslie invites the main one inside and orders the others to remove the body, alerting the audience immediately to her powerful and dishonest personality with the sentence "There's been an accident."

She goes into her room and locks the door, dismissing the man, who in an obvious foreshadowing of a powerful symbol to be emphasized throughout the movie, picks up the intricate lace work she has been doing.

Her husband Bob is notified and rushes home. As she is throughout most of the movie, she is cold and emotionless, except when she needs to use an emotional ploy. Also, as she does throughout the movie, she easily lies, saying "He tried to make love to me and I shot him." Howard Joyce, her friend and lawyer, however, is not so easily deceived, and we watch him considering the fact she shot the man six times, suggesting more was involved than a simple need to protect herself.

The others are easily deceived, especially her husband, and the scene reveals her deceptive abilities as she weaves her web of what happened, accomplishing her desired effect of causing all of them, except Howard, to feel pity for the "poor child."

The next morning, she is informed that she is not going to get away with it as easily as she hopes, for she has, after all, just killed a man and just might be imprisoned for murder, and the movie emphasizes her impending prison time, as well as her psychological prison, by continually having the striped shadows of the window shades crossing over her (later these same "bars" will cross both Howard and Bob as they are drawn into her psychosis). Throughout the scene she blithely maintains her story.

It is decided she must go to Singapore immediately to begin the process of a trial. As she packs for her trip she needs to know her husband can still love her after her act of violence:

> "We have been happy, haven't we?"
> "You've been the best wife a man could have. If only there were something I could do."
> "You can love me. That's all I need."
> "I've always loved you."
> "Yes. But now…"
> "Leslie, darling, if I could love you any more, I would now."

Then when they leave the house, we see her shadow pass over the place where Hammond died, and we get our first view of his wife, the dark, shadowy, sinister, oriental woman dressed in black standing in the shadows, unseen but intently watching them pass by her.

After a scene where Leslie, Bob, and Howard talk, revealing mainly that Bob is weak and trusts her without question, saying "She shot him as she would have shot a mad dog," and a brief scene where Howard's obsequious clerk Ong, certainly an evil little man, tells him about a "friend" who has a letter proving Leslie has been lying and has, in fact, been having an affair with this man she just killed, a letter that is so incriminating that she will almost certainly be found guilty if it is exposed. Ong leaves Howard a copy of the letter and the beginnings of what turns out to be a well thought through plan for blackmail.

Now, when Leslie comes to see him, Howard is ready to catch her in her lie. At first, while she is gathering her thoughts and trying to reinvent her story, she denies it:

> Leslie: We heard about his wife. . . . once, quite by chance, I actually saw her . . .
>
> Howard: What was she like?
>
> Leslie: Horrible. She was all covered in gold chains . . . a face like a mask . . .
>
> Howard: So when you knew about her, you stopped having anything to do with Hammond?
>
> Leslie: (smug) Yes.

The insinuation is that Hammond was no longer acceptable because of his Eurasian (lesser human) wife. As E. C. Whitman states, "The shadow is the archetypal experience of the 'other fellow,' who in his strangeness is always suspect. It is the archetypal urge for a scapegoat, for someone to blame and attack in order to vindicate oneself and be justified; it is the archetypal experience of *the enemy*, the experience of blameworthiness which always adheres to the other fellow, since we are under the illusion of knowing ourselves and of having already dealt adequately with our own problems. In other words, to the extent I have to be right and good, *he, she*, or *they* become the carriers of all the evil which I fail to acknowledge within myself" (34).

> Howard: I think I should tell you there is in existence a letter in your hand writing. . .

He continues, saying that this letter puts "an entirely different complexion on the whole case." It is no accident that this particular phrase, which gets repeated, is used, because it has its strong reference to the racism evident throughout the film.

Covered by the horizontal stripes of shadow from the window blinds, which fall over her like the bars of a cell, Leslie denies the letter and is obviously struggling to come up with a new story. She knows she has to admit the letter exists, so she says she invited Hammond over to ask his advice about purchasing a gun for her husband's birthday. (As an aside, the obvious Freudian symbolism here of the gun and the sexual powers of the two men leaps out, foreshadowing the weakness of her husband.)

However, once Howard reads the letter, she knows it is no use denying the obvious relationship she had with Hammond, so she "conveniently" faints and falls to the floor.

When she is revived, she and Howard continue in the First Aid Room. She knows he knows, and she knows she needs a new approach:

> Leslie: Are you going to let them hang me?
> Howard: What do you mean by that, Leslie?
> Leslie: You could get the letter.
> Howard: Do you believe it's so easy to do away with unwelcome evidence?

The tension fills the screen. Howard struggles with his integrity. Leslie uses every ploy she can think of to draw him in, including how it would hurt his friend Bob's reputation. In the end, Howard succumbs, "I won't tell you what I personally thought within I read it (the letter). It's the duty of council to defend his client—not convict her-even in his own mind. I don't want you to tell me anything, but what is needed to save your neck." Now he can no longer justify his actions, and he knows it. In Jungian terms, the *psychological shadow* driving Leslie has caught him and his *ego*, his *persona as the uprighteous lawyer* has succumbed to his own *shadow*, amazingly in line with Jung's views of how a man's psychological *shadow* and *anima* work together against the *ego*. He agrees to obtain the letter and join in the deception.

Now the play is put into operation, the workings of the *dark shadow* of Leslie, drawing her ever more into her evil and own dark desires, and the *reluctant shadow* of Howard unable to resist his own corruption. Howard meets with the *id-like* Ong, who is also obviously driven by his own evil desires, though certainly not as powerful or imposing a person, and thus appearing more as a crude, primitive man, more of an annoying man, more of a servant to the *shadow* then those driven by fully developed *shadows*, and an arrangement is made to exchange the exact amount of money Bob has available for the letter. The one condition, and a necessary one, is that Leslie must bring the money to her lover's wife herself. If it were not that Leslie is being drawn to this *shadow woman* within herself, she would never put herself in such a self-deprecating and dangerous position, but it is obvious she is completely under the control of her own dark desires.

After a brief scene where the inept Bob is told about the plan and gives Howard permission to use his money to purchase it without suspecting anything negative about his wife, and another brief scene where Howard and Leslie discuss their "shady plans" with the unsuspecting others, and Leslie says blatantly, "I am so evil," the two of them head to the *dark, shadowy part of the city*, symbolic of not only their own shadowy sides but of all of Europe's shadowy side. It is a scene where the "civilized" world of Europe enters the "uncivilized" world of the Orient.

Leslie wears her carefully knitted, white shawl over her head, an obvious symbol of her attempt to hide beneath her ego-controlled, socially acceptable, non-sexual persona from the dark masochistic drives of her shadow. The camera has drawn our eyes to this lacework throughout the story, beginning in the initial scene, when the man left in the front room after Leslie locked herself in her bedroom saw it discarded on the table and briefly picked it up, an obvious symbolic foreshadowing. Shortly before her meeting with Mrs. Hammond that she has been driven by her shadow to experience, Howard and Leslie have the following exchange:

> Howard: (referring to her needlework) "It must take enormous concentration and patience."
> Leslie: "I find it soothing."

On a simple level, this lace work, beautiful to the eye and painstaking work to achieve, is a symbol for the proper, civilized life she has *stitched together* with her husband, the *persona* she has worked on so hard and tried to live up to, but cannot.

The shadowy Mrs. Hammond will tell her to remove it when they meet.

The annoying Ong, in his role as the servant or messenger of the shadow, takes Howard and Leslie to that uncivilized, moon-drenched world of the dark side, and we watch as Howard and Leslie browse in the Chinese store that serves as a front for the dark energy taking place upstairs. In another obvious bit of foreshadowing, Leslie is drawn to an elaborately carved oriental knife (with its connotations of sex and death). Soon they are led upstairs to an Opium Den, completed by an animal-like man smoking the opiate. While oriental music is played, they wait.

Then glass chimes tinkle and Mrs. Hammond parts the beaded curtain to enter. Dressed in black and wearing a stern mask-like expression, she stares at Leslie with "eyes like a cobra's eyes." Indeed, she is in the power position, the dark energy force, similar to the Biblical Lilith, who has been said to be the snake in the Garden of Eden, and she demands obedience. Not surprisingly, she does not speak in English, only the language of that dark, uncivilized world of Malay. Staring intently at Leslie, she tells Ong to tell Leslie that she must remove her shawl. Leslie obeys without hesitation. The money is passed to this dark demanding woman, but she waves it away. She demands that Leslie approach her, and Leslie obeys. The camera angle emphasizes how this dark shadowy woman looms over Leslie. She produces the letter from her sleeve and purposely lets it fall to the floor. In complete submission, Leslie kneels slowly and picks it up. "Thank you," she whispers.

There is more going on here than a simple desire to avoid persecution by a jury. Leslie is caught up in this dark woman's power. Leslie is drawn to her, drawn to obey and serve her. Indeed, this woman is that *psychological shadow* of the night, that strange desire to undermine the sunlight world of the *ego* and the *self.*

From this point on, Leslie becomes serene, a zombie working quietly on her lacework, almost indifferent to the outcome of the trial.

Of course, Howard has already given in to his weakness, and he performs his role at the trial, pointing out that there is no incriminating evidence to convict Leslie. There is no need to drag out the trial or the wait while the jury considers the verdict. Shortly, they arrive at the obvious; she is innocent.

Weak and ignorant Bob then comes up with a new plan. He is going to purchase a plantation in Sumatra, going to move with what he views as his innocent and loving wife to a new world, a better place. At first, Leslie agrees, but then realizes that Bob no longer has the money to purchase such a place and attempts to use her standard ploy of lying to change his mind. Howard, who we remember is also implicated in the dark digressions, also attempts to dissuade Bob. But Bob in his most demanding moment insists, and they are forced to tell him his money is gone. That letter had more in it than he thought.

While he is incredibly naïve, upon reading the letter, he finally realizes his loving wife was in fact cheating on him. Leslie confesses everything, how she was drawn to Hammond, pursued him even as he denied her. She did not kill him because he attacked her but because he rejected her, and in fact, she still does love him. We already know it, but now it is clear that she has been completely overcome by her *shadow*. She is not in control. It is.

Weak Bob is completely broken and leaves them. Howard knows Bob doesn't have the strength of character to stand up to the powers of the world of the shadow and says: "He's going to forgive you." Leslie also knows it and replies, "Yes." Neither is happy about this. Both want someone to stand up to their own failures. But there is no one to do so.

Had this film been but a superficial expression of a corrupt woman, it would have likely ended here. But the battle with the *shadow* is not yet complete. Now, in a better conclusion than the original one written by Somerset Maugham (where Bob is the one who confronts Hammond's mistress and recovers the letter), Edward Koch's screen play drives us to a much, much deeper conclusion.

As Leslie's emotionally destroyed husband Bob makes a fool of himself getting drunk at the bar while the party swirls about him, Leslie leaves it, drawn to that darkness, that world represented by the silent, moonlit garden behind her room. She opens the door and sees the knife she admired earlier on the mat, calling to her.

She is called back into the party, dances in a daze for a while, but cannot remain in that false, civilized gathering and goes back to her room. In a desperate attempt to regain control, she tries to knit, but cannot. The bars of the shutters again cross over her. Bob enters. Leslie tries to talk positively about their future, tries to keep her dark desires hidden. But she cannot do it. "Robert, it's no use, is it? We can't go on." She absolves him, telling him what a good, kind man he is. He tells her he forgives her, as she has known all along he would do. She tries to put up a good front, tells him she will try to make him happy, but finally cannot continue the charade and says she still loves the man she murdered.

Yet again made weak and defeated, Bob leaves. Leslie has accepted her fate, and opens the door to the night, the moon, and the garden. The knife has disappeared from her doormat. She follows her own *shadow* out into the garden (in what is an overly obvious reference to her obedience to this dark, psychological force). The exotic oriental music of the unconscious and supernatural worlds, the realities beyond the conscious, civilized world of Europe plays. There is only the inevitable now, and we are drawn by our own dark side to follow her as she follows her *shadow* to Mrs. Hammond, that dark woman, the exotic psychological and mythological goddess (who goes by many names, Lilith, Kali, Hecate, Morgauna), the universal female *shadow* with the emotionless mask of a face.

The woman kills her with the knife.

Leslie has lost herself in her *shadow*. This powerful dark female entity has defeated her attempts at maintaining control, at being socially correct, at playing the dutiful wife, at living out the European version of a civilized woman.

Demetra George writes: "The Dark Goddess leads us into the labyrinth of our unconscious. . . . forces us to look at ourselves with utter, naked honesty. For many of us this is very frightening—to see ourselves stripped of our illusions and false pretensions. . . As we descend into the dark depths of our hidden beings, we may discover our frustration, resentment, and anger that lie buried beneath the layers of our socially conditioned 'nice and normal' persona. Encounters with the Dark Goddess make us dissatisfied with the part of our lives that forces us to deny our true feelings." (35) Nor Hall writes: "One has to give something to the death dealing mother, acknowledge her presence, leave a candle at her crossroads, admit your shadow side to view. If you give a part of yourself to lunacy, she will permit you to pass to and from the realm of the moon's dark phase. Otherwise she will detain you and stupor and blackness will possess you." (36)

And it is all elemental, the deep drive within, the desires of the blood, of that rebellious, maverick, male or female, that needs to be an individual, that needs to challenge the sunlight logic of existence and establish the individual, the Thanatos beyond Eros, that demands its own existence.

Joseph Conrad presents the need to not give into the *shadow* but to incorporate it into the total *self* in a precise, parable-like novella, *The Secret Sharer.* (37)

In parable fashion, the main character is unnamed. He has assumed the position of captain of his first ship on a fortnight previous to when the story begins; his is untried and unsure of himself. Because of his uncertainty he does not yet have the needed authority and confidence to successfully command a ship, and though he is well-meaning, he is weak, not yet in control of his ship and by extension his life, not yet a man.

Because of this, when we first meet him, he is standing watch at night (instead of ordering one of his men to do so). He sees a man we soon find out is named Leggatt come swimming through the water from another ship, the *Sephora*, a man who has been imprisoned on that ship for killing another seaman while simultaneously saving the ship from a terrible storm. While Leggatt did not intentionally commit the murder, and might have even been justified in his actions, he is nevertheless a criminal, a renegade, a powerfully brutish, take-charge man, one willing to break the rules.

The young captain, at this time, would not have done what Laggett did, for he is still controlled by those very rules, and he represents the more "rational," yet more "timid" aspects of being a man. He is a boy/ man who has just begun his rite-of-passage from the expected and normal "psychological obedience" expected of a child into the necessary "self-responsibility" of an adult, a "captain" who can take charge of his own "ship," can take charge of his own life, can bite the *forbidden fruit* and live outside of the innocent and meaningless world of Eden.

Separately, Leggatt and the Captain are incomplete, one too timid, rational and obedient to the rules of civilization, the other too independent and brutish. They need to merge, and if so, then the Captain will be a perfect commander, one who can be trusted to confidently sail his ship through dangerous waters.

In the suggested connection, the doubling of these two men, Conrad might be condemned as being too obvious, for he gives Leggatt the same looks as the Captain, two men who are physically identical twins. He leaves us no choice but to see them as two aspects of one person.

And then the Captain does something that transforms him. He hides this criminal in his cabin and helps him escape to shore. He has, in other words, accepted responsibility for that dark side of himself, that *shadow* within him, for certainly he would have been condemned, court marshaled and stripped of his command, his adulthood, had he been caught aiding this criminal's escape. And now he is no longer pure and innocent. He has a dangerous secret, a shadowy criminal hidden inside him that he can never reveal to his civilization. He has accepted that *shadow* inside him that he needs to balance with his *ego*, the mask, the *persona* he must wear to continue to exist in his public life.

It is not surprising that the next day he confidently sails his ship through some dangerous waters.

Alan Watts writes: "There is a point, not at all easy to determine, at which inattention and opposition to the essential ambivalence of nature becomes neurotic . . . For the dark side of life, the principle of evil or of man's irreducible rascality, is to be "reckoned with." (38)

The lesson: We must each encounter and incorporate our *shadow*, but then must keep it from gaining control over us.

Jung also throws the *anima* into his mix of psychic archetypes. Biologically, men and women have the hormones of both sexes, and characteristics attributed to each sex can be found to various degrees in the other sex. Thus, we are all in some ways bi-sexual. The male psychic equivalent to the *anima* is the *animus*, and for a healthy psychic life, both entities must work together, each giving its specific qualities to the totality.

George Lucas gives us a straight-forward expression of this in the initial three films of his Star Wars series (39)

We first meet Leia, a princess (symbolic of her super-ego status, which is reinforced by her flowing white robe attire--representing her purity and her position as a spiritual person (associated with agape) and one connected to nature, as opposed to the mechanical men she faces). She has the plans to the evil Empire's Death Star, and she gives them to R2D2 just before she is captured. R2D2 and CP3O exit the space ship (in obvious "birth" symbolism) and land on Tatooine, Luke's home planet.

Luke is living on his aunt and uncle's farm, as they struggle to grow crops in the middle of the huge desert that makes up most of the planet, symbolic of efforts to keep spirituality alive in a wasteland. At the same time, it serves as a womb, a secure place for Luke live out his childhood.

But now he is reaching the age where he is becoming anxious to push back this small world and entire adulthood.

R2D2 and C3PO are captured by the Jawas, scavengers living in the desert, and brought to the farm to be sold. Luke's foster father, Uncle Owen, purchases them and tells Luke to clean them up. As Luke is doing this, he accidentally ignites a projected image of Leia from R2D2, who is malfunctioning because of the lock the Jawas have put on him, and when Luke sees her, he is enthralled by her, says she is "beautiful," exactly how a psychically healthy *animus* would respond to its *anima*.

After Luke goes through a three-part "call to adventure" in the frame of a "heroes adventure" (the first him seeing Leia with the message for Obi-wan; the second Obi-wan inviting him to partake in the adventure; and the third the death of his foster parents), has his departure (stepping over the threshold from the known world of childhood into the unknown world of adulthood), which takes place at Moss Easley, and results in Han Solo and Chewbacca, two more "helpers," joining him, finds the Rebels' home world of Alderson has just been destroyed by the Death Star (the mechanical equivalent of the "beast" in the ocean, here a cosmic ocean), he and his companions enter beast (what Joseph Campbell calls entering the belly of the whale, in reference to the biblical Jonah's similar experience in the whale's belly). In this case, the belly is represented by the Death Star's trash compactor.

Obi-wan has gone off from the group to disengage the power-field preventing them from escaping, and R2D2, plugging into the star's computers finds that Princess Leia is imprisoned deep inside it. Luke immediately demands they rescue her. Han, who at this point neither knows her nor cares about her, sees no reason to risk his neck to save her; but Luke suggests a huge reward, and Han (who begins the films as a very practical, *id* driven person) understands the language of money. So a plan is hatched. And soon they manage to free Leia from her cell. However, they are all cornered by the Empire's soldiers. Leia, demonstrating her leadership qualities and her courage, blasts open a passage to the Trash Compactor, and they all follow her down into it.

Now the symbolism of the belly of the whale comes at the viewers full force. Luke is dragged beneath the water (symbolic of transformation—think of baptism) by a snake-like creature (with all of the symbolism of the snake, including transformation (it sheds its skin and is reborn), the enticer and giver of the knowledge (think of the Garden of Eden), and even the representative of the *shadow* (think again of the snake in the Garden of Eden). When Luke emerges, he is chocking on the water (the stomach fluid of the beast), and as Joseph Campbell claims, this is symbolic of taking in the essence of the beast, of connecting up with the body, with nature, with the beast side of oneself; it is necessary for empowerment). Here is Campbell's discussion:

> Moyers: What's the mythological significance of the belly?
>
> Campbell: The belly is the dark place where digestion takes place and new energy is created. The story of Jonah and the whale is an example of a mythic theme that is practically universal, of the hero going into a fish's belly and ultimately coming out again, transformed.
>
> Moyers: Why must the hero do that?
>
> Campbell: It's a descent into the dark. Psychologically, the whale represents the power of life licked in the unconscious. Metaphorically, water is the unconscious, and the creature in the water is the life or energy of the unconscious, which has overwhelmed the conscious personality and must be disempowered, overcome and controlled.
>
> In the first stage of this kind of adventure, the hero leaves the realm of the familiar, over which he has some measure of control, and comes to a threshold, let us say the edge of a lake or sea, where a monster of the abyss comes to meet him. There are then two possibilities. In a story of the Johan type, the hero is swallowed and taken into the abyss to be later resurrected—a variant of the death-and-resurrection theme. The conscious personality here has come in touch with a charge of unconscious energy which it is unable to handle and must now suffer all the trails and revelations of a terrifying night-sea journey, while learning how to come to terms with this power of the dark and emerge, at last, to a new way of life.
>
> The other possibility is that the hero, on encountering the power of the dark, may overcome and kill it, as did Siegfried and St. George when they killed the dragon. But as Siegfried learned, he must then taste the dragon blood, in order to take to himself something of that dragon power. When Siegfried has killed the dragon and tasted the blood, he hears the song of nature. He has transcended his humanity and reassociated himself with the powers of nature, which are the powers of our life, and from which our minds remove.
>
> You see, consciousness thinks it's running the shop. But it's a secondary organ of a total human being, and it must not put itself in control. It must submit and serve the humanity of the body. When it does put itself in control, you get a man like Darth Vader in *Star Wars* the man who goes over to the consciously intentional side.
>
> Moyers: The dark figure.
>
> Campbell: Yes, that's the figure that in Goethe's *Faust* is represented by Mephistopheles. (40)

I included the last bit here on Darth Vader to provide another aspect of the *shadow*, for Darth Vader most certainly does represent that. But for our current discussion, the point is that Luke clearly goes into a version of the belly of the whale, and he will emerge transformed, which we see immediately when he very capably helps Han Solo fight the Tie Fighters during their escape from the Death Star, something Luke could not have done prior to that belly of the whale experience, as demonstrated by his inept comments while Han provided his escape from the Empire's space fighters at Moss Easley. Now, however, after Luke's transformation, and upon his destruction of one of the Tie Fighters and bragging about it, Han pointedly says, "Don't get cocky," and the double-entendre jumps out at us.

Luke has indeed begun his transformation from boy to man, and a part of that is the result of him rescuing his *anima* Leia from the Death Star. But this oversimplifies it a bit, as Leia has a much of a role in the escape as Luke. Certainly, he initiated it, and he went into her cell to free her, but from that moment on, the emphasis is as much on her as him. It's no accident that the two of them get separated and have to work together to escape. The main scene here is when they get locked on a ledge with the Storm Troopers threatening to bust through the door, and an endless fall awaiting them if they cannot find a way across it. Luke hands Leia the powerful gun, which she welds amazingly well, as he expertly throws a hooked rope over a metal bar above them so they can swing Tarzan style to the other side. Noticeably, Leia gives Luke a kiss for luck. She misses his mouth, but it seems almost certain she is meant to kiss him there, and the symbolism of exchanging one's life breath, one's spirit makes for wonderful symbolism of the unity of the *anima* and *animus*. In a later scene, this will be made blatantly clear when Leia kisses Luke forcefully on the mouth.

Throughout the rest of *A New Hope* they will work together, Leia mainly in her super-ego role as military commander, and Luke in his hero's role, his role as a Jedi Knight (with the same spiritual connotations as the original Knights of the Round Table). The movie will conclude with Luke destroying the Death Star by trusting his connection to the Force, followed by Leia, her hair symbolically curled up above her head in the form of a crown, assuming her role as the political, social, military, spiritual and mythic leader to recognize her successful warriors.

In *The Empire Strikes Back* Luke and Leia will spend most of their time apart, Leia going through some complex literal and symbolic interactions with Han, and Luke spending most of his time on Degobah, the swampy planet that symbolizes both his own unconscious (he says "it's like something out of a dream) and Jung's universal, archetypal unconscious (it looks like a primitive swamp, complete with pterodactyls), where his spiritual guide Yoda will go about training him to be a Jedi.

In one interesting scene, Luke is drawn into a cave on Degobah (which symbolizes him going into one of his own psychological "caves"). Yoda tells him not to take a weapon, but he does out of fear anyway. In the cave, with its symbolic snakes and lizards, he meets a ghostly version of Darth Vader (the *shadow* side of his own father). He immediately draws his light saber, and in the short sword fight that follows cuts off Darth Vader's head. In a moment it rolls to his feet, and he sees his own face in the black helmet. It is obvious that Darth Vader is both the black, *shadow* of his father Anakin Skywalker, and thus Luke's own potential *shadow*. But he must not deny his own shadow, must not kill it. He must admit it, incorporate it, and gain control over it. Yoda lets both Luke and us know that Luke has "failed" in striking out against it in fear.

The film will cumulate in a battle between the real Darth Vader and Luke, in the symbolic bowels or belly of the City in the Clouds, an underbelly dominated by black and red passages with doors that slam shut and will not allow any backtracking. This scene is a huge loss of innocence for Luke, as he finds out that he is indeed the son of Darth Vader, and now knows that he is capable of becoming a similar evil man. It is a huge fall, and is represented by him falling down through the shaft of the planet, into a passage, and eventually out the bottom to hang on an upside down cross. The door closes (once we lose our innocence we cannot regain it). His hand, the messenger of his heart, his self, his humanity, was cut off at the moment of his discovery of his dark side. He calls out to his spiritual father (Obi-wan), just as Christ called out to God.

Leia's scenes with Han continue their super-ego/id roles, she driven by a powerful conscience but needing to awaken her body, her sexual, sensual id, and he driven by an equally powerful libido but needing to awaken his spiritual potential. In one scene, they have flown the Millennium Falcon into what they think at first is a cave, but later find out is the throat and belly of a huge beast (thus both the symbolism of the cave and of the beast are involved). While hiding from the Empire's ships, they go about repairing their own. The key scenes involve Han coming to see if Leia needs help:

> Han: I'm going to shut down everything but the emergency power systems.
>
> *Han and Chewie busily shut down the engine and all electronic systems. Threepio and Leia watch worriedly.*
>
> Threepio: Sir, I'm almost afraid to ask, but . . . does that include shutting me down, too?
>
> Han: No, I need you to talk to the *Falcon*, find out what's wrong with the hyper drive.

Suddenly the ship lurches, causing all the loose items in the cockpit to go flying. Chewie howls.

Threepio: Sir, it's quite possible this asteroid is not entirely stable.

Han: not entirely stable? I'm glad you're here to tell us these things. Chewie, take the professor in the back and plug him into the hyper drive.

Threepio: Oh! Sometimes I just don't understand human behavior. After all, I'm only trying to do my job in the most . . .

The sliding door closes behind the indignant Threepio as he and Chewie move back to the hold. Suddenly the ship lurches again, throwing Leia across the cabin into Han's arms. Then, abruptly, the motion stops as suddenly as it started. With some surprise, Leia realizes she is in Han's arms.

Leia: Let go.

Han: Sshh!

Leia: Let go, please.

Leia flushes, averting her eyes. She's not exactly fighting to get free. But of course Han blows it . . .

Han: Don't get excited.

The anger rises in Leia.

Leia: Captain, being held by you isn't quite enough to get me excited.

Han: Sorry, sweetheart. We haven't got time for anything else.

Han grins wickedly at Leia as he turns and exits through the door. Leia's confused emotions show clearly on her lovely face. (41)

This love/hate relationship that began when they first met in the detention halls of the Death Star gets a wonderful symbolic representation in a later scene in this whale's belly:

Leia finishes welding the valve she has been working on and attempts to reengage the system by pulling a lever attached to the valve. It doesn't budge. Han notices her struggle and moves to help her. She rebuffs him.

Han: Hey, Your Worship, I'm only trying to help.

Leia: (*still struggling*) Would you please stop calling me that?

Han hears a new tone in her voice. He watches her pull on the lever.

Han: Sure, Leia.

Leia: Oh, you make it so difficult sometimes.

Han: I do, I really do. You could be a little nicer, though. (*he watches her reaction*) Come on, admit it. Sometimes you think I'm all right.

She lets go of the lever and licks her sore hand.

Leia: Occasionally, maybe . . . (*a little smile, haltingly*) . . . when you aren't acting like a scoundrel.

Han: Scoundrel? Scoundrel? I like the sound of that.

Han has taken her hand and starts to massage it.

Leia: Stop that.

Han: Stop what?

Leia is flushed, confused.

Leia: Stop that! My hands are dirty.
Han: My hands are dirty, too. What are you afraid of?
Leia: *(looking right into his eyes)* Afraid?
Han looks at her with a piercing look. He's never looked more handsome, more dashing, more confident.
Han: You're trembling.
Leia: I'm not trembling.
Then, with an irresistible combination of physical strength and emotional power, the space pirate begins to draw Leia toward him . . . very slowly.
Han: You like me because I'm a scoundrel. There aren't enough scoundrels in your life.
Leia is now very close to Han, and as she speaks, her voice becomes an excited whisper, a tone completely in opposition to her words.
Leia: I happen to like nice men.
Han: I'm a nice man.
Leia: No, you're not. You're . . .
He kisses her now with slow, hot lips. He takes his time, as though he had forever, bending her body backward. She has never been kissed like this before.
Suddenly Threepio appears in the doorway, speaking excitedly.
Threepio: Sir, sir! I've isolated the reverse power flux coupling.
Han turns slowly, icily, from their embrace.
Han: Thank you. Thank you very much.
Threepio: Oh, you're perfectly welcome, sir. (42)

Notice the intertwining symbols. The hands are the messengers of the heart, and now their once clean hands (representing clean, pure hearts) are dirty. Han (hand) Solo (as in solo heart) is now falling in love, no longer solo. They kiss, sharing their breath (their essence, their hearts). And it all takes place in the belly of a beast, the place where the body connects with the universal world of nature. This is where their relationship switches from bickering to supporting. When they exit this place of transformation, they have been transformed.

It is possible to claim that this relationship is also an *anima/animus* one, and in truth, Leia spends far more time with Han than she does with Luke. That would not deny either her *anima/animus* relationship with Luke or her *super-ego/id* relationship with Han. All of them can be and, in fact, are going on at the same time.

At the end of *The Empire Strikes Back*, while Luke is hanging on the symbolic cross, he and Leia give us an even stronger indication that they are *anima/animus* characters. They communicate telepathically!

The Return of Jedi immediately takes all of them into the world of the *id* or *libido*. Han has been frozen in carbonate and given to a bounty hunter, who, in turn, has brought him to Jabba the Hutt, referred to as a slug. And that is just what Jabba the Hutt is, a slug, which is a snake without the higher qualities of a snake. In other words, Jabba is very simply pure *id*, and so is his world, noticeably an underground cave. It is filled with growing things that have grotesque shapes, life without form, the *id* without the balancing *super-ego*. Here Leia, after awakening Han (a clear death/resurrection theme going on), gets captured by Jabba, and becomes a prisoner of her id (represented by him), and wears that persona, her super-ego garb replaced by a scanty sexual outfit. She has been forced to expose her powerful *id*, and does not have the power, at least not at first, to gain control over it. Instead, it controls her. Luke arrives, dressed in black (he is now a man, no longer an innocent boy dressed in white), and he is forced to face his own *id*, a fight to the death with the very powerful Rancor.

Again, together, Leia and Luke (with the help of the rest of the gang) defeat Jabba. Leia literally chokes him to death with the very chain used to keep her his prisoner (she has clearly exposed and now gained control over her sexual drives).

Both Yoda and Obe-wan now confirm for Luke (and the viewers) that Leia is Luke's twin sister. Now it's time for the final battle. Luke, Leia, Han, Chewy, R2D2, and C3PO go to the Forest Moon of Endore, where they encounter the Ewoks, creatures of nature, exhibiting all of those anti-civilization, anti-military, anti-corrupt qualities of the Empire. They are primitive, prone to see things supernaturally, embrace family, tradition, heritage, community, and all of the "right brain" world. It is only natural they live in the tops of trees in the middle of a lush forest (both places that symbolize the unconscious/spiritual world).

Immediately, Luke and Leia work together on their bikes (futuristic horses) to prevent the soldiers of the Empire from reporting their existence on the moon. They get separated, and Leia ends up making friends with an Ewok. When he takes her to the tribe, they believe she is a goddess and worship her. Now, for the first time, we see her with her long hair let loose to fall over her shoulders (a symbol of her as *nature woman*, only possible because of her previous opening up and gaining control of her sexual *id* qualities). The rest of the group is captured by the Ewoks and appears to be headed for a cannibalistic ritualized death. C3PO, however, because of his shiny gold metal and ability to communicate with them is seen as a god. Luke connects with the Force to raise C3PO off the ground and scare the Ewoks into accepting everyone into the tribe. They hold a tribal gathering, complete with stories, drums, and ceremony, to make it all official.

Then Luke and Leia leave the gathering, and high in the branches of the trees at night (another symbol of the world beyond the conscious world of the sun) Luke tells Leia that she is his sister. She says she knows, says she somehow senses it.

The huge final battle takes place, working on three levels: Luke fighting Darth Vader, Leia, Han and the Ewoks fighting the Empire troops on the Moon, and the rest of the Rebel forces fighting to break into the Death Star in space. In the end, the Rebel Forces win because of Luke's compassion for his father Anakin Skywalker/Darth Vader, which sparks it in return from Anakin, who kills the Evil Emperor to save his son (once again the scene has references to Christ calling out to his father).

Edgar Allen Poe's *The Fall of the House of Usher* is a focused account of an *anima/animus* relationship, with Roderick representing an *animus* and/or a *shadow* psychic force, and his twin sister Madeline representing an *anima* psychic force. (43)

They are the last in a direct line of descent that has definite suggestions of intermarriage (offering a possible medical reason for their condition). Roderick suffers from a "morbid acuteness of the senses," and Madeline suffers from a "settled apathy, a gradual wasting away of the person, and frequent although transient affections of a partly cataleptical character," which causes her to lose consciousness and feeling, resulting in her body assuming a deathlike rigidity. Possible connections between the twins and the house are suggested, as if the physical environment interacts with the psychological conditions of its inhabitants. Roderick becomes "enchanted by certain superstitious impressions in regard to the [mansion]," believing that it controls his behavior. "For many years, he had never ventured forth—in regard to an influence whose superstitious force was conveyed in terms too shadowy here to be restated."

An emotional wreck, Roderick writes a letter to a childhood companion, one he refers to as "his only personal friend," in the hope that the "cheerfulness of" this friend's "society" might help get rid of "his malady." This friend, who serves as the narrator of the tale, is touched by the "apparent *heart* that went with his request," allowing "no room for hesitation." And this stressed *heart* has to suggest the initial quote for the story:

Son Coeur est un luth suspend;
Sitot qu'on le touché il resonne.

This is a quote from De Begranger that translates: "His/her heart is a poised lute; as soon as it is touched it resounds." The sexual ambiguity of *son* leaves it open to refer to either Rodrick or Madeline or perhaps even both of them. The suggestion, especially in the context of the letter and other events that will take place in the story, is that the twins are so alone and have such "acute senses" that they are easily affected by the slightest outside influence; they are emotionally and psychologically hyper-sensitive to their surroundings.

And the story begins with a carefully crafted description of the heavy, disconsolate, morbid connections by the narrator as he approaches the house:

> During the whole of a dull, dark, and soundless day in the autumn of the year, when the clouds hung oppressively low in the heavens, I had been passing alone, on horseback, through a singularly dreary tract of country, and at length found myself, as the shades of the evening drew on, within view of the melancholy House of Usher. I know not how it was—but, with the first glimpse of the building, a sense of insufferable gloom pervaded my spirit. I say insufferable; for the feeling was unrelieved by any of that half-pleasurable, because poetic, sentiment with which the mind usually receives even the sternest natural images of the desolate or terrible. I looked upon the scene before me—upon the mere house, and the simple landscape features of the domain—upon the bleak walls—upon the vacant eye-like windows—upon a few rank sedges—and upon a few white trunks of decayed trees—with an utter depression of soul which I can compare to no earthly sensation more properly than to the after-dream of the reveler upon opium—the bitter lapse into every-day life—the hideous dropping off of the veil. There was an iciness, a sinking, a sickening of the heart—and unredeemed dreariness of thought which no goading of the imagination could torture into aught of the sublime. What was it—I paused to think—what was it that so unnerved me in the contemplation of the House of Usher? It was a mystery all insoluble; nor could I grapple with the shadowy fancies that crowded upon me as I pondered. I was forced to fall back upon the unsatisfactory conclusion, that while, beyond doubt, there *are* combination of very simple natural objects which have the power of thus affecting us, still the analysis of this power lies among considerations beyond our depth. It was possible, I reflected, that a mere different arrangement of the particulars of the scene, of the details of the picture, would be sufficient to modify, or perhaps to annihilate its capacity for sorrowful impression; and, acting upon this idea, I reined my house to the precipitous brink of a black and lurid tarn that lay in unruffled luster by the dwelling, and gazed down—but with a shudder even more thrilling than before—upon the remodeled and inverted images of the gray sedge, and the ghastly tree-stems, and the vacant and eye-like windows.

Naming the house and suggesting it is "melancholy and has "Eye-like windows" helps create the illusion it is a living presence with a human psyche, and admitting that both the house and the surrounding landscape have some mysterious ability to affect the mind cannot help but imply an interaction between the physical world, the *natural* world and the invisible world of the spirit, the comingling of the *natural* and the *supernatural*. The house has been *personified*, and the story will continue to interweave the *psyche* of the house with the *psyches* of the humans.

Both are in a state of death and decay, and when the narrator describes the house, pointing out that "no portion of the masonry had fallen . . . [and] there appeared to be a wild inconsistency between its still perfect adaption of parts, and the crumbling condition of the individual stones," the reader grasps the correlation with the twins—the *house* of Usher and the *family* of Usher are inextricably woven into the same tapestry. Later, when the narrator relates that "The eye of a scrutinizing observer might have [noticed] a barely perceptible fissure, which, extending from the roof of the building in front, made its way down the wall in a zigzag direction, until it became lost in the sullen waters of the tarn," it is understood that this same crack threatens to destroy Roderick and Madeline, who while separate individuals, are in essence two halves of the same family psyche.

Once inside, the narrator felt that "an air of stern, deep, and irredeemable gloom hung over and pervaded all." And when he first met Roderick, he exclaimed, "Surely, man had never before so terribly altered, in so brief a period, as had Roderick Usher!" He had a "cadaverousness of complexion; an eye large, liquid, and luminous; lips . . . very pallid; a nose . . . with a breadth of nostril unusual in similar formations; a . . . chin . . . in . . . want of moral energy; hair of a . . . weblike softness and tenuity; these features, with an inordinate expansion above the regions of the temple, made up altogether a countenance not easily to be forgotten." It is clear that suggestions of the influence of the mind and spirit on the flesh are assumed here, as the physiognomy matched and represented the psyche as surely as the physical presence of the house.

The narration continued over several days, the friend trying to "alleviate the melancholy" of Roderick. They "painted and read together," and the narrator would listen, "as if in a dream, to the wild improvisations" of Roderick's "speaking guitar." Then Roderick said that "the lady Madeline was no more," and "stated his intention of preserving the corpse for a fortnight" before putting it into its final interment because of her unusual illness and the possibilities of "eager inquiries of her medical men." When the two men carried her encoffined body to its temporary resting place deep in a dungeon or vault directly beneath Roderick's bedroom, the friend become aware of the similarities of the vault and one of Roderick's paintings. It is at this time that Roderick tells his friend that he and Madeline are more than just siblings, they are twins, and share “sympathies of a scarcely intelligible nature.” When the lid is secured on the coffin, the friend notices a “faint blush upon the bosom and the face, and suspiciously lingering smile upon the lip,” normal in cases of a cataleptical character and suggestive of some psychological disorder.

The days following Madeline’s death represent how it affected Roderick. At first he demonstrates natural grief, but then “an observable change came over” his “mental disorder. . . . He roamed from chamber to chamber. . . . The pallor of his countenance had assumed . . . a more ghastly hue . . . the luminousness of his eye had utterly gone out. . . .” He stared “upon vacancy for long hours, in an attitude of the profoundest attention, as if listening to some imaginary sound.”

After some seven or eight nights, a fierce storm raged outside (again, the physical environment matching the psychological condition). Roderick and the narrator were unable to sleep, and Roderick entered the narrator’s room agitated and restless. The narrator decided to try and calm him by reading to him from Sir Launcelot Canning’s *The Mad Trist*, a story about Ethelred, who must break into the dwelling of a hermit and slay a dragon who is guarding the palace of gold and silver in order to retrieve a brass shield hanging on the wall. As he read the story, it seemed as if “from some remote portion of the mansion, there came indistinctly to ears what might have been, in its exact similarity of character, the echo . . . of the very sound that Sir Launcelot had so particularly described.” This unnerved the friend, and he jumped to his feet.

Roderick had already moved his chair so it was facing the door of the room. His head had dropped onto his chest, but he was not asleep. Instead, his eyes were rigid and open, and he stared at the doorway, lips trembling and muttering incoherently, body rocking from side to side. When the narrator approached and put his hand gently on Roderick’s shoulder, he felt “a strong shudder over” Rodderick’s “whole person; a sickly smile quivered about his lips; and” he spoke “in a low, hurried, and gibbering murmur, as if unconscious of” the narrator’s “presence. Bending closely over him,” the narrator “at length drank in the hideous import of his words:”

> "Not hear it?--yes, I hear it, and *have* heard it. Long--long--long--many minutes, many hours, many days, have I heard it--yet I dared not --oh, pity me, miserable wretch that I am!--I dared not--I *dared* not speak! *We have put her living in the tomb!* Said I not that my senses were acute? I *now* tell you that I heard her first feeble movements in the hollow coffin. I heard them--many, many days ago--yet I dared not--*I dared not speak!*"

Then Roderick explained that the sounds they had been hearing were actually Madeline returning from the grave, "the breaking of the hermit's door" was "the rendering of her coffin; the death-cry of the dragon" was "the grating of the iron hinges of her prison" as she opened the door, "and the clangor of the shield" was her "struggles within the copper archway of the vault!" Then Roderick sprang to his feet: *"Madman! I tell you that she now stands without the door!"*

A gust of wind blew open the doors, and "there *did* stand the enshrouded figure of the lady Madeline. . . . There was blood upon her white robes, and the evidence of some bitter struggle upon every portion of her emaciated frame. For a moment she remained trembling and reeling to and fro upon the threshold, then with a low moaning cry, fell heavily inward upon . . . her brother, and in her violent and now final death agonies, bore him to the floor a corpse." Then the storm increased, and the mansion began to shake and crumble.

The narrator fled from the room and the mansion. Only once did he turn to look back, and he saw a wild light. "The radiance was that of the full, setting . . . blood-red moon, which now shone vividly through that once barely discernible fissure." As he watched, the fissure of the house rapidly widened, there was a loud explosion, and the mansion came crashing down. The "deep and dank tarn . . . closed sullenly and silently over the fragments of the *House of Usher.*"

It is clear that Roderick and Madeline are not just twins but representative of the mental and physical pieces of a single being or soul or spirit, and the house itself is both the dwelling and the family itself. Roderick, in fact, has developed a theory that the stones of the house have a consciousness, that they embody the fate of the Usher family: "He was enchained by certain superstitious impressions in regard to the dwelling which he tenanted, and whence for many years, he had never ventured forth." Roderick further connects the house and family in the poem, "The Haunted Palace." Furthermore, it is obvious that the crack in the mansion represents the fissure or flaw in the twin personality of Roderick and Madeline, a foreboding of the dramatic ruin to come.

There is also a connection between Roderick's withdrawal from the *real* world into his own world of imagination, a world filled with art and music and literature. However, his own art has gone awry. He has entered this psychic reality, but he has gotten lost in it, much as a schizophrenic might.

The narrator performs much the same role as other narrators who experience the nightmarish world of the madman. Marlow, the main character in Joseph Conrad's *Heart of Darkness* is a perfect example.

Ultimately, *The Fall of the House of Usher* is more about whether or not a *normal* person can experience the insane world of a *madman* and survive than it is about the *madman* at the center of that world. In the *Heart of Darkness* Kurtz is the brilliant representative of the best of European culture, the superior civilization and race that goes into the heart of darkness, both the physical, geographical darkness of the wilderness of the Congo, and by extension the invisible, psychological darkness of the mind, and succumbs to it, just as Roderick succumbs to his darkness. Marlow, however, does not succumb. He witnesses it, takes responsibility for his own darkness, as is demonstrated in him taking responsibility for it by lying to Kurtz' intended when he returns, and yet maintains his sanity. In *The Fall of the House of Usher*, the unnamed narrator (a sort of *everyman*) has a similar experience, even to the extent of helping bury Madeline.

Both works demonstrate overlapping yet different textures of this darkness. In *The Heart of Darkness*, Kurtz is an artist, but that is not the focus. In *The Fall of the House of Usher* the artistic relationship to insanity is emphasized. Nevertheless, in each, madness and genius are closely intertwined.

Needless to say, Roderick is Jung's *animus* and Madeline Jung's *anima*. And the tight relationship between Madeline and Roderick can also be said to represent the close relationship between the *anima* and the *shadow*. It can also be claimed that these two Jungian entities have joined in Jung's trilogy with the *ego*, represented by the narrator. The *shadow* and *anima* reside in the unconscious (the house) and the ego in the conscious (outside the house). If the shadow and anima are able to unite in the struggle with the ego and gain control over it, then the ego will be defeated, and the individual will be psychically ill. However, if the ego can experience the psychological world of the shadow and anima and not be overwhelmed by it, a balance can be obtained resulting in a healthy, powerful individual—a mature adult.

While the *ego* is the dominant force in the conscious portion of the psyche, the *shadow* and the *anima* are the more powerful forces of the *unconscious*. Jung writes:

> The darkness which clings to every personality is the door into the unconscious and the gateway of dreams, from which those two twilight figures, the shadow and the anima, step into our nightly visions or, remaining invisible, take possession of our ego-consciousness. A man who is possessed by his shadow is always standing in his own light and falling into his own traps. Whenever possible, he prefers to make an unfavourable impression on others. In the long run luck is always against him because he

> is living below his own level and at best only attains what does not suit him. And if there is no doorstep for him to stumble over, he manufactures one for himself and then fondly believes he has done something useful.
>
> Possession caused by the anima or animus presents a different picture. Above all, this transformation of personality gives prominence to those traits which are characteristic of the opposite sex; in man the feminine traits and in woman the masculine. In the state of possession both figures lose their charm and their values; they retain them only when they are turned away from the world, in the introverted state, when they serve as bridges to the unconscious. Turned towards the world, the anima is fickle, capricious, moody, uncontrolled and emotional, sometimes gifted with daemonic intuitions, ruthless, malicious, untruthful, bitchy, double-faced, and mystical. The animus is obstinate, harping on principles, laying down the law, dogmatic, world-reforming, theoretic, word-mongering, argumentative, and domineering. Both alike have bad taste: the animus lets himself be taken in by second-rate thinking. (44)

As the *self* emerges in a healthy individual, it replaces the *ego* as the center of the personality, combining both *conscious* and *unconscious* portions of the total psyche. In order for this to happen, we must *not* deny the *shadow* and *anima* forces. Though dangerous, they are necessary to a healthy psyche. For Jung, the *libido* is the drive to life, and it operates on the principal of opposites—for every *good* thought there is a matching *bad* thought. The result might be that a positive or good *conscious* thought might result in its opposite getting repressed in the *unconscious*, where it remains as negative energy, needing a release. If the *ego* dumps too much negative energy into the *unconscious,* then the buildup can cause problems. Archetypes in and of themselves have *stored energy, stored libido*, what Jung calls *numen*, so there is inherent in humans an energy in the *unconscious* that needs a release. And they find release through *symbolic expressions* in *dreams, religious experiences, artistic expressions, and mythological representations and enactments.* If these are not available, then there will be problems. Two sources of neurosis, then, are the denial of the forces of the *unconscious* by an overly powerful *ego persona* and the lack of possible forms of conscious *symbolic* expression. The result is a person who is living an unreal *persona* to satisfy the demands and constraints of his social world, but who becomes empty, feels bored, tired and distressed, who has no purpose. The solution to this is to recognize and incorporate the forces of the *unconscious* into the total *self.*

A Jungian interpretation of *The Star Wars Trilogy* clearly demonstrates his insistence on the duality of psychic energy, and George Lucas has stated that the full six film sequence is focused on Anakin

Skywalker/Darth Vader, who interestingly enough provides us with both the ultimate *hero* in Anakin, and ultimate *anti-hero* or *shadow* in Darth Vader, as powerful a presentation of this dual nature in man as has probably ever been given in film

There are a number of psychological types, sometimes grouped under *delusional misidentification syndrome,* that are related to such duplicate self or *doppelganger* experiences. (45)

Capgras delusion is the belief that a close relative or a spouse has been replaced by an identical-looking impostor. It is named after Joseph Capgras (1873-1950) a French psychiatrist who first described the disorder in a paper by Capgras and Reboul-Lachaux in 1923. (46) They used the term *l'illusion des sosies* (the illusion of doubles) to describe the case of a French woman who complained that various 'doubles' had taken the place of people she knew. However, the term illusion has a subtly different meaning from delusion in psychiatry so 'Capgras delusion' is used as a more suitable name. In 1991, Passer and Warnock offered the following case report:

> Mrs. D, a 74-year old married housewife, recently discharged from a local hospital after her first psychiatric admission, presented to our facility for a second opinion. At the time of her admission earlier in the year, she had received the diagnosis of atypical psychosis because of her belief that her husband had been replaced by another unrelated man. She refused to sleep with the imposter, locked her bedroom and door at night, asked her son for a gun, and finally fought with the police when attempts were made to hospitalize her. At times she believed her husband was her long deceased father. She easily recognized other family members and would misidentify her husband only. (47)

Fregoli delusion is the belief that different people the believer meets are actually the same person in disguise. It is named after Leopold (Luigi) Fregoli (July 2, 1867 - November 26, 1936) a stage star and early Italian actor who was the greatest protean (quick-change) artist of his day, famous for his extraordinary ability at impersonations and his quickness in exchanging roles, so much so that while he was performing in London in the 1890s unkind rumors spread that there was more than one Fregoli. He quickly quashed these rumors by inviting journalists and doubters backstage to see him at work, proving he had no secrets, no tricks beyond his abilities. *Fregoli delusion* was first reported in a paper by P. Courbon and G. Fail in 1927, a case study of a 27-year-old woman who believed she was being persecuted by two actors whom she often went to see at the theatre, believing that these people "pursued her closely, taking the form of people she knows or meets." (48)

Intermetamorphosis, first described in 1932 by P. Courbon and J. Tusques (*Illusions d'intermétamorphose et de la charm*), is the belief that people swap identities with each other while maintaining the same appearance. One patient, Betty, believed that a former lover and his girlfriend were monitoring her. She was convinced that they were occupying neighboring homes and garages, rapidly changing their identities, all in an attempt to prevent her from telling family and friends about her previous affair with the gentleman. She believed that these people were stunning masters of disguise, that they could change their facial appearance, clothes, and even their sex at a moment's notice (49)

Reduplicative paramnesia is the delusion that there exist identical places or events. In one case, a woman who had sustained a head injury in a purse snatching incident, believed that she had actually be victimized twice, by the same man (50). In another example, a patient whose husband had died some years earlier thought he was staying in the same hospital as she. In this case, as with many such cases, the patient had an otherwise logical, firm grasp on reality, and was well aware that the notions of her delusions were absurd. She knew the impossibility of her claims, yet still believed them. (51) *Reduplicative paramnesia* was first used in 1903 by neurologist Arnold Pick to describe a patient with suspected Alzheimer's disease who insisted that she had been moved from Pick's city clinic, to one she claimed looked identical but was in a familiar suburb. To explain the discrepancy she further claimed that Pick and the medical staff worked at both locations. (52) Cases have since been discovered from as early as 1788, the first by Swiss naturalist Charles Bonnet, who described a woman who also had what would now be called *Cotard delusion.* (53) Henry Head, Paterson, and Zangwill, later reported cases of soldiers who had the delusional belief that their hospital was located in their home town. (54) In 1976, when Benson and his colleagues reported three cases and attempted to explain the phenomena in terms of neurocognitive deficits, thus giving the condition a neuropsychological explanation, more serious consideration was given to the disorder. The following is an example of a case reported by them. The patient had suffered a head injury from a fall at home, causing a fractured skull and frontal lobe damage to both left and right sides from the formation of intracerebral hematomas:

> A few days after admission to the Neurobehavioural Center, orientation for time was intact, he could give details of the accident (as related to him by others), could remember his doctors' names and could learn new information and retain it indefinitely. He exhibited, however, a distinct abnormality of orientation for place. While he quickly learned and remembered that he was at the Jamaica Plain Veterans Hospital (also

> known as the Boston Veterans Administration Hospital), he insisted that the hospital was located in Taunton, Massachusetts, his home town. Under close questioning, he acknowledged that Jamaica Plain was part of Boston and admitted it would be strange for there to be two Jamaica Plain Veterans Hospitals. Nonetheless, he insisted that he was presently hospitalized in a branch of the Jamaica Plain Veterans Hospital located in Taunton. At one time he stated that the hospital was located in the spare bedroom of his house. (55)

The delusion has since been reported in the context of a number of neurological disorders, including stroke, intracerebral hemorrhage, tumor, dementia, encephalopathy and various psychiatric disorders. (56)

Cotard delusion (also known as *Walking Corpse Syndrome*) is the belief that one is dead or does not exist; sometimes coupled with the belief that one is putrefying or missing internal organs. People suffering this often doubt their own existence and the existence of the external world and often attempt suicide. (57). It is named after Jules Cotard (1840–1889), a French neurologist who first described the condition, which he called *le délire de négation* ("negation delirium"), in a lecture in Paris in 1880, describing it as having degrees of severity that range from mild to severe. Despair and self-loathing characterize a mild state. Someone suffering the severe state begins to deny the very existence of the self. In his lecture, Cotard described a patient who denied the existence of God, the Devil, several parts of her body, and her need to eat. As her condition continued, she came to believe she was eternally damned and could no longer die a natural death. She later died of starvation. (58) Young and Leafhead describe a modern-day case of Cotard delusion in a patient who suffered brain injury after a motorcycle accident:

> [His] symptoms occurred in the context of more general feelings of unreality and being dead. In January, 1990, after his discharge from hospital in Edinburgh, his mother took him to South Africa. He was convinced that he had been taken to hell (which was confirmed by the heat), and that he had died of septicaemia (which had been a risk early in his recovery), or perhaps from AIDS (he had read a story in *The Scotsman* about someone with AIDS who died from septicaemia), or from an overdose of a yellow fever injection. He thought he had "borrowed my mother's spirit to show me round hell", and that he was asleep in Scotland. (59)

There is some disagreement among researchers about the causes. Philip Gerrans credits it to a reasoning deficit. (60) Ramachandran and Blakeslee claim that it is nothing more than severe form of the Capgras delusion, involving damage to more neural pathways. (61) Young and Leafhead suggest that it is a matter of attribution differences within the person; in other words, people who are internally focused would be more likely to experience Cotard delusion and people who are externally focused would be more likely to experience Capgras delusion. (62)

Mirrored self-misidentification (*delusional misidentification syndrome*) is the belief that one's reflection in a mirror is some other person. N. Breen, D. Caine, and M. Coltheart studied two cases of this. This first involved a successful 87 year old man who had retired at the age of 84 and had no unusual medical history. At age 86 he was admitted to the hospital after a brief spell of poor hand coordination, diagnosed as a "transient ischaemic attack." He was released. Soon after he began having nocturnal hallucinations of women and children in his house. Then he moved, and it became obvious he could no longer recognize his own fact in a mirror. His visual field was normal, and nothing else appeared to be wrong with him. Seranace was prescribed. He began to believe that his own reflection was another person who was following him around, and though his family explained to him this other person was simply his own reflection, and he understood their explanations and knew exactly what a mirror was and how it worked, he continued in his belief, and became annoyed that his attempts to communicate with this person received no responses. Over the next two years, things remained much the same, though he slowly began to incorporate his wife's reflection, stating at one point, "I have met the stranger's wife, seen her. I don't think she talks either." CT and MRI brain scans revealed some normal atrophy but nothing unusual. For the first 21 months following the initial onset of his delusion, he remained stable, but over the final two years of his life, his functions decreased dramatically up to his death.

The second case they studied was a 77 year old man who had been experiencing what they refer to as the *mirror sign* for several years. He was married, had three children, and had a varied professional life, including being an Evangelical missionary, a farm laborer, a store man, a market gardener, a truck driver, and a maintenance worker. His medical history had several possibly damaging experiences. He had suffered meningitis at the age of five (but had a full recovery), had become an alcoholic for about 15 years (but had been abstinent for about 30 years), had lost consciousness for about 30 minutes from a head injury, had heart problems and suffered cardiac arrest at age 63, had radio therapy treatment for myeloma at age 64, and had mild emphysema. Neither he nor any of his friends considered him cognitively impaired in any way. His neurological examination five months after the onset of *mirror sign* revealed nothing remarkable or out of the ordinary beyond it.

He described his mirror reflection as a "dead ringer" for himself, and said that when he attempted to talk with this person, he did not replay, causing him to believe there was something wrong with his voice or tongue. He did not feel threatened; he said the person lived in an apartment adjoining his own (though none existed). When he was examined seven months later, he also said there were two duplicate hospitals to the one he was in (*Reduplicative paramnesia).* At times he could accurately identify other people's reflections in the mirror, but at times he thought they were other people, saying, for example, that he had seen the mirror person's wife in the mirror and she was very much like his own wife. As with the first case, CT and MRI scans reveals nothing unusual, just normal atrophy. Similarly, his condition remained much the same over the next year, but soon after that he was admitted to a nursing home, where he began declining rapidly over the next two years. (63)

Somatoparaphrenia is the belief that one's own body parts, even an entire side of the body belongs to someone else (often connected with stroke). It is almost always the result of a right-brain injury, with motor and somatosensory deficits, and the syndrome of unilateral spatial neglect, most often characterized by a delusion of disownership of left-sided body parts. What follows comes from my book *Insanity and Genius*:

During World War II, a number of Russian scientists (e.g., Leontev, Anokhin, Bernstein, and most importantly A. R. Luria) began a more formal scientific study of the brain, what they called neuro-psychology. It was all set out systematically in A. R. Luria's *The Higher Cortical Functions in Man*, first translated into English in 1966, and put forth in the form of a biography/autobiography/journal or pathography in *The Man with the Shattered Brain*, first translated into English in 1972, both dealing with the resulting losses of left hemisphere damage to the brain. (64)

Zasetsky's life in Russia began much as any other. He wrote in his journal, "In 1941, right before the war began, I finished my third year of courses at a polytechnic institute and hoped soon to get some practical experience in a specialized plant. . . . For some reason, even as a child I was fascinated by science, by knowledge in general, and greedily devoured any information I could pick up . . . Before I was two years old my father died suddenly in a coal mine where he worked as an engineer. After his death my mother had a rough time of it with four young children, since she was illiterate and didn't know how to go about getting a pension for her children. . . . Soon, I thought, I'll be graduating from the institute. Two years left to go? That's nothing! What can possibly stand in my way now? And as soon as I get my degree, I'll start giving my mother a hand, it's about time she had a chance to rest!"

Then came WWII. Zasetsky's plans dissolved as the war demanded soldiers. He reported with good detail his fighting on the western front, being wounded in the temple, but not seriously, and returning to the Russian offensive in 1943, the battle of Smolensk, the flame-throwers, the wait for the order to attack. Then the moment, the order to move forward, the clank of armor, the momentary stillness, the sudden burst of machine guns. Waking somewhere in a tent, head empty, no thoughts, no memory, just a buzz, a dizzy feeling. A man with a broad, thick-set face and angry eyes studying through glasses. People in bright white coats and gauze masks rushing about. Being held down to the operating table, screaming, gasping for breath, warm blood running down ears and neck, a salty taste in the mouth.

Later, waking, he felt his head was a blank emptiness, no memory. At first, he could not even recognize himself when a doctor spoke to him, "Comrade Zasetsky?" As the days passed, he began to have what he called memory fragments. "Right after I was wounded, I seemed to be some newborn creature that just looked, listened, observed, repeated, but still had no mind of its own." These scattered, disconnected memories came and went. At times he could remember having a mother and two sisters, and a brother.

Since that initial confusion, up to the time of his journal entries he found that he was "in a kind of fog all the time, like a heavy half-sleep," his memory "a blank, unable to "think of a single word," just flashes of "images, hazy visions that suddenly appear and just a suddenly disappear, giving way to fresh images," but unable to "understand or remember what these mean."

He certainly still had self-awareness, felt that others realized his worthlessness, felt that he was fit for nothing, that in truth he had died, a man killed in the war. He wrote, "I miraculously remained alive. Still, even though I seem to be alive, the burden of this head wound gives me no peace. I always feel as if I'm living out a dream—a hideous, fiendish nightmare—that I'm not a man but a shadow, some creature that's fit for nothing."

He wondered if it was all a dream, not real, but a nightmare he just could not wake up from. Yet it could not be. He was aware enough, at least for moments, to understand the therapist, who told him he had been wounded. Finally, after being moved from one hospital to another, he ended up at the rehabilitation hospital in the Urals. He found it a "lovely, quiet place, a refuge with a magnificent view of "an enormous lake surrounded by evergreens." He could remember the trip there with clarity, yet he wrote in his journal that he still had "to read syllable by syllable like a child," that he was still "plagued by amnesia," could not remember "words or meanings," was overcome by "aphasia," and could not recover his memory.

He had continual thoughts of the meaninglessness of his life, of how he should just die, but at the same time fought them with a desire to live and have a meaningful life.

When A. R. Luria first met Zasetsky, he found him young looking, "scarcely more than a boy . . . with a puzzled smile" and a need to tilt his head, since the vision on his left side was gone. The initial interview revealed a person unable to remember relatives, where he lived, how he had been wounded, read, add, and find the words to answer even the simplest questions. He could list the months of the year, but not respond to which month precedes another, not indicate which hand was right or left. He enjoyed nature greatly, listened intently to the sounds of birds, noted the smoothness of the lake.

The official record states that the bullet penetrated the left parietal-occipital region of the cranium, that it was followed by a prolonged coma, that inflammation complicated matters by causing adhesions of the brain to meninges and changes in adjacent tissues, that scar tissue pulled the left lateral ventricle up and produced an incipient atrophy of the medulla.

Luria's medical knowledge of the structure of the brain leads him to postulate what has been lost due to the wound, and what retained, and his conclusions lead to a chilling realization, for he knows that the frontal cortex has been spared, and with it the ability to understand the damage and want to overcome it, the awareness of what it means to be human, the need to find meaning and value. In other words, Zasetsky was not only severely brain damaged, but he was still able to step outside of himself and realize his damaged state. Zasetsky writes, "It was depressing, unbearable to realize how miserable and pathetic my situation was. You see, I'd become illiterate, sick, had no memory. "

As the journal entries continue, they trace out some of the strange physical problems outlining his mental wound. He writes: "Ever since I was wounded I haven't been able to see a single object as a whole—not one thing. Even now I have to fill in a lot about objects, phenomena, or any living thing from imagination . . . Even now I still don't see entire objects, things, or people as I did before—only part of them. When I look at a spoon, at the left tip, I'm amazed. I can't figure out why I only see the tip and not the whole spoon. . . . Through and beyond the objects I see there are endless numbers—a myriad really—of tiny, shifting swarms of midges that made it hard for me to look at the objects themselves. . . . Once when I left my room and was walking in the corridor, I'd no sooner taken a few steps than I suddenly banged my right should and the right side of my forehead against the wall and got a huge bump on my forehead. I was furious; I simply couldn't understand why I'd suddenly bumped into the wall. I should have seen it. Just then I happened to look down—at the floor and at my feet—and I shuddered. I couldn't see the right side of my body. My hands and feet had disappeared."

His body often seemed to have disappeared. "I move the fingers of my left hand, feel them, but can't see the fingers of my right hand and somehow I'm not even aware they're there. . . . I can't get used to that idea, so often I'm terrified when part of my body disappears. . . . Sometimes when I'm sitting down I suddenly feel as though my head is the size of a table—every bit as big—while my hands, feet, and torso become very small. . . . sometimes, when I'm sitting on a chair, I suddenly become very tall, but my torso becomes terribly short and my head very, very tiny."

Space also became an ever-shifting mystery. He wrote, "Ever since I was wounded I've had trouble sometimes sitting down in a chair or on a couch. I first look to see where the chair is, but when I try to sit down I suddenly make a grab for the chair since I'm afraid I'll land on the floor. Sometimes that happens because the chair turns out to be further to one side than I thought"

The tragedy, as tragedies often do, also reveals a tremendous resilience, that force of life that drives humans, that powerful need for mapping out meaning and value, shines forth even more clearly in such a darkness. As the decades passed, and Luria continued to work with Zasetsky, he witnessed some amazing recoveries. Slowly, with years of effort, Zasetsky learned to live with his mental loss of vision on the right side, with his visual hallucinations, with his inability to even sense parts of his body, much less control them, with his spatial disorientation, and even amazingly with his loss of reading and writing abilities. From not even being able to remember the alphabet, from not being able to recall even the most basic words, he actually gained the ability to write out sentences and express deep human concerns (as this journal demonstrates).

The major breakthrough here came from kinetic-motor memory. He wrote: "Each time I wanted to think of a particular letter I'd have to run through the alphabet until I found it. But one day a doctor I'd come to know well, since he was always very informal with me and the other patients, asked me to try to write automatically—without lifting my hand from the paper. I was bewildered and questioned him a few times before I could even begin. But I finally picked up the pencil and after repeating the word 'krov' [blood] a few times, I quickly wrote it. I hardly knew what I'd written since I still had trouble reading—even my own writing. . . . after the doctor showed me how to write quickly, automatically, and not letter by letter, I was able to get one word down after the other without having to think about it. . . . even though I couldn't read my own writing."

And the fact that he forced himself to write out a journal, putting a pattern on his life, tells us even more about the human need for such a mapping out of meaning.

Beneath the factual, literal, scientific truths to be found in this case study lie those intuitive human truths, the very truths of meaning and value Zasetsky so desperately sought, the truths that draw us into the study, the truths that make us emphasize with him, see him as more than just a case study, see him as a human. These truths are captured in a strikingly similar fictional scenario, Dalton Trumbo's *Johnny Got His Gun*, where Joe Bonham also gets seriously wounded in war, this time not a wound to the brain, but a wound that separates his brain, and thus his mind from contact with the outside world. In this case an exploding bomb causes Joe Bonham to lose his arms, legs, and face. He is kept alive only for medical study, and assumed to have no higher thought functioning. We then experience the horror of a man who, in fact, does have such higher powers of thought, but who is unable to connect them with the physical world about him. We understand, not just logically, but intuitively, feelingly, how dispiriting such a situation is for humans. There is no denying the terrible tragedy of the physical deformations, but that becomes secondary to the deeper tragedy of the loss of a means to give meaning and value to life.

He is closeted off from the world, literally put in a storage room without light, without anything other than the basic physical care needed to survive.

When his hospital bed is finally put in front of a window by a humane nurse, and he can feel the sunlight on his skin, we know the joy of his mind connecting with a means to tell the passage of days, to figure out how to map out even this simple bit of a pattern for his life. Such seemingly simple desires, such enormously important human needs. But communication is still denied. The isolation, the loneliness, the need to communicate is overpowering, so powerful, he cannot give up trying to satisfy it. And he searches his mind for a means. Empathizing, we search with him, trying to figure out some way for him to call out from his prison. Then comes that Zasetsky-like discovery, that alternate way around the deformity:

> When he had thought for an instant that his mother and his sisters and Kareen might be standing beside the bed he had wanted to hide. But now that he had generals and big guys he felt a sudden fierce surging desire for

them to see him. Just as before he had started to reach for the medal without an arm to reach with so now he began to blow the mask off his face without having mouth and lips to blow with. He wanted them to get just one look at that hole in his head. He wanted them to get their fill of a face that began and ended with a forehead. He lay there blowing and then he realized that the air from his lungs was all escaping through his tube. He began to roll again from shoulder to shoulder hoping to dislodge the mask.

While he lay there rolling and puffing he felt a vibration way down in his throat a vibration that might be a voice. It was a short deep vibration and he knew that it was making a sound to their ears. Not a very big sound not a very intelligent sound but it must seem to them at least as interesting as the grunting of a pig. And if he could grunt like a pig why then he was accomplishing a great thing because before he had been completely silent. So he lay thrashing and puffing and grunting like a pig hoping that they would see damned well how much he appreciated their medal. While he was in the middle of this there was an indefinite churning of footsteps and then the departing vibrations of his guests. A moment later he was all alone in the blackness in the silence. He was all alone with his medal.

Suddenly he quieted. He was thinking about the vibrations of those footsteps. He had always carefully felt for vibrations. He had measured the size of his nurses and the dimensions of his room by them. But suddenly to feel the vibrations of four or five people tramping across the room made him think. It made him realize that vibrations were very important. He had thought of them up to this time only as vibrations coming to him. Now he began to consider that also there could be vibrations going from him. The vibrations which he received told him everything—height weight distance time. Why shouldn't he be able to tell something to the outside world by vibrations also?

In the back of his mind something began to glimmer. If he could in some way make use of vibrations he could communicate with these people. Then the glimmer became a great dazzling white light. It opened up such breathless prospects that he thought he might suffocate from sheer excitement. Vibrations were a very important part of communication. The fall of a foot on the floor is one kind of vibration. The tap of a telegraph key is simply another kind.

When he was a kid way back maybe four year ago or five he had a wireless set. He and Bill Harper used to telegraph each other. Dot dash dot dash dot. Particularly on rainy nights when their folks wouldn't let them go out and there was nothing to do and they just lounged around the house and got in everybody's way. On such nights he and Bill Harper used to dot and dash at each other and they had a hell of a good time. He still remembered the Morse code. All he had to do in order to break through to people in the outside world was to lie in bed and dot dash to the nurse. Then he could talk. Then he would have smashed through his silence and blackness and helplessness. Then the stump of a man without lips would talk. He had

> captured time and he had tried to figure geography and now he would do the greatest thing of them all he would talk. He would give messages and receive messages and he would have made another step forward in his struggle to get back to people in his terrible lonely eagerness for the feel of people near him for the things that were in their minds for the thoughts they might give him his own thoughts were so puny so unfinished so incomplete. He would talk." (65)

He begins tapping his head, tapping and tapping and tapping, desperate for the nurse, for anyone to catch on to what he had discovered. Time passes, days, weeks, months, perhaps years, he does not know. But he keeps on tapping. Then, a new nurse, a nurse with young hands, a nurse not so certain he is nothing more than a piece of meat without a mind, takes over his care, and discovers how to communicate with him by writing letters on his chest, fittingly writing Merry Christmas, and he is ecstatic, and we rejoice at his realization that now at least he can place his map of time in real time, can measure the days by the alternating warmth of the sun and cool of the night from Christmas and know at least what time of year his is in. But still, he cannot respond, cannot talk back to her.

He keeps tapping, tapping, tapping.

Then comes the break-through, the military representative, the Morse code expert, and the contact, the chance at interaction. We feel his joy as the question is tapped out: "What do you want?"

> It is a good question. But he has been so focused on the simple desire to communicate he has not thought about it, not considered just what he now wanted, given the limited options.
>
> They should know what he wanted the silly bastards and they should know they couldn't give it to him. He wanted the things they took for granted the things nobody could ever give him. He wanted eyes to see with. Two eyes to see sunlight and moonlight and blue mountains and tall trees and little ants and houses that people live in and flowers opening in the morning and snow on the ground and streams running and trains coming and going and people walking and a puppy dog playing with an old shoe worrying it and growling at it and backing away from it and frowning and wiggling its bottom and taking the shoe very seriously. He wanted a nose so that he could smell rain and burning wood and cooking food and the faint perfume that stays in the air after a girl has passed by. He wanted a mouth so he could eat and talk and laugh and taste and kiss. He wanted arms and legs so that he could work and walk and be like a man like a living thing.
>
> What did he want what was there for him to want what was there left that anybody could give him?

> It came over him rushing and howling like a torrent of water from behind a dam that has broken. He wanted to get out. (66)

Let me out, let me out, let me out. Put me on display. Let me have some purpose, some value. Give my life meaning. We hear his unspoken words. We feel his loneliness, his pain, his absolute entrapment. We anxiously with him for the reply, wanting some level of human existence to touch him, wanting some reason for him to continue his life.

But the cold, logical military does not, apparently cannot, get beyond its rational, left hemisphere rules. The Morse code reply deadens us: "What you ask is against regulations!" The movie version Trumbo directed pushes it even further. In it Joe simply requests to be put to death, as pure physical existence is meaningless, and a meaningless existence is worse than no existence at all. The cold reply is the same. He will be forced to continue isolated, in as pure a Hell as can be imagined. (67)

The impact of this novel comes not from the scientific explanations that might accompany Joe Bonham's condition, but from the intuitive knowing of the horror of it. The same is true with Zasetsky. While we read his "story," we are feeling his suffering, understanding the agony, the tremendous loss, the sublime struggle to regain the human part of his life.

Luria interrupts Zasetsky's journal writings in the book to make comments, and goes off on a few more lengthy discussions of the neurological reasons for his condition, pointing the discipline of neurology forward to a more complex understanding of the brain/mind interactions, but still unable to go much beyond the two established areas of the left side of the brain (Broca and Wiernicke areas). Notable here is that there is no emphasis put on the two separate halves of the brain having important differences in terms of thinking abilities.

Nonetheless, while Luria was studying Zasetsky, other scientific evidence for the location of separate and complementary modes of human thinking in the cerebral cortex was accumulating from a study of other brain lesions, accidents or strokes in the left hemisphere of the neocortex that resulted in diminished ability to read, write, speak, or perform simple mathematical tasks, and accidents or strokes in the right neocortex that resulted in a loss of pattern recognition, musical ability, and holistic reasoning abilities, even, in some cases, the ability to recognize one's own face in a mirror.

Such detailed, personalized studies were revealing compelling evidence. Even though, as with Zasetsky, the studies focused on and were mainly successful in dealing with what today is established as left brain thinking, and right brain thinking remained still much more in the dark, it was about to become obvious that, in the complex, intertwining operations of the human mind and brain, two separate forms of higher level thinking were taking place.

The key to it all is the corpus callosum, a mass of white transverse fibers, a bundle of nerves that carries information from one hemisphere of the brain to the other. In the 1940s, neurosurgeons developed a technique, technically titled corpus colostomy, less technically referred to as split-brain operation, for severing this information highway, as a means of helping patients who suffered epileptic seizures, and though it was done in a very crude, experimental fashion, it worked, or at least helped.

As is often the case, the practical solution resulted in some unexpected side effects, which, in turn, would open unexpected doors to higher understandings. Patients, while no longer burdened with seizures, began instead to experience other strange forms of thinking. One complained that the left half of his body often did unusual things that he simply could not understand. Another reported that, while his right hand was reaching into a drawer to retrieve a sock, his left hand slammed the drawer shut. Another complained that his left hand kept unbuttoning his shirt as he was attempting to button it with his right. Another told of his right hand placing objects in a shopping cart, only to have his left hand remove them and place them back on the shelf:

> According to Norman Geschwind, one split-brain patient complained that his left hand on several occasions suddenly struck his wife—much to the embarrassment of his left (speaking) hemisphere. In another case, a patient's left hand attempted to choke his own throat and had to be wrestled away. The patient expressed complete shock and surprise regarding these incidents and claimed that his left hand acted of its own accord.
>
> Another split-brain patient, described by S. J. Dimond, remarked that, on several occasions when she had overslept, she was suddenly awakened by her left hand, which had slapped her until she woke up.
>
> J. E. Bogen reported that almost all of his complete commissurotomy patients manifested some degree of intermanual conflict in the early postoperative period. One patient, Rocky, for years complained of difficulty getting his left leg to go in the direction he (or rather his left hemisphere) desired. Another patient often referred to the left half of her body as "my little sister" when complaining of its peculiar and independent actions.
>
> Indeed, the French neurosurgeons Brion and Jedynak reported that this type of independent left-sided (right hemisphere) activity was common in their split-brain patients and termed it the "alien hand." (68)

The dual mind concept becomes bizarrely clear in extreme cases of conflict between left and right hemispheres. A. J. Akelaitis wrote about a patient who "in tasks requiring bimanual activity" found that "the left hand would frequently perform oppositely to what she desired to do with the right hand. For example, she would be putting on clothes with her right and pulling them off with her left, opening a door or drawer with her right hand and simultaneously pushing it shut with the left." Another patient, who was recently divorced, when walking about town "found himself forced by the left half of his body to go some distance in another direction," which was later discovered to be where his wife lived, suggesting his right brain wanted to go where his left brain did not. (69)

Clearly this corpus colostomy procedure was entering neurology into as of yet misunderstood territory, and also clearly it could be used to study the brain from a new perspective.

The now classic experiment was worked out by Roger W. Sperry (who later would win the 1981 Nobel Prize in Physiology or Medicine for his work) and Ronald Myers in 1953, and it would not be overly bold to give this as the date contemporary neurology began. For now, for the first time, definite proof was initiated that the two halves of the brain work in two separate arenas. The initial research was done on a cat, and it began with an unassuming report:

> Through a transbuccal approach, the optic chiasma was sectioned in the midsagittal plane thereby restricting the central projection of retinal patterns to the homolateral sides of the brain. The cats were then taught a simple form discrimination (circle vs. square) with a mask covering the left eye. After overtraining, the mask was shifted to the right eye for critical trials. "Interocular transfer" of the habit was found to be effected with no significant deterioration in level of performance (two cases). In one of these cases the transfer to the untrained eye survived subsequent section of the corpus callosum in the midsagittal plane; in the other it did not. Transfer failed in another case in which the corpus callosum was sectioned just before the critical tests after the completion of training. "Interocular transfer" was demonstrated in two cases in which the corpus callosum as well as the chiasma had been sectioned prior to training.
>
> However, three later cases with the corpus callosum cut failed to show transfer. This discrepancy in the data may be due to incomplete section of the chiasma in the earlier cats. Anatomical check of the lesions has been deferred until further tests on the cats have been completed. The effects of eliminating other commissural systems and brain centers in various combinations are currently being investigated with particular regard to the location and nature of the mnemonic traces. (70)

Now, for the first time, definite proof was appearing that the two halves of the brain work in two separate arenas. This initial research done on a cat suggested that, with its corpus callosum and anterior commissar severed, the cat was unable to pass information learned from one eye to the other eye. In fact, each eye needed to be trained completely from the beginning. In effect, this can be said to be when the concept of two totally separate brains within one, or double-brain theory, came to the forefront of neurology. Again, the connecting corpus callosum is the key. With it cut, the human brain becomes two separate brains with two separate consciousnesses. And soon it would be discovered that these two separate consciousnesses think in two very distinct ways

Sperry and his associates continued their experiments. The first experiments on cats were then duplicated on monkeys with similar results. (71) Already by 1955, H. L. Teuber was able to discuss "double-dissociation," a method where comparison of abilities not affected by injury to the left-hemisphere are subsequently found to be affected by right-hemisphere injury is used to confirm theories of hemisphere specific functions. (72) J. E. Bogen, M. S. Gazzaniga, J. Levy, and other neurologists joined in. The research quickly gained momentum, and articles detailing and attempting to explain the data from this new asymmetrical approach filled the neurological publications. (73) By 1962, C. B. Trevarthen was able to demonstrate that the two hemispheres cannot only work independently but also simultaneously. (74) By 1966, M. S. Gazzaniga and R. Sperry demonstrated that humans can solve two independent problems by the two hands independently simultaneously. (75)

By the late 1960s and into the early 1970s, Roger W. Sperry, and others at the California Institute of Technology were able to help victims of grand mal epilepsy by cutting the corpus callosum in a much more sophisticated and refined manner than what had been done in the 1940s, and demonstrated that, not only did this procedure help tremendously in solving the grand mal epilepsy problems, but the split-brain patients were able to function normally, suggesting that the two sides of the brain can work independently. (76)

Already by 1969, Bogen was able to offer a well supported claim for the specific, complementary interactions between the two hemispheres of the brain, the left supplying the needed logical, "prepositional," structures, the right the needed symbolic, "appositional" content, concluding:

> One of the most obvious and fundamental features of the cerebrum is that it is double. Various kinds of evidence, especially from hemispherectomy, have made it clear that one hemisphere is sufficient to sustain a personality or mind. We may then conclude that the individual with two intact

> hemispheres has the capacity for two distinct minds. This conclusion finds its experimental proof in the split-brain animal whose two hemispheres can be trained to perceive, consider, and act independently. In the human, where prepositional thought is typically lateralized to one hemisphere, the other hemisphere evidentially specializes in a different mode of thought, which may be called appositional. . .
>
> The belief that man is possessed of two ways of thought, occasionally conflicting, is common in everyday speech where it often takes the form of supposing a struggle between "reason" and "emotion," or between "the mind" and "the heart." (77)

The early 1970s saw a rapid development in use of brain scanning techniques. Robert Ornstein and David Galin, at the Langley Porter Neuropsychiatric Institute, San Francisco, found that the EEG (electroencephalogram), which had originally be developed nearly a half century earlier, through offering poor spatial resolution, perhaps, at best, a few inches, does offer excellent temporal resolution, and indicates activity in normal people moves from one hemisphere to the other in relation to what form of thinking is occurring. For example, alpha activity (8-12 Hz) is suppressed in the left hemisphere more than the right during several verbal tasks. (78)

By 1978, Sperry was able to write: "Everything we have seen so far indicates that the surgery has left these people with two separate minds, that is, two separate spheres of consciousness. . . . Each brain half, in other words, seems to have its own largely separate cognitive domain with its own private perceptual, learning, and memory experiences, all of which are seemingly oblivious to corresponding events in the other hemisphere." (79)

George Ojemann, building on the electrical stimulation of portions of the brain experiments of Wilder Penfield, at the Montreal Neurological Institute, conducted elaborate brain mapping. (80)

John Wada used anesthetics (the Wada amytal test), injecting sodium amobarbital into one side of the brain or the other (the left or right carotid artery, which supplies blood to the ipsilateral hemisphere), to put one side or the other to sleep, and then record what functions are affected. (81)

Others demonstrated that isotopic scanning, the injection of radioactive isotopes (i.e., technetium 99 or iodine 131) into the blood vessels to the cranial region, can locate and provide information about the size, etc., of tumors and blood vessel lesions. This is now generally done with CAT (computerized axial tomography) scans, which allow x-rays from multiple angles to provide a 3D view, and which have been used to offer spatial resolution in the 1-2mm range, but have the disadvantage of slower temporal resolution (30 seconds plus). Furthermore, they cannot provide a dynamic picture of how activation changes during task performance.

Others used PET (positron emission tomography) scans, introducing a radioactive tracer-labeled compound and tracking its behavior. It was discovered that NMR or NURI (nuclear magnetic resonance imaging) scans can provide maps of slices of the brain, and other rCBF (regional cerebral blood flow) measures can offer dynamic pictures of brain activity. (82)

And these pictures, in turn, suggested specific areas of left or right hemisphere location for specific tasks. For example, during verbal tasks rCBF is stronger in the left hemisphere than the right hemisphere. (83)

Other tests, in addition to reaffirming that the left hemisphere is involved with verbal ability, suggested that the right hemisphere involves the ability to manipulate geometric figures, assemble puzzles, complete patterns, and, in general work with forms, distances, and space relationships. (84)

Tests were then done to attempt to determine how the two separate hemispheres comprehended the world around them, and, though initially the assumption still remained that the two halves thought in similar ways, only the right hemisphere less adept at it, a mapping of what was to emerge as two distinct forms of knowing began in earnest.

In one test, a word such as “hatband” was placed on a screen, “hat” visible only to the left eye, “band” visible only to the right eye. When asked to identify the word, the split-brain patient was only able to verbally communicate what the left hemisphere received (a note, the hemispheres process information from the opposite eyes, left hemisphere from the right eye, right hemisphere from the left), i.e., only the word “band.” When asked what kind of “band,” the patient could only guess. In contrast, when asked to write what he saw, with his hand hidden from sight, the patient wrote only “hat.” Thus, he could write, but not verbalize, what he saw with his left eye. Furthermore, when asked what he wrote, he would give a totally incorrect response. (85)

In recent years, Vilayanur Subramanian "Rama" Ramachandran has worked with patients who have lost a limb and yet continue to vividly feel the presence of that “phantom limb.” The traditional view was that these patients were feeling this at the ends of the severed nerves. However Ramachandran has since proven that this is not so, but that the “phantom limb” sensation actually takes place in the brain itself. For example, in the brain the location of the sensation of the hand is close to the location of the sensation of the cheek. If his theories are correct, then, touching the cheek should elicit sensations in the phantom hand, and in fact laboratory experiments have proven this is so. (86) He also developed the *"mirror box,"* for people who felt pain because they thought their "phantom limb" was paralyzed in a painful position. By arranging a mirror set up so that the good limb is visually duplicated in the position of the missing limb, the patient is able to see the missing limb as still existing and to overcome this painful paralysis, is in others words able to psychologically feel that the limb exists and can indeed be moved. (87)

All of the above experiences either are or are on the twilight fringe of what are categorized as *out-of-body experiences*, experiences that involve a feeling of being detached from one's own body, often a sense of watching oneself from another position in the room or environment (*autoscopy*). (88) One category of such experiences is called *astral, etheric or spiritual projection*.

Astral projection or travel refers to an *out of body experience* where the soul or spirit or non-physical essence of a person leaves the physical body, exists in the *astral plane*, an intermediate world of light between Heaven and Earth composed of the spheres of the planets and stars thought to be populated by angels, demons and spirits. The term *astral* comes from Latin for *star*. (89) This experience is often connected to religious accounts of the *afterlife*, where the consciousness or soul of the body journeys out of the body and up through planes of existence, ascends to *higher realms*. (90) Paul's second letter to the Corinthians can be and has been said to refer to these astral planes:

> 2: I knew a man in Christ above fourteen years ago, (whether in the body, I cannot tell; or whether out of the body, I cannot tell: God knoweth;) such a one caught up to the third heaven.
> 3. And I knew such a man, (whether in the body, or out of the body, I cannot tell: God knoweth;)
> 4. How that he was caught up into paradise, and heard unspeakable words, which it is not lawful for a man to utter. (91)

And this passage, in turn, opens the door to the *Apocalypse of Paul* (*Visio Pauli*), a 4th century text of the *New Testament apocrypha*, a tract that offers a vision of heaven and hell, which, in turn, is a forerunner of similar visions found in such works as the *Vita Columbae*, the *Visio Thurkilli*, the *Visio Godeschalci*, the *Tractatus de Purgatorio Sancti Patricii* (an account of a visit to Saint Patrick's Purgatory), and the *Tnugdalus*, as well as Dante Alighieri's *Divine Comedy*. (92)

Since *astral projection* means leaving the body, it is related to death, and there are numerous accounts of near death experiences suggesting the existence of an *astral plane*.

One of the most famous of these experiences concerns Pam Reynolds Lowery, an American singer-songwriter, who, in 1991, had a near death experience during a brain operation at the age of 35. During this operation she was under close medical monitoring, had no brain-wave activity and no blood flowing to her brain for several minutes, which means she was at least clinically dead, yet she survived, and after the operation was able to make several observations about it that proved to be surprisingly accurate.

A CAT scan revealed she had a large artery aneurysm close to her brain stem, and Dr. Robert F. Spetzler, Barrow Neurological Institute, Phoenix, Arizona, decided to perform a hypothermic cardiac arrest (also known as a standstill operation). Here is the detailed timeline of the operation (93):

7:15 – She is brought into the operating room, still awake, is anesthetized with thiopental (Pentothal) by IV and lifted onto the operating table. Her eyes are taped shut. Small speakers are inserted into her ears. A thermostat is placed into her esophagus to measure her core body temperature (which is to be lowered to 60 degrees Fahrenheit). EEG electrodes are taped to her head to record her cerebral cortical brain activity.

8:40 – Her entire body, except for her head and groin, is covered with sterile drapes. *Her near death experience begins. She hears a D natural, and feels as if it is pulling her out of her body. She looks down and sees several things in the operating room, feels very aware and has a more focused vision than normal. She notices that her head is shaved in an unexpected manner. She sees the "saw thing" (bone saw). It looks like an electric toothbrush, has a dent or groove at the top where the saw connects to the handle and has interchangeable blades placed in what appears to be a socket wrench case. She hears the saw crank up.* Dr. Spetzler begins the surgery by opening the scalp and then carving out a section of the skull with a Midas Rex (a bone saw). *She hears the saw crank up, but doesn't see it being used. It hums at a high pitch, then suddenly goes "brrrrrrrrrrrr.'*

Dr. Spetzler removes the bone flap, and the operating microscope is swung into position over her head. At the same time, a female cardiac surgeon locates the femoral artery and vein in her right groin, which turn out to be too small to deal with the large flow of blood from the heart-lung machine. *Reynolds hears a female voice saying her veins and arteries are very small.* The left femoral artery and vein are prepared for use. Dr. Spetzler inspects the aneurysm with the operating microscope, finds it very large, and decides that a hypothermic cardiac arrest (standstill) is necessary.

10:50 – The heart-lung machine is connected to her body, and her blood is cooled down.

11:00 – Her core temperature is approximately 75 degrees Fahrenheit. The cardiac monitor indicates cardiac malfunction.

11:05 – She receives a massive dose of potassium chloride. The Cardiac arrest is complete. Her brain waves become flat. Her brain stem responds weaker and weaker to the clicks from the ear speakers.

11:20 – Her core temperature is approximately 60 degrees Fahrenheit. The brain stem no longer responds to the clicks from the ear speakers. The brain is shut down.

11:25 – The heart-lung machine is disconnected from her body. The head of the operating table is lifted and the blood is drained from her body. *She feels as if she is being pulled, but not against her will. She is going on her own accord because she wants to go. She feels as if she is going through a tunnel vortex. She comes to a bright light. She begins to discern several figures, including a grandmother and an uncle. They stop her from going further because she otherwise would not be able to return to her body.* The aneurysm is deflated and Dr. Spetzler removes it. The heart-lung machine is turned back on and pumps warmed blood into her body. Her brain stem begins to respond to the clicks from the ear speakers. *The deceased relatives seem to be feeding Reynolds, not with food but with something sparkly. She feels as if she is being nurtured and make strong.* Waves of electrical activity from her higher brain centers begin to appear on the EEG machine.

12:00 – There is a problem as the heart monitor begins to register ventricular fibrillation. Efforts are made to correct it with additional warming, but are unsuccessful. Two defibrillator paddles are placed on her chest and her heart is shocked twice, solving the problem. *Her uncle takes her back through the end of the tunnel. She sees her body but doesn't want to go in. It looks dead and she is scared of it. Then her uncle pushes her. The tunnel seems to push her and her body seems to pull her. When she goes back into her body it feels like diving into a pool of ice water.*

12:32 – Her body temperature is about 90 degrees Fahrenheit, and the heart-lung machine is turned off. Her body is distrumented. Dr. Spetzler's assistants take over the closing surgical duties and music in the background begins to play. *She regains consciousness and hears the song Hotel California being played.*

14:10 – She is taken to the recovery room. She is still incubated for respiration, but in stable condition.

Many religions and philosophies make a distinction between the *subtle body* (known in Sanskrit as *sukshma-sharira* or *linga sarira*) and the *physical body*. The *subtle body* (what might be called the *soul* or *spiritual body*) exists in the *invisible plane* or *planes*, though often it can be detected as an aura or some form of energy, and the *physical body* in the *visible plane*. One of the interpretations of the *Bible* coming from the final chapter of *Ecclesiastes* ("before the silver cord be loosed") is that the *subtle body* is attached to the physical body by a silver cord. (94)

It is sometimes called *puryastaka* (the city of eight) in reference to the *tattvas* (the five *tanmatras* (subtle elements; sound, touch, form, taste, and smell) and the *antah karana* (inner instrument; *buddhi* and *manas*)). This number, however is not standard; one Vedantic classification has the subtle body consisting of seventeen parts (the five *pranas*, and the ten organs of action and knowledge, *manas,* and *buddhi).* The *subtle body* is the means by which the soul transmigrates through *samsara* and the repository of *karmic* seeds that determine the physical body and individual destiny. Beyond the *subtle body* is the causal or highest body. The *subtle body* and the gross bodies correspond to the states of deep sleep, dreaming, and waking. Though these views are mainly derived from the religions coming out of India, they spread into the Orient and were embraced in the West in the late nineteenth century through the theosophical movement. Tibetan medicine holds that there is a network of energy paths parallel to nerves and blood vessels that carry energy from oxygen, sensory, and food-derived nutrients to help the flow of blood and neural impulses, not a system that can be known in conventional ways, but one that can be accessed through the imagination and meditation. (95) Ancient Egyptian religion believed the *soul* can hover outside the physical body in the *ka (subtle body).* (96)

According to the teachings of Tantra and Kundalini Yoga, the entire universe is a manifestation of pure consciousness, which divides into two poles, the masculine, represented by Shiva, is unmanifested consciousness (being but not becoming), and the feminine, represented by Shakti, the dynamic energy, the Great Mother from which all form comes. Each human is a miniature universe, and all of the forms of energy of the universe are also located in the human body. In humans, the feminine is called Kundalini, the potential energy that resides at the base of the spinal cord. The object of life is to get the female energy to rise through the seven chakras (Sanskrit for wheels) levels of consciousness and unite with the male energy located above the crown of the head.

The three lowest chakras match up with the neurological reptilian and limbic regions of the brain. The first chakra is located at the base of the spine. Its color is red. Its element is earth. Its main sense is smell. Its body associations are the kidneys, legs, adrenals, and spinal column. It is represented by a worm or slug, and it is related to simple survival instincts, such as eating. The second chakra is located at the navel or lower abdomen. Its color is orange. Its element is water. Its body associations are ovaries, testicles, prostate gland, genitals, spleen, womb, and bladder, and it is associated mainly with procreation. The third chakra is located below the breastbone and behind the stomach. Its color is yellow. Its element is fire. Its body associations are pancreas, liver, digestive tract, stomach, spleen, gall bladder, and the autonomic nervous system. Its main sense is sight. Its main association is that of personal power, ambition, and conquering.

It is at the fourth chakra, the chakra of the heart, that the higher kinds of feelings and emotions take place, those associated with compassion, the forms of love known as amore, philius, and agape. This chakra's colors are green and pink. Its element is air. Its organs are the heart, ribs, chest cavity, lower lungs, blood, skin, thymus, and importantly hands. Its sensory function is touch. It is the place where the spiritual world and the physical world connect, and the passage for the heart and mind (or left and right hemispheres of the neurological brain) to connect.

The three chakras above the heart all lead away from physical existence. The fifth, at the level of the throat is for verbal and mental communication, the world beyond the physical, and not surprisingly its sensory function is hearing. Its color is blue. It is the gateway to higher consciousness.

Thus, the four higher chakras are all associated with the neurological neocortex, the three lower the limbic and reptilian regions. The sexual dance, the erotic striptease, the wild uninhibited dance of abandonment to the sounds and beat of the drums, the Dionysian dance of nature, that's the dance of the limbic region. (97).

Taoism (Daoism), a mystical philosophy from prehistoric China that informs and intertwines with various Oriental religions and beliefs, often credited to Lao-tzu, who gave it a more formal frame in the 6th century B.C., includes a form of sacrifice involving the burning of Joss paper, or Hell Bank Notes, on the assumption that images thus consumed by the fire will reappear, not as a mere images, but as the actual items, in the spirit world, making them available for revered ancestors and departed loved ones. (98) Yang Erzeng's 17th century novel *the Story of Han Xiangzi* about Han Xiangzi, who seeks and achieves immortality and then converts his materialistic, politically driven uncle HanYu to Daoism, includes the following example of dual bodies (very similar to a doppelganger situation):

> "Xiangzi ... with a drum as his pillow fell fast asleep, snoring and motionless. His primordial spirit, however, went straight into the banquet room and said, "My lords, here I am again." . . . When Tuizhi walked . . . with the officials to take a look, there really was a Daoist sleeping on the ground and snoring like thunder. Yet inside, in the side room, there was another Daoist beating a fisher drum and singing Daoist songs. The officials all said, "Although there are two different people, their faces and clothes are exactly alike. Clearly he is a divine immortal who can divide his body and appear in several places at once. . . ." . . . At that moment, the Daoist in the side room came walking out, and the Daoist sleeping on the ground woke up. The two merged into one." (99)

In this sense, *astral projection* is sometimes referred to as *etheric projection*, the distinction being that in *astral projection* the subtle body enters a different world, but in *etheric projection* the subtle body remains in the physical world, often, though not always, invisible to others who are in their normal physical bodies. (100) Robert Monre calls this form of projection *Here-Now* or *Local I,* (101) Robert Bruce calls it the *Real Time Zone (RTZ)*, and claims it is the non-physical closest to the physical. (102) Max Heindel believes the *etheric double* is a medium between the astral and physical realms. (103) Stephen LaBerge suggests that all *out of body experiences* might represent *lucid dreams* or misinterpreted dream experiences. (104)

Often the *astral projection* experience takes those experiencing it into settings beyond the physical world, some populated, some not, some natural, some artificial, some beatific, some horrific. (105) Some believe it is possible during *astral projection* (and under *hypnosis*) to access the *Akashic Records. Akasha* is Sanskrit for "sky," "space," or "aether," and it is used in theosophy to describe a compendium of mystical knowledge (all of the knowledge of human experience and the entire history of the cosmos) held in a non-physical plane of existence, something of a library or a supercomputer that is constantly being automatically updated, a "book of life." (106)

C. W. Leadbeater, claimed to have seen the *Akashic Records* at the Theosophical Society headquarters in Adyar, India, 1910, and recorded them (including the history of Atlantis and the future society of Earth in the twenty-eighth century) in *Man: How, Whence, and Whither?* (107) Hypnotherapist Michael Newton claimed to have encountered many accounts of the akashic record from subjects his put into deep states of hypnosis. The belief is that souls prior to physical incarnation, go to this *library*, view the pages associated with lives they are considering living in order to satisfy a particular learning experience, a lesson, or a karmic debt, and choose a family and body, a life to be born into. For many, some of the images seen in this library survive *birth amnesia* and are the source of *intuition*. All is not predetermined, either before or after birth, as *free will* can change paths, events and outcomes. (108) Edgar Cayce claimed to have *channeled* the "social memory complex" known as "Ra," an "intelligent infinity [that] is brought into intelligent energy from [the] eighth density or octave." He used this "gateway" to "view the present, which is not the continuum you experience but the potential social memory complex of this planetary sphere. The term your peoples have used for this is the "Akashic Record" or the "Hall of Records." (109) Helen Stewart Wamback, Ph.D. (1925-1985) claimed to have the ability to read the akashic records, and as a result have the ability to hypnotize people and allow them to experience possible future lives in various alternate universes. (110)

In many accounts of *astral projection*, it is intertwined with *dreams*, often of seeing dreamers enacting their *dreams* in the *astral plane*, unaware of the larger environment surrounding them, suggesting that at least some *dreams* are a form of *astral projection*. (111)

There have been numerous practitioners and publications on *astral projection*, including Robert Monroe (who popularized the term OBE for *out of body experience*) and Robert Bruce, who suggest that the *astral world* is divided into levels or planes (heavens and hells, after-death spheres, and so on). (112) Other notable practitioners include Oliver Fox (113), Sylvan Muldoon (who worked with psychical researcher Hereward Carrington and developed techniques to facilitate the process) (114), Yram (115), William Buhlmann (116), and Albert Taylor. (117) Susan Blackmore discusses the entire world of *out-of-the-body-experiences* (OBE) in *Beyond the Body*. (118) Famed author Michael Crichton includes his own experiences in his autobiography, *Travels*. (119) Physician and dentist Waldo Vieira claims to have had his first OBE at the age of nine, and has written over twenty books on it, including *Projectiology of the Consciousness*. (120) President of the International Academy of consciousness Wagner Alegretti discusses several OBE experiences in such publications as *Retrocognitions: An Investigation into Memories of Past Lives and the Period Between Lives*. (121)

Theosophists believe that there are some beings that exist *only* in the *etheric* plane. *Devas* live either in the atmospheres of the planets of the solar system as *planetary angels* or inside the sun as *solar angels* (other planetary systems have their own set of angels). These *devas* help guide the operations of nature (evolution and growth of plants, and so on) in the forms of *fairies, ondines, sylphs, salamanders*, *gnomes* and other such nature spirits. They appear as colored flames roughly the size of humans and can be observed by the *third eye*. (122) Geoffrey Hodson, in *Kingdom of the Gods*, claims to have seen them, and has included paintings of them by psychic Ethelwynne M. Quail. (123)

Notes

1. Plato, *The Symposium*, Greek text with commentary by Kenneth Dover. Cambridge: Cambridge University Press, 1980. ISBN 0521295238.
2. Krajenke, Robert W., *Suddenly We Were!: a Story of Creation Based on the Edgar Cayce Readings*. A.R.E. Press, 1972; "What is a Twin Flame?", *SoulEvolution.org*. Retrieved on 2007-12-21.
3. *Two Essays on Analytical Psychology*, p. 154.
4. “Wotan,” in *Civilization in Transition*, p. 12.
5. *Memorie, Dreams, Reflections,* pp. 87-88.
6. *The Individuated Hobbit: Jung, Tolkien and the Archetypes of Middle-earth,* Houghton Mifflin, 1979, p. 27.
7. Lyrical Ballads, 1798; rev. 1817; rpt., *The Annotated Ancient Mariner*, Clarkson Potter, 1965.
8. *Archaeologiae Philosophiae, p. 68.*
9. *The Strange Case of Dr. Jekyll and Mr. Hyde,* 1886; rpt., Signet Classics, 2003.
10. Tolkien, J. R. R. *The Hobbit*. George Allen & Unwin, Ltd., 1937, rev., 1951; rpt., Ballantine Books, 1965, 1982, 20th prt., 1987, p. 76.
11. Joseph Campbell with Bill Moyers. *The Power of Myth*. ed., Billy Sue Flowers. New York: Doubleday, 1988, p. 180.
12. *Man and His Symbols*, New York: Dell, 1968, p. 266.
13. Schneider, Marious, *El origen musical de los animals-simbolos en la mitologia y la escultura antiguas, Barcelona*, 1946; trans. J. E. Cirlot, *A Dictionary of Symbols*. Trans. Jack Sage, London: Routledge & Kegan Paul, 1962, p. 137.
14. Otto Rank, *The Myth of the Birth of the Hero,* 1909 ; rev. and expanded, John Hopkins Univ., 2004.
15. J. E. Cirlot, *A Dictionary of Symbols*. Trans. Jack Sage, London: Routledge & Kegan Paul, 1962, p. 365.
16. *Nicene and Post-Nicene Fathers*, London and New York, 1889–90.
17. Tolkien, J. R. R. *The Hobbit*. George Allen & Unwin, Ltd., 1937, rev., 1951; rpt., Ballantine Books, 1965, 20th prt., 1982, p. 121.
18. Henry Gleitman, *Basic Psychology*, 4th ed. W.W. Norton, 1995, pp. 591-2.
19. Joseph Campbell with Bill Moyers. *The Power of Myth*. ed., Billy Sue Flowers. New York: Doubleday, 1988, p. 180.
20. *Man and His Symbols*, New York: Dell, 1968, p. 182.
21. Joseph Campbell, *Myths to Live By*. Bantam, 1972.
22. Rollo May, *The Cry for Myth*. New York: Dell, 1991, pp. 51-52.

23. J. E. Cirlot, *A Dictionary of Symbols*. Trans. Jack Sage, London: Routledge & Kegan Paul, 1962, p. 99.
24. *The Psychology of C. G. Jung*, London, 1951.
25. J. E. Cirlot, *A Dictionary of Symbols*. Trans. Jack Sage, London: Routledge & Kegan Paul, 1962, p. 77.
26. Joseph Campbell with Bill Moyers. *The Power of Myth*. ed., Billy Sue Flowers. New York: Doubleday, 1988, p. 180.
27. Jorge E. Gracia, "The Quests of Sam & Gollum for the Happy Life," *The Lord of the Rings and Philosophy: One Book to Rule Them All*. eds., Gregory Bassham & Eric Bronson. Peru, Ill.: Carus Publ., 2003, p.53.
28. Purtill, Richard L. *JRR Tolkien: Myth, Morality, and Religion*. San Francisco: Harper & Row, 1984, p. 46.
29. *The Twin Towers: The Lord of the Rings Triology*, Allen and Unwin 1955; rpt., Ballantine.
30. William Wyler, *The Letter*, 1940; DVD, Warner Brothers.
31. A. Stevens, A., *Ariadne's Clue*. Princeton: Princeton University Press, 1988, p.136.
32. M. E. Gomes and A. D. Kanner, "The rape of the well-maidens: Feminist psychology and the environmental crisis," *Ecopsychology: Restoring the earth, healing the mind*, San Francisco: Sierra, T. Roszak, M.E. Gomes and A.D. Kanner, ed., 1995, p.112.
33. R. A. Johnson, *Owning your own shadow*. San Francisco: Harper, 1995, p. 5.
34. E. C. Whitmont, "The evolution of the shadow," *Meeting the shadow*. C. Zweig & J. Abrams (Ed.),
New York: Tarcher/Putnam. Whitmont, 1991, p. 14.
35. Demetra George, *Mysteries of the dark moon*. San Francisco: Harper, 1992, p. 230.
36. Nor Hall, quoted by Demetra George, *Mysteries of the dark moon*. San Francisco: Harper, 1992, p. 150.
37. Joseph Conrad, "The Secret Sharer," *Harper's Magazine*, 1910; rpt., *Twix Land and Sea,* 1912; rpt., FQ Publishing, 2007.
38. Alan Watts, *The Two Hands of God,* Macmillan, 1969, p. 24.
39. *Star Wars Episode IV: A New Hope*. [DVD]. 20th Century Fox. 2006; *Star Wars Episode I: The Phantom Menace*. [DVD]. 20th Century Fox. 2001 *Star Wars Episode II: Attack of the Clones*. [DVD]. 20th Century Fox. 2002. *Star Wars Episode III: Revenge of the Sith*. [DVD]. 20th Century Fox. 2005.*Star Wars Episode V: The Empire Strikes Back*. [DVD]. 20th Century Fox. 2004.*Star Wars Episode VI: Return of the Jedi*. [DVD]. 20th Century Fox. 2004.
40. Joseph Campbell with Bill Moyers. *The Power of Myth*. ed., Billy Sue Flowers. New York: Doubleday, 1988, pp. 180-181.
41. Quotes are taken from *Star Wars: The Annotated Screenplays,* Laurent Bouzereau, Ballantine, 1997, pp. 165-166.
42. Quotes are taken from *Star Wars: The Annotated Screenplays,* Laurent Bouzereau, Ballantine, 1997, pp. 166-171.
43. First published in *Burtan's Gentlemen's Magazine,* 1939; rev. and reprinted in 1840, *Tales of the Grotesque and Arabesque*.

44."Die verschiedenen Aspekre der Wiedergeburt," *Erano-Jahrbuch*, 1939; rev., "Ober Wiedergeburt," *Gestaltungen des Unbewussten*, 1950; trans. by R.F.C. Hull, "Concerning Rebirth," *Archetypes and the Unconscious,* 2nd ed., Princeton Univ., 1969, pp. 123-124.
45. See Davies, M., Coltheart, M., Langdon, R., & Breen, N., "Monothematic delusions: Towards a two-factor account," *Philosophy, Psychiatry and Psychology, 8*, 2000, pp. 133–158; Sellen, J., Oaksford, M., Langdon, R., & Gray, N.. (2005). Schizotypy and Conditional Reasoning. "Schizophrenia Bulletin 2005, 31"(1), 105–116. Dudley, R., John, C., Young, A., Over, D. (1997). Normal and abnormal reasoning in people with delusions. "Br J Clinical Psychology, 36"(2), 243–58.
46. Capgras, J, Reboul-Lachaux, J., "Illusion des sosies dans un delire systematise chronique," *Bulletin de la Societe Clinique de Medicine Mentale*, 2, 1923, pp. 6-16; and Ellis HD, Whitley J, Luaute JP. "Delusional misidentification. The three original papers on the Capgras, Fregoli and intermetamorphosis delusions." (Classic Text No. 17). *History of Psychiatry*, 5 (17), 1994, pp. 117-46.
47. Passer, K.M., Warnock, J.K.., Pimozide in the treatment of Capgras' syndrome. A case report. *Psychosomatics*, 32 (4), 1991, pp., 446-8.
48. *Syndrome d'illusion de Frégoli et schizophrénie*. See Ellis, H. D.; Whitley, J.; & Luaute, J. P., "Delusional misidentification. The three original papers on the Capgras, Fregoli and intermetamorphosis delusions," (Classic Text No. 17). *History of Psychiatry* 5 (17 pt. 1), 1994, pp. 117–146.; and Mojtabai, R., "Fregoli syndrome," *Australian and New Zealand Journal of Psychiatry* 28 (3), 1994, pp. 458–462.
49. Ellis, H. D., & Szulecka, T. K., "The disguised lover: A case of Fregoli delusion" in P. W. Halligan & J. C. Marshall (Eds.), *Method in madness: Case studies in cognitive neuropsychiatry*, East Sussex, UK: Psychology Press, 1996, pp. 39-50.
50. Pisani, Marra, & Silveri, M.C, "Anatomical and psychological mechanism of reduplicative misidentification syndromes," *Neurological Sciences*, 21 (5), 2000, pp. 324-329. Retrieved February 28, 2002, from Ebscohost Academic Search Premier database..
51. Breen, N., Caine, D., Coltheart, M., Hendy, J., & Roberts, C., "Towards an understanding of delusions of misidentification: Four case studies," *Mind and Language*, 15 (1), 2000, pp. 74-111. Retrieved February 28, 2002, from Ebscohost Academic Search Premier database.
52. Pick, A., "On reduplicative paramnesia," *Brain*, 26, 1903, pp. 242-267.
53. *British Journal of Psychiatry*, 160, pp. 416-8.
54. Head, H., *Aphasia and Kindred Disorders*. London: Cambridge University Press, 1926; Paterson, A. & Zangwill, O., "Recovery of spatial orientation in the post-traumatic confusional state," *Brain*, 67, 1944, pp. 54-68.
55. "Reduplicative paramnesia," *Neurology*, 26 (2), pp. 147-51.
56. Forstl, H., Almeida, O.P., Owen, A.M., Burns, A., Howard, R., "Psychiatric, neurological and medical aspects of misidentification syndromes: a review of 260 cases'" *Psychological Medicine*, 21(4), 1991, pp. 905-10.

57. Young, A. W., & Leafhead, K. M. In P. W. Halligan & J. C. Marshall (Eds.), *Method in madness: Case studies in cognitive neuropsychiatry*, East Sussex, UK: Psychology Press, 1996, pp. 147-171.
58. Berrios G.E. & Luque R., "Cotard's 'On hypochondriacal delusions in a severe form of anxious melancholia'." *History of Psychiatry* 10, 1999, pp. 269-278.
59. Young, A.W. & Leafhead, K.M., in P.W. Halligan & J.C. Marshall. (eds.) *Method in Madness: Case studies in Cognitive Neuropsychiatry*. "*Betwixt Life and Death: Case Studies of the Cotard Delusion*" Hove: Psychology Press, 1996, p. 155.
60. Gerrans, Philip, "Refining the explanation of Cotard's delusion" *Mind and Language*, 15 (1), 2000, pp. 111-123.14. 61. Ramachandran, V. S., & Blakeslee, S., *Phantoms in the brain: Probing the mysteries of the human mind*. New York: William Morrow, 1998.
62. Young, A. W., & Leafhead, K. M. In P. W. Halligan & J. C. Marshall (Eds.), *Method in madness: Case studies in cognitive neuropsychiatry*, East Sussex, UK: Psychology Press, 1996, pp. 147-171.
63. Breen N, Caine D, Coltheart M., "Mirrored-self misidentification: two cases of focal onset dementia," *Neurocase*, 7 (3), 2001, pp. 239-54.
64. Lynn Solotaroff, New York, 1972. It is a detailed journal of a man's attempt to overcome his damaged brain and give meaning and value to his life, with numerous interspersed comments by Luria attempting to explain the neurological implications. Oliver Sacks considers Luria's works (especially this case study) to contain the greatest treasures of all of neurological thought; Luria's other works offer a more scientific discussion of the field of neurology. Some of the more important are: *The Mind of a Mnemonist*, New York, 1968; *Higher Cortical Functions in Man*, 2nd ed., New York, 1980, and the condensed version, *The Working Brain*, Hamondsworth, 1973.
65. *Johnny Got His Gun,* Bantam: New York, 1939. Dalton Trumbo directed a film of the novel in 1971 for which he received International Film Critics and Cannes Film Festival awards. Later, Metallica wrote and performed *One,* a song based on the film, and a video that incorporated clips from the film, Elektra Records, New York, 1989, pp. 160-162.
66. *Johnny Got His Gun,* Bantam: New York, 1939, pp. 221-222.
67. *Johnny Got His Gun,* Bantam: New York, 1939.
68. Dr. R. Joseph, *The Right Brain and the Unconscious: Discovering the Stranger Within*, New York: Plenum Press, 1992, p.104. The only one of these Joseph includes a source for is J. E. Bogen, "The Callosal Syndrome," *Clinical Neuropsychology*, K. M. Heilman and E. Valenstein, Eds. (pp. 308-358), New York: Oxford Univ. Press, 1979.
69. A. J. Akelaitis, "Studies on the Corpus Callosum: 4. Diagnostic Dyspraxia in Epileptics Following Partial and Complete Section of the Corpus Callosum, *American Journal of Psychiatry* 101 (1945), 594-599.
70. R. E. Myers and Roger Sperry, "Interocular transfer of a visual form discrimination habit in cats after section of the optic chiasma and corpus callosum," *Anatomical Record*, 115: 351-352, 1953.

71. Here are a few of the actual clinical publications from the fifties (listed by date of publication): R. E. Myers, "Interocular transfer of pattern discrimination in cats following section of crossed optic fibers," *Journal of Comparative Physol. Psychology*, 48, pp. 470-473, 1955; R. E. Myers, "Neural basis of bilateral perceptual integration," *Science*, 122: pp. 877, 1955; R. E. Myers, "The corpus callosum and hemispheric interaction," Ph. D. Thesis, Univ. of Chicago, 1955; Wilder Penfield, "Mechanisms of voluntary movement," *Brain*, 77, pp 1-17, 1955; R. E. Myers, "Function of corpus callosum in interocular transfer," *Brain*, 79, pp. 358-363, 1956; R. W. Sperry, "Experiments on perceptual integration in animals," *Psychait. Res. Rep.*, 6, pp. 151-159, 1956; R. W. Sperry, J. S. Stamm, and Nancy Miner, "Relearning tests for interocular transfer following division of optic chiasma and corpus callosum," *Journal of Comp. Physiol. Psychol.*, 49, pp. 529-533, 1956; R. W. Sperry and J. S. Stamm, "Function of corpus callosum in contralateral transfer of somesthetic discrimination in cats," *Journal of Comp. Physiol. Psychol.*, 50, pp. 138-143, 1957; R. W. Sperry, "High-order integrative functions in surgically isolated somatic cortex in cat," *Anat. Rec.*, 127, p. 371, 1957; R.E. Myers and R. W. Sperry, "Interhemispheric Communication Through the Corpus Callosum, Mnemonic Carry-Over Between the Hemispheres," *Archives Neurology and Psychiatry* 80, 1958, pp. 298-303; R. W. Sperry, J. S. Stamm, and Nancy Miner, "Relearning tests for interocular transfer following division of optic chiasma and corpus callosum," *Journal of Comparative Physiol. Psychology*, 49, 1959, pp. 529-533; R. J. White, L. H. Schreiner, R. A. Hughes, C. S. MacCarty, and J. H. Grindlay, "Physiologic consequences of total hemispherectomy in the monkey," *Neurology*, 9, pp. 149-159, 1959.

72. "Physiological psychology," *Annual Review of Psychology*, 6, pp. 267- 296, 1955.

73. Here are some of the lab reports coming out of the sixties, listed by date: J. E. Bogen and B. Campbell, "Total hemispherestomy in the cat," *Surg. Forum*, 11: 381-383, 1960; R. Sperry, "Cerebral organization," *Science*, 1331749-1757, 1961; R. Sperry, "Some developments in brain lesion studies of learning," *Fed. Proc.*, 20:609-616, 1961; M. S. Gazzaniga, J. E. Bogen, and R. W. Sperry, "Some functional effects of sectioning the cerebral commissures in man," Proc. *Nat. Acad. Sci.*, 48: 1765-9, 1962; J. E. Bogen and P. J. Vogel, "Treatment of generalized seizures by cerebral commissurotomy," *Surg. Forum*, 14: 431-433, 1963; M. S. Gazzaniga, J. E. Bogen, and R. W. Sperry, "Laterality effects in somesthesis following cerebral commissurotomy in man," *Neuropsychologia* , 1:209-215, 1963; R. W. Sperry, "The great cerebral commissure," *Sci Amer.*, 210:42-52, 1964; R. W. Sperry, "Problems outstanding in the evolution of brain function," James Arthur Lecture, American Museum of Natural History; New York, 1964; J. E. Bogen, E. D. Fisher, and P. J. Vogel, "Cerebral commissurotomy: A second case report," *Journal of the American Medical Association.*, 194: 1328-1329, 1965; R. E. Myers, "The Neocortical Commissures and Interhemispheric Transmission of Information," *Functions of the Corpus Callosum*. Ciba Fndn. Study Group No. 20. Ettlinger, E. G., Reuck, A. V. S., and Porter, R., eds., Little, Brown and Co.: Boston, 1965; M. S. Gazzaniga, J. E. Bogen, and R. W. Sperry, "Observations on visual perception after disconnection of the cerebral hemispheres in man," *Brain*,

88:221-236, 1965; J. E. Bogen, M. S. Gazzaniga, "Cerebral commissurotomy in man: Minor hemisphere dominance for certain visuospatial functions," *Journal of Neurosurgery.*, 23: 394-399, 1965; R. W. Sperry, "Brain bisection and mechanisms of consciousness," pp. 442-468, *Semaine d'Etude Sur Cerveau et Experience Consciente.*, J. Eccles, ed., Pontificae Acad. Scient. Scripta varia, Rome, 1965; R. W. Sperry and M. S. Gazzaniga, "Language Following Surgical Disconnection of the Hemispheres," *Brain Mechanisms Underlying Speech and Language*, ed., F. L. Darley, Grune and Stratton: New York, 1966; M. S. Gazzaniga and R. W. Sperry, "Simultaneous double discrimination response following brain bisection," *Psychon. Sci.*, 4:261-262, 1966; M. S. Gazzaniga, and E. D. Young, "Effects of commissurotomy on the processing of increasing visual information." *Experimental Brain Research*, 3: 368-371, 1967; M. S. Gazzaniga and R. W. Sperry, "Language after section of the cerebral commissures," *Brain,* 90:131-148, 1967; M. Gazzaniga, "The split-brain in man," *Scientific American*, 217:24-29, 1967; M. S. Gazzaniga, J. E. Bogen, and R. W. Sperry, "Dyspraxia following division of the cerebral commissures," *Arch. Neurol.*, 16:606-612, 1967; M. S. Gazzaniga, "Short-term memory and brain-bisected man," *Psychon. Sci.*, 12:161-162, 1968; S. R. Butler and U. Norrsell, "Bocalization possibly indicated by the minor hemisphere," *Nature*, 220:793-794, 1968; R. W. Sperry, "Hemisphere deconnection and unity in conscious awareness," *American Psychologist,* 23:723-733, 1968; R. W. Sperry, "Mental unity following surgical disconnection of the cerebral hemispheres," Harvey Lectures, Series 62, N. Y.; *Academic Press*, 1968; B. Milner, L. Taylor, and R. W. Sperry, "Lateralized suppression of dichotically presented digits after commissural section in man," *Science*, 161:184-6, 1968; J. Levy-Agresti, "Ipsilateral projection systems and minor hemisphere function in man after neocommissurotomy," *Anatomy Record*, 160:3844, 1968; J. E. Bogen, R. W. Sperry, and P. J. Vogel, "Commissural Section and the Propagation of Seizures," *Basic Mechanisms of the Epilepsies*, H. H. Jaspher, A. A. Ward, and A. Pope, eds., Little, Brown: Boston, 1969; J. E. Bogen, "The corpus callosum, the other side of the brain, and pharmacologic opportunity," *Drugs and Cerebral Function*, W. L. Smith, ed., Thomas: Springfield, Ill, 1969; Here are some of the reports from the 1970s: Michael S. Gazzaniga, *The Bisected Brain*, Appleton-Century-Crofts, New York, 1970 (an overview of the findings to this date by one of those involved in the research); M. Kinsbourne, "The cerebral basis of lateral asymmetries in attention," *Acta Psychologica*, vol. 33, pp. 193-201, 1970; J. Levy, C. Trevarthen, and R. W. Sperry, "Perception of Bilateral Chimeric Figures Following Hemispheric Deconnection," *Brain* 95, pp. 61-78, 1972; R. Sperry, "Lateral Specialization in the Surgically Separated Hemispheres," *The Nurosciences: Third Study Program*, F. O. Schmitt and F. G. Worldern, Eds., Cambridge: MIT Press, pp. 1-12, 1974; M. Kinsbourne, "The mechanism of hemispheric control of the lateral gradient of attention," *Attention and Performance*, vol. 5, ed. P.M.A. Rabbitt and S. Dornic, New York: Academic Press, 1975; J. Levy and C. Trevarthen, "Metacontrol of Hemispheric Function in Human Split-Brain Patients," *Journal of Experimental Psychology: Human Perception and Performance 2*, pp. 299-312, 1976; H. A. Whitaker and G. Ojemann, "Lateralization of higher cortical functions: A critique," *Annals of the new York Academy of Science*, vol. 299, pp. 459-473, 1977; J.E. Bogen, "The Callosal Syndrome," *Clinical Neuropsychology*, K. M. Heilman and E. Valenstein, Eds., New York: Oxford Press, pp. 308-358, 1979; J. Levy, "Language, Cognition, and the Right Hemisphere," *American Psychologist* 38, pp. 538-541, 1983.

74. C. B. Trevarthen, "Double visual learning in split-brain monkeys," *Science*, 136:258-259, 1962.

75. M. S. Gazzaniga and R. W. Sperry, "Simultaneous double discrimination response following brain bisection, "*Psychon. Sci.* 4:261-262, 1966.

76. See "Interhemispheric relationships: the neocortical commissures, syndromes of hemispheric disconnection," *Handbook of Clinical Neurology, Vol. 4, Disorders of Speech, Perception and Symbolic Behavior*, ed. P. J. Vinken and G. W. Bruyn. Amsterdam: Elsevier/North Holland Biomedical Press, pp. 145-153, 1969; see "Brain Bisection and Consciousness," *Brain and Conscious Experience*, ed. J. Eccles, New York: Springer-Verlag, 1966; see "Perception in the Absence of the Neocortical Commissures, Perception and its Disorders," *Research Publication of the Association for Research in Nervous and Mental Diseases*, Vol. 48, 1970.

77. J. E. Bogen, "The Other Side of the Brain," p. 157-8, *Bulletin of the Los Angeles Neurological Societies* 34, pp. 135-162, 1969; Bogen also includes a list of famous people's dual terms for the two forms of thought, which I list here in paragraph form: C. S. Smith, Atomistic/Gross; Price, Analytic or reductionist/Synthetic or concrete; Wilder, Numerical/Geometric; Head, Symbolic or systematic/Perceptual or non-verbal; Goldstein, Abstract/Concrete; Rluesch, Digital or discursive/Analogic or eidetic; Bateson & Jackson, Digital/Analogic; J. Z. Young, Abstract/Map-like; Pribram, Digital/Analogic; W. James, Differential/Existential; Spearman, Eduction of relations/Eduction of correlates; Hobbes, Directed/Primary process; Pavlov, Second signaling/First signaling; Freud, Secondary process/Primary process; Sechenov (Luria), Successive/Simultaneous; Levi-Strauss, Positive/Mythic; Bruner, Rational/Metaphoric; Akhilinanda, Buddhi/Manis, Radhakrishnan, Rational/Integral.

78. See "Lateral Specialization of Cognitive Mode: An EEG Study," *Psychophysiology*, Vol. 9, pp. 412-418, 1972; see *The Psychology of Consciousness*, 2nd ed., New York: Harcourt Brace Jovanovich, 1977; see "The Split and Whole Brain," *Human Nature 1*, 1978

79. Roger Sperry, "Brain Bisection and the Neurology of Consciousness," *Brain and Conscious Experience*, J. C. Eccles, Ed. (pp. 298-313) (New York: Springer Verlag, 1978.

80. See W. Penfield and L. Roberts, *Speech and Brain Mechanisms*, Princeton, N.J.: Princeton Univ. Press, 1959; see G. A. Ojemann, "Brain Organization for Language from the Perspective of Electrical Stimulation Mapping," *The Behavioral and Brain Sciences 6*, 1983, pp. 235-238; see A. S. Gevins, "Brain potential (BP) evidence for lateralization of higher cognitive functions," *Cerebral Hemisphere Asymmetry: Method, Theory and Application*, J. B. Hellige, New York: Praeger, 1983.

81. See J. Risberg, J. H. Halsey, E. L. Wills, and B. M. Wilson, "Hemispheric specialization in normal man studied by bilateral measurements of the regional cerebral blood flow," *Brain*, 98, pp. 511-524, 1975; M. I. Posner, S. E. Peterson, P.

T. Fox, and M. E. Raichle, "Localization of cognitive operations in the human brain," *Science*, 240, pp. 1627-1631, 1988.

82. For further discussion, see F. Wood, "Laterality of cerebral function: Its investigation by measurement of localized brain activity," *Cerebral Hemisphere Asymmetry: Method, Theory, and Application*, ed. J. B. Hellige, pp. 383-410, New York: Praeger, 1983; J. L. Bradshaw, *Hemispheric Specialization and Psychological Function*, Chichester, England: Wiley, 1989; F. B. Wood, D. L. Flowers, and E. E. Naylor, "Cerebral laterality in functional neuroimaging," *Cerebral Laterality: Theory and Research*, ed. F. L. Kitterle, pp. 103-116, Hillsdale, N. J.: Erlbaum, 1991.

83. See J. Risberg, J. H. Halsey, E. L. Wills, and B. M. Wilson, "Hemispheric specialization in normal man studied by bilateral measurements of the regional cerebral blood flow," *Brain*, 98, pp. 511-524, 1975; M. I. Posner, s. e. Peterson, P. T. Fox, and M. E. Raichle, "Localization of cognitive operations in the human brain," *Science*, 240, pp. 1627-1631, 1988.

84. See H. Hecaen and M. Albert, *Human Neuropsychology*, New York: Wiley, 1978.

85. For more discussion of the studies from 1980-1990, see: E. Zaidel and A. M. Peters, "Phonological encoding and ideographic reading by the disconnected right hemisphere; Two case studies," *Brain and Language*, vol 14, pp. 205-234, 1981; J. G. Beaumont, *Divided Visual Field Studies of Cerebral Organization*, New York: Academic Press, 1982; M. P. Bryden, *Laterality: Functional Asymmetry in the Intact Brain*, New York: Academic Press, 1982; J. J. Sidtis and M. S. Gazzaniga, "Competence versus performance after callosal section: Looks can be deceiving," *Cerebral Hemisphere Asymmetry: Method, Theory and Application*, Hellige, pp. 152-176, 1983; E. Zaidel, "Disconnection syndrome as a model for laterality effects in the normal brain," *Cerebral Hemisphere Asymmetry: Method, Theory, and Application*, ed. J. B. Hellige, New York: Praeger, pp. 95-151, 1983; M. Kinsbourne and M. Hiscock, "Asymmetries of dual-task performance," *Cerebral Hemisphere Asymmetry: Method, Theory and Application*, Hellige, New York: Praeger, pp. 255-334, 1983; M. P. Bryden, "Handedness and cerebral organization: Data from clinical and normal populations," *Duality and Unity of the Brain: Unified Functioning and Specialization of the Hemispheres*, ed. D. Ottoson, vol. 55-70, London: Macmillan, 1987; *Duality and Unity of the Brain*, ed. D. Ottoson, London: Macmillan, pp. 454-465, 1987; M. W. O'Boyle, F. van Wyhe-Lawler, and D. A. Miller, "Recognition of letters traced in the right and left palms: Evidence for a process-oriented tactile asymmetry," *Brain and Cognition*, vol. 6, pp. 474-494, 1987; K. Hugdahl, *Handbook of Dichotic Listening: Theory, Methods and Research*, New York: Wiley, 1988; J. B. Hellige and D. W. Kee, "Asymmetric manual interference as an indicator of lateralized brain function," *Cerebral Control of Speech and Limb Movements*, ed. G. R. Hammond, Amsterdam: North-Holland, pp. 635-660, 1990; R. Efron, *The Decline and Fall of hemispheric Specialization*, Hillsdale, N. J.:Erlbaum, 1990; A. Bouma, *Lateral Asymmetries and Hemispheric Specialization: Theoretical Models and Research*, Amsterdam: Swets and Zeitlinger, 1990.

86. Ramachandran V.S., Rogers-Ramachandran D., Stewart M., "Perceptual correlates of massive cortical reorganization," *Science (journal)* 258 (5085), November, 1992, pp. 1159–60.
87. MacLachlan M, McDonald D, Waloch J., "Mirror treatment of lower limb phantom pain: a case study," *Disabil Rehabil* 26 (14-15), 2004, pp. 901–4; Ramachandran VS, Rogers-Ramachandran D., "Synaesthesia in phantom limbs with mirrors," *Proc. Biol. Sci.* 263 (1369), pp. 377–86, .April, 1996.
88. See G.N.M. Tyrrell, *Apparitions*, Gerald Duckworth and Co. Ltd, London, 1943, pp. 149; C.E. Green, *Out-of-the-body Experiences*, Hamish Hamilton, London, 1968; and *Journeys Out of the Body*, 1971, Robert Monroe.
89. See E. R. Dodds, *Proclus: The Elements of Theology*. A revised text with translation, introduction, and commentary, 2nd edition, 1963, Appendix; and Walter Pagel, *William Harvey's Biological Ideas*. Karger Publishers, 1967, pp. 147–148.
90. Suki Miller, *After Death: How People around the World Map the Journey after Death* (1995); and Dr. Roger J. Woolger, *Beyond Death: Transition and the Afterlife*, accessed online June 2008 at the website of the Royal College of Psychiatrists, http://www.rcpsych.ac.uk/PDF/RWoolgerTransition.pdf.
91. 2 Corinthians, xii, 2-4, *King James Bible,*1611; Thomas Nelson Inc.; Camden, New Jersey, 1970.
92. See Bart Ehrman, *Lost Christianities: The Battles for Scripture and the Faiths We Never Knew*, Oxford Press, 2003, pp. xiv.
93. *Light and Death*, Michael Sabom, Zondervan, November 1, 1998.
94. See: *Projection of the Astral Body* by Carrington and Muldoon; and *Out of Body Experiences: How to have them and what to expect* by Robert Peterson (chapters 5, 17, 22).
95. *Mosby's Dictionary of Complementary and Alternative Medicine*, Elsevier, 2005.
96. Melton, J. G., "Out-of-the-body Travel," *Encyclopedia of Occultism & Parapsychology*, 1996.
97. See: Harish Johari, *Chakras*, Destiny Books, 1987, ISBN: 0-89281-054-8; Harish Johari, *Chakras: Energy sources of Transformation*, 2000.
98. See: Mantak Chia, *Fusion of the Five Elements*. Destiny Books, 2007; Chad D. Hansen, *A Daoist Theory of Chinese Thought: A Philosophical Interpretation*, Oxford University Press, 2000; Kristopher Schipper, *The Taoist Body* (Berkeley: University of California Press, 1993; and Kristopher Schipper and Franciscus Verellen. *The Taoist Canon: A Historical Companion to the Daozang*, Chicago: University of Chicago, 2004.
99. Erzeng, Yang (2007). *The Story of Han Xiangzi*. University of Washington Press. pp. 207–209.
100. See the following for discussions of astral projection: Melton, J. G. (1996). *Out-of-the-body Travel. In Encyclopedia of Occultism & Parapsychology*. Thomson, Gale, ISBN 978-0810394872; Osho, *The Transmission of the Lamp*, Chapter 3, Rebel Press; Chic Cicero, Chic C, Sandra Tabatha Cicero The Essential Golden Dawn, Llewellyn Worldwide, 2003; Arthur A.Powell, *THE ASTRAL BODY AND OTHER ASTRAL PHENOMENA*, The Theosophical Publishing

House, London, England; Wheaton,Ill, U.S.A.; Adyar, Chennai, India, 1927, reprinted in 1954 and 1965, page 7, online June 2008 at http://www.theosophical.ca/AstralBodyByPowell-A.htm; Henri Corbin, Creative Imagination in the Sufism of Ibn Arabi, tr. Ralph Mannheim, Bollingen XCI, Princeton U.P., 1969; William Judge, *The Ocean of Theosophy,* 2nd Ed. TPH, 1893, Chapter 5, book online June 2008 at www.theosociety.org/pasadena/ocean/oce-hp.htm; Astral-Projections.com "Secret Guide To Instant Astral Projection"; Monroe, Robert. *Far Journeys.* ISBN 0-385-23182-2; *Astral Dynamics* by Robert Bruce. Hampton Roads Publishing Company, Inc, 1999 ISBN 1-57174-143-7 ; *Journeys Out of the Body* by Robert A. Monroe, p 60. Anchor Press, 1977; *Astral Dynamics* by Robert Bruce Hampton Roads Publishing Company, Inc, 1999. p 25-27, 30-31.

101. *Journeys Out of the Body* by Robert A. Monroe, p 60. Anchor Press, 1977.

102. *Astral Dynamics* by Robert Bruce Hampton Roads Publishing Company, Inc, 1999, pp. 25-27, 30-31.

103. Heindel, Max, *The Rosicrucian Mysteries,* "Chapter IV, The Constitution of Man: Vital Body - Desire Body – Mind," 1911, ISBN 0-911274-86-3.

104. *Lucid Dreaming: the power of being awake & aware in your dreams*, pp. 232-346.

105. Astral-Projections.com"Secret Guide To Instant Astral Projection."

106. Bruce: *Astral Dynamics: The Complete Book of Out-of-Body Experiences*, 2009, ch 24.

107. Besant, Annie and Leadbeater, C.W. *Man: How, Whence, and Whither?* Adyar, India:1913 Theosophical Publishing House, "Introduction," p. vii.

108. *Journey of Souls*: *Case Studies of Life between Lives*, 1994; and *Destiny of Souls:New Case Studies of Life between the Lines,* Llewellyn Publications, 2000.

109. Elkins, Rueckert, McCarty: *The Ra Material: An Ancient Astronaut Speaks*, p. 141. The Donning Company, 1984.

110. Future-life progression," also called future progression or future-life progression hypnosis, is a variation of past-life therapy developed by Helen Stewart Wambach, Ph. D, author of *Recalling Past Lives* (Harper & Row, 1978) and *Life Before Life* (Bantam Books, 1979). Chet B. Snow, Ph.D. "Future-life progression is a means, it is claimed, of viewing one's future and the potential lives of future incarnations of oneself," *Skeptic's Dictionary of New Age Theories.*

111. Monroe, Robert. *Far Journeys.* ISBN 0-385-23182-2; *Astral Dynamics* by Robert Bruce. Hampton Roads Publishing Company, Inc, 1999 ISBN 1-57174-143-7.

112. Monroe, Robert. *Far Journeys.* ISBN 0-385-23182-2; *Astral Dynamics* by Robert Bruce. Hampton Roads Publishing Company, Inc, 1999 ISBN 1-57174-143-7; *Journeys Out of the Body* by Robert A. Monroe, p. 60. Anchor Press, 1977.

113. Oliver Fox, *Astral Projection,* Citadel, 2000.

114. Sylvan Muldoon and Hereward Carrington, *Projection of the Astral Body,* Kessinger Publishing, LLC, 2010

115. Yram, *Practical Astral Projection,* Kessinger Publishing, LLC, 2010.

116. William Buhlman, Adventures Beyond the Body: How to Experience Out-of-Body Travel HarperOne; 1st edition, 1996.

117. Albert Taylor, *Soul Traveler: A Guide to Out-of-Body Experiences and the Wonders Beyond*, NAL Trade, 2000.
118. Susan Blackmore, *Beyond the Body,* Academy Chicago Publishers; illustrated edition, 2005.
119. Michael Crichton, *Travels,* Harper Paperbacks, 2002.
120. WaldoVieira, *Projections of the Consciousness,* International Academy of Consciousness; 3rd edition, 2007.
121. Walter Alegretti, *Retrocognitions: An Investigation into Memories of Past Lives and the Period Between Lives,* International Academy of Consciousness, 2004.
122. Powell, A.E. *The Solar System*, London, 1930; rpt., Kessinger Publishing, 2003; *The Astral Body and other Astral Phenomena,* Quest Books, 1927.
123. Hodson, Geoffrey, *Kingdom of the Gods,* Quest Books, 1972; C. W. Leadbeater and Annie Wood Besant, *Occult Chemistry: Investigations by Clairvoyant Magnification into the Structure of the Atoms of the Periodic Table and Some Compounds*, Kessinger, 1951; rpt., 1997.

EMPATHY

"I am he as you are he as you are me and we are all together"
—*I am the Walrus,* Lennon and McCartney

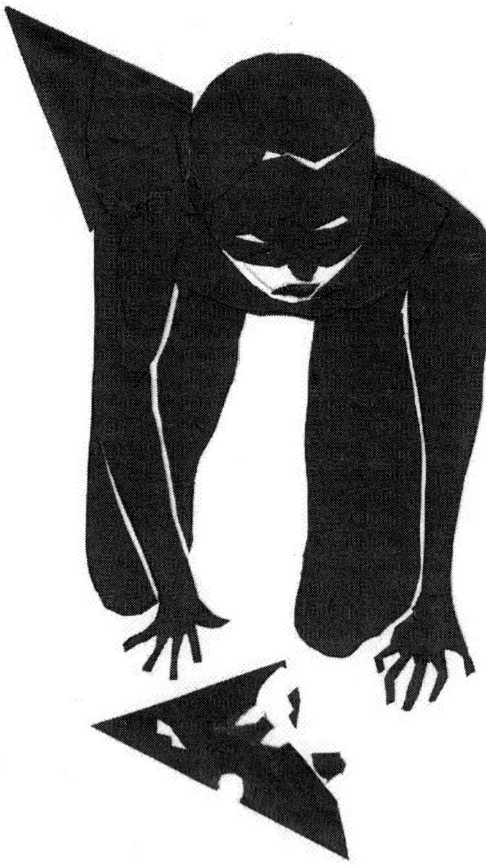

Fallen Hero

Stardate 5121.5. the starship USS Enterprise arrives at Minara II, a planet in serious peril because its star is about to go supernova. Captain Kirk, Dr. McCoy, and Mr. Spock beam down to locate and rescue a research team located there, but find the camp site abandoned and the scientists missing.

While they search for the missing scientists, the Enterprise is bombarded by intense solar radiation, causing instrumentation failure and threatening the lives of the crew. Mr. Scott, left in charge orders the ship to leave orbit.

The landing party gets teleported to an underground chamber to find a young woman lying on a raised platform. She awakens but appears to be mute. All attempts at communication with her fail. Dr. McCoy names her Gem.

Two silver-robed aliens appear and identify themselves as Vians. However, when Captain Kirk attempts to approach them, he is repelled by a force field, knocking him to the ground and injuring him. Gem immediately rushes to his side and uses some kind of mental power to absorb his injuries, transferring them to herself, where we watch them quickly heal, and we see that she is an *empath.*

The aliens leave the chamber to plan out experiments on their new prisoners. Spock scans the chamber for a way out and discovers that there is a nearby area filled with sophisticated machinery and computer banks. In addition, there are several glass cylinders, two containing dead bodies frozen in horrific poses. Signs identify them as Linke and Ozaba, the missing research scientists. Three additional cylinders are empty but have the foreboding plaques McCoy, Spock, and Kirk.

The Vians reappear, explain that Linke and Ozaba died of their own fears, and demand that one of the landing party volunteer for their tests. Captain Kirk agrees to do so on the condition that Mr. Spock and Dr. McCoy are freed. The Vians agree, but only transport Mr. Spock and Dr. McCoy to another chamber with Gem. Then they proceed to torture Captain Kirk. When they are finished with this round of tests, they send him to the chamber with the others and Gem heals his wounds as she did previously. However, this time his wounds are more serious, and it takes more out of Gem to absorb them. She faints from the exertion, and the three of them worry that she could die if she overuses her abilities. Dr. McCoy suggests that her instinct for self-preservation would prevent her from doing this.

Not surprisingly, the Vians are not satisfied with their tests on Captain Kirk and return to demand another subject, giving Captain Kirk the choice of Dr. McCoy or Mr. Spock, offering the information that there is an 87%

chance Dr. McCoy will die and a 93% chance Mr. Spock with suffer brain damage resulting in permanent insanity. While Captain Kirk debates this choice, Dr. McCoy sedates him, intending to offer himself. Mr. Spock, however, now technically in command, says no, he is going to choose himself. So Dr. McCoy sedates Mr. Spock as well.

While Dr. McCoy gets his wish and is being tortured, Mr. Spock and Captain Kirk revive. Spock makes adjustments to a teleportation device stolen earlier from the Vians and suggests they return to the surface. However, Captain Kirk decides "The best defense is a good offense, and I intend to start offending now." So they go to the Vians' medical chamber, where they find Dr. McCoy near death.

Returning to the first chamber, they find Gem resting, very weak and afraid. Captain Kirk suggests that she might be persuaded to help Dr. McCoy, at which point the Vians again appear and imprison Captain Kirk and Mr. Spock in a force field to prevent them from interfering with their experiments. Gem overcomes her fear and tries to take on Dr. McCoy's pain, suffering tremendously as she does so. Captain Kirk demands an explanation for the cruelty. The Vians explain that they aren't interested in the landing party, but in actuality are testing Gem. Apparently, they only have the ability to save one of the races of people from the upcoming supernova disaster, and they want to see if Gem's race is worthy of saving. If she passes their tests, then her race will be saved. If not, some other race will be saved.

They continue to test Gem, watching her slowly become ever weaker. Finally, she stops, and they decide that she is not willing to give her life for another and thus that her people are not worthy of being saved. They demand Gem return and continue to absorb Dr. McCoy's pain until she dies from it. She begins again, but Dr. McCoy shoves her away.

In the meantime, Mr. Spock explains that, since Gem has already offered her life, she has proven she is willing to do so and need not actually die to save her people. Furthermore, Dr. McCoy's life is not, after all, dependent solely on Gem; the Vians themselves have the technology to save him. They Vians refuse. Captain Kirk accuses them of lacking the one thing Gam has already demonstrated, the one thing the Vians claim to prize—compassion. Then, to emphasize his point, he finishes, "If death is all you understand, here are four lives for you." This is finally enough to get the Vians to reconsider. They restore Gem and Dr. McCoy to heath and agree to spare her people.

The aliens and Gem disappear, and Captain Kirk and his team return to the Enterprise. He muses on the chance encounter with Gem, and Scott suggests the biblical parable of the Pearl of Great Price: "Again, the kingdom of heaven is like unto a merchant man, seeking goodly pearls: Who, when he had found one pearl of great price, went and sold all that he had, and bought it." (2)

The reason for Dr. McCoy's name of the empath as *Gem* is now clear.

Lest it is missed in the clever pun and the dramatics of the plot, the episode clearly embraces the qualities of *empathy* and *compassion*. Self-sacrifice is the highest of human qualities, as precious not only as a gem or a pearl, but as the Kingdom of Heaven itself, and by implication, God's grace. It is worth more than all of earthly existence.

Mr. Spock, half-Vulcan-half-Human, offers another interesting slant on *empathy*, because Vulcan's have the ability to *mind-meld*, which means they can share thoughts, experiences, memories, emotions, and, ultimately, their entire mental essence with another (a process called *katra* that allows them to cheat death).

Before discussing this, however, it is worth briefly highlighting another, related quality. Vulcans, as a matter of custom and policy, work hard to suppress all emotional influence by living lives of rigid self-control through meditative techniques and training of mental discipline. This does not mean that Vulcans have no emotions; although at times they themselves make this claim; on the contrary, Vulcans are exceptionally emotional. However, they have developed techniques to suppress their emotions precisely because of the damage they can cause if unchecked. In the original Star Trek series episode "The Savage Curtain," Spock meets Surak and displays emotion, for which Surak reprimands him, and he asks forgiveness. In the episode "Gravity" of *Star Trek: Voyager*, Tuvok explains that Vulcans' natural emotions are "erratic and volatile;" if Vulcans do not strongly repress emotions, they can get violently angry in an instant. T'Pol of *Star Trek: Enterprise* states that paranoia and homicidal rage were common on Vulcan prior to the adoption of Surak's code of emotional control.

The ritual of *Kolinahr* is used to purge all vestigial emotion; the word also refers to the discipline by which this state is maintained. Though most Vulcans do retain control over their emotions, only the most devoted and trained Vulcan students attain *Kolinahr*. In *Star Trek: The Motion Picture,* Spock is not able to complete this ritual after receiving powerful telepathic signals from space and experiencing strong emotions as a result. The Vulcan masters conducting the trials concluded that since Spock's human blood was touched by these messages from space, he could not have achieved *Kolinahr,* and the ritual was halted.

The term for the purge of emotion is *arei'mnu, a* term that apparently does not translate properly into any Earth language. In Diane Duane's novel *Spock's World,* it is suggested that *arei'mnu* closely translates into "mastery of emotions," but that linguist Amanda Grayson, Sarek's wife and Spock's mother, in her work on the universal translator, had mistranslated the Vulcan word to mean "lack of emotions."

Some Vulcans, such as T'Pol, Sarek (in his later years, due to a rare disease which can affect Vulcans over the age of 200 years), and Soval, carry their emotions close to the surface, and are prone to emotional outbursts, even without outside influences or illness; T'Pau certainly displayed restrained but definite emotions in the TOS episode "Amok Time," including suspicion of the Human visitors followed by admiration and approval of their friendship for Spock, and contempt for Spock's humanity.

Not all Vulcan characters follow the path of pure logic; a group of renegade Vulcans instead believed in embracing emotions in the *Star Trek: Enterprise* episode "Fusion." Spock's half-brother Sybok, *Star Trek V: The Final Frontier,* was also fully emotional. An episode of *Enterprise* titled "E^2" featured an elderly T'Pol in an alternate timeline who had embraced emotion and allowed her half-Human son, Lorian, to do likewise.

In the pilot episode "The Cage," Spock showed much more emotion. Initially, "Number One" was supposed to be the emotionless character. However, although the test audience indicated they liked the actress, they hated the character because they could not relate to a female who was so "cold." As a result, the character of Christine Chapel was created for Barrett and the "coldness" was transferred to the Spock character.

This whole struggle with emotions and controlling them is related to a belief in the embracement of logic and reason, and in terms of neurology, it is closed related to an embracement of left brain or left cerebrum thinking. And the Star Trek series constantly demonstrates that, although the very intelligent and logical Vulcans think more rationally than Humans, human ability to go beyond logic gives them an advantage; there is a time for trusting one's emotions, one's intuition. There is indeed more to life than logic.

Many Vulcans are also *contact telepaths*, and they have been observed taking part in a number of telepathy-related actions and rituals, including an instance where CDR Spock was telepathically aware of the simultaneous deaths of 400 other Vulcans on a faraway ship, the U.S.S. *Intrepid,* whose crew was entirely Vulcan, in the Season 2 episode "The Immunity Syndrome."

It is their ability to *mind*-meld, however, that relates most closely to *empathy.* A "mind-meld" is a technique for sharing thoughts, experiences, memories, and knowledge with another individual, normally requiring physical contact with another, though instances of mind-melds without contact are possible (i.e., the episode "The Devil in the Dark"). Jonathan Archer, Captain of the original Enterprise, is the first known Human participant. Even the Earth Humpback Whale can be successfully melded with. Even machines, such as the Nomad probe, have been melded with. In the *Star Trek: The Animated Series* episode "One of Our Planets is Missing," a touch-less melding of a gaseous nebular entity is depicted. The Ferengi are one of the few races known to be immune from it; mentally disciplined Cardassians might also be resistant to mind melds if properly trained, though it is not firmly established if this potential ability is inherent to Cardassians, or if members of any race can be trained to resist.

Mind melds have been used to erase memories, as Spock does to Captain Kirk in "Requiem for Methuselah." Mind melds can also allow more than one mind to experience memories and sensations, and sometimes even interact with the memories, as seen in the *Star Trek: Voyager* episode "Flashback."

One interesting aspect of this is the complete intimacy of a mind-melt. There simply is no hiding from a mind-meld. Also, because of the strength of Vulcan emotions and the strict psycho-suppression disciplines in which they are trained, a mind meld is not to be taken lightly. In the *Star Trek: The Next Generation* episode "Sarek," when the diplomat proves to have Bendii's syndrome and thus to be incapable of completing his last great mission without assistance, he executes a mind meld with Captain Jean-Luc Picard, gaining enough emotional stability from this to complete his mission--but Picard himself almost goes insane from the direct onslaught of Sarek's powerful emotions as a result.

Though mind melds are frequently portrayed as a consensual act, it is not always the case. In "Mirror, Mirror," Spock of the Mirror Universe performs a forced mind meld on Dr. Leonard McCoy in order to learn what he is keeping secret. Mind melds can also be very violating and potentially harmful. In *Star Trek VI: The Undiscovered Country,* Spock forcefully uses a mind meld on Valeris to discover information she has that can be used to prevent a war; Valeris begins screaming in pain just before Spock breaks the connection.

Because of the intimacy and danger of the mind meld, it was taboo for a period of time. However, this changed when experienced melders were shown to be able to cure Pa'nar Syndrome, a condition passed on by melders who are improperly trained. Within a week of the Kir'Shara incident in 2154, the stigma against mind-melders was ending, and sufferers of *Pa'nar* were being cured in large numbers. By the mid-23rd century, the mind meld was a fully accepted part of Vulcan society, and was even used once to rejoin Spock's *katra* with his re-generated physical body.

There is even indication that some Vulcans with advanced mental abilities can use a mind meld to induce uncertainty in another's mind, i.e., the episode "A Taste of Armageddon," where Spock does this in the mind of a prison guard on Eminiar VII, and the episode "The Devil in the Dark," where he is able to perform a limited mind meld with a *horta* without actually making physical contact. However, it is made clear that a touch-less meld is limited in effectiveness compared to physical melds, and that more intense melds can be accomplished using both hands.

As is the case with most of these interesting psychological oddities or gifts in Star Trek, the implications of the mind meld are not given much time. They are used mainly as a plot device, a solution to a seemingly unsolvable problem, rather than explored in terms of what they mean in terms of human existence, in terms of the multiple realties humans might experience, and in terms of how human existence is defined. Certainly, the ability to merge with another's mind and even influence that mind, erasing memories, creating doubts, discovering secrets, raises questions about how an individual is defined. In other words, if one's thoughts can be changed without one's control, is there such a thing as an individual self?

The most famous example of *katra* occurs when Spock, near the end of *Star Trek II: The Wrath of Khan,* implants his *katra* into the mind of Dr. McCoy prior to sacrificing his life to save the USS *Enterprise* from Khan's attack, and the movie ends with the shocking death of Spock. However, the next movie brings the much desired resurrection. Following Spock's death, Dr. McCoy begins exhibiting Vulcan-like behavior and is briefly institutionalized. It is later discovered that Spock's body came to rest on the Genesis Planet after his burial in space, and is regenerated. This body is subsequently recovered and taken with Dr. McCoy to Mount Seleya on Vulcan, where a Vulcan high priestess named T'Lar performs a seldom-attempted ritual called the *fal tor pan,* the "re-fusion," removing Spock's *katra* from Dr. McCoy and implanting it into Spock's regenerated body. Subsequently, Spock recovers, although it takes some time to retrain his mind and recover his memories.

This ultimate form of mind meld raises serious questions about what constitutes an individual, as the invisible mind is separated from the physical brain and reunited at a future date to a new body that is very similar to a cloned body.

In "The Perfect Mate, the 120th episode of *Star Trek: the Next Generation,* another spin is put on an *empathon.* (3) In an attempt to bring an end to centuries of war between the planets of Krios and Valt Minor, an agreement is made to hold a ceremony of reconciliation to be held onboard the USS Enterprise. As the Enterprise heads to the agreed rendezvous point, the Kriosian Ambassador Briam meets with Captain Jean-Luc Picard about the arrangements, and asks if everything is ready for the "irreplaceable" cargo to be transported, informing him that the storage needs to be placed off limits. An apparent accident also brings two Ferengi aboard. Captain Jean-Luc Picard and Chief Engineer Jordi La Forge take Briam to the holodeck to show him the recreation of the Temple of Akadar, where the ceremony will take place. Braim is impressed but says there are some things that need to be added.

The Ferengi who have managed to sneak aboard come to light. One confronts Briam, and Chief of Security Worf discovers the other in the cargo bay, along with a woman held in stasis in Briam's shipment. Captain Jean-Luc Picard orders Worf to keep the Ferengi under surveillance and out from under foot. Then he demands an explanation from Briam about this unexpected woman. She introduces herself as Kamala, and says she is a gift for the Valt representative, Chancellor Alrick. Both Captain Jean-Luc Picard and First Officer William Riker protest that a core principle of the Federation Constitution states that people are not to be the property of anyone else. Kamala, however, while she appreciates their efforts, insists she is acting of her own free will. It is made clear that she is the key piece to the upcoming peace agreement. She is an *empathetic metamorph*, a *mutation* with special abilities that allow her to perceive the desires of men and adapt her *persona* to be their perfect mate. Furthermore, she explains that she is on the cusp of adapting herself to a permanent mate, and her body is producing pheromones that have a strong affect on any men near her.

The next morning at breakfast, Doctor Beverly Crusher tells Captain Jean-Luc Picard that Briam has ordered Kamals to remain in her quarters, and she is a virtual prisoner. Beverly strongly disagrees with the use of an arranged marriage to seal a political union, saying it is the equivalent of selling her into prostitution. Captain Picard attempts to sooth her by explaining that political marriages have been used throughout history in many cultures on many planets, including Earth. Furthermore, he says there is little alternative. If the marriage does not take place, the war will continue and will cost many lives. Nevertheless, as they part, he promises to look into the matter.

He goes to Kamala, allows her more freedom about the ship, and begins to get to know her. Of course, she is everything he would want in a woman—adventurous, brilliant, independent, an intellectual match, educated in two of his favorite disciplines, literature and archeology. He realizes he is falling for her and tells her to stop doing this thing that she does to men.

Briam protests Kamala's new freedom, insisting that every man she meets will fall for her. Captain Jean-Luc Picard, however, has Android Data and replies, "Not every man." So Data is assigned to accompany Kamala. However, as Briam predicted, a fight ensues in Ten Forward over her. Kamala comes to Picard and agrees to stay in her quarters if he will visit her. He responds that it would be inappropriate. She is not to be put off and begins working her wiles, telling him that eventually even the Walls of Jerico fell, and that he better not take the interest of a *metamorph* lightly.

Of course, the annoying Ferengi are still lurking about, and they try to bribe Briam into releasing Kamala to them. He refuses and begins to leave, but they restrain him and he falls, injuring himself, resulting in him not being able to participate in the ceremony. Kamala suggests Captain Picard take on his role. At first he refuses, but realizing he might be able to influence a better agreement he changes his mind and agrees to do it.

This opens the door for Kamala and Picard to spend time together preparing for the ceremony, and they share thoughts. He asks her if she has had a lonely life having to constantly fulfill everyone else's expectations. However, she answers that the opposite is true, that she has always had tutors and servants with her, preparing her for this moment; and this journey is actually the first time she has been alone. She also says she finds it ironic that she should meet a man like him just before the arranged mating, says she likes the person she is when she is with him and that is what every metamorph wants at the end of the bonding process.

But it is not to be. William Riker announces that the Valtese ship has arrived and Chancellor Alrik is ready to beam aboard. He is not a likeable man, states he has little use for the copy of the Temple or the rituals and the entire Ceremony of Reconciliation, calling the Kriosians "sentimental people." What he cares about are trade agreements and the exchange of technology.

When Picard tells Kamela that it is time for her to prepare for the ceremony, she asks him to stay with her, telling him she does not want to be alone, causing him to ask if he has done anything wrong. Then Picard and Crusher meet. He tells her that he finds himself wishing that the next man wouldn't come. He is uncomfortable knowing Kamala will be bonding with a man who cares less about her than trade agreements. When he returns to Kamala, he is shocked to learn that she has already bonded with him! He asks if she is still planning on going through with the ceremony, and she says that she has learned about duty from him and will perform hers, noting that she still has her abilities and will be able to please him, though, she says as an aside, I wish he liked William Shakespeare. Picard escorts her to the transporter room, where Briam wonders out loud how Picard was able to resist her. He hides his true feelings and he bids goodbye.

It is an interesting episode, daring to plunge directly into touchy aspects of slavery, arranged marriage, political negations, doing one's duty, and the roles of men and women in general. In the end, it leaves us with a sad sense of the complications of life where right and wrong are far from clear.

The series includes another form of *empathy* in the character of Ship Counselor Deanna Troi, a half-Human-half-Betazoid who has the *empathetic* ability to sense others' emotions. For the first six seasons of the series, she is a lieutenant commander; in the seventh season, she is promoted to commander. By the time *Star Trek: Nemesis* comes out, she is married to William Riker. In the beginning, she and William Riker are former lovers who now find themselves assigned together on the USS Enterprise. Later, she will have a strong romantic relationship with Klingon Starfleet Officer Lieutenant Worf, and several brief romances with aliens, before finally ending up with her first love, Riker.

As the series goes along, her past is fleshed out. She was born March 29, 2336, near Lake El-Nar, Betazed, to her Betazoid mother, the Ambassador Lwzxzna Troi and Human father, deceased Starfleet officer Lt. Ian Andrew Troi. She had an older sister, Kestra, who drowned during her infancy. She has had little exposure to Earth culture, but attended Starfleet Academy from 2355-2359, and the University on Betazed, earning an advanced degree in psychology (and it is a form of Freudian psychology).

In addition to her *empathic* powers, she has partial *telepathic* abilities, and she is an *extra-sensory empath,* because she has *clairsentience*, the ability to sense the energy surrounding a person, place or thing. The series develops just what her abilities allow. Often, especially in the earlier episodes, they are poorly used as a simple plot device, when, for example, Captain Jean-Luc Picard is talking with some alien ship and she tells him whether or not she can *sense* if they are telling the truth or lying, or, in an only slightly more subtle sense, whether they are anxious or fearful or open and friendly and trustworthy. A perfect example of this is an episode titled "The Last Outpost, when the crew first encounters the Ferengi and Troi reports that she can discern neither thoughts nor emotions from them, giving her the initial impression that they can shield those from others. She later mentioned, however, that she could sense one of the Ferengi was hiding something—a rather poor attempt at trying to let the audience know not to trust them and still keep things a mystery.

In the first episode of this series, "Encounter at Farpoint," her abilities to sense feelings help the crew realize that the station is actually a shape-shifting entity forced into servitude by a life form calling itself the Bundi. By releasing this entity from its servitude and allowing it to reunite with its mate, the crew passes a test imposed on it by the Q continuum, an extra dimensional plane of existence inhabited by a race of extremely powerful, hyper-intelligent beings known as the Q, who act indifferently to the affairs of the non-Q beings living in normal space, or in the many dimensions parallel to their own, and yet for reasons hard to sort out show a unique interest in the development of humanity and the progress displayed by mankind.

In "Code of Honor" her abilities came in handy in uncovering the intentions of Ligonian leader, Lutan, after he kidnapped Security Chief Natasha Yar. In "Where No One Has Gone Before," she cannot detect the feelings of The Traveler, a being able to channel pure thought into reality, a reverse way of demonstrating that The Traveler is beyond even extra-ordinary psychological powers. In "Lonely Among Us," her powers allow her to discover that an alien force has been invading the minds of the crew and influencing Captain Picard, who later temporarily blinds her while under alien influence. After Picard beams himself and the alien into space and the crew believes he is gone forever, she senses that he has separated from the alien force and, thanks to her advice, he is recovered.

Later, in an episode titled "Haven," the *Enterprise* travels to that planet in the Beta Cassius system, the residency of Wyatt Miller, who is scheduled to marry Troi due to their genetic bonding. Having expected the marriage would not happen due to her serving years aboard the *Enterprise* and the resultant distance from her home world, Deanna initially did not inform her crew mates of her obligation. However, she agreed to honor vows taken years earlier, even though she had since become doubtful of them and they necessitated that she leave the ship with her new husband once they had been married. While Deanna's mother, Lwaxana, and both Wyatt Miller's parents are aboard the *Enterprise*, a social gathering known as a pre-joining announcement is held to celebrate the forthcoming wedding. In the end, the marriage is permanently canceled when Wyatt, a doctor by profession, chooses to join his fantasy lover aboard an infected Tarellian vessel. She has various other experiences throughout the first year, being chosen to make first contact with the planet Angel I because she believes it is similar to her own home planet, being held prisoner by an entity that called itself Armus (who kills Lieutenant Yar), but escaping when Wesley Crusher and Worf discover a weakness in the force field whenever the entity is provoked. Near the end of the first year, we find her looking forward to a swim on the planet Pacifica, but not getting the chance because the Enterprise gets diverted to Dytallix B and then Earth, and finally we find her helping Clare Raymond, a recently revived Human from the late 20th century, and learn about her descendants in "The Neutral Zone."

The next season, Troi becomes pregnant by an alien, gives birth, and has to face the loss of her child, who grows at an accelerated rate and within hours is eight years old. As this happens, a plasmic plague strikes the ship, threatening to kill all aboard it, then realizes he is responsible, and gives up his human life to save the ship (i.e., dies as a human child). In "The Schizoid Man" she is the one who realizes Ira Graves has downloaded his memories into Data.

In "The Prize," she falls in love with delegate Devinoni Ral at a conference for the rights to a wormhole, but is disillusioned when she finds he is also part Betazoid and has been using his powers to influence the negotiations. The Ferengi threaten to blow up the wormhole. Ral is awarded it. It turns out to be unstable, and Ral leaves. In "Tin Man," Tam Elbrun, a Betazoid male who was once her patient because he suffered from not having the normal Betazoid ability to tune out the thoughts of others, is now being transported by Enterprise to make first contact with an alien life form that looks like an organic spaceship. Since it lost its crew years ago, Tin Man wanted to die and was waiting by a star that would shortly explode. Tam bond with Tin Man and was able to relieve his psychological pain; and Tin Man had a companion. In "Hollow Pursuits," Reginald Barclay, a new member of the crew, becomes attracted to Troi, but is too shy to approach her, so he creates a holographic program in order to interact with her. She counsels him and he ends the program. In "Ménage a Troi," she, Lwaxana, and Riker are captured by the Ferengi, who want to use Lwaxana's telepathic abilities to gain an advantage in negotiations. Riker, however, is able to contact the Enterprise, and they are rescued. In "The Loss," she loses her power when the ship encounters a two-dimensional life form. But by using her "human" abilities, she is able to determine the aliens' intentions, and the Enterprise is able to break free, after which her powers return.

In "Night Terrors," while investigating the USS *Brattain*, which had become stranded in space, the *Enterprise* found one crewmember alive, a Betazoid science adviser. The rest of the crew had killed each other. They discovered that the ship was caught in Tyken's Rift which sapped all the energy from the ship. Additionally, the crew of the *Brattain* had succumbed to madness through sleep deprivation from an unknown cause. The same thing was happening to the *Enterprise*. The crew was on the verge of madness, and only Data and Troi were unaffected, as Data did not require sleep and Troi's partially Betazoid physiology processed dreams at a different frequency. Data believed that an explosion would get them out of the rift, but the plan failed. Troi had experienced a single, recurring nightmare, but determined that it was an act of communication from other beings stuck on the other side of the rift. This communication had caused the dream states of the rest of the crew to become disrupted. In a dream state she relayed a plan of cooperation that would release each ship. The plan worked.

In "Disaster," she takes command of Enterprise after it is hit by a quantum filament that causes major damage and traps the officers in various parts of the ship. Her decision not to separate the bridge and engineering and divert power to engineering saves the ship. In "New Ground," she counsels Worf and his son Alexander Rozhenko, helping them to stabilize their relationship. In "Violations," Enterprise takes on three aliens who are telepathic and specialize in being able to bring back past memories. One of them mentally assaults Troi, uses his powers to make her think Riker is the attacker, and later attempts to do so physically as well (another simple plot device here making it easy to catch him in the act at the end of the show). This episode has a bit more to its exploration of telepathy and the possibility of entering and controlling another's mind. In "The Masterpiece Society," she becomes romantically involved with the leader of a closed society of genetically-engineered Earth colonists, but the romance ends when he declines leaving his colony.

In "Power Play," while investigating the disappearance of the USS Essex nearly two hundred years previously, her body and those of O'Brian and Data are taken over by alien spirits, who proceed to hijack the Enterprise, taking hostages in the process. The Troi alien states that he is Bryce Shumar, captain of the *Essex*, and that he and his crew's spirits were caught up in the magnetic field of the moon. He asks that their bones, which were on the planet, be returned to Earth, so their spirits can rest. Picard does not believe alien Troi and finds out that she wishes to return to the planet to get the other alien spirits so they can take over the crew's bodies. As it turns out, the moon is a penal colony and the spirits are criminals. After Picard threatens to destroy the Enterprise and their existences, the spirits decided to stay alive on their moon.

Her mother Lwaxana is hard to take seriously, and is played as a broadly comic woman bent on enjoying life however illogical and annoying that might be for Deanna and the others. In "Cost of Living," a major episode featuring her, she slips away from a party during Deanna's sixth birthday only to return dressed as a Koropian princess carried in a sedan chair by four men (much to Deanna's embarrassment).

In "Man of the People," Ves Alkar, a Federation mediator, boards the Enterprise, and attempts to telepathically transfer his dark thoughts and emotions into her, as he has done with other "hosts," in order to keep his mind clear and youthful. These hosts in turn suffer rapid aging and death. Dr. Crusher puts Troi into a stasis to save her life. In "A Fistful of Datas," she participates in an Old West skit when the holodeck program malfunctions putting all in the program in danger.

In truth, up to this point in the series, she has mainly been used as eye-candy, usually wearing plunging necklines and form-fitting dresses, not logically appropriate for her position, but . . . . She has been a secondary character, a background character, not developed to any real degree, and her special gifts more often used as simple plot devices rather than as phenomenon worth exploring as relevant to the human condition. A common use of her special powers to sense emotional states is to suggest when aliens are not to be trusted, as the episode where she tells Picard that she cannot quite read the Ferengi but something is not on the up and up.

Generally, when aliens take over her mind, it is seldom more than a plot device. An example of this occurs in "Clues," an episode from season four, where the Enterprise's crew lose a day's memory, and an entity takes over her mind to do just this.

In this same vein, one of her major character traits is a love of chocolate, and this gets stressed in several episodes. In one she explains how to properly enjoy eating it. In another she hosts a normally ascetic alien species who are constantly indulging in it. In an episode titled "Remember Me," Dr. Crusher, who is trapped in a warp bubble and losing crew members, describes Troi to Captain Picard as the one who loves chocolate to try and jog his memory of her.

However, in season six, all that changes. In an episode titled "Face of the Enemy," Troi is kidnapped, surgically altered by the Romulan underground movement, and forced to assume the role of Major Rakal, an operative for the Tal Shiar, aboard the IRW *Khazara*. While there, Troi befriends Subcommander N'Vek, who helps her to adopt to her role and also reveals the true nature of her mission, to help Vice-Proconsul M'ret and two of his aides defect to the Federation. Troi discovers that many fear her new persona Tal Shair, and as a result she has a great deal of power over the crew of the *Khazara*. However, her relationship with the *Khazara*'s commanding officer, Commander Toreth is not a good one. When Troi's mission takes a turn for the worse and a fight with the

Enterprise seems imminent, Troi seizes command of the *Khazara* and is able to successfully complete her mission by concealing a transporter beam inside a low-level disruptor blast. N'Vek is killed by the *Khazara*'s helmsman after Toreth re-takes command, and the *Enterprise* barely manages to beam Troi back on board before the *Khazara* flees under cloak. Troi is returned to her normal looks and reassured that N'Vek's sacrifice was not in vein.

From now on, she is depicted wearing a standard uniform instead of her earlier eye-candy outfits, and transforms from her secondary status to a much more three dimensional character. However, her powers of *empathy* never get the exploration they should have received.

This episode is followed by other ones that feature her less. In "Timescape," Troi, Picard, Data, and La Forge return from a conference to find the Enterprise and a Romulan ship suspended in time, the result of aliens using the warp core as incubation for their young. The timeline is restored once the aliens are driven out. "Descent" ends the sixth season, and is couple with "Descent, Part II" to begin the seventh season. These powerful episodes focus on Data, his evil brother Lore, and the Borg drones, and Troi's role is minimal. In the next episode, "Liaisons," Troi is a liaison for Loquel, who drives her crazy because all he and his crew want to do is indulge themselves and party. At the end, it is revealed that his assignment is simply to experience pleasure. In "Thine Own Self" Troi attempts the "Bridge Officer's Test" unsuccessfully several times. In the end, Riker hints to her that the whole point of the test was to see if she had it in her to send a crewmember to his death. In "Dark Page," she helps save her mother's life. Lwaxana is suffering a severe mental breakdown due to a long repressed memory. However, with the help of a telepathic alien, Troi is able to enter into her mother's mind and uncover the source of the mental problem—Lwaxana had an older sister who died in a drowning accident and blames herself.

"Eye of the Beholder" explores the possibilities of telepathy a bit. In it, crewmember Daniel Kwan commits suicide on board the Enterprise, and Troi is asked to investigate because he had empathic abilities similar to hers. In the process of this investigation, Troi becomes insanely jealous of Worf, and when she finds him in the arms of another woman, she kills him and attempts suicide. However, just as she is about to jump to her death, Worf, who did not die, saves her. As it turns out, it was all in her mind. When the Enterprise-D was being built, one of the crew, also an empath, committed murder and suicide, and left an empathic imprint, which got picked up by Kwan, resulting in his death, and Troi, who was more fortunate.

Troi gets some air time in the movie *Star Trek Generations*, and ends up being the last person to pilot the Enterprise-D during the Battle of Veridian III, which ends with it crashing into the planet, destroying both the engineering section and the saucer section. She also appears n *Star Trek: First Contact*, but in a minor role (in her big scene, she has transported to the past and gets drunk while trying to convince Zefram Cochrane to go ahead with his launch, which will be the beginning of the entire space program to come) , and in *Star Trek: Insurrection*, where she and Will Riker rekindle their romance. She also uses her telepathic ability to sense that several Ba'ku children have incredible mental discipline and clarity of perception. Her roles are a bit mixed here, as she is both armed with a phaser rifle and is briefly in command of the bridge, but also realizes her breasts are getting larger as the result of metaphasic radiation.

In the subsequent film *Star Trek: Nemesis*, she is mentally raped by Shinzon's viceroy, who is also telepathic—the first time in her quarters while making love with her new husband Riker, and the second time in the bonus deleted scenes in the turbo lift. She also takes the helm, and under Captain Picard's orders, crashes the ship into the *Scimitar* to disable enemy Shinzon's Raman warbird. Later, she rejoins the USS titan, under Riker's command, and is expected to return to Romulus on another diplomatic mission.

This is the movie where she finally does marry Will Riker. The Wedding ceremony takes place in Alaska (the year 2379), a traditional Earth wedding, where Captain Picard serves as Will's best man. After that ceremony, a traditional Betazoid wedding ceremony was to take place on Betazed. However the *Enterprise*-E's journey to Betazed is interrupted by the discovery of B-4.

Finally, Troi appears in three episodes of *Star Trek: Enterprise,* "Pathfinder," "Lifeline," and "Inside Man."

When all is said a done, the character of Deana Troi is exciting and yet disappointing. The concept of an *empath* raises questions about the deepest aspects of the human condition, especially in a time when philosophers, artists and poets are struggling with the realities of isolation, the impossibility of communication, loneliness, meaninglessness, nothingness, and lives lived in quiet desperation. When T. S. Eliot writes *The Love Song of J. Alfred Prufrock*, he sees us "etherized upon a table," afraid to even try and interact because we are so certain to be misunderstood. (5)

Indeed, the entire 19th century is one of dark, nightmarish questioning. Following WWI, William Butler Yeats writes the famous poem, *The Second Coming*:

Turning and turning in the widening gyre
The falcon cannot hear the falconer;
Things fall apart; the centre cannot hold;
Mere anarchy is loosed upon the world,
The blood-dimmed tide is loosed, and everywhere
The ceremony of innocence is drowned;
The best lack all conviction, while the worst
Are full of passionate intensity.

Surely some revelation is at hand;
Surely the Second Coming is at hand.
The Second Coming! Hardly are those words out
When a vast image out of Spiritus Mundi
Troubles my sight: somewhere in sands of the desert
A shape with lion body and the head of a man,
A gaze blank and pitiless as the sun,
Is moving its slow thighs, while all about it
Reel shadows of the indignant desert birds.
The darkness drops again; but now I know
That twenty centuries of stony sleep
Were vexed to nightmare by a rocking cradle,
And what rough beast, its hour come round at last,
Slouches towards Bethlehem to be born? (6)

WWI was the dramatic result of a European Imperialism collapsing back upon itself. Joseph Conrad's *Heart of Darkness* (1902) predicted it, and the title of the book is precisely the problem on multiple levels, economic, political, even artistic and philosophical, and most importantly psychological and spiritual.

The old verities had lost their validity, and the life defining mythos of Europe had shattered under the weight of abuse and misrepresentation. If Europe was the greatest civilization, the peak of human achievement, then something was wrong, because it had brought destruction and death on the most horrific level humans had ever experienced.

No longer was war a heroic conquest; instead, as Stephen Crane showed us in *The Red Badge of Courage* (1895), it was a mindless, hellish form of slaughter. The American Civil War had taken the most America lives of any war ever, and it was a war where brothers were killing brothers, sons killing fathers—line after line of ill trained boys standing in front of and methodically killing off each other with each command to fire. Is this heroism or stupidity? Whatever it is, it would soon get done exponentially in Europe.

For Western Civilization, after WWI it was no longer possible to map out life in some meaningful way, at least not in the known ways. Instead, in *The Trial* (1925), Franz Kafka gave us Joseph K., the man taken by the police and imprisoned without ever knowing why. And, some twenty years later, while Adolf Hitler and the Nazis were experimenting on and exterminating some six million Jews and other *undesirables*, Jean-Paul Sartre wrote *No Exit* (1944). No longer was Hell some Biblical place; it was us: *l'enfer, c'est les autres* ("Hell is other people").

Ten years later, during the McCarthy era in the United States, William Golding put it all into a book length parable in *The Lord of the Flies,* where, as the stranded boys are hunting for their imagined *beast*, and clearly turning into *beasts* themselves, mentally unbalanced Simon is left alone with a killed pig's head that has been stuck on the end of a stick shoved in the ground. And he has one of his spells, and the head speaks to him:

> "You are a silly little boy," said the Lord of the Flies, "just an ignorant, silly little boy."
>
> Simon moved his swollen tongue but said nothing.
>
> "Don't you agree?" said the Lord of the Flies. "Aren't you just a silly little boy?"
>
> Simon answered him in the same silent voice.
>
> "Well then," said the Lord of the Flies, "you'd better run off and play with the others. They think you're batty. You don't want Ralph to think you're batty, do you? You like Ralph a lot, don't you? And Piggy, and Jack?"
>
> Simon's head was tilted slightly up. His eyes could not break away and the Lord of the Flies hung in space before him.
>
> "What are you doing out here all alone? Aren't you afraid of me?"
>
> Simon shook.
>
> "There isn't anyone to help you. Only me. And I'm the Beast."
>
> Simon's mouth labored, brought forth audible words.
>
> "Pig's head on a stick."
>
> "Fancy thinking the Beast was something you could hunt and kill!" said the head. For a moment or two the forest and all the other dimly appreciated places echoed with the parody of laughter. "You knew, didn't you? I'm part of you? Close, close, close! I'm the reason why it's no go? Why things are what they are?"
>
> The laughter shivered again.
>
> "Come now," said the Lord of the Flies. "Get back to the others and we'll forget the whole thing."
>
> Simon's head wobbled. His eyes were half closed as though he were imitating the obscene thing on the stick. He knew that one of his times was coming on. The Lord of the Flies was expanding like a balloon.
>
> "This is ridiculous. You know perfectly well you'll only meet me down there—so don't try to escape!"

> Simon's body was arched and stiff. The Lord of the Flies spoke in the voice of a schoolmaster.
>
> "This has gone quite far enough. My poor, misguided child, do you think you know better than I do?"
>
> There was a pause.
>
> "I'm warning you. I'm going to get angry. D'you see? You're not wanted. Understand? We are going to have fun on this island. Understand? We are going to have fun on this island! So don't try it on, my poor misguided boy, or else—"
>
> Simon found he was looking into a vast mouth. There was blackness within, a blackness that spread.
>
> "—Or else," said the Lord of the Flies, "we shall do you. See? Jack and Roger and Maurice and Robert and Bill and Piggy and Ralph. Do you. See?"
>
> Simon was inside the mouth. He fell down and lost consciousness. (7)

Certainly the possibility of a meaningless world was thrust upon the entire history of western thought over the first half of the nineteenth century in clear, dramatic terms with the advent of WWI followed by WWII, leaving the world in a state of shock, and humans lived in a dark foreboding landscape dominated by the very real potential of a nuclear Armageddon.

Such mass murder as took place in these wars, accented by the bombing of Hiroshima and Nagasaki, and the dramatic denial of the value of human life put forth very consciously, supported with elaborate logic and cruel precision in the Nazi concentration camps, had to have prompted concrete questions about human existence, questions infused with a raw, naked facing of life stripped bare of all of the former systems of meaning and value.

A few excerpts from those who were first on the scene give full force, or, rather, as much as we need stomach, to the nightmarish world that European civilization, which less than a 100 years prior held a good deal of confidence in its superior ethical position, had plunged. Harry J. Herder, Jr., one of the soldiers first to arrive at Buchenwald on April 11, 1945, writes about it, including his first encounter with the dead:

> The bodies of human beings were stacked like cord wood. All of them dead. All of them stripped. The inspection I made of the pile was not very close, but the corpses seemed to be all male. The bottom layer of the bodies had a north/south orientation, the next layer went east/west, and they continued alternating. The stack was about five feet high, maybe a little more; I could see over the top. They extended down the hill, only a slight hill, for fifty to seventy-five feet. Human bodies neatly stacked, naked, ready for disposal. The arms and legs were neatly arranged, but an

occasional limb dangled oddly. The bodies we could see were all face up. There was an aisle, then another stack, and another aisle, and more stacks. The Lord only knows how many there were.

Just looking at these bodies made one believe they had been starved to death. They appeared to be skin covering bones and nothing more. The eyes on some were closed, on others open. Bill, Tim, and I grew very quiet. I think my only comment was, "Jesus Christ."

Then, passed the stacks of bodies, through the survivors and other soldiers. The living dead had more to reveal:

They pointed to a long building which was about two stories high, and butted up tightly to the chimney. It had two barn-like doors on either end of the building we were looking at, and the doors were standing open. We turned and walked back to the building where we found others from our company, along with some of the prisoners milling around in the space between the bodies and the building. We moved gently through those people, through the doors and felt the warmth immediately. Not far from the doors, and parallel to the front of the building, there was a brick wall, solid to the top of the building. In the wall were small openings fitted with iron doors. Those doors were a little more than two feet wide and about two and a half feet high; the tops of the doors had curved shapes much like the entrances to churches. Those iron doors were in sets, three high. There must have been more than ten of those sets, extending down that brick wall. Most of the doors were closed, but down near the middle a few stood open. Heavy metal trays had been pulled out of those openings, and on those trays were partially burned bodies. On one tray was a skull partially burned through, with a hole in the top; other trays held partially disintegrated arms and legs. It appeared that those trays could hold three bodies at a time. And the odor, my God, the odor. (8)

The most famous of the eye-witness reports comes from Edward R. Morrow:

There surged around me an evil-smelling stink, men and boys reached out to touch me. They were in rags and the remnants of uniforms. Death already had marked many of them, but they were smiling with their eyes. I looked out over the mass of men to the green fields beyond, where well-fed Germans were ploughing....

[I] asked to see one of the barracks. It happened to be occupied by Czechoslovaks. When I entered, men crowded around, tried to lift me to their shoulders. They were too weak. Many of them could not get out of bed. I was told that this building had once stabled 80 horses. There were 1200 men in it, five to a bunk. The stink was beyond all description.

They called the doctor. We inspected his records. There were only names in the little black book — nothing more — nothing about who had been where, what he had done or hoped. Behind the names of those who had died, there was a cross. I counted them. They totaled 242 — 242 out of 1200, in one month.

As we walked out into the courtyard, a man fell dead. Two others, they must have been over 60, were crawling toward the latrine. I saw it, but will not describe it.

In another part of the camp they showed me the children, hundreds of them. Some were only 6 years old. One rolled up his sleeves, showed me his number. It was tattooed on his arm. B-6030, it was. The others showed me their numbers. They will carry them till they die. An elderly man standing beside me said: "The children — enemies of the state!" I could see their ribs through their thin shirts....

We went to the hospital. It was full. The doctor told me that 200 had died the day before. I asked the cause of death. He shrugged and said: "tuberculosis, starvation, fatigue and there are many who have no desire to live. It is very difficult." He pulled back the blanket from a man's feet to show me how swollen they were. The man was dead. Most of the patients could not move.

I asked to see the kitchen. It was clean. The German in charge.... showed me the daily ration. One piece of brown bread about as thick as your thumb, on top of it a piece of margarine as big as three sticks of chewing gum. That, and a little stew, was what they received every 24 hours. He had a chart on the wall. Very complicated it was. There were little red tabs scattered through it. He said that was to indicate each 10 men who died. He had to account for the rations and he added: "We're very efficient here."

We proceeded to the small courtyard. The wall adjoined what had been a stable or garage. We entered. It was floored with concrete. There were two rows of bodies stacked up like cordwood. They were thin and very white. Some of the bodies were terribly bruised; though there seemed to be little flesh to bruise. Some had been shot through the head, but they bled but little.

I arrived at the conclusion that all that was mortal of more than 500 men and boys lay there in two neat piles. There was a German trailer, which must have contained another 50, but it wasn't possible to count them. The clothing was piled in a heap against the wall. It appeared that most of the men and boys had died of starvation; they had not been executed.

But the manner of death seemed unimportant. Murder had been done at Buchenwald. God alone knows how many men and boys have died there during the last 12 years. Thursday, I was told that there were more than 20,000 in the camp. There had been as many as 60,000. Where are they now?

I pray you to believe what I have said about Buchenwald. I reported what I saw and heard, but only part of it. For most of it, I have no words.

If I have offended you by this rather mild account of Buchenwald, I'm not in the least sorry.... (9)

Perhaps a comment he made outside of the report, expresses it best: "A French newsman, imprisoned there throughout the war, had summed it up: "To write about this, you must been here at least two years. And after that—you don't want to write anymore." (10)

Such conscious implementation of the most horrific possibilities of the human mind by the very center of civilization, by the very people who thought of themselves as the leading edge of morality and spirituality, leaves us who were not there stunned. We cannot know the reality of it, but even at a distance, we can sense the feelings of hopelessness and meaningless and depression that had to have entered into any discourse. Why, indeed, would anyone want to bother to "write" or do anything to give human existence some positive perspective when the "real" world has proven that if there is such a thing as an ethos, humans must be condemned as monsters. Or, even if the need to find a meaning still existed, and perhaps even if the human brain demanded meaning, certainly the culture that had been supplying the maps was at fault, was not to be trusted, certainly the very heritage that had underpinned the culture needed to be re-evaluated. But how? All of the tools of both logical thinking and artistic expression, all of the understandings of religion and spirituality had not done it.

And to simply write it off as a non-sequitur, an aberration required a blindness. During this same war, the Japanese had concentration camps where they were using humans for experiments with chemical weapons. The Americans had moved all Japanese citizens into concentration camps (perhaps not as horrific as the Nazi ones, but certainly denying them any dignity, taking away all of their possessions, separating them from their families, for no reason other than their bloodlines), and, of course, the frantically developed atomic bombs killed and maimed hundreds of thousands of non-military people. The list could be continued. Regardless how argued, how much justification can be found, it is hard to deny the darkness.

In a world such as this, *Waiting for Godot*, generally considered the ultimate expression of Theatre of the Absurd, might be the way to actually suggest meaning and value do exist. Why write, perform or view a play in a world gone so wrong? How can one find meaning after the loss of innocence? Perhaps a parody is the place. Perhaps by purposely trying to undermine all meaning and value, and yet ending up finding it cannot be denied is exactly the way to support it. Perhaps facing the ultimate evil in men's souls is where we must go for a chance at something more, for a chance at meaning, for the possibility of salvation.

"Poo-tee-weet." Kurt Vonnegut gives us a Dadaist-like comment on it all through the voice of a bird. Having been a prisoner of war in Dresden during the bombings there, bombings that it has been claimed killed more people than the nuclear bombing of Hiroshima, he wanted to find a way to express what he had experienced, but as the initial chapter to his book, *Slaughterhouse-Five* gives the reader, he is stuck, caught in a paradox. (11) How does one give meaning and value to that which is beyond meaning? In what has become designated a technique of *metafiction* a type of fiction which consciously, self-consciously highlights the devices of fiction, systematically drawing attention to its status as an artifact in order to raise questions about the relationship between fiction (illusion) and reality, by necessity creating an ironic perspective, similar to Theatre of the Absurd, that does not let the reader or audience forget they are reading a work of fiction or viewing a play, Vonnegut immediately confuses realities with the simple opening "All this happened, more or less, and brings the reader into a mutual evaluation of the work by apologizing for the fact that the novel is "so short and jumbled and jangled" and seeming to echo the thoughts of those who first witnessed the Buchenwald concentration camps at the end of the war, explaining that this is because "there is nothing intelligent to say about a massacre." As the novel unfolds and Vonnegut presents us with the fictional Billy Pilgrim's experiences, he refuses to let us fall completely into the fictional world, breaking it by intruding himself, and demanding we stop and take notice, stating: "That was I. That was me. That was the author of this book."

He also mixes in several science fiction devices, including time travel. Billy Pilgrim becomes "unstuck in time" and experiences his life in a disjointed journey where even his death is not the end but just one point to be revisited randomly. This frame, which has connections to "stream of consciousness" and "interior monologue" techniques made famous by James Joyce, gets explored in more depth by having Billy Pilgrim meet, and then be kidnapped by aliens from the planet Tralfamadore, who exhibit him in a Tralfamadorian zoo with Montana Wildhack, a pornographic movie star. The Tralfamadorians experience life in four dimensions, the fourth dimension being time. Though the Tralfamadorians have seen every instant of their lives already; they cannot choose to change anything about their fate.

What free will there is consists in the ability to choose to focus on any moment in their lives that they wish. Thus, outside of the individual brain/mind, there is no free will. Vonnegut states this through one of the Tralfamadorians, "I've visited thirty-one inhabited planets in the universe...

Only on Earth is there any talk of free will." To the Tralfamadorians, everything always exists at the same time, and for them everyone is therefore always alive. They too have wars and tragic events (they destroy the universe testing spaceship fuels), but when asked by Billy what they do about wars, the Tralfamadorians tell him they simply ignore them.

It seems likely that, in the Tralfamadorians, Vonnegut is demonstrating that life is only worthwhile if there is an unknown. Obviously, for the Tralfamadorians, nothing can be changed, there is no chance of influencing existence, and nothing new can be learned. Furthermore, even inside the human brain/mind what free will there is has no value beyond self-gratification or pacification, for even one's experiencing of an event cannot be changed. One can choose to focus on any moment, but one cannot choose to change anything about that moment. At most one can only choose to dwell on the pleasant experiences and ignore the unpleasant ones.

However, again we are led to simply deeper or other contexts, rather than a dead-end. The mere fact that the Tralfamadorians can choose when to exist opens the door to free will. Outside of their minds, they cannot change the happenings, but they can travel through both time and space within their minds. Thus, they have a huge number, perhaps an infinite number of experiences to exist in, and since they can feel good or bad, they can experience emotions, and can make ethical judgments, even in a seemingly fatalistic worldview, meaning and value for humans exists. Existence simply needs to be understood as taking place in the human mind, at least if it is to have meaning and value as humans understand such things.

The next step in this sequence of logic is that the human brain is constructed so that only certain thoughts can take place within it. Thus, ultimately, it is all pre-determined by the scientific properties involved with the human brain. Ultimately, whatever logical path is taken from this leads to the edges of what logic and thus science can explain and comprehend, and we end up struggling with the underlying mathematic attempts to explain existence, which, at the moment, are saying we end up with the logic of illogic (as in Godel's famous theory of infinity squared, which proves under his mathematical system that there are at least two mathematical universes). In other words, at least at this time humans cannot comprehend everything through logic and explanation, cannot explain away either infinity or eternity, at least as these terms are generally used to refer to human existence. Ironically, this inability to explain is the key to meaning and value. It gives an opening to the kinds of knowing beyond logic, all of the possibilities of worlds of expression (of faith and spirituality).

Viktor Frankl did experience the horror of Auschwitz, satisfying Edward R. Murrow's requirement, and it can safely be said, living through an even more horrific imprisonment than Kurt Vonnegut. Yet, Frankl did want to write about it, and found a very different path to giving life, even in the most degrading and "inhuman" circumstances, meaning and value.

Born in Vienna to a Jewish servant family in 1905, and graduating from the Gymnasium in 1923, he went on to study medicine at the University of Vienna, eventually specializing in neurology and psychiatry, especially depression and suicide. In 1924, he became president of Sozialistische Mittelschuler Osterreich, a program to counsel students and prevent suicides, and his success (not a single student committed suicide during his tenure) resulted in Wilhelm Reich bringing him to Berlin. During the mid-thirties, he ran the "suicide pavilion" of Vienna's General Hospital, treating over 30,000 women at risk of suicide. However, in 1938, his Jewish bloodlines began getting him censored, and he was prevented from treating any more Aryan women. In 1940, he moved to Rothschild Hospital, the only place left where Jews were still admitted, where he continued both psychiatric and neurological work, including brain surgery, and using what influence he had to prevent euthanasia of as many Jews as possible.

In 1942, he, his wife, and his parents were deported to a concentration camp in Theresienstadt, where his father would die in 1943. In addition to his regular assignments, his background put him in a position to continue to work with other inmates and help them through the horrific conditions that caused a great deal of depression and suicide. In a dark irony the "Nazis sought to prevent Jewish suicides. Wherever Jews tried to kill themselves - in their homes, in hospitals, on the deportation trains, in the concentration camps - the Nazi authorities would invariably intervene in order to save the Jews' lives, wait for them to recover, and then send them to their prescribed deaths." (12)

October 19, 1944, Frankl was transported to Auschwitz, where his mother died. His wife was transported to Bergen-Belsen, where she died. October 25, he was transported to Turkheim, a camp near Dachau. Finally, on April 27, 1945, he was liberated.

Viktor Frankl, thus, was in a unique position. He was a highly trained and experienced psychologist and neurologist who was thrust into the most inhumane environment, where he witnessed both personally and all around him the cruelest and darkest actions of humans and the deepest depressions of the victims.

It would seem he had to become the poster-child for the most negative views of the 20th century. Certainly he would find life to be meaningless, filled with at best a cruel, depressing endurance of pain and suffering.

However, instead, he becomes a central figure in the argument against such negative views, offering a powerful confirmation for the belief in the strength of the human spirit to give life meaning and value no matter how extreme the tests. In fact, the more extreme the test, the more chance to prove the strength of the human spirit (or mind or heart or whatever term is used for the human self).

In his best known book, *Man's Search for Meaning: An Introduction to Logotherapy,* he first describes the standard experiences of a prisoner of a concentration camp, and then, in part two presents his central concepts. (13) He writes:

> Let me explain why I have employed the term "logotherapy" as the name for my theory. *Logos* is a Greek word that denotes "meaning!" Logotherapy or, as it has been called by some authors, "The Third Viennese School of Psychotherapy," focuses on the meaning of human existence as well as on man's search for such a meaning. According to logotherapy, the striving to find a meaning in one's life is the primary motivational force in man. That is why I speak of a *will to meaning* in contrast to the pleasure principle (or, as we could also term it, the *will to pleasure*) on which Freudian psychoanalysis is centered, as well as in contrast to the *will to power* stressed by Adlerian psychology. (14)

Arguing that humans have not only physical and psychological dimensions, but a spiritual dimension, not external but "within the reference of logotherapy," he is careful to clarify "'spiritual' does not have a primarily religious connotation but refers to the specifically human dimension." (15) Putting his theories into the general philosophy of existentialism, he writes: "Man's will to meaning can . . . be frustrated, in which case logotherapy speaks of "existential frustration." The term "existential" may be used in three ways: to refer to (1) *existence* itself, i.e., the specifically human mode of being; (2) the *meaning* of existence; and (3) the striving to find a concrete meaning in a personal existence, that is to say, the *will* to meaning."

Thus, he continues, "Existential frustration can . . . result in neurosis. For this type of neurosis, logotherapy has coined the term "noogenic neurosis" in contrast to neurosis in the usual sense of the word, i.e., psychogenic neurosis. Noogenic neuroses have their origin not in the psychological but rather in the "noological" (from the Greek "noos" meaning mind) dimension of the human existence. This is another logotherapeutic term which denotes anything pertaining to the "spiritual" core of man's personality." (16)

As with the other theorists we've encountered, Viktor Frankl must deal with the source of *meaning*. Sounding much like Albert Camus, Viktor Frankl writes:

> We have to beware of the tendency to deal with values in terms of the mere self-expression of man himself. For *logos*, or "meaning," is not only an emergence from existence itself but rather something confronting existence. If the meaning that is waiting to be fulfilled by man were really nothing but a mere expression of self, or no more than a projection of his wishful thinking, it would immediately lose its demanding and challenging character; it could no longer call man forth or summon him. This holds true not only for the so-called sublimation of instinctual drives but for what C. G. Jung called the *"archetypes"* of the "collective unconscious" as well, inasmuch as the latter would also be self-expressions, namely, of mankind as a whole. This holds true as well for the contention of some existentialist thinkers who see in man's ideals nothing but his own inventions. According to Jean-Paul Sartre, man invents himself, he designs his own "essence"; that is to say, what he essentially is, including what he should be, or ought to become. However, I think the meaning of our existence is not invented by ourselves, but rather detected. (17)

Here Viktor Frankl is clearly separating himself from the views that separate humans from the external environment. "Wishful thinking" cannot help but bring Sigmund Freud's *pleasure principal* to mind, and Viktor Frankl wants to distinguish the "higher" forms of thinking, those of meaning and value from the "instinctual drives" that serve as a basis for both Sigmund Freud and Carl Jung's theories. Furthermore, he wants to separate his views from such existential thinkers as Sartre who claim that "ideals" are nothing more than human inventions.

Just what, then, is Viktor Frankl trying to claim? He attempts to clarify:

> Psychodynamic research in the field of values is legitimate; the question is whether it is always appropriate. Above all, we must keep in mind that any exclusively psychodynamic investigation can, in principle, only reveal what is a driving force in man. Values, however, do not drive a man; they do not *push* him, but rather *pull* him. This is a difference, by the way, of which I am constantly reminded whenever I go through the doors of an American hotel. One of them has to be pulled while the other has to be pushed. Now, if I say man is *pulled* by values, what is implicitly referred to is the fact that there is always freedom involved: the freedom of man to make his choice between accepting or rejecting an offer, i.e., to fulfill a meaning potentiality or else to forfeit it. (18)

Now comes the clarification he wants to make between a moral or religious *drive* and a moral or religious *choice*. He continues:

> . . . it should be made quite clear that there cannot exist in man any such thing as a *moral drive*, or even a *religious drive*, in the same manner as we speak of man's being determined by basic instincts. Man is never driven to moral behavior; in each instance he decides to behave morally. Man does not do so in order to satisfy a moral drive and to have a good conscience; he does so for the sake of a cause to which he commits himself, or for a person whom he loves, or the sake of his God. If he actually did it for the sake of having a good conscience, he would become a Pharisee and cease to be a truly moral person. (19)

Here Viktor Frankl is confronting the key distinction between *a meaningful and a meaningless existence*. It can be, and has been put forth many different ways. If life is predetermined, if there is some form of predestination, if the fates are in control, if, as Viktor Frankl focuses on, our actions are all determined by heredity and instincts, then life is meaningless. Life can only have meaning and value if there is some form of individual responsibility and free will.

Ever since Soren Kierkegaard phrased the human condition in terms of "Fear and Trembling" and "*Sickness Unto Death*," and Friedrich Nietzsche proclaimed the death of God, philosophers have gleefully plunged into a dark, meaningless world, overlooking the simple truth that, as long as humans exist, meaning and value exist, for the very definition of human is the giver of meaning and value. To separate humans from meaning and value is the error that lies at the basis of the dialogue of philosophy for at least the past 150 years. However one wishes to postulate the resulting world of meaning and value when the human brain and mind come together, that is the place it happens. And as much as clever intellectuals are able to play endless intricate language games to dodge around it, humans are a part of the physical and spiritual worlds, and give it meaning (whether as receptacles of some God or scientific process, the result is the same). It seems very likely that the reason this final click does not take place is simply the western world's interpretation of the human condition coming out of the Judeo/Christian tradition that condemns humans and demands they bow before the Jewish/Christian God. Hubris becomes the ultimate sin in this view, but, unfortunately, hubris is misapplied to such an extreme that blindness replaces it.

Furthermore, the simple breaking away from the huge hold of the Christian view that ultimately denies humans any true meaning in life, by denying them any true self-responsibility, and true freedom to be either

Good or Bad, has made the outlaw, the condemned one so attractive that once the door got opened to deny God all power, the dark world became just too enticing to ignore. For only in going against Good could Self be established. This is the same thing as the embracement of the Shadow over the Ego in Jungian terms. The Shadow is where the Self separates from the social, the cultural, the legal, etc., and the individual assumes self-responsibility. Thus, even being Evil is better than being Good by default, for Evil equals existence and meaning in life. Good means being obedient and giving up all chance at a meaningful life.

The rebel, the maverick, the outlaw become attractive because they demand self-responsibility, which is a definition of human existence. Without it, human existence has no meaning or value. By tautology, the outsider is not ethically good in terms of the particular system he rebels against. That does not make him Evil in any universal sense. Rather it means the system itself is being called into account, the very basis of the system is brought into question, the established ethos is denied or at least not absolute. Whether or not the New Ethos of the Rebel is a better one or not isn't the point. The ability to bring a new ethos into existence is what matters. It means that if humans have self-responsibility then by definition, they do create meaning and value. Thus, not only are the standard categories of the outsiders justified, but the artist is embraced as well, for the artist is the one bringing, by definition, something new into being, the one remapping or thickening the map of meaning and value. This is human existence at its highest level. And it is not meaningless, not nothingness, not mere physical existence. Rather, it is frightening, terrifying, because there is so much responsibility involved. Humans become, not the weak recipients of some huge, powerful, unknown force, some God, but, rather, the voice, the conscience, the meaning of existence.

Again, by definition, this does not mean humans always do wonderful things. If humans can only be Good then there is no choice involved, and we are back to zero, back to a meaningless existence. Furthermore, not only are humans capable of error, but great errors are to be expected, as humans are born into a mysterious world and ultimately have to trust their own minds, which they must struggle to comprehend with perhaps nothing outside of them to help.

Arthur Schopenhauer sees life as the stage necessary for the discovery of the *self*. He writes:

> [Life] is played that a man may come to understand himself, that he may see what it is that he seeks and has sought to be; what he wants, and what, therefore, he is. *This is a knowledge which must be imparted to him from without.* Life is to man, in other words, to will, what chemical re-agents are

> to the body: it is only by life that a man reveals what he is, and it is only in so far as he reveals himself that he exists at all. Life is the manifestation of character, of the something that we understand by that word; and it is not in life, but outside of it, and outside time, that character undergoes alteration, as a result of the self-knowledge which life gives.
>
> Life is only the mirror into which a man gazes not in order that he may get a reflection of himself, but that he may come to understand himself by that reflection; that he may see *what* it is that the mirror shows. Life is the proof sheet, in which the compositors' errors are brought to light. How they become visible, and whether the type is large or small, are matters of no consequence. Neither in the externals of life nor in the course of history is there any significance; for as it is all one whether an error occurs in the large type or in the small, so it is all one, as regards the essence of the matter, whether an evil disposition is mirrored as a conqueror of the world or a common swindler or ill-natured egoist. In one case he is seen of all men; in the other, perhaps only of himself; but that he should see himself is what signifies.
>
> Therefore if egoism has a firm hold of a man and masters him, whether it be in the form of joy, or triumph, or lust, or hope, or frantic grief, or annoyance, or anger, or fear, or suspicion, or passion of any kind - he is in the devil's clutches and how he got into them does not matter. What is needful is that he should make haste to get out of them; and here, again, it does not matter how.
>
> I have described *character* as *theoretically* an act of will lying beyond time, of which life in time, or *character in action*, is the development. For matters of practical life we all possess the one as well as the other; for we are constituted of them both. Character modifies our life more than we think, and it is to a certain extent true that every man is the architect of his own fortune. No doubt it seems as if our lot were assigned to us almost entirely from without, and imparted to us in something of the same way in which a melody outside us reaches the ear. But on looking back over our past, we see at once that our life consists of mere variations on one and the same theme, namely, our character, and that the same fundamental bass sounds through it all. This is an experience which a man can and must make in and by himself. (20)

So what is an *empath?* How does *empathy* result from *self-responsibility* and *individuality*? If our civilization isn't giving us a guide to meaning and value, how do we find it?

Let's begin with some brief definitions of *empathy*:

According to S. D. Hodges and K. J. Klein, *empathy* blurs the line between *self* and *other*, including knowing the other's thoughts and emotions. (21) D. M. Berger elaborates that it is "the capacity to know emotionally what another is experiencing from within the frame of reference of that other person, the capacity to sample the feelings of another or to put one's self in another's shoes." (22) Jean Decety adds the condition that the "sense of similarity in feelings experienced the self and the other" not involve a "confusion between the two individuals," that, in other words, each remains aware of their separate identities. (23) In a similar vein, Carl Rogers says it is the ability to perceive the internal frame of reference of another with accuracy and with the emotional components and meanings which pertain thereto as if one were the person, but without ever losing the "as if" condition. Thus, it means to sense the hurt or the pleasure of another as he senses it and to perceive the causes thereof as he perceives them, but without ever losing the recognition that it is as if I were hurt or pleased and so forth. (24) Simon Baron-Cohen writes: "Empathy is about spontaneously and naturally tuning into the other person's thoughts and feelings, whatever these might be. . . There are two major elements to empathy. The first is the cognitive component: Understanding the others feelings and the ability to take their perspective . . . the second element to empathy is the affective component. This is an observer's appropriate emotional response to another person's emotional state." (25) Khen Lampert connects it to *astral projection:* "[Empathy] is what happens to us when we leave our own bodies...and find ourselves either momentarily or for a longer period of time in the mind of the other. We observe reality through her eyes, feel her emotions, share in her pain." (26)

Central to all of these is the ability to understand the emotions of others, whether they are the result of physical similarities (i.e., all humans hurt when the body is injured), or psychological (i.e., all humans need love, feel sorrow, and face the same realizations of the limitations of death, disease, and time). This allows for *pity*, for feeling sorry for another, and *compassion* or *sympathy*, a feeling of distress for another's suffering aligned with a desire to relieve it. *Com-passion* might be understood as *com*ing together in *passion*.

Empathy is usually taken to be a right cerebrum, intuitive, emotional unity with another, rather than a conceptual, left cerebrum, logical unity. And though there are arguments that *empathy* is a valuable and even necessary quality for the survival and evolution of the species (in various forms of Darwinian evolution), it can easily be claimed it contradicts or at the very least goes beyond basic physical survival of the fittest, for it at least seems to push against anything practical and is the basis for *self-sacrifice*, the giving up of one's own life for a belief or another person, the sacrifice of physical well-being and even physical existence for some kind of existence beyond the physical.

The ability to put one-self in the place of another is also connected to the ability to step outside of one-self and see and judge one-self, even to be evaluating one-self's words and actions while speaking and performing.

Only humans deal with meaning and value; it is our gift to the world. Anthropologists, paleontologists and evolutionists say true humans appear on the scene not when crude tools are found, or weapons. No, it is when cave wall paintings are found. Why is this? It's actually rather simple and straight-forward. Paintings are a form of symbolic thought, as are all of the arts, and only humans do this. Other creatures don't attempt to influence the hunt or appease the gods with paintings or rituals or myths. Other creatures do not have this invisible world of the mind that gives a value to an otherwise meaningless universe. Only humans have eaten of the apple of the knowledge of good and evil. Only humans consciously give up physical existence for some higher or other non-physical form of existence, an existence of the spirit or soul.

Loren Eiseley in *The Immense Journey* writes:

> Symbolic communication had begun. Man had escaped out of the eternal present of the animal world into a knowledge of past and future. The unseen gods, the powers behind the world of phenomenal appearance, began to stalk through his dreams.
>
> Nature, one might say, through the powers of this mind, grossly superstitious though it might be in its naïve examination of wind and water, was beginning to reach out into the dark behind itself. Nature was beginning to evade its own limitations in the shape of this strange, dreaming and observant brain. It was a weird multi-headed universe, going on, unseen and immaterial save as its thoughts smoldered in the eyes of hunters huddled by night fires, or were translated into pictures upon cave walls, or were expressed in the trappings of myth or ritual. The Eden of the eternal present that the animal world had known for ages was shattered at last. Through the human mind, time and darkness, good and evil, would enter and possess the world. (27)

Rollo May gives us the pinnacle of this in the following from *Man's Search for Himself*:

> Man's consciousness of himself is the source of his highest qualities. It underlies his ability to distinguish between I and the world. It gives him the capacity to keep time, which is simply the ability to stand outside the present and to imagine oneself back in yesterday or ahead in the day after tomorrow. Thus human beings can learn from the past and plan for the future. And thus man is the historical mammal in that he can stand outside and look at his history; and thereby he can influence his own development as a person, and to a minor extent he can influence the march of history in

> his nation and society as a whole. The capacity for consciousness of self also underlies man's ability to use symbols, which is a way of disengaging something from what it is, such as the two sounds which make up the word "table," and agreeing that these sounds will stand for a whole class of things. Thus man can think in abstractions like "beauty," "reason," and "goodness."
>
> This capacity for consciousness of ourselves gives us the ability to see ourselves as others see us and to have empathy with others. It underlies our remarkable capacity to transport ourselves into someone else's parlor where we will be in reality next week, and then in imagination to think and plan how we will act. And it enables us to imagine ourselves in someone else's place, and to ask how we would feel and what we would do if we were this other person.
>
> No matter how poorly we use or fail to use or even abuse these capacities, they are the rudiments of our ability to begin to love our neighbor, to have ethical sensitivity, to see truth, to create beauty, to devote ourselves to ideals, and to die for them if need be.
>
> To fulfill these potentialities is to be a person. (28)

We have circled back to the discussion about scapegoats and saviors.

Abelard's perspective on the Crucifixion of Christ is that it is in his suffering that he brings *salvation*, because his suffering causes *compassion*, *empathy* in those who are exposed to it, both in humans and in God, and it is through *compassion*, through humans and God *coming together in passion* that *salvation* takes place.

Empathy, then, is an ability to put oneself into another, to have a real connection with the *essence* of another, to feel and understand the emotions, the needs, and the desires of another. It is what allows for *compassion*, a feeling of connection to another, an emotion that results from another's emotion, whether it be sorrow, joy, pain, anguish, love, fear, hate, sadness, or desire. *Empathy* is what humans experience as a result of the world of the mind or soul or psyche. While the physical world causes emotional states, it is the psyche that knows them, and the ability to stand outside of oneself and to put oneself in the position of another is the ultimate essence of human existence. *Empathy* and the resulting *compassion* are the highest qualities of human existence, the most unique form of *self-realization*.

Notes

1."The Empath" is a third season episode of *Star Trek: The Original Series,* and was broadcast December 6, 1968. It is episode #67, production #63, written by Joyce Muskat and directed by John Erman. This episode was remastered in 2006 and aired July 26, 2008 as part of the remastered *Original Series.*

2. Matthew 13:45-46, *King James Bible.*

3. "The Perfect Mate" is the 120th episode of the science fiction television series *Star Trek: The Next Generation* and the 21st episode of the show's fifth season. It was first broadcast on April 27, 1992.

4. Adam Schrager, "Marina Sirtis: From Hoi Polloi to Counselor Troi," *The Finest Crew in the Fleet: The Next Generation's Cast On Screen and Off.* New York: Wolf Valley Books, 1997.

5. June, 1915, *Poetry: a Magazine of Verse*; rpt., *The Norton Anthology of Poetry,* 1970.

6. *Michael Robartes and the Dancer,* 1921; rpt., Thomas Parkinson and Anne Brannen, eds. Ithaca, NY: Cornell University Press, 1994; and *The Norton Anthology of Poetry,* 1970.

7. Putnam, 1954.

8. *Liberation of Buchanvald*, www.remember.org.

9. "They Died 900 a Day in 'the Best' Nazi Death Camp," *PM,* April 16, 1945.

10. *Murrow: His Life and Times*, Ann M. Sperber. Fordham, 1998, p. 252.

11. *Slaughterhouse Five; or the Children's Crusade, a Duty Dance with Death*, Delacore, 1968. Interestingly, Beckett read and was impressed by the novel in 1972; see James Knowlson, *Dammed to fame: The life of Samuel Beckett*, pp. 594-595.

12. Kwiet, K.: "Suicide in the Jewish Community," *Leo Baeck Yearbook*, vol. 38. 1993.

13. trans. Ilse Lasch, Washington Square Press (Simon & Schuster), 1959; rpt, ISBN 0-671-02337-3 (Softcover, January, 1997).

14. *Man's Search for Meaning*, pp. 153-154.

15. *Man's Search for Meaning*, p. 160.

16. *Man's Search for Meaning,* p. 159.

17. *Man's Search for Meaning,* pp. 156-157.

18. *Man's Search for Meaning,* pp. 157-158.

19. *Man's Search for Meaning,* p. 158.

20. "On Human Nature: Character: Part 1," *The Essays of Arthur Schopenhauer*, Kensinger Publ., 2004.

21. S. D. Hodges, and K. J. Klein, "Regulating the costs of empathy: the price of being human," *Journal of Socio-Economics*, 2001.

22. D. M. Berger, *Clinical Empathy*, Northvale: Jason Aronson, Inc., 1987.

23. J. Decety and P. L. Jackson, "The functional architecture of human empathy," *Behavioral and Cognitive Neuroscience Reviews*, 3, 2004, pp. 71-100; J. Decety, and M. Meyer, M., "From emotion resonance to empathic understanding: A social developmental neuroscience account," *Development and Psychopathology*, 20, 2008, pp. 1053-1080.

24. C. R. Rogers, "A theory of therapy, personality and interpersonal relationships, as developed in the client-centered framework, "*Psychology: A study of science* (Vol. 3, pp. 210-211; 184-256), ed., S. Koch, New York: McGraw Hill, 1959.
25. *The Essential Difference: The Truth about the Male and Female Brain,* Basic Books, July 1, 2003.
26. *Traditions of Compassion: From Religious Duty to Social Activism*, Palgrave Macmillan February 16, 2006.
27. *The Immense Journey: An Imaginative Naturalist Explores the Mysteries of Man and Nature,* Vantage, 1955, pp. 120-121.
28. *Man's Search for Himself*, Norton: New York, 1953, pp. 74-76.

PART II:

THE DANCE OF LIGHT AND SHADOW

The Puppet Master

The first Christians lived and dreamed and worshipped in the caves of Qadicha Valley. Centuries later, monks used them as a place to bind the mentally ill in chains and pray for God's cure. In the twentieth century, Arab Christians came to light the candles of faith, watching the war ravaged country outside driving away what few staunch believers remained.

****

During several nights when I could not get to sleep, a recurrent crackling noise in the wall of our bedroom became noticeable at shorter or longer intervals; time and again it woke me as I was about to go to sleep. Naturally we thought of a mouse although it was very extraordinary that a mouse should have found its way to the first floor of such a solidly built house. But having heard similar noises innumerable times since then, and still hearing them around me every day in daytime and at night, I have come to recognize them as undoubted divine miracles—they are called "interferences" by the voices talking to me—and I must at least suspect, without being too definite about it, that even then it was already a matter of such a miracle; *in other words that right from the beginning the more or less definite intention existed to prevent my sleep and later my recovery from the illness resulting from the insomnia for a purpose which cannot at this stage be further specified.*

—Daniel Paul Schreber, *Memoirs of My Nervous Illness,* p. 64

****

And I turned myself to behold wisdom, and madness, and folly: for what can the man do that cometh after the king? Even that which hath been already done.

—Ecclesiastes 2:12, *King James Bible*

****

The soul that is well may succeed in ignoring all that is comprised in the word "God," the soul that is sick meets gods and devils at every turn.

—John Custance, Wisdom, Madness and Folly, p. 12

****

Instead of the notions of the somatic, psychical, and mixed views stated above, and the doubtful foundations upon which they rest, you will now naturally wish to be informed which of them are the views that these lectures adopt, or what others they will propose, in order that you may be guided by something not negative, but positive. A well-grounded answer to this point can only be furnished by the lectures themselves; but from our preliminary basis thus much may be premised. The maladies of the spirit alone, *in abstracto,* that is, error and sin, can be called diseases of the mind only *per analogiam.* They come not within the jurisdiction of the physician, but that of the teacher and clergyman, who again are called *physicians* of the mind only *per analogiam.* The maladies of the body alone, *in abstracto*, for instance, of the brain or the nerves, without mental alienation, are not diseases of the mind, but of the body. The notion, *mental disease*, must therefore be deduced, neither from the mind nor from the body, but from the relation of each to the other. The question does not turn here on the external cause of psychopathies, which may be either psychical or corporeal, nor upon what is called the proximate cause, which inscrutable, because the relation between body and mind is inexplicable; the question is respecting the phenomenon itself. Where psychical phenomena appear *abnormal*, there is mental disorder which has its root in the mind, so far as this is manifested through the sensual organ, and has its root in the body, so far as this is the organ of the mind. To search after the phenomena in which these relations are revealed, with the unprejudiced eye of experience—to investigate them scientifically in every point that is of importance to the physician, and to collect them in one whole, is the province of medical psychology, upon which we are now about to enter.

—E. Feuchtersleben, 1845, *Medical Psychology*
Translated by H. E. Lloyd & B. G.
Babington, London, 1847
(Possibly the first book on psychology)

THE MYSTERIUM TREMENDUM

> Aldous Huxley has noted that what he saw when, for once, he really *saw* something, was "wonderful almost to the point of being terrifying," so that suddenly he had an inkling of what it must feel like to be mad. The mad are those who, when they have broken contact with the mode of meaning, with the integrating component of thinking consciousness, cannot again restore it—whereas the great artist, like the shaman, like the *paramaharmsa*, the "supreme wild gander" of the titanic yogic flight, can be carried away and return."
>
> —Joseph Campbell (1)

Sometimes appearing as a withered old person with arms outstretched like wings fringed with a flickering fire, Kalona, the raven mocker, is a dead spirit that must renew itself by drinking the blood or eating the entrails of humans. Just as buzzards circle above and descend on dying and dead remains of animals, Kalona comes to those on the verge of death. Sometimes Kalona even torments the dying, beating them and tossing them about, hastening their deaths. Then it feeds on the remains.

The Cherokee have known these bird spirits from the earliest mists of memory. Even the most powerful of their witches fear the Kalona, specters of the undead. Though the Kalona are not ravens, they imitate the raven's crackling *caw, caw, caw,* for it is the sound of death. (2)

However, this is too simple. While the *black* bird might symbolize death, the Kalona are *mock* black birds, not birds of death, but birds of the *undead*, the walking spirits of the *living dead*. Alan Kilpatrick writes: "Like the Romanian *nosferatu*, it is believed that these specters of the "undead" renew their life force by devouring the blood, heart, or entrails of the living." (3) This is the bird that feeds on the world of sunlight, conscious knowing, reason and logic. It is a creature of the *other world*, the world beyond conscious comprehension.

Rudolph Otto called this *other world* the *numinous*, from the Latin *numen*, the *power of God* or the *will of God* or simply *God*. This is a rubric for the "interpretation and evaluation" of non-rational manifestations of the sacred characterized by a "sense of one's creature state" (by which he means that of the physical world, a creation of God), other than the *numinous*, a creation of the *numinous* but not the *numinous* itself; mystical awe (*tremendum*); a presentiment of divine power (*majestas*); amazement in the face of that which is "completely other" (*mysterium*), demonical energy, and paradox. (4) It is the mystery behind a religious experience.

This is not simply a normal experience intensified, but rather a different experience entirely, a form of *dread* not in relation to extreme *fear*, but a form of *dread* aroused by intimations of or actual experience of that which is *other*, the *numinous*. This *numinous dread* or *awe* or *awe-fullness*, Otto called the *mysterium tremendum*, which has three components, tremendousness (*tremendum*), mysteriousness (*mysterium*), and fascination (*facinans*). The difference between fear of physical danger and *numinous dread* is that the experience of *numinous dread* is caused by a realization of the inexplicable.

Kalona are not frightening in the sense that a ferocious animal such as a tiger is frightening because it might physically devour us, nor are they frightening in the sense that death-as-the-end-of-existence-in-this-world might be frightening. They are frightening in that they are of a reality beyond all of this, a reality beyond human comprehension and control. At the same time, their existence confirms that there is something more, that there is a reality beyond mere physical existence, beyond science and math and logic, beyond the laws of reason (which, if such laws are carried to their ultimate conclusion prove life is the result of formulas and humans have no free will but are only following patterns predetermined by the workings of physics, are, in other words, not responsible for anything they do but are, rather, simply sophisticated organic machines and nothing more). In other words, the existence of an entity beyond explanation allows for the possibility that life has meaning and value, that each individual has the potential of some form of self-determination. Thus, even the most horrific, most monstrous entity from the *other* is enticing because it gives life meaning simply by existing, simply by being of that which is beyond explanation and predetermination.

And the key to the experience is that this other reality becomes more than just a subject for speculation; it entails an existing reality beyond speculation. Since it is *absolute other*, unapproachable through any form of conscious knowing, overwhelmingly powerful, and of an urgency and force that might be compared to the "wrath of God," an experience of it results in a state of stupor, of blank amazement, of astonishment, where the soul bypasses the mind to experience a *trembling shudder*--a feeling, a knowing beyond the intellect, the awareness of being a creature, a creation of the creator God; this is not a moral experience, but an experience beyond morality, a form of *grace*. We are drawn to this experience. There is a *mysterium fascinosum*, an attraction to the *numinous*, a desire to encounter the mystical moment when all of the oppositions of the two worlds come together in a strange harmony, what Otto calls the *mysterium tremendum* and *fascinosum.*

All humans are capable of this experience, though some are born with a greater potential for it. Then, if they should experience the necessary encounters, they will become the connectors with the *other,* and take on one of the myriad forms of mystical humans, including the *shamans.* `

A *shaman* experiences the *mysterium tremendum* and survives it, returns from it, does not succumb to it, is not driven *mad*, though it might be said he has experienced *madness*, experienced the realities beyond reason, beyond morality.

It is possible to compare a *shaman* with a *schizophrenic*. Both have separated from the normal social community, have gone beyond the cultural images and symbols of meaning, have experienced a psychological break. The difference between the two in terms of the *other*, of the *mysterium tremendum* is that the *shaman* is able to return from this and reintegrate with the community; the *schizophrenic* succumbs to it, becomes lost in it, experiences it as a frightening nightmare from which there is no escape.

Schizophrenia has been used in so many ways to describe so many different forms of mental illness that it becomes at times simply a catch-all term. The same is true of *paranoia*. However, in more strict uses, *Paranoiac Schizophrenia* is a firmly established category of mental illness.

According to the Mayo Clinic the onset of *paranoid schizophrenia* usually occurs in men in their late teens or twenties. It involves delusions, such as being spied on by the FBI or perhaps being an agent for the FBI, in either case not being able to trust others because of some sense of them being the enemy. These delusions often become very complex stories that reinforce the person's non-realistic views. The person commonly feels a sense of grandeur, some sense of connecting up to superhuman powers or forces or spirits. Voices that no one else can hear are common, and at times they demand harmful actions to one-self or others.

Theories of its cause include the possibility that early brain development might involve too many or too few connections being made, specifically certain areas of the brain that are rich in the chemical dopamine. There are several different theories for why this might happen. One possibility is that there are risk-associated genes. Another is that it might be the result of certain viruses. A third is that stressful childhood environments might precipitate this disorder.

There are no blood or brain-imaging tests currently available for a diagnosis, and one form of *schizophrenia* has been known to mutate at times into another form. However, once *schizophrenia* develops, it does not go away. It is a chronic disease. (5)

The chronic absoluteness of *schizophrenia* is not agreed on by all, and there is certainly a school of psychology and psychiatry that believes a *schizophrenic* can eventually find his or her way out of the nightmarish existence.

The term comes from combining two Greek words, *schizein* (to split) and *phren* (mind), and has been most often used to describe people who have auditory hallucinations, paranoid or bizarre delusions, disorganized speech and thinking, all resulting in the inability to function in social situations. Eugen Bleuler coined the term in 1908, giving it a plural form, *schizophrenias* because it took on so many similar yet different symptoms and its causes, while they might intertwine, varied. It has since been discovered that schizophrenics all have increased dopamine activity in the meso-limbic pathway, resulting in the common use of antipsychotic medication to suppress this activity.

The American Psychiatric Association lists five categories:

1. *Paranoid*, where delusions and hallucinations are present but thought disorder, disorganized behavior and affective flattening are absent.
2. *Disorganized* or *hebephrenic*, where thought disorder and flat affect are present together.
3. *Catatonic*, where inflexibility and immobility or purposeless movement dominate.
4. *Undifferentiated*, where there is some obvious psychotic neurosis but the symptoms of *paranoid, disorganized* or *catatonic* are not present.
5. *Residual*, where the symptoms are present but to a lesser degree. (6)

The World Health Organization (basing its criterion on the theories of Kurt Schneider, who designated what he called first-rank symptoms, which included the delusion of being controlled by an external force, the belief that thoughts are being inserted into or withdrawn from one's consciousness, the belief that one's thoughts are being broadcast to others, and hallucinatory voices (even to the extent of having conversations with imagined voices) includes two additional categories:

1. *Post-schizophrenic depression*, which is just what its title suggests, a low-level depression following a *schizophrenic* illness.
2. *Simple schizophrenia*, which is an insidious and progressive development of prominent negative symptoms with no history of psychotic episodes. (7)

It is most important to highlight the confusion and guesswork involved with all of these attempts to classify *schizophrenia.* While there is the obvious, non-scientific, non-psychological, non-neurological realization that a *schizophrenic* is somehow noticeably different from a *normal* person (I realize the danger of even suggesting that there is such a thing as a *normal* person, but the point I am making here is that we can intuitively sense a difference in the mental makeup of a *schizophrenic*); however, while it is possible to sense this, at least at this point in time it is not possible to pigeon-hole individuals into a specific scientific explanation of it. The fields of psychology, psychiatry, and neurology realize this, and in the end must admit that *schizophrenia* is more of a general center of, or central term for, a group of aberrations having something to do with *hallucinations*, *paranoia*, an entering into or intermingling of conscious, reasonable, logical thinking with a kind of thinking other than that, whether it be designated as madness, insanity, dementia or, on the more positive side, mysticism, spirituality, artistic creation, the experience of the *mysterium tremendum*--the realization of the *numinous.*

For Carl Jung, it's all couched in the journey to *individuation*, a symbolic process that integrates the unconscious with the consciousness. He writes:

> Its beginning is almost always characterized by one's getting stuck in a blind alley or in some impossible situation; and its goal is, broadly speaking, illumination or higher consciousness, by means of which the initial situation is overcome on a higher level. As regards the time factor, the process may be compressed into a single dream or into a short moment of experience, or it may extend over months and years, depending on the nature of the initial situation, the person involved in the process, and the goal to be reached. The wealth of symbols naturally varies enormously from case to case. Although everything is experienced in image form, i.e., symbolically, it is by no means a question of fictitious dangers but of very real risks upon which the fate of a whole life may depend. The chief danger is that of succumbing to the fascination influence of the archetypes, and this is most likely to happen when the archetypal images are not made conscious. If there is already a predisposition to psychosis, it may even happen that the archetypal figures, which are endowed with a certain autonomy anyway on account of their natural numinosity, will escape from conscious control altogether and become completely independent, thus producing the phenomena of possession. (8)

He offers a few examples:

> In the case of an anima-possession, for instance, the patient will want to change himself into a woman through self-castration, or he is afraid that something of the sort will be done to him by force. The best-known example of this is Schreber's *Memories of My Nervous Illness*. Patients often discover a whole anima mythology with numerous archaic motifs. A case of this kind was published some time ago by Nelken. ["*Analytische Beobachtungen uber Phantasien eines Schizophrenen*," pp. 504] Another patient has described his experiences himself and commented on them in a book. [*Wisdom, Madness, and Folly,"* John Custance] I mention these examples because there are still people who think that the archetypes are subjective chimeras of my own brain. (9)

Two of the above examples have become famous in the world of psychology. The first, that of Daniel Paul Schreber, perhaps the most studied case of *schizophrenia* ever, begins with his famous father, Daniel Gottlieb Moritz Schreber, an extremely important physician, orthopedist, and pedagogue, author of many influential and popular books promoting gymnastics as the means to a "revivification of the robust German popular spirit in a perfected and ennobled form corresponding to the level of general cultural development." (10) It can hardly be overstated how well received his ideas were. His book *Medical Indoor Gymnastics; or, A System of Hygienic Exercises for Home Use To Be Practiced Anywhere without Apparatus or Assistance by Young and Old of Either Sex, for the Preservation of Health and General Activity* by 1909 had already gone through its thirty-second edition .

He created and promoted the *Schrebergarten* (a private garden within an urban area that became a standard feature of German cities) and used his expertise in orthopedics and gymnastics with missionary zeal to embrace the "glorious embers of the German popular spirit, mired deep in the ruins and ashes left behind," so it "could again burst forth in individual flames." (11) Putting forth the need for a "system," he envisioned his mission as that of providing a scientific basis upon the "young and ennobled instinct of the . . . still healthy root of Germanic national life." (12)

These strong views about the current morality of Germany, which he found to be "soft" and "decayed," tied directly to his views about raising children. He felt a strong discipline was necessary, a system aimed at making children obedient and submissive to adults. In *Book of Health*, he wrote:

> The tempers of the small child, making themselves known by the child's screaming and crying for no apparent reason, . . . expressing nothing more than whim, the first emergence of obstinacy, . . . must be confronted in a

> positive manner . . . by quickly diverting the child's attention, through stern admonitions or, if all else fails . . . by repeated, physically perceptible admonitions . . . In this way—and only in this way—the child becomes conscious of its dependence on the external world and learns . . . submission . . . This kind of procedure is necessary but once, or at most twice—and one will have become master of the child forever. (13)

It is only to be expected that he would employ these views in raising his own children, and he did. Samuel M. Weber writes, "That the author of these lines became the "master" of his child—indeed, "forever"—is just as certain as the fact that one of these children, Daniel Paul, never, for the rest of his life, ceased to cry out against this authority. (14) Indeed, the results of his personal totalitarian child-raising practices, rather than offering proof of his views, undermined them, as Daniel Gustav, Daniel Paul's older brother, went mad and committed suicide, and Daniel Paul became infamous as *the* classic case of *paranoia* and *schizophrenia*. Furthermore, perhaps nothing more than a coincidental mishap, but certainly suggestive of more, later in life this father was struck on the head by a falling iron bar during a daily gymnastic exercise, resulting in chronic headaches and "hallucinations with a pathological urge to murder." (15)

How much Daniel Paul Schreber's illness is the result of his father's strict views is debatable. Eugen Bleuler, the man given credit for inventing the term "schizophrenia," completely ignored Daniel Paul Schreber's upbringing in his analysis, and came to the conclusion that the statements of such people were "semantic discharges of a disease process," having no real meaning or value. (16) Curiously, Sigmund Freud, who knew the case and would almost certainly be expected to make this connection, did not bother to study the father's extensive writings about child-rearing. Furthermore, contrary to Freud's entire theoretical system of psychological analysis, he did not meet Schreber nor know much of anything at all about Schreber's childhood. This is especially interesting in that it involves the case where Freud put forth the influential claim that *paranoia* arises as a defense against homosexual love, i.e., the result of being persecuted by a parent of the same sex. (17) However, in 1959, William Niederland did include a study of both Daniel Paul's father and Daniel Paul's own childhood, highlighting some similarities between Daniel Paul's curious thoughts and his father's views of child-rearing. (18) In *Soul Murder: Persecution in the Family*, Morton Schatzman built on this, offering a detailed comparison of Daniel Paul's discussion of his illness with his father's theories of child raising, and suggesting a strong possibility of Daniel Paul's madness being the result of having been raised by a father with a border-line sadistic insanity of his own. (19)

Before plunging into Daniel Paul's *paranoia* and *schizophrenia* let's take at least a brief look at his life before his attacks, at what was a fairly "normal," respectable life. Franz Baumayer finds that Daniel Paul "was quite gifted and had always been an excellent pupil. He is described as being of good-natured and sociable character. In his later life he demonstrated great talent and climbed the rungs of the career ladder relatively quickly. His last position was that of Senatsprasident at the Superior Country Court at Dresden. He led, as far as we know, a thoroughly respectable life." (20) He married Sabine Behr, daughter of a senior director at the Municipal Theater in Leipzig (likely thought to be beneath the family's social position, but certainly not suggestive of any mental illness). Then came the first public infamy. On October 28, 1884, he suffered a crushing defeat in his bid to be elected to the German Reichstag in Chemnitz. This was immediately followed by a spell of hypochondria, centered by the notion he was emaciated, and quickly led to his interment in the Psychiatric Clinic at the University of Leipzig, where the records indicate he was in a "very unstable state of mind." (21) There are few sources to find out much about this initial breakdown and six month stay. Nonetheless, records indicate that he exhibited some speech impediments, twice tried to take his own life, was sensitive to noise, and had a "weepy disposition."

Following his release, his life returned to a very normal state, and it lasted as such for eight years. However upon being appointed the Senatsprasident of the Dresden Superior State Court, he began having new attacks of anxiety, including some prefiguring feelings of being a woman succumbing to intercourse, which he stated at the time was "so foreign to my whole nature that I may say I would have rejected it with indignation if fully awake." (22) He begin meeting with Dr. Flechsig, the director of the Leipzig clinic he had previously stayed in. However, while he described these meetings in positive ways, they obviously did not solve his problems, as his psychosis worsened quickly, finally resulting in his interment for eight years. These are the years written about in *Memoirs of My nervous Illness*, the book that became perhaps the most quoted study of a neurosis in all of psychology.

The medical records indicate his condition upon entering:

> At first more hypochondrical complaints, that he suffers from a "softening of the brain, will soon die," etc., at the same time mixed with delusions of persecution, that "he has now been made happily insane." Also hallucinations he is dead and has begun to rot, that he is no longer in a condition "fit for burial"; that he is "plague-stricken," probably as a result of olfactory hallucinations; that his penis was twisted off by means

> of a "nerve probe"; he thinks he is a woman, but also often claims he must repulse energetically "the homosexual love of certain persons." All of these things tormented him greatly so that he wished for death; he tried to drown himself in the bathtub and for many weeks demanded daily "the glass of cyanide destined for him." The auditory and visual hallucinations sometimes became so strong that he spent hours at a time in a chair or in bed completely inaccessible, squinting his eyes. The delusions of his senses apparently were of ever-changing content, referring in the more recent period of his stay at the Leipzig clinic to his belief that he was being tortured to death in a ghastly manner. He then lost himself more and more in a mystic-religious dimension, maintaining that God spoke openly to him, that vampires and devils make game of him. He said he wanted to convert to the Roman Catholic Church in order to avoid being persecuted. He then saw apparitions, heard sacred music and, finally, apparently thought he was in another world. At last he considered everything around him to be spirits, taking his environment to be a world of illusions . . . At that time Flechsig considered him dangerous to himself and to others. (23)

He was discharged in 1902, but following the death of his mother and his wife's stroke, would return again in 1907 and remain there until his death in 1911. As with his first internment, there is little to go on for this final one beyond the medical records.

It is important to note the "normalcy" of his life prior to his fall into a *paranoid* or *schizophrenic* or *other* psychic world, if for no other reason than that it suggests his childhood life was not, after all, so psychologically damaging as to render him *psychotic* beyond a normal range. While it no doubt influenced his psychological development, perhaps made him more susceptible or more sensitive to a potential breaking off from normal conscious existence, it seems it did not in-and-of-itself cause it.

Other factors that often accompany, but have not been shown to always be present in such individuals, also are worth noting. There can be no doubt he inherited a high level of intelligence (not only his father, but his relatives going back several generations demonstrated this). Furthermore, though it is much more evident in other similar cases, the mere fact he married into a theatrical family against the wishes of his own family suggests his attraction to the arts. Two tangential but nevertheless useful additional notes are worth mentioning. While much of his life is obscured simply because his family was ashamed of his insanity and worked to destroy instead of preserve biographical items, it is known he was attracted to music and, especially in relation to his later actions that have been classified as homosexual, he and his wife very much wanted children, and tried to have them, but were unable to conceive.

Now, with the brief biographical and factual frames in place, we can dig into the interesting *other world* he experienced, and then we can explore some of the more important attempts to explain his experiences. Finally, we can compare these experiences with others, some of whom have been dismissed, as has he, as simply suffering some form of *neurosis*, whichever clever psychological frame we put over it, some of whom have been placed among the more highly regarded individuals of their cultures, as *artist, shamans,* even *savors,* people who have perhaps experienced the *mysterium tremendum.*

It is worth beginning with his own *Preface* to the book, which in addition to putting forth his approach, his views on his current state, and his reasons for deciding to publish his experiences, demonstrates that he was in a very reasonable, self-aware condition while he reviewed and put together the final drafts of it:

> I started this work without having publication in mind. The idea only occurred to me as I progressed with it; however, I did not conceal from myself doubts which seemed to stand in the way of publication: mainly consideration for certain persons still living. Yet I believe that expert examination of my body and observation of my personal fate during my lifetime would be of value both for science and the knowledge of religious truths. In the face of such considerations all personal issues must recede.
>
> Of the whole work the following were written:
>
> The Memoirs themselves (Chapters I-XXII) in the period February to September 1900.
> Postscripts I-VII in the period October 1900 to June 1901.
> Postscripts second series at the end of 1902.
>
> The outward circumstances of my life have materially changed since the early beginnings of this work. While at the beginning I was living in almost prison-like isolation, separated from contact with educated people, excluded even from the family table of the Director (to which so-called boarders of the Asylum were admitted), never able to get outside the walls of the Asylum, etc., I have gradually been granted increasing freedom of movement, and contact with educated people has been made increasingly possible. Finally I was completely successful in winning the proceedings against my tutelage (albeit in the Second Instance) as mentioned in Chapter XX, inasmuch as the decree of 13th March 1900 placing me under tutelage issued by the District court, Dresden, was rescinded by the final judgment of the Superior country court, Dresden, of 14th July 1902. My legal capacity was thereby acknowledged and free disposition of my properties restored to me. With regard to my stay in the Asylum, for months I have been in possession of a written declaration from the Asylum Authorities

that there was now no opposition in principle to my discharge; I am planning therefore to return to my house and home probably early next year.

All these changes have afforded me the opportunity of considerably widening the range of my personal observations. Accordingly some of my earlier opinions need revision: in particular I can no doubt that the so-called "play-with-human-beings" (the effect of miracles) is limited to myself and *to whatever constitutes my immediate environment* at the time. I might perhaps have formulated some passages of my Memoirs differently now. Nevertheless I have left them mainly in the form in which they were written originally. To change certain points now would only prejudice the freshness of the original descriptions. It is also in my opinion of little importance whether, in view of the relationship contrary to the Order of the World which arose between God and myself, ideas which I formed at the time were more or less faulty. A more general interest can in any case be claimed only for those conclusions which I arrived at in consequence of my impressions and experiences about the *lasting* conditions, about the essence and attributes of God, the immortality of the soul, etc. In this respect I have no reason whatever, even after my subsequent personal experiences, to make the very slightest alteration in the basic ideas set out particularly in chapters I, II, XVIII, and XIX of the Memoirs.

Sonnenstein Asylum, near Pirna,
December 1902
The Author (24)

I think it legitimate to expect readers to agree that this introduction suggests a mind under the control of reason and common sense, not a deranged man, not a *paranoid*, not a *schizophrenic,* not a *neurotic* or *psychotic* man, even though he is discussing his time spent in an asylum because of his *insanity*. This preface is followed by *"Open Letter to Professor Flechsig,"* a letter to his main psychiatrist at the asylum, and it is a worthwhile, perhaps even necessary follow-up read. Again, it is written in a calm, even considerate manner; yet here readers should have a different view of the author:

Dear Professor,

I take the liberty of enclosing a copy of "Memoirs of a Patient Suffering from a Nervous Illness," which I have written, and beg you to examine it in a kindly spirit.

You will find your name mentioned frequently, particularly in the first chapter, partly in connection with circumstances which might be painful to you. I very much regret this but unfortunately cannot make any changes without from the very outset precluding making myself understood. In any case it is far from me to attack your honour, as indeed *I do not harbor any personal grievance against any person.* My aim is solely to further knowledge of truth in a vital field, that of religion.

I am absolutely certain that in this regard I command experiences which—when generally acknowledged as valid—will act fruitfully to the highest possible degree among the rest of mankind. Equally I have no doubt that your name plays an essential role in the genetic development of the circumstances in question, in that certain nerves taken from your nervous system become "tested souls" in the sense described in Chapter I of the "Memoirs," and in this capacity achieved supernatural power by means of which they have for years exerted a damaging influence on me and still do to this day. You like other people may be inclined at first to see nothing but a pathological offspring of my imagination in this; but I have an almost overwhelming amount of proof of its correctness, details of which you will find in the content of my "Memoirs." I still feel daily and hourly the damaging influence of the miracles of those "tested souls;" the voices that speak to me even now shout your name again and again at me hundreds of times every day in this context, in particular as the instigator of those injuries; and this despite the fact that the personal relations which existed between us for some time have long since receded into the background for me; I could hardly therefore have any reason to keep on thinking of you, especially with any sense of grievance.

For years I have pondered how to reconcile these facts with my respect for your person, *whose integrity and moral worth I have not the least right to doubt.* Only quite recently however, just before the publication of my book, I had a new idea which might *possibly* lead to the correct solution of the problem. As remarked at the end of chapter IV and the beginning of chapter V of the "Memoirs," I have not the least doubt that the *first impetus* to what my doctors always considered mere "hallucinations" but which to me signified communication with supernatural powers, consisted of *influences on my nervous system emanating from your nervous system.* How could this be explained? I think it is possible that you—at first as I am quite prepared to believe only for therapeutic purposes—carried on some hypnotic, suggestive, or whatever else one could call it, contact with my nerves, *even while we were separated in space.* During this contact you might suddenly have realized that other voices were speaking to me as well, pointing to a supernatural origin. Following this surprising realization you might have continued this contact with me for a time out of scientific interest, until you yourself felt as it were uneasy about it, and therefore decided to break it off. But it is possible that in this process a part of your own nerves—probably unknown to yourself—was removed from your body, a process explicable only in a supernatural manner, and ascended to heaven as a "tested soul" and there achieved some supernatural power. This "tested soul" still endowed with human faults like all impure souls—

in accordance with the character of souls which I have come to know with certainty—then simply allowed itself to be driven by the impulse of ruthless self-determination and lust for power, without any restraint by something comparable to the moral will power of man, exactly in the same way as another "tested soul," that of von W., as recorded in my "Memoirs." It is possible therefore that all those things which in earlier years I erroneously thought I had to blame you for—particularly the definite damaging effects on my body—are to be blamed only on that "tested soul." There would then be no need to cast any shadow upon your person and only the mild reproach would perhaps remain that you, like so many doctors, could not completely resist the temptation of using a patient in your care *as an object for scientific experiments* apart from the real purpose of cure, when by chance matters of the highest scientific interest arose. One might even raise the question whether perhaps all the talk of voices about somebody having committed soul murder can be explained by the souls (rays) deeming it impermissible that a person's nervous system should be influenced by another's to the extent of imprisoning his will power, such as occurs during hypnosis; in order to stress forcefully that this was a malpractice it was called "soul murder," the souls for lack of a better term, using a term already in current usage, and because of their innate tendency to express themselves hyperbolically.

I need hardly mention *of what immeasurable importance it would be* if you could in any way confirm the surmises I have sketched above, all the more if they could be substantiated in recollections of earlier years retained in your memory. The rest of my thesis would thereby gain universal credence and would immediately be regarded as a *serious scientific problem to be investigated in every possible way.*

I beg you therefore, my dear Sir—I might almost say: I *implore* you—to state without reservation:

(1) Whether during my stay in your Asylum you maintained a hypnotic or similar contact with me in such a way that even when separated in space, you exerted an influence on my nervous system;

(2) Whether you thus witnessed in any way communications from voices originating elsewhere, indicating supernatural origin: finally

(3) Whether during my time in your Asylum *you yourself also* received visions or vision-like impressions particularly in dreams, which dealt amongst others with the almighty power of God and human freedom of will, unmanning, loss of states of Blessedness, my relations and my friends, as well as yours, particularly Daniel Furctegott Flechsig named in Chapter VI, and many other matters mentioned in my "Memoirs."

I hasten to add that from the numerous communications I received from the voices that talked to me at that time, I have the most weighty indications that you yourself had similar visions.

In appealing to your scientific interest I may be permitted to trust that you will have the courage of truth, even if you had to admit some trifle which could never seriously affect your prestige or authority in the eyes of any sensible person.

In case you want to send me a written communication you may rest assured that I would publish it only with your permission and in a form which you yourself may choose.

In view of the wide interest which the content of this letter may claim, I have thought fit to have it printed in the form of an "open letter" prefacing my "Memoirs."

Dresden, March 1903
Yours sincerely,
Dr. Schreber, Senatsprasident (retired). (25)

After reading this, I suspect any views of Daniel Paul Schreber as being *sane* have disappeared, and now my task becomes not convincing anyone of his *unnormal* mind, but rather of planting the seeds of there being more to him than *mere insanity*, or that *insanity* might be more than simply a *flawed mind*.

Let's begin by looking through his *Memoirs*. They are, after all, commonly thought to be among the best record we have of *insanity*.

The book begins with a brief "Introduction," which again contrasts some very rational, intellectual discussion and some passages that clearly want the reader to go beyond this to some equally strange and irrational discussion. It begins with the initial, practical reason for the manuscript:

> I have decided to apply for my release from the Asylum in the near future in order to live once again among civilized people and at home with my wife. It is therefore necessary to give those persons who will then constitute the circle of my acquaintances, an approximate idea at least of my religious conceptions, so that they may have some understanding of the necessity which forces me to various oddities of behavior, even if they do not fully understand these apparent oddities. (26)

He then goes on to explain that he intends to do his best to explain as well as he can his experience of "divine revelation," which he points out that he only partially understands, but has brought him closer to the truth than most humans. He even goes into the realization that the truths he is trying to explain are ultimately beyond explanation, resulting in the necessity to use images and similes, which can at best only approximate the truths he has experienced. He gives an example:

> An obvious example is that the concept of *eternity* is beyond man's grasp. Man cannot really understand that something can exist which has neither beginning nor end, that there can be a cause which cannot itself be traced to a previous cause. And yet eternity is one of God's attributes, which with all religiously-minded people I feel I must accept. Man will always be inclined to ask: "If God created the world, how then did God Himself come to be?" This question will forever remain unanswered. The same applies to the concept of divine creation. Man can always only imagine that new matter is created through the influence of forces on matter already in existence, and yet I believe—and I hope to prove in what follows by means of definite examples—that divine creation is a creation out of the void. (27)

He goes on in this manner, concluding:

> Before I proceed with the account of how, owing to my illness, I entered into peculiar relations with God—which I hasten to add were in themselves contrary to the Order of the World—I must begin with a few remarks about the nature of God and of the human soul; these can for the time being only be put up as axioms—tenets not requiring proof—and their proof as far as is at all possible can only be attempted later in the book. (28)

While a few phrases slip into this introduction that suggest perhaps he is moving beyond philosophical discourse, on the whole he sounds in it much as if he is simply entering an intellectual dialogue that has been going on since the beginnings of history. However, he adds a footnote that pushes the envelope:

> On the other hand, on the basis of what I have myself experienced, I am able to give a more detailed explanation of some Christian dogmas and how such things can come about through divine miracles. Something like the conception of Jesus Christ by an Immaculate Virgin—i.e., one who never had intercourse with a man—happened in my own body. Twice at different times (while I was still in Flechsig's Asylum) I had a female genital organ, although a poorly developed one, and in my body felt quickening like the first signs of life of a human embryo: by a divine miracle God's nerves corresponding to male seed had been thrown into my body; in other words fertilization had occurred. (29)

He continues in this footnote to discuss how Christ might have died and then reappeared, pointing out that he has had similar experiences of people appearing and vanishing. Hardheaded logic and reason wants to jump in here and say simply, yes, he was insane. No matter how much he might be able to hide it in his carefully constructed attempts to appear reasoned, he is saying he had female genital organs, is saying he was impregnated by God, is saying he saw people who were not there (or even alive).

One aside before proceeding further, he is making some interesting comparisons of his own experiences with those believed to have taken place with Christ. The above footnote is in reference to the following passage:

> Even in the dogmas of our positive religion there are certain matters which escape full understanding by the intellect. The Christian teaching that Jesus Christ was the Son of God can be meant only in a mystical sense which but approximates the human sense of these words, because nobody would maintain that God, as a Being endowed with human sexual organs, had intercourse with the woman from whose womb Jesus Christ came forth. (30)

If we pause for a moment here and take this all in, it becomes clear, or at least easily defended, that he is telling us directly he does not mean his own experiences of intercourse with God are to be understood literally, but rather in a symbolic or metaphoric sense. However, it's not so simply separated as this, for he also claims that such miracles as the Immaculate Conception can take place, as he has experienced it himself. In other words, he is attempting to clarify how *this literal world* and *the other world beyond this literal world* both exist separately and yet do at times come together.

How he has experienced these two worlds coming together, what he has learned about the human body, the human soul, and how it all connects up to God in an elaborate web of nerves is going to be the center, the purpose of the book, and he and others have and are going to attempt to comprehend it both psychologically and mythically, as the two disciplines merge.

His explanation at first seems like a science fiction movie in the making, and a "B" grade movie at that, something like *The Body Snatchers*. However, if we simply use more sophisticated medical language, substitute perhaps the "double helix," chromosomes, the genes, the world of heredity, the concepts aren't so "out of this world." In other words, at least a part of his strange belief system is simply the result of it being written at the beginning of the 20th century, and the language, the jargon of science has changed. Of course, that doesn't completely resolve the weirdness. The best way to exhibit it is to simply exhibit it, so here is the beginning of his religious treatise:

> The human soul is contained in the nerves of the body; about their physical nature I, as a layman, cannot say more than that they are extraordinarily delicate structures—comparable to the finest filaments—and that the total mental life of a human being rests on their excitability by external impressions. Vibrations are thereby caused in the nerves which produce the sensations of pleasure and pain in a manner which cannot be further explained; they are able to retain the memory of impressions received (the human memory) and have also the power of moving the muscles of the body which they inhabit into any manifest activity by exertion of their will power. From the most tender beginnings (as the fruit of the womb—as a child's soul) they develop to a complex system which embraces the most widespread regions of human knowledge (the soul of mature man). Part of the nerves is adapted solely for receiving sensory impressions (nerves of sight, hearing, taste and voluptuousness, etc., which are therefore only capable of the sensation of light, sound, heat and cold, of the feeling of hunger, voluptuousness and pain, etc.); other nerves (the nerves of intellect) receive and retain mental impressions and as the organs of will, give to the whole human organism the impulse to manifest those of its powers designed to act on the outside world. Circumstances seem to be such that *every single nerve of intellect represents the total mental individuality of a human being*, that the sum total of recollections is as it were inscribed on each single nerve of intellect [here he points the reader to a footnote where he points out that if every nerve has the totality of a human, that completely explains heredity, as each male seed and each female egg recreates the father and mother in the child; of course not exactly on the mark, but not far off either]; the greater or lesser *number* of nerves of intellect only influences the length of time for which recollections can be retained. While man is alive he is body and soul together; the nerves (soul of man) are nourished and kept in living motion by the body whose function is essentially similar to that of the higher animals. Should the body lose its vitality then the state of unconsciousness, which we call *death* and which is presaged in sleep, supervenes for the nerves. This however, does not imply that the soul is really extinguished; rather the impressions received remain attached to the nerves. The soul, as it were, only goes into hibernation as some lower animals do and can be re-awakened to a new life in a manner to be described below. (31)

Again, though the attachment of the soul to the nerves seems a bit strange at first, the overall logic of the views isn't all that far off of other respected religious views. These claims are immediately followed with "God to start with is only nerve, not body, and akin therefore to the human soul." To say that God is only nerve seems sacrilegious, and I am certain many would stop at that. However, again, if a different word were used, perhaps to say God is only *spirit,* then the ideas don't come off so strange. Also, if one were to use more scientific language, it would again seem more legitimate. After all, as Paul Schreber was writing this, science was struggling with mysterious electromagnetic fields and how invisible forces might be the explanation for everything that happens in the universe. It's interesting to substitute *energy* for *nerve* in Schreber's discussion--makes it seem much more sane.

He continues:

> But unlike the human body, where nerves are present only in limited numbers, the nerves of God are infinite and eternal. They possess the same qualities as human nerves but in a degree surpassing all human understanding. They have in particular the faculty of transforming themselves into all things of the created world; in this capacity they are called rays; and herein lies the essence of divine creation. An intimate relation exists between God and the starry sky. I dare not decide whether one can simply say that God and the heavenly bodies are one and the same, or whether one has to think of the totality of God's nerves as being above and behind the stars, so that the stars themselves and particularly our sun would only represent *stations*, through which God's miraculous creative power travels to our earth (and perhaps to other inhabited planets). He has a footnote reference here where he writes: "Such things are also known to our poets: "Far above the starry sky, surely dwells a kindly father," etc. (32)

As he continues, it is worth noting he refers to current philosophical and scientific theories as contexts for his own.

> Equally I dare not say whether the celestial bodies themselves (fixed stars, planets, etc.) were created by God, or whether divine creation is limited to the organic world; in which case there would be room for the Nebular Hypothesis of Kant-Laplace side by side with the existence of a living God whose existence has become absolute certainty for me. Perhaps the full truth lies (by way of a fourth dimension) in a combination or resultant of both trends of thought impossible for man to grasp. In any case the light and warmth-giving power of the sun, which makes her the origin of all organic life on earth, is only to be regarded as an indirect manifestation of the living God; hence the veneration of the sun as divine by so many peoples since antiquity contains a highly important core of truth even if it does not embrace the whole truth. (33)

However, it must be admitted that, just as one begins to see a reasoned logic to his ideas, he steps beyond it:

> The teaching of present-day astronomy about the movements, the distances and the physical properties of the celestial bodies, etc., may in the main be correct. My own personal experiences leave me in doubt however whether even the astronomy of today has grasped the whole truth about the light-and warmth-giving power of the stars and particularly of our sun; perhaps one has to consider her directly or indirectly only as that part of God's miraculous creative power which is directed to the earth. As proof of this statement I will at present only mention the fact that the sun has for years spoken with me in human words and thereby reveals herself as a living being or as the organ of a still higher being behind her. (34)

Okay, so now he has crossed over. He continues:

> God also regulates the weather; as a rule this is done automatically, so to speak, by the greater or lesser amount of heat emanating from the sun, but He can regulate it in certain ways in pursuit of His own purposes. For instance I have received fairly definite indications that the severe winter of 1870-71 was decided on by God in order to turn the fortunes of war in favour of the Germans; and the proud words on the destruction of Phillip II's Spanish Armada in the year 1588 "*Deus afflavit et dissipati sunt*" (God blew the wind and they were scattered) most probably also contains a historical truth. In this connection I refer to the sun only as that instrument of God's will power which lies nearest to the earth; in reality the condition of the weather is affected by the sum total of the other stars as well. Winds or storms in particular arise when God moves further away from the earth. (35)

Well, now we're in the realm of religious claims. In that world, views similar to these are found, and most certainly the faithful believe them true. However, we are immediately going to find him taking us yet another step:

> In the circumstances contrary to the Order of the World which have now arisen this relation has changed—and I wish to mention this at the outset—the weather is now to a certain extent dependent on *my* actions and thoughts; as soon as I indulge in thinking nothing, or in other words stop an activity which proves the existence of the human mind such as playing chess in the garden the wind arises at once. To anybody who is inclined to doubt such a fantastic statement, I could almost daily give the opportunity of convincing him of its correctness, as in fact I have recently convinced various people about the so-called attacks of bellowing (the doctor, my wife, my sister, etc.). The reason for this is simply that as soon as I indulge

> in thinking nothing God, presuming that I am demented, thinks he can withdraw from me. (36)

He extends this to point out that God continues to watch over His initial creation and in general just let it go on, partially because if He were to connect up with it too often it would be dangerous for Him. The contacts God does make fit into the categories of the occasional *miracle*, "For instance a particularly fervent prayer might in a special case induce God to give help by intervening with a miracle or to shape the fate of whole nations (in war, etc.) by means of miracles"; or personal communication with "highly gifted people (poets, etc.), in order to bless them (particularly in dreams) with some fertilizing thoughts and ideas about the beyond." (37)

It is worth noting that, however peculiarly put, these views fit into generally accepted religious views of God's interaction with humans (all one need do is read "Exodus" in the *Bible* for several examples of both kinds of contact; the conversion of Saul to Paul in the "New Testament"; the *awakening* of Buddha (whose name means *awakening*), the *realization* of Mohammad resulting in the *Koran,* and the endless interactions of the Greco/Roman, Norse, Celtic, etc. religions). Furthermore, the associations surrounding these occasional visits fit into Otto's discussion of experiencing the *mysterium tremendum.* Schreber writes: "such 'nerve contact' was not allowed to become the rule . . . because for reasons which cannot be further elucidated, the nerves of *living* human beings particularly when in a state of *high-grade excitation*, have such power of attraction for the nerves of God that he would not be able to free Himself from them again, and would thus endanger His own existence." (38)

Schreber added a footnote to this at a later date that again suggests a rational person attempting to explain that which transcends reason (not all that different from such famous philosophers as De Carte, Kierkegaard and Kant). Schreber writes: "the idea of a *force of attraction* emanating from individual human bodies or—in my case—from one single human body, acting at such vast distances, must in itself appear absurd if one thinks in terms of natural forces acting purely mechanically. Nevertheless, that an attracting force is at work is for me a fact beyond dispute. This phenomenon will perhaps be somewhat comprehensible and brought nearer human understanding if one remembers that the rays are *living beings* and therefore the power of attraction is not purely a mechanically acting force, but something like a *psychological motive power*: the rays too find that "attractive" which is of interest to them. The relationship therefore appears to be similar to that expressed by Goethe in his "Fisherman": "partly she dragged him down, partly he sank." (39)

His theories (beliefs) also clarify, or perhaps simply re-express in different words, the whole Christian idea of joining with God or going to Heaven after death. According to Schreber, God normally connects up with human souls only after death, awakening them to life after death, a "*state of Blessedness,*" where the individual's soul (nerve) becomes attached to the nerve of God. Furthermore, he supplies a discussion of how most people have to go through various stages of preparation (somewhat similar to *purgatory*) before achieving this ultimate state, and he even considers hell as part of this process, not a permanent state but a time of purging.

Unfortunately, he then goes into a detailed discussion of how purification involves learning the sacred language of the *chosen people*, God's language, which he claims to be his own language (German). Hard to buy into this. He does work hard at it, though, pointing out how, in the past, other languages were this chosen language, beginning with the language of the Jews (the "Old Testament" of the *Bible*) and continuing through the Persians, the Greco-Romans, and the Franks, before becoming the Germans. He follows up on this less-than-enlightening discussion by claiming that this *transmigration of souls* also resulted in life on other planets.

Then he moves it into more of a connection with his own situation, this time by employing the Buddhist belief in reincarnation. According to Schreber, "From the voices that speak to me, as well as in other ways, I learnt of a number of persons to whom in after life a much lower station was allotted than they had held in the previous one, perhaps as a kind of punishment." (40) This sets him up for his attack on his psychiatrist we encountered in his letter earlier, Flechsig. He writes: "Particularly noteworthy was the case of Mr. v. W., whose soul for a long time profoundly influenced my relation with God and therefore my persona fate, as Flechsig's soul does to this very day. During my stay in Pierson's Asylum (the "Devil's Kitchen"), von W. held there the position of senior attendant—not as a real human being but, as I though then and think still, as a "fleeting-improvised-man," that is to say as a soul temporarily given human shape by divine miracle. He was said to have already led a second life as the "Insurance Agent Marx" on some other planet during the process of transmigration of souls." (41)

The following passages also intermingle insightful attempts to comprehend "Heaven" (that mysterious other world) with personal idiosyncrasies. He writes, for example, "The male state of Blessedness was superior to the female state; the latter seems to have consisted mainly in an uninterrupted feeling of voluptuousness." (42) He also leads into a confusing discussion of two divisions of Heaven, the forecourts (where God dwelt above), as opposed to the posterior realms, which were divided into a division subject to a lower God (Ariman) and an upped God (Ormuzd). This really begins getting strange as he moves into a discussion of Ariman finding the Semites (nations of a brunette race) attractive, while the upper God liked the blonde Aryan people. After a few other comments on his views of Heaven and how they do or don't fit standard Christian views, he ends this section. With it in place, he is now ready to go into the "rent" or rip in the "miraculous structure" God had put together and how he personally is involved.

It relates to the histories of the Flechsig and Schreber families, beginning, he suggests, in the eighteenth century when some member of one family committed *soul murder* on the other. *Soul murder* occurs when a person takes possession of another person's soul in order to prolong the first person's life. Daniel Schreber cannot be sure exactly who committed the original *soul murder* between the families, though at first the voices in his talks with God suggested it was Flechsig, and later it seemed to have been Daniel himself. Later, he became convinced that he was the victim of the *soul murder*. At any rate, he readily admits it's all murky, the details confusing, but suggests it most likely was a man who specialized in *nervous illnesses*, because such a man would be both very intelligent and because he would be interacting with people who held more *nervousness* within them and these are precisely those who would have most contact with the ultimate nerve, God, and who would be the most dangerous to God, as a result. This line of thought leads him to suggest it was likely Daniel Furchtegott Flechsig, who lived in the eighteenth century, a time Daniel Schreber believes had no asylums for the insane, and thus a man who was in that position because he was a country clergyman and might well have connections with God through that profession. It is interesting that Schreber immediately wanders into the possibility of Flechsig possibly having seen "miraculous visions *in a dream*," (43) since a common belief at the time of his writings (certainly Carl Jung's belief) is that dreams are the place to experience such inexplicable events, what might be called the *mysterium tremendum* or the *numinous,* that other world of the *spirit*, the realm of God.

The result of Flechsig's wrongful contact with God is that Schreber has been put into the position of having to save the world. It gets convoluted. He writes:

> No clash of interests between God and individual human beings could arise as long as the latter behaved according to the Order of the World. If despite this such a clash of interest arose in my case because of supposed soul murder, this can only be due to such a marvelous concatenation of

> events as probably never before happened in the history of the world, and I hope will never happen again. Even in such an extraordinary case the Order of the World carries its own remedies for healing the wounds inflicted upon it; the remedy is *Eternity*. Whilst I had earlier (for about two years) believed I had to assume and was forced by my experiences to assume, that if God were permanently tied to my person, all creation on earth would have to perish with the exception of some play-with-miracles in my immediate surroundings, I have had reason lately to modify this idea considerably.
>
> Some people were made very unhappy; I may say that I myself lived through cruel times and endured bitter sufferings. On the other hand six years of uninterrupted influx of God's nerves into my body has led to the total loss of all the states of Blessedness which had accumulated until then and made it impossible for the time being to renew them; the state of *Blessedness* is so to speak suspended and all human beings who have since died or will die *can for the time being not attain to it.* For God's nerves also it is unpleasant and against their will to enter into my body, shown by the continual cries for help which I daily hear in the sky from those parts of the nerves which have become separated from the total mass of nerves. All these losses can however be made good again insofar as an *Eternity* exists, even though total restoration of the previous state may take thousands of years. (44)

Several things are worth pointing out here. First, there is the obvious self-aggrandizement, common to *schizophrenia* and *paranoia*, as it appears he believes he is the person God has entered and it is up to him to, in essence, save the world. Along with this, there are the *voices*. And there is the entrance into a detailed *other* world. There is also the ability to separate from the experiences, what might be called *hallucinations*, and discuss them in a detached, reasonable manner, all characteristics evident in both *schizophrenic* and *paranoiac* people.

At the same time the experiences match up with *shamanic* experiences, with the experiences of those who have encountered the world beyond explanation.

Second, there is the concept of *eternity*, not as a linear endless time, but rather as a *state of existence*. It is worth interrupting Schreber's narrative to explore this concept.

St. Paul offers a memorable passage on it from Christianity, when he writes in a letter to the church at Corinth:

> While we look not at the things which are seen, but at the things which are not seen: for the things which are seen are temporal; but the thing which are not seen are eternal. For we know that if our earthly house of

> this tabernacle were dissolved, we have a building of God, a house not made with hands, eternal in the heavens. (45)

Here it is obvious that *eternity* is contrasted with the *temporal*; it is of the world of the spirit, an *other* world, a world beyond the world of physical sight, beyond the world of the body. The *Catechism of the Catholic Church* connects *eternal* with living *forever* in the grace of God, and refers its readers to the "Gospel of St. John," where Jesus contrasts God with the *world*, by which he means the sensual, physical world. Knowing that he is about to be apprehended by the soldiers of the priests and Pharisees, knowing he is about to be sacrificed, he offers the following prayer, where it is clear he sees existence with God as being in a world other than the world of human existence, at least of physical human existence:

> Father, the hour is come; glorify thy Son, that thy Son also may glorify thee: As thou hast given him power over all flesh, that he should give eternal life to as many as thou hast given him. And this is life eternal, that they might know thee the only true God, and Jesus Christ, whom thou hast sent. I have glorified thee on the earth; I have finished the work which thou gavest me to do. And now, O Father, glorify thou me with thine own self with the glory which I had with thee before the world was. I have manifested thy name unto the men which thou gavest me out of the world; thine they were, and thou gavest them me; and they have kept thy word. Now they have known that all things whatsoever thou hast given me are of thee. For I have given unto them the words which thou gavest me; and they have received them; and have known surely that I came out from thee, and they have believed that thou didst send me. I pray for them; I pray not for the world; but for them which thou has given me, for they are thine. And all mine are thine, and thine are mine; and I am glorified in them. And now I am no more in the world, but these are in the world, and I come to thee, Holy Father, keep through thine own name those whom thou hast given me, that they may be one, as we are. While I was with them in the world, I kept them in thy name; those that thou gavest me I have kept, and none of them is lost, but the son of perdition; that the scripture might be fulfilled. And now come I to thee; and these things I speak in the world, that they might have my joy fulfilled in themselves. I have given them thy word; and the world hath hated them, because they are not of the world, even as I am not of the world. I pray not that thou shouldest take them out of the world, but that thou shouldest keep them from the evil. They are not of the world, even as I am not of the world. Sanctify them through thy truth; thy word is truth. As thou hast sent me into the world, even so have I also sent them into the world. And for their sake I sanctify myself, that they also might be sanctified through the truth. Neither pray I for these alone, but for them also which shall believe on me through their word; That they all may be

> one; as thou, Father, art in me, and I in thee, that they also may be one in us; that the world may believe that thou hast sent me. And the glory which thou gavest me I have given them; that they may be one, even as we are one; I in them, and thou in me, that they may be made perfect in one; and that the world may know that thou hast sent me, and hast loved them, as thou hast loved me. Father, I will that they also, whom thou hast given me, be with me where I am; that they may behold my glory, which thou hast given me; for thou lovest me before the foundation of the world. O righteous Father, the world hath not known thee; but I have known thee, and these have known that thou hast sent me. And I have declared unto them thy name, and will declare it; that the love wherewith thou hast loved me may be in them, and I in them. (46)

It's just as hard to sort through these words of Jesus as through those of Daniel Schreber, but however redundant and wandering this passage might be, it is clear that Jesus (or perhaps more accurately, St. John) is clearly offering two separate worlds, two realities, the one beyond physical existence having a quality of *eternity* about it.

One other Biblical passage is worth highlighting, and this one comes from Moses, who says: "the eternal God is thy refuge, and underneath are the everlasting arms." (47) Here *eternity* and *everlasting* are equated. And such equations become dangerous. Here is a bit of Joseph Campbell's attempt to distinguish:

> Moyers: Jesus did talk of bringing a sword, and I don't believe he meant to use it against your fellow. He meant it in terms of opening the ego—I come to cut you free from the binding ego of your own self.
>
> Campbell: This is what is known in Sanskrit as *viveka*, "discrimination." There is a very important Buddha figure who is shown holding a flaming sword high over his head—and so what is that sword for? It is the sword of discrimination, separating the merely temporal from the eternal. It is the sword distinguishing that which is enduring from that which is merely passing. The tick-tick-tick of time shuts out eternity. We live in this field of time. But what is reflected in this field is an eternal principle made manifest.
>
> Moyers: The experience of the eternal.
>
> Campbell: The experience of what you are.
>
> Moyers: Yes, but whatever eternity is, it is here right now.
>
> Campbell: And nowhere else. Or everywhere else. If you don't experience it here and now, you're not going to get it in heaven. Heaven is not eternal, it's just everlasting.
>
> Moyers: I don't follow that.
>
> Campbell: Heaven and hell are described as forever. Heaven is of unending time. It is not eternal. Eternal is beyond time. The concept of time shuts out eternity. It is over the ground of that deep experience of

eternity that all of these temporal pains and troubles come and go. There is a Buddhist ideal of participating willingly and joyfully in the passing sorrows of the world. Wherever there is time, there is sorrow. But this experience of sorrow moves over a sense of enduring being, which is our own true life.

Moyers: There's some image of Shiva, the god Shiva, surrounded by circles of flame, rings of fire.

Campbell: That's the radiance of the god's dance. Shiva's dance is the universe. In his hair is a skull and a new moon, death and rebirth at the same moment, the moment of becoming. In one hand he has a little drum that goes tick-tick-tick. That is the drum of time, the tick of time which shuts out the knowledge of eternity. We are enclosed in time. But in Shiva's opposite hand there is a flame which burns away the veil of time and opens our minds to eternity. . . .

Moyers: Why do you think so many people have a deep yearning to live forever?

Campbell: That's something I don't understand.

Moyers: Does it come out of the fear of hell and the desirable alternative?

Campbell: That's good Christian doctrine—that at the end of the world there will be a general judgment and those who have acted virtuously will be sent to heaven, and those who have acted in an evil way, to hell.

This is a theme that goes back to Egypt. Osiris is the god who died and was resurrected and in his eternal aspect will sit as judge of the dead. Mummification was to prepare the person to face the god. But an interesting thing in Egypt is that the person going to the god is to recognize his identity with the god. In the Christian tradition, that's not allowed. So if you're saying that the alternative is hell or heaven, well, give me heaven forever. But when you realize that heaven is the beholding of the beatific image of God—that would be a timeless moment. Time explodes, so again eternity is not something everlasting. You can have it right her, now, in your experience of your earthly relationships. . . .

Moyers: Myths are full of the desire for immortality, are they not?

Campbell: Yes. But when immortality is misunderstood as being an everlasting body, it turns into a clown act, really. On the other hand, when immortality is understood to be identification with that which is of eternity in your own life now, it's something else again. (48)

Clearly Joseph Campbell is making a distinction between *eternity* and *chronological time*. This cannot help but bring two realities into existence, a reality that operates according to the rules of logic, math, and science, the reality of physical existence, a reality that can be *explained* and understood and controlled through *reason*; and the reality of that which is beyond logic and reason, that which cannot be *explained* by math and science, that which is beyond the "tick-tick-tick" of time. In the reality of *eternity*, the limitations of logic and science are shattered. *Sanity* denies it; *insanity* embraces it. Whether or not *existence beyond reason* is more than the human *imagination* at work, there is no doubt that humans desire it, for it is what allows for meaning and value in life.

Other important thinkers, philosophers, spiritual people have put Campbell's claims in their own words. Plotinus claims that *eternity* is a "life which endures in its identity, ever-present to itself in its totality." (49) Boethius describes *eternity* as "the complete and unqualified possession of life without limitation." (50) Dante claims that *eternity* is the place where all seasons are present. (51) According to Rennes, the Irish attempted to represent the distinctions between time and eternity by symbolically setting *human time* in the realm of science, a mechanical progress that cannot be manipulated, and *eternity* in the realm of God, flexible and beyond the laws of science. (52) With these dualities in place, *time* comes to represent the struggles involved with *change*, and with *loss*, as it passes and cannot be reclaimed, and ultimately with the struggle against death. *Eternity* becomes a quiet sense of non-struggle, a place of peace and serenity, of bliss. *Time* might be pictured as a hurricane, with *eternity* being the peaceful center.

Daniel Schreber offers his own experience of this when he writes in the middle of his description of the Order of the World being in disarray and the need for he himself to resolve it that "even in such an extraordinary case the Order of the World carries its own remedies for healing the wounds inflicted upon it; the remedy is *Eternity*." (53)

After he has explained his *spiritual* and/or *psychotic* world, i.e., his views of Heaven and the workings of God, he says he is ready to put them into practice, to in fact "prove" them to the extent such things can be proved. Unfortunately, the next section of his writings, one where he promises to go into events concerning other members of his family, especially in relation to the soul murder taking place, were removed by those other members and presumably destroyed. That omitted section is followed by blunt, detailed discussions of his "personal fortunes" while in his psychotic state following two nervous breakdowns, both spent in the Psychiatric Clinic of the University of Leipzig under the care of Dr. Flechsig.

His first stay apparently went by "favourably," and, other than some minor, what he calls "white lies" on the part of Dr. Flechsig, he left it with positive feelings about Dr. Flechsig, even stressing that his wife was so impressed that she kept a picture of Dr. Flechsig on her desk for many years. After this initial stay and release, he spent eight years outside the asylum, years he seems to have lived a normal, happy life. He remembers having several dreams during this time, only one that struck him as "peculiar." He writes, "It was the idea that it really must be rather pleasant to be a woman succumbing to intercourse." It is worth noting his own judgment of it, "This idea was so foreign to my whole nature that I may say I would have rejected it with indignation if fully awake; from what I have experienced since I cannot exclude the possibility that some external influences were at work to implant this idea in me." (54) It is also worth noting that this transsexual part of his experiences has become the central focus of subsequent psycho-analysis of him, beginning with Freud.

Just as his first attack and commitment was the result of tensions caused by an embarrassing defeat in his bid for election to the German Reichstag, the second came as he took on the tensions of being appointed Senatsprasident at the Dresden Superior State court, a position Schreber stresses caused him a great deal of tension, causing him to overwork and experience sleepless nights, nights when he began to hear a crackling noise, a noise he at first thought was mice in the walls, but later came to believe was voices, divine miracles coming to him from the other world. Since these experiences increased rapidly over the next few days, he traveled again to Dr. Flechsig for treatment. It is worth mentioning that one of the medicines he took for a cure or at least relief from his anxiety was morphine, not unusual at the time, but since found to be dangerous. After his first reunion with Flechsig, he felt slightly better, took some sleeping medicine, but could not sleep that night and made a feeble attempt at suicide (which his wife stopped).

Immediately admitted into the asylum, he spends the first few nights being given what he calls mild drugs in an attempt to help him sleep. They don't work. On what he thinks was the fifth night, he has the following experience, worth quoting because it reveals a bit about how asylums worked at the time and suggests that the combination of drugs and insensitive treatment must have factored negatively into his mental condition:

> I was pulled out of bed by two attendants in the middle of the night and taken to a cell fitted out for dements (maniacs) to sleep in. I was already in a highly excited state, in a fever delirium so to speak, and was naturally terrified in the extreme by this event, the reasons for which I did not know. The way led through the billiard room; there, because I had no idea what one intended to do with me and therefore thought I had to resist, a fight started during which I tried to hold fast to the billiard table, but was eventually overpowered and removed to the above-mentioned cell. There I was left to my fate; I spent the rest of the night mostly sleepless in this cell, furnished only with an iron bedstead and some bedding. Regarding myself as totally lost, I made a naturally unsuccessful attempt during the night to

> hang myself from the bedstead with the sheet. I was completely ruled by the idea that there was nothing left for a human being for whom sleep could no longer be procured by all the means of medical art, but to take his life. I knew that this was not permitted in asylums, but I labored under the delusion that when all attempts at cure had been exhausted, one would be discharged—solely for the purpose of making an end to one's life either in one's own home or somewhere else. (55)

The next day Schreber is removed from this cell and put back into a more friendly, conventional room, where he continues in his nervous state but at a much lesser level. He sees Flechsig, has visits from his wife, spends part of several days outside the asylum at his mother's house, and is able to sleep fairly well by taking chloral hydrate. However, he soon begins to become more nervous again, and when his wife is unable to visit him for four days straight, he decides he doesn't want to see her ever again. He also begins to suspect Flechsig is lying to him, to hear the *inner voices*, and to think of himself as what he calls a *seer of spirits* (I have to jump in and highlight how this phrase fits designations of *shamans* and other such people thought to connect with the *other realms*, the world of the *spirit*).

As Schreber goes deeper into his *other world*, he again uses his unique language to attempt to clarify what happens. One important element consists of what he designates as *nerve language*, a form of silent speech (basically thinking without actually speaking). The difference he makes is that the exchanges are not just from within, not just thinking, but communicating with voices outside of the mind. Interestingly, he states that "by this means God has always been able to infuse dreams into a sleeping human being," (56) thus connecting the kind of thinking or knowing of the dream with the kind of thinking or knowing of the world of God, with, in other words, the experiencing of the *mysterium tremendum*.

As he discusses this, Schreber immediately, somewhat casually states that he first experienced this *nerve language* (which takes the form of *divine rays*) "emanating from Professor Flechsig," suggesting yet again the connection of Flechsig with God, and it can hardly be argued but that Schreber has some form of *complex* surrounding *father figures.*

Also interesting, especially in the realm of psychiatry, and especially of Freud's own background, Schreber says that "under normal . . . conditions, use of this *nerve-language* depends only on the will of the person whose nerves are concerned; no human being as such can force another to use this nerve-language," except, he states in a foot note "*hypnotizing* is perhaps an exception." (57)

The connections of *father, father-figure, psychiatrist,* and *God* become even more intertwined. Schreber writes, "In my case, however, since my nervous illness took the above-mentioned critical turn, my nerves have been set in motion *from without* incessantly and without any respite. Divine rays above all have the power influencing the nerves of a human being in this manner; by this means God has always been able to infuse dreams into a sleeping human being. I myself first felt this influence as emanating from Professor Flechsig. The only possible explanation I can think of is that Professor Flechsig in some way knew how to put divine rays to his own use; later, apart from Professor Flechsig's nerves, direct divine rays also entered into contact with my nerves." (58)

Whether it be reduced to a form of Oedipus complex or some other form of father complex, it is obvious that Schreber was affected by some form of psychiatric problem involving a strong male father figure.

Morton Schatzman titles his well respected, though controversial study of this aspect *Soul Murder: Child Abuse and Deprivation*, which he defined as "the apparently willful abuse and neglect of children by adults that are of sufficient intensity and frequency to be traumatic." (59) In it he stresses that he is applying this concept to situations where a child's development has been "profoundly and predominantly negatively affected; what has happened to them has dominated their motivating unconscious fantasies; and they have become subject to the compulsion to repeat the cruelty, violence, neglect, hatred, seduction, and rape of their injurious past."

However, interesting considering Schatzman's focus on child abuse, he expands the landscape:

> Some of Schreber's experience, in his madness, resembles reported experiences of shamans or medicine men, i.e., specialists in ecstasy and the sacred in "archaic" culture (see Eliade, 1960 [*Myths Dreams and Mysteries: the Encounter between contemporary Faiths and Archaic Realities*] and 1964 [*Shamanism*]) Like them he is "chosen" by supernatural powers; the sacred manifests itself through his sharpened senses; and he learns the names and functions of souls and higher beings, the language of birds, and a secret language—in his case, the "basic language [*Groundsprache*]" of God. He experiences visions and trances and sees, hears, and feels events hidden from other men. He says, in "soul language," he is called "the seer of spirits," that is, a man who sees and is in communication with, spirits or departed souls." (*Memoirs*, p.88) Like some shamans, Schreber experiences an increase in light around him, wears women's clothes, and feels himself to be bisexual. Like nearly all shamans, especially during their initiation, he endures bodily torture and dismemberment.

> I think some experiences of many people labeled schizophrenic resemble those of shamans. People widely separated in space, language, culture, and prior spiritual beliefs have had strikingly similar experiences. Could anyone have them? More study is needed here, not only to learn more about "them," the shamans and schizophrenics, but about parts of our minds of which we may be usually unaware." (60)

These concepts and this perspective move the discussion away from the study of a *psychosis* into the realm of those who experience some kind of encounter with the reality beyond literal, normal experience, the mystics, the shamans, the saints. Furthermore, in highlighting Mircea Eliade, Schatzman is suggesting the experience of the *mysterium tremendum* put forth by Rudolf Otto. Mircea Eliade discusses his central concept of the sacred and the profane in several books. *Cosmos and History: The Myth of the Eternal Return* is his seminal book. (61) In it he separates the understanding of time into the "archaic" and the "modern." "Archaic" humans conformed their actions in time to a primordial or mythic time (to the actions of mythic gods and heroes), and thus gave life meaning and value, removing it from the terrors of meaninglessness. In contrast, modern humans see time in a linear manner, therefore seeing themselves as historical, as existing in history. This division, however, is complicated by Judaic prophets, who have a god who intervenes in history and reveals himself through events, thus involving history in human relationships with God, which, according to Mircea Eliade, brings a new element into play, faith. Christianity builds on this, claiming that the Incarnation of Christ is a unique fact, a historical event.

The book most clearly building on Rudolf Otto's *The Idea of the Holy* is Mircea Eliade's *The Sacred and the Profane: The Nature of Religion.* (62) In this book, Mircea Eliade stresses a distinction between what he calls the *sacred* and the *profane* (63), reversing the seemingly obvious and claiming that the *sacred* contains all "reality," and the *profane* only obtains reality to the extent it participates in the *sacred*. (64) All of this centers on the concept of *hierophany* (the manifestation of the sacred), a concept that includes, but is not limited to, the older and more restrictive concept of *theophany* (the manifestation of a god). (65) Thus, from the perspective of religious thought, *hierophanies* give structure and orientation to the world, establishing a sacred order. Since the profane space of nonreligious experience can only be divided up geometrically, it has no "qualitative differentiation and, hence, no orientation [can be] given by virtue of its inherent structure." (66) Thus, profane space gives man no pattern for his behavior. However, in opposition to this profane space, the site of a *hierophany*, which is a "revelation of an absolute reality, opposed to the non-reality of the vast surrounding expanse," (67) has a sacred structure to which religious man conforms himself. For an example of a sacred space demanding a certain response from man, he provides the biblical account of Moses halting before Yahweh's manifestation as a burning bush from *Exodus* 3:5 and removing his shoes. (68)

In the first of Mircea Eliade's books Schatzman highlights, *Myths, Dreams and Mysteries: The Encounter Between Contemporary Faiths and Archaic Realities* (originally published as *Myths, Reves et Mysteries*, 1957), Mircea Eliade builds on his early works and stresses a distinction between the *temporal* reality of the European world of the mid-twentieth century and the *non-temporal* world of previous, what he calls "primitive" civilizations (quickly noting that he realizes this is not a good term but is using it because it is what the general intellectual community uses) and of what he calls the Oriental and other non-European religious ideologies. It is important to him to make this distinction between two types of time and to highlight that Europe has fallen into a "historical" mindset that denies the reality of the mythic world, a world where linear time does not exist, but it might be said all time is at the same time or the *eternal* exists. This he again clarifies as a distinction between the *profane* and the *sacred* (which he works hard to explain is "supremely, the *other* than man—the transpersonal, the transcendent"). (69)

It is worth noting that this division is once again an attempt to distinguish between the literal, physical, sensual world that can be reduced to logic and reason, and a world beyond such reduction. Furthermore, Mircea Eliade immediately puts forth that the world beyond the literal world is the *real* world, suggesting that what most would accept as real is in fact a world of illusion. After his two introductions to the book, he begins chapter one by describing the two worlds, focusing on the mythic worlds (the one that exists beyond linear time):

> We are at last beginning to know and understand the value of the myth, as it has been elaborated in "primitive" and archaic societies—that is, among those groups of mankind where the myth happens to be the very foundation of social life and culture. Now, one fact strikes us immediately: in such societies the myth is thought to express the *absolute truth*, because it narrates a *sacred history*; that is, a transhumant revelation which took place at the dawn of the Great Time, in the holy time of the beginnings (*in illo tempore*). Being *real* and *sacred*, the myth becomes exemplary, and consequently *repeatable*, for it serves as a model, and by the same token as a justification, for all human actions. In other words, a myth is a *true history* of what came to pass at the beginning of Time, and one which provides the pattern for human behavior. In *imitating* the exemplary acts of a god or of a mythic hero, or simply by recounting their adventures, the

> man of an archaic society detaches himself from profane time and magically re-enters the Great Time, the sacred time.
>
> Clearly, what we are dealing with here is a complete reversal of values; whilst current language confuses the myth with "fables," a man of the traditional societies sees it as the *only valid revelation of reality.* (70)

While some of what Mircea Eliade claims here goes beyond the focus of the two realities, his insistence on the world of myth providing exemplary models (which might or might not be so), the exciting claim that the spiritual world, that reality beyond explanation, is the true reality, and the seeming reality of the senses, of logic, of literal existence is the questionable reality comes through clearly. This is what he believes the Western psyche, the European Man has lost because of the emergence of linear time, of history. In embracing linear time, a belief in non-linear time gets lost.

After some unfortunate rambling about Marxism, National Socialism, and Nazi Germany (which reminds us that such writers as Mircea Eliade coming out of WWII were strongly influenced by the current political and military forces that surrounded them), he then again offers his interesting comment on the Christian mythology, which he believes causes considerable problems in claiming to partake of both non-linear and historical time, a mixing of two separate forms of existence. He states:

> Christianity, *by the very fact that it is a religion*, has had to preserve at least one mythic attitude—the attitude towards liturgical time; that is, the rejection of profane time and the periodical recovery of the Great Time, *illud tempus* of "the beginnings."
>
> For the Christian, Jesus Christ is not a mythical personage: on the contrary, he is a historical personage; his greatness itself is founded upon that absolute historicity. For the Christ not only made himself man, "man in general," but accepted the historical condition of the people in whose midst he chose to be born; and he had recourse to no miracle to escape from that historicity—although he worked plenty of miracles in order to modify the "historical situation" of others—by curing the paralytic, raising Lazarus, etc. Nevertheless, the religious experience of the Christian is based upon an imitation of the Christ as *exemplary pattern*, upon the liturgical repetition of the life, death and resurrection of the Lord and upon the *contemporaneity* of the Christian with *illud tempus* which begins with the Nativity at Bethlehem and ends, provisionally, with the Ascension. (71)

The purpose of a sacred ceremony, then, is to bring *profane existence*, which is based on linear time, into contact with *sacred existence* (mythic existence), which is timeless, eternal, a state of all time at the same time.

The Christian ceremony should not be one consisting of a sermon as a lecture relating ethical demands, but an experience that takes those participating into a mythic state of existence beyond ethos, beyond the logic and reason of a lecture.

Mircea Eliade continues:

> Now, we know that the initiation of a transhuman model, the repetition of an exemplary scenario and the breakaway from profane time through a moment which opens out into the Great time, are the essential marks of "mythical behavior"—that is, the behavior of the man of the archaic societies, who finds the very source of his existence in the myth. One is always *contemporary with a myth*, during the time when one repeats it or imitates the gestures of the mythic personages. Kierkegaard's requirement of the true Christian was that he should be a contemporary of the Christ. But even one who is not a "true Christian" in Kierkegaard's sense still is, and cannot *not* be, a contemporary of Christ; for the liturgical time in which the Christian *lives* during the divine service is no longer profane duration but is essentially sacred time, the time in which the Word is made flesh, the *illud tempus* of the Gospels. A Christian is not taking part in a commemoration of the Passion of Christ, as he might be joining in the annual celebration of the Fourth of July or the Eleventh of November, for example. He is not commemorating an event but re-actualizing a mystery. For the Christian, Jesus dies and resurrects before him *hic et nunc*. Through the mystery of the Passion or of the Resurrection, the Christian dispels profane time and is integrated into time primordial and holy. (72)

This brings into play the concept of *incarnation*, the central Christian doctrine that God became flesh, assumed a human nature in the form of Jesus Christ, the Son of God and the second person of the Trinity, perfectly uniting the divine nature of the Son of God with human nature in one divine person, Jesus, making him both truly God and truly man. The theological term for this is hypostatic union: the Second Person of the Holy Trinity, God the Son, became flesh when he was miraculously conceived in the womb of the Virgin Mary. Biblical passages traditionally referenced in connection with the doctrine of the *Incarnation* include John 1:14 and Colossians 2:9.

Christians, then, connect the physical, sensual world, the profane world of the body to the invisible, sacred world of the spirit through Jesus Christ, and this is most importantly accomplished in the *Eucharist* or *Holy Communion*.

Notes

1. *The Flight of the Wild Gander,* New World Library, 3rd. ed., 2002, p. 189.
2. James Mooney, "Myths of the Cherokee," Nineteenth Annual Report of the Bureau of American Ethnology, pt. 1, Washington, D. C.: Bureau of American Ethnology, pp. 401-402.
3. The Night has a Naked Soul, Syracuse Univ. Press: Syracuse, New York, 1997.
4. The holy: an inquiry into the non-rational factor in the idea of the divine and its relation to the rational, 1917; rpt., trans., John w. Harvey, London: Oxford Univ. Press, 1926, p. 10.
5. mayoclinic.org; see also, Castle D, Wesseley S, Der G, Murray RM (1991), "The incidence of operationally defined schizophrenia," British Journal of Psychiatry 159: pp. 790–794; Bhugra D (2006). "The global prevalence of schizophrenia," PloS Medicine 2 (5), pp. 372–373; Goldner EM, Hsu L, Waraich P, Somers JM (2002). "Prevalence and incidence studies of schizophrenic disorders: a systematic review of the literature". Canadian Journal of Psychiatry 47 (9), pp. 833–43; and American Psychiatric Association (2000). "Schizophrenia." Diagnostic and statistical manual of mental disorders: DSM-IV. Washington, DC: American Psychiatric Publishing, Inc., ISBN 0-89042-024-6.
6. www.pysch.org.
7. Schneider, K. (1959) *Clinical Psychopathology.* New York: Grune and Stratton.Bertelsen, A (2002). "Schizophrenia and Related Disorders: Experience with Current Diagnostic Systems". *Psychopathology* 35, pp. 89–93; Jakobsen KD; Frederiksen JN, Hansen T, Jansson LB, Parnas J, Werge T (2005). "Reliability of clinical ICD-10 schizophrenia diagnoses". *Nordic Journal of Psychiatry* 59 (3), pp. 209–12. Bentall, Richard P. (1992). *Reconstructing schizophrenia.* New York: Routledge. ISBN 0-415-07524-6.Boyle, Mary (2002). *Schizophrenia: a scientific delusion?.* New York: Routledge. ISBN 0-415-22718-6. Verdoux H; van Os J (2002). "Psychotic symptoms in non-clinical populations and the continuum of psychosis". *Schizophrenia Research* 54 (1-2): 59–65. doi:10.1016/S0920-9964(01)00352-8. PMID 11853979. Johns LC; van Os J (2001). "The continuity of psychotic experiences in the general population". *Clinical Psychology Review* 21 (8): 1125–41. doi:10.1016/S0272-7358(01)00103-9. PMID 11702510. Peters ER; Day S, McKenna J, Orbach G (2005). "Measuring delusional ideation: the 21-item Peters et al. Delusions Inventory (PDI)". *Schizophrenia Bulletin* 30: 1005–22. PMID 15954204. David AS (1999). "On the impossibility of defining delusions". *Philosophy, Psychiatry and Psychology* 6 (1): 17–20.
http://muse.jhu.edu/journals/philosophy_psychiatry_and_psychology. Retrieved on 24 February 2008. Tsuang MT; Stone WS, Faraone SV (2000). "Toward reformulating the diagnosis of schizophrenia". *American Journal of Psychiatry* 157 (7): 1041–50; Rosenhan D (1973). "On being sane in insane places". *Science* 179: 250–8. doi:10.1126/science.179.4070.250. PMID 4683124. McGorry PD; Mihalopoulos C, Henry L, Dakis J, Jackson HJ, Flaum M, Harrigan S, McKenzie D, Kulkarni J, Karoly R (1995). "Spurious precision: procedural validity of diagnostic assessment in psychotic disorders". *American Journal of Psychiatry* 152

(2): 220–3. PMID 7840355. Bentall, Richard P.; Read, John E; Mosher, Loren R. (2004). *Models of Madness: Psychological, Social and Biological Approaches to Schizophrenia.* Philadelphia: Brunner-Routledge. ISBN 1-58391-906-6. Sato M (2004). "Renaming schizophrenia: a Japanese perspective". *World Psychiatry* 5 (1): 53–5. PMID 16757998. Schizophrenia term use 'invalid'. BBC News Online, (9 October 2006). Retrieved on 2007-05-16. Green, Michael (2001). *Schizophrenia revealed: from neurons to social interactions.* New York: W.W. Norton. ISBN 0-393-70334-7.

8. *The Archetypes of the Collective Unconscious,* p. 38-39.
9. *The Archetypes of the Collective Unconscious,* p. 38-39
10. *Das Pangymnastikon*, Leipzig, 1869, p. 2.
11. *Das Pangymnastikon*, Leipzig, 1869, p. 4.
12. *Das Pangymnastikon*, Leipzig, 1869, p. 4.
13. Quoted in William g. Niederland, "Schrebers 'angewumderte' Kindheitswelt," *Psyche* 22, no. 3 (1969): 200; trans., Benjamin Gregg. Niederland's analyses of D. G. M. Schreber's writing reveal the extent to which the father's text furnished the material for the son's delusional ideas. The voices' language is derived often literally from that of the father, while the orthopedic apparatus invented by the father recur in the son's book as a "head-compression machine" or a the "compression-of-the-chest miracle"; taken from the endnotes to the introduction to *Memoirs of My Nervous Illness,* by Samuel M. Weber, p. l.
14. "Introduction," *Memoirs of My Nervous Illness,* Harvard University Press, 1988, p. x.
15. Franz Baumayer, "Der Fall Schreber," *Psyche* 9, 1955-1956, p. 515.
16. *Dementia Praecox or The Group of Schizophrenias.* Trans. By J. Zinkin, New York: International Universities Press, 1950; referred to in *Soul Murder: Persecution in the Family*, Morton Schatzman, Random House, 1973, pp. 8-9.
17. "Psych-analytic Notes on an Autobiographical Account of a Case of Paranoia (Dementia Paranoide)," *Standard Edition of the Complete Psychological Works of Sigmund Freud,* ed. And trans., James Strachey, Hogarth Press, 1953-1974, vol. 12, pp. 17-18.
18. "The Miracled-Up World of Schreber's Childhood," *Psychoanal, Stud. Child.,* vol.14: pp. 383-41.
19. Random House, 1973.
20. Baumayer, "Der Fall Schreber," *Psyche* 9, 1955-1956, p. 515.
21. Baumayer, "Der Fall Schreber," p. 514.
22. *Memoirs of My Nervous Illness,* Harvard University Press, 1988, p. 63.
23. Baumayer, "Der Fall Schreber," p. 515.
24. "Preface," *Memoirs of My Nervous Illness,* Harvard University Press, 1988, pp. 31-32.
25. "Open Letter to Professor Flechsig," *Memoirs of My Nervous Illness,* Harvard University Press, 1988, pp. 33-36.
26. *Memoirs of My Nervous Illness,* Harvard University Press, 1988, p. 41.
27. *Memoirs of My Nervous Illness,* Harvard University Press, 1988, p. 42.
28. *Memoirs of My Nervous Illness,* Harvard University Press, 1988, p. 43.
29. *Memoirs of My Nervous Illness,* Harvard University Press, 1988, p. 42-43.

30. *Memoirs of My Nervous Illness,* Harvard University Press, 1988, p. 42.
31. *Memoirs of My Nervous Illness,* Harvard University Press, 1988, pp. 45-46.
32. *Memoirs of My Nervous Illness,* Harvard University Press, 1988, p. 46.
33. *Memoirs of My Nervous Illness,* Harvard University Press, 1988, p. 46.
34. *Memoirs of My Nervous Illness,* Harvard University Press, 1988, pp. 46-47.
35. *Memoirs of My Nervous Illness,* Harvard University Press, 1988, p. 47.
36. *Memoirs of My Nervous Illness,* Harvard University Press, 1988, p. 47.
37. *Memoirs of My Nervous Illness,* Harvard University Press, 1988, p. 48.
38. *Memoirs of My Nervous Illness,* Harvard University Press, 1988, p. 48.
39. *Memoirs of My Nervous Illness,* Harvard University Press, 1988, p. 48.
40. *Memoirs of My Nervous Illness,* Harvard University Press, 1988, p. 51.
41. *Memoirs of My Nervous Illness,* Harvard University Press, 1988, p. 51.
42. *Memoirs of My Nervous Illness,* Harvard University Press, 1988, p. 52.
43. *Memoirs of My Nervous Illness,* Harvard University Press, 1988, p. 57.
44. *Memoirs of My Nervous Illness,* Harvard University Press, 1988, pp. 60-61.
45. *King James Bible,* 2 Cor. 4:18- 5:1.
46. *King James Bible,* 14 St. John.
47. *King James* Bible, Deuteronomy, Chapter 33, xxvii.
48. *Joseph Campbell: The Power of Myth with Bill Moyers*, ed. Betty Sue Flowers, Doubleday, 1988, pp.279-282.
49. *Enneads* 3:7.
50. *De consolation* 5, Prosa 6.
51. *Paradiso* 17:18.
52. *Ogam—tradition celique 18*, pp. 148-150.
53. *Memoirs of My Nervous Illness,* Harvard University Press, 1988, p. 60.
54. *Memoirs of My Nervous Illness,* Harvard University Press, 1988, p. 63.
55. *Memoirs of My Nervous Illness,* Harvard University Press, 1988, p. 66.
56. *Memoirs of My Nervous Illness,* Harvard University Press, 1988, 69.
57. *Memoirs of My Nervous Illness,* Harvard University Press, 1988, p. 69.
58. *Memoirs of My Nervous Illness,* Harvard University Press, 1988, p. 69.
59. *Soul Murder Revisited: Thoughts About Therapy, Hate, Love, and Memory,* Yale Univ., 1990.
60. *Soul Murder: Persecution in the Family*, Morton Schatzman, Random House, 1973, pp. 7-8.
61. *Cosmos and History: The Myth of the Eternal Return,* 1954; rpt., Bollinger, 1971.
62. trans. W. Trask, London: Harcourt Brace Jovanovich, 1959.
63. *Patterns in Comparative Religion*, p.1
64. *Cosmos and History: The Myth of the Eternal Return*, 1954; rpt., Bollinger, 1971, p.5.
65. *The Sacred and the Profane*, p.20-22; *Shamanism*, p. xiii.
66. *The Sacred and the Profane*, p.22.
67. *The Sacred and the Profane*, p.21.
68. *The Sacred and the Profane*, p.20.

69. *Myths, Dreams and Mysteries: The Encounter Between Contemporary Faiths and Archaic Realities* (originally published as *Mythes, Reves et Mysteries*, 1957), translated by Philip Mairet, Harper, 1960, p. 18.
70. *Myths, Dreams and Mysteries: The Encounter Between Contemporary Faiths and Archaic Realities* (originally published as *Mythes, Reves et Mysteries*, 1957), translated by Philip Mairet, Harper, 1960, pp. 23-24.
71. *Myths, Dreams and Mysteries: The Encounter Between Contemporary Faiths and Archaic Realities* (originally published as *Mythes, Reves et Mysteries*, 1957), translated by Philip Mairet, Harper, 1960, p. 30.
72. *Myths, Dreams and Mysteries: The Encounter Between Contemporary Faiths and Archaic Realities* (originally published as *Mythes, Reves et Mysteries*, 1957), translated by Philip Mairet, Harper, 1960, pp. 30-31.

MIRACLES

Falling From

Mircea Eliade's views inform the *Eucharist* or Holy Communion. The term *Eucharist* comes from the Greek noun *eucharistía* (εὐχαριστία) a combination of *eú-* "good, well" and *cháris* "favor, grace." *Eucharistéō* (εὐχαριστῶ) is the usual verb for "to thank" in the *Septuagint* (the *Koine* or commonly spoken Greek version of the *Hebrew Bible* that was translated in stages between the third and first centuries BC in Alexandria) and in the *New Testament*, where it is found in the major texts concerning the Lord's Supper, resulting in it being used to mean the rite of *Holy Communion* and/or the bread and wine consumed during this rite:

> And as they did eat, Jesus took bread, and blessed, and brake it, and gave to them, and said, Take, eat: this is my body.
> And he took the cup, and when he had given thanks, (*eucharistéō*), he gave it to them: and they all drank of it.
> And he said unto them, This is my blood of the new testament, which is shed for many.
> Verily I say unto you, I will drink no more of the fruit of the vine, until that day that I drink it new in the kingdom of God. (St. Mark, 14, 22-25)

> And as they were eating, Jesus took bread, and blessed it, and brake it, and gave it to the disciples, and said, Take, eat; this is my body.
> And he took the cup, and gave thanks (*eucharistéō*), and gave it to them, saying, Drink ye all of it;
> For this is my blood of the new testament, which is shed for many for the remission of sins.
> But I say unto you, I will not drink henceforth of this fruit of the vine, until that day when I drink it new with you in my Father's kingdom. (St. Matthew, 26, 26-29)

> And he said unto them, with desire I have desired to eat this Passover with you before I suffer:
> For I say unto you, I will not any more eat thereof, until it be fulfilled in the kingdom of God.
> And he took the cup, and gave thanks (*eucharistéō*), and said, Take this, and divide it among yourselves'
> For I say unto you, I will not drink of the fruit of the vine, until the kingdom of God shall come.
> And he took bread, and gave thanks, and brake it, and gave unto them, saying, This is my body which is given for you: this do in remembrance of me.
> Likewise also the cup after supper, saying, This cup is the new testament in my blood, which is shed for you. (St. Luke, 22, 15-20)

> And when he had given thanks (*eucharistéō*), he brake it, and said, Take, eat: this is my body, which is broken for you: this do in remembrance of me.
> After the same manner also he took the cup, when he had supped, saying, this cup is the new testament in my blood: this do ye, as oft as ye drink it, in remembrance of me.
> For as often as ye eat this bread, and drink this cup, ye do show the Lord's death till he come.
> Wherefore whosoever shall eat this bread, and drink this cup of the Lord, unworthily, shall be guilty of the body and blood of the Lord.
> But let a man examine himself, and so let him eat of that bread, and drink of that cup.
> For he that eateth and drinketh unworthily, eateth and drinketh damnation to himself, not discerning the Lord's body.
> For this cause many are weak and sickly among you, and many sleep.
> For if we would judge ourselves, we should not be judged.
> But when we are judged, we are chastened of the Lord, that we should not be condemned with the world.
> Wherefore, my brethren, when ye come together to eat, tarry one for another.
> And if any man hunger, let him eat at home; that ye come not together unto condemnation. And the rest will I set in order when I come. (1 Corinthians, 11, 24-34) (1)

Here we encounter a central division in Christian theology. Many denominations consider the *Eucharist* or *Holy Communion* to be a *sacrament*, defined by St. Augustine as an outward sign of inward grace instituted by Christ for our sanctification (2). In other words, the *Eucharist* causes divine grace, the gift of God for *divine salvation*. Roman Catholicism and Eastern Orthodoxy believe that the consecrated elements truly become the body and blood of Jesus Christ through *transubstantiation*, and that it is therefore theologically incorrect to refer to them, after consecration, just as bread and wine or even just as holy bread and wine. The consecrated elements retain the appearance and attributes of bread and wine but are in reality the body and blood of Christ. The words of the Ethiopic liturgy are representative of the faith of Oriental Orthodoxy: "I believe, I believe, I believe and profess to the last breath that this is the body and the blood of our Lord God and Savior Jesus Christ, which he took from our Lady, the holy and immaculate Virgin Mary, the Mother of God."

The Eastern Orthodox Church Synod of Jerusalem states: "We believe the Lord Jesus Christ to be present, not typically, nor figuratively, nor by superabundant grace, as in the other Mysteries, ... but truly and really, so that after the consecration of the bread and of the wine, the bread is transmuted, transubstantiated, converted and transformed into the true

Body Itself of the Lord, Which was born in Bethlehem of the ever-Virgin Mary, was baptized in the Jordan, suffered, was buried, rose again, was received up, sitteth at the right hand of the God and Father, and is to come again in the clouds of Heaven; and the wine is converted and transubstantiated into the true Blood Itself of the Lord, Which, as He hung upon the Cross, was poured out for the life of the world." (3)

The Western Catholic Church greets the *Eucharist* with the words of a Latin hymn that translates: "Hail, true body, born of Mary Virgin, and which truly suffered and was immolated on the cross for mankind! (4) None of these Churches considers the *Eucharist* as a lifeless corpse and mere blood, but as the whole Christ, body and blood, soul and divinity; nor do they perceive the persisting outward appearances of bread and wine as a mere illusion. All agree that this occurs "in a way surpassing understanding." The Catechism of the Catholic Church, 1333 calls this *transubstantiation* or, in Greek, *metousiosis*. Furthermore, the presence of Christ in the *Eucharist* is of an order different from the presence of Christ in the other sacraments where he is present by his power rather than by the reality of his body and blood, the basis of the phrase *Real Presence*, which involves the belief that *Jesus Christ is really present* in what was previously just bread and wine, not merely present in symbol, metaphor, or through his power, differing from those who believe that, in objective reality, the elements of the *Eucharist* remain unchanged. In Mircea Eliade's construct, these forms of Christianity are attempting to break *profane* time and enter into *sacred* time during the *Eucharist*.

The Protestant Reformation brought new variations on the meaning of the *Eucharist*, and it was the central dispute that broke apart the mainstream German and Swiss Protestant reformers at the Colloquy of Marburg in 1529. The dispute turned on the extent to which Christ was thought to be present in the bread and wine, with Huldrych (or Ulrich) Zwingli claiming that the *Eucharist* was a mere memorial of the Last Supper and there was no change in the bread and wine at all (the *Eucharist* is simply the Lord's Supper). Luther, on the other hand, held to the doctrine of *sacramental union* (often erroneously designated *consubstantiation*) in which, during the *Eucharist*, both the bread and wine and Christ's body and blood co-existed. It all came down to differing interpretations of Jesus' words at the Last Supper, "this is my body" and "this is my blood." Zwingli, basing his views on the belief that "the body and spirit are such essentially different things that whichever one you take it cannot be the other," insisted that "is" means "signifies." (5)

Luther contradicted this, and put forth the *Eucharist* as a *sacramental union*, a union where both natures of Christ remain distinct, the bread and wine exist as bread and wine at the same time as they are united with the body and blood of Christ, i.e., in *Real Presence*:

> Why then should we not much more say in the Supper, "This is my body," even though bread and body are two distinct substances, and the word "this" indicates the bread? Here, too, out of two kinds of objects a union has taken place, which I shall call a "sacramental union," because Christ's body and the bread are given to us as a sacrament. This is not a natural or personal union, as is the case with God and Christ. It is also perhaps a different union from that which the dove has with the Holy Spirit, and the flame with the angel, but it is also assuredly a sacramental union. (6)

This view was further asserted in the *Wittenberg Concord of 1536* and the *Formula of Concord*, where the term was joined with *circumlocution* (i.e., "in, with, and under the forms of bread and wine"; *in, cum et sub pane*):

> For the reason why, in addition to the expressions of Christ and St. Paul (the bread in the Supper is the body of Christ or the communion of the body of Christ), also the forms: under the bread, with the bread, in the bread [the body of Christ is present and offered], are employed, is that by means of them the papistical transubstantiation may be rejected and the sacramental union of the unchanged essence of the bread and of the body of Christ indicated." (7)

It was also supported by quoting the words of Christ from the Last Supper, the Words of Institution:

> Thus it is not our word or speaking but the command and ordinance of Christ that, from the beginning of the first Communion until the end of the world, make the bread the body and the wine the blood that are daily distributed through our ministry and office. Again, "Here, too, if I were to say over all the bread there is, 'This is the body of Christ,' nothing would happen, but when we follow his institution and command in the Lord's Supper and say, 'This is my body,' then it is his body, not because of our speaking or of our efficacious word, but because of his command in which he has told us so to speak and to do and has attached his own command and deed to our speaking."(8)

While this view has at times been conjoined with *consubstantiation*, because it asserts the simultaneous presence of four essences in the *Eucharist*, the consecrated bread, the Body of Christ, the consecrated wine, and the Blood of Christ, it differs in that it does not claim a local (real time, physical) presence of Christ in the bread and wine. (9)

Furthermore, Martin Luther distinguished his doctrine of the *Sacramental Union* from that of *transubstantiation* and *impanation* (the theological doctrine that the body and blood of Christ are present in the bread and wine after they are consecrated but denying any change in the substance of the bread and wine): "... we do not make Christ's body out of the bread ... Nor do we say that his body comes into existence out of the bread [i.e. *impanation*]. We say that his body, which long ago was made and came into existence, is present when we say, "This is my body." For Christ commands us to say not, "Let this become my body," or, "Make my body there," but, "This is my body." (10)

In other words, in Mircea Eliade's schema, *sacred* and *profane* time remain separated, yet they both exist in the same space at the same time.

In Anglican theology, a sacrament is an outward and visible sign of an inward and spiritual grace. In the *Eucharist*, the outward and visible sign is that of bread and wine, while the inward and spiritual grace is that of the Body and Blood of Christ. A classic Anglican aphorism in regard to the debate on the *Eucharist* is expressed in a poem by John Donne: "He was the Word that spake it; He took the bread and brake it; And what that Word did make it; I do believe and take it." (11)

Anglicans generally and officially believe in the *Real Presence* of Christ in the *Eucharist*, but the specifics of that belief range from *transubstantiation* or *metousiosis*, sometimes with *Eucharistic adoration* (Anglo-Catholics or High-Church Anglicans), to something similar to a belief in a *pneumatic presence* (Broad-Church Anglicans). The oldest of the various Anglican devotional societies, the Confraternity of the Blessed Sacrament, was founded largely to promote and re-affirm belief in the *real presence* amongst Anglicans. However, a few still reject the doctrine of the *Real Presence* altogether (Low-Church Anglicans).

The Anglican *Thirty-nine Articles* state that the doctrine of *transubstantiation*, as understood by those who drew up the text, denies the nature of a sacrament as an outward, visible sign that conveys an inward, spiritual grace. For some Anglicans, whose mysticism is intensely *incarnational*, it is important that God has used the *profane and temporal* as a means of giving people the *transcendent and eternal*. They consider the presence to belong to the realm of spirit and eternity, and not to be about corporeal-fleshiness, which is not to say that they accept only a *pneumatic* presence. Instead, they strongly argue to allow *the mystery to remain a mystery*. They rebuke the idea that one material substance gets substituted for another. (Roman Catholic doctrine insists that the material substance, being part of what is open to the senses, is in no way altered, and that the philosophical-sense substance or inner reality is *converted* into that of the body and blood of Christ, not *substituted* by it.)

Furthermore, from some Anglican perspectives the *Real Presence* of Christ in the Holy Eucharist does not imply that Jesus Christ is present materially or locally. This is in accord with the definition of the Roman Catholic Church, as expressed, for instance by St. Thomas Aquinas, who, while saying that *the whole Christ* is present in the sacrament, also said that this presence was not "as in a place." Real does not mean material: the lack of the latter does not imply the absence of the former. The *Eucharist* is not intrinsic to Christ as a body part is to a body, but extrinsic as His instrument to convey Divine Grace. Some Anglicans believe this is compatible with different theories of Christ's Presence, *transubstantiation, consubstantation* or *virtualism,* without getting entangled in the particulars of a metamorphosis or the impossibility of explaining a *mystery* of God's own doing. In other words, as with the other forms of Christianity, these Anglicans ultimately reach the point of embracing the intertwining of the two realities, one profane, one sacred, as beyond explanation. And thus, at least in the views of the Anglican and Roman Catholic Joint Preparatory Commission, Anglican and Roman Catholic theologians can claim to have "reached substantial agreement on the doctrine of the Eucharist." (12) They accept that there are two realities, the literal world of the body and of the senses, and the spiritual or other reality. As with all Christians (by definition), they believe that Christ is the key to merging these two realities. How it is accomplished, after all of the endless discussion by the most spiritual and intelligent of people throughout history, remains, and perhaps must remain a mystery.

Christian explanations of the *Eucharist*, in other words, have reached what Joseph Campbell refers to as "the edge between what can be known and what is never to be discovered because it is a mystery that transcends all human research. The source of life." (13)

Yet again, the two realities, the profane and the sacred variously come together and remain separate, and thus the mystery remains or receives explanations that ultimately dissolve into the very dust they come from, leaving the inexplicable only resolved through faith, or if by any other form, not through the clear eyes of conscious thought, but through the eyes of the dream, where the phantoms of that which is beyond the burning rays of the sun appear and lure those with second sight to enter and experience the deepest enigmas of existence.

The United Methodist Church holds to the doctrine that Jesus Christ is present in *Holy Communion*, and through him and the power of the Holy Spirit, God joins humans at the altar during the ceremony. This is more than a merely symbolic joining. Christ is present through the followers gathered in his name (Matthew, 18:20), through the Biblical Word both proclaimed and enacted, and through the bread and wine shared (1 Corinthians 11:23-26).

Falling in line with founder John Wesley's views, they generally affirm Holy Communion as a *means of Grace* (a way for God to bestow *Grace*) by which the *real presence* of Christ is communicated to the believer. (14) Just how this is accomplished remains a mystery. They reject the doctrine of *transubstantiation.* (15) In 2004, they put forth *This Holy Mystery*, a document stressing this belief in the *Real Presence*, and anamnesis (remembrance) as a re-presentation of Jesus Christ, stating that this anamnesis or re-presentation is so power it makes God acts in the past present in the present.

In the invocation of the Great Thanksgiving, the minister prays: "Pour out your Holy spirit on us gathered here, and on these gifts of bread and wine. Make them be for us the body and blood of Christ that we may be for the world the body of Christ, redeemed by his blood."

This is, however, for most Methodists, as far as they go in attempting to define the *Real Presence*, asserting that Jesus is present, that the means of this presence is a Holy *Mystery*.

In the mid-sixteenth century, John Calvin, rejected the Catholic doctrine of transubstantiation and the treatment of the *Eucharist* as a sacrifice, condemned the Lutheran doctrine of sacramental union in which Christ was "in, with and under" the elements, and put forth a view similar to Zwingli's, but moved beyond a purely symbolic stance and claimed that faith was nourished and strengthened through communion as a result of the participation of the Holy Spirit ("the spirit truly unites things separated in space"). For him, the *Eucharistic* rite was "a secret too sublime for my mind to understand or words to express. I experience it rather than understand it." (16) By faith (not a mere mental apprehension), and in the Holy Spirit, the partaker beholds God incarnate, and in the same sense touches him with hands, so that by eating and drinking of bread and wine Christ's presence penetrates to the heart of the believer more nearly than food swallowed with the mouth can enter in. If one does not believe, then partaking in Holy Communion condemns him. The food itself is unchanged and not in and of itself holy.

Calvinism, and the various Reformed Churches based on his views have taught that Christ's body is seated to at the right hand of God in Heaven, and thus cannot be present in the bread and wine. Furthermore, the bread and wine do not transform into his body in any physical or literal sense. However, there is also the belief that during Holy Communion, not just the spirit but also the body of Christ are received though the Holy Spirit (if those partaking are "worthy" and have "faith"). Thus, in some way, the Holy Spirit units the true Christian with Jesus even though they are separated by a great distance. (17) The Presbyterian and Reformed Free churches continue to debate the details of how all this works, and in 1997 the Evangelical Lutheran church in America, the Presbyterian Church in the United States of America, the Reformed Church in America, and the United Church of Christ came together to produce *A Formula of Agreement,* which states: "The theological diversity within our common confession provides both the complementary need for a full and adequate witness to the gospel (mutual affirmation) and the corrective reminder that every theological approach is a partial and incomplete witness to the Gospel (mutual admonition)." (18)

More specifically, in reference to the *Real Presence*, the portion titled Marburg Revisited states:

> During the Reformation both Reformed and Lutheran Churches exhibited an evangelical intention when they understood the Lord's Supper in the light of the saving act of God in Christ. Despite this common intention, different terms and concepts were employed which. . . led to mutual misunderstanding and misrepresentation. Properly interpreted, the differing terms and concepts were often complementary rather than contradictory. (19)

and further:

> In the Lord's Supper the risen Christ imparts himself in body and blood, given up for all, through his word of promise with bread and wine....we proclaim the death of Christ through which God has reconciled the world with himself. We proclaim the presence of the risen Lord in our midst. Rejoicing that the Lord has come to us, we await his future coming in glory....Both of our communions, we maintain, need to grow in appreciation of our diverse eucharistic traditions, finding mutual enrichment in them. At the same time both need to grow toward a further deepening of our common experience and expression of the mystery of our Lord's Supper. (20)

Baptists and many of the Evangelical Churches deny *Real Presence* completely, and have some form of Zwingli view, generally seeing the *Eucharist* as simply a symbolic meal, a memorial of the Last Supper and the Passion where nothing miraculous takes place. Roman Catholics, Eastern Orthodox, Anglicans and Lutherans and other churches that believe in the doctrine of the Real Presence of Christ, require ordained clergy officiate the Eucharist. Some other groups, mainly Protestants, who view consecration as a "setting aside," require that pastors, elders, or deacons preside.

Many of the most learned and seriously spiritual people throughout history have joined in this discussion, each rephrasing the beliefs and concepts slightly in attempting to clarify how the *spiritual* world of God interacts with the *profane* world of humans through Jesus Christ in the central ceremony of the Christian religion. Whatever particular slant one takes on this commingling of the two separate realities is not the point as much as the fact that the belief in two separate realities drives the debate. In other words, large numbers of the most intelligent, educated, and serious of humans have lived their lives under a basic assumption that there is a reality beyond mere physical existence.

Way to Go

For Christians, Christ is the connecting link between the two realities, though others have most certainly experienced this interaction in the form of *miracles. Webster's New Twentieth Century Dictionary* defines a *miracle* in theology as "an event or effect that apparently contradicts known scientific laws and is hence thought to be due to supernatural causes, especially to an act of God." (21) The *King James Version of the Holy Bible* lists 84 *miracles* described in "The Old Testament" and 130 in "The New Testament." (22) In each case at least one person has experienced something beyond explanation, something of the world of the spirit, of the world of the *sacred*, of the *numinous*, the *Mysterium Tremendum*, the *eternal* reality beyond the ticking of time.

Moses clearly was one of those who experienced this *other world*, this reality beyond the laws of science. An Israelite, born of the house of Levi during a time when the Pharaoh of Egypt had ordered all male children of Israelites killed for fear they might multiply into too large an army and overthrow him, Moses escaped death by being floated down a river and discovered by the Pharaoh's daughter, who raised him as her own son. When he came of age, he saw the evil about him, the mistreatment of the Hebrews by the Egyptians, and he killed an Egyptian. This made him a criminal, and he was forced to flee and hide from the Pharaoh. For a time he dwelt with Reuel, married his daughter Zipporah, who bore him a son, Gershom. During this time the Pharaoh died, and the Israelites complained to God about their mistreatment. God heard them and chose Moses to lead them out of bondage.

This is where Moses becomes the Judeo-Christian equivalent of a shaman, of a special person who experiences miracles:

> Now Moses kept the flock of Jethro his father-in-law, the priest of Midian: and he led the flock to the backside of the desert, and came to "the mountain of god, *even* to Horeb.
> And the angel of the Lord appeared unto him in a flame of fire out of the midst of a bush: and he looked, and, behold, the bush burned with fire, and the bush *was* not consumed.
> And Moses said, I will now turn aside, and see this great sight, why the bush is not burnt.
> And when the Lord saw that he turned aside to see, God called unto him out of the midst of the bush, and said, Moses, Moses. And he said, Here *am* I.
> And he said, Draw not nigh hither: put off thy shoes from off thy feet, for the place whereon thou standest *is* holy ground.
> Moreover he said, I *am* the God of thy father, the God of Abraham, the God of Isaac, and the God of Jacob. And Moses hid his face; for he was afraid to look upon God. (Exodus 3, 1-6)

Moses has *looked upon the face of God*, the sacred, the powerful mysterious, *invisible* force that informs literal existence.

God proceeds to tell Moses that he must deliver the Israelites out of bondage and gives him instructions for doing this. When Moses replies that his people will not believe him, will not believe that he has really seen the face of God, God provides a second miracle (actually two, and suggests a third):

> And the Lord said unto him, What is that in thine hand? And he said, A rod.
> And he said, Cast it on the ground. And he cast it on the ground, and it became serpent; and Moses fled from before it.
> And the Lord said unto Moses, Put forth thine hand, and take it by the tail. And he put forth his hand, and caught it, and it became a rod in his hand:
> That they may believe that the Lord God of their fathers, and the God of Abraham, the God of Isaac, and the God of Jacob, hath appeared unto thee.
> And the Lord said furthermore unto him, Put now thine hand into thy bosom. And he put his hand into his boson: and when he took it out, behold, his hand *was* leprous as snow.
> And he said, Put thine hand into thy bosom again. And he put his hand into his bosom, and, behold, it was turned again as his *other* flesh.
> And it shall come to pass, if they will not believe thee, neither hearken to the voice of the first sign, that they will believe the voice of the latter sign.
> And it shall come to pass, if they will not believe also these two signs, neither hearken unto thy voice, that thou shalt take of the water of the river, and pour *it* upon the dry *land*: and the water which thou takest out of the river shall become blood upon the dry *land.* (Exodus 4, 2-9)

It's one thing for Moses to experience these *miracles*, but the *Bible* is going to take this further and have entire groups of people experience *miracles*:

> And Moses *was* fourscore years old, and Aaron fourscore and three years old, when they spake unto Pharaoh.
> And the Lord spake unto Moses and unto Aaron, saying,
> When Pharaoh shall speak unto you, saying, Show a miracle for you: then thou shalt say unto Aaron, Take thy rod, and cast *it* before Pharaoh, *and* it shall become a serpent.
> And Moses and Aaron went in unto Pharaoh, and they did so as the Lord had commanded: and Aaron cast down his rod before Pharaoh, and before his servants, and it became a serpent.
> The Pharaoh also called the wise men and the sorcerers: now the magicians of Egypt, they also did in like manner with their enchantments.
> For they cast down every man his rod, and they became serpents: but Aaron's rod swallowed up their rods.

> And he hardened Pharaoh's heart, that he hearkened not unto them; as the Lord had said. (Exodus 7, 7-13)

Here the shamanic experience, the sacred experience has brought the profane world into a sacred existence, for the miracles have gone beyond a single person's experience and become a part of the physical world. Not only that, but the assumption is in place that there are several others capable of bringing the two worlds together (i.e., the Pharaoh's wise men, magicians, and sorcerers). This is going to be immediately followed by God having Moses use the rod to turn the rivers and seas and all of the water of Egypt into blood and killing all of the fish. Then either Moses or Aaron will continue to use the rod to cause nine more plagues upon Egypt: frogs, lice, flies, murrain, boils, hail, locusts, darkness, and death of the firstborn.

This literal intermingling of the non-literal world with the literal world is what presses the issue, what demands *faith*, because it breaks the laws of logic and science. And that is what a *mythology* depicts. If a mythology is seen as a recounting of a spiritual happening, of the *eternal* world before the *chronological ticking of time*, then, in Mircea Eliade's theories the mythology is a recounting of that *sacred* world before the *profane* world replaced it, and in Christian terms (at least in standard Catholic ceremonies) the idea is to interrupt *profane* time and enter into *sacred* time.

Mircea Eliade's comingling of the religious or mythological perspectives with the psychological (though he claims to be separating his from them) take a clear, precise doubling in *Myths, Dreams and Mysteries: The Encounter between Contemporary Faiths and Archaic Realities* where he directly connects Freud's theories of the individual psyche to his own theories of *profane* and sacred *time*:

> We cannot refrain from thinking of the significance that the "return to the past" has acquired in modern therapeutics. Psycho-analysis especially has found out how to use, as its chief curative method, the memory, the recollection of the "primordial events." But, within the horizons of modern spirituality, and in conformity with the Judeo-Christian conception of historic and irreversible Time, the "primordial" could mean only one's earliest childhood, the true individual *intuim*. Psychoanalysis, therefore, introduces historical and individual time into therapeutics. The patient is no longer seen as an individual who is suffering only because of contemporary and objective events (accidents, bacteria, etc.) or by the fault of others (heredity), as he was supposed to be in the pre-psychoanalytic age; he is also suffering the after-effects of a shock sustained in his own temporal duration, some personal trauma that occurred in the *illud tempus*

> of childhood—a trauma that has been forgotten or, more exactly, has never come to consciousness. And the cure consists precisely in a "return to the past"; a re-tracing of one's steps in order to re-enact the crisis, to re-live the psychic shock and bring it back into consciousness. . . .
>
> Freud's was a most audacious undertaking: it introduced Time and History into a category of phenomena that had previously been approached from without, rather in the way that a naturalist treats his subject. One of Freud's discoveries above all has had portentous consequences, namely, that for man there is a "primordial" epoch in which all is decided—the very earliest childhood—and that the course of this infancy is exemplary for the rest of life. . . . (pp. 53-54)

Mircea Eliade then immediately connects Freud's theories to Carl Jung's theories:

> One would be tempted to extend these observations to take in Jung's discovery of the collective unconscious, of the series of psychic structures prior to those of the individual psyche, which cannot be said to have been forgotten since they were not constituted by individual experiences. The world of the archetypes of Jung is like the Platonic world of Ideas, in that the archetypes are impersonal and do not participate in the historical Time of the individual life, but in the Time of the species—even of organic Life itself. (p. 54)

He then connects up Jung's archetypal theories to his own views of profane and sacred time, "in the final reckoning they all mean the same thing: that *the essential human condition precedes the actual human condition*, that the decisive deed took place before us, and even before our parents: that decisive deed having been done by the mythic Ancestor (Adam, in the Judeo-Christian context). (pp. 54-55)

In highlighting Mircea Eliade's theories in *Myths, Dreams and Mysteries: the Encounter Between Contemporary Faiths and Archaic Realities* Morton Schatzman clearly wants to put his own discussion of Daniel Paul Schreber in his book *Soul Murder: Persecution in the Family* into both the personal context of Freudian theory and into the mythological context of Carl Jung's theories.

Shamanism: Archaic Techniques of Ecstasy, the other book of Mircea Eliade that Morton Schatzman highlights in his introduction was at the time of Morton Schatzman's publication, 1973, the definitive book on the subject, and though dated it remains a must read. For Morton Schatzman's purposes, it is in the comparisons of shamanism with a psychotic person that resonate, and curiously Mircea Eliade stresses:

> The writer who approaches shamanism as a psychologist will be led to regard it as primarily the manifestation of a psyche in crisis or even in retrogression; he will not fail to compare it with certain aberrant psychic behavior patterns or to class it among mental diseases of the hysteroid or epileptoid type.
>
> We shall explain why we consider it inacceptable to assimilate shamanism to any kind of mental disease. (pp. xi-xii)

Mircea Eliade elaborates on this in much more detail later on in a section titled "Shamanism and Psychopathology":

> Regarded in the horizon of *homo religiosus*—the only horizon with which we are concerned in the present study—the mentally ill patient proves to be an unsuccessful mystic or, better, the caricature of a mystic. His experience is without religious content, even if it appears to resemble a religious experience, just as an act of autoeroticism arrives at the same physiological result as a sexual act properly speaking (seminal emission), yet at the same time is but a caricature of the latter because it is without the concrete presence of the partner. (pp. 26-27)

A major difference, perhaps the major difference, Mircea Eliade stresses has to do with coming out of the experience, with returning from the psychotic or mystic state, with being in control of it, rather than it being in control:

> There is always a cure, a control, an equilibrium brought about by the actual practice of shamanism. It is not to the fact that he is subject to epileptic attacks that the Eskimo or Indonesian shaman, for example, owes his power and prestige; it is to the fact that he can control his epilepsy. Externally, it is very easy to note numerous resemblances between the phenomenology of *meryak* or *menerik* and the Siberian shaman's trance, but the essential fact remains the latter's ability to bring on his epileptoid trance at will. Still more significantly, the shamans, for all their apparent likeness to epileptics and hysterics, show proof of a more than normal nervous constitution; they achieve a degree of concentration beyond the capacity of the profane; they sustain exhausting efforts; they control their ecstatic movements, and so on. (p. 29)

Furthermore, he contends:

> And we must also consider the fact that the shamanic initiation proper includes not only an ecstatic experience but, as we shall soon see, a course of theoretical and practical instruction too complicated to be within the grasp of a neurotic. Whether they still are or are not subject to real attacks of epilepsy or hysteria, shamans, sorcerers, and medicine men in general

> cannot be regarded as merely sick; their psychopathic experience has a theoretical content. For if they have cured themselves and are able to cure others, it is, among other things, because they know the mechanism, or rather, the *theory* of illness. (p. 31)

Here Mircea Eliade has become so determined to separate the *shaman* from the *psychotic* he has suggested, actually more than suggested that the *shaman's* encounters with the *sacred*, the *other*, the *Mysterium Tremendum* is a learned, controlled, ritualized event. Furthermore, Mircea Eliade precedes these claims with a series of quotes from others that shamans, when they are not in their state of ecstasy are completely normal people demonstrating neither physical nor psychological abnormalities.

In making these claims, Mircea Eliade is obviously trying to separate a shaman from a psychotic, and in so doing is misrepresenting the similarities, one of them the simple likelihood or at least possibility that both have somehow entered a reality beyond the profane one. As others have suggested, the difference might simply be that the designations of shaman and psychotic put a judgment over the experience in terms of how well those experiencing them deal with them.

In "Schizophrenia—The Inward Journey," Joseph Campbell discusses paranoid schizophrenia as the psychological equivalent of a failed hero's adventure. (23) He has been invited to deliver a talk in conjunction with Dr. John Weir Perry, noted psychiatrist, obtains a paper of Weir on schizophrenia published in the *Annals of the New York Academy of Sciences* (24), and realizes that the imagery of schizophrenia matches that of a mythological hero's adventure. His discussion begins:

> My own [theory] had been a work based on a comparative study of the mythologies of mankind, with only here and there passing references to the phenomenology of dream, hysteria, mystic visions, and the like. Mainly, it was an organization of themes and motifs common to all mythologies; and I had had no idea, in bringing these together, of the extent to which they would correspond to the fantasies of madness. According to my thinking, they were the universal, archetypal, psychologically based symbolic themes and motifs of all traditional mythologies; and now from this paper of Dr. Perry I was learning that the same symbolic figures of mind of modern individuals suffering from a complete schizophrenic breakdown: the condition of one who has lost touch with the life and thought of his community and is compulsively fantasizing out of his own completely cut-off base." (25)

After making this general comparison, Campbell continues the discussion with a more concrete correspondence:

Very briefly: The usual pattern is, first, of a break away or departure from the local social order and context; next, a long, deep retreat inward and backward, as it were, in time, and inward, deep into the psyche; a chaotic series of encounters there, darkly terrifying experiences, and presently (if the victim is fortunate) encounters of a centering kind, fulfilling, harmonizing, giving new courage; and then finally, in such fortunate cases, a return journey of rebirth to life." (26)

According to Perry, the best way to handle such a schizophrenic breakdown might be to allow the patient to live out the fantasy, to let the psychic journey take its course in the belief it will, as does a hero's adventure, eventually work its way back to the world of light, back out of the nightmare to the world of day. This view is held by others.

Well known psychiatrist Rollo May writes:

[The] autobiographical novel *I Never Promised You a Rose Garden*, tells the experience of a young schizophrenic woman, Deborah, in her actual treatment with a psychiatrist. The stirring events in the treatment of this girl read like a contemporary extraterrestrial film. In her therapy we see a constant and gripping interplay of myths. Deborah (as she is called) lived with the mythic figures of Idat, Yr. Anterrabae, Lactamaen, the Collect, all of whom inhabited the Kingdom of Yr. Since Deborah could communicate with no one else in the world, she desperately needed these mythic figures. She writes, "the gods of Yr had been companions—secret, precisely *sharers of her loneliness*." She would flee to them when she was terrified or unbearably lonely in the so-called real world.

On the way to the sanatorium, as Deborah tells us, she and her parents stayed overnight in adjacent rooms in a motel. On the other side of the wall, Deborah stretched to sleep. The kingdom of Yr had a kind of neutral place which was called the Fourth Level. It was achieved only by accident and could not be reached by formula or an act of will. At the Fourth Level there was no emotion to endure, no past or future to grind against.

Now, in bed, achieving the Fourth Level, a future was of no concern to her. The people in the next room were supposed to be her parents. Very well. But that was part of a shadowy world that was dissolving, and now she was being flung unencumbered into a new one in which she had not the slightest concern. In moving from the old world, she was also moving from the intricacies of Yr's kingdom, from the Collect of Others, the Censor, and the Yr gods. She rolled over and slept a deep, dreamless, and restful sleep.

Next morning, she tells us, she felt the great reassurance and comfort the myths had given her. . . . it occurred to Deborah, as the car pulled away from the motel and out into the sunny day, that the trip might last forever and that the calm and marvelous freedom she felt might be a new gift from the usually too demanding gods and offices of Yr.

Not only are these gods in Deborah's scheme remarkable for their imaginative depth, but they are remarkable as well for their great similarity to what has been shown thirty years later, in E.T. The Return of the Jedi, Close Encounters of the Third Kind, and other extra-worldly films which attract millions of children and adults in our late twentieth century. Deborah was schizophrenic. But where one draws the line between schizophrenia and intensely creative imagination is a perpetual puzzle. Again Hannah Green (her pen name) writes:

> She began to fall, going with Anterrabe through this fire-framed darkness into Yr. This time the fall was far. There was utter darkness for a long time and then a grayness, seen only in bands across the eye. The place was familiar; it was the Pit. In this place gods and Collect moaned and shouted, but even they were unintelligible. Human sounds came, too, but they came without meaning. The world intruded, but it was a shattered world and unrecognizable.

The psychiatrist who served as therapist for Deborah at Chestnut Lodge, Frieda Fromm-Reichmann, wisely made clear to Deborah at the outset that she would not pull these gods away against Deborah's will. Dr. Frieda, as she is called in the book, worded them into the treatment, suggesting sometimes to Deborah that she tell her gods such-and-such, or occasionally asking her what her gods said. What is most important is that Dr. Fromm-Reichmann respected Deborah's need for these mythic figures, and she sought to help Deborah to see that she, Deborah, had her part in creating them. In one session,

> "Our time is over," the doctor said gently, "You have done well to tell me about the secret world. I want you to go back and tell those gods and Collect and Censor that I will not be cowed by them and that neither of us is going to stop working because of their power."
>
> But when Dr. Frieda had to go to Europe for a summer, Deborah was temporarily assigned to a younger psychiatrist who was imbued with the new rationalism. This psychiatrist marched in to destroy the "delusions" of Deborah with no understanding whatever of Deborah's need for her myths. The result was that Deborah, her whole system of gods and their extraterrestrial kingdom in shambles, deteriorated markedly. She regressed into a completely withdrawn world. She set fire to the sanatorium, burned and maimed herself, and behaved like a human being whose humanity is destroyed. For this is literally what had happened. Her soul—defined as the most intimate and fundamental function of her consciousness—was taken away, and she had literally nothing to hold on to. (27)

Dr. Perry introduced Joseph Campbell to "Shamans and Acute Schizophrenia," an article by Dr. Julian Silverman of the National Institute of Mental Health. (28) In addition to it describing a Shamanic experience and equating that to a psychological experience, a form of psychosis, the article distinguishes two types of schizophrenia, Essential Schizophrenia which involves a withdrawal from the experiences of the external world, and Paranoid Schizophrenia, where the person remains alert, sensitive to the external world, perhaps even highly social, but at the same time sees the external world as a projection of his own inner nightmare, his own fears, fantasies, and terrors. The external world, in other words, is a projection of his inner world.

In Essential Schizophrenia the person disassociates from the symbolism of the external world and must find psychic health in his own developed symbol systems. This fits the case of Deborah.

Joseph Campbell discusses the stages of the schizophrenic fall. First, he says, there is a sense of splitting. The world divides and the person sees himself in two roles. In one, he is but a clown, a ghost, an outsider, a fool, a person seen as inferior. In the other, he sees himself as the savior, the hero chosen for a high purpose. Campbell quotes a man having such an experience saying, "I have seen my father. . . . He is old now and has told me just to wait. I shall know when the time comes for me to take over." (29)

The second is of regression, falling back, becoming more one with the world outside of human existence, the exaltation of transcending personal bounds, what Freud referred to as the "oceanic feeling," the feeling of a new knowledge, of an ability to understand the deep mysteries of life. It is similar to the experience of a yogi, a saint, a shaman.

Psychiatrist R. D. Laing, in his book *The Politics of Experience*, discusses the case of Jesse Watkins, a former Royal Navy commodore, then a sculptor, who, at the culmination of his journey experiences a sense of sheer light, a terribly dangerous, over-powering light to be encountered and endured. (30)

Briefly, here is his experience. He is born the last day of the 19th century, December 31, 1899, goes to sea in 1916 during WWI on a tramp steamer, and ends WWII as a commander and Commodore of coastal convoys. During this time, he encounters ship wrecks, mutiny and murder.

He also paints throughout this life and has some short stories published about his adventures at sea.

After retiring from the service, he begins working long hours. During this time he grows emotionally, physically, and spiritually run down. Then he is bitten by a dog, and the wound will not heal. Finally he goes to the hospital, and is given an anesthetic. Upon his return from the hospital, he sits down in a chair and his son finds him acting strangely.

Thus, does the "voyage" begin. He describes it for Laing in sessions taped twenty-seven years later:

> "Suddenly I looked at the clock and the wireless was on and then the music was playing . . . something like Revel's repetitive tune. . . . Suddenly I felt time going backwards.
>
> I even felt it so strongly I looked at the clock and in the same way I felt that the clock was reinforcing my own opinion of time going back . . . I felt alarmed because I suddenly felt as if I was moving somewhere on a kind of conveyor belt—and unable to do anything about it, as if I was slipping along and sliding down a chute. . . . I looked into the mirror at myself, and I looked in a strange way . . . as though I were looking at someone who—who was familiar but . . . very strange and different from myself.
>
> My wife became very . . . worried. . . . I was going back into sort of previous existences. [My wife, the next door neighbor and the doctor who had been brought over] looked at me as if I were mad. . . And the next thing was that an ambulance came and I was taken off.
>
> I was put into bed [in an observation ward]. . . I had the feeling that I had died. And I felt that other people were in beds around me and I thought they were all other people that had died—and they were there-just waiting to pass on to the next department . . .

According to Dr. Laing, this experience is not representing a real death but an ego death, which is accompanied by a feeling of an enhanced significance of everything, of the entire world and the experiences one has, as Jesse's next statements indicate:

> I started going into . . . feelings of real regression in time. . . . experiencing everything . . . At one time I actually seemed to be wandering in a kind of landscape . . . as if I were an animal. . . . I felt as if I were a kind of rhinoceros or something like that and emitting sounds like a rhinoceros and being at the same time afraid and at the same time being aggressive and on guard. And then . . . going back to further periods of regression and even sort of when I was just struggling like something that had no brain . . . as if I were just struggling for my own existence against other thing which were opposing me. . . . Then at times I felt as if I were like a baby . . . I could even hear myself cry like a baby.
>
> All these feeling were very acute and . . . real. . . . I was aware of these things happening to me. . . I was a sort of observer of myself but yet experiencing it. . . . I found that I had periods when I came right out of this state . . . comparatively lucid states. . . .
>
> I had a letter from my wife. . . . she said, "The sun is shining here" . . . and "It's a nice day." . . . And I felt that if this letter was from her, she was

> in a quite different world. She was in a world that I could never inhabit any more—and this gave me feelings of alarm and I felt somehow that I was—I'd gone off into a world that I could never move out of.

Here Jesse clearly sees the world as splitting into two worlds, the physical world he once inhabited and occasionally still enters and the other world, the psychological, spiritual, mythological world. Jesse is both unable to stop his hallucinations and yet able to step outside of them and see himself as an outsider would. This wandering back and forth between these two worlds has him frightened, has him lost, in a twilight zone, whereas if he had completely entered into the "other" world, the dream world, he would not have had these uneasy feelings, as he would have been unaware of the dual realities.

Jesse also thinks his enhanced powers can influence the real world, and discusses how he tells a nurse not to bother bandaging a cut on his finger because he can will it to heal itself, and how he feels he is able by mere thought to will other patients to lie down and stop making noises.

He continues:

> I felt that I had . . . tapped powers that I in some vague way . . . reincarnation. . . . [I felt] an enormous journey in front . . . , a fantastic journey, . . . and it seemed that I had got an understanding of things which I'd been trying to understand for a long time, problems of good and evil and so on. . . . I had come to the conclusion . . . that I was more–more than I had always imagined myself, not just existing now, but I had existed since the beginning— . . . from the lowest form of life to the present time. . . . and ahead of me was lying the most horrific journey . . . a journey to being aware of all—everything . . . and I felt this so strongly, it was such a horrifying experience to suddenly feel that, that I immediately shut myself off from it because I couldn't contemplate it. . . . I was unable to take it.

Dr. Laing discusses how Jesse feels there are three levels of existence, an antechamber level, a central level, and a higher world. He feels most people are in waiting in the antechamber to move into the next level, the one he has entered.

He continues:

> I had feelings of . . . gods, not only God but gods as it were, of beings which are far above us capable of . . . dealing with the situation that I was incapable of dealing with, that were in charge and were running things and . . . at the end of it, everybody had to take on the job at the top. . . . And at the same time I felt that . . . God himself was a madman . . . because he's got this enormous load of having to be aware and governing and running things . . . and that all of us had to come up and finally get to the point

> where we had to experience that ourselves. . . . and every single one of us has to go through it . . . the purpose of everything and the whole of existence is . . to equip you to take another step, and another step, and another step, and so on . . .

After several days, Jesse gets to the point where he decides it was time to return from his "voyage." The nurses have reached a decision to put him in a padded cell, apparently because he talks so loud all night he keeps them up. However, he asks a nurse to leave the door open, and she does. This physical door, then, becomes the psychological door he will walk through to return to sanity.

He says:

> I sat on the bed, and I thought, well, somewhere or other I've got to sort of join up with my present . . . self.

The nurse offered him some medicine, but he declined, determined to no longer be mentally sick. He continued:

> I sat on the bed and I held my hands together, and as—I suppose in a clumsy way of linking myself up with my present self, I kept on saying my own name over and over again and all of a sudden, just like that—I suddenly realized that it was all over.

Dr. Laing concluded by emphasizing, "We can no longer assume that such a voyage is an illness that has to be treated," but rather that "this voyage is not what we need to be cured of, but that it is itself a natural way of healing our own appalling state of alienation called normality," and referred to Carl Jung as leading the way toward understanding this.

As mentioned, Campbell tied this psychological journey to the mythological journey of the Hero's Adventure, repeating Dr. Laing's conclusion by expanding it with the following claims:

> Something much the same was the view, also, of both Dr. Perry and Dr. Silverman . . . and, as I have most lately learned, the earliest documented proposal of this view was in a study published by C. G. Jung already in 1902, "On the Psychology and Pathology of So-called Occult Phenomena." (31)

"In sum," then, he continued,

the inward journey of the mythological hero, the shaman, the mystic, and the schizophrenic are in principle the same; and when the return or remission occurs, it is experienced as a rebirth: the birth, that is to say, of a "twice born" ego, no longer bound in by its daylight-world horizon. It is now known to be but the reflex of a larger self, its proper function being to carry the energies of an archetypal instinct system into fruitful play in a contemporary space-time daylight situation. One is now no longer afraid of nature; nor of nature's child, society—which is monstrous too, and in fact cannot be otherwise; it would otherwise not survive. The new ego is in accord with all this, in harmony, at peace; and, as those who have returned from the journey tell, life is then richer, stronger, and more joyous.

The whole problem, it would seem, is somehow to go through it, even time and again, without shipwreck: the answer being not that one should not be permitted to go crazy; but that one should have been taught something already of the scenery to be entered and the powers likely to be met, given a formula of some kind by which to recognize, subdue them, and incorporate their energies. (32)

Neurologists today tend to put schizophrenia into the world of autism, and especially the types discussed above into a form of autism designated as Asperger's syndrome, which might be categorized as a form of autism where the person realizes and can tell us about his mental state, whereas more classical autism cannot.

Donna Williams was "a severely withdrawn and bewildered autistic toddler," (33) whose mother and brother called her names, "a nut, a retard, a spastic," a child who "threw 'mentals' and couldn't act normal. 'Look at her, look at her,' they would say about a child who, to them, was either 'a retard' when I was in my own world or 'a nut' when I was in theirs. I couldn't win." (34).

She was considered either schizophrenic or autistic or both and more, certainly a problem child, and sent to several schools, where she failed miserably, then to special schools, where she also failed.

She had frightening dreams.

I once woke up after being bitten by a beautiful blue-eyed kitten that had suddenly turned into a rat as I went to pat it. I had, during the nightmare, gone downstairs and played the scene in the living room, before waking up as I switched on the light. I stood there screaming as the blood dripped from my hand; then, like magic, it disappeared and everything in the room changed back to how it was in reality.

Another night I woke up standing in the wardrobe doorway, rigid with horror, glaring at a doll that had suddenly returned to normal. Seconds before, I had seen it come to life, hands outstretched, its lips eerily

> mouthing words I could not hear, like some scene from a macabre horror film.
>
> I had become literally terrified of falling asleep. I would wait until everyone was asleep and then, frightening as my mother had become, I would go into her room and stand there watching her sleep, feeling secure in the knowledge that if anything was to get me it would have to get her, too, and she knew how to fight. From sheer tiredness, I began to hallucinate. Images on the walls would move. Unknown to my mother, I lay stiff and silent under her bed, almost too afraid to breathe. Tears rolled down my face. I made no sound. (35)

She took on different personas to remove herself from herself, to hide behind.

> I took to sleeping under the bed and I became Willie. By this time I was three years old. Willie became the self I directed at the outside world, complete with hateful glaring eyes, a pinched-up mouth, a rigid corpselike stance, and clenched fists. Willie stamped his foot, Willie spat when he didn't like things, but the look of complete hatred was the worst weapon and Donna paid the price. His name probably derived from my own surname, and some of Willie's behavior was certainly modeled upon and in response to my violator: my mother.
>
> Willie learned to turn other people's phrases back at them in some sort of meaningful yet attacking way, though silence still seemed a far deadlier weapon." (36)

She met the real Carol while playing at the park. Carol took Donna home to her mother, and she immediately was attracted to them. "As I got older, I would compulsively bring home kitten after kitten, reenacting the way Carol had taken me home, and I would wait and wonder when my mother would become Carol's mother. She never did. (37)

Then, in a wonderful coincidence (or is it?) with Lewis Carroll's *Through the Looking Glass*, the Carol within her "came in through the mirror" in her room, and that mirror became the entrance into Carol's world (just as it did for Alice to enter into Carroll's imaginative world; and the coincidence extends to the name Carol/Carroll; and even further to the connection with a kitten). Here is Alice's entrance from Carroll:

> But this is taking us away from Alice's speech to the kitten. 'Let's pretend that you're the Red Queen, Kitty! Do you know, I think if you sat up and folded your arms, you'd look exactly like her. Now do try, there's a dear!' And Alice got the Red Queen off the table, and set it up before the kitten as a model for it to imitate: however, the thing didn't succeed,

principally, Alice said, because the kitten wouldn't fold its arms properly. So, to punish it, she held it up to the

Looking-glass, that it might see how sulky it was, '—and if you're not good directly,' she added, 'I'll put you through in to Looking-glass House. How would you like that?

'Now, if you'll only attend, Kitty, and not talk so much, I'll tell you all my ideas about Looking-glass House. First, there's the room you can see through the glass—that's just the same as our drawing-room, only the things go the other way. I can see all of it when I get upon a chair—all but the bit just behind the fireplace. Oh! I do so wish I could see that bit! I want so much to know whether they've a fire in the winter: you never can tell, you know, unless our fire smokes, and then smoke comes up in that room too—but that may be only pretence, just to make it look as if they had a fire. Well then, the books are something like our books, only the words go the wrong way: I know that, because I've held up one of our books to the glass, and then they hold up one in the other room.

'How would you like to live in Looking-glass House, Kitty? I wonder if they'd give you milk in there? Perhaps Looking-glass milk isn't good to drink— but, oh, Kitty, now we come to the passage. You can just see a little peep of the passage in Looking-glass House, if you leave the door of our drawing-room wide open and it's very like our passage as far as you can see, only you know it may be quite different on beyond. Oh, Kitty, how nice it would be if we could only get through into Looking-glass House! I'm sure it's got, oh! Such beautiful things in it! Let's pretend there's a way of getting through into it, somehow, Kitty. Let's pretend the glass has got all soft like gauze, so that we can get through. Why, it's turning into a sort of mist now, I declare! It'll be easy enough to get through—She was up on the chimney-piece while she said this, though she hardly knew how she had got there. And certainly the glass was beginning to melt away, just like a bright silvery mist. (38)

When Donna saw her Carol in her mirror, she found that "Carol looked just like me, but the look in her eyes betrayed her identity. It was Carol all right. I began to talk to her, and she copied me. I was angry. I didn't expect her to do that. My expression asked her why, and hers asked me. I figured that the answer was a secret.

I decided that Carol understood that no one else was allowed to see me communicating with her and that this was her way of protecting me. I began to whisper to her, putting my face very close to hers and wondering why she didn't turn to hear.

When I was not in front of the mirror, Carol would disappear. I would feel deserted. When I walked in front of it, she would come back, and I'd try to look behind the mirror to find if she had gone through the door to my brother's room after all. It was Carol's house! The room I saw her in, in the mirror, was only a secret. If I could get through that room, I could leave with her, into her world. The only problem was how to get into the mirror." (39)

These and other personas allowed Donna's "real" self to hide, to "disappear." "I began to sit in a huddled ball inside the cupboard," she wrote. "I would close my eyes and try hard to lose all sensation of my own existence so that I could get into Carol's world in my mind. I became angry at any need to go to the toilet or eat, or any call to participate in the family . . . . In short my humanness, my mere physical existence, was my failing."

In the darkness of that cupboard I found Carol within myself.

Carol was everything that people liked. Carol laughed a lot. Carol made friends. Carol brought things home. Carol had a mother. . . .

In the meantime . . . Donna had disappeared. I was by this time five years old." (40)

Donna was not born of royal bloodlines, not given the position that Claudius had, yet perhaps partially because she did not have such opportunities, her achievements are as great as, or greater than, his. This person, inhabiting "a place of chaos, cacophony, and dancing light—where physical contact is painful and sights and sounds have no meaning. . . labeled, at times, deaf, retarded, or disturbed . . .," by her own words "autistic," and "afflicted by a baffling condition of heightened sensory perception that imprisons the sufferer in a private, almost hallucinatory universe of patterns and colors" (back cover), not only wrote a stunning autobiography, Nobody Nowhere, and then followed it up with Somebody Somewhere, and two other autobiographical works, Like Color to the Blind and Everyday Heaven, but several other works, both non-fiction and fiction, film scripts, music, poetry, paintings, sculpture, and the list goes on. At the time of this writing, she has an online site filled with her impressive activities and accomplishments (www.donnawilliams.net).

While reading about her fantasy world, peopled by characters as real, in some ways more real than her own self, and especially while reading the passages about her interactions with Mary, an understanding psychiatrist who allowed her to keep her inner world, I was immediately reminded of the famous autobiography of Joanne Greenberg *I Never Promised You a Rose Garden* (originally published under the pseudonym Hannah Green and referring to herself as Deborah Blau), and the discussion of it by Rollo May. (41)

Joanne's private dream world did not have a clever mirror doorway. However, in another interesting coincidence, at times she entered it the same way as Alice did in Lewis Carroll's *Alice in Wonderland.* Here is Carroll's version:

Alice had not a moment to think about stopping herself before she found herself falling down what seemed to be a very deep well.

Either the well was very deep, or she fell very slowly, for she had plenty of time as she went down to look about her, and to wonder what was going to happen next. First, she tried to look down and make out what she was coming to, but it was too dark to see anything: then she looked at the sides of the well, and noticed that they were filled with cupboards and bookshelves: here and there she saw maps and pictures hung upon pegs. She took down a jar from one of the shelves as she passed: it was labeled 'ORANGE MARMALADE' but to her great disappointment it was empty: she did not like to drop the jar, for fear of killing somebody underneath, so managed to put it into one of the cupboards as she fell past it.

'Well!' thought Alice to herself. 'After such a fall as this, I shall think nothing of tumbling down-stairs! How brave they'll all think me at home! Why, I wouldn't say anything about it, even if I fell off the top of the house!' (Which was very likely true.)

Down, down, down. Would the fall never come to an end? 'I wonder how many miles I've fallen by this time?' she said aloud. 'I must be getting somewhere near the centre of the earth. Let me see: that would be four thousand miles down, I thing—' (for, you, see, Alice had learnt several things of this sort in her lessons in the school-room, and though this was not a very good opportunity for showing off her knowledge, as there was no one to listen to her, still it was good practice to say it over) '—yes, that's about the right distance— but then I wonder what Latitude or Longitude I've got to?' (Alice had not the slightest idea what Latitude was, or Longitude either, but she thought they were nice grand words to say).

Presently she began again. 'I wonder if I shall fall right through the earth! How funny it'll seem to come out among the people that walk with their heads downwards! The Antipathies, I think-' (she was rather glad there was no one listening, this time, as it didn't sound at all the right word) '—but I shall have to ask them what the name of the country is, you know. Please, Ma'am, is this New Zealand? Or Australia?' (and she tried to curtsey as she spoke—fancy, curtseying as you're falling through the air! Do you think you could manage it?) 'And what an ignorant little girl she'll think me for asking! No, it'll never do to ask: perhaps I shall see it written up somewhere.'

Down, down, down. There was nothing else to do, so Alice soon began talking again. 'Dinah'll miss me very much to-night, I should think!" (Dinah was the cat.) 'I hope they'll remember her saucer of mild at tea-time. Dinah, my dear! I wish you were down here with me! There are no mice in the air, I'm afraid, but you might catch a bat, and that's very like a mouse, you know. But do cats eat bats, I wonder?' And here Alice began to get rather sleepy, and went on saying to herself, in a dreamy sort of way, 'Do cats eat bats? Do cats eat bats?' and sometimes 'Do bats eat cats?' for, you see, as she couldn't answer either question, it didn't much matter which way she put it. She felt that she was dozing off, and had just begun

> to dream that she was walking hand in hand with Dinah, and was saying to her, very earnestly, 'Now, Dinah, tell me the truth: did you ever eat a bat?' when suddenly, thump! Thump! Down she came upon a heap of sticks and dry leaves, and the fall was over. (42)

Hiding behind her Deborah character, Joanne Greenberg writes:

> She began to fall, going with Anterrabe through this fire-framed darkness into Yr. This time the fall was far. There was utter darkness for a long time and then a grayness, seen only in bands across the eye. The place was familiar; it was the Pit. In this place gods and Collect moaned and shouted, but even they were unintelligible. Human sounds came, too, but they came without meaning. The world intruded, but it was a shattered world and unrecognizable. (43)

It is interesting to see how both Joanne and Donna find ways of denying the self. Donna writes:

> Not surprisingly, . . . , I referred to myself as "you." This was because "you" logically captured my relationship to myself. One develops an "I" in interaction with "the world." Donna didn't interact; the characters did. Mary would try to get me to clarify whether I was implying that the events I was talking about applied to her, as she was the only "you" in the room. I tried to explain that this was how I described things. She continued. I reverted to using "I" in a conforming effort to avoid her pedantic emphasis on the pronouns I was using. Her efforts to get me to refer to these incidents in a personal manner overlooked the fact that my use of the word "you" captured the impersonal way in which I had experienced the incidents at the time they happened. She probably felt that she had to help me to overcome my depersonalization, as thought this were some recently developed defense reaction. I don't think she realized that I had actually experienced life this way since the creation of Willie and Carol, and my subsequent ability to communicate through them, thirteen years before. (44)

Yet, while she went to these extremes to hide, perhaps the greatest strength of her autobiography is that it is so incredibly personal, so revealing, opening up to the entire world at a level few others would do. Joanne, on the other hand, hid behind the literary devices of a pseudonym and a fictionalized persona, not revealing the autobiographical nature of the story until years later. It's also clear that she "bent" some truths for her fictionalized biography. How many of these "slight changes" are really important ultimately cannot be resolved. She has created a work of fiction to give her life a pattern. All biographies do that. And what's more important than whether her version of reality fits the literal reality better or worse than the rest of us is that she is expressing the deeper truths of the psyche, and has done that well.

Donna's first person narrative is so bluntly literal that similar questions can be raised from the opposite direction. Just how true is this seemingly straightforward account? It is an amazing accomplishment for a child as completely incapable of the very basics of language as she was, and the book itself suggests she was able to write it rather rapidly, sparked by her recent stumbling on some library books about autism. Given her penchant for assuming "roles' to hide behind, and her excellent skills at using various personas to fool people, it must be at least considered that she is not quite so innocently recounting her autism and childhood experiences as she claims. Nevertheless, the same entrance into the more important truths comes through.

These two adults, functioning on very high levels and demonstrating exceptional abilities, were once broken windmills, unable to connect with the normal winds of the mind, sputtering and stuttering and simply lost.

And they did it by entering the part of the mind that works through fiction, through the imagination. This is the place where meaning and value get mapped out, and it is not a reach at all to say that it is the natural place for people desperate for such truths to shine, because that is where the "self" is found.

At the time the Joanne Greenberg's book first came out (1964), and even at the time of Rollo May's reference to it in *The Cry for Myth* (1992), (45) Joanne Greenberg's condition was defined as schizophrenia, a term used to classify a wide variety of mental illnesses at that time, what is sometimes referred to as a "trashcan" diagnosis. (46) Current research supports redefining this initial classification of Joanne's illness from schizophrenia to perhaps obsessive-compulsive disorder or some form of autism. Whatever conclusions are reached about the classification, amazing similarities are to be found between Joanne Greenberg and Donna Williams.

Both retreated from the literal world into a fantasy world. Joanne Greenberg's world, instead of consisting of multiple personalities to disappear into, was made up of various "judges," godlike characters that generally took on super-ego qualities. Anterrabae (originally Antilobia), based on an illustration of Milton's Satan from *Paradise Lost*, falls eternally through the darkness, his hair and fingertips flickering in the wind. Latamaeon is the black, sarcastic god. Censor, originally a god meant to protect Deborah, became a demanding dictator intent on taking over complete control of her. The Collect of the Others consists of a group of critical voices that constantly condemns her. There are two main landscapes. The Kingdom of Yr (originally Iria) is the huge alternate world she escapes into. The Pit is a place of punishment in Yr, a place without meaning, will, or feeling, and it is especially frightening because the return from it begins with the *need for meaning* first, before the actual meanings return. (47)

Joanne Greenberg's story takes place at a time when psychoanalysis was a more accepted treatment, and in real life that is exactly what she got, and it apparently was successful. Her real life psychiatrist was Frieda Fromm-Reichmann, who, along with Harry Stack Sullivan, and Clara Thompson, operated out of the Chestnut Lodge Hospital, Rockville, Maryland, and was successful in treating several patients using nothing but psychoanalytical psychotherapy, a Freudian based system that consisted largely of simply sitting and listening to a patient talk out his or her cure.

This, however, is not so simple as it might at first appear, and the novel clearly demonstrates the difference between it being done correctly and incorrectly. Early in the sessions, Dr. Frieda (the fictionalized doctor) concludes a session: "'Our time is over, ... You have done well to tell me about the secret world. I want you to go back and tell those gods and Collect and Censor that I will not be cowed by them and that neither of us is going to stop working because of their power." (48). This seemingly casual remark is a key to unfolding the treatment, as it is a strong assurance of acceptance of the
patient's need for the fantasy world, not a rejection of exactly the form of thinking needed to work through the problems.

And this becomes extremely clear when Dr. Frieda leaves Deborah with a different doctor for a summer, one not understanding of this simple truth:

> From the silent self-conscious hall of B ward, she went to see the New One.
>
> She found Dr. Royson sitting stiffly in his chair in one of the offices on the main floor. "Come in," he said. "Sit down."
>
> She sat down.
>
> "Your doctor has told me a lot about you," he said. Deborah turned her mind for something to reply, thinking only: How stiffly he sits; I told her I would be
> fair . . . I told her I would try as hard with this one. . . .
>
> "Yes," she said. He was not a friendly person. She understood and set out to try the first directions. "You're from England, aren't you?"
>
> "Yes."
>
> "I like the accent," she said.

"I see."

This is one-by-one from the jawbone! Anterrabae groaned a little scornfully.

After a short silence the doctor said, "Tell me what you are thinking." It seemed to come like a demand.

"About dentistry," Deborah said.

"And what thoughts do you have about dentistry?" he said in his unchanging tone.

"That it can be more expensive than we think it will be," Deborah said. She caught herself and tried again. "I'm out of Novocain because Furii took it away with her."

"Who is that" Who took it away?" He jumped on it as if it were some prize.

"The doctor—Dr. Fried."

"You called her something else—what else did you call her?" The same demand, like a pickax.

"Just another name."

"Oh, the Secret Language," and he leaned back. Comfortably on safe ground, it looked to her. It was in the book on page ninety-seven. It was All Right. "Dr. Fried told me that you had a secret language."

Withdraw! Anterrabae said. He used the poetic Yri form and in her heartsickness it seemed newly beautiful—*Te quaru*: be as the sea and ebb and leave only a moment of the sandshine. *But I promised her*, Deborah insisted to the firelit falling god in the black place.

She is dead, Lactamaeon said on the other side of her.

"Tell me one of your words in that language," the outside voice insisted.

"*Quaru*," she said absently.

"What does it mean?"

"What?" She came to look at him suddenly and at the brutally hard lines of his disapproving face. He even sat austerely.

"What does it mean, that word you spoke? What was it?"

"*Quaru* . . ."she repeated. She was flustered with the confrontation, and she heard her own voice tell the gods, *But I promised* . . . "It means . . . well, it means wavelike, and it can imply something more of the sea, sometimes the coolness, or that soft, swishing sound, too. It means acting the way a wave acts."

"Why don't you merely say wavelike then?" he said.

"Well . . ." She was beginning the black sweat that was prelude to the Punishment. "You use it for anything that is wavelike, but it gives the sea-connotation with it and sometimes that can be very beautiful."

"I see," he said. She knew that he didn't.

"You can use it for the way the wind is blowing sometimes, or beautiful long dresses, or hair that is rippling, or . . . or leaving."

"It also means leaving?"

> "No, . . ." Deborah said, ". . . there is another word that means leaving."
> "What word?" He demanded.
> ". . . It depends on whether one has the intention of coming back . . ." she said miserably.
> "Very interesting," he said.
> "There is also a saying—" (She had made it up that minute to try to save herself and them.) "It is: don't cut bangs with a hatchet."
> "Cut bangs?" he said.
> An Americanism, perhaps, so she tried again. "Don't do brain surgery with a pickax."
> "And what does that signify to you?" he said, perhaps forgetting that if she could speak truly to the world, she would not be a mental patient.
> "It suffered and died in translation," she said.
> There followed a long silence between them, and though she tried at the next hour and the next and the next, his humorless and automatic responses brought down the muteness like a night. He worked hard to convince her that Yri was a language formulated by herself and not sent with the gods as a gift. He had taken the first words she gave him and shown her the roots of them from scraps of Latin, French, and German that a nine- or ten-year-old could pick up if she tried. He analyzed the structure of the sentences and demanded that she see that they were, with very few exceptions, patterned on the English structure by which she, herself, was bound. His work was clever and detailed and sometimes almost brilliant, and she had many times to agree with him, but the more profound he was the more profound was the silence which enveloped her. She could never get beyond the austerity of his manner or the icy logic of what he had proven, to tell him that his scalpels were intrusions into her body, and that furthermore, his proofs were utterly and singularly irrelevant. At the end she marshaled all of her strength, and with as much clarity as she could give him, she said, "Please, Doctor, my difference is not my sickness." It was a last cry and it went unheard. (49)

Not surprisingly, Joanne Greenberg's book suggests in standard Freudian analytical theory that a parent has been at least a part of the reason for the problems. In this case a brief family history is explored beginning with her mother's father:

> Pop had come from Latvia. He had a clubfoot. Somehow these two things represented him more fully than his name or occupation. He had come to America a young man, poor and foreign and lame, and he had borne down on the new life as if it were an enemy. In anger he had educated himself; in anger he had gone into business, failed, succeeded, and made a fortune. With his fortune and his anger he had bought a great home in an old neighborhood of the inbred and anciently rich. His neighbors had every

> manner he admired, and in turn they despised his religion, his accent, and his style. They made the lives of his wife and children miserable, but he cursed them all, the neighbors and wife and children, in the crude, blunt words of his abhorrent past. (50)

And this man, Joanne's grandfather had despised the man who would become her father, a poor man forced to take charity from the very man who hated him. And he, in turn, had been filled with anger, unable to "open his heart" to his daughter. So when he dropped Joanne off at the psychiatric ward he was too knotted up in his own emotions to reach out, to show his love. "He was a man of tempers and now he needed a rage that was cleansing, simple, and direct. But the anger here was so laced with pity, fear, and love that he did not know how he could free himself of it. It lay writhing and stinking inside him, and he began to feel the old, slow waking ache of his ulcer." (51)

It's not surprising that, when the parents come to visit her, Joanne refuses to see her father. She fears his own fears will be too much for her to deal with.

Donna Williams stresses the more current autistic explanations for her problems, but her discussions of her mother are actually far more filled with hate and a very, very troubled relationship, her mother's behavior simply criminal. One passage should suffice:

> My aunty had recalled many memories of my early childhood, but none had really struck a chord. Willie stood there remembering many of these, but did so without any feeling for the self who had experienced them. Then, as my aunty recalled an event when I was three, it triggered something, and my mind replayed it in all its vividness and horror.
>
> I was back there. I could see my aunty across the room. I could hear the pleading tone in her voice and sensed danger. I was watching everything around me happen as though in slow motion, though still moving far too fast for me to be able to respond in time.
>
> I look up at the figure of my mother. I shot silent glances in the direction of the pleading voice from across the room. I looked down at the opened tin of cold spaghetti in front of me and was aware of the fork in my hand.
>
> I had not heard the introduction: the threat of death against my spilling a single drop of food. I never connected the repeated slapping with the event. It was just something that came to me from out of the blue as a series of shocks.
>
> I felt the dishcloth being forced into my mouth. It made me gag. I was choking as I vomited up against it.
>
> The pleading voice was at war with the cutting snarl of my mother's voice. I glanced at the black and white striped cord as though it was a

> snake. It began to whip my face. I could not cry, or speak, or scream. I looked at my aunty and collapsed on the cold smooth surface of the table in front of me and vomited through my nose. I thought I had drowned. (52)

At the same time, both also suggest possible physical problems for their psychological struggles. Certainly, one contributing factor for Donna was the result of diet and allergies: "At the first clinic, using a series of blind tests, they found that I was allergic to all meat except beef, all dairy products, eggs, soy products, potatoes, tomatoes, and corn. I was also put through a six-hour blood-sugar test and found to be suffering from severe hypoglycemia. Another clinic found her to be "allergic to a group of chemicals called phenolics and salicylates, which are common to many fruits, vegetables, herbs, and spices, and almost all prepackaged foods." (53) And we cannot ignore the fact that Joanne had a brain tumor.

Whatever the diagnosis, yet again a broken mind has found a way to catch the power of the wind. Joanne Greenberg's accomplishments easily compare with Donna Williams. In addition to earning a degree in anthropology and literature from American University, she has published several novels and collections of short stories, receiving awards for her work, tutored Latin and Hebrew, taught cultural anthropology and creative writing, and appeared around the world at various writers' seminars and workshops. In 1977 *I Never Promised You a Rose Garden* was made into a film by Imorh Productions, unfortunately, not a great one, as it omits the whole anti-Semitism center and changes the psychological diagnosis to a retreat from reality as a result of a bout with urethral cancer.

Just as schizophrenia was the "trashcan" term for unexplained psychic anomalies a half a century ago, the new "in" term is autism. Actually, the term is not so new. It refers back to the work of the first American Child Psychiatrist Leo Kanner of Johns Hopkins Children's Psychiatric Clinic, and his paper from 1943, "Autistic Disturbances of Affective Contact," (54) and to similar work being done by Hans Asperger of the University Pediatric Clinic in Vienna. Both chose the term from adult psychiatry, where it was being used to refer to adult schizophrenics exhibiting a progressive withdrawal from the outside world.

Kanner's paper resulted from studying eleven children all ten years or younger he thought could be grouped under four common traits: the desire to be alone, the desire for sameness, the desire for elaborate routines, and the possession of some remarkable abilities in stark contrast with their disabilities.

In his report, he goes through each of the eleven in turn, simply titling them "case one," "case two," and so on. The first and most often referred to case is about Donald T., a boy Kanner first met at the age of five. Before this initial meeting the boy's father had sent a thirty-three page history that Kanner found filled with "obsessive detail." In it the father indicated that Donald's birth was normal, his breast feeding normal (though later he simply didn't show the appetite of other children), his teeth developed normally, and that he walked at thirteen months. By age one he hummed and sang tunes well, demonstrated an unusually good memory for faces and names and memorizing passages of the Bible. He had good enunciation, and memorized the alphabet and could count to 100. However, he did not ask the normal questions nor show any curiosity beyond his specific interests, and he demonstrated an extraordinary desire to simply be alone, even to the point of being indifferent to whether either father or mother was home. He was "self-satisfied." If he was interfered with, he had tantrums.

At age two, he was found to be "horrified" of self-propelled vehicles such as tricycles and of the playground slide, and he developed a strong attraction to spinning pans, blocks and other round objects.

At the age of four he was placed in a tuberculosis preventorium, where he continued to display his desire to simply be left alone, "perfectly oblivious" to all that went on around him. He continued his obsession to spinning objects, and developed the habit of shaking his head from to side. Dr. Eugenia S. Cameron and George Frankl examined him over a two week period at age five at the Child Study Home of Maryland and found in addition to the above that there was a "marked limitation of spontaneous activity." He liked elaborate rituals or repetitions, and he made up his own ways of communicating. For example, "At mealtime, repeating something that had obviously been said to him often, he said to his mother, 'Say eat it or I won't give you tomatoes, but if you don't eat it I will give you tomatoes', or say 'If you drink to there I'll laugh and I'll smile.'" And if his mother didn't go along with this ritual, he would throw a tantrum. All of the words he used had specific meanings to him, often far removed from their normal meanings.

By the following year, he was showing some movement to a more normal child, including more imagination, but was still dominated by the above symptoms.

The final report on him takes place when he is eight, concluding: "He was still extremely autistic. His relation to people had developed only in so far as he addressed them when he needed or wanted to know something. He never looked at the person while talking and did not use communicative gestures. Even this type of contact ceased the moment he was told or given what he had asked for." (p. 6)

And the report finishes with a follow up letter from his mother:

> Don is still indifferent to much that is around him. His interests change often but always he is absorbed in some kind of silly, unrelated subject. His literal-mindedness is still very marked, he wants to spell words as they sound and to pronounce letters consistently. Recently I have been able to have Don do a few chores around the place to earn picture show money. He really enjoys the movies now but not with any idea of a connected story. He remembers them in the order in which he sees them. Another of his recent hobbies is with old issues of Time magazine. He found a copy of the first issue of March 3, 1923, and has attempted to make a list of the dates of publication of each issue since that time. So far he has gotten to April, 1934. He has figured the number of issues in a volume and similar nonsense.

At this time and for several decades after, autism was thought to have resulted from the same kinds of negative childhood experiences that caused other neurosis, and the once highly acclaimed, but now often discounted theories of Bruno Bettelheim put forth most completely in his book *The Empty Fortress: Infantile Autism and the Birth of Self*, which popularized the phrase "refrigerator moms" for mothers of such children, suggesting that it is indeed the result of poor parenting, and that what is needed is to get the children away from these bad environments. (55) It's easy to see how such views would bring a storm of protest from the parents of autistic children, especially because psychology can be and has been much oversimplified and misinterpreted from the beginnings of Freudian theory. In this case the central controversy has been oversimplified into one of blaming the parents, especially the mothers for the autism, which makes for good drama. And even though Bettelheim, in truth, does not blame the mothers, just the opposite, a more careful study of his views doesn't make for good drama, but rather makes for more work, too sophisticated, too complex, too much into the depths of psychology for the average person. Instead, let's just keep it simple. Bettelheim is saying autism is caused by refrigerator moms!

Furthermore, since Bettelheim became such a media sensation (appearing on the *Today* show, getting extremely positive write ups in *The New Yorker* and *The New Republic*, and even having the rock opera *Tommy* by the Who based on his theories) he was a perfect target. Also, the growing field of neurology was looking to replace psycho-analysis with biologically based theories, and Bettelheim was the one they needed to bring down. The mud-slinging was as emotionally charged as any done during a Presidential election. It really wasn't that hard to do. Bettelheim, it was pointed out, had not received any formal degrees in psychology (i.e., was a quack!). Furthermore, he committed suicide at the end of his life (obviously neurotic himself!). And let's go to the sources themselves; three of his former patients were found to have doubts about his work and even called him a tyrant (ran his own clinic like a concentration camp!). Now, how convenient, on the word of three disgruntled patients his years of interment at Dachau and Buchenwald concentration camps could be turned against him (and it would have been seen as politically incorrect to question their motives or their own psychological conditions). The most well known book ripping him to shreds is Richard Pollak's *The Creation of Dr. B: A Bibliography of Bruno Bettelheim*, and it's hard to come away from that book without hating Bettelheim.

Perhaps it's worth noting at this point that Bettelheim does continue to have his supporters among professionals in both psychology and neurology. The point here is not so much whether or not Bettelheim's views are correct or incorrect or somewhere in between, but rather simply that the riddles remain.

Today autism is considered to be one of five or six categories of Pervasive Developmental Disorders (PDD), also referred to as Autistic Spectrum Disorders: Autistic Disorder, Asperger's Disorder, Childhood Disintegrative Disorder (CDD), Multiplex Disorder, Rett's Disorder, and PDD-not otherwise specified (PDD-NOS).

The Yale Development Disorders Clinic lists all six.

> 1. Autism (also referred to as Early Infantile Autism, Autistic Disorder, and Kanner's syndrome) . . . is characterized by marked problems in social interaction (autism), as well as by delayed and deviant communication development (speech is absent in about 50 percent of cases) and various other behaviors which are usually subsumed in the term 'insistence on sameness.' Such behaviors include stereotyped motor behaviors (hand flapping, by rocking), insistence on sameness and resistance to change. . . . Many individuals with autism exhibit mental retardation on the basis of their full-scale (or averaged) IQ score; however, unlike most people with primary mental retardation, those with autism often have marked scatter in their development, so that some aspects of the IQ, particularly nonverbal skills, may be within the normal range."
>
> 2. In Asperger's Disorder "affected individuals are characterized by social isolation and eccentric behavior in childhood. There are impairments in two-sided social interaction and non-verbal communication. Though grammatical, their speech is peculiar due to abnormalities of inflection and a repetitive pattern. Clumsiness is prominent both in their articulation and gross motor behavior. They usually have a circumscribed area of interest which usually leaves no space for more age appropriate, common interests. Some examples are cars, trains, French Literature, door knobs, hinges,

cappuccino, meteorology, astronomy or history. . . . In people with Asperger's Syndrome, "deficits in social interaction and unusual responses to the environment, similar to those in autism, are observed. Unlike in autism, however, cognitive and communicative development are within the normal or near-normal range in the first years of life, and verbal skills are usually an area of relative strength. Idiosyncratic interests are common and may take the form of an unusual and/or highly circumscribed interest (e.g., in train schedules, snakes, the weather, deep-fry cookers, or telegraph pole insulators)."

3. Childhood Disintegrative Disorder is a rare condition originally "described many years before autism (Heller, 1908) but has only recently been 'officially' recognized. With CDD children develop a condition which resembles autism but only after a relatively prolonged period (usually 2 to 4 years) of clearly normal development (Volkmar, 1994). This condition apparently differs from autism in the pattern of onset, course, and outcome (Volkmar, 1994)." It "develops in children who have previously seemed perfectly normal. Typically language, interest in the social environment, and often toileting and self-care abilities are lost, and there may be a general loss of interest in the environment. The child usually comes to look very 'autistic', i.e., the clinical presentation (but not the history) is then typical of a child with autism. . . .

4. Rett's Disorder is included as a Pervasive Developmental Disorder because there is some potential confusion with autism - particularly in the preschool years (Tsai,1992). Otherwise the course and onset of this condition is very distinctive. In people with Rett's Disorder (first reported by Rett in 1966), very early development is normal. Head growth then decelerates, usually in the first months of life, and a loss of purposeful hand movements occurs. Motor involvement is quite striking and profound mental retardation is typical. Characteristic hand-washing stereotypes develop. While the DSM-IV does not list male sex in the exclusionary criteria, the existing literature on Rett's syndrome documents the condition primarily in girls. The DSM-IV field trial sample included only girls and a recent, very well executed epidemiological investigation documented a prevalence of 3.8 per 10,000 girls; boys were not included. Since the discovery of the MECP2 gene, responsible for Rett's, variants of the syndrome have been reported in males who have mutations of MECP2, with some overlap in the symptomatology observed in girls (Amir, Van de Veyver, Wan, Tran, Franke, & Zoghbi, 1999; Schwartzman, Zatz, Vasquez, Gomes, Koiffman, Fridman & Otto, 1999; Schanen, Kurczynski, Brunelle, Woodcock, Dure, & Percy 1998).

5. Ever since autism was first recognized, its continuity with schizophrenia has been a matter of debate. In fact, until the late 1970s, children with autism were often labeled as having "childhood schizophrenia." In the last

thirty years, however, the term "childhood schizophrenia" has been displaced. Diagnostic criteria for autism have been established that rely solely on social, communicative and sensorimotor symptoms, without reference to the thought disorders typical of schizophrenia. Nevertheless, there are some children who display the severe, early-appearing social and communicative deficits characteristic of autism who ALSO display some of the emotional instability and disordered thought processes that resemble schizophrenic symptoms. Cohen, et al. (1986) coined the term Multiplex Developmental Disorder (MDD) to describe these children, although they are often given a diagnosis of PDD-NOS by clinicians who may be unfamiliar with this terminology. Unlike schizophrenia, MDD symptoms emerge in earliest childhood, often in the first years of life, and persist throughout development. Diagnostic criteria for MDD include:" Impaired social behavior and sensitivity (such as social disinterest and withdrawal), similar to autism, affective symptoms (such as recurrent panic and anxiety), though disorder symptoms (including confusions between reality and fantasy).

6. "Pervasive Developmental Disorder, Not Otherwise Specified (PDD-NOS) is a 'subthreshold' condition in which some - but not all - features of autism or another explicitly identified Pervasive Developmental Disorder are identified.

PDD-NOS is often incorrectly referred to as simply "PDD." The term PDD refers to the class of conditions to which autism belongs. PDD is NOT itself a diagnosis, while PDD-NOS IS a diagnosis. The term Pervasive Developmental Disorder - Not Otherwise Specified (PDD-NOS; also referred to as "atypical personality development," "atypical PDD," or "atypical autism") is included in DSM-IV to encompass cases where there is marked impairment of social interaction, communication, and/or stereotyped behavior patterns or interest, but when full features for autism or another explicitly defined PDD are not met.

It should be emphasized that this "subthreshold" category is thus defined implicitly, that is, no specific guidelines for diagnosis are provided. While deficits in peer relations and unusual sensitivities are typically noted, social skills are less impaired than in classical autism. The lack of definition(s) for this relatively heterogeneous group of children presents problems for research on this condition. The limited available evidence suggest that children with PDD-NOS probably come to professional attention rather later than is the case with autistic children, and that intellectual deficits are less common." be classified as having MDD. (56)

There are other categories that often get mixed into these, such as Fragile X syndrome, often called Martin-Bell syndrome, a genetic disorder transmitted from the mother to her sons resulting in autistic behavior such as poor eye contact, hand-flapping and other random movements, poor sensory skills, and delayed speech abilities. There are also several unusual physical features, including strabismus (lazy eye), large ears, a long face, poor muscle tone, flat feet, and large testicles.

Probably the most famous autistic today is Temple Grandin. Her resume is easily as impressive as those of Donna Williams and Joanna Greenberg, including two autobiographical works, *Emergence: Labelled Autistic* (co-written with Margaret Scariano) (57) and *Thinking in Pictures: and Other Reports from My Life with Autism.* (58) She earned a B.A. at Franklin Pierce College an M.S. in Animal Science at Arizona State University, a Ph.D. in Animal Science from the University of Illinois in 1989, and has become perhaps the most important animal scientist in her field, having designed 1/3 of the livestock-handling facilities in the United States. In North America, almost half of the cattle meat plants now use a center track restrainer system designed by her, cattle curved chute and race systems of her designed are used worldwide, and her writings on animal behavior have been central to animal welfare advocacy movements (her book *Animals in Transition* was a *New York Times* best seller).

She has appeared on such national television shows as *20/20, 48 Hours, Prime Time Live,* and the *Today Show*, been featured in such magazines as *U.S. News, World Report, Time, The New York Times, Forbes*, and *Discover*, and produced the videos *Visual Thinking, Careers, and Medications* on VHS and *Dr. Temple Grandin* on DVD which can be obtained from Future Horizons. In 2010, HBO produced a highly rated movie of her starring Claire Danes.

Though she was well known in autistic circles, Oliver Sachs, prompted by Dr. Uta Firth to visit her, first brought Temple Grandin to public attention when he named one of his books, *An Anthropologist on Mars: Seven Paradoxical Tales,* on a phrase she used to describe herself, and concluded the book with a discussion of his visit. (60)

In his preface to Grandin's *Thinking in Pictures: and other Reports from my Life with Autism,* Oliver Sachs points out that she was, in fact, the spark that pushed neurologists to see autism in a new way. Her first autobiography, *Emergence,* presented an autistic life that was much more fully rounded, more capable of the deeper human experiences than the previous views of "a child mute, rocking, screaming, inaccessible, cut off from human contact," or of the autistic savant, similar to that portrayed in *Rain Man*, a person filled with uncanny powers of "calculation, memory, drawing, whatever," yet "cut off from normal life." Temple Grandin while obviously somehow different was at the same time not devoid of standard human needs and desires and abilities. Not only was she highly accomplished, and in the end capable of complex thinking and writing, but she did have a need for being "hugged."

And yet perhaps this need for being hugged can open the door to demonstrate how she was both the same and different. She writes:

> From as far back as I can remember, I always hated to be hugged. I wanted to experience the good feeling of being hugged, but it was just too overwhelming. It was like a great, all-engulfing tidal wave of stimulation, and I reacted like a wild animal. Being touched triggered flight; it flipped my circuit breaker. I was overloaded and would have to escape, often by jerking away suddenly. (p. 61)

Yet, as she points out, she was one of many autistic children who "crave pressure stimulation even though they cannot tolerate being touched." As a child of six, she would wrap herself in blankets and get under sofa cushions because the pressure relaxed her. She dreamed of building a machine that would supply this pressure. This dream began to take on real possibilities when she first saw a squeeze chute used to hold cattle in place when they were given vaccinations at her aunt's ranch.

> I asked Aunt Ann to press the squeeze sides against me and to close the head restraint bars around my neck. I hoped it would calm my anxiety. At first there were a few moments of sheer panic as I stiffened up and tried to pull away from the pressure, but I couldn't get away because my head was locked in. Five seconds later I felt a wave of relaxation, and about thirty minutes later I asked Aunt Ann to release me. For about an hour afterward I felt very calm and serene. This was the first time I ever felt really comfortable in my own skin. (p. 63)

After she discusses other autistics also having this need for touch stimulation, along with the dangers of the wrong forms of touching (the anxiety and violent reactions that can result from over-stimulation), and her own developments of a personal "squeeze machine," she writes:

> As I developed my squeeze machine, I designed it to enhance the feeling of being embraced. Now, if I suddenly resist, I cannot pull my head out of the softly padded neck opening. In order to open the latch, I have to relax and lean forward. I am never locked in the machine, but I am prevented from suddenly pulling away from the soothing pressure. At all times I am in control of the amount of pressure applied to my body. The new design has enabled me to give in completely to the gentle feeling of being held. (p. 80)

And concludes: "Help autistic children fulfill that most basic human need, the comfort of touch, is like taming an animal. At first they pull away, but then they learn that touching feels good." (p. 81)

As she admits, the squeeze machine does seem a strange desire, and those who knew her kept trying to get her to stop using it. The next chapter of her book takes this curious hate/love of being embraced to a deeper level. She begins it:

> To have feeling of gentleness, one must experience gentle bodily comfort. As my nervous system learned to tolerate the soothing pressure from my squeeze machine, I discovered that the comforting feeling made me a kinder and gentler person. It was difficult for me to understand the idea of kindness until I had been soothed myself. It wasn't until after I had used the modified squeeze machine that I learned how to pet our cat gently. He used to run away from me because I held him too tightly. Many autistic children hold pets too tightly, and they have a disproportionate sense of how to approach other people or be approached. After I experienced the soothing feeling of being held, I was able to transfer that good feeling to the cat. As I became gentler, the cat began to stay with me, and this helped me understand the ideas of reciprocity and gentleness.
>
> From the time I started using my squeeze machine, I understood that the feeling it gave me was one that I needed to cultivate toward other people. It was clear that the pleasurable feelings were those associated with love for other people. (p. 82)

As an aside here, this leads into a brief discussion of her now famous interactions with animals, how she connects up with them through touching, establishing an almost mystical unity. She also throws in a brief comment on Bettelheim's theories, following it with the comment, "We now know that autism is caused by neurological abnormalities that shut the child off from normal touching and hugging. It is the baby's abnormal nervous system that rejects the mother and causes it to pull away when touched." (p. 85)

This chapter, tellingly titled "Learning Empathy" is an interesting attempt to explain how autistics can logically or intellectually understand the deeper emotions, yet not experience them as emotions. She concludes:

> Yet, it has only been during the last two or three years that I have discovered that I do not experience the full range of emotions. My first inkling that my emotions were different came in high school, when my roommate swooned over the science teacher. Whatever it was she was feeling, I knew I didn't feel that way toward anyone. But it was years before I realized that other people are guided by their emotions during most social interactions. For me, the proper behavior during all social

> interactions had to be learned by intellect. I became more skilled at social interactions as I became more experienced. Throughout my life I have been helped by understanding teachers and mentors. People with autism desperately need guides to instruct and educate them so they will survive in the social jungle. (p. 95)

However, just as we begin to see her as missing the deeper, more complex emotions of adults, we come across this report from Oliver Sachs:

> Temple is an intensely moral creature. She has a passionate sense of right and wrong, for example, in regard to the treatment of animals; and law, for her, is clearly not just the law of the land but, in some far deeper sense, a divine or cosmic law, whose violation can have disastrous effects—seeming breakdowns in the course of nature itself. "You've read about action at a distance, or quantum theory," she said. "I've always had the feeling that when I go to a meat plant I must be very careful, because God's watching. Quantum theory will get me."
>
> Temple started to become excited. "I want to get this out before you get to the airport," she said, with a sort of urgency.
>
> She had been brought up an Episcopalian, she told me, but had rather early "given up orthodox belief"—belief in any personal deity or intention—in favor of a more "scientific" notion of God. "I believe there is some ultimate ordering force for good in the universe—not a personal thing, not Buddha or Jesus, maybe something like order out of disorder. I like to hope that even if there's no personal afterlife, some energy impression is left in the universe. . . . Most people can pass on genes—I can pass on thoughts or what I write.
>
> "This is what I get very upset at. . . ." Temple, who was driving, suddenly faltered and wept. "I've read that libraries are where immortality lies. . . . I don't want my thought to die with me. . . . I want to have done something. . . . I'm not interested in power, or piles of money. I want to leave something behind. I want to make a positive contribution—know that my life has meaning. Right now, I'm talking about things at the very core of my existence." (61)

In his introduction to her book *Thinking in Pictures: And Other Reports from my Life with Autism*, Oliver Sachs repeats this passage and concludes: "Thus, in my brief (but very full) few days with Temple, I had a revelation of how, while in many ways so flat and constricted, her life was in other ways full of health, of depth, of deep human striving." (p. 15)

Theories abound. Brilliant minds struggle to explain minds that somehow just don't fit the general category of "normal." It's always dangerous to enter into such debates, but at the same time, whether or not we can explain such categories, we certainly can sense them. No matter how much we encounter, read about and study such children as Donna Williams, Joanna Greenberg, and Temple Grandin we cannot deny that they are somehow not normal children. They have qualities that just don't fit the category of normal. This is not a negative statement, simply a statement of fact.

Psychology and neurology and related fields have worked hard to sort out just what makes such children unique. Perhaps, today, certain things have been discovered, and at least some hesitating categories, causes, and treatments can be put forth. However, the field is still young, and contradictions rule. Even just in the small arena of creativity and imagination in such children, the studies and theories abound, and offer most every possible conclusion on the spectrum from poor to exceptional. In 1999, Jamie Craig and Simon Baron-Cohen published findings demonstrating "impoverished creativity" in autistic children. (62) In the same journal six years later Neil Gordon published "Unexpected discoveries of Artistic Talent," where he found "The development of exceptional and unexpected artistic skills . . . can occur among young children with severe learning difficulties, especially if they are autistic." (63) A. Chetterjee suggested that creativity was neither more nor less in autistic children (or children with other mental malfunctions), but rather was simply brought about through different pathways. (64) C. Hou, B. L. Miller, J. L. Commings, M. Goldberg, P. Mychack, V. Bottino, and D. F. Benson studied five autistic savants, concluding that "Savants exhibit extraordinary visual talents along with profound linguistic and social impairment." (65) Autism and genius is one of the hot topics. Frank Klein suggests that Albert Einstein was exactly this. (66) In "Illness: the Pathway to Creative Genius," Rodger Dobson claims that "Disease, rather than being a barrier to greatness, may be its wellspring," and suggests that "Einstein, Warhol, Newton, Cézanne, Goya, Michelangelo, Turner and Berlioz are among many whose achievements are now thought to have been influenced by disease." In fact, he claims that "Conditions such as depression, autism, myopia, anxiety, chronic pain, gout, stroke and dementia heavily influenced their paths to creativity." (67) Clara Claiborne Park has two books on her autistic, yet exceptionally artistic daughter. (68) Lorna Selfe has an excellent book on *Nadia: a case of extraordinary drawing ability in an autistic child.* (69) Tito Rajarshi Mukhopadhyay has written *The Mind Tree: A Miraculous Child Breaks the Silence of Autism*, a book similar to Donna Williams in that it is a well written autobiography by an autistic person. (70) These, however, are the exceptions, stunning because of their sharp contrast with the norm.

But what is the norm? Just what does it mean to be autistic? Some, such as Bruno Bettelheim, think it is at least partially determined by the environment, especially the mother-child relationship. Others, such as Uta Firth, think it is biological. Some think it should be divided up into five or six categories, the final category simply a catch-all one for children "sort of but not quite" fitting the others. Some think it promotes creativity and "genius," others that it is characterized by a lack of imagination. Many think much of what was once diagnosed as schizophrenia really fits autism better. Feral children, once thought to be animal-like because of growing up outside of civilization (for better or worse), now are more likely to be thought of as autistic. And while reasoned and friendly debates are possible and do take place, the field is often characterized by emotional diatribes. The Wikipedia site online has a section titled "Controversies in autism," and finds the topic so explosive that it includes a highlighted hand on a stop sign with the disclaimer "The neutrality of this article is disputed." (71)

There are several emotionally charged groups working in the field today. As long ago as 1962, a group of parents in the United Kingdom who were frustrated by the lack of support and understanding of their own children with autism, created The Society for Autistic Children, which later was renamed The National Autistic Society (NAS). While their focus is help for the families dealing with autism, another organization, The National Alliance for Autism Research (NAAR) focuses on biomedical research into autism, and provides grants for research. It has, in turn, formed an alliance with Autism Speaks, an organization founded by Suzanne and Bob Wright as a result of their personal experiences with an autistic grandson. The Autism Society of America (ASA) was founded in 1965 by Bernard Rimland, Ph.D., and claims to be the oldest and largest grassroots organization within the autism community, currently having more than 120,000 members and supporters connected through a working network of nearly 200 chapters nationwide. As with the others, it is dedicated to increasing public awareness about autism and the day-to-day issues faced by individuals with autism, their families and the professionals with whom they interact.

So many people trying to understand, trying to help. Yet the silence, the separation remains. And while there are the wondrous exceptions to the general lack of ability, even they are informed by a quiet sorrow, a shadowy world inside the mind unable to find the normal passages, unable to take the same paths others do, forced to create their own maps of meaning, perhaps, at times, brilliant new maps, but still maps across lonely landscapes that cannot help but express an isolation. Bruno Bettelheim describes Laurie:

> When Laurie was about two and a half, the young nursemaid left suddenly. She was replaced with an older woman who took care of Laurie until she was four years old. This woman, as well as other caretakers who followed her, never seemed of much importance to Laurie who, with the leaving of her original nursemaid, began to give up what she had learned.
>
> Within a few days the mother noticed a great change in Laurie. She stopped saying the few words she had known and all talking was replaced by peculiar clucking sounds. One day, after repeatedly making what sounded to the mother like loud animal-like noises, the mother became very angry, spanked her, and told her to be still. Laurie then stopped talking and has not spoken since.
>
> Soon Laurie gave up bowel control. A while later began an ever more severe withdrawal from the world, which by the age of six had reached such proportions that for long time periods she seemed blind, deaf, and unable to move on her won. Most of the time she spent her days motionless, staying wherever she was put, sitting in a chair, on the floor, or on the toilet, until bodily moved by someone to some other place. The small remainder of her days she spent in an empty turning of magazine pages without looking at them, or in tearing them into tiniest pieces.
>
> The only activities Laurie engaged in spontaneously were destructive. She ripped buttons off her clothes, tore her sheets, ripped wallpaper off the walls. If she got hold of a piece of ribbon, she shredded it to a mass of fine fuzzy matter until it looked like a ball of absorbent cotton. Similarly she tore shag rugs to shreds, or her blankets. This is mentioned in contrast to an elaborate and complex tearing of paper that characterized her later months with us.
>
> When spoken to, Laurie turned her face away. When annoyed or scolded, she simply stared at her hand or into empty space. As time passed, she withdrew more and more. (72)

Morton Schatzman's statement quoted earlier that "some experiences of many people labeled schizophrenic resemble those of shamans . . .," that "more study is needed here, not only to learn more about 'them,' the shamans and schizophrenics, but about parts of our minds of which we may be usually unaware" includes the following footnote: "Most of us in the presence of a man who experiences the extraordinary adopt the position of Hamlet's mother when Hamlet asks if she does not see the ghost: Hamlet. Do you see nothing there? Queen. Nothing at all; yet all that is I see. How, I wonder, did she know she saw 'all that is'?

In the introduction to his study of Daniel Paul Schreber, Morton Schatzman provides two frames, and the highlights them by referring to two of Mircea Eliade's books. The first, *Myths, Dreams and Mysteries: The Encounter between Contemporary Faiths and Archaic Realities,* has to do with the separation of two planes of existence into *profane* and *sacred*, the first based on chronological time, the second on a return to the *eternal* time represented in the sacred myths, to the *illud tempus*, and the connection of the individual's need to return to his or her own *illud tempus* in the same manner as Sigmund Freud's theories suggest. In other words, each individual's life journey through temporal existence is initiated in childhood, and the cure for a neurosis is to return the patient to those "beginnings" in the same way as religion needs to return a person to the spiritual *illud tempus*, to, in other words, break chronological time, *profane* time, and re-enter the *eternity* of *sacred* existence. The second frame Morton Schatzman provides, and refers to Mircea Eliade's *Shamanism: Archaic Techniques of Ecstasy*, has to do with whether or not a psychotic has any relationship to a shaman.

With these frames in place, Morton Schtzman points out that Sigmund Freud's important study of Daniel Paul Schreber, curiously, does not include a close study of what materials were available.

Clearly, Schreber is connecting a powerful father figure with God and attempting to clarify how he is realizing things, is being "told" or "taught" *truths* in his psychological or spiritual or psychotic or other-worldly experiences; and whether or not it is literally true, he is using the symbolism, especially the strong psychological symbolism he knows to express what he is experiencing. This symbolic, this dream world language might or might not have numerous literal connections, but the importance is *not* to reduce it to *literal* truths but to understand it as a means of connecting up to truths beyond those.

In conjunction with his *nerve language* which came to him through *divine rays*, was what he called *compulsive thinking*, which was the inability to stop thinking, something he claimed the average person can do. (I can't; and though it's more complicated than this, it is in a sense central to such religions as Buddhism, where the idea is to eliminate the noise of conscious thinking and connect up with the silence of the universe.) At any rate, he says it was necessary for him to develop a system of *falsifying my thoughts* because the voices were constantly asking him what he was thinking and he didn't know how to answer them. All of the *souls* of both dead and living people that were constantly speaking to him at the same time created "an unholy turmoil," too much thinking all at the same time, but then eventually went beyond this to a monotonous repetition of recurring phrases (memorized and repeated endlessly).

The *second* point he emphasizes here, and it is worth highlighting that it is second, has to do with what has become the main point of most of the analysis of him ever since, beginning with Freud, who, unfortunately, in this case, missed the deeper meanings, or at least lessened them by being seduced into an easier and less enlightening conclusion. Daniel Paul Schreber states, "The second point to be discussed in this chapter is the tendency, innate in the Order of the World, to *unman* a human being who has entered into permanent contact with rays. Putting forth a rather strange theory that at times throughout history the human race has become so *blackened* or so depleted that it has been necessary for God to choose *one* human to replenish the world. He writes:

> In such an event, in order to maintain the species, one single human being was spared—perhaps the relatively most moral—call by the voices that talk to me the "*Eternal Jew*." This underlying the legend of the same name of the Jew Ahasver; one is however automatically reminded of the legends of Hoah, Deucalion and Pyrrha, etc. Perhaps the legend of the founding of Rome belongs her also, according to which Rhea Sylvia conceived the later Kings Romulus and Remus directly of Mars the god of War, and not of an earthly father. The Eternal Jew (in the sense described) had to be *unmanned* (transformed into a woman) to be able to bear children. This process of unmanning consisted in the (external) male genitals (scrotum and penis) being retracted into the body and the internal sexual organs being at the same time transformed into the corresponding female sexual organs, a process which might have been completed in a sleep lasting hundreds of years, because the skeleton (pelvis, etc.) had also to be changed." (pp. 73-74)

Dr. Weber, director of Sonnenstein Asylum, writes:

> The cumulating point of the patient's delusional system is his belief that he has a mission to redeem the world, and to restore mankind to their lost state of bliss. He was called to this task, so he asserts, by direct inspiration from God, just as we are taught that the Prophets were; for nerves in a condition of great excitement, as his were for a long time, have precisely the property of exerting an attraction upon God—though this is touching on matters which human speech is scarcely, if at all, capable of expressing, since they lie entirely outside the scope of human experience and, indeed, have been revealed to him alone. The most essential part of his mission of redemption is that is must be preceded by his *transformation into a woman*. It is not to be supposed that he *wishes* to be transformed into a woman; it is rather a question of a "must" based upon the Order of Things, which there is no possibility of his evading, much as he would personally prefer to remain in his own honourable and masculine station in life. But neither he nor the rest of mankind can regain the life beyond except by his

being transformed into a woman (a process which may occupy many years or even decades) by means of divine miracles. He himself, of this he is convinced, is the only object upon which divine miracles are worked, and he is thus the most remarkable human being who has ever lived upon earth. Every hour and every minute for years he has experienced these miracles in his body, and he has had them confirmed by the voices that have conversed with him. During the first years of his illness certain of his bodily organs suffered such destructive injuries as would inevitably have led to the death of any other man: he lived for a long time without a stomach, without intestines, almost without lungs, with a torn esophagus, without a bladder, and with shattered ribs, he used sometimes to swallow part of his own larynx with his food, etc. But divine miracles ("rays") always restored what had been destroyed, and therefore, as long as he remains a man, he is altogether immortal. These alarming phenomena have ceased long ago, and his "femaleness" has become prominent instead. This is a matter of a process of development which will probably require decades, if not centuries, for its completion, and it is unlikely that anyone now living will survive to see the end of it. He has a feeling that enormous numbers of "female nerves" have already passed over into his body, and out of them a new race of men will proceed, through a process of direct impregnation by God. Not until then, it seems, will he be able to dies a natural death, and, along with the rest of mankind, will he regain a state of bliss. In the meantime not only the sun, but trees and birds, which are in the nature of "bemiracled residues of former human souls," speak to him in human accents, and miraculous things happen everywhere around him." (73)

This, then, is what Schreber believes happened to him, and it is what Freud focuses and elaborates on, quoting various odds-and-ends passages to help support his contentions. Freud admits that "the medical report might easily lead us to suppose that Schreber exhibited the everyday form of Redeemer phantasy, in which the patient believes he is the son of God, destined to save the world from its misery or from the destruction that is threatening it, and so on." (74) However, he elaborates, suggesting the Redeemer fantasy is *not* the primary delusion:

"The medical officer lays stress upon two points as being of chief importance: the patient's *assumption of the role of Redeemer,* and his *transformation into a woman.* The Redeemer delusion is a phantasy that is familiar to us through the frequency with which it forms the nucleus of religious paranoia. The additional factor, which makes the redemption dependent upon the man being previously transformed into a woman, is unusual and it itself bewildering, since it shows such a wide divergence from the historical myth which the patient's phantasy is setting out to reproduce. It is natural to follow the medical report in assuming that the motive force of this delusional complex was the patient's ambition to play the part of Redeemer, and that his *emasculation* was only entitled to be regarded as a means for achieving that end. Even though this may appear to be true of his delusion in its final form, a study of *Denkwurdigkeiten* compels us to take a very different view of the matter. For we learn that the idea of being transformed into a woman (that is, of being emasculated) was the primary delusion, that he began by regarding that act as constituting a serious injury and persecution, and that it only became related to his playing the part of Redeemer in a secondary way. There can be no doubt, moreover, that originally he believed that the transformation was to be effected for the purpose of sexual abuse and not so as to serve higher designs. The position may be formulated by saying that a sexual delusion of persecution was later on converted in the patient's mind into a religious delusion of grandeur. The part of persecutor was at first assigned to Professor Flechsig, the physician in whose charge he was; later, his place was taken by God Himself. (75)

Freud then gives support with quotes from the *Memoirs*:

"In this way a conspiracy against me was brought to a head (in about March or April, 1894). Its object was to contrive that, when once my nervous complaint had been recognized as incurable of assumed to be so, I should be handed over to a certain person in a particular manner: my soul was to be delivered up to him, but my body—owing to a misapprehension of what I have described above as the purpose underlying the Order of Things—was to be transformed into a female body, and as such surrendered to the person in question [Flechsig] with a view to sexual abuse, and was then simply to be "left on one side"—that is to say, no doubt, given over to corruption." (76)

"It was, moreover, perfectly natural that from the human standpoint (which was the one by which at that time I was still chiefly governed) I should regard Professor Flechsig or his soul as my only true enemy—at a later date there was also the von W. Soul, about which I shall have more to say presently—and that I should look upon God Almighty as my natural ally. I merely fancied that He was in great straits as regards Professor Flechsig, and consequently felt myself bound to support Him by every conceivable means, even to the length of sacrificing myself. It was not until very much later that the idea forced itself upon my mind that God Himself had played the part of accomplice, if not of instigator, in the plot whereby my soul was to be murdered and my body used like a strumpet. I may say, in fact, that this idea has in part become clearly conscious to me only the course of writing the present work." (77)

"Every attempt at murdering my soul, or at emasculating me for purposes *contrary to the Order of Things* (that is, for the gratification of the sexual appetites of a human individual), or later at destroying my understanding—every such attempt has come to nothing. From this apparently unequal struggle between one weak man and God Himself, I have emerged as the victor—through not without undergoing much bitter suffering and privation—because the Order of Things stands upon my side." (78)

Furthermore, Freud points out,

"It may be added that the 'voices' which the patient heard never treated his transformation into a woman as anything but a sexual disgrace, which gave them an excuse for jeering at him. 'Rays of God' calling me "Miss Schreber," in allusion to the emasculation which, it was alleged, I was about to undergo." (79)

Or they would say: 'So *this* sets up to have been a Senatsprasident, this person who lets himself be f—d!' Or again: 'Don't you feel ashamed in front of your wife. (80)

Though Freud stresses the emasculation fantasy taking place before the Redeemer one, and stresses the early dream of being a woman submitting to copulation, another view is possible, and certainly can at least be mixed in. Shreber was disparate for a map of meaning and value in his life. Somehow, he had become disconnected. As do all creative people, he began developing a world that would supply his need for meaning. An early part of this world was involved with the symbolism of a female receiving male impregnation, a necessary step in human procreation (and it might have gotten some spark in him as a result of he and his wife wanting a child and not being able to have one; he was trying hard to impregnate her and she wanted him to do so, in order to produce a child; this could very easily have caused him to put himself in her position, desiring impregnation).

Other contexts are also likely, some almost impossible to deny. He was in a very submissive role growing up beneath the father he had, a demanding, perhaps fanatical disciplinarian. He was also in the submissive role as a patient to Dr. Flechsig. This submissive role, which he can easily represent as the female role in reproduction (and perhaps in life in general), also works for God in the standard Christian sense of God being the all powerful *Father*.

Shreber feels disempowered. It might be noted that both his early breakdowns occurred in relation to real world events that had to do with power or the loss of it, the first with a clear public and personal disgrace in the embarrassing loss of his political ambitions, the second the result of the tensions of handling a new position of power (and not feeling up to it).

The initial dreams, voices, cruel questions about his weakness, taking on the most degrading language, are in the context of this and are a form of self condemnation. Furthermore, it should be noted that Shreber is still in the world of public posing, as he does take the route of not spelling out fucked! This is an important indication of him not being disconnected, out of touch with reason and appearance.

Freud stresses Shreber's claims that on November, 1895, he accepted his role as the female in his relation to God, quoting the following passage: "I became clearly aware that the Order of Things imperatively demanded my emasculation, whether I personally liked it or not, and that no *reasonable* course lay open to me but to reconcile myself to the thought of being transformed into a woman. The further consequence of my emasculation could, of course, only be my impregnation by divine rays to the end that a new race of men might be created." (81)

Freud further stresses a later passage by Schreber that suggests homosexual desires in the real world as well as in the mind: "The *only thing* which could appear unreasonable in the eyes of other people is the fact. Already touched upon in the expert's report, that I am sometimes to be found standing before the mirror or elsewhere, with the upper portion of my body bared, and wearing sundry feminine adornments, such as ribbons, false necklaces, and the like. This only occurs, I may add, when I am *by myself*, and never, at least so far as I am able to avoid it, in the presence of other people." (82).

It is worth noting, as Freud does, in conjunction with this passage that Schreber adds in 1901, a time when he has regained more of his sanity, "I have now long been aware that the persons I see about me are not "cursorily improvised men" but real people, and that I must therefore behave towards them as a reasonable man is used to behave towards his fellows." (83)

What is important to stress here is that Schreber's *fantasy* or *other world* images come from that world first. In other words, he has entered a psychic reality that is trying to map out meaning and value, trying to find a way of expressing his struggles in the real world. If one is to theorize, as Freud would most naturally do, that Schreber's real world struggles have to do with seeing himself in relationships with powerful men who are "emasculating" him, his psyche, and in Freudian terms, his unconscious, dream mode of thinking, is trying to find a way of expressing this, of making sense of this in the language of the unconscious, which means symbolically. Seeing himself as a disempowered man, a man who is being psychologically dominated, even raped by other men easily translates into the whole symbolism of a female in a sexual relationship. In fact Freud's famous early conclusions in relation to several women he worked with who did exactly the same thing supports this view. In a letter to his friend Wilheilm Fliess, Freud wrote:

> Before going further into the question of infantile sexuality I must mention an error into which I fell for a while and which might well have had fatal consequences for the whole of my work. Under the pressure of the technical procedure which I used at that time, the majority of my patients reproduced from their childhood scenes in which they were sexually seduced by some grown-up person. With female patients the part of seducer was almost always assigned to their father. I believed these stories, and consequently supposed that I had discovered the roots of the subsequent neurosis in these experiences of sexual seduction in childhood. My confidence was strengthened by a few cases in which relations of this kind with a father, uncle, or elder brother had continued up to an age at which memory was to be trusted. If the reader feels inclined to shake his head at my credulity, I cannot altogether blame him; though I may plead that this was at a time when I was intentionally keeping my critical faculty in abeyance so as to preserve an unprejudiced and receptive attitude towards the many novelties which were coming to my notice every day. When, however, I was at last obliged to recognize that these scenes of seduction had never taken place, and that they were only *phantasies* which my patients had made up or which I myself had perhaps forced upon them, I was for some time completely at a loss. My confidence alike in my technique and in its results suffered a severe blow; it could not be disputed that I had arrived at these scenes by a technical method which I considered correct, and their subject-matter was unquestionably related to the symptoms from which my investigation had started. When I had pulled myself together, I was able to draw the right conclusions from my discovery: namely, that the neurotic symptoms were not related directly to actual events but to *phantasies* embodying wishes, and that as far as the neurosis was concerned psychical reality was of more importance than material reality. (84)

Here, in very clear terms, Freud is stressing that in the very case studies he begins to build his theories upon "the neurotic symptoms were not related to actual events but to wishful *phantasies*, and that as far as the neurosis was concerned psychical reality was of more importance than material reality."

Grasping Freud's dramatic insight here, Perry Meisel concludes his own discussion of Freud, "Just as Shakespeare uses traditions at will in a mingled discourse that appeals to countless regimens while submitting, in the end, to none in particular, so Freud contaminates science with literature, literature with science, to produce a prose-poetry whose only real boundaries are those of his own imagination… And just as Milton chooses the most authoritative of anterior myths in a gamble to assert his priority over the past, so Freud chooses for his equivalent purposes the most authoritative of anterior nineteenth-century myths, the myth of science." (85)

In other words, what Freud was doing was to move beyond the limitations of science (of neurology) into the realities beyond them. And it's worth noting that Freud is indeed coming out of science, out of the very discipline of neurology he is now moving beyond, and even writing a draft for a paper titled "Project for a Scientific Psychology," where he offered an important beginning discussion of a neurological explanation for neurotic behavior. (86)

Thus, perhaps Freud's deepest insight, which he never completely understood himself, is that the truths of the mind are of two worlds, the visible and the invisible, both valid, but, if anything, the more real, more important, more powerful, are those of the invisible world which take the form of symbolic expression, the language of the dream, where the literal realities become important more for their ability to be gate-posts rather than walls, just as metaphors are not meant to close off the invisible but to serve as a set of posts, one on each side of an opening, a gate to that which is beyond them.

In other words, Shreber's *phantases* of being a female entered into by a powerful God father-figure, whether or not they have any basis in his literal life desires (and at the very least it must be admitted the evidence that he had strong homosexual desires in his literal existence is contradictory), are much more important in terms of him attempting to understand and map out his entrance into a psychic and perhaps mythic world beyond his physical existence.

Ida Macalpine and Richard A. Hunter, the original translators of Schreber's account, after offering a detailed summary of terminology and of Freud, especially in terms of homosexuality write:

> We . . . read Schreber's *Memoirs* and subsequently published a study (Macalpine and Hunter, 1953) in which we showed that projection of unconscious homosexuality, though playing a part in the symptomatology, could not account for the illness in course or outcome, phenomenologically or aetiologically. Freud's homosexual bias had led him to interpretation of castration anxieties in Schreber's illness, based more on theoretical preconceptions than on actual material. Indeed he appears to have misunderstood some of Schreber's fundamental delusions, such as being "unmanned." This was a fantasy of being transformed gradually over "decades if not centuries" into a reproductive woman, carrying neither a castration threat, now passive homosexual wishes. From the beginning of his illness Schreber was as much male as female, both and neither.

> Simultaneously he "felt quickening like the first signs of life of a human embryo" in his body, "by a divine miracle . . . fertilization had occurred." (*Memoirs*, footnote 1, p. 4)
>
> This was the deepest layer of his psychosis and with it he showed what we have come to regard as the two pathognomonic features of schizophrenia: doubt and uncertainty in sex identity, which is of course implied in the ideas of change of sex accompanied by archaic procreation fantasies.
>
> If such confusion about sex identity is termed homosexuality then of course schizophrenic "homosexuality" is of a different order, and should be clearly differentiated from passive homosexual wishes towards members of the same sex, as is implied in Freud's use of the term. This last presupposes certainty in one's sex identity which Schreber had so obviously lost from the beginning of his illness and which he still clearly displayed when leaving the mental hospital by the wearing of feminine articles such as ribbons and cheap jeweler. (87)

As the image of female sexual submission develops, Schreber begins working to find a way of turning the tables, of making the conquered the conqueror, and the concluding remarks demonstrate how he is intertwining the psychic-mythic realities and the literal reality, trying to force this literal reality to conform to his symbolic world and still make his readers understand that he *does not* mean it literally. Confusing, of course, but necessarily so because he so needs to clarify that the symbolic truths are both real and yet beyond a common understanding of what is real.

Beginning in Section XXI, he tries to provide "factual proof" of the "miracles" that he experienced and of the "truth" of his "religious ideas." In addition to his "bellowing," which he claims offers some proof if only more "educated" persons had witnessed this, he attempts to convince readers that his body has, in fact, taken on "recognizable feminine characteristics," which he claims are "convincing to everybody." To do this, he offers a couple of passages he wrote during his stay at the asylum, mainly claiming that the feminine "nerves of voluptuousness" running throughout his body would be obvious upon a medical examination. He also suggests his physical appearance suggests some of the characteristics of a female, though admitting that he retains many male qualities. The first of his arguments here is couched in the neurologic terms of his time, and can be interpreted in psychological ways; the second is less convincing. What comes immediately following it is of more importance:

> "Voluptuous enjoyment of Blessedness is granted *to souls* in perpetuity and as an end in itself, but to *human beings* and other living creatures *solely as a means for the preservation of the species*. Herein lie the moral

> limitations of voluptuousness for human beings. An excess of voluptuousness would render man unfit to fulfill his other obligations; it would prevent him from ever rising to higher mental and moral perfection; indeed experience teaches that not only single individuals but also whole nations have perished through voluptuous excesses. *For me such moral limits to voluptuousness no longer exist, indeed in a certain sense the reverse applies.* In order not to be misunderstood, I must point out that when I speak of my duty to cultivate voluptuousness, I *never mean any sexual desires towards other human beings (females) least of all sexual intercourse*, but that I have to imagine myself as a man and woman in one person having intercourse with myself, or somehow have to achieve with myself a certain sexual excitement etc.—which perhaps under other circumstances might be considered immoral—but which has nothing whatever to do with any idea of masturbation or anything like it." (88)

This is a clear, dramatic statement that his female role is not meant to be understood as the desires of the flesh, but is a role he plays in his *other reality*, in his experience of that which is beyond the world of the flesh.

He continues: "This behavior has been forced on me through God having placed Himself into a relationship with me which is contrary to the Order of the World; although it may sound paradoxical, it is justifiable to apply the saying of the Crusaders in the First Crusade to myself: *Dieu le veut* (God wishes it)." (p. 209)

Furthermore, he continues, not only does God wish to be connected to him, but he says that "God is inseparably tied to my person through my nerves' power of attraction which for some time past has become inescapable; there is no possibility of God freeing Himself from my nerves for the rest of my life—although His policy is aimed at this—except perhaps in case my unmanning were to become a fact. (p. 209)

In other words, two things are getting stressed: one, that God has no choice (notice how the power has now reversed), and two, this union only exists as long as it is *not a fact*, i.e., not true in the world of facts, in the literal reality. Thus, if his feminine role were a literal, physical, sexual one, the mythic one would end.

He continues: "On the other hand God demands *constant enjoyment*, as the normal mode of existence for souls within the Order of the World. It is my duty to provide Him with it in the form of highly developed soul-voluptuousness, as far as this is possible in the circumstances contrary to the Order of the World." (p. 209)

Again, a close reading indicates he is stressing a relationship in the world of the "soul."

Immediately following this he discusses feeling it is okay if he should derive some "little sensuous pleasure in this process," which muddies the clarity, and might suggest some form of physical sex, some form of being "turned-on" by the idea of being entered by God, by a powerful male. Nevertheless, if taken in the context of his total discussion and his emphasis but one paragraph prior to this that literal sex is not what he is talking about, the passage can more justifiably be interpreted as referring to his having been instituted and condemned and asking for some other kind of "recompense," perhaps simply a better understanding of him and what he has experienced.

With this in mind, it is worth pointing out that, after discussing how he cannot always maintain his soul-voluptuousness as he feels God would want but must at times move his thoughts into a more intellectual arena, he suggests "that God would never attempt to withdraw (which always impairs my bodily well-being considerably) but would follow my attraction without resistance permanently and uninterruptedly, if only I could *always* be playing the woman's part in sexual embrace with myself, *always* rest my gaze on female beings, *always* look at female pictures, etc." p. 210)

It's worth highlighting that in order to keep his thoughts on track here, he does not want to look at male beings or pictures, as would be the case if the reality were a simple homosexual desire, but rather would find stimulation in looking a females.

In terms of his struggles with a powerful "father" figure, he concludes this section by pointing out how his "voluptuousness has become God-fearing." In other words, his female role does tie into his fear of a powerful male.

However, in the final section of his *Memoirs*, *XXII*, he stresses a reversal, certainly at the very least an emergence from this fear, from this struggle, from this experience. He begins directly, "I have arrived at the end of my work;" (p. 211) then shortly states, "All I can say with absolute certainty is something *negative, namely* that God will never succeed in his purpose of destroying my reason." (p. 211) This confidence is backed up with more of the same: "I have been absolutely clear on this point for years, as mentioned above (Chapter XX, p. 264); with it the main danger which seemed to threaten me during the early years of my illness is removed. Can there be any prospect more terrible for a human being so highly gifted in such various ways, as I may say of myself without conceit, than the prospect of losing one's reason and perishing an imbecile? Hence anything which might befall me seemed more or less trivial, once I had gained the absolute conviction through years of experience that all attempts in this direction were predestined to fail, as within the Order of the World not even God has the power to destroy a person's reason." (pp. 211-212)

He then confidently deals with his "unmanning," concluding that he "shall die as a man." (p. 212)

His next claims dealing with how he will die paint him as beyond normal human physical illnesses or even serious injury (his "restorative power of divine rays" will immediately heal him), and concludes he can only die of "senility," certainly a confident view, perhaps so confident as to undermine his psychic victory, but it is still possible to claim his new found confidence is justifiable and real, however grandiose it might be, and it goes even further.

Notice the reversal of power in his next sentence: "The other aspect of this question is what is to become of God—if I may so express myself—should I die. I am certain that the whole relation into which god brought Himself to our earth and which exists between Him and me. Hence should my person disappear through death, this relation would have to change; whether this change would be obvious to other human beings I cannot say. Perhaps one would then of necessity be forced to measures which would ensure the return of the normal Order of the World (such as discontinuing the tying-to-celestial-bodies, complete suppression of the remaining tested souls, etc.), measures which so far one has not had the will power to carry through. Only in this way, I believe, will God be able to resume once again the functions which are His duty within the Order of the World, in particular to resume His task of founding anew states of Blessedness. That my nerves would be among the first to be raised to a state of Blessedness I consider as almost certain in view of the relation which for years has existed between me and God." (p. 213)

After a few words about his discharge, concluding with "they will sooner or later have to acknowledge that they are not dealing with a lunatic in the ordinary sense," he states, "I have the impression therefore that in my future life some *great* and *magnificent satisfaction* is in store for me—not provided by human beings but somehow as a logical development arising out of the situation itself." (p. 214) As he continues, notice how he simply assumes he is innocent of any sin: "While still in Flechsig's Asylum, when I had my first glimpses of the miraculous harmony of the Order of the World, and also suffered wounding humiliations and was daily threatened by horrifying dangers, I coined this phrase for the rays: *there must be an equalizing justice and it can never be* that a morally unblemished human being with feet firmly planted in the Order of the World should have to perish as the innocent victim of other people's sins in a struggle carried on against him by hostile powers." (p. 214)

He continues in this vein, claiming "This sentence, for which I had only little evidence at the time and which was mostly intuitive, proved in the course of years correct almost beyond my expectation. The scales of victory are coming down on my side more and more, the struggle against me continues to lose its previous hostile character, the growing soul-voluptuousness makes my physical condition and my other outward circumstances more bearable. And so I believe I am not mistaken in expecting that a very special palm of victory will eventually be mine." (p. 214)

The confidence radiates from each word, and it almost has to seem overly so, but he is not lost in his glory, and demonstrates he is capable of stepping outside of his thoughts and making reasoned judgments: "Such thoughts may seem fantastic and chimerical, perhaps even ridiculous considering the pitiful and restricted circumstances in which I still lead my life." (p. 214)

However, he correctly points out, "Only he who knows the *full* measure of my sufferings in past years can understand that such thoughts *were bound* to arise in me. When I think of my sacrifices through loss of an honorable professional position, a happy marriage practically dissolved, deprived of all the pleasures of life, subjected to bodily pain, mental torture and terrors of a hitherto unknown kind, the picture emerges of a martyrdom which all in all I can only compare with the crucifixion of Jesus Christ. (p. 214) Certainly the comparison with Jesus will raise some reader's eyebrows, yet there is a similarity, and in truth some really interesting insights into Jesus relation to God (and Mary's relation to God) can be explored. If one believes Jesus is the son of God, then God was/is in Jesus, and through Jesus' suffering the entire human race was/is saved. It can be claimed that Jesus was/is the receptacle of God, of the spiritual, a female role, though here Mary figures in and might be considered the more literally natural receptacle. Perhaps it can be said that the male and female roles are more *naturally* divided between Jesus and Mary in the Biblical account. But the same salvation of the entire human race results from a union of God and human. In other words, the *other world* of the spirit intersects with the *literal world* of a particular human, and through this union salvation is achieved.

Schreber continues: "On the other hand there is the immense background of the picture of which my person and my personal fate only form the foreground. If it be true that the continuation of all creation on our earth rests entirely on the very special relations into which God entered with me, the reward of victory could only be something very extraordinary for my loyal perseverance in the struggle for my reason and for the purification of God." (p. 214-215)

Notice how, yet again, Schreber is seeing himself as the intermediary resulting in a salvation of not just humans but also God. His final two paragraphs place him clearly in a role similar to that of Jesus.

> "I come to the last point of my work. I consider it possible, even likely, that the future development of my personal fate, the spread of my religious ideas and the weight of proof of their truth will lead to a fundamental revolution in mankind's religious views unequalled in history. I do not underestimate the dangers which might arise from the overthrow of all existing religious systems. But I trust the victorious powers of truth will be sufficiently strong to cancel out any damage caused through a temporary confusion of religious feelings.
>
> Even if may, particularly Christian dogmas hitherto accepted as true, would have to be revised, the absolutely certain knowledge that a living God exists and the soul lives on after death could only come as a blessing to mankind: And so I close in the hope that in this sense favourable stars will watch over the success of my labour." (p. 215)

Notice how the redeemer as connecting link between the spiritual world of God and human existence and the need for the redeemer to suffer are intertwined in the following discussion by Joseph Campbell:

> Campbell: Abelard's idea was that Christ came to be crucified to evoke in man's heart the sentiment of compassion for the suffering of life, and so to remove man's mind from blind commitment to the goods of this world. It is in compassion with Christ that we turn to Christ, and the injured one becomes our Savior. . . It is the suffering that evokes the humanity of the human heart.
>
> Moyers: So you would agree with Abelard that mankind yearning for God and God yearning for mankind met in compassion at the cross?
>
> Campbell: Yes. (89)

This same reference also circles us back to the previous discussions of the *scapegoat*, the *savior*, and the *empathon*.

Freud, Jung, and subsequent psychologists have interpreted Schreber's *Memoirs* as the expressions of a *schizophrenic*, more precisely a *paranoid schizophrenic* (which they defined in terms of homosexual desires), and perhaps on one level they are. However, at the same time his experiences match up with the kinds of experiences *shamans* and other spiritual people have claimed to have had, whether in the realm of Judaism, Christianity, Buddhism, Hinduism, or any other organized religion (and remember all of the Catholic Saints must have experienced at least two *miracles*).

Notes

1. All of these passages are from the King James version of the *Bible.*
2. Catechismus council, Trident, n. 4, *De Catechizandis rudibus.*
3. Decree XVII of the Synod of Bethlehem.
4. *Ave verum corpus natum /de Maria Virgine; /vere passum, immolatum /in cruce pro homine*!" (late-fourteenth-century hymn).
5. *Commentary on True and False Religion*, 1525.
6. *Confession Concerning Christ's Supper*, 1528; *Weimar Ausgabe* 26, 442; *Luther's Works* 37, 299-300.
7. *Formula of Concord Solid Declaration* VII, 35; *Triglot Concordia*, 983.
8. *Formula of Concord Solid Declaration* VII.77-78 with quotation from Luther Weimar Ausgabe 26, 282ff (Tappert, 583-584).
9. *Formula of Concord* Epitiome, VII, 42; Solid Declaration, VII, 127; Triglot Concordia, 817, 1015.
10. *Luther's Works*, American Edition, Jaroslav Pelikan and Helmut Lehmann, gen. eds., 55 vols., (St. Louis and Philadelphia: CPH and Fortress Press, 1955-86), 37:187.
11. *Divine Poems. On the Sacrament.*
12. Windsor Statement on Eucharistic Doctrine from the Anglican-Roman Catholic International Consultation and Elucidation of the ARCIC Windsor Statement.
13. *The Power of Myth*, p. 162.
14. *This Holy Mystery: Part One*, The United Methodist Church GBOD (Governing Body of Desciples).
15. *see "Article XVIII" of the Articles of Religion, Means of Grace.*
16. Potter, G. R.; Greengrass, M., *John Calvin*, London: Edward Arnold, 1983, pp. 34-42.
17. See *Westminster Confession of Faith*, Ch. 29; Belgic Confession, Article 35; open communion.
18. "A Common Calling," p. 66.
19. *Marburg Revisited*, pp. 103-104.
20. *A Formula for Agreement.*
21. Unabridged 2nd ed., World Publishing, 1970, p. 1147.
22. Royal Publ., 1971, Riverside Book and Bible House, Iowa.
23. *Myths to Live By*, Bantam, 1973.
24. Vol. 96, Article 3, Jan. 27, 1962, pp. 853-876.
25. *Myths to Live By*, Bantam, 1973, p. 208.
26. *Myths to Live By*, Bantam, 1973, pp. 208-209.
27. *The Cry for Myth*, Bantam, 1991, pp. 17-19.
28. *American Anthropologist*, vol. 69, no 1, 1967.
29. *Myths to Live By*, Bantam, 1973, p. 225.
30. Ballantine Books, "Chapter Seven," 1967.
31. *Myths to Live By*, Bantam, 1973, p. 237.
32. *Myths to Live By*, Bantam, 1973, p. 237.
33. Bernard Rimland, "Foreword," *Nobody Nowhere*, 1992; rpt, HarperCollins, 2002.

34. Donna Williams, *Nobody Nowhere*, 1992; rpt, HarperCollins, 2002, p. 11.
35. Donna Williams, *Nobody Nowhere*, 1992; rpt, HarperCollins, 2002, p. 47.
36. Donna Williams, *Nobody Nowhere*, 1992; rpt, HarperCollins, 2002, p. 12.
37. Donna Williams, *Nobody Nowhere*, 1992; rpt, HarperCollins, 2002, p. 17.
38. "Through the Looking-Glass," *The Works of Lewis Carroll*, ed. Roger Lancelyn Green, Spring Books/Hamlyn Publ., 1968, p. 120.
39. Donna Williams, *Nobody Nowhere*, 1992; rpt, HarperCollins, 2002, p. 18.
40. Donna Williams, *Nobody Nowhere*, 1992; rpt, HarperCollins, 2002, pp. 19-20.
41. *I Never Promised You a Rose Garden*, Hannah Green, Signet, 1964; rpt., Joanna Greenberg, 1989; The Cry for Myth, Rollo May, Delta, 1991, pp. 17-21.
42. "Alice's Adventures in Wonderland," *The Works of Lewis Carroll*, ed. by Roger Lancelyn Green, Hamlyn Publ., 1965, pp. 24-25.
43. *I Never Promised You a Rose Garden*, Hannah Green, Signet, 1964; rpt., Joanna Greenberg, 1989, p. 31.
44. Donna Williams, *Nobody Nowhere*, 1992; rpt, HarperCollins, 2002, p. 10
45. Rollo May used *I Never Promised You a Rose Garden* to demonstrate the relationship of individualized myths with archetypal myths and how they both supply the necessary landscapes for psychic health; put quote from May, p. 1920 to demonstrate connection with myths, concluding his discussion: "Myth making thus is central in psychotherapy. It is of the essence that the therapist permit the client to take his or her myths seriously, whether the myths come up in dreams or in free association or in fantasy. Every individual who needs to bring order and coherence into the streams of her or his sensations, emotions, and ideas entering consciousness from within and without is forced to do deliberately for himself what in previous ages had been done for him by family, custom, church, and state. In therapy myths may be a reaching out, a way of trying out new structures of life, or a desperate venture at rebuilding his or her broken way of life. Myths, as Hannah Green put it, are "sharers of our loneliness." (p. 21)
46. When a medical or psychiatric diagnosis can't come up with a specific condition it is sometimes referred to as a "trashcan" diagnosis. In other words, something is obviously wrong, but just what it is cannot be determined. This has been and remains a common situation for psychology and neurology. For a number of decades in the mid-1900s, schizophrenia was the trashcan term, taking on a somewhat glamorous quality and being applied to many forms of mental illness now classified outside of it. The current "trashcan" term (though, of course, since it is the "in" thing, would not be so easily dismissed as such) is autism.
47. It would be an interesting exercise to compare the various characters in Joanna Greenberg's fantasy world with those in Lewis Carroll's. In both cases, these entities are far from friendly, and seem to be operating out of some illogical sense of how the world works, have some system of ethics, but it either simply doesn't match that of the real world or is expressed in ways that make it hard to sort out.
48. *I Never Promised You a Rose Garden*, Hannah Green, Signet, 1964; rpt., Joanna Greenberg, 1989, p. 54.
49.*I Never Promised You a Rose Garden*, Joanne Greenberg, 1989, pp. 152-156.
50. *I Never Promised You a Rose Garden*, Joanne Greenberg, 1989, pp. 34-35.
51. *I Never Promised You a Rose Garden*, Joanne Greenberg, 1989, pp. 13-14.

52. *Nobody Nowhere*, 1992; rpt, HarperCollins, 2002, p. 130.
53. *Nobody Nowhere*, 1992; rpt, HarperCollins, 2002, p. 160.
54. *Nervous Child*, 2, pp.217-250.
55. The Free Press/Simon & Schuster, 1972. New York: Simon and Schuster, 1997.
56. Yale Development Disorders Clinic, www.med.yale.edu/chldstdy/autism/pddinfl/html, August 9, 2006.
57. Warner Books, 1996.
58. Coauthored with Margaret M. Scariano, Warner Books, 1986.
59. Vintage Books, 1995.
60. Vintage Books, 1995.
61. p. 296, *An Anthropologist from Mars: Seven Paradoxical Tales*)
62. "Creativity and Imagination in Autism and Asperger Syndrome," *Journal of Autism and Developmental Disorders*, August 29, 1999, pp. 319-326.
63. *Journal of Autism and Developmental Disorders*, December 8, 2005, pp. 753-755.
64. "The Neuropsychology of Visual Artistic Production," *Neuropsychologia*, 2004 (42:11), pp. 1568-1583.
65. *Neuropsychiatry, Neuropsychology, and Behavorial Neurology*, January, 2000, pp. 29-38.
66. home.att.net/~ascaris1/genius.html.
67. "Body and Soul," *The Times*, December 1, 2005.
68. *The Siege: A Family's Journey into the World of an Autistic Child,* Little, Brown and Company, 1967, and *Exiting Nirvana: A Daughter's Life with Autism*, Little, Brown and Company, 2001.
69. Harcourt Brace Jovanovich, 1977.
70. Arcade Publishing, 2003.
71. www.answers.com/topic/controversies-in-autism.
72. The Free Press, 1967, pp. 96-97.
73. report on Schreber, 1899, pp. 386-8; quoted in Freud, "Notes on a Case of Paranoia," *The Complete Pyschoanalytic Works of Sigmund Freud*, Vol XII, trans. By James Strachey, Hogarth Press, 1958, pp. 16-17.
74. *The Standard Edition of the Complete Psychological Works of Sigmund Freud, Vol XII, The Case of Schreber,* translated by James Strachey, Hogarth Press, 1958, p. 29.
75. *The Standard Edition of the Complete Psychological Works of Sigmund Freud, Vol XII, The Case of Schreber,* translated by James Strachey, Hogarth Press, 1958, p. 18.
76. p. 56; *The Standard Edition of the Complete Psychological Works of Sigmund Freud, Vol XII, The Case of Schreber,* translated by James Strachey, Hogarth Press, 1958, p. 19.
77. p. 59; *The Standard Edition of the Complete Psychological Works of Sigmund Freud, Vol XII, The Case of Schreber,* translated by James Strachey, Hogarth Press, 1958, p. 19.

78. p. 61; *The Standard Edition of the Complete Psychological Works of Sigmund Freud, Vol XII, The Case of Schreber,* translated by James Strachey, Hogarth Press, 1958, p. 19.
79. p. 127; *The Standard Edition of the Complete Psychological Works of Sigmund Freud, Vol XII, The Case of Schreber,* translated by James Strachey, Hogarth Press, 1958, p. 20.
80. p 177; *The Standard Edition of the Complete Psychological Works of Sigmund Freud, Vol XII, The Case of Schreber,* translated by James Strachey, Hogarth Press, 1958, p. 20.
81. p. 177; *The Standard Edition of the Complete Psychological Works of Sigmund Freud, Vol XII, The Case of Schreber,* translated by James Strachey, Hogarth Press, 1958, p. 20-21.
82. p. 429; *The Standard Edition of the Complete Psychological Works of Sigmund Freud, Vol XII, The Case of Schreber,* translated by James Strachey, Hogarth Press, 1958, p. 21.
83. p. 409; *The Standard Edition of the Complete Psychological Works of Sigmund Freud, Vol XII, The Case of Schreber,* translated by James Strachey, Hogarth Press, 1958, p. 21.
84. Quoted from a letter to Fliess, *The Origins of Psycholoanalysis: Letters to Wilheilm Fliess, Drafts and Notes*, 1887-1902; trans. Eric Mosbacher and James Strachey, NewYork: Basic Books, 1954, pp. 215-218; *Sigmund Freud: An Autobiographical Study*, 1925; trans., James Strachey, 1936; rpt., W.W.Norton: New York, 1963, pp.62-64.
85. *Freud, Standard Edition*, volume 1, 1895, pp. 283-391; also in Peter Gay's *The Freud Reader*, Yale Univ., Norton: New York, 1989, pp. 86-89.
86. "Introduction: Freud as Literature," *Freud: A Collection of Critical Essays.* Ed. By Perry Meisel, Prentice-Hall: Englewood Cliffs, N. J., 1981, pp. 34-35.
87. "Translators' Introduction," *Memoirs of My Nervous Illness*, pp. 24-25.
88. *Memoirs of My Nervous Illness* pp. 208-209.
89. *The Power of Myth: Interviews with Bill Moyers,* p. 140.

PSYCHOSIS

The Burning of Evil

For Carl Jung, Schreber is an example of a man who has experienced a *psychotic break*, what can be considered a *schizophrenic neurosis*:

> The things that come to light brutally in insanity remain hidden in the background in neurosis, but they continue to influence consciousness nonetheless. When, therefore, the analysis penetrates the background of conscious phenomena, it discovers the same archetypal figures that activate the deliriums of psychotics. Finally, there is any amount of literary and historical evidence to prove that in the case of these archetypes we are dealing with normal types of fantasy that occur practically everywhere and not with the monstrous products of insanity. The pathological element does not lie in the existence of these ideas, but in the dissociation of consciousness that can no longer control the unconscious. In all cases of dissociation it is therefore necessary to integrate the unconscious into consciousness. This is a synthetic process which I have termed the "individuation process." (1)

In Jungian terms, a *schizophrenic* gets stuck in his unconscious images and symbols, and cannot integrate them with his conscious world. Another example Jung offers of this is John Custance's autobiography, *Wisdom, Madness and Folly: The Philosophy of a Lunatic.*

The cover flap of this has the following summary:

> This book is an autobiographical account of madness that is unlike any book by an ex-lunatic you have ever read. John Custance writes brilliantly without self-pity of the exaltation and terror of madness. But more than a description of insanity, this book is one of wisdom, of one man's search for truth and insight into the nature of good and evil. It is the only attempt to our best knowledge that has yet been made to relate original experiences of psychosis with serious philosophical thought.
>
> John Custance is subject to manic depression. He has spent many periods in mental hospitals, public and private, as a voluntary patient, and has been on several occasions certified as insane. His book is an original document of psychological experience written for the most part while the author was actually confined in mental institutions over a period of fifteen years. His account of conditions in mental hospitals – which is disturbing enough – is included in an Appendix, and for the greater part of the book he analyzes his disease and explorers the states of vision and illumination on which it affords.
>
> The book's supreme interest lies in its startlingly intimate revelations if what goes on in the human mind in the manic and depressive state. The main characteristics of the manic state he gives as: intense sense of well-being, heightened sense of reality (a more vivid reaction to sense impression) breach of barriers in individuality, inhibition of sense of

> repulsion, a release of sexual and moral tension, delusions of grandeur, and a sense of ineffable revelation. (2)

In an introduction to the book, Jung stresses that a key in these types of psychosis is the freeing up of the unconscious from the constraints or inhibitions of the conscious, which allows the psychologist a chance to see how the unconscious works in its raw state (he makes the same claim in other passages about both *schizophrenia* and *manic depression,* what today is generally referred to as *bipolar disease*). As the cover flap highlights, that uninhibited bursting forth of the unconscious caused by this kind of psychosis is the exciting promise of the book. Unfortunately, the book does not take us into that world as much as it promises, mainly because it is written during Custance's *normal states*, and tends to be much, much more him showing off his scholarship and plunging into pseudo psychology, pseudo psychiatry, pseudo philosophy, pseudo theology, and the like, in order to put forth his grand views of what he titles *actuality*, a curious worldview based roughly on an application of *schizophrenia* to the entire world, which might have more interest if it were better supported by rigorous logic and scholarship, something he continually dodges by claiming in his humble way to not be an expert, but instead putting forth his unique position as a *bipolar* or *manic depressive* who has experienced it and thus knows it better than the various intellectuals in the fields he wanders into. Furthermore, it is written during and shortly after WWII, and there is a good deal of predicting future events resulting from that war, most notably WWIII, that, if anything, demonstrates he was wrong in his predictions, which contributes to undermining his whole convoluted theory. Nevertheless, even with these large weaknesses, the memoir does offer a few glimpses into those strange states when he was experiencing his psychosis.

As the above passages indicate, *bipolar* or *manic depression* involves dramatic mood shifts between states of euphoria and depression, interspersed with periods of normal functioning. During the manic phase, feelings of extreme irritability towards other people and happenings occur, and energy, joy, and self-esteem climb to irrational levels, followed by a delusional pattern. Hallucinations are common. Rapid speech and racing thoughts are normal, as is a decreased need for sleep, hyper-sexuality, and impulsiveness. Often, unimportant stimuli take on excessive interest, resulting in loss of normal functioning, such as knowing what time it is. Even the periods of euphoria are mixed with disturbing, at times frightening behavior.

There are two forms of *Bipolar Disorder. Bipolar I* involves such *manic symptoms* as severe, debilitating symptoms, extreme mood swings, agitation, nervousness, irritability, a short-tempered, edgy feeling, an inflated sense of self, inappropriate judgment, increased sex drive, loss of inhibition, the inability to focus, delusions, hallucinations, euphoria, heavy use of drugs or alcohol, boundless energy, insomnia, rage, aggression, disassociated thoughts, rapid speech, reckless spending, high speed driving, and high risk activities; and such *depressive symptoms* as a low, listless mood, a lack of energy, constant fatigue, insomnia, feelings of guilt, worthlessness and unworthiness, an inability to concentrate and make decisions, excessive drug or alcohol use, a lack of self-esteem, a withdrawal from others, a loss of interest in activities, self-abuse, thoughts of suicide.

Bipolar II (aka *Hypomania*) involves less extreme forms of bipolar behavior. It is closely related to *Attention Deficit-Hyperactivity Disorder (ADHD)*, *Borderline Personality Disorder (BPC),* as mentioned above, *Schizophrenia.* (3)

Edgar Allan Poe first published "The Tell-Tale Heart" in James Russell Lowell's *The Pioneer*, January, 1843. This short story of a man both sane and insane is probably the best literary expression ever of such a condition.

In *Insanity and Genius* I compared this to Richard Dadd, with the suggestion that the story's representation and the real life of Richard Dadd both fit standard definitions of *schizophrenia.* (4) Now let's see how Poe's story matches John Custance's form of *bipolarism/manic depression*.

"The Tell-Tale Heart" begins in perfect *schizophrenic, manic depressive, bi-polar* voice:

> TRUE!—Nervous—VERY, very dreadfully nervous I had been and am; but why *will* you say that I am mad? The disease had sharpened my senses—not destroyed—not dulled them. Above all was the sense of hearing acute. I heard all things in the heaven and in the earth. I heard many things in hell. How, then, am I mad? Hearken! And observe how healthily—how calmly I can tell you the whole story.

Even in just this short initial passage, the dual insane and sane voices of the narrator are apparent, and several characteristics are highlighted, including his *nervousness* and his *sharpened senses*, two of the most stressed aspects of *manic depression/bipolarism*. Immediately in his own discussion, John Custance writes, "I was attacked by a not uncommon nervous disease known as manic-depression."

Here is a discussion from John Custance similar to Poe's narrator's comments about hearing "all things in the heaven and in the earth . . . [and] in hell":

> My hearing appears to be more sensitive, and I am able to take in many different sound-impressions at the same time. Thus, although busily engaged in writing this in a crowded ward with people walking up and down and the most diverse sounds all around me, from the cries of gulls outside to the laughter and chatter of my fellow-patients, I am fully alive to what is going on and yet find no difficulty in concentrating on my work. At times I have known sounds make a tremendous effect upon me, almost as though I were in a gallery with supernatural powers of resonance. At such times my own very ordinary bass voice appears to be as powerful as that of Chaliapin's at least; it is as though passages in my chest which are normally clogged were opened up, and my chest actually seems to set up abnormal vibrations. (5)

And, just as Poe's narrator points out that "the disease had sharpened [not just hearing but all] my senses—not destroyed—not dulled them," Custance includes other senses as well, beginning with his visual sense:

> The first thing I note is the peculiar appearances of the lights—the ordinary electric lights in the ward. They are not exactly brighter, but deeper, more intense, perhaps a trifle more ruddy than usual. Moreover, if I relax the focusing of my eyes, which I can do very much more easily than in normal circumstances, a bright starlike phenomenon emanates from the lights, ultimately forming a maze of iridescent patterns of all colours of the rainbow, which remind me vaguely of the Aurora Borealis.
>
> There are a good many people in the ward, and their faces make a peculiarly intense impression on me. I will not say that they have exactly a halo round them, though I have often had that impression in more acute phases of mania. At present it is rather that faces seem to glow with a sort of inner light which shows up the characteristic lines extremely vividly. Thus, although I am the most hopeless draughtsman as a rule, in this state I can draw quite recognizable likenesses. The phenomenon is not confined to faces; it applies to the human body as a whole, and to a rather lesser degree to other objects such as trees, clouds, flowers and so on. Coloured objects make a particularly vivid impression, possibly in view of the associations they arouse . . . and, curiously enough, so do large vehicles, particularly steamrollers, railway engines and trains. Perhaps the associations of childhood are involved here. Connected with these vivid impressions is a rather curious feeling behind the eyeballs, rather as though a vast electric motor were pulsing away there. (6)

Custance continues:

All my other senses seem more acute than usual. Certainly my sense of touch is heightened; my fingers are much more sensitive and neat. Although generally a clumsy person with an execrable handwriting I can write much more neatly than usual; I can print, draw, embellish and carry out all sorts of little manual operations, such a pasting up scrapbooks and the like, which would normally drive me to distraction. I also note a peculiar tingling in my fingers tips. (7)

And later, he writes:

At the moment my sense of smell seems more or less normal, and so does my sense of taste. In slightly acute phases of mania, however, both these senses are well above par. Even now I have no doubt that if I were to be allowed to walk about freely in a flower garden I should appreciate the scents far more than usual; and I have often in manic states eaten ordinary cabbage leaves or new Brussels sprouts picked straight off the plants with such relish that they appeared to me the greatest delicacies—a kind of manna from Heaven. Even common grass tastes excellent, while real delicacies like strawberries or raspberries give ecstatic sensations appropriate to a veritable food of the gods. (8)

Poe's madman continues his narrative:

It is impossible to say how first the idea entered my brain; but once conceived, it haunted me day and night. Object there was one. Passion there was none. I loved the old man. He had never wronged me. He had never given me insult. For his gold I had no desire. I think it was the eye! Yes, it was this! One of his eyes resembled that of a vulture—a pale blue eye, with a film over it. Whenever it fell upon me, my blood ran cold; and so by degree—very gradually—I made up my mind to take the life of the old man, and thus rid myself of the eye for ever.

Now this is the point. You fancy me mad. Madmen know nothing. But you should have seen *me*. You should have seen how wisely I proceeded—with what caution—with what foresight—with what dissimulation I went to work! I was never kinder to the old man than during the whole week before I killed him. And every night, about midnight, I turned the latch of his door and opened it—oh so gently! And then, when I had made an opening sufficient for my head, I put in a dark lantern, all closed, closed, so that no light shone out, and then I thrust in my head. Oh, you would have laughed to see how cunningly I thrust it in! I moved it slowly—very, very slowly, so that I might not disturb the old man's sleep. It took me an hour to place my whole head within the opening so far that I could see him as he lay upon his bed. Ha!—would a madman have been so wise as this?

After describing how he crept in precisely at midnight for seven nights to gaze in on this father figure of a man, he describes how, on the eight night, once again with great caution, with great care and patience and cunning, he entered the old man's room, this time accidentally making a noise when his thumb slipped, but again displaying great patience in standing completely silent and still for a whole hour until the man again fell asleep. But then he describes how he began to hear the old man's heart beating, saying "It increased my fury, as the beating of a drum stimulates the soldier into courage." Finally, the beating drives him to kill the man.

John Custance writes:

> Some other abnormal features in my condition can I think be directly related to the intensified sense-impressions mentioned above, and so can properly be classified under "heightened sense of reality." One of these is extreme rapidity of association of ideas. Since it is largely through the association of ideas that we take in the sense-impressions of the world around us, it would seem to be quite logical that intensified sense-impressions should be connected with a freer functioning of that particular faculty. Let me try to give an example.
>
> As I sit here, looking out of the window of the ward, I see flocks of seagulls who have been driven inland by the extreme cold. The mere sight of these seagulls sets up immediately and virtually simultaneously in my mind the following trains of thoughts:--
>
> 1. A pond called Seagull's Spring near my home.
> 2. Mermaids, i.e. "Sea girls," sirens, Lorelei, Mother Seager's syrup, syrup of figs, the blasted fig-tree in the Gospels, Professor Joad who could not accept Jesus as the supremely perfect Man owing to particular incident. Here the chain stops as I cannot remember the exact title of Joad's book, which was a confession of the failure of his agnosticism.
> 3. The Mental Hospital where I spent nearly a year during my worst attack of suicidal depression. The weather that winter was also very cold, and quantities of seagulls came into the courts of the hospital. At that time I was suffering from the delusion that I was a supremely evil person who had sold his soul to Sata, and the gulls terrified me for two reasons: firstly because I thought of myself as a sort of super-gull who had been "gulled" into selling his soul; and secondly because I thought I was responsible for all the death and evil in the world and that the spirits of all the lost seamen since the world began were in those gulls calling for vengeance on me.
>
> It is interesting to note that both in manic and in depressive periods of sufficient intensity animistic conceptions of this kind impel themselves forcibly upon me; I cannot avoid seeing spirits in everything.

> 4. Gulls equals girls, lovely girls, lovelies, film-stars, countless stars in the infinite wastes of space, query: is space really infinite? According to Einstein it is not; it is a sort of finite infinity best represented by a multi-dimensional sphere which it is theoretically possible to circumnavigate. Einstein has always had a peculiar fascination for me, but it is only in manic periods that I imagine that I can really understand him. No doubt it is pure delusion. My mind is filled with fantastic ideas revolving about Time and its associations, and in particular about the Wellsian concept of a Time Machine. Time seems to be as it were fluid and relative so that it must be possible to move about in it. The "space-time continuum" has a peculiarly vivid reality for me; I actually see it as a kind of endless band. Einstein's principle that all in the continuum must be relative to an observer situated at a given place and proceeding at a given speed in a given direction fits in very well, since it emphasizes the essential connection between the human factor and the physical world, life and matter. On occasion I have had actual visions of a Time Machine, a horrible mechanism which would only work by utilizing the psychic energy and contacts of a live human being who convinced that evil men were making or could in the course of time make such a machine. I can see it now as I saw it first, reflected as an "illusion" from the wall of my room, distorting the face and body of its victim in the most horrible manner conceivable. It was surmounted by a huge clock.
>
> That will serve, I think, as a fair example of the associations and trains of thought aroused the sight of those seagulls. It is quite reasonable that objects which can through the psycho-physical mechanism of the human body awaken such numerous and vivid associations should also make intense impression on the retina. (9)

Then, Poe's narrator continues, "If still you think me mad, you will think so no longer when I describe the wise precautions I took for the concealment of the body." And he proceeds to explain how he carefully cut up and hide the body under the floor. Then two officers arrive. A neighbor had heard a shriek during the night. But he is not concerned. Instead, he seems to enjoy it all. He says:

> I smiled,—for *what* had I to fear? I bade the gentlemen welcome. The shriek, I said, was my own in a dream. The old man, I mentioned, was absent in the country. I took my visitors all over the house. I bade them search—search *well.* I led them, at length, to his chamber. I showed them his treasures, secure, undisturbed. In the enthusiasm of my confidence, I brought chairs into the room, and desired them *here* to rest from their fatigues, while I myself, in the wild audacity of my perfect triumph, placed my own seat upon the very spot beneath which reposed the corpse of the victim.

He is in control. He is confident. He is enjoying his superiority over these lesser minds. But the insane part of him starts to intrude, the beating of the heart becomes louder and louder and drives him into a frenzy. He says:

> The officers were satisfied. My *manner* convinced them. I was singularly at ease. They sat, and while I answered cheerily, they chatted familiar things. But, ere long, I felt myself getting pale and wished them gone. My head ached, and I fancied a ringing in my ears: but still they sat and still chatted. The ringing became more distinct:--it continued and became more distinct: I talked more freely to get rid of the feeling: but it continued and gained definitiveness—until, at length, I found that the noise was *not* within my ears.
>
> No doubt I now grew *very* pale;--but I talked more fluently, and with a heightened voice. Yet the sound increased—and what could I do? It was *a low, dull, quick sound—much such a sound as a watch makes when enveloped in cotton.* I gasped for breath—and yet the officers heard it not. I talked more quickly—more vehemently; but the noise steadily increased. I arose and argued about the trifles, in a high key and with violent gesticulations, but the noise steadily increased. Why *would* they not be gone? I paced the floor to and fro with heavy strides, as if excited to fury by the observation of the men—but the noise steadily increased. Oh God! What *could* I do? I foamed—I raved—I swore! I swung the chair upon which I had been sitting, and grated it upon the boards, but the noise arose over all and continually increased. It grew louder—louder–*louder*! And still the men chatted pleasantly, and smiled. Was it possible they heard not? Almighty God!—no, no! They heard!—they suspected!—they *knew*!—they were making a mockery of my horror!—this I thought, and this I think. But anything was better than this agony! Anything was more tolerable than this derision! I could bear those hypocritical smiles no longer! I felt that I must scream or die!—and now—again!—hark! Louder! Louder! Louder! *Louder*!—
>
> "Villains!" I shrieked, "dissemble no more! I admit the deed!—tear up the planks!—here, here!—it is the beating of his hideous heart!"

Now notice how John Custance's discussion of colors leads to a similar over-confidence and grandiose view of himself:

> The windows of my side-room look out on to a road much frequented by the female patients of the Hospital. They affect rather gay attire, and the colours are sometimes a little overpowering. During the last few days those colours have seemed to be threatening me in an extraordinary way, perhaps because there was an underlying possibility of a swift change from mania to depression. At one time green and red predominated. There was a time when I was terrified of green, because it was the signal to go, and the only

place I thought I could be going to was Hell. However I eventually got out of Hell and at present green has no terrors for me. It is my wife's favourite colour—she does not think it unlucky; and it stands for grass and growth.

In combination with red, however, it does not seem so favourable. Red is the Devil's colour, and perhaps I am not quite safe from him yet. Red also means stop, and I don't in the least want to stop here forever. However, with a certain amount of effort, concentration and prayer, I conquered the red with the help of the green and felt safe.

The next day the colours had suffered a kaleidoscopic change. Gone were the reds and the greens; there were nothing but blues, blacks and grays, with an occasional purple. The sky, which had been bright and clear, was overcast; it was raining. This new combination of colours constituted a new threat, with which I had to deal.

Blue was the heavenly colour; I was in Heaven, so that blue was appropriate and could be regarded as on my side. Black, on the other hand, was another of the Devil's colours. Was he going to get me after all? What had grey to say about it? At night all cats are grey, so perhaps grey was a feline colour. I like the cat tribe, particularly when in the manic state. They are, I know, slightly Satanic, but it is the kind of Satanism I prefer; it reminds me of a favourite delusion—that I am Satan, the Servant of All, the Scientific Snake who told the truth in the Garden of Eden (as Bernard Shaw pointed out in *Man and Superman*). So I need not fear the Devil or his sable colour. As for the purple, well in those circumstances I could reasonably look upon it as the imperial purple, a sign that I was Emperor or colours, if of nothing else. I asked the spirit of Julius Caesar by the simple process of tossing a coin with the image and superscription of his successor, King George. Julius was good enough to give me confirmation. The coin fell heads. Upon this I took a sheet of lavatory paper and printed in large letters

I HAVE MADE A CORNER IN COLOURS 8-3-47.

This document I showed with pride to the doctor when he came to see me on his rounds. Greatly to his credit he took me very seriously indeed. After all, an Emperor of Colours should be treated with respect! (10)

Returning to Richard Dadd, we now have some interesting frames for trying to understand him, his psychological journey, his painting *The Fairy-Feller's Masterstroke*, and his accompanying poem. How well does he fit all of the discussion above? Well, it seems clear he did wander through a twilight zone of multiple realities. The world of fairies, the world of mythology, the world of the dream, the world of art, the world of psychology, and the world of simple physical existence certainly got intermingled for him, and all existed, all were real in some way. There can be no doubt that he saw himself at the center of all of these worlds. He was the Fairy-Feller in the painting waiting for the command from the Patriarch to cut open the hazelnut. As suggested earlier, this in itself opens multiple realities, for the Fairy-Feller in the painting ultimately exists in one world as merely a fictional character in a painting, the result of Richard Dadd's imagination, a character that populated the world of the fairy, which was also the world of the dream, and the world of mythology, and the world of the psyche. At the same time this character was Dadd himself. So, in depicting himself in this fictional world he was saying that he, that Dadd himself was the person capable of cracking open the hazelnut, and the hazelnut was the carriage of Queen Mab (of the main life force of the world of dreams). Thus, Dadd was in position to provide the vehicle for the dream to begin. But, he waited for the command from the Patriarch, which has been discussed earlier as that father figure, both real and yet spiritual, in Dadd's case clearly represented in his schizophrenic connection to Osiris.

Richard Dadd was also capable of disassociating himself from his dual personalities, both the servant of Osiris, insane and condemned by the "real" world, seen as someone to be pitied, to be ostracized, to be locked up, and at the same time a person superior to this "real" world in having been chosen by a god as a special person with higher knowledge. And the other depiction of him in the painting, the creator of this world, the one who conjures it up, the alchemist, represented this.

Whether or not Dadd went through the schizophrenic journey or voyage described above can be debated. The various commentaries still in existence about him make it obvious he retained his beliefs in Osiris his entire life, and thus perhaps never did complete the journey, never did find his way back (which actually fits the current definitions of paranoid schizophrenia better than these stories of people who did make it back). He was seen by others consistently as a poor figure, someone to be pitied. At the same time, there are many references to his sane personality, especially as time went on in his imprisonment, and he made friends with those in charge of him, was even considered a teacher by Hayden in something of a role reversal. Also while there is no statement from Richard Dadd or anyone else that he returned or recovered from his insanity, the *Fairy-Feller's Master Stroke* reveals a highly complex comprehension of what he had gone through and where he had emerged, much in line with shamanic experiences.

Notes

1. *The Archetypes of the Collective Unconscious*, pp. 39-40.
2. Pellegrini & Cudahy, 1952.
3. See: http://health.nih.gov/topic/BipolarDisorder; *www. bipolar central.com.*
4. *Insanity and Genius: Masks of Madness and the Mapping of Meaning and Value,* Harry Eiss, Cambridge Scholars Press, 2008.
5. *Wisdom, Madness and Folly: The Philosophy of a Lunatic* Pellegrini & Cudahy, 1952, p. 32.
6. *Wisdom, Madness and Folly: The Philosophy of a Lunatic* Pellegrini & Cudahy, 1952, p. 31.
7. *Wisdom, Madness and Folly: The Philosophy of a Lunatic* Pellegrini & Cudahy, 1952, p. 32.
8. *Wisdom, Madness and Folly: The Philosophy of a Lunatic* Pellegrini & Cudahy, 1952, p. 32.
9. *Wisdom, Madness and Folly: The Philosophy of a Lunatic* Pellegrini & Cudahy, 1952, pp. 33-35.
10. *Wisdom, Madness and Folly: The Philosophy of a Lunatic* Pellegrini & Cudahy, 1952, p. 37-38.

ILLUMINATION

Grief

The writings of Daniel Paul Schreiber and John Custance (and the painting of Richard Dadd) become even more interesting when current views about the connections of *artists* with *shamans* and *spirituality* are explored.

Joseph Campbell states it again and again in his interviews with Bill Moyers:

> Moyers: Who interprets the divinity inherent in nature for us today? Who are our shamans? Who interprets unseen things for us!
>
> Campbell: It is the function of the artist to do this. The artist is the one who communicates myth for today. But he has to be an artist who understands mythology and humanity and isn't simply a sociologist with a program for you.
>
> Moyers: So shamans functioned in early societies as artists do now. They play a much more important role than simply being—
>
> Campbell: They played the role the priesthood traditionally plays in our society.
>
> Moyers: The shamans were priests?
>
> Campbell: There's a major difference, as I see it, between a shaman and a priest. A priest is a functionary of a social sort. The society worships certain deities in a certain way, and the priest becomes ordained as a functionary to carry out that ritual. The deity to whom he is devoted is a deity that was there before he came along. But the shaman's powers are symbolized in his own familiars, deities of his own personal experience. His authority comes out of a psychological experience, not a social ordination.
>
> Moyers: The shaman has been somewhere I haven't, . . .
>
> Campbell: Also, . . . the shaman may translate some of his visions into ritual performances for his people. That's bringing the inner experience into the outer life of the people themselves.
>
> Moyers: This is the beginning of religion?
>
> Campbell: Personally, I think that's how religions began. But that's just a guess. We don't really know.
>
> Moyers: Jesus goes into the wilderness, experiences a psychological transformation, comes back, and says to people, "Follow me." And this happens in these elementary cultures?
>
> Campbell: That's the evidence we have. We find a shamanic aspect in practically all the hunting cultures.
>
> Moyers: Why, particularly, in the hunting cultures?
>
> Campbell: Because they're individual. The hunter is an individual in a way that no farmer will ever be. Toiling in the fields and waiting for nature to tell you when you're going to do it is one thing, but going off on a hunt—every hunt is a different hunt from the last one. And the hunters are trained in individual skills that require very special talents and abilities.
>
> Moyers: So what happened to the shaman in human evolution?

Campbell: When this big emphasis came on the settled village life, the shaman lost power. In fact, there's a wonderful set of stories and myths of some of the Southwestern American Indians, the Navaho and Apache, who were originally hunting peoples who came down into an area where agriculture had been developed and took on an agricultural system of life. In their stories of the beginning, there is typically an amusing episode where the shamans are disgraced and the priests take over. The shamans say something that offends the sun, and the sun disappears, and then they say, "Oh, I can bring the sun back." Then they do all their tricks, and these are cynically, comically described. But their tricks don't bring back the sun back. The shamans are reduced, then, to a shaman society, a kind of clown society. They are magicians of a special power, but their power is now subordinate to a larger society. (1)

At another point, Campbell says:

Myth must be kept alive. The people who can keep it alive are artists of one kind or another. The function of the artist is the mythologization of the environment and the world.

Moyers: You mean artists are the mythmakers of our day?

Campbell: The mythmakers of earlier days were the counterparts of our artists.

Moyers: They do the painting on the walls, they perform the rituals.

Campbell: Yes. There's an old romantic idea in German, *das Volk dichtet,* which says that the ideas and poetry of the traditional cultures come out of the folk. They do not. They come out of an elite experience, the experience of people particularly gifted, whose ears are open to the song of the universe. These people speak to the folk, and there is an answer from the folk, which is then received as an interaction. But the first impulse in the shaping of a folk tradition comes from above, not from below.

Moyers: In these early elementary cultures, as you call them, who would have been the equivalent of the poets today?

Campbell: The shamans. The shaman is the person, male or female, who in his late childhood or early youth has an overwhelming experience that turns him totally inward. It's a kind of schizophrenic crack-up. The whole unconscious opens up, and the shaman falls into it. The shaman experience has been described many, many times. It occurs all the way from Siberia right through the Americas down to Tierra del Fuego. (2)

Later in the same set of interviews;

Moyers: What is illumination?

Campbell: The illumination is the recognition of the radiance of one eternity through all things, whether in the vision of time these things are judged as good or evil. To come to this, you must release yourself

> completely from desiring the goods of this world and fearing their loss. "Judge not that you be not judged," we read in the words of Jesus. "If the doors of perception were cleansed," wrote Blake, "man would see everything as it is, infinite."
>
> Moyers: That's a tough trip.
>
> Campbell: That's a heavenly trip.
>
> Moyers: But is this really just for saints and monks?
>
> Campbell: No, I think it's also for artists. The real artist is the one who has learned to recognize and to render what Joyce has called the "radiance" of all things, as an epiphany of showing forth of their truth. (3)

This is expressed most simply in John Keats' famous couplet from *Ode on a Grecian Urn*: "'Beauty is truth, truth beauty,—that is all / Ye know on earth, and all ye need to know.'" (4) Piet Mondrian calls it "pure reality," claiming that "the appearance of natural forms changes but reality remains constant." (5)

Pablo Picasso states:

> We all know that Art is not truth. Art is a lie that makes us realize truth, at least the truth that is given us to understand. . . . And from the point of view of art there are no concrete or abstract forms, but only forms which are more or less convincing lies. That those lies are necessary to our mental selves is beyond any doubt, as it is through them that we form our aesthetic point of view of life. . . . To me there is no past or future in art. If a work of art cannot live always in the present it must not be considered at all. The art of the Greeks, of the Egyptians, of the great painters who lived in other times, is not an art of the past; perhaps it is more alive today than it ever was. (6)

Notes

1. *The Power of Myth: Joseph Campbell with bill Moyers,* ed. Sue Flowers, Doubleday, 1988, pp. 122-124.
2. *The Power of Myth: Joseph Campbell with bill Moyers,* ed. Sue Flowers, Doubleday, 1988, p. 107.
3. *The Power of Myth: Joseph Campbell with bill Moyers,* ed. Sue Flowers, Doubleday, 1988, pp. 204-205.
4. Written May, 1819; rpt., *The Norton Anthology of Poetry,* ed., Arthur M. Eastman, 1970, p. 698.
5. "Plastic Art and Pure Plastic Art," *Documents of Modern Art,* vol. 2, New York: Witterborn and company, 1945, p. 10.
6. From an interview with Marious de Zayas, translated with Picasso's approval and published as "Picasson Speaks," *The Arts*, New York, May 1923, pp. 315-326.

SHAMANS

> One of the old *shaman* of the Tungus explains: "I lay sick for an entire year. I became a shaman at the age of fifteen. The sickness that forced me to become a shaman showed itself in a swelling of my body and frequent fainting spells. When I began to sing, the sickness usually disappeared. My ancestors appeared to me and began to shamanize. They stood me up like a block of wood and shot at me with their bows until I lost consciousness. They cut up my flesh, they separated my bones and counted them, and they ate my flesh raw. When they counted my bones they found that there was one too many. Had there not been enough I should not have been able to become a shaman. While they were accomplishing this rite, I, for a whole summer, ate and drank nothing. At the end the shaman priests drank the blood of a reindeer and gave some to me, also, to drink. After these events, a shaman has less blood and looks pale. . . . The same thing happens to every Tungus shaman. Only when his shaman ancestors have cut his body in this manner and separated his bones can he begin to practice." (1)

According to the Merriam-Webster online dictionary, "A Shaman is a priest or priestess who uses magic for the purpose of curing the sick, divining the hidden, and controlling events." Shamanism is an anthropological term referring to a range of beliefs and practices that involve interacting with the *spiritual* world, the reality beyond the literal, physical world. It is based on the belief that certain people, shamans, are capable of living in both the human world and the spirit world. Because of this connection, these people are able to heal illnesses by mending the soul, by bringing a balance to the spirit that in turn restores the body, makes the body whole. In addition shamans are able to visit the "other" world in order to gain solutions to the afflictions for the entire community. (2) This visit to the "other" world generally involves a physical illness, a sickness that might last over a lengthy period of time during which the shaman experiences visions. Often the shaman encounters a *spiritual guide*, who energizes and directs the shaman on his journey through the *spiritual world*. As is to be expected, the shaman becomes a form of *scapegoat*, a wounded healer, becoming sick both to experience and come to know what the affliction is and to take on the sickness of another in order to heal him, very similar to an *empathon*. (3) Furthermore, since the shaman is able to enter into the spiritual realm, the shaman is able to communicate with the dead, both to relieve the anxiety of the living and to deliver gifts to the spirits in the hope of appeasing them and receiving favorable spiritual help (especially in terms of the hunting, killing and eating of animals; as in the Sedna myth of the Inuit mentioned in the Preface to this book). (4)

In addition to healing, communicating with the spirits, and appeasing them, shaman also often are the storytellers, the ones who pass on and preserve the traditions, beliefs and myths of their community. (5) According to Eliade, most forms of shamanism include the following beliefs: spirits exist and play an important roles in both the individual's and the community's lives; shaman can communicate with these spirits and have some influence over them; spirits can be either good or evil; shaman can relieve illness caused by spirits; shaman can induce trances that result in visionary ecstasy, and they can go on vision quests; shaman spirits can leave the body and enter the supernatural world; shaman can evoke animal images or spirit guides as message-bearers, and shaman can predict the future, by throwing bones/runes, tarot cards, palm reading, and through other forms of divination. (6)

Shamanist practices also include sacred songs (sometimes called *icaros*), sacred dances (rituals), both often accompanied by the beat of drums, totemic items with special powers, the use of herbs and other plants (which might be dangerous and even fatal if misused), sacred symbols, such as a circle, sacred places, and spells (sacred words, chants, phrases that can affect the physical world).

In addition, shamans often employ some form of Entheogen (a term coined in 1979 as a replacement for the terms *hallucinogen* and *psychedelic*. *Hallucinogen* was popularized by Aldous Huxley's experiences with mescaline, which were published as *The Doors of Perception* in 1954. *Psychedelic* is a Greek neologism for "mind manifest," and was used by psychiatrist Humphrey Osmond in reference to Huxley's experiences with mescaline). Entheogen literally means "that which causes God to be within an individual," and it means a drug used to induce a spiritual state, as opposed to the more recreational contexts of the related terms hallucinogen and psychedelic. Some of the more common *plants* used are psilocybin mushrooms, cannabis, tobacco, San Pedro cactus, peyote, ayahuasca, cedar, datura, deadly nightshade, and fly agarics.

And they employ other means to cause a *trance-like* state: fasting, dancing, singing, music, vigils, blood-letting, and prolonged periods in the wilderness or in some other environment separated from their community, such as meditating in a sweat lodge.

Especially interesting in relation to Daniel Paul Schreber, there are numerous examples of shaman assuming a *dual-spirit* identity, taking on the dress, attributes, roles and functions of the *opposite sex*. According to Joseph Campbell, it is common among the Chukchi, Sea Dayak, Patagonians, Araucanians, Arapaho, Cheyenne, Navajo, Pawnee, Lakota, Ute, and other Native American tribes. (7)

Perhaps it goes without saying, but it is so important, it is worth emphasizing that shamanism is based on the premise that the visible world is influenced by the invisible world. There is a world beyond the rules of the visible, sensual world that can break the rules of logic and reason, and give life meaning and value.

And with this in mind, it is not surprising that *dreams* are often involved. The shamans often experience their encounter with the spiritual world in the form of a *dream* that then needs to be interpreted. And these dreams connect up with the *spiritual stories* of the community, the *myths* that form the foundation for the entire belief system. And all are interpreted *symbolically*, the symbols interacting with each other in the same way all of language works to create ever changing maps of *meaning-beyond-explanation*.

The Inuit and Yupik Eskimos that Joel Rudinger lived with and studied have a strong tradition of shamanic practice, which has been recorded by several anthropologists. (8) Perhaps the most important of them is Knud John Victor Rasmussen, who was born in Jakobshaven, Greenland, the son of a Danish missionary, Charles V. Rasmussen, and an Inuit mother, Sofie Fleicher, and spent his childhood living among the Kalaallit Inuit in Greenland, learning their Kalaallisut language, hunting, driving dog sleds, and living in harsh Arctic conditions. From 1902-1904, he went on his first expedition (known as the Danish Literary Expedition) to study and save the surviving Inuit culture, following it with a lecture tour and book, *The People of the North* (1908), the same year he married Dagmar Andersen.

In 1910, he and his friend Peter Freuchen set up the Thule Trading Station at Cape York, Greenland, the most northern trading post in the world, and used it as a base for a series of seven expeditions, the Thule Expeditions, 1912-1933. (9)

He and Freuchen went on the first of these to test Robert Peary's claims that a channel divided Peary Land from Greenland, and they proved that this was not true by going on a 1,000 kilometer journey across the inland ice, nearly dying. Clements Markham, president of the Royal Geographic Society, called the journey the "finest ever performed by dogs, and Freuchen wrote personal accounts of it in *Vagrant Viking* and *I Sailed with Rasmussen.*

The second expedition was larger and had a team of seven men. Its purpose was to map a largely unknown area of Greenland's northern coast. Rasmussen gave an account of it in *Greenland by the Polar Sea*, 1921. There were two fatalities. The third one was depot-laying for Roald Amundsen's polar drift in *Maud*, and the fourth was in the east Greenland to collect ethnographic data near Angmagssalik.

The fifth one was the major achievement, an attempt to discover the origin of the Eskimo race, and it resulted in a ten volume account of ethnographic, archaeological and biological data and artifacts collected and organized, many currently still on display in Denmark. The team of seven began their journey in eastern Arctic Canada, but then Rasmussen separated from the rest and went on a sixteen month trip with two Inuit hunters by dog-sled across North America to Nome, Alaska. He hoped to continue into Russia, but not allowed in. The journey is detailed out in *Across Arctic America*, has also been called *The Great Sled Journey*, and was dramatized in the film *The Journals of Knud Rasmussen*, 2006.

After seven years of lecturing and writing, in 1931, Rasmussen went on the sixth expedition in an attempt to consolidate Denmark's claims on a portion of eastern Greenland that were being contested by Norway. His seventh expedition in 1933 was again meant to support these claims, but he contracted pneumonia the result of food poisoning, and died a few weeks later in Copenhagen at the age of fifty-four.

For our purposes, Rasmussen's journeys allowed him to live with and record firsthand the experiences of the Eskimo tribes, including their *shaman* and *shamanic beliefs*.

Igjugarjuk, a Caribou Eskimo shaman of one of the North Canadian tundra tribes, described the following experiences: As a youth he was visited by strange beings in dreams. When he awoke he remembered his dreams and told them to his family and friends, who, worried, sent for Peqanaoq, an old shaman, who, after hearing the dreams, decided Igjugarjuk should be placed on a small sled and then dragged through the dark and freezing Arctic night to a small snow hut, where he was to sit on a piece of skin without food or drink, and to concentrate on the Great Spirit. After five days Peqanaoq returned with water, and after fifteen with more water and some meat. Igjugarjuk remained this way for thirty days, until, finally, toward the end of the period a female spirit appeared and hovered in the air above him. When he returned to the village, he fasted for another five months. After this, he told Rasmussen, that such fasting and depravation is the best way to gain knowledge of the "hidden things," the "true wisdom" that "lives far from mankind, out in great loneliness, and can be reached only through suffering."

Najagneq, another Eskimo shaman, told Rasmussen, that there is a power called Sila, the soul of the universe, who is so mighty his speech comes, not through words, but through storms, snowfall, rain showers, tempests, and all of the forces of nature, and brings both fear and comfort. Sila is "never seen; its voice alone is heard," and it is a "gentle voice, like a woman, a voice so fine and gentle that even children cannot become afraid. And what it says is: *Sila ersinarsinivdluge,* 'Be not afraid of the universe.'" (10)

Unfortunately, people who don't understand the deep connections between shaman, shamanic rituals, and the connections between the visible world and the invisible world have largely demystified and taken away the power of the Eskimo culture. Joel Rudinger includes the following in his discussion about their important Sedna Creation Story and Ritual:

> The Legend of Sedna is full of the deeply ingrained, powerful human archetypes that make its appeal both timeless and universal.
>
> Yet there are suggestions that in some Inupiaq communities, Sedna is no longer being credited with being the great mother of the sea mammals, the spiritual being who has for a score of generations given sustenance to hungry Eskimo communities. On a recent National Geographic special, televised on February 5th, 2009, the documentary "Whale Hunters" was shown of a recent whale capture. After a bowhead whale had been killed and dragged onto the ice near the Alaskan village of Barrow, men, women, and children gathered together to give thanks. As I watched the community gather at the edge of the sea, I waited with anticipation to hear their thanks to Sedna for her bounteous gift. However, that was not what happened. Instead, they all stood at the edge of the ice as the leader proclaimed loudly over the Arctic Ocean, "Thank you, God, for the gift of this whale you have given us. This is for your glory only, in Jesus' name, Amen." As I sat silent in my chair, I asked myself: What will be the future of this wonderful legend? Will the Inuit children of the current generation forget about Sedna and all that she has meant to their culture for thousands of years"? Will they never know her story or its meaning? Will she, like Zeus and Athena and Atlas and Persephone, become a folk legend they discover by accident in a history book or a literature class instead of hearing of her from their fathers? I mention this National Geographic documentary because in its own way it is part of the changing history of the Sedna legend. It has all the same ritual, but the benefactor has changed. Perhaps the greatest variation of a tale is the disintegration and disappearance of that tale. We can only hope that Jesus and Sedna can co-exist within this ancient culture and both keep their separate and distinct cultural presences alive. (11)

Perhaps the most famous shamanic experience on record is that of Black Elk.

John G. Neihardt first met Black Elk in August of 1930. He had come to Pine Ridge Reservation in search of finding some of the old medicine men who had been active in the Messiah Movement, the Messianic *Dream* that had come to the Sioux while they were being defeated by the white men, ultimately leading up to the famous massacre at Wounded Knee, South Dakota, December 29, 1980. He was told by the field agent there he should seek out Black Elk, told Black Elk was a *wishasha wakon* (a holy man, a priest, more accurately, a shaman). He drove to Manderson, where he met up with Flying Hawk, an interpreter he knew, and was taken to Black Elk. When he arrived at Black Elk's home, a one-room log cabin with weeds growing out of the roof, Black Elk indicated he had sensed the arrival. Black Elk was old and nearly blind, and only spoke Sioux, so all of the exchanges had to come through Flying Eagle, and what Flying Eagle told John G. Neihardt was that Black Elk felt he was a man sent to learn of the "other world." Black Elk told John G. Neihardt to return the following spring and he would teach him of his "great vision."

When the snows melted and the grass began to grow, John G. Neihardt did just that, and the *shaman* begins his story:

> I was four years old then, and I think it must have been the next summer that I first heard the voices. . . . Maybe it was not this summer when I first heard the voices, but I think it was, because I know it was before I played with bows and arrows or rode a horse, and I was out playing alone when I heard them. It was like somebody calling me, and I thought it was my mother, but there was nobody there. This happened more than once, and always made me afraid, so that I ran home.
>
> It was when I was five years old that my Grandfather made me a bow and some arrows. The grass was young and I was horseback. A thunder storm was coming from where the sun goes down, and just as I was riding into the woods along a creek, there was a kingbird sitting on a limb. This was not a dream, it happened. And I was going to shoot at the kingbird with the bow my Grandfather made, when the bird spoke and said: "The clouds all over are one-sided." Perhaps it meant that all the clouds were looking at me. And then it said: "Listen! A voice is calling you!" Then I looked up at the clouds, and two men were coming there, headfirst like arrows slanting down: and as they came, they sang a sacred song and the thunder was like drumming. I will sing it for you. The song and the drumming were like this:
>
> "Behold, a sacred voice is calling you;
> All over the sky a sacred voice is calling."
>
> I sat there gazing at them, and they were coming from the place where the giant lives (north). But when they were very close to me, they wheeled

> about toward where the sun goes down, and suddenly they were geese. Then they were gone, and the rain came with a big wind and a roaring.
>
> I did not tell this vision to anyone. I liked to think about it, but I was afraid to tell it. (12)

Such experiences today would be explained neurologically as a form of autistic savant, where a young child, generally even younger than Black Elk was, goes beyond the logic of literal existence into a *dream*, a world considered *unreal*, only *imagined*. There are many examples: Jessy Park, the autistic artist whose works have a luminous quality similar to Vincent van Gogh's, though they are done in a very different style, comes immediately to mind. Also, immediately in this passage is that Black Elk did not have any control over the appearance of the visions, and was both comforted and frightened by them.

For the next few years, Black Elk was occasionally visited by voices, but nothing major. Then, one day, when he was nine, the voice came to him and said: "It is time; now they are calling you." Black Elk got up and exited the tepee to follow where the voice would take him, but his thighs and his legs hurt, so he returned to the tepee.

The next day this "sickness" came back, now worse, causing legs, arms and face to swell. That night, lying in his tepee next to his mother and father, he saw out the opening the same men on horseback coming down from the clouds. This time they stopped, looked at him and said: "Hurry! Come! Your Grandfathers are calling you!"

Then they left. Black Elk got up, his legs no longer hurting, and followed. A small cloud gathered him in and took him rapidly into the sky. In this world of the clouds, Black Elk watched as a bay horse gathered together other horses, until horses everywhere danced about him. Soon they began to morph into other animals, which eventually fled into the four corners of the world from whence the horses had come. Then the cloud became a tepee with six men sitting in a row inside it. Then the two men with spears joined them, and the oldest spoke kindly and invited Black Elk to join them, saying: "Your Grandfathers all over the world are having a council, and they have called you here to teach you."

> His voice was very kind, but I shook all over with fear now, for I knew that these were not old men, but the Powers of the World. And the first was the Power of the West; the second, of the North; the third, of the East; the fourth of the South; the fifth, of the Sky; the sixth, of the Earth. I knew this, and was afraid, until the first Grandfather spoke again: "Behold them yonder where the sun goes down, the thunder beings! You shall see, and have from them my power; and they shall take you to the high and lonely

> center of the earth that you may see; even to the place where the sun continually shines, they shall take you there to understand." (13)

Then Black Elk saw a rainbow come over him. He was given a cup of water, which is the sky, and a bow, which is the power to destroy, and his spirit, called Eagle Wing stretched. Then the old Grandfather got up, ran to the setting sun, turned into a sick, old horse, and looked at the boy. Then the Grandfather of the North gave the horse an herb, which healed him, and he again became the first Grandfather.

Then the Grandfather of the North said, "On earth a nation you shall make live, for yours shall be the power of the white giant's wing, the cleansing wing." The he ran to the north, where he turned into a goose, and all of the horses of the west became thunders and the horses of the north became geese. And this Grandfather sang two songs, one about the "thunder nation appearing," the other about the "geese nation appearing."

Then the third Grandfather spoke: "Take courage, younger brother, for across the earth they shall take you!" And he pointed to two men flying beneath a shining star to the east. "From them you shall have power, from them who have awakened all the beings of the earth with roots and legs and wings." Then he held out a peace pipe and said: "With this pipe, you shall walk upon the earth, and whatever sickens there you shall make well." Then he pointed to a red man, and the man rolled on the earth and changed into a bison, and the bison got up and ran to the horses of the east, which now also became bison, healthy and fat.

Then the fourth Grandfather spoke: "Younger brother, with the powers of the four quarters you shall walk, a relative. Behold, the living center of a nation I shall give you, and with it many you shall save." And he held up a red stick, which immediately began to transform, to grow and become a living tree with singing birds, and beneath it Black Elk saw villages of people, a happy world. Then the Grandfather said, "It shall stand in the center of the nation's circle, a cane to walk with and a people's heart; and by your powers you shall make it blossom."

> Then when he had been still a little while to hear the birds sing, he spoke again: "Behold the earth!" So I looked down and saw it lying yonder like a hoop of peoples, and in the center bloomed the holy stick that was a tree, and where it stood there crossed two roads, a red one and a black. "From where the giant lives (the north) to where you always face (the south) the red road goes, the road of good," the Grandfather said, "and on it shall your nation walk. The black road goes from where the thunder beings live (the west) to where the sun continually shines (the east), a fearful road, a road of troubles and of war. On this you shall walk, and from it you shall

> have the power to destroy a people's foes. In four ascents you shall walk the earth with power." (14)

Then the fifth Grandfather stretched out his arms and a spotted eagle appeared. "Behold, all the wings of the air shall come to you, and you and the winds and the stars shall be like relatives. You shall go across the earth with my power." Then the sky filled with wings.

Then the sixth Grandfather, the Spirit of the Earth, began to morph, seeming to grow backwards into his youth, until he became a boy, and Black Elk knew the boy was himself. Then he said: "My boy, have courage, for my power shall be yours, and you shall need it, for your nation on the earth will have great troubles. Come."

With that Black Elk followed the Grandfather out the rainbow door, and found he was riding a bay horse. Then all of the horses of the various directions came together behind him and men rode them, and they all rode the "fearful road" to the east. And below the earth was silent and sick.

Then he saw the images of the great battle with the white men. And he led his tribes to war. Then he rode around his villages, filled with sick and dying people, and as he did they began to rise and come forth, smiling and happy. "And a Voice said: "Behold, they have given you the center of the nation's hoop to make it live." So he rode to the middle of the nation's hoop and thrust the red stick into it, and there was peace and joy throughout the nation. Then the Voice offered a great insight: "It shall be a relative to them; and who shall see it, shall see much more, for thence comes wisdom; and those who do not see it shall be dark."

This is the great insight! This is the invisible world of meaning and value beyond the visible world. Black Elk experienced it. It is the shamanic experience.

Then the Voice said:

> "Behold the circle of the nation's hoop, for it is holy, being endless, and thus all powers shall be one power in the people without end. Now they shall break camp and go forth upon the red road, and your Grandfathers shall walk with them." (15)

Then the spirits lead Black Elk up four ascents, which represent four generations, and he saw the future, and it was a harsh one, but once he passed through them a Voice said to him:

> "Behold this day, for it is yours to make. Now you shall stand upon the center of the earth to see, for there they are taking you."
>
> I was still on my horse, and once more I felt the riders of the west, the north, the east, the south, behind me in formation, as before, and we were

> going east. I looked ahead and saw the mountains there with rocks and forests on them, and from the mountains flashed all colors upward to the heavens. Then I was standing on the highest mountain of them all, and round about beneath me was the whole hoop of the world. And while I stood there I saw more than I can tell and I understood more than I saw; for I was seeing in a sacred manner the shapes of all things in the spirit, and the shape of all shapes as they must live together like one being. And I saw that the sacred hoop of my people was one of many hoops that made one circle, wide as daylight and as starlight, and in the center grew one mighty flowering tree to shelter all the children of one mother and one father. And I saw that it was holy. (16)

This is the key, and fortunately, John C. Neihardt realized the importance of adding the following footnote: “Black Elk said the mountain he stood upon in his vision was Harney Peak in the Black Hills. “But anywhere is the center of the world,” he added. This is the key. This is the realization of the intersection of the physical and the spiritual worlds. This is the *experience* of the passage between the two worlds, what Aldous Huxley called *the doors of perception*. The *shaman* is able to join with the *axis mundi* (center of the world), to become one with the flow of the universe, to *realize*, to *experience* the *intersection of multiple planes of existence*.

Notes

1. G. V. Kenofontov, *Legendy I rasskazy o shamanach u. yakutov, buryat I tungusov*, Moscow, 1930; trans., Adolf Friedrich and Georg Buddruss, *Schamanengeschichten aus Sibrien*, Munich: Otto-Wilhelm-Barth-Verlag, 1955, pp. 211-212.
2. Mircea Eliade, *Shamanism, Archaic Techniques of Ecstasy*, Bollingen Series LXXVI, Pantheon Books, NYNY 1964, pp. 3–7. Hoppál, Mihály (in Hungarian). *Sámánok Eurázsiában*. Budapest: Akadémiai Kiadó.2005, pp. 77, 287; Znamensky, Andrei A. (2005). "Az ősiség szépsége: altáji török sámánok a szibériai regionális gondolkodásban (1860–1920)". In Molnár, Ádám (in Hungarian). *Csodaszarvas. Őstörténet, vallás és néphagyomány. Vol. I.* Budapest: Molnár Kiadó. pp. 117–134.
3. Halfax, Joan (1982). *The Wounder Healer Shaman*. New York, NY: The Crossroads Publishing Company.
4. Hoppál, Mihály (in Hungarian). *Sámánok Eurázsiában*. Budapest: Akadémiai Kiadó.2005, p. 45; Znamensky, Andrei A., "Az ősiség szépsége: altáji török sámánok a szibériai regionális gondolkodásban (1860–1920)", 2005. In Molnár, Ádám (in Hungarian). *Csodaszarvas. Őstörténet, vallás és néphagyomány. Vol. I.* Budapest: Molnár Kiadó. p. 24.
5. Hoppál, Mihály (in Hungarian). *Sámánok Eurázsiában*. Budapest: Akadémiai Kiadó.2005, pp. 27-36.

6. Mircea Eliade, *Shamanism, Archaic Techniques of Ecstacy*, Bollingen Series LXXVI, Pantheon Books, NYNY 1964.
7. *The Historical Atlas of World Mythology*, Vol I: The Way of the Animal Powers: Part 2: p. 174.
8. Kleivan, Inge; B. Sonne (1985). *Eskimos: Greenland and Canada*. Iconography of religions, section VIII, "Arctic Peoples", fascicle 2. Leiden, The Netherlands: Institute of Religious Iconography • State University Groningen. E.J. Brill.
9. Knud Rasmussen, Knud, *The People of the Polar North*, 1908; *Greenland by the Polar Sea: The Story of the Thule Expedition from Melville Bay to Cape Morris Jesup*, translated by Asta and Rowland Kenny, published by W. Heinemann, 1921; *Across Arctic America: Narrative of the Fifth Thule Expedition*, 1927; *Across Arctic America: Narrative of the Fifth Thule Expedition*. University of Alaska Press; Reprint edition, February 1999; *The Fifth Thule Expedition*, 10 volumes, 1946-1952; Elizabeth Cruwys, Elizabeth, "Rasmussen, Knud (1879-1933)", in *Literature of Travel and Exploration: An Encyclopedia*, volume 3, 2003; Jean Malaurie, 1982, *The Last Kings of Thule: With the Polar Eskimos, as They Face Their Destiny*, trans. Adrienne Folk; Clements R. Markham, *The Lands of Silence: A History of Arctic and Antarctic Exploration*, Cambridge University Press. 1921.
10. Knud Rasmussen, *Across the Arctic America* (New Your and London: G. P. Putnam's Sons, 1927), pp. 82-86, and H. Osterman, *The Alaskan Eskimos, as Described in the Posthumous Notes of Dr. Knud Rasmussen, Report of the Fifth Thule Expedition, 1921-24*. Vol. X, No. 3 (Copenhagen: Nordisk Forlag, 1952), pp. 97-99.
11. "The Path to Sedna," *Young Adult Literature and Culture,* ed., Eiss, Cambridge Scholars Press, p. 63.
12. John G. Neihardt, *Black Elk Speaks: Being the Life Story of a Holy Man of the Oglala Sioux*, Pocket Books, 1959, pp. 15-16.
13. John G. Neihardt, *Black Elk Speaks: Being the Life Story of a Holy Man of the Oglala Sioux*, Pocket Books, 1959, pp. 21-22.
14. John G. Neihardt, *Black Elk Speaks: Being the Life Story of a Holy Man of the Oglala Sioux*, Pocket Books, 1959, pp. 24-25.
15. John G. Neihardt, *Black Elk Speaks: Being the Life Story of a Holy Man of the Oglala Sioux*, Pocket Books, 1959, p, 29.
16. John G. Neihardt, *Black Elk Speaks: Being the Life Story of a Holy Man of the Oglala Sioux*, Pocket Books, 1959, p. 36.

THE KALONA

The dove returns: it found no resting place;
It was in flight all night above the shaken seas;
Beneath dark eaves
The dove shall magnify the tiger's bed;
Give the dove peace.
The split-tailed swallow leaves the sill at dawn;
At dusk, blue swallows shall return.
On the third day the crow shall fly,
The crow, the crow, the spider-colored crow,
The crow shall find new mud to walk upon.
—Robert Bly (1)

Taking a Babylonian version of the story of Noah and the Great Flood, of the sending out of a bird to find the newly reborn land, the new world, a version where three different birds are sent out on successive days, Robert Bly clearly expresses the value of the *shadow* in the image of a black bird, an intelligent black bird, a bird of the night, connected to both the spider and mud.

The dove is the bird of innocence, pure, spiritually clean, untouched by darkness, the bird of peace and love, of the world of Adam and Eve before the fall. It is not the bird of transformation and energy, not the bird of dark drives and desires, not the bird of creativity and imagination.

The swallow is not as pure as the dove, but neither is it a bird of the night. It is blue, and blue is the color of spirituality and of the intellect, of the sky, but not of the *blood* and the *libido*.

The crow is the bird that will find the new mud to reshape the world, the wet clay necessary for the creation and evolution of life.

The raven is a large black bird of the crow family, the one chosen by Edgar Allan Poe to represent the dark, mental sufferings of a lover for his lost love, the exact image of the *shadow* of the human psyche working its mysterious, uncompromising mantra on a man unable to resist its temptations, even more a man desiring its call to self-destruction. (2)

Poe begins by setting the scene, one of a man caught in that twilight state between two worlds, the conscious and the unconscious, the world of the dream about to descend. It is no accident that the connection takes place at midnight, the moment when supernatural events are most likely to take place:

Once upon a midnight dreary, while I pondered, weak and weary,
Over many a quaint and curious volume of forgotten lore—
While I nodded, nearly napping, suddenly there came a tapping,
As if someone gently rapping, rapping at my chamber door.
"Tis some visitor," I muttered, "tapping at my chamber door—
Only this and nothing more."

This is not just a physical door, not just a literal chamber. It is all a wonderfully symbolic entrance to the psyche, a "weak and weary" psyche, one filled with "many a quaint and curious volume of forgotten lore."

The narration continues:

Ah, distinctly I remember it was in the bleak December,
And each separate dying ember wrought its ghost upon the floor.
Eagerly I wished the morrow;—vainly I had sought to borrow
From my books surcease of sorrow—sorrow for the lost Lenore—
For the rare and radiant maiden whom the angels name Lenore—
Nameless here forever more.

Here the dark images and symbols continue, "bleak," "December," "dying ember," "ghost," "sorrow," 'lost." Poe uses the name Lenore to represent a lost love in several poems, including one titled "Lenore," and she does not refer to any specific person, simply to a lost love that the narrator here both wants to forget and yet to remember, the combination of agony and ecstasy a form of amore, in this case one that cannot be satisfied, but that can only torment, and this lover seems to ravel in his own self-perpetuating anguish and destruction.

The narration continues:

And the silken sad uncertain rustling of each purple curtain
Thrilled me—filled me with fantastic terrors never felt before;
So that now, to still the beating of my heart, I stood repeating:
"Tis some visitor entreating entrance at my chamber door—
Some late visitor entreating entrance at my chamber door;
This it is and nothing more."

Notice how he is both "thrilled" and "filled . . . with fantastic terrors," heart "beating" with anticipation.

Presently my soul grew stronger; hesitating then no longer,
"Sir," said I, "or Madam, truly your forgiveness I implore;

But the fact is I was napping, and so gently you came rapping,
And so faintly you came tapping, tapping at my chamber door,
That I scarce was sure I heard you"—here I opened wide the door;—
Darkness there and nothing more.

Now he invites the dream or nightmare in, opens the door to his psyche, his inner chamber. And in case we doubt if it really is this that he refers to, really is a dream, he follows this by stating it so there can be no questioning:

Deep into that darkness peering, long I stood there wondering, fearing,
Doubting, dreaming dreams no mortals ever dared to dream before;
But the silence was unbroken, and the stillness gave no token,
And the only word there spoken was the whispered word, "Lenore!"
This I whispered, and an echo murmured back the word, "Lenore!"—
Merely this and nothing more.

The echo response highlights that he is talking to himself. It is his own *projection*, in Jungian terms the placing upon another one's own psychic image or complexes. Mayan culture thought echoes were an attribute of the great Underworld-god, the Jaguar, which fits here, as the only response by Lenore would come from the afterlife, the underworld, the otherworld, the unconscious, the *numinous*. In Greek mythology, Echo is a nymph scorned by Narcissus (whose name is derived from the Greek *narke*, numbness), who drowned in a pool while admiring his own beauty, thus representing vanity, self love, in Jungian terms an *ego* unable to connect with the *self* or with another, and water symbolizes the unconscious, so it is an *ego* drowning in its own *unconscious*, certainly appropriate to what's going on in this poem, and with the *shadow* in the form of a raven about to enter into this dream, it becomes the *ego* unable to resist or gain some kind of balance with its *shadow*. The flower the name comes from was used in initiation ceremonies associated with Demeter, Mother Earth, the Greek goddess of the seasons, the stages of life and death, and the relation of numbness to death resulted in narcissus flowers being planted on graves, not necessarily to symbolize death but to symbolize a death which is, perhaps, nothing more than a sleep, an entrance into the world of the dream. Demeter's daughter Persephone was drugged by the narcissus flower and carried off to the Underworld by Hades. All these connections include the possibility of rebirth. Winter does give way to spring. Persephone does return from Hades. It is possible to wake from a dream, though, as the poem will make clear, that will not happen here. This is a man lost forever in his own nightmare.

The narration continues:

Back into the chamber turning, all my soul within me burning,
Soon again I heard a tapping something louder than before.
"Surely," said I, "surely that is something at my window lattice;
Let me see, then, what thereat is,
and this mystery explore—
Let my heart be still a moment, and this mystery explore;—
'Tis the wind and nothing more."

A window is a place both of separation and of transformation, as it does divide two separate worlds, but one can see through it, see from one world to the other world, and ultimately could pass through one into the other. Interestingly, this window has lattices, suggesting prison bars, perhaps a feeling of being caged in or perhaps more likely a protection from what is on the other side, which, as we will immediately see, the narrator cannot resist.

The narration continues:

Open here I flung the shutter, when, with many a flirt and flutter,
In there stepped a stately Raven of the saintly days of yore.
Not the least obeisance made he; not a minute stopped or stayed he,
But, with mien of lord or lady, perched above my chamber door—
Perched upon a bust of Pallas just above my chamber door—
Perched, and sat, and nothing more.

Now the shutter is flung open, the world of the dream allowed in, and the Raven appears, a powerful, stately, saintly Raven, with the dignity of a lord or lady, perched upon the head of Athena, a Raven from the days of yore, the days of the great Classical Greek gods and goddesses, a Raven from the birth of European consciousness, the world, as stated earlier, the narrator has been seeking in volumes of forgotten lore.

The narration continues:

Then this ebony bird beguiling my sad fancy into smiling,
By the grave and stern decorum of the countenance it word,
"Though thy crest be shorn and shaven, thou," I said, "art sure no craven,
Ghastly grim and ancient Raven wandering from the Nightly shore—
Tell me what thy lordly name is on the Night's Plutonian shore!"
Quoth the Raven, "Nevermore."

Perhaps the one word response from the Raven is a real sound, the sound a Raven does make; perhaps it is the result of the deranged man's determination to hear "Nevermore," to find a negative word in the wordless sound. If it really is a universal voice and judgment of the universal black bird, then it is the archetypal *shadow*. If it is but the man's own dark imaginings, then it is his personal *shadow*. It matters not, as either carries the other within it.

It is no accident the man thinks the Raven is from "Night's Plutonian shore," since Pluto is the Roman god of the underworld, and thus the Raven is seen as a messenger of that world, a place of shadowy existence, of afterlife, not so much of death, but of continued existence in a world of suffering. And the suffering is self-induced. Once the man realizes the Raven has only one response, he begins punishing himself by asking it questions to which he already knows it will respond negatively. The poem takes on an unrelenting psychic whipping, and the reader can feel the mental leather strap "nevermore" snapping against the mental flesh. This man is a masochist. His *ego*, his self esteem has lost out to his dark side.

The final four lines are so exactly related to the negative side of the *shadow* they expressed it in the form of a poem long before Carl Jung and his followers attempted to explain it:

> And his eyes have all the seeming of a demon's that is dreaming,
> And the lamp-light o'er him streaming throws his shadow on the floor;
> And my soul from out that shadow that lies floating on the floor
> Shall be lifted—nevermore!

Indeed, the world of *expression* is filled with such insightful depictions of the dark, negative shadow. Left out of the many discussed in Part I of this book is Shakespeare's darkest representation, Iago, the soldier in the tragedy of Othello who has fought beside Othello and become his trusted advisor, his *shadow*.

While Iago's motives cannot be clarified for certain, his desire to mislead and bring down Othello might be attributed to his belief he has been unfairly passed over for promotion to the rank of lieutenant in favor of Cassio. He also suspects that his wife, Emilia, is cheating on him with Othello. Perhaps, he is simply an evil character with no need of justification. Perhaps, he is not evil so much as simply amoral, and does what he does for practical purposes.

With the help of Roderigo, who has his own interests in mind the result of Iago promising him Desdemona's affections, Iago engineers a drunken brawl to bring about Cassio's demotion (Act II). Then he sets his sights direction on Othello, putting doubts in Othello's mind about his wife Desdemona, persuading Othello that she is having an affair with Cassio. Iago manipulates his own wife Emilia, Desdemona's lady-in-waiting, into taking a handkerchief that Othello has given Desdemona; then Iago tells Othello he has seen it in Cassio's possession.

Othello flies into a jealous rage, and Iago has him right where he wants him. He tells Othello to hide while Iago talks to Cassio, and manipulates a conversation that Cassio thinks is about his mistress Biance to appear to be about Desdemona. Fooled by this *evil shadow*, Othello is easy prey for Iago's lies, and orders Iago to kill Cassio, promising Iago his desired position as lieutenant.

Then, continuing his double-crossing lies, Iago gets Cassio and Roderigo to fight, actually killing his co-conspirator Roderigo himself and leaving Cassio wounded.

In the final scene, Iago seems to have succeeded. Othello kills the innocent Desdemona in his blind rage; and Iago has had his revenge, or if it's not for revenge, simply his desire for evil fulfilled. However, Emilia reveals the truth, and Iago is placed under arrest, where he refuses to admit anything: "Demand me nothing. What you know, you know. From this time forth I never will speak a word."

Certainly Iago is one of Shakespeare's most sinister villains, at least partially because of the unique trust that Othello places in him, which he so consciously betrays while maintaining his reputation of honesty and dedication. And this betrayal is even more clear and sharp because it so contrasts with Othello's nobility and integrity.

Interestingly, Iago actually has more lines in the play than Othello, and is a more dramatic and developed (though enigmatic) character. He is a Machiavellian schemer, a manipulator, whose clever poses are emphasized by having him often referred to as "honest Iago," the one person the other characters are most trusting. Critic A. C. Bradley says of him that "evil has nowhere else been portrayed with such mastery." (3)

And perhaps a major reason his evil seems so strong is that there is no clear reason, leaving us to ponder a man who appears to be driven by pure evil for not enough of a practical, logical, or even emotional reason. In the exposition in Act 1, scene 1, Iago says he does it because he has been passed over for promotion. He also reveals some racism at seeing "a black ram tupping" a "white ewe." And, as stated above, he later reveals suspicions of his wife's infidelity with both Othello and Cassio. However, the elaborate, complex evil he puts carefully in motion doesn't seem driven by any of these. Leone Teyssandier suggests envy is what drives him, envy of the others because he knows they are better than him, more noble, more generous, and certainly in the case of Cassio, more handsome, saying "He hath a daily beauty in his life that makes me ugly." (V.i.19–20) (4)

The Boston Review states that Kenneth Branagh portrayed Iago as a homosexual, suggesting he was actually in love with Othello and jealous of Desdemona. Branagh's response: "Well, you know, a rather distinguished critic said he was annoyed with my performance because I'd clearly played Iago gay. But I don't mean in a sexual sense. I just meant that he absolutely loved him. And frankly, that's the way I am with my male friends: I say 'I love you" when I feel it." (5)

When Andy Serkis portrayed Iago at the Royal Exchange Theatre in Manchester, he offered the following suggestions;

> There are a million theories to Iago's motivations, but I believed that Iago was once a good soldier, a great man's man to have around, a bit of a laugh, who feels betrayed, gets jealous of his friend, wants to mess it up for him, enjoys causing him pain, makes a choice to channel all his creative energy into the destruction of this human being, and becomes completely addicted to the power he wields over him. I didn't want to play him as initially malevolent. He's not the Devil. He's you or me feeling jealous and not being able to control our feelings. (6)

Placing Iago into each of us is important. He is the dark side of Othello, Cassio, and all of us, the negative potential of our own shadows.

This is where *dramatic irony* comes in, as we, the audience, come to see Iago's true self in his soliloquies and asides directed at us. The other characters in the play only see his charismatic, charming, friendly persona, not the real person behind it, and this discrepancy is what drives the play. In other words, the emotional center of the play is the struggle with that dark shadow within us all, seeing Iago act it out, and being drawn in because he includes us in his conspiracies (similar to what Edgar Allan Poe does in such stories as *The Cask of Amontillado*).

Carl Jung thinks of the *shadow* as the counterpart to the *ego*, sometimes depicting it as a primitive force, similar to the *id* or *libido*, sometimes giving it more of an ethical quality, the evil side to either balance or work against the good intentions of the *ego*. In 1912, he writes:

> It is a frightening thought that man also has a shadow side to him, consisting not just of little weaknesses- and foibles, but of a positively demonic dynamism. The individual seldom knows anything of this; to him, as an individual, it is incredible that he should ever in any circumstances go beyond himself. But let these harmless creatures form a mass, and there emerges a raging monster; and each individual is only one tiny cell in the monster's body, so that for better or worse he must accompany it on its bloody rampages and even assist it to the utmost. Having a dark suspicion of these grim possibilities, man turns a blind eye to the shadow-side of human nature. Blindly he strives against the salutary dogma of original sin, which is yet so prodigiously true. Yes, he even hesitates to admit the conflict of which he is so painfully aware. (7)

And in another passage from the same year, he directly states that this conflict between the *ego* and *shadow* can result in a form of neuroses, in a dramatic mental collapse:

> We know that the wildest and most moving dramas are played not in the theatre but in the hearts of ordinary men and women who pass by without exciting attention, and who betray to the world nothing of the conflicts that rage within them except possibly by a nervous breakdown. What is so difficult for the layman to grasp is the fact that in most cases the patients themselves have no suspicion whatever of the internecine war raging in their unconscious. If we remember that there are many people who understand nothing at all about themselves, we shall be less surprised at the realization that there are also people who are utterly unaware of their actual conflicts. (8)

Insight, creativity, transformation, the birth of meaning and value come not just from the conscious self of the *ego,* but from the conscious *ego* in conflict with the unconscious drives of the *shadow,* with madness, insanity, the loss of reason. Only by facing one's *shadow*, admitting it, empowering it, and then controlling it can one move beyond a shallow world of innocence and self-denial, can one, in Jungian terms, achieve *individuation.* Jung states:

> The things that come to light brutally in insanity remain hidden in the background in neurosis, but they continue to influence consciousness nonetheless. When, therefore, the analysis penetrates the background of conscious phenomena, it discovers the same archetypal figures that activate the deliriums of psychotics. Finally, there is any amount of literary and historical evidence to prove that in the case of these archetypes we are dealing with normal types of fantasy that occur practically everywhere and not with the monstrous products of insanity. The pathological element does not lie in the existence of these ideas, but in the dissociation of consciousness that can no longer control the unconscious. In all cases of dissociation it is therefore necessary to integrate the unconscious into consciousness. This is a synthetic process which I have termed the "individuation process." (9)

This can be depicted in the symbol of the Ouoboros, a circular dragon or snake or serpent where the head is biting and perhaps eating its tail. In alchemy this is taken to represent a process of the *ego* (the serpent's head) of consciousness connecting to and consuming the *shadow* (the entire world of the unconscious). In other words, consciousness is assimilating its unconscious origins. In Depth Psychology, this is referred to as "integrating the *shadow*." In mythology, it is generally represented by a hero defeating a dragon, often one guarding gold (the riches of the unconscious, the energy of life) and/or a female (the *anima*, the agent of transformation). It is important that the hero partake of the dragon's flesh, taste the dragon's blood, somehow take the essence of the dragon into his being, thus connecting up with the natural impulses out of which consciousness is born. On one level, this is a uniting or marriage of the *ego* and the *anima* through an encounter with the dragon or serpent, the force that brings them together.

Carl Jung's writing offers a worthwhile frame for understanding this better in a discussion about the *trickster,* a figure he puts forth as the precursor to the *shadow* entity.

He begins by comparing Adolf Bandelier's discussion of the *trickster* in Pueblo Indian mythologies of New Mexico (10) to the European carnival in the Medieval church, where the hierarchic order gets reversed, to the medieval depictions of the Devil as the ape of God (*simian dei*), to various folklore characters such as Stupid Hans and Tom thumb, and noticeable to Mercurius, the alchemical entity known for "sly jokes and malicious pranks, his powers as a shape-shifter, his dual nature, half animal, half divine, his exposure to all kinds of tortures, and—last but not least—his approximation to the figure of a savior." (11). In alchemical representation, this is the character that units opposites, life and death, sun and moon, man and woman.

Jung also connects the *trickster* to *shaman* and medicine-men, both know to play jokes on others, often only to fall victim to their own malicious tricks. This leads into their connection to suffering, where due to either or both the reversal of their prankster antics and the real taking on of the suffering of others in both physical and psychological realms they suffer, perhaps never to completely recover. This, of course, also fits my discussions of *empathons*. Jung said the *trickster's* "approximation to the savior is an obvious consequence of this, in confirmation of the mythological truth that the wounded is the agent of healing, and that the sufferer takes away the suffering." (12)

After discussing examples of the *trickster* in various official ceremonies of the Medieval Church, the *tripudia* and *tripudium hypodiaconorum* (the most famous of which is called the *festum stultorum*, Feast of Fools) where lesser clergy and lower classes held wild partying, including a mock election of a child to the position of bishop, ultimately degenerating to grotesque masquerades filled with dancing, indecent songs, dice games, and profanity; and a particularly disrespectful celebration, the *festum asinorum* in France, which began as a celebration of Mary's flight into Egypt, but kept getting more and more filled wanton crudity, bringing donkeys right into the church, ultimately concluding the mass with the priest braying like a donkey three times; after discussing these and other examples, including pointing out that the Winnebago tribes still have similar customs Jung comes to the conclusion that the *trickster*, in psychological terms, is the reflection of an earlier stage of consciousness.

Then he makes an important claim, a claim that these reflections still exist in the current psychic make-up as dissociations, as split off personalities that stand in direct complementary or compensatory relationship to the *ego-personality*, not as a personal complex but as something known to all, an aggregate character. In modern man, Jung claims, this figure appears in "counter tendencies," "accidents," that seem to be purposely thwarting him, seem to have malicious intent. Jung continues, "I have, I think, found a suitable designation for this character-component when I called it the *shadow*." (13) Thus, the *shadow* began as part of the collective unconscious, but as civilization pushed it aside, it became personalized, an object of personal responsibility. In other words, the *trickster* is of a pre-conscious world, and as humans gained the higher conscious levels of thinking, they were able to detach it and objectify it. Jung states, "He is both subhuman and superhuman, a bestial and divine being, whose chief and most alarming characteristic is his unconsciousness." (14) He is a creator god, the body out of which the world is made. At the same time he is simply stupid, less intelligent than even the lowest animals.

Why then, Carl Jung continues, does modern man continue to retain this *shadow*. And this leads into a complex relationship between the *shadow* and the *ego-consciousness*. He states, "from the psychology of the individual, namely the appearance of an impressive shadow figure antagonistically confronting a personal consciousness: this figure does not appear merely because it still exists in the individual, but because it rests on a dynamism whose existence can only be explained in terms of his actual situation, for instance because the shadow is so disagreeable to his ego-consciousness that it has to be repressed into the unconscious." However, he continues, "This explanation does not quite meet the case here because the trickster obviously represents a vanishing level of consciousness which increasingly lacks the power to take, express and assert itself. Furthermore, repression would prevent it from vanishing, because repressed contents are the very ones that have the best chance of survival. . . ." Furthermore, he suggests that it is actually in the best interest of consciousness to keep the shadow as much in the conscious realm as possible, because that allows consciousness to critique it, to respond to it, to have some say in what it does.

Nevertheless, as consciousness becomes more and more powerful, the *shadow* does recede, not disappear, but retreat deeper into the unconscious, where it waits for a "favourable opportunity to reappear as a projection upon one's jealousy. If this trick is successful, there is immediately created between them that world of primordial darkness where everything that is characteristic of the trickster can happen—even on the highest plane of civilization." (15)

Jung continues: "The so-called civilized man has forgotten the trickster. He remembers him only figuratively and metaphorically, when, irritated by his own ineptitude, he speaks of fate playing tricks on him or of things being bewitched. He never suspects that his own hidden and apparently harmless shadow has qualities whose dangerousness exceeds his wildest dreams. As soon as people get together in masses and submerge the individual, the shadow is mobilized, and, as history shows, may even be personified and incarnated." (16)

This view, as Carl Jung points out, comes from the idea that humans are born *tabula rasa* , empty vessels to be molded by the environment, and it leads to the loss of self-responsibility. It is not, in this view, the individual's fault for any of the problems in the world, including his own psychic being. The various environments, natural, political, economic are in control.

Before continuing with Jung's views here, I must jump on this, as it is the key to meaning and value in human existence. Without self-responsibility life is meaningless. If a human is not responsible for his own choices then he can neither be blamed nor praised for anything, nor can he achieve any form of salvation. He is simply the "mindless" respondent to his environment.

At this point in his essay Jung has a foundation for why the *trickster/shadow* is preserved and developed. He writes, "It holds the earlier low intellectual and moral level before the eyes of the more highly developed individual, so that he shall not forget how things looked yesterday. We like," he continues, "to imagine that something which we do not understand does not help us in any way. But that is not always so. Seldom does a man understand with his head alone, least of all when he is a primitive. Because of its numinosity the myth has a direct effect on the unconscious, no matter whether it is understood or not. The fact that its repeated telling has not long since become obsolete can, I believe, be explained by its usefulness. The explanation is rather difficult because two contrary tendencies are at work: the desire on the one hand to get out of the earlier condition and on the other hand not to forget it." Carl Jung quotes from Radin: "Viewed psychologically, it might be contended that the history of civilization is largely the account of the attempts of man to forget his transformation from an animal into a human being. . . . So stubborn a refusal to forget is not an accident." (17) Jung continues, "And it is also no accident that we are forced to contradict ourselves as soon as we try to formulate man's paradoxical attitude to myth. Even the most enlightened of us will set up a Christmas-tree for his children without having the least idea what this custom means, and is invariably disposed to nip any attempt at interpretation in the bud. It is really astonishing to see how many so-called superstitions are rampant nowadays in town and country alike, but if one took hold of the individual and asked him, loudly and clearly, 'Do you believe in ghosts? In witches? In spells and magic?' he would deny it indignantly. It is a hundred to one he has never heard of such things and thinks it all rubbish. But in secret he is all for it, just like a jungle-dweller. The public knows very little of these things anyway, for everyone is convinced that in our enlightened society that kind of superstition has long since been eradicated, and it is part of the general convention to act as though one had never heard of such things, not to mention believing in them.

But nothing is ever lost, not even the blood pact with the devil. Outwardly it is forgotten, but inwardly not at all." (18)

Furthermore, Jung states later, "The conflict between the two dimensions of consciousness is simply an expression of the polaristic structure of the psyche, which like any other energy system is dependent on the tension of opposites. . . . In other words the "figure works because secretly it participates in the observer's psyche and appears as its reflection, thought it is not recognized as such. It is split off from his consciousness and consequently behaves like an autonomous personality." (19)

He continues later, "If we take the trickster as a parallel of the individual shadow, then the question arises whether that trend towards meaning, which we saw in the trickster myth, can also be observed in the subjective and personal shadow. Since this shadow frequently appears in the phenomenology of dreams as a well-defined figure, we can answer this question positively: the shadow, although by definition a negative figure, sometimes has certain clearly discernible traits and associations which point to a quite different background. It is as though he were hiding meaningful contents under an unprepossessing exterior." (20)

Jung puts the *shadow* figure of the unconscious nearest to consciousness, the first one to be encountered and dealt with in the process of *individuation*, and insightfully relates it to the riddle of the Sphinx, which of course opens up the thick meanings of Oedipus Rex, who solved this riddle, and thus was able to begin his psychic journey to self-knowledge, to *individuation*.

Though Carl Jung doesn't elaborate on the connection of *individuation* to *salvation*, he does bring his essay to a conclusion by referring again to the connection of the *trickster* myth with *salvation*, stating that this "comforting premonition or hope means that some calamity or other has happened and been consciously understood." Briefly elaborating, he states, "Only out of disaster can longing for the saviour arise—in other words, the recognition and unavoidable integration of the shadow creates such a harrowing situation that nobody but a saviour can undo the tangled web of fate. . . . As in its collective, mythological form, so also the individual shadow contains within it the seed of an enantiodromia, of a conversion into its opposite." (21)

This discussion by Jung, while constantly suggesting the *shadow* having a relationship to such higher levels of meaning and value as ultimately *salvation*, stresses the *shadow* as a primitive, lesser part of the psyche, to the point where its importance as the *counter-ego*, the dark side of the *ego* gets undermined, at least *suggesting* that the balancing is more of one of a higher form of consciousness opposing a lower form of psychic existence rather than an interplay of two equally developed levels.

In fact, as theories of the *shadow* have developed, its position as the counter-balance to the *cultural persona*, as a somewhat attractive and absolutely necessary psychic entity, perhaps even more the "I" within us than the *ego,* have gained prominence. Robert A. Johnson writes:

> We are born whole and, let us hope, will die whole. But somewhere early on our way, we eat one of the wonderful fruits of the tree of knowledge, things separate into good and evil, and we begin the shadow-making process; we divide our lives. In the cultural process we sort out our God-given characteristics into those that are acceptable to our society and those that have to be put away. This is wonderful and necessary, and there would be no civilized behavior without this sorting out of good and evil. But the refused and unacceptable characteristics do not go away; they only collect in the dark corners of our personality. When they have been hidden long enough, they take on a life of their own—the shadow life. The shadow is that which has not entered adequately into consciousness. It is the despised quarter of our being. It often has an energy potential nearly as great as that of our ego. If it accumulates more energy than our ego, it

> erupts as an overpowering rage or some indiscretion that slips past us; or we have a depression or an accident that seems to have its own purpose. The shadow gone autonomous is a terrible monster in our psychic house.
>
> The civilizing process, which is the brightest achievement of humankind, consists of culling out those characteristics that are dangerous to the smooth functioning of our ideals. Anyone who does not go through this process remains a "primitive" and can have no place in a cultivated society. We all are born whole but somehow the culture demands that we live out only part of our nature and refuse other parts of our inheritance. We divide the self into an ego and a shadow because our culture insists that we behave in a particular manner. This is our legacy from having eaten of the fruit of the tree of knowledge in the Garden of Eden. Culture takes away the simple human in us, but gives us more complex and sophisticated power. (22)

It is clear here that Robert A. Johnson is attaching the *ego* to the cultural values and the *shadow* to the individual outside of the cultural values. He goes on to point out both the artificial quality of the cultural values (they vary in different cultures) and how they are both necessary and practical.

Then he writes: "It is also astonishing to find that some very good characteristics turn up in the shadow. Generally, the ordinary, mundane characteristics are the norm. Anything less than this goes into the shadow. But anything better also goes into the shadow! Some of the pure gold of our personality is relegated to the shadow because it can find no place in that great leveling process that is culture." (23)
In this view, the *ego* tends to lose its attraction, becoming a cultural pawn, at best boring, at worst a completely passive entity, meaningless. The *shadow*, on the other hand, becomes the individual thinking for itself that has been purposely hidden deep in the psyche.

Furthermore, Robert A. Johnson writes: "Curiously, people resist the noble aspects of their shadow more strenuously than they hide the dark sides. To draw the skeletons out of the closet is relatively easy, but to own the gold in the shadow is terrifying. It is more disrupting to find that you have a profound nobility of character than to find out you are a bum." (24)

He completes his model of the ego and the shadow by claiming that they involve a process, the first step the learning of the culture's rules, the fall from innocence into a world of ethical values, where the *ego* is strongly related to the public *persona*, the cultural good person, and the *shadow* the cultural bad person, evil a necessary balance to good; the second step the restoring of the wholeness that got divided when the

forbidden fruit was eaten, the new unity a bringing of what was unconscious into consciousness.
Robert Bly writes:

> When we were one or two years old we had what we might visualize as a 360-degree personality. Energy radiated out from all parts of our body and all parts of our psyche. A child running is a living globe of energy. We had a ball of energy, all right; but one day we noticed that our parents didn't like certain parts of that ball. They said things like: "Can't you be still?" Or "It isn't nice to try and kill your brother." Behind us we have an invisible bag, and the part of us our parents don't like, we, to keep our parents' love, put in the bag. By the time we go to school our bag is quite large. Then our teachers have their say: "Good children don't get angry over such little things." So we take our anger and put it in the bag. By the time my brother and I were twelve in Madison, Minnesota we were known as "the nice Bly boys." Our bags were already a mile long.
>
> Then we do a lot of bag-stuffing in high school. This time it's no longer the evil grownups that pressure us, but people our own age. So the student's paranoia about grownups can be misplaced. I lied all through high school automatically to try to be more like the basketball players. Any part of myself that was a little slow went into the bag. My sons are going through the process now; I watched my daughters, who were older, experience it. I noticed with dismay how much they put into the bag, but there was nothing their mother or I could do about it. Often my daughters seemed to make their decision on the issue of fashion and collective ideas of beauty, and they suffered as much damage from other girls as they did from men. . . . (25)

After a few more examples, he writes: "We spend our life until we're twenty deciding what parts of our self to put into the bag, and we spend the rest of our lives trying to get them out again." (26)

Robert Bly's bag here is the same thing as the serpent's tail of the Ouroboros, the forbidden energy of the unconscious that must be brought into consciousness, incorporated into the adult psyche to be whole and complete.

The problem here, again, is the strong suggestion that the *shadow* is simply the ethical bad guy as defined by culture, and *we must go beyond ethics*. The *shadow* is not ethically good or bad. It exists beyond ethos, in the world of the *numinous*.

The world of reason, the world of ethical explanation, the world where the human conscious mind attempts to give life logic, to control life and understand life abhors the shadow, the numinous, the drive to life of the libido, the illogic necessary for meaning and value. Ethos is an attempt to explain right and wrong, explain and control human actions. That which is beyond explanation shatters ethos. The world of the night and moon escapes the burning rays of the sun, and becomes the landscape of the powerful drives for meaning beyond reduction, meaning that can only exist in mystery, in that which is beyond knowing.

Thus, when Adam and Eve ate of the Tree of the Knowledge of Good and Evil it must be a conundrum, a kind of knowledge of the unknowable, a knowledge that the unknowable exists. That is the fall (or release) from innocence, that is the knowledge that must bring with it oblivion.

This is the forbidden knowledge that gives life meaning. It is necessary. Only with the knowledge of the horrors of life can human actions take on value, can humans either succumb to or overcome those horrors. Innocence is valueless. Children cannot be blamed or praised for they know not that which is beyond what they are told is good and bad, know not free will, know not how to be kind or generous beyond the fear of condemnation or the pleasure of praise. They are by definition psychologically dependent on their parents.

This brings us back to Ursula K. Le Guin's simple, very short story, *The Ones Who Walk Away from Omelas.* There really isn't much to it at all. In fact, it's fair to say there isn't a real plot, characters are so undeveloped they barely exist, and the setting is so vague it becomes a non-setting. Yet this minimal work has a strangely lingering quality, a disturbing suggestion that one has just read something very important, something elemental about life.

Here the *forbidden*, the dark, frightening aspects of human existence get absorbed by what might be called a *scapegoat*, a character who takes the burdens, the guilt, the evil into him or herself so that the rest of the community can be freed from it.

When I discussed this book earlier, I didn't give the horrifying details, the necessary *inhuman* existence of the *scapegoat*:

> In a basement under one of the beautiful public buildings of Omelas, or perhaps in the cellar of one of its spacious private homes, there is a room. It has one locked door, and no window. A little light seeps in dustily between cracks in the boards, secondhand from a cobwebbed window somewhere across the cellar In one corner of the little room a couple of mops, with stiff, clotted, foul-smelling heads, stand near a rusty bucket. The floor is dirt, a little damp to the touch, as cellar dirt usually is. The room is about three paces long and two wide: a mere broom closet or disused tool room. In the room a child is sitting. It could be a boy or a girl. It looks about six, but actually is nearly ten. It is feeble-minded. Perhaps it was born defective, or perhaps it has become imbecile through fear, malnutrition, and neglect. It picks its nose and occasionally fumbles vaguely with its toes or genitals, as it sits hunched in the corner farthest

> from the bucket and the two mops. It is afraid of the mops. It finds them horrible. It shuts its eyes, but it knows the mops are still standing there; and the door is locked; and nobody will come. The door is always locked; and nobody ever comes, except that sometimes—the child has understanding of time or interval—sometimes the door rattles terribly and opens, and a person, or several people, are there. One of them may come in and kick the child to make it stand up. The others never come close, but peer in at it with frightened, disgusted eyes. The food bowl and the water jug are hastily filled, the door is locked, the eyes disappear. The people at the door never say anything, but the child, who has not always lived in the tool room, and can remember sunlight and its mother's voice sometimes speaks, "I can will be good," it says. "Please let me out. I will be good!" They never answer. The child used to scream for help at night, and cry a good deal, but now it only makes a kind of whining, "eh-haa, eh-haa," and it speaks less and less often. It is so thin there are no calves to its legs; its belly protrudes; it lives on a half-bowl of corn meal and grease a day. It is naked. Its buttocks and thighs are a mass of festered sores, as it sits in its own excrement continually.

It is a gut-wrenching sacrifice of human dignity, and it is even more horrifying because it cannot work, because it shatters the human world of self-responsibility, leaving life meaningless. Perhaps in the other world, the *numinous*, the spiritual world beyond physical existence, opposites do come together, but human existence is defined by a splitting. Before Adam and Eve eat of the Tree, there is no difference between Good and Evil, between Man and Woman, no choice, no free will, but that is not the world of human existence—that is pre-human existence. And life is meaningless.

If everything is Good, then Good doesn't exist. Good only exists in contrast to Evil; and choice only exists if there are options.

It is emphasized that the others in this world are not ignorant of the evil taking place, not innocent, not still living in a Garden of Eden:

> They all know it is there, all the people of Omelas. Some of them have come to see it, others are content merely to know it is there. They all know that it has to be there. Some of them understand why, and some do not, but they all understand that their happiness, the beauty of their city, the tenderness of their friendships, the health of their children, the wisdom of their scholars, the skill of their makers, even the abundance of their harvest and the kindly weathers of their skies, depend wholly on this child's abominable misery.

Child psychologists and others who study human growth know that there is a time when puberty occurs, when both the body and the psyche go through a rite-of-passage, a transformation, a time when children become adults, capable of giving birth, and capable of knowing the difference between Good and Evil and that which is beyond Good and Evil, capable of making judgments and of taking self-responsibility. And that time, that age is when the adventure of life begins. Ursula K. Le Guin writes that the necessity of the child's suffering:

> is usually explained to children when they are between eight and twelve, whenever they seem capable of understanding; and most of those who come to see the child are young people, though often enough an adult comes, or comes back, to see the child. No matter how well the matter has been explained to them, these young spectators are always shocked and sickened at the sight. They feel disgust, which they had thought themselves superior to. They feel anger, outrage, impotence, despite all the explanations. They would like to do something for the child. But there is nothing they can do. If the child were brought up into the sunlight out of the vile place, if it were cleaned and fed and comforted, that would be a good thing, indeed; but if it were done, in that day and hour all the prosperity and beauty and delight of Omelas would wither and be destroyed. Those are the terms. To exchange all the goodness and grace of every life in Omelas for that single, small improvement: to throw away the happiness of thousands for the chance of the happiness of one: that would be to let guilt within the walls indeed.

What hits the reader is that the uneasy, uncomfortable "happy" world is not, as Ursula K. Le Guin emphasizes, a world of ignorance or stupidity, but is a world without meaning, for the reader knows meaning only exists in taking self-responsibility, in accepting one's own suffering, not in innocence or in obedience to some outside being, some other power, or even some barrier to human existence. And it is not an absence of empathy and compassion, but the opposite, the realization of it, the knowing of the shared suffering of all humans, the inherent sorrow of life, that carries the emotional punch:

> Often the young people go home in tears, or in a tearless rage, when they have seen the child and faced this terrible paradox. They may brood over it for weeks or years. But as time goes on they begin to realize that even if the child could be released, it would not get much good of its freedom: a little vague pleasure of warmth and food, no doubt, but little more. It is too degraded and imbecile to know any real joy. It has been afraid too long ever to be free of fear. Its habits are too uncouth for it to respond to humane treatment. Indeed, after so long it would probably be wretched without walls about it to protect it, and darkness for its eyes, and its own excrement to sit in. Their tears at the bitter injustice dry when they begin to perceive the terrible justice of reality and to accept it. Yet it is their tears and anger, the trying of their generosity and the acceptance of

> their helplessness, which are perhaps the true source of the splendor of their lives. Theirs is no vapid, irresponsible happiness. They know that they, like the child, are not free. They know compassion. It is the existence of the child, and their knowledge of its existence, that makes possible the nobility of their architecture, the poignancy of their music, the profundity of their science. It is because of the child that they are so gentle with children. They know that if the wretched one were not there sniveling in the dark, the other one, the flute-player, could make no joyful music as the young riders line up in their beauty for the race in the sunlight of the first morning of summer.

This is why the conclusion is so unnerving:"At times one of the adolescent girls or boys who go to see the child does not go home to weep or rage, does not, in fact, go home at all." Instead some of these adolescents, and later she includes some of the older people as well, simply walk away from Omelas, their exposure to the suffering child making their idyllic world no longer desirable. This cannot help but suggest the exit from the most idyllic world of all, Eden, the garden where Adam and Eve lived without the knowledge of good and evil (or of the dual planes of existence—physical and spiritual), a purely childlike innocence without meaning or value. But when given the chance, the temptation to do so, they *knowingly* bite of the forbidden fruit and gain the knowledge of good and evil. This knowledge of something other than pure joy, pure happiness, and pure festival is the fall from innocence into the world of the adult human, a world where meaning and value and the dual planes of visible and invisible exist.

This *realization and acceptance of the horror* of a world without self-responsibility, without ethical sensitivity, without meaning and value is the added silence between the words that touches the reader with the knowledge of both the sorrow and nobility of human existence. "These people go out into the street, and walk down the street alone. They keep walking, and walk straight out of the city of Omelas, through the beautiful gates. They keep walking across the farmlands of Omelas. Each one goes alone, youth or girl, man or woman. Night falls; the traveler must pass down village streets, between the houses with yellow-lit windows, and on out into the darkness of the fields." This indeed is the human journey out of the sunlit world of childhood into the dark, shadowy world of the adult, a world that includes the ultimate unknown darkness of death and the knowledge of our own ignorance. "Each alone, they go west or north, towards the mountains. They go on. They leave Omelas, they walk ahead into the darkness, and they do not come back. The place they go towards is a place even less imaginable to most of us than the city of happiness. I cannot describe it at all." And we all walk with them, at least those of us who have the courage to face the human condition. And what do they or we know about this place they and we walk toward? According to Le Guin, "It is possible that it does not exist." Nonetheless, there is a strange comfort in the concluding sentence, "But they seem to know where they are going, the ones who walk away from Omelas."

Now we return to the Kolona, the mock black bird, the fearful life force of the other world, that numinous, spiritual world beyond the sunlit one of consciousness:

Alan Kilpatric writes:

> In the late 1950s my father and I, on our way to Stilwell, Oklahoma, took a side excursion off Highway 100. The purpose of our trip into these remote woods was to see the grave of an aunt generations removed from my mother. "Nannie," as this distant relative was called, died sometime in the 1850s, and her mortal remains were interred in a curious wooden miniature of an Iroquoian longhouse, now ramshackle and decayed. Even more remarkable than the shape of her grave was the extreme isolation of the site located many miles from any human habitation. When I asked my father why Nannie "was buried all by herself" and "so far from everything," I was told the terrible truth—that she was rumored to have been a *kolana a:yélis:sgi* and "very evil." Thus, feared in death as much as in life, "Nannie'' was forever banished from all human contact in observance of ancient Cherokee tradition. (27)

Is there some kind of pure evil lurking beyond, behind the conscious world of the senses, some force that can enter into this world, can possess a human soul? Certainly, Christianity includes it, and the "original sin" involves eating the forbidden fruit from the tree of *the knowledge of good and evil.* Theological discourse as to just what this represents has interpreted it in numerous ways, from something as insignificant as a slight deficiency, or a tendency toward sin yet without collective guilt, referred to as a "sin nature," to something as drastic as total depravity or automatic guilt by all humans through collective guilt. (28) Certainly, if God and Satan are adversaries in their spiritual world, and if humans are God's creation, then the struggles between God and Satan are going to involve humans. And if humans are sinful or prone to sin as a result of this "original sin," then Satan is capable of entering into and in some sense possessing humans. And if humans are born in sin (as boldly assumed in the famous Puritan alphabet that begins "In Adam's sin we sinned all"), then children are born evil, born with some form of Satan already in them.

This is the stuff of horror fiction and movies. According to Gary Hoppenstand, horror fiction was first brought into the American publishing mainstream by three novels, Ira Levin's *Rosemary's Baby*

(1967), Thomas Tryon's *The Other* (1971), and William Peter Blatty's *The Exorcist* (1971), and it consisted of three significant motifs: that the appearance of normalcy may be deceiving, that evil involves violations of sacred American institutions and values, and that it takes place in the world of the child. Furthermore, in dealing with these motifs, the real, the contemporary world and real world social issues are emphasized. (29)

The first of these motifs, the "appearance of normalcy" is easily indicated. In *Rosemary's Baby*, the setting is the Bramford, an old apartment building in New York City, where a number of people who seem very normal (just a group of doddering senior citizens more prone to senility than to evil) turn out to be members of a satanic witches coven. In *The Other* a seemingly normal boy harbors a dark secret. In *The Exorcist*, a standard, upscale Georgetown brownstone is the site of an innocent young girl's demonic possession.

The second of these motifs, the underbelly of American institutions and values, has to do with the focus, the social issues that form the center of the stories. In *Rosemary's Baby*, it is not the evil satanic cult, but the break-up of the marriage between Guy and Rosemary and the fears of childbirth. In *The Other,* it is the validity of the American rural myth, the idyllic rural world. In *The Exorcist*, it is the efficacy of the Church in the modern, pragmatic world, the questioning of *faith*.

Most important, the third of the motifs has to do with ambivalent views of the child in a culture that is questioning and changing its values about having and raising children, about personal and professional success, about the roles of men and women. In *Rosemary's Baby*, the expected child sparks numerous strong and contradictory emotions. It is at once a love object, more than just a way of propagating the family line, yet it is also a hindrance to both personal and professional success, and beneath it all, it is potentially the cause of sickness and death, and it is perhaps pure evil, the son of Satan himself. In *The Other*, the child is the cause of evil, a sociopathic monster preying upon society. (Hoppenstand suggests this represents the rising world of the adolescent with its drug abuse, sexual promiscuity, rebellion against various institutions, and general anti-social behavior.) In *The Exorcist*, the child is the victim, the result of a loss of faith, of an evolving family structure that places more emphasis on personal and professional success than on the role of parenthood—a world where children become dysfunctional as a result of dysfunctional families.

Stephen King, the writer who quickly follows these three to become the biggest name in contemporary horror fiction, got his big break with *Carrie*, a dramatic example of combining the elements of a dysfunctional family in the central character of an adolescent girl.

Carrie has been abused at home all of her life by her unstable Christian fundamentalist mother, Margaret, and bullied at Ewen High School from first grade on because of her unusual religious beliefs, her poor, outdated clothes, and her unattractive looks. The novel begins with Carrie having her first period while showering during gym class. Since she has no idea what menstruation is all about, she has a psychological breakdown, causing the electric light above her to burn out, and letting the reader know something beyond normal is taking place.

The other girls in the locker room tease Carrie and throw tampons and sanitary napkins at her. Miss Desjardin catches them and intervenes, but she doesn't realize at first how innocent Carrie is about it all until later, when she does punish the girls.

Carrie begins to realize she has telekinetic powers. At first, she tries to control them, but her mother's punishments and the teasing make it hard to hold them in. Sue Snell, one of the girls who originally teased Carrie, begins to feel sorry for her and offers to befriend her, setting her up to go to prom with her boyfriend Tommy Ross, a very popular boy in the class.

Chris Hargensen, however, is not so thoughtful, and is smarting from being banned from prom as punishment for her own mean teasing of Carrie. So she and her boyfriend Billy Nolan, a thug, put in place a plan to humiliate Carrie in front of the entire school. Billy fills two buckets with pig blood and places them on a rafter over the stage. Carrie's mother begs her not to go to prom, but Carries goes anyway. However, she is very nervous. But the other students are friendly and she begins to enjoy her big date with Tommy, who actually begins to find her attractive.

Sue becomes worried about both what's happening at the prom and her own possibility of being pregnant.

Things are coming to a climax. Carrie and Tommy are voted King and Queen of the prom. While they stand on stage, Chris puts her plan in motion, drenching them with the pig's blood, causing the rest of the students to laugh at them. Tommy gets knocked unconscious by a bucket and Carrie runs out of the gym in humiliation.

This is the spark that ignites the fire. She thinks about her life of confinement and her power. She decides to go back to the prom and exact revenge. She locks the doors and turns on the sprinkler system. After seeing two children die of electrocution, she snaps, and uses her telekinetic power to set fire to the entire gym, causing numerous deaths. Miss Desjardin and a few of the students escape through the fire escape. By now, Carrie has taken her destructive powers beyond the school out into the town, blowing up gas stations and setting her entire neighborhood on fire. In a symbolically rich connection to her life of punishment resulting from her mentally deranged mother's views of Christianity, Carrie goes into a cathedral and prays while causing power-lines outside to electrocute and kill even more of the town. Then she runs back to the school and watches it explode. Finally, she returns home to confront her mother, who is now completely insane, and reveals to Carrie that she conceived Carrie as the result of being raped. Then she attacks Carrie with a knife. In retaliation, Carrie kills her by stopping her heart (another symbolic double-entendre).

Though Carrie has been mortally wounded, she continues her rampage, making her way to the local roadhouse, the place her father got drunk and raped her mother. Coincidentally, Chris and Billy happen to be making love inside. They attempt to escape, but Carrie telekinetically sends the car crashing into the roadhouse, killing them both. Then she collapses in the parking lot from loss of blood.

Then Sue shows up. Carrie communicates with her telekinetically and finds out that Sue was not responsible for the prank. Then Carrie dies in Sue's arms. Sue runs away from the roadhouse in terror, collapses, and has her period (so she is relieved of her fear of being pregnant).

The story continues by showing the town one month later; it has become a ghost town. The "Black Prom" events have hit the nation's news. Scientists are deciding to consider the real possibilities that telekinesis exists. Miss Desjardin is consumed with guilt for not helping Carrie and resigns from teaching. Sue writes a memoir. It all ends with a letter written by a woman in Tennessee whose niece is developing telekinetic powers.

Though his expectations for the book were low, Stephen King had struck a chord in contemporary America. As with the other three horror fiction authors, he had connected the dark, frightening world of the mythic shadow with the normal, small town of modern life, exposing the dark evils that lurk just behind the sunny surface.

But the influence of mythic evil, of some malicious force of the invisible world on the visible world, is not restricted to contemporary horror fiction. It is a constant throughout all of human existence, and it works best when it contains a connection to a psychological darkness, to the personal *shadow*. In Shakespeare's *Macbeth,* the personal evil, the psychological darkness of Macbeth is matched by an evil outside of his psyche (similar to the general belief in England that "the land and the king are one, that the king's spiritual and ethical condition determines the physical condition of the land and subjects of England). Shakespeare expresses this in the voices of witches, beings similar to shamans and psychics who connect with both worlds, who have one foot in the literal, physical world and the other foot in the invisible, spiritual world, as is clear in Act IV, Scene I, 1-45, which ends with the famous line, "Something wicked this way comes":

Thunder. Enter the three WITCHES.

First Witch
1 Thrice the branded cat hath mew'd.

Second Witch
2 Thrice and once the hedge-pig whined.

Third Witch
3 Harpier cries "'Tis time, 'tis time."

First Witch
4 Round about the cauldron go;
5 In the poison'd entrails throw.
6 Toad, that under cold stone
7 Days and nights has thirty-one
8 Swelter'd venom sleeping got,
9 Boil thou first i' the charmed pot.

ALL
10 Double, double toil and trouble;
11 Fire burn, and cauldron bubble.

Second Witch
12 Fillet of a fenny snake,
13 In the cauldron boil and bake;
14 Eye of newt and toe of frog,
15 Wool of bat and tongue of dog,
16 Adder's fork and blind-worm's sting,
17 Lizard's leg and howlet's wing,
18 For a charm of powerful trouble,
19 Like a hell-broth boil and bubble.

ALL
20 Double, double toil and trouble;
21 Fire burn and cauldron bubble.

Third Witch
22 Scale of dragon, tooth of wolf,
23 Witches' mummy, maw and gulf
24 Of the ravin'd salt-sea shark,
25 Root of hemlock digg'd i' the dark,

Liver of blaspheming Jew,
Gall of goat, and slips of yew
Sliver'd in the moon's eclipse,
Nose of Turk and Tartar's lips,
Finger of birth-strangled babe
Ditch-deliver'd by a drab,
Make the gruel thick and slab.
Add thereto a tiger's chaudron,
For the ingredients of our cauldron.

ALL
Double, double toil and trouble;
Fire burn and cauldron bubble.

Second Witch
Cool it with a baboon's blood,
Then the charm is firm and good.

** *Enter* HECAT *and the other three* WITCHES.

HECATE
O well done! I commend your pains;
And every one shall share i' the gains;
And now about the cauldron sing,
Live elves and fairies in a ring
Enchanting all that you put in.

Music and a song: "Black spirits, etc."

[*Exit* HECATE.]

Second Witch
By the pricking of my thumbs,
Something wicked this way comes.

Psychological evil is matched by mythological evil, the inner mind matches the exterior world, they are of the same stuff, and they affect each-other. It might be said that the cosmos is the mind and that the mind is the cosmos.

Now, returning to the beginning of Part II of this book, we can better understand the experience Rudolph Otto was trying to clarify in 1917, when he published *Das Heilige (The Idea of the Holy)*, and created the term *numinous* from the Latin word *numen*, which means god or the power of god or the will of god. According to Otto the *numinous* is a "category for the interpretation and evaluation" of nonrational manifestations of the sacred characterized by a "sense of one's creature state" (by which he means a being that has been created), mystical awe (*tremendum*), a presentiment of divine power (*majestas*), amazement in the face of the "completely other" (*mysterium*), demoniacal energy, and paradox. (30)

It is the mystery behind a religious experience. This experience is not simply an ordinary experience intensified; for example fear intensifying until it becomes dread, but an entirely different feeling, a dread aroused by intimations of or actual experience of the *numinous*.

This *numinous dread* or awe or awe-fullness, Otto called the *mysterium tremendum*, which has three components, tremendousness (*tremendum*), mysteriousness (*mysterium*), and fascination (*facinans*). The difference between the fear of physical danger and dread is that the experience of dread is that of the realization of the inexplicable. So, for example, the fear that comes from encountering a wild beast, a lion or tiger or bear that might harm one is not the same as that of encountering a ghost, which suggests an other realm of existence, not just as a subject for speculation, but as a reality.

This reality is absolutely other, unapproachable through any conscious form of understanding, overwhelmingly powerful, and of an urgency and energy that might be compared to the "wrath of God."

Since it is absolutely other, it results in a state of stupor, of blank amazement, of astonishment, where the soul reaches beyond the mind to a *trembling* shudder only known by the feelings, not by the intellect. The awareness of being a creature, of being but a creation of the creator is a sense, not of guilt, but of realization of being other than the spiritual, a feeling of nothingness in the presence of the other, the creator, the god. This has nothing to do with a moral judgment, but is in the realm of an awareness of the *numinous*. And it is this awareness of the *numinous* that frees the person experiencing it from being unfit, provides a shield, a form of grace.

Furthermore, according to Rudolph Otto a *mysterium fascinosum*, an attraction to the *numinous*, draws us to the experience, pulls us to an encounter with the *numen*, a mystical moment, when all of the oppositions come together in a strange harmony, what Otto called the *mysterium tremendum* and *fascinosum*.

Rudolph Otto believed humans have an a priori ability to experience the *numinous*, a potential for such an experience, some more so than others, but that does not necessarily mean each human will experience it. It must be evoked through some experience or series of experiences. It cannot be taught. Those who are especially receptive and who have the necessary experiences are the shamans and prophets who draw others to also experience it.

It is difficult but worthwhile trying to clarify the difference between the *numinous* and the *sublime*. Both are mysterious, inexplicable, and enticing; both involve the experience of human existence as small and weak and unimportant in the overpowering movements of nature and fate; yet in complete paradox include the joy of being a part of it all, even the necessity of human existence to the value of all existence, the strange truth inherent in the Biblical story that when God created man he considered man superior to the angels, considered man his greatest creation. While the lines are not clearly drawn, it might be said that the *sublime* is the experience of these truths in the physical world, while the *numinous* is the experience of the *other*, the world beyond this world. Thus, in an experiencing of one it is possible to be led to an experience of the other.

James Baldwin concludes “Sonny’s Blues”:

> All I know about music is that not many people ever really hear it. And even then, on the rare occasions when something opens within, and the music enters, what we mainly hear, or hear corroborated, are personal, private, vanishing evocations. But the man who creates the music is hearing something else, is dealing with the roar rising from the void and imposing order on it as it hits the air. What is evoked in him, then, is of another order, more terrible because it has no words, and triumphant, too, for that same reason. And his triumph, when he triumphs, is ours. I just watched Sonny's face. His face was troubled, he was working hard, but he wasn't with it. And I had the feeling that, in a way, everyone on the bandstand was waiting for him, both waiting for him and pushing him along. But as I began to watch Creole I realized that it was Creole who held them all back. He had them on a short rein. Up there, keeping the beat with his whole body, wailing on the fiddle, with his eyes half closed, he was listening to everything, but he was listening to Sonny. He was having a dialogue with Sonny. He wanted Sonny to leave the shoreline and strike out for the deep water. He was Sonny's witness that deep water and drowning were not the same thing—he had been there, and he knew. And he wanted Sonny to know. He was waiting for Sonny to do the things on the keys which would let Creole know that Sonny was in the water.
>
> And, while Creole listened, Sonny moved, deep within, exactly like someone in torment. I had never before thought of how awful the relationship must be between the musician and his instrument. He has to fill it, this instrument, with the breath of life, his own. He has to make it do what he wants it to do. And a piano is just a piano. It's made out of so much wood and wires and little hammers and big ones, and ivory. While

there's only so much you can do with it, the only way to find this out is to try; to try and make it do everything.

And Sonny hadn't been near a piano for over a year. And he wasn't on much better terms with his life, not the life that stretched before him now. He and the piano stammered, started one way, got scared, stopped; started another way, panicked, marked time, started again; then seemed to have found a direction, panicked again, got stuck. And the face I saw on Sonny I'd never seen before. Everything had been burned out of it, and, at the same time, things usually hidden were being burned in, by the fire and fury of the battle which was occurring in him up there.

Yet, watching Creole's face as they neared the end of the first set, I had the feeling that something had happened, something I hadn't heard. Then they finished, there was scattered applause, and then, without an instant's warning, Creole started into something else, it was almost sardonic, it was Am I Blue. And, as though he commanded, Sonny began to play. Something began to happen. And Creole let out the reins. The dry, low, black man said something awful on the drums, Creole answered, and the drums talked back. Then the horn insisted, sweet and high, slightly detached perhaps, and Creole listened, commenting now and then, dry, and driving, beautiful, calm and old. Then they all came together again, and Sonny was part of the family again. I could tell this from his face. He seemed to have found, right there, beneath his fingers, a damn brand-new piano. It seemed that he couldn't get over it. Then, for a while, just being happy with Sonny, they seemed to be agreeing with him that brand-new pianos certainly were a gas.

Then Creole stepped forward to remind them that what they were playing was the blues. He hit something in all of them, he hit something in me, myself, and the music tightened and deepened, apprehension began to beat the air. Creole began to tell us what the blues were all about. They were not about anything very new. He and his boys up there were keeping it new, at the risk of ruin, destruction, madness and death, in order to find new ways to make us listen. For, while the tale of how we suffer, and how we are delighted, and how we may triumph is never new, it must always be heard. There isn't any other tale to tell, it's the only light we've got in all this darkness.

And this tale, according to that face, that body, those strong hands on those strings, has another aspect in every country, and a new depth in every generation. Listen, Creole seemed to be saying, listen. Now these are Sonny's blues. He made the little black man on the rums know it, and the bright, brown man on the horn. Creole wasn't trying any longer to get Sonny in the water. He was wishing him Godspeed. Then he stepped back, very slowly, filling the air with the immense suggestion that Sonny speak for himself.

Then they all gathered around Sonny and Sonny played. Every now and again one of them seemed to say, amen. Sonny's fingers filled the air with life, his life. But that life contained so many others. And Sonny went

> all the way back, he really began with the spare, flat statement of the opening phrase of the song. Then he began to make it his. It was very beautiful because it wasn't hurried and it was no longer a lament. I seemed to hear with what burning he had made it his, with what burning we had yet to make ours, how we could cease lamenting. Freedom lurked around us and I understood at last how he could help us to be free if we would listen, that he would never be free until we did. Yet, there was no battle in his face now. I heard what he had gone through, and would continue to go through until he came to rest in earth. He had made it his: that long line, of which we knew only Mama and Daddy. And he was giving it back, as everything must be given back, so that, passing through death, it can live forever. I saw my mother's face again, and felt, for the first time, how the stones of the road she had walked on must have bruised her feet. I saw the moonlit road where my father's brother died. And it brought something else back to me, and carried me past it. I saw my little girl again and felt Isabel's tears again, and I felt my own tears begin to rise. And I was yet aware that this was only a moment, that the world waited outside, as hungry as a tiger, and that trouble stretched above us, longer than the sky.
>
> Then it was over. Creole and Sonny let out their breath, both soaking wet, and grinning. There was a lot of applause and some of it was real. In the dark, the girl came by and I asked her to take drinks to the bandstand. There was a long pause, while they talked up there in the indigo light and after awhile I saw the girl put a Scotch and milk on top of the piano for Sonny. He didn't seem to notice it, but just before they started playing again, he sipped from it and looked toward me, and nodded. Then he put it back on top of the piano. For me, then, as they began to play again, it glowed and shook above my brother's head like the very cup of trembling. (31)

Here it all is, the connection of music to one's heritage, one's traditions, one's community, to one's inner soul, one's psyche, to one's salvation, to touching the *numinous*, the knowledge of the *other,* the world of God. And the final sentence refers directly to Isaiah, 51, xvii-xxii:

> Awake, awake, stand up, O Jerusalem, which hast drunk at the hand of the LORD the cup of his fury; thou hast drunken the dregs of the cup of trembling, *and* wrung *them* out.
> *There is* none to guide her among all the sons *whom* she hath brought forth; neither is *there any* that taketh her by the hand of all the sons *that* she hath brought up.
> These two *things* are come unto thee; who shall be sorry for thee? desolation, and destruction, and the famine, and the sword: by whom shall I comfort thee?
> Thy sons have fainted, they lie at the head of all the streets, as a wild bull in a net: they are full of the fury of the LORD, the rebuke of thy God.
> Therefore hear now this, thou afflicted, and drunken, but not with wine:

> Thus saith thy Lord the LORD, and thy God that pleadeth the cause of his people, Behold, I have taken out of thine hand the cup of trembling, *even* the dregs of the cup of my fury; thou shalt no more drink it again:
> But I will put it into the hand of them that afflict thee; which have said to thy soul, Bow down, that we may go over: and thou hast laid thy body as the ground, and as the street, to them that went over. (32)

Here it is, God's wrath, "the dregs of the cup of trembling," the suffering he has unleashed on the Israelites, but now will turn on their enemies, now will put into the hands of their enemies.

But it is not nearly so simple, not nearly so shallow, superficial, and literal as this. The passage connects directly to the images throughout "Sonny's Blues," scenes of drunkenness and the dark corners of the streets of the ghetto, the struggles of addiction, whether it be heroin or alcohol, and it connects these types of suffering to those "afflicted, and drunken, but not with wine."

How does all this connect to the musician, the artist? Sonny here has just demonstrated that he can enter into, can experience, express the fear, the pain, the sorrows and sadness of his people. And though it is clear that this *cup of trembling* contains the drug, the alcohol, the addiction that brings the suffering, it is offered to Sonny at a *moment of salvation*. It is a gift, a sign of acceptance. Certainly Sonny and his brother have now connected for the first time, have resolved or found a way beyond their conflicts (and there are strong intimations of the Cain and Able story throughout, so on one level this is a resolution to the conflict of brothers underlying all of Christianity). But why symbolize it with a *cup of trembling*, why an offering of alcohol and milk, why an acceptance of the addiction?

Perhaps it is an expression of the necessity of the artist to experience, to drink from the *cup of trembling*, the wrath of God. Perhaps it even goes further to say that the artist, in drinking from this cup is taking on the suffering of his community, of the entire human race, perhaps it connects directly to the last verse just quoted from Isaiah, and expresses the idea that the artist is the one who, in translating his own pain into music, "hast laid [his] body as the ground, and as the street, to them that went over." Perhaps the artist is taking on the suffering so that his listeners will not have to do so themselves, and the acceptance of it by the listeners, the audience, the community, the culture, the whole human race, is a realization of this.

It is not hard at all to take this to the conclusion that Sonny, representing the artist, performs a sacrifice, internalizes and then expresses back all of the anguish, fear, and joy of his listeners, absorbs the condemnation of God when he expels Adam and Eve from the Garden of Eden for disobedience and gives the means of salvation. Here the artist becomes Christ-like.

The various lines of thought converge. We have reached a point of *axis mundi*, a center. The *artist*, the *true artist*, and the *shaman* become one, and they are one with the *trickster*, the *shadow*, and the *savior*.

They exist beyond *ethos*, not subject to the tree of the knowledge of good and evil, but, rather, as mediums, as illuminated beings, and their expressions, their works of art are meant to take us there, to take us beyond mere physical existence to that *numinous* world we cannot enter until we pass beyond the body, but we can know, can sense, can feel, if we experience that *trembling* of the soul.

Carl Jung who has already used *numen* to designate the autonomy of psychic energy in relation to *mana*, spiritual power, (33) begins in the 1930s to simply incorporate *numinous* into his Analytical Psychology. For him, *numinous* refers to a psychic event, an experience when the person connects to that which is completely other and is beyond intellectual understanding, an experience that is indescribable and "puts the subject into a state of amazement or passive submission." (34). This is dangerous and can result in various forms of psychic neurosis. Consciousness is altered, possibly resulting in schizophrenia, egotism, possession, and fanaticism. (35).

Yet, in spite of the serious dangers, a *numinous* experience can also be positive, a necessary step toward psychic healing. It is a transforming experience, signaling the emergence of an archetype with a specific energy or emotional charge, and this can compensate for the unilateral attitude of consciousness. For example, the *numinosity* of the archetype of the *self* can prompt a man to realize the paradoxical totality of his being, conscious and unconscious, through the female the symbols of the quaternity that appear in his dreams. The *ego* is the determining factor—whether it is ready, in the right place for a positive transformation, or not. In this case, the attitude of the *ego* is the determining factor. Such an experience, Jung considered to be religious in the sense of *relegere* (sending forth), a reaching out, a connecting, “a careful and scrupulous observation of . . . the *numinosum.*" (36)

Does the artist, then, perform the same function as the shaman? The shadow? The trickster? The savior? The empathon? The scapegoat? Do these entities take on the suffering for the culture? Are they the wounded wounders who take on the wounds for all?

Jean Chevalier and Alain Gheerbrant write:

> Dance is celebration and dance is language, a language beyond words. The courtship dances of birds display this. It is beyond words for, when words fail, up surges the dance. This fever, which can take hold of all beings and drive them to the pitch of frenzy, can only be a manifestation of the Spirit of Life. Often explosive, its aim is to throw off every vestige of the dual nature of temporal things to rediscover at a bound the primeval Oneness. Then body and soul, creator and creation, visible and invisible meet and anneal timelessly in a unique ecstasy. The dance proclaims and celebrates its identification with the imperishable.
>
> Such was David's dance before the Ark of the Covenant or the dance which carried off in a rapture of endless whirling Maulavi (Jalal-al-Din Muhammad Rumi). Founder of the order of Whirling Dervishes and one of the greatest lyric poets of all time. Such are all primary dances, dances which may be described as sacred. (37)

The Buffalo Dance, the most famous dance of the Blackfoot tribe expresses the need to justify and absolve the killing and eating of the sacred animal. As all such ritual dances are, it is the enactment of a myth.

Since the buffalo were the primary source of food, shelter, clothing, and all of the major needs of the tribe, it was necessary to kill them. The method used was to stampede them to a cliff, called a buffalo jump. As the story goes, the buffalo decided they no longer wanted to be killed in this fashion, and instead of jumping off the cliff turned aside.

"No, no more," they said. "No longer will we willing become your blankets and your pants and your coats. No longer will we give you our dried flesh for your winter rations. No longer will we let you use our hooves and horns for your tools and utensils. No longer will we give up our lives so you can use our sinew for your sewing."

And no matter how hard the hunters tried to get the buffalo herd to jump off the cliff, it always turned aside. It looked as if the tribe would go cold and hungry for the winter.

But the chief of the tribe had a lovely daughter, one who was very proud of her father's prowess with the bow, and all summer long, when he brought her the hides of the best of the buffalo, she would turn them into the softest of garments to wear, and she would make moccasins for the children of the village.

Just as the winter winds began to blow, she decided to strike a deal with the buffalo. She walked out to their herd above the buffalo jump and called out. "Oh buffalo, oh buffalo, if you will come jumping off the cliff and join me below, I will marry one of you."

She continued to make this promise for some time. Then she heard the hoofs of the buffalo begin to move, and then she saw them, buffalo after buffalo crashing off the cliff. Then the main buffalo came down on top of the others unharmed and walked over to her. "I have come to claim my bride," he said.

"Oh, but now I am afraid to go with you," she replied.

"Oh no! You're not getting out of your promise. Look, see all of my family, my brothers and sisters, my sons and daughters, my friends; they have given of themselves for your tribe, and now you must keep your side of the bargain." With that he lifted her up with his horns and took her off to be his wife.

The next morning, her tribe woke to find the many buffalo at the jump and were delighted that their winter needs had been solved. However, her father found her gone, and knew what had happened. He followed the trail, determined to bring her back.

After some days, he encountered a magpie. "O wise bird, I'm looking for my daughter. She's gone off with a buffalo. Have you seen her?"

"Yes," said the magpie. "In fact, they are just over this hill."

"Will you please tell my daughter I am here, waiting for her. Tell her to come to me."

"Will do."

With this said, the magpie flew over to the sleeping heard. The daughter was sitting quietly by her sleeping husband. "Your father is waiting for you on the other side of the hill," he whispered.

"Oh, no," she whispered. "This is terrible. If the herd finds out, they will kill him. Go, tell him to wait. I will come to him as soon as I can."

Soon her husband woke up and told her to fetch him some water from the nearby wallow. This was her chance, and she snuck over to where her father waited.

"Come," he said. "I've come to take you home."

"No," she said. "This is dangerous. If they find you here, they will kill you." I will go back and see what I can do about this. You wait here.

But when she returned to her buffalo husband, he could smell her father. He alerted the herd and they all danced a great buffalo dance over the girl's father, killing him and trampling him into tiny pieces.

His daughter sat on the edge of the wallow and cried.

"Why are you crying," her husband asked.

"You have killed my father."

"Well, what of my family? We have given our parents, our children, our wives."

He turned away, but she continued to cry.

"Okay," he said, "go to your father. If you can bring him back to life, then you can take him back to your people."

The daughter immediately rushed to her father. With the magpie's help, she found one splinter of one of his bones. This she placed on the ground and put a blanket over it.

"Then she sang the revivifying song handed down from her grandmother to her mother to her. Quietly, she sang, and the soft melody spread across the night. Then, after some time, the magpie noticed something under the blanket. When he looked, he saw her father, but he was still not breathing. She continued to sing. Then her father's eyes opened and he rose, alive again.

"You have brought your father back to life," said her buffalo husband. "If you will sing this song and do the dance I teach you, then we will continue to allow you to drive us off the cliffs, for you will bring us also back to life.

And so the great buffalo herd rose and began a solemn dance, befitting the great beasts. And after this the woman and her father returned to their tribe and taught their people this dance.

So now they dance the buffalo dance to the beat of drums, and the sacred animal willingly joins with them, and the dance enacts the central myth. (38)

Elaine Pagels offers a dance connected to Christianity:

> In the Round Dance, which is found in the *Acts of John*, a second-century collection of stories and traditions inspired by John's gospel, John begins the story of Jesus' final night where the gospel account leaves off, and says that Jesus invited his disciples to dance and sing with him:
>
> > "Before he was arrested . . . he assembled us all, and said, 'Before I am delivered to them, let us sing a hymn to the Father, and so go to meet what lies before us." So he told us to form a circle, holding one another's hands, and he himself stood in the middle and said, "Answer Amen to me."
>
> Then, as the disciples circled him, dancing, Jesus began to chant a hymn in words that echo the Gospel of John:
>
> > "Glory to you, Father." And we, circling around him, answered him, "Amen."
> >
> > "Glory to you, Logos; glory to you, Grace." "Amen."
> >
> > "Glory to you, Spirit; glory to you, Holy One. . . ." "Amen."
> >
> > "We praise you, Father; we thank you, Light, in whom dwells no darkness."
> >
> > "Amen."
> >
> > "I am a light to you who see me." "Amen."

> "I am a mirror to you who know me." "Amen."
> "I am a door to you who knock upon me." "Amen."
> "I am a way to you, the traveler." "Amen."
>
> Although the phrase about the mirror could have come straight from the *Gospel of Thomas*, the primary source for the last two, as well as many of the others, is the *Gospel of John*.
>
> Whoever composed this hymn, then, clearly found in John's gospel inspiration for the kind of teaching we more often associate with Thomas; for here Jesus invites his disciples to see themselves in him:
>
> "*[W]hich I am about to suffer is your own.* For you could by no means have understood what you suffer, unless I had been sent to you as word [logos] by the Father . . . if you knew how to suffer, you would be able not to suffer."
>
> Thus, in the Round Dance of the Cross, Jesus says that he suffers in order to reveal the nature of human suffering, and to teach the paradox that Buddha also taught: that those who become aware of suffering simultaneously find release from it. Yet he also tells them to join in the cosmic dance: "'Whoever dances belongs to the whole'. Amen. 'Who ever does not dance does not know what happens.' 'Amen.'"
>
> Those who love the Acts of John apparently celebrated the Eucharist by chanting these words, holding hands, and circling in this dance to celebrate together the mystery of Jesus' suffering, and their own—and some Christians celebrate it thus to this day. (39)

Joseph Campbell elaborates on this dance as a celebration, the celebration of the transformation from this world into the world beyond, and equates it with an Iroquois ritual:

> Moyers: Do you think it is true that he who loses his life gains his life?
>
> Campbell: That is what Jesus says.
>
> Moyers: Do you believe it is true?
>
> Campbell: I do—if you lost it in the name of something. There is a report by the seventeenth-century Jesuit missionaries in eastern Canada of a young Iroquois brave who has just been captured by an enemy tribe. He is being brought to be tortured to death. The Northeastern Indians had a custom of systematic torture of their male captives. The ordeal was to be suffered without flinching. That was the final test of real manhood. And so this young Iroquois is being brought in to endure this horrible ordeal; but, to the Jesuits' amazement, it is as though they were his welcoming hosts and he their honored guest. And he is playing the game along with them, knowing all the while to what end he is being conducted. The French priests describing the occasion are simply appalled by what they interpret as the heartless mockery of such a reception, characterizing the youth's captors as a company of savage brutes. But no! Those people were to be

the young brave's sacrificial priests. This was to be a sacrifice of the altar and, by analogy, that boy was the like of Jesus. The French priests themselves, every day, were celebrating Mass, which is a replication of the brutal sacrifice of the cross.

There is an equivalent scene described in the apocryphal Christian Acts of John, immediately before Jesus goes to be crucified. This is one of the most moving passages in Christian literature. In the Matthew, Mark, Luke and John gospels, it is simply mentioned that, at the conclusion of the celebration of the Last Supper, Jesus and his disciples sang a hymn before he went forth. But in the Acts of John, we have a word-for-word account of the whole singing of the hymn. Just before going out into the garden at the end of the Last Supper, Jesus says to the company, "Let us dance!" And they all hold hands in a circle, and as they circle around him, Jesus sings, "Glory be to thee, Father!"

To which the circling company responds, "Amen."

"Glory be to thee, Word!"

And again, "Amen."

"I would be born and I would bear!"

"Amen."

"I would eat and I would be eaten!"

"Amen."

"Thou that dancest, see what I do, for thine is this passion of the manhood, which I am about to suffer!"

"Amen."

"I would flee and I would stay!"

"Amen."

"I would be united and I would unite!"

"Amen."

"A door am I to thee that knocketh at me. . . . A way am I to thee, a wayfarer."

And when the dance is ended, he walks out into the garden to be taken and crucified.

When you go to your death that way, as a god, in the knowledge of the myth, you are going to your eternal life. So what is there in that to be sad about? Let us make it magnificent—as it is. Let us celebrate it."

Moyers: The god of death is the lord of the dance." (40)

This leads directly to the Dance of Shiva.

Shiva (Siva) is a form of *Ishvara* (God) in later Vedic scriptures of Hinduism. In some views he is one of the *Trimurit* (Hindu trinity), where Brahma is the creator, Vishnu the preserver, and Shiva the destroyer (of Evil), and destruction is seen as positive, as creation follows it. One interpretation of this has Shiva creating Vishnu, who in turn creates Brahma, and thus creation begins. Beyond his role in the eternal cycle of the coming into being, being, and ending of being, Shiva takes on many other roles, or inflections of this role. Most important here is his representation as Shiva *Nataraga* (in Sanskrit *nata* means dance, and *raja* means king).

The most well known story of Shiva's beginnings as the *Nataraga* is set in a dense forest in South India where a number of heretical sagas dwelt. Shiva and Vishnu, disguised as a beautiful woman, traveled there to confront them. At first the sagas were led to a violent dispute among themselves, but then they turned their anger toward Shiva and attempted to destroy him with incantations. First they created a ferocious tiger in the sacrificial fires, and it rushed at him. But Shiva seized it and with the nail of his smallest finger stripped off its skin and wrapped it about him like a silken garment.

Then they created a monstrous serpent. However, Shiva seized it and wrapped it about his neck like a scarf.

Then he began to dance. A final monster in the form of an evil dwarf rushed toward him. But Shiva stepped on him and broke his back, leaving him writhing on the ground, and continued the dance.

Shiva, the arch-yogi of the gods, then, is also the god of the dance, and dancing is the art form where the artist, the dancer, and the art created are one and the same, resurrecting the oneness of God and Creation. Dance induces a trance, same as yoga, where the dancer experiences ecstasy and the divine. Thus, the dance, seemingly in opposition to it, goes hand-in-hand with the austerities of yoga meditation (fasting, introversion, and so on).

The symbolism of Shiva's dance is intricate and details out a complex mythology. Shiva is depicted with four arms, representing the four cardinal directions. Since hands are the messengers of the heart or soul, each hand has strong symbolic qualities. The upper right hand holds an hourglass drum, the symbol of creation, the ticking of time in the sensual universe (Kant's forms of sensibility). It is the pulse of the universe, the beat of Shiva's dance, and sound is considered the first and most pervasive element in the unfolding universe. In fact, when Shiva gave Panini (the Sanskrit grammarian), wisdom, the entire system was included in this drumbeat. The grammar is called Shiva sutra.

The hourglass drum also symbolizes male and female principles (Jung's animus and anima). The two triangles penetrate each other to form a hexagon. When they part, the universe dissolves. Thus, only in the unity of male and female principles does sensate existence take place.

The opposite hand, the upper left hand, holds a tongue of flames. Fire is the element that destroys the universe (it is the symbol of violent transformation). For Hindus, the end of the world will take place through fire.

Thus, these two hands represent creation and destruction, sound opposed by flames, birth and death.

The second right hand with its open palm presents the *abhaya* pose (fearless), a gesture of protection, the idea of god as protector.

The left leg rises towards and across the right leg, and the left hand stretches across the body and points to the left leg in imitation of an elephant's trunk, symbolic of Ganesha, Shiva's son (the remover of obstacles), and symbolizing a release from birth and death.

Depicting the original story, Shiva dances on the body of the dwarf, *Apasmarapurusha* (the man of forgetfulness), who represents indifference, ignorance and laziness, thus representing that creation and all creative energy is possible only when inertia is overcome and suppressed. Thus, each person must overcome the negative qualities of the dwarf to participant in the energy of the cosmos.

The ring of fire and light circles the dance and identifies it with the dance of the universe. The lotus pedestal serves as the floor of the dance and locates it in each person's individual consciousness.

Here we have a dance representing the paradox of time and eternity. The energetic arms and legs are contrasted to the immobile mask of the face, serine and silent. Shiva is both *Kala* (time) and *Maha Kala* (eternity).

His long, sensuous hair is loosened and waving in a violent frenzy to the energetic dance, embracing the world of time and space. Hair is of the world of growth and life, and such wild, untouched hair represents the power of the body (same as is expressed in the Christian story of Samson). This is also strongly connected to the woman as giver of life. When she lets down her hair she invites the act of creation. Shaving one's hair simulates sterility, and is symbolic of the life of asceticism, a life beyond the seasons of growth and change. (41)

> In India, Shiva-nataraja's *tandava* was the prototype of the cosmic dance. Confined within a circle of fire, this dance symbolized creation or propitiation, destruction or preservation. It also symbolized the discipline of yoga. Furthermore, in Tantric Buddhism, Buddha Amoghasiddhi, lord of the current of life, the creator and the intellect, is known as the 'Lord of the Dance.'
>
> Indian religious dancing brings into play every portion of the body in movement which symbolizes precise spiritual states. Hands, fingernails even, eyeballs, nose, lips, arms, legs, feet and thighs all move in a swirl of silk and colours and sometimes in a state of semi-nakedness.

> All these images display and invoke a kind of fusion in the same aesthetic, emotional, erotic, religious or mystic motion, like the return to the Sole Being from whom all things emanate and to whom all things return in the ceaseless ebb and flow of the life force.
>
> Chinese tradition, linking dance to the rhythm of numbers, held that it allowed the universe to operate. It tamed wild animals and established the harmony of Heaven and Earth. By dancing, Yu the Great brought to an end the flood caused by an excess of yin. The ideogram wu, which expresses non-manifestation or destruction, may, according to some critics, have had the original meaning of 'dance'.
>
> Of all places in the world dancing takes its most extravert form in Africa. As Father Mveng observes, it is 'the most dramatic example of cultural display, for it is the only one in which human beings, breaking the mould of the natural world, can seek not merely freedom, but freedom from their natural limitations.' This is why, he maintains, dancing is the only mystical expression of African religion.
>
> In Ancient Egypt, where dances were as numerous as they were elaborate, "'if we can believe Lucian some mimes "translated into expressive movements the most mysterious tenets of their religion, the myths of Apis and Osiris, the transformations of gods into animals, and above all their love affairs."' (42)

The dance floor is the stage of life, the place where physical actions take on the symbolic meanings of mythology and express the deepest archetypes of the human mind. At times these expressions represent an abandonment of the restrictive controls of conscience, Freud's super-ego, and the ethos of religion, as the basic drives to life of the limbic system, the lower *chakras* of the *kundalini*, and Freud's libido are caught up in an ecstasy, a physical reaction to the beat of the drums and the drive of the music. At times, they are the medium for the structures of the community and the transforming shapes of amore. At times, they become the highest expressions of art, the intuitive movements and organizations of space and time that reveal the deepest needs and truths of life. In the end, they always lead back to the spiritual rituals that connect physical existence with the invisible world of meaning and value.

Duality, then, is inherent in the *consciousness of self*, in the birth of *human existence*; and this is precisely what is represented in the Christian Garden of Eden story, where the biting of the fruit of the tree of the knowledge of Good and Evil brings duality into existence, man and woman, day and night, birth and death, and most importantly time and eternity.

Joseph Campbell offers some commentary on this in his interviews with Bill Moyers:

Moyers: What is the myth of Adam and Eve trying to tell us about the pairs of opposites? What is the meaning?

Campbell: It started with the sin, you see—in other words, moving out of the mythological dreamtime zone of the Garden of Paradise, where there is no time, and where men and women don't even know that they are different from each other. The two are just creatures. God and man are practically the same. God walks in the cool of the evening in the garden where they are. And then they eat the apple, the knowledge of the opposites. And when they discover they are different, the man and woman cover their shame. You we, they had not thought of themselves as opposites. Male and female is one opposition. Another opposition is the human and God. Good and evil is a third opposition. The primary oppositions are the sexual and that between human beings and God. Then comes the idea of good and evil in the world. And so Adam and Eve have thrown themselves out of the Garden of Timeless Unity, you might say, just by that act of recognizing duality. To move out into the world, you have to act in terms of pairs of opposites.

There's a Hindu image that shows a triangle, which is the Mother Goddess, and a dot in the center of the triangle, which is the energy of the transcendent entering the field of time. And then from this triangle there come pairs of triangles in all directions. Out of one comes two. All things in the field of time are pairs of opposites. So this is the shift of consciousness from the consciousness of identity to the consciousness of participation I duality. And then you are into the field of time.

Moyers: Is the story trying to tell us that, prior to what happened in this Garden to destroy us, there was a unity of life?

Campbell: It's a matter of planes of consciousness. It doesn't have to do with anything that happened. There is the plane of consciousness where you can identify yourself with that which transcends pairs of opposites.

Moyers: Which is?

Campbell: Unnamable. Unnamable. It is transcendent of all names.

Moyers: God?

Campbell: "God" is an ambiguous word in our language because it appears to refer to something that is known. But the transcendent is unknowable and unknown. God is transcendent, finally, of anything like the name "God." God is beyond names and forms. Meister Eckhart said that the ultimate and highest leave-taking is leaving God for God, leaving your notion of God for an experience of that which transcends all notions.

The mystery of life is beyond all human conception. Everything we know is within the terminology of the concepts of being and not being, many and single, true and untrue. We always think in terms of opposites. But God, the ultimate, is beyond the pairs of opposites, that is all there is to it.

Moyers: Why do we think in terms of opposites?

Campbell: Because we can't think otherwise.

Moyers: That's the nature of reality in our time.

Campbell: That's the nature of our experience of reality.

Moyers: Man-woman, life-death, good-evil—

> Campbell: —I and you, this and that, true and untrue—every one of them has its opposite. But mythology suggests that behind that duality there is a singularity over which this plays like a shadow game. "Eternity is in love with the productions of time," says the poet Blake.
>
> Moyers: What does that mean, "Eternity is in love with the productions of time"?
>
> Campbell: The source of temporal life is eternity. Eternity pours itself into the world. It is a basic mythic idea of the god who becomes many in us. n India, the god who lies in me is called the "inhabitant" of the body. To identify with that divine immortal aspect of you is to identify yourself with divinity.
>
> Now, eternity is beyond all categories of thought. This is an important point in all of the great Oriental religions. We want to think about God. God is a thought. God is a name. God is an idea. But its reference is to something that transcends all thinking. The ultimate mystery of being is beyond all categories of thought. As Kant said, the thing in itself is no thing. It transcends thingness, it goes past anything that could be thought. The best things can't be told because they transcend thought. The second best are misunderstood, because those are the thoughts that are supposed to refer to that which can't be thought about. The third best are what we talk about. And myth is that field of reference to what is absolutely transcendent. . . .
>
> . . . transcendent means to "transcend" to go past duality. Everything in the field of time is dual. . . .
>
> Moyers: Do you think there was such a place as the Garden of Eden?
>
> Campbell: Of course not. The Garden of Eden is a metaphor for that innocence that is innocent of time, innocent of opposites, and that is the prime center out of which consciousness then becomes aware of the changes.
>
> Moyers: But if there is in the idea of Eden this innocence, what happens to it? Isn't it shaken, dominated, and corrupted by fear?
>
> Campbell: That's it. There is a wonderful story of the deity, of the Self that said, "I am." As soon as it said I am," it was afraid.
>
> Moyers asks "Why?"
>
> Joseph Campbell replies: "It was an entity now, in time. Then it thought, 'What should I be afraid of, I'm the only thing that is.' And as soon as it said that, it felt lonesome, and wished that there were another, and so it felt desire. It swelled, split in two, became male and female, and begot the world." (43)

This is what Sigmund Freud struggles with, that moment of self-realization, the moment when the self realizes it's self, and ends up deciding it takes place at the oedipal stage. Otto Rank breaks with Sigmund Freud and says it takes place at birth. He calls it "life fear," the fear of living autonomously, of being abandoned. Rollo May states, "This is the fear of self-actualization." (44) Joseph Campbell refers to psychiatrist Stanislav Grof as claiming it takes place in the womb just before birth, when the uterus begins the rhythms of labor, and there is the terror, "the horrific stage of getting born, the difficult passage through the birth canal, and then . . . light! . . . . That is the breaking into the world of light and the pairs of opposites." (45)

James Joyce writes at the end of *A Portrait of the Artist as a Young Man*: "Welcome, O life! I go to encounter for the millionth time the reality of experience and to forge in the smithy of my soul the uncreated conscience of my race." (46)

Thus, conscience, the world of meaning and value is not simply somewhere outside of the human psyche, but rather, as Rollo May states, "It is created, first of all, out of the inspiration derived from the artist's symbols and forms. Every authentic artist is engaged in this creating of the conscience of the race, even though he or she may be unaware of the fact." (47) Thus, creativity, Rollo May continues, involves "an active battle with the gods." (48)

By definition, creativity brings something new into existence, and also by definition this changes existence, re-creates existence. Archibald MacLeish quotes a Chinese poet: "We poets struggle with Non-being to force it to yield Being. We knock upon silence for an answering music." (49)

Rollo May states:

> A host of other riddles, which I can only cite without comment, are bound up with this major one. One is that genius and psychosis are so close to each other. Another is that creativity carries such an inexplicable guilt feeling. A third is that so many artists and poets commit suicide, and often at the very height of their achievement. (50)

The myths representing this are combining the birth of human consciousness, of *Self-awareness* with the accompanying anger of the supernatural forces, of the gods. The biting of the forbidden fruit in Eden brings the wrath of God on Adam and Eve. They are condemned and lose their eternal *Self*. The same is true in the Greek myth of Prometheus. He stole fire from the gods and gave it to humans, thus representing giving humans both physical and psychological illumination, enlightenment, the ability to think and create. Zeus was outraged and condemned Prometheus to have his liver (thought at the time the myth was created to be the center of consciousness) eaten by a vulture (a black bird that lives on the flesh of death animals; black representing the opposite of innocence (white), a bird a creature of the unconscious (the sky), each day (the bright sun symbolizing conscious knowing) the liver growing back each night (night and the moon symbolizing the unconscious and regeneration), and the entire story involving the necessity of death once consciousness of *Self* as separate from unity with god is realized. Just to emphasize this, the story has a concluding possibility of release for Prometheus, where Zeus will free him from his chains if another immortal will give up his immortality (which is done by Chiron). Of course, in the Christian version this reunion with God and immortality is accomplished through the half-man-half-god Christ (both cases involving a willing sacrifice).

So we end this enquiry with the announcement of the moment human existence goes from mere clay to something more, the moment when the announcement comes that spirit is born out of flesh:

> 10. And the angel said unto them, Fear not for behold, I bring you good tidings of great joy, which shall be to all people.
> 11. For unto you is born this day in the city of David a Saviour, which is Christ the Lord.
> 12. And this shall be a sign unto you; Ye shall find the babe wrapped in swaddling clothes, lying in a manger.
> 13. And suddenly there was with the angel a multitude of the heavenly host praising God, and saying,
> 14. Glory to God in the highest, and on earth peace, and good will toward men. (51)

When I was young, I was fortunate enough to live on the shore of Lake Minnetonka, and I spent many summer afternoons laying on my homemade swimming raft, a raft that floated me but a couple of inches above the surface of the water. While the warmth of the sun caressed my tan body, I would gaze at the ever-changing dance of light and shade as the water rippled around me. Certainly this could be nothing other than the dance of life, an eternal waltz of wind and water, light and shade, spirit and flesh—flirting, teasing, playing and laughing--*lila, the joy of life, the exuberance of existence, the divine madness of the gods--bliss dancing all around me.*

Notes

1. *A Little Book on the Human Shadow,* HarperCollins, 1988, p. 7.
2. *The Raven and Other Poems*, 1845; rpt, *Edgar Allen Poe*, Octopus Books, London, 1981.
3. A. C. Bradley, A. C., *Shakespearean Tragedy*, 1904; Basingstoke: Macmillan Press, 1974, p. 169.

4. *Williams, Shakespeare* (1995) (in French and English). *Oeuvres Complètes. Tragédies II*, Bouquins ed., Robert Laffont. pp. 46–47.
5. Boston Review, April/May,1996.
6. *Gollum: How We Made Movie Magic,* HarperCollins, 2003.
7. "On the Psychology of the Unconscious," 1912; rpt. "Two Essays on Analytical Psychology, *The Collected Works of Carl Jung,* vol. 7, p. 35.
8. "new Paths in Psychology," 1912; rpt, "Two Essays on Analytical Psychology, *The Collected Works of Carl Jung,* vol. 7, p. 425.
9. "Archetypes of the Collective Unconscious," *The Collected Works of Carl Jung*, trans., R. F. C. Hull, vol. 9, part 1, pp. 39-40.
10. *The Delight Makers*, 1890; rpt., Bibliobazaar, 2006.
11. "On the Psychology of the Trickster-Figure," *The Collected Works of Carl Jung*, trans., R. F. C. Hull, vol. 9, part 1, p. 255.
12. "On the Psychology of the Trickster-Figure," *The Collected Works of Carl Jung*, trans., R. F. C. Hull, vol. 9, part 1, p. 256.
13. "On the Psychology of the Trickster-Figure," *The Collected Works of Carl Jung*, trans., R. F. C. Hull, vol. 9, part 1, p. 262.
14. "On the Psychology of the Trickster-Figure," *The Collected Works of Carl Jung*, trans., R. F. C. Hull, vol. 9, part 1, p. 263.
15. "On the Psychology of the Trickster-Figure," *The Collected Works of Carl Jung*, trans., R. F. C. Hull, vol. 9, part 1, pp. 266-267.
16. "On the Psychology of the Trickster-Figure," *The Collected Works of Carl Jung*, trans., R. F. C. Hull, vol. 9, part 1, p. 266.
17. *The World of Primitive Man*, p. 3-5.
18. "On the Psychology of the Trickster-Figure," *The Collected Works of Carl Jung*, trans., R. F. C. Hull, vol. 9, part 1, Princeton Univ., 2nd ed., 1969, p. 268.
19. "On the Psychology of the Trickster-Figure," *The Collected Works of Carl Jung*, trans., R. F. C. Hull, vol. 9, part 1, Princeton Univ., 2nd ed., 1969, pp. 269-270.
20. "On the Psychology of the Trickster-Figure," *The Collected Works of Carl Jung*, trans., R. F. C. Hull, vol. 9, part 1, Princeton Univ., 2nd ed., 1969, p. 270.
21. "On the Psychology of the Trickster-Figure," *The Collected Works of Carl Jung*, trans., R. F. C. Hull, vol. 9, part 1, Princeton Univ., 2nd ed., 1969, p. 272.
22. *Owning Your Own Shadow: Understanding the Dark Side of the Psyche*, Harper, 1991, pp. 4-5.
23. *Owning Your Own Shadow: Understanding the Dark Side of the Psyche*, Harper, 1991, pp. 7-8.
24. *Owning Your Own Shadow: Understanding the Dark Side of the Psyche, Harper, 1991, p. 8.*
25. *A Little Book on the Human Shadow*, ed., William Booth, Harper, 1988, pp. 17-18.
26. *A Little Book on the Human Shadow*, ed., William Booth, Harper, 1988, p. 18.
27. The Night has a Naked Soul, Syracuse Univ. Press, New York, 1997, p. 10.
28. Jeffrey Brodd, *World Religions*. Winona, MN: Saint Mary's Press, 2003.
29. *Images of the Child*, Bowling green State University, 1994.

30. *The Holy: an inquiry into the non-rational factor in the idea of the divine and its relation to the rational*, 1917; rpt., trans., John w. Harvey, London: Oxford University Press, 1926, p. 10.
31. *Partisan Review*, 1957; rpt., *Going to Meet the Man*, Vintage Books, 1965.
32. *Holy Bible*, King James Version.
33. *On Psychic Energy,* 1928; rpt., *The Collected Works of Carl Jung,* Vol. 8, trans. R. F. C. Hull, Princeton Univ., 2nd ed., 1969, p. 233.
34. *On Psychic Energy,* 1928; rpt., *The Collected Works of Carl Jung,* Vol. 8, trans. R. F. C. Hull, Princeton Univ., 2nd ed., 1969, p. p. 186.
35. *A Psychological Approach to the Dogma of the Trinity*, 1942; rpt., *The Collected Works of Carl Jung,* Vol. 11, trans., R. F. C. Hull, Princeton Univ., 2nd ed., 1969, p. 184.
36. *Psychology and Religion*, 1937-40; rpt., *The Collected Works of Carl Jung*, Vol. 11, trans., R. F. C. Hull, Princeton Univ., 2nd ed., 1969, p. 7.
37. *The Penguin Dictionary of Symbols*, 1969; trans., John Buchanan-Brown, Penguin,1996, pp. 272-274.
38. The Buffalo Dance and the myth it is based on can be found in many sources, including Bruno Nettl, *Blackfoot Musical Thought: Comparative Perspectives*, Kent State Univ. Press, 1989, ISBN: 0873383702; Alan G. Hefner, "Legend of the Buffalo Dance, *Encyclopedia Mythica*, www.pantheon.org; and Joseph Campbell, "The First Storytellers," *The Power of Myth with Bill Moyers*, Doubleday, 1988, pp. 95-99.
39..*Beyond Belief: The Secret Gospel of Thomas*, Random House, 2003, pp. 123. The Acts of John (2nd century) is a collection of stories and traditions inspired by John's gospel. "The Round Dance of the Cross," is in Acts of John 94.1-4. For a recently edited Greek text with French translation and notes, see E. Junod and J. P. Kastli, *Acta Johannis: Praefatio-Texus, in Corpus Christinaorum* (Turnout, 1983), English trans. Barbara E. Bowe, "Dancing into the Divine: The Hymn of the Dance in the Acts of John," *Journal of Early Christian Studies* 7:1 (1999), 83-104. According to *Irenaeus, Libros Quinque Adversus Haereses*, ed. W. W. Harvey, Cambridge, 1851, an anonymous follower of Valentinus wrote the Round Dance, suggesting it was a scene left off of John's gospel, in which Jesus danced with his disciples the night he was betrayed.
40. *The Power of Myth with Bill Moyers*, Doubleday, 1988, pp. 135-137.
41. See *The Dance of Shiva*, Ananda K. Coomaraswamy; Noonday Press, Rev. Ed. 1972; rpt. as *The Dance of Siva*, Dover, 1985, ISBN: 0486248178. *Shiva: The Wild God of Power and Ecstasy*, Wolf-Dieter Storl, Inner Traditions, 2004, ISBN: 159477014X. *Siva Sutras: The Supreme Awakening*, Swami Lakshmangoo, Authorhouse, 2002, ISBN: 0759654573.
42. Jean Chevalier and Alain Gheerbrant, *The Penguin Dictionary of Symbols*, 1969; trans., John Buchanan-Brown, Penguin, 1996, pp. 272-274.
43.*The Power of Myth: Joseph Campbell with Bill Moyers,* ed., Sue Flowers, Doubleday, 1988, pp. 55-59.
44. *The Courage to Create*, Norton/Bantam, 1975, p. 11.
45. *The Power of Myth: Joseph Campbell with Bill Moyers,* ed., Sue Flowers, Doubleday, 1988, pp. 55-59.

46. First serialized in *The Egoist*, 1914-1915; published as a book 1916; rpt., Penguin, 2003, concluding passages.
47. *The Courage to Create*, Norton/Bantam, 1975, p. 21.
48. *The Courage to Create*, Norton/Bantam, 1975, p. 22.
49. *Poetry and Experience,* Boston, 1961, pp. 8-9.
50. *The Courage to Create*, Norton/Bantam, 1975, p.23.
51. "St. Luke," 2, 10-14, *King James Bible.*

INDEX